A WODEHOUSE HANDBOOK

The World and Words of P.G. Wodehouse

Revised Edition

Volume Two

THE WORDS OF WODEHOUSE

Quotations and References

Also by N.T.P. Murphy

In Search of Blandings

One Man's London

A True and Faithful Account of the Amazing Adventures of The Wodehouse Society on Their Pilgrimage July 1989

The Reminiscences of the Hon. Galahad Threepwood

Three Wodehouse Walks

One Man's London: Twenty Years On

A WODEHOUSE HANDBOOK

The World and Words of P.G. Wodehouse

Revised edition

By

N.T.P. Murphy

Volume Two

THE WORDS OF WODEHOUSE

Quotations and References

Sybertooth Inc
Sackville, New Brunswick
Litteris Elegantibus Madefimus

Revised second edition published 2013 by Sybertooth Inc.
59 Salem Street
Sackville, NB
E4L 4J6
Canada
www.sybertooth.ca

The paper in this edition is acid free and meets all ANSI standards for archival quality; see the publisher's website for information on the paper's sustainable forestry & forest stewardship certification.

Library and Archives Canada Cataloguing in Publication

Murphy, N. T. P., author
A Wodehouse handbook : the world and words of P.G. Wodehouse / by N.T.P. Murphy. -- Revised edition.

Includes bibliographical references and index.
Contents: Volume 1. The world of Wodehouse -- Volume 2. The words of Wodehouse : quotations and references.
ISBN 978-1-927592-00-7 (v. 1 : pbk.).--ISBN 978-1-927592-01-4 (v. 2 : pbk.)

1. Wodehouse, P. G. (Pelham Grenville), 1881-1975--Criticism and interpretation. 2. Wodehouse, P. G. (Pelham Grenville), 1881-1975--Characters. I. Title.

PR6045.O53Z797 2013 823'.912 C2013-901774-7

Contents

Illustrations

Introduction

> I imagine there must be quite a few aspects of my stuff which the new generation of reader doesn't understand. Let me put it this way. When I was a boy reading all those Greek and Latin authors, the one who appealed to me the most was Aristophanes. He was a very funny fellow. But, you know, he must have seemed ever so much funnier to the Greeks. That is the point I want to make. I suppose we miss eighty per cent of Aristophanes' humour. Some line that means nothing to us might have been a wonderful dig at Cleon.
>
> P.G. Wodehouse, quoted in
> *The World of P.G. Wodehouse*
> by Herbert Warren Wind (1981)

Wodehouse quoted from more sources than any other writer — from the Bible through Homer and Shakespeare to popular songs, clichés, political slogans, British and American topical catchphrases and advertisements of the late nineteenth and early twentieth centuries. He did so because he knew his readers would appreciate them — when he wrote them.

It is significant that in his last ten or so books, Wodehouse gave the source of many quotations because, as he also said to Wind, he had realised the readership of the 1960s was not as familiar with the Bible, the Classics and Shakespeare as he was. I should also point out that much of his humour lay in the deliberate, splendid mis-quotations perpetrated by Bertie, Bingo and the rest of them. They added to the fun — readers laughed because they appreciated the mistakes, as Wodehouse knew they would. A cause for occasional confusion is that subsequent editors, subeditors and proofreaders did not recognise certain references, misread them or failed to check them. I note, for example, that the latest UK issue of *Tales of St Austin's* has changed the word 'push' to 'posh', presumably because the editors had not bothered to check that 'push' was a perfectly good expression that Wodehouse had used correctly and that I, for one, was still using in the 1960s. I am grateful to Tony Ring for demonstrating that incorrect Biblical references in the book version of the Anselm Mulliner stories exist because proofreaders simply misread the correct allusions in the original magazine stories.

I spent many months working my way through Wodehouse's quotations and references. I did so for eight reasons. The first is that, since I wrote *In Search of Blandings* thirty years ago, I have received many letters from people asking what Wodehouse was referring to when he wrote a certain passage or the source of a character he mentioned in another.

Secondly, I have never forgotten the comment made by my Dutch friend Rob Kooy, who attended the first Wodehouse Pilgrimage in 1989. He said that unless one was a native-born English speaker, one missed ninety per cent of Wodehouse's references. I am sure he was right. Indeed, I now believe that unless one was born in 1881, studied Classics at an English public school and read every author of the time, good and bad, that you could lay your hands on, even a native-born English speaker still misses many of the jokes. On one occasion I was startled to be asked by an American enthusiast what was the origin of the title of the golf story 'Those in Peril on the Tee'? I thought he was joking. He was an educated man, surely he knew that the official hymn of the American (and Royal) Navy ends each verse with the words "For those in peril on the sea"?

Thirdly, Wodehouse wrote in both English and American English. I don't think he did so consciously, though he often had to 'anglicise' his books, and there are surprising differences in some editions. I believe he simply absorbed the phraseology and popular quotations of England and America and forgot they were peculiar to one country. I have therefore had to include references which every Briton has known since childhood and their transatlantic equivalents which every American knows just as well. I wonder how many English readers pick up "Fire when ready, Gridley", "A big stick" or "Fight it out on these lines if it takes all summer"? Conversely, how many Americans get the point of "one of the ruins that Cromwell knocked about a bit", "Loose Chippings" or "that sinking feeling"? And how many people of either nation know the origin of one of his favourite phrases — "just like mother makes"?

Fourthly, I happen to be of an age when, like the young Wodehouse, I trilled 'Cherry Ripe' as a boy treble (as well as the 'Volga Boatman'), reluctantly mastered 'The Wreck of the Hesperus', and worked my way through Caesar's *Gallic Wars* and Xenophon's *Anabasis.* The books in my parents' house were much the same as they would have been in his. He read the *Odyssey* at six; I read it at eight and I still recall the illustrations vividly. It was on the shelves with Dickens, Scott, Conan Doyle, W.W. Jacobs, Tennyson, Twain, Bret Harte, Anthony Hope and the rest of them. One just read them and absorbed them — as he did.

....

> Two final thoughts; first, Wodehouse is, with the possible exception of Joyce, the most literary of our great novelists. He is not only highly allusive, but his work offers a continuous succession of various themes from the Bible, Shakespeare and other poets. This is perhaps the one obstacle to his survival for, the way education is going, it must be doubtful if anyone will be able to understand him in a couple of generations without the myriad footnotes now provided for works like the *Dunciad*.
>
> Finally, he is not only the most literary, but — again Joyce is the only rival — the most completely devoted to literature.
>
> Review by Alan Massie of Wodehouse's
> 'Uncle Fred' stories, *The Scotsman*, 14 January 1984

....

I cannot stress too strongly that Wodehouse's knowledge of the Bible, the Classics and Shakespeare was of a standard one rarely meets today. He grew up in an age when schoolboys attended chapel twice a day and when his aunts had family prayers before breakfast. Along with *Hymns Ancient and Modern* and the superb rhythms of the *Book of Common Prayer*, the Bible sank into his subconscious as it did into that of most people of his time. When Freddie Widgeon, Catsmeat Potter-Pirbright and other Drones quoted the Bible, they were simply reflecting the then-typical upbringing of middle-class and upper-class children.

Fifthly, I still remember from my schooldays a footnote on the word 'costard' in a Shakespeare text. It ran: "Costard, an apple. Mostly grown in Kent, those who brought them into London for sale were known as costermongers." I have never forgotten that footnote and I am still grateful to the person who wrote it. It taught me a new word and explained another. I hope that some of the quotations and references I have traced will be as useful to readers as that footnote was to me.

Sixthly, I have read Wodehouse for sixty years and much has changed in that time. The English language has changed, slang has changed, popular music has changed and the once well-known magazine advertisements he quoted so often have vanished forever. Though his language and slang seem old-fashioned today, he made a point of keeping up to date. In nearly every book, there are topical references which he knew his readers would appreciate. He referred to contemporary fads, fashions and advertisements all his life and quoted from musical hits of the day that everybody knew. Most readers today pick up "Beatle, Beatle and Beatle of Liverpool" ('Life with Freddie') and many appreciate "there is nothing like a dame" (*The Girl in Blue*). The "celebrated Maisie" of *Tales of St Austin's* (1903) was just as up-to-date — *then*. As Wodehouse said of Aristophanes, he is even funnier if you knew the chaps he was joking about.

Seventhly, there are private and semi-private jokes scattered through the novels. I would put Rodney Spelvin's surname in the semi-private category, but Miss Eustacia Pulbrook and writing a life of Talleyrand are far more obscure. There are few things more tedious than explaining jokes, but I have tried to make the explanations as succinct as possible.

Eighthly, I read a piece recently about the historian A.L. Rowse. Written by the eminent Shakespearean scholar Stanley Wells, it described Rowse's career, his academic quarrels and the dreadful errors he sometimes made, but ended by praising him for explaining an obscure Latin joke in *Love's Labours Lost* that had puzzled critics for centuries. Professor Wells made the point that this was no small achievement. I am no Rowse but I hope the following pages will be of some use to Wodehouse enthusiasts.

It has been firmly pointed out to me that not everyone has a copy of the Authorised Version of the Bible or a complete Shakespeare/Tennyson/Byron/Browning/Scott to hand. For that reason, where Wodehouse altered or amended a reference, I have set out the original quotation.

Finally, my thanks for their corrections to this edition go to Fr Rob Bovendeaard,

Charles Gould, Dr Tim Healey, Murray Hedgcock, David Jasen, David Landman, Jim Linwood, Hetty Litjens, David McDonough, Ian Michaud and Richard Vine –and others. I owe a special debt to Neil Midkiff, who picked up more errors than anybody.

N.T.P. Murphy

Notes

NOTE 1. To save space, I have used certain abbreviations:

B = Bible[1]
BCP = Book of Common Prayer
D = Dickens
G&S = Gilbert & Sullivan
S = Shakespeare
T = Tennyson

NOTE 2. A quotation/reference followed by, for example, '31 p24' indicates it is to be found on page 24 of *my* copy of *The Inimitable Jeeves*. I am well aware that page numbers change with different editions, but at least it gives an indication of its general position in the book. The numbering of book titles is set out below. Where a phrase or quotation is used frequently in PGW, I have simply indicated 'frequent' or 'often'.

NOTE 3. I have chosen to use the 'word by word' method of alphabetization, meaning that alphabetizing ends after the first space; for example, 'As worn' is placed before 'Ashburton'. Apostrophes and hyphens, however, are ignored; for example, *Nature's* is treated as if spelled *Natures* and *A-weary* as if spelled *Aweary*. For readers accustomed to letter-by-letter alphabetization, please note: names beginning 'Mc' are incorporated with those beginning 'Mac' and abbreviated saints' names (e.g. St Ambrose) are treated as if they are spelled out 'Saint'. Finally, though most names, real or fictional, are found under the surname (e.g., Bassett, Madeline), there are some exceptions (e.g. Captain Coe, Colonel Bogey and titles of books such as *David Copperfield*).

NOTE 4. Much as I would have liked to, I found it impossible to follow the normal rules of indexing by the main noun or verb. Time and again, the reader's recognition of a quotation depends on one or two key words and will be found under those. 'Hot time in the old town tonight' is a quotation people recognise with that order of words — and no other — and is therefore indexed under 'Hot time'. 'Came the dawn' is another example and is under 'Came'. 'He wants his pound of flesh', on the other hand, is under 'Pound of flesh, he wants' because 'pound of flesh' are the words that are familiar. 'When you admonish a congregation, it stays

[1] I have used the Authorised Version of the Bible (King James), which I am sure was the version with which Wodehouse grew up. It should be noted, however, that the Book of Common Prayer often uses different wording for the psalms.

admonished' is under 'Admonish a congregation' for the same reason. I apologise for any confusion this may cause and I have attempted to alleviate matters with frequent cross-references in SMALL CAPS (e.g., 'See MADE IT SO'). To those who would still carp at my method, I would ask them to look at the entries under 'Thingummy' and 'Tiddley-om-pom' in the hope they will view my indexing with a less critical eye.

Numbering of Book Titles and Editions Used

It can be a source of great irritation among Wodehouse enthusiasts that so many Wodehouse books have different titles in the UK and the USA. In his Preface to the 1974 edition of *French Leave*, Wodehouse wrote:

> Changing titles is an occupational disease with American publishers. As A.A. Milne said when they altered the title of his Autobiography from *It's Too Late Now* to *What Luck*, "This is a habit of American publishers. I fancy that the Order of Installation — taken (as I see it) in shirt sleeves, with blue pencil upheld in right hand, ends 'And I do solemnly swear that whatsoever the author shall have called any novel submitted to me, and however suitable his title shall be, I will immediately alter it to one of my own choosing, thus asserting by a single stroke the dignity of my office and my own independence.'"

Because of this, I have numbered the books in order of publication, as set out below. The edition shown beside it is the version I used. An alphabetical list of titles (both UK and US) follows with its corresponding number.

1.	*The Pothunters*	(1902 on title page; in fact 1915 UK edition)
2.	*A Prefect's Uncle*	(1924? 1925? UK edition)
3.	*Tales of St Austin's*	(1903 UK edition)
4.	*The Gold Bat*	(1904 UK edition)
5.	*William Tell Told Again*	(1907 edition)
6.	*The Head of Kay's*	(1928 UK edition)
7.	*Love Among the Chickens*	(1921 rewritten UK ed.)
8.	*The White Feather*	(1972 UK edition)
9.	*Not George Washington*	(1907 First edition signed by Westbrook!)
10.	*The Globe By the Way Book*	(1985 Heineman edition)
11.	*The Swoop*	(1909 UK edition)
12.	*Mike*	(1924 UK edition)

13.	*A Gentleman of Leisure / The Intrusion of Jimmy*	(1910 US edition; 1921 UK edition)
14.	*Psmith in the City*	(1928 UK edition)
15.	*The Prince and Betty*	(1912 US edition, US version)
15A.	*Psmith Journalist*	(1923 UK edition, 1941 reprint)
16.	*The Prince and Betty*	(1926? UK edition, UK version)
17.	*The Little Nugget*	(1950 UK edition)
17A.	*A Man of Means*	(1991 UK edition)
18.	*The Man Upstairs*	(1928? UK edition)
19.	*Something Fresh / Something New*	(1933 15th UK edition)
20.	*Uneasy Money*	(1969 UK re-issue ed.)
21.	*Piccadilly Jim*	(Prob 1931? UK edition)
22.	*The Man with Two Left Feet*	(1932 UK edition)
23.	*My Man Jeeves*	(1919?/1920 UK edition)
24.	*The Coming of Bill / Their Mutual Child*	(1922 UK edition)
25.	*A Damsel in Distress*	(Prob 1923 UK edition)
26.	*Jill the Reckless / The Little Warrior*	(1922 UK edition)
27.	*Indiscretions of Archie*	(1940 UK edition)
28.	*The Clicking of Cuthbert / Golf Without Tears*	(1923 UK edition)
29.	*The Girl on the Boat / Three Men and a Maid*	(1922 UK edition)
30.	*The Adventures of Sally / Mostly Sally*	(1923 UK edition)
31.	*The Inimitable Jeeves / Jeeves*	(1923 UK edition)
32.	*Leave It to Psmith*	(1924 UK edition)
33.	*Ukridge / He Rather Enjoyed It*	(1924 UK edition)
34.	*Bill the Conqueror*	(1924 UK edition)
35.	*Carry On, Jeeves*	(1925 UK edition)
36.	*Sam the Sudden / Sam in the Suburbs*	(1925 UK edition)
37.	*The Heart of a Goof / Divots*	(1938 UK edition)
38.	*The Small Bachelor*	(1927 UK edition)
39.	*Meet Mr Mulliner*	(1927 UK edition)
40.	*Money for Nothing*	(1933 5th? UK printing)
41.	*Mr Mulliner Speaking*	(1929 UK edition)
42.	*Summer Lightning / Fish Preferred*	(1929 UK edition)
43.	*Very Good, Jeeves*	(1930 UK edition)

44.	*Big Money*	(1931 US edition)
45.	*If I Were You*	(1931 UK edition)
46.	*Louder and Funnier*	(1932 UK edition)
47.	*Doctor Sally*	(1932 UK edition)
48.	*Hot Water*	(1932 UK edition)
49.	*Mulliner Nights*	(1933 US edition)
50.	*Heavy Weather*	(1933 UK edition)
51.	*Thank You, Jeeves*	(1934 UK edition)
52.	*Right Ho, Jeeves / Brinkley Manor*	(1934 UK edition)
53.	*Blandings Castle*	(1935 UK edition)
54.	*The Luck of the Bodkins*	(1935 UK edition)
55.	*Young Men in Spats*	(1936 UK edition)
56.	*Laughing Gas*	(1936 UK edition)
57.	*Lord Emsworth and Others / Crime Wave at Blandings*	(1937 UK edition)
58.	*Summer Moonshine*	(Prob 1949; Fourth printing UK ed.)
59.	*The Code of the Woosters*	(1938 UK edition)
60.	*Uncle Fred in the Springtime*	(1939 UK edition)
61.	*Eggs, Beans and Crumpets*	(1940 UK edition)
62.	*Quick Service*	(1940 UK edition)
63.	*Money in the Bank*	(1947 UK edition)
64.	*Joy in the Morning*	(1947 UK edition)
65.	*Full Moon*	(1947 UK edition)
66.	*Spring Fever*	(1948 UK edition)
67.	*Uncle Dynamite*	(1948 UK edition)
68.	*The Mating Season*	(1949 UK edition)
69.	*Nothing Serious*	(1950 UK edition)
70.	*The Old Reliable*	(1951 UK edition)
71.	*Barmy in Wonderland / Angel Cake*	(1952 UK edition)
72.	*Pigs Have Wings*	(1952 UK edition)
73.	*Ring for Jeeves / The Return of Jeeves*	(1953/4? Second UK ed.)
74.	*Bring on the Girls*	(1954 UK edition signed by Guy Bolton!)
75.	*Performing Flea / Author! Author!*	(1953 UK edition)
76.	*Jeeves and the Feudal Spirit / Bertie Wooster Sees It Through*	(1954 UK edition)
77.	*French Leave*	(1955 UK edition)

78. *Over Seventy /America, I Like You* (1957 UK edition)
79. *Something Fishy / The Butler Did It* (1957 UK edition)
80. *Cocktail Time* (1958 UK edition)
81. *A Few Quick Ones* (1959 UK edition)
82. *Jeeves in the Offing / How Right You Are, Jeeves* (1960 UK edition)
83. *Ice in the Bedroom / The Ice in the Bedroom* (1961 UK edition)
84. *Service with a Smile* (1961 UK edition)
85. *Stiff Upper Lip, Jeeves* (1963 UK edition)
86. *Frozen Assets/Biffen's Millions* (1964 UK edition)
87. *Galahad at Blandings / The Brinkmanship of Galahad Threepwood* (1965 UK edition)
88. *Plum Pie* (1966 UK edition)
89. *Company for Henry / The Purloined Paperweight* (1967 UK edition)
90. *Do Butlers Burgle Banks?* (1968 UK edition)
91. *A Pelican at Blandings / No Nudes Is Good Nudes* (1969 UK edition)
92. *The Girl in Blue* (1970 UK edition)
93. *Much Obliged, Jeeves / Jeeves and the Tie That Binds* (1971 UK edition)
94. *Pearls, Girls and Monty Bodkin / The Plot That Thickened* (1972 UK edition)
95. *Bachelors Anonymous* (1973 UK edition)
96. *Aunt Aren't Gentlemen / The Catnappers* (1974 UK edition)
97. *Sunset at Blandings* (1977 UK edition)
98. *The Parrot and Other Poems* (1988 UK edition)
99. *Tales of Wrykyn and Elsewhere* (1997 UK edition)

Alphabetical Listing of Titles, Both UK and US

№	Title
30	*The Adventures of Sally*
78	*America, I Like You*
71	*Angel Cake*
96	*Aunts Aren't Gentlemen* 75

75 *Author! Author!*
95 *Bachelors Anonymous*
71 *Barmy in Wonderland*
76 *Bertie Wooster Sees It Through*
86 *Biffen's Millions*
44 *Big Money*
34 *Bill the Conqueror*
53 *Blandings Castle*
74 *Bring on the Girls*
52 *Brinkley Manor*
87 *The Brinkmanship of Galahad Threepwood*
79 *The Butler Did It*
35 *Carry on, Jeeves*
96 *The Catnappers*
28 *The Clicking of Cuthbert*
80 *Cocktail Time*
59 *The Code of the Woosters*
24 *The Coming of Bill*
89 *Company for Henry*
57 *Crime Wave at Blandings*
25 *A Damsel in Distress*
37 *Divots*
90 *Do Butlers Burgle Banks?*
47 *Doctor Sally*
61 *Eggs, Beans and Crumpets*
81 *A Few Quick Ones*
42 *Fish Preferred*
77 *French Leave*
86 *Frozen Assets*
65 *Full Moon*
87 *Galahad at Blandings*
13 *A Gentleman of Leisure*
92 *The Girl in Blue*
29 *The Girl on the Boat*
10 *The Globe By the Way Book*
4 *The Gold Bat*
28 *Golf Without Tears*

23	*My Man Jeeves*
91	*No Nudes Is Good Nudes*
9	*Not George Washington*
69	*Nothing Serious*
70	*The Old Reliable*
78	*Over Seventy*
98	*The Parrot and Other Poems*
94	*Pearls, Girls and Monty Bodkin*
91	*A Pelican at Blandings*
75	*Performing Flea*
21	*Piccadilly Jim*
72	*Pigs Have Wings*
94	*The Plot That Thickened*
88	*Plum Pie*
1	*The Pothunters*
2	*A Prefect's Uncle*
15	*The Prince and Betty* (US version)
16	*The Prince and Betty* (UK version)
14	*Psmith in the City*
15A	*Psmith Journalist* (UK version)
89	*The Purloined Paperweight*
62	*Quick Service*
73	*The Return of Jeeves*
52	*Right Ho, Jeeves*
73	*Ring for Jeeves*
36	*Sam in the Suburbs/Sam the Sudden*
84	*Service with a Smile*
38	*The Small Bachelor*
79	*Something Fishy*
19	*Something Fresh/Something New*
66	*Spring Fever*
85	*Stiff Upper Lip, Jeeves*
42	*Summer Lightning*
58	*Summer Moonshine*
97	*Sunset at Blandings*
11	*The Swoop*
3	*Tales of St. Austin's*

A

(MTT = My thanks to)

A1. Frequent. First class, in excellent condition. Originally from the insurance classification of ships at Lloyd's of London. The letters A, B, C refer to the condition of the hull; the figures 1, 2, 3 describe its fittings and cargo. A2 meant the hull was sound but the fittings, cables, anchors, etc. were second-rate. Lloyd's introduced this classification back in 1777 and it was used in this sense until the First World War. In March 1916, military service was made compulsory in the UK, and the Army authorities adopted the same classification for their medical examination of the men coming forward. A1 meant a man was fit and healthy, C3 meant he was not fit/strong enough for army service. By transference, A1 came to mean someone felt fine, on top of the world, while C3 was used to describe someone useless at their job or someone who felt rotten. I am informed that the equivalent American service grading for recruits is 1A for those well suited down to 4F for those rejected on medical grounds.

Abbreviations. Frequent. Eggs and b. (eggs and bacon) 43 p15; f.c.f. (finely chiselled features) 52 p98; pure as the driven s. (driven snow) etc. PGW did not develop this use of abbreviation till well into the stories narrated by Bertie Wooster. However, he had noted the idea in his *Phrases & Notes* notebook back in 1905, when he referred to a friend, 'JEG': "Instead of saying 'All was joy, jollity and song', J.E.G. says 'all was j.j. and s.'."

Abby, Dear. 89 p119. US agony aunt (newspaper advice columnist) Abigail Van Buren 1950s-onwards. Her twin sister, Ann Landers, was agony aunt for a rival chain and syndicated in 1,000 US newspapers.

ABC shops. 4 p229 and often later. The Aerated Bread Company opened their tea-shops in London in 1861. They were an alternative to the chop-houses and taverns of the time and offered cheap meals and snacks (tea, coffee, buns and sandwiches etc.).

Abelard & Heloise. 94 p118. A famous *affaire d'amour* of 12th-century France that ended tragically. See any good literary encyclopaedia.

Abercrombie & Fitch/ Sir Abercombie Fitch. 45 p199; 65 p39; Sir Roderick Glossop's fictional locum 91 p169. A famous and expensive New York outfitters till the 1990s, the organisation has now become a retail clothing chain.

Abide our question. See OTHERS ABIDE OUR PLEASURE.

Abimilech begat Jazzbo and Jazzbo begat Zacharaiah. 55 p49. I regret to say that these words will not be found in the Bible's Book of Genesis, though many like them will.

Abney, Arnold. See Chap. 3.

Abou Ben Adhem, his name led all the rest, and others in Wodehouse "whose name led all the rest". Frequent from 25 p77 onwards. From Leigh Hunt's poem 'Abou Ben Adhem and the Angel': "Abou Ben Adhem (may his tribe increase!), / Awoke one night from a deep dream of peace … / And lo! Ben Adhem's name led all the rest."

About his bath and about his bed and spying out all his ways. See Spying.

Abraham. Press it to his bosom like Abraham 66 p176. B. Luke 16.22: "And it came to pass that the beggar died, and was carried by the angels into Abraham's bosom …"

Absalom. 48 p46; would have liked being bald 60 p223. B. 2 Samuel 18.9–15. Absalom, son of David, king of Israel, led a rebellion to become king in David's place. While riding through a wood, his long hair caught in the branches and pulled him off his mule. One of David's soldiers found him there helpless and killed him, despite David's orders that his son was not to be harmed.

Absence makes the heart grow fonder. 24 p139 and later. A line in the song 'Isle of Beauty' by Thomas Haynes Bayly (1797–1839). As the title of a popular song of 1900 by Gillespie and Dillea, the phrase became a familiar one, and two more songs with the same title came out in 1921 and 1929.

'Absent Treatment'. 23 p107. I understand this is a Christian Science term used for those occasions when a Christian Science practitioner cures somebody, though not actually present, by using Christian Science principles. MTT Bennett Quillen.

Absurd, as Euclid would say. 2 p172. When I learned geometry at school, 'Quid absurdum est' ('which is absurd') was the term used to describe a fallacy or erroneous conclusion. See also Euclid.

Abyssinia, apostolic claims of the Church of. 55 p246; 70 p157; 79 p88; 91 p175. Abyssinia became Christian in the 1st century A.D. but, because of the Islamic conquest of north Africa, it was cut off from European Christianity till the 19th century. During the intervening period, it developed certain rituals and practices that caused considerable disquiet in European ecclesiastical circles when it re-established contact. The validity of the ordination of Abyssinian clerics was a subject of heated discussion in the Church of England during PGW's youth. See Chap. 11.

Acacia Road, Dulwich. 14 p23. See Chap. 9.

Academy, at the. 23 p128 and jokes about it later, especially from Lancelot Mulliner ('The Story of Webster'). The Royal Academy of Arts, founded in 1768, is the oldest society in England devoted to the fine arts. In the late 19th century its painting classes had become stereotyped, and it was fashionable to mock its 'old-fashioned' techniques and teaching. Its exhibitions favoured portraits, landscapes or paintings that told a story ('The Emigrant's Farewell'), pointed a moral ('Love Locked Out') or depicted some scene of English life (Frith's 'Derby Day' etc.). This is why the New English Art Club (NEAC) was founded in opposition in 1886.

In 1892 an NEAC man became Professor of Art at London University and started to use 'live' (i.e. nude) models. Shock, horror at the Academy, but they were forced to do so as well. British art students no longer had to go to Paris to draw from life and we saw fewer books/plays in England about *la vie Bohème* in Paris with students falling in love with pretty, golden-hearted midinettes (see TRILBY). Emboldened by the success of the NEAC, new artistic Societies became the fashion. The last list I saw has some twenty, including such bodies as the British Society of Enamellers, the British Water-Colour Society, the Society of Women Artists, Society of Wildlife Artists and United Society of Artists.

Somewhere PGW writes of artists founding a new movement: 'The Five', 'The Seven' or some such title. This was his recollection of 'The Eight', a famous Greenwich Village group around 1910 or so. The founder was John Sloan (1871–1951), a self-taught painter who rejected European influences and 'traditional Art' and set out to establish 'modern' art in the USA. They were known colloquially as The Black Gang, Apostles of Ugliness or The Ash-Can School.

Accidents. Moving a. by flood and field 79 p144. S. *Othello* 1.3: "Wherein I spake of most disastrous chances, Of moving accidents by flood and field."

Accommodation for man and beast. 25 p89 and often later. Until 1914, this was a common advertisement on English country inns since many still travelled on horseback and drovers walked their cattle and sheep to market. Many inns in the North of England still have strips of land (usually car parks today) where the animals were kept overnight.

Accoutred as he was, he plunged in. 84 p59. S. *Julius Caesar* 1.2. "Upon the word, Accoutred as I was, I plunged in, And bade him follow."

Ace of Spades. 80 p154. In the 1920s, English thriller writers loved giving their villains names like this. One thriller by this name came out in 1919 and another in 1930. Wodehouse was parodying a fashion all his English readers recognised. See also SECRET NINE.

Achilles. 12 p89; his heel 18 p66 and later. He was the bravest of the Greeks in Homer's account of the siege of Troy. Because he had been dipped in the river Styx as a child, he could not be injured except in his heel, by which he was held during the river-dipping. He took offence easily, sulked in his tent instead of helping his Greek comrades, and was eventually killed by an arrow in his heel. "His/her Achilles' heel" became a standard expression for someone's weak point.

Ack emma. Frequent. 'Ack emma' and 'pip emma' are from the phonetic alphabet used by radio signallers in the First World War to denote A.M. and P.M. The phonetic alphabet then began 'Ack, Beer, Charlie'. The present commonly-used (NATO) phonetic alphabet (Alfa, Bravo, Charlie, Delta) is only about 50 years old.

Ackleton, Earl of. 25 p267. See Chap. 35.

Acre, battle of. 84 p84 and elsewhere. Acre was taken by Richard Coeur de Lion in 1191 during the Third Crusade. See also Joppa.

Across the pale parabola of joy. 32 p116. I believe this reflects PGW's view of the avant-garde poets of his time, especially Gertrude Stein (1874–1946). Her style of writing was "intended as a verbal counterpart to Cubism", which she claimed to have created, and "to liberate language and thinking from the bonds of convention". Her best-remembered lines are "Rose is a rose is a rose" and "Not enough can be enough and being enough quite enough is enough and being enough enough is enough and being enough it is that". Pale parabolas are child's play to that.

Act of God. Like an earthquake or waterspout or any other Act of God 63 p8. A dictionary definition is "a result of natural forces, unexpected and not preventable by human foresight". It came into popular usage in the UK with household insurance policies that would cover you for fire, burglary etc., but specifically excluded Acts of God (typhoons and earthquakes, which are rare in the UK). I have a vague memory of a law case some years ago when insurance companies were forced to drop the exclusion.

Acting of a dreadful thing and the first motion … nature of an insurrection. 64 p166. S. *Julius Caesar* 2.1. PGW gave us three long quotations on this page, two from *Julius Caesar* and one from S. *Henry V*.

Action then became, as it were, general. 51 p79. See Fighting became general.

Actium. Cleopatra's pep talk before the Battle of Actium 72 p71. In 31 B.C., Octavius fought Antony at Actium. PGW was referring to S. *Antony and Cleopatra* 3.7, where Cleopatra announced she would lead the Egyptian fleet to fight alongside Antony's fleet against Octavius.

Acts of kindness, unremembered, and of love. As done by Boy Scouts including, all too often, young blighted Edwin. 12 p244; 15A p179; 35 p21 and later. Baden-Powell set down the daily act of kindness as a rule for Boy Scouts, but the phrase comes from Wordsworth's 'Lines Composed above Tintern Abbey': "His little, nameless, unremembered acts, / Of kindness and of love." See also Little acts.

Adam, the old. Frequent. Memories of/desire to repeat the sins and indiscretions of youth. BCP. The Ministration of Publick Baptism of Infants has the words: "God grant that the old Adam in this child may be so buried, that the new man may be raised up in him."

Addams, Charles. Looked like something C.A. might have thought up 88 p63. This American cartoonist (1912–88) created the Addams family of ghouls for the *New Yorker*, and they are still to be seen on TV. One English newspaper ended Addams' obituary with: "He was thrice married. The third marriage took place in a pets' cemetery with Addams' dog Alice B. Cur as the only attendant. The bride wore black."

Adder, deaf. He could understand how those Old Testament snake charmers must have felt who tried to ingratiate themselves with the deaf adder and did not get to first base 91 p141-2; play it never so wisely 4 p118 and elsewhere. B. Psalms 58.4–5: "Their poison is like the poison of an adder; they are like the deaf adder that stoppeth her ear. Which will hearken not to the voice of charmers, charming never so wisely."

Adders. Bite like serpents and sting like adders 2 p171 and later. Wodehouse applied the term often to a headmaster's cane or home-brew beer. The latter references are particularly appropriate since B. Proverbs 23.31–32 inveighs against drinking too much with the words: "Look not thou upon the wine when it is red, when it giveth his colour in the cup, when it moveth itself aright. And at the last it biteth like a serpent and stingeth like an adder."

Addington. 33 p153 and elsewhere. See Chap. 27.

Ade, George. Quoted at 7 p129 ('The Fable of the Author Who Was Sorry for What He Did to Willie'); his *Fables* admired by Cloyster 9 p95. This American humorous writer and playwright (1866–1944) was famous for his use of American vernacular and slang, some of which he coined himself. 'Rubbernecking' is one of his. Wodehouse admired him and Ring Lardner for "writing the way Americans spoke". It was Ade who began the fashion of musical comedies based on Americans getting into embarrassing situations in foreign countries. See also MARTINIS and THIRTY CENTS.

Adieu, he cried and waved his lily hand. 79 p27. From John Gay's 'Sweet William's Farewell to Black-Eyed Susan': "Adieu, she cries! and wav'd her lily hand."

Admirable Bashville, in Bernard Shaw's phrase he was total gules. 90 p182. Shaw's play *The Admirable Bashville* came out in 1901. 'Total gules' (red) is from S. *Hamlet* 2.2. describing the death of Pyrrhus: "Head to foot, Now he is total gules."

Admonish a congregation. When you admonish a congregation, it stays admonished 61 p148. BCP. The Publick Baptism of Infants begins: "The people are to be admonished."

Adonis. 21 p25. A young man in Greek mythology who was too good-looking for his own good.

Adullam. Hosea addressing the people of A. 61 p154. See HOSEA.

Adventure of the Five Orange Pips. 92 p132. See FIVE ORANGE PIPS.

Adventure of the Maharajah's Ruby. 22 p1; Adventure of the Wand of Death 19 p9. PGW's *The Luck Stone* was on the same lines. See GREEN EYE.

Adventure of the Ship's Bore. 30 Dedication. See Chap. 17.

Aeneid. Quoted 3 p4 & p240. After Caesar's *Gallic Wars*, Virgil's *Aeneid* used to be the most commonly taught Latin text in English schools.

Aequam memento rebus in arduis servare mentem, Horace's. 29 p275; 63 p134 and later. From Horace's *Odes* 2.3.1. Wodehouse's translation in *The Girl on the Boat* is as accurate as you can get. ("Take my tip, preserve an unruffled mind in every crisis.")

Aeroplanes. See Chap. 17.

Aeschylus is a demon. 3 p240; 4 p232; tells Euripides that you can't beat inevitability 67 p154. After fighting at Marathon, Salamis and Plataea, Aeschylus (525–456 B.C.) went on to write some ninety tragedies and was the first to introduce two characters on stage. Wodehouse's description reflects the difficulty he had had with him at Dulwich. Aeschylus' style was obscure and he is generally considered to be the most difficult of Greek writers.

After you, my dear Alphonse. "After you, my dear Alphonse" was a catchphrase, and a song, from F.B. Opper's (US) cartoon strip 'Gaston & Alphonse', which began in 1902. In 1922, when George Grossmith (see Chap. 13) and PGW were in New York working on their next show, *The Cabaret Girl*, with Jerome Kern, the Ziegfeld Follies show had two famous comedians (Gallagher and Shean) singing: "Positively, Mr Gallagher." "Absolutely, Mr Shean." PGW and Grossmith put it into *The Cabaret Girl* as "After you, Mr Gravvins." "No, after you, Mr Gripps." MTT Neil Midkiff.

Agag. A blow that landed like Agag among butterflies 9 p124; descended the stairs mincingly like Agag 67 p126. B. 1 Samuel 15.32: "And Agag came unto him delicately, And Agag said, surely the bitterness of death is past."

Agamemnon. Watchman in A. who whistled 3 p41 & p237; 4 p232. The watchman in Aeschylus' *Agamemnon* opens the play by telling the audience what is going on and concludes with the words: "I try to whistle or hum to ease the hours."

Age of miracles had returned. 12 p297. S. *All's Well That Ends Well* 2.3: "They say miracles are past."

Age or sex. Sparing neither/irrespective of/regardless of a. or s. 39 p205 and often later. The only source I can find for this phrase is in history books where it is often used to describe massacres. Thus, an account of the Sicilian Vespers uprising of 30 March 1282 says that the Sicilians rose against the Normans who ruled the island and "put them to the sword without regard to age or sex".

Aged man a-sitting on a gate, I saw an. 3 p 166. The White Knight's poem 'The Aged, Aged Man' in Lewis Carroll's *Alice Through the Looking-Glass*.

Aged Parent. 60 p100. In D. *Great Expectations*, Mr Wemmick always referred to his father by this term. MTT David McDonough. See also CHARLES, HIS FRIEND.

Agesilaus. 14 p107. A brave king of Sparta, died 362 B.C.

Agincourt, battle of. "So had an Emsworth advanced on the foe at Agincourt" 42 p298 (though he had also taken cover there — see 53 p47); a Sieur de Wooster fought with vim there 52 p22 and later. Many English families are proud of an ancestor who fought at Agincourt (1415, we walloped the French — see S. *Henry V* for a dramatic account), including the Wodehouse family. Their coat of arms has the motto 'Agincourt', granted to them by Henry V with the knighthood he gave to John Wodehouse for his valour on that day. PGW may have written lightly of such things, but occasionally his pride in his own forebears comes through. My favourite of such references is at 60 p130, where

Lord Ickenham dismisses Pongo's suggestion they should clear out by proudly reviewing the family involvement at Crécy, Agincourt, Blenheim, Malplaquet and Waterloo, finishing with the inspiring words: "We Twistletons do not clear out, my boy. We stick around, generally long after we have outstayed our welcome." See also Chap. 2.

Agley ... the way things have ganged. See MICE AND MEN.

Agonizing reappraisal. 84 p191; 86 p187. PGW picked up this cliché very quickly. From memory, it came into use around 1955–58 and 'after an agonizing reappraisal' became a common phrase among UK politicians explaining why they could not keep election pledges. It had become a cliché in the 1960s and '70s in Whitehall, where I cut it out of the drafts of my senior officers' speeches whenever I saw it, but they always put it back.

Agony, a strong smoker in his. See STRONG SMOKER.

Agony had/has abated. 21 p50 and frequent later up to PGW's last book. The phrase originated with Thomas Babington Macaulay (1800–59), one of the intellectual giants of the 19th century. He is said to have learned Latin at the age of four and Greek at the age of five. Having banged his head or bruised his leg when he was four years old, he was asked by a lady if it still hurt. He replied: "Thank you, Ma'am. The agony is abated." The phrase dug itself into the intellectual consciousness of Britain and agony *always* abated until about 1970. Among the older age group (mine), it still does.

'Ahead of Schedule'. 18 p217. Common phrase in the UK when a train arrives early.

A-hunting we will go, pom pom. 68 p60. Traditional hunting song, now thought to have been written by Henry Fielding (1707–54), though five more with the same title were published between 1911 and 1937.

Aid and comfort, to lend him. 34 p108; 52 p167 and later. The only source I know for this phrase is the definition in English law for treason which, amongst other categories, used to include "giving aid and comfort to the enemy in time of war". I think it became well known during the Boer War (1899–1902) when some firms were accused of trading with the Boers.

Aid of the party. 4 p273 and later. See NOW IS THE TIME.

Aim to please, we. 20 p23 and later. Cliché commonly used as actors took their bow. A possible origin is S. *Twelfth Night*, last line: "our play is done, And we'll strive to please you every day."

Ainus, Hairy (at the White City). 18 p63. A party of Ainus, aboriginal inhabitants of Japan, were a big attraction at the White City Exhibition (London) in 1908. They were indeed notable for their hirsute growth.

Airy light, as the poet Milton so beautifully puts it. 41 p29. Milton's *Paradise Lost* has: "When Adam wak't, so custom'd, for his sleep was airy light."

Airy nothing a local habitation and a name, giving. 72 p27. S. *Midsummer Night's Dream* 5.1: "the poet's pen Turns them to shapes, and gives to airy nothing, A local habitation and a name."

Aix to Ghent, good news from. See GOOD NEWS.

Ajax defying the lightning. 18 p169; 42 p222. A famous statue, based on the legend of Ajax, the Greek hero who, at the siege of Troy, boasted that even the gods could not kill him. Jupiter's bolts of lightning didn't, but Neptune's storm at sea did.

Alarm and despondency. Causing a. and d. 34 p 13 and later. This phrase from the (British) Army Act came into popular use during World War I when almost every young man went into uniform. As well as the normal criminal law, soldiers are subject to the Army Act, which has to be passed by Parliament every year and covers military offences. It was, and probably still is, an offence in the Army to "spread alarm and despondency". *The Manual of Military Law* has illustrative examples to describe each offence. My favourite was that given for "disobeying a lawful order". If memory serves, it was on the lines of: "In that he, Private —— at —— Barracks, on —— (date), when ordered to pick up his rifle by a superior officer, refused to do so and threw his belt to the ground, saying as he did so: 'You may say what you please. I will soldier no more', or words to that effect."

I have always thought this use of "or words to that effect" one of the finest euphemisms in the language. See also WORDS TO THAT EFFECT.

Alas, poor Phipps. 70 p99. S. *Hamlet* 5.1: "Alas, poor Yorick. I knew him, Horatio." As this is, alphabetically, one of the first of the quotes from *Hamlet* I have found in PGW, it seems appropriate to mention the observation made by my wife Charlotte years ago. An enthusiastic crossword-solver with a remarkable knowledge of English literature, she said once that half the quotations people use in Britain seem to come from Hamlet — and half of those are from the 'To be or not to be' speech. Having now worked my way through PGW's usages, I reckon she wasn't exaggerating. See also FELLOW OF INFINITE JEST.

Alastor. Like A. on the long Chorasmian shore, he paused 34 p222; a sombre figure like Shelley's A. 86 p124. SHELLEY's poem 'Alastor': "At length upon the lone Chorasmian shore, he paused."

Albany, the. 18 p20. Bill Bates lives here, as does Freddie Rooke in 26. This elegant 18th-century building in Piccadilly was divided into apartments in 1802. It is still one of London's smartest addresses.

Albert Hall. 41 p179; falling on the Crystal Palace 43 p193. This enormous building in London, completed in 1870, was built from the profits of the Great Exhibition of 1851. Someone once said of it (very accurately, in my opinion) that it looked like 'a Christmas pudding that has not properly set.' My own favourite description is attributed to Queen Victoria, who said its appearance reminded her of the British Constitution. It took me a long time to work it out, but I think she was right. See also CRYSTAL PALACE.

Alcala. See 'IN ALCALA'.

Alcatraz. 70 p21. This famous prison on an island in San Francisco Bay opened in 1934 and closed in 1963.

Aldermaston. We march from A., protesting like a ton of bricks 88 p121. In the 1960s, the annual march by British anti-nuclear protesters from Aldermaston (a nuclear plant) to London was a regular feature of the Easter holiday.

Aldershot. 1 p13; 6 p57; 8 p116. Aldershot, an army garrison town 35 miles west of London, was the headquarters of the APTC (Army Physical Training Corps) and hosted the Public Schools boxing championships for many years. PGW reported on them several times for *The Captain* magazine (see Chap. 4). From about 1870, most English public schools had a voluntary Army cadet corps who received basic military training from retired sergeant-majors. The annual camp at Aldershot was the culmination of the training year.

Aldwych Site. 11 p55. The demolition of many old streets to create today's Kingsway and Aldwych was central London's biggest re-building project of the period. It lasted from 1900 to 1905, and Londoners became thoroughly fed up with it. The last office buildings along Kingsway were not completed till 1916.

Alexander. Like A. you have no more worlds to conquer 28 p113. From a comment by the historian Plutarch that, when told by an astronomer there were many worlds other than this, Alexander the Great (356–323 B.C.) had wept because he had not conquered even one. Somehow, probably from a bad translation, historians came to believe Alexander had wept because there were no more worlds for him to conquer and the phrase became popular.

Alexander of the *Times*. 26 p267. Another topical reference. The dramatic critic of the *New York Times* at the time was Alexander Woollcott (1887–1943), probably best remembered today as being the original of Sheridan Whiteside of *The Man Who Came to Dinner*. The 1939 play by Kaufman and Hart became a successful 1942 film with Monty Woolley playing the main role. After his initial fury, Woollcott forgave Kaufman and Hart and played the part himself on tour for a period.

Like Cole Porter's *Anything Goes*, the play is full of topical references which mean little today. Woollcott, Kaufman and Hart were all habitués of the Algonquin Round Table, and other characters in *The Man Who Came to Dinner* were allegedly based on Dorothy Parker, Gertrude Lawrence and Noel Coward. 'Banjo' was certainly based on Harpo Marx, who appeared in the West Coast production. In an essay, 'Colossal Bronze', Woollcott expressed his appreciation of the hospitality he had received when visiting Leonora Wodehouse and her husband.

Alexander's Ragtime Band. 22 p87. First big hit (1911) by Irving Berlin. Alexander was real enough, a cornet player and bandleader, and Berlin had written a song about him, 'Alexander and His Clarinet', the previous year. For the sequels that quickly followed, See Chap. 36.

Alger, Horatio. 67 p55. Horatio Alger (1834–99) wrote hundreds of stories of poor, honest American boys who worked hard, won through and became rich, famous and respected by all. In Britain we had Samuel Smiles doing the same thing. See SMILES.

Alice Blue Gown. 58 p175. This popular song comes from the show *Irene* (1919). 'Alice' was President Theodore Roosevelt's daughter, who always liked to wear blue and made 'Alice Blue' the fashionable colour of the day.

***Alice in Wonderland* (and the Mad Hatter's Tea party) is nothing to what happens in musical comedy.** 26 p222. See *ALICE THROUGH THE LOOKING-GLASS*.

Alice through the Looking-Glass. 14 p30. Lewis Carroll's two immortal Alice stories need no introduction. If you have not read them, I advise you to do so. Otherwise you will miss a lot of Wodehouse allusions — as well as a landmark of English literature. At 48 p255 Soup Slattery finds the White Rabbit somewhat perplexing, but no doubt he worked it out in due course. (Note. The title of the book is *Through the Looking-Glass* but, like everybody else, PGW used the *Alice* prefix to make the reference clear.)

All but he had fled. 65 p 187. See 'CASABIANCA'.

All Clear blown. 53 p125; 59 p61 and elsewhere. In the First and Second World Wars, when Britain was being bombed, the signal to show an air raid was over was the 'All Clear' on the sirens, a long single note.

All dressed up and nowhere to go. 34 p163 and later. The popular 1913 song 'When You're All Dressed Up and No Place to Go' became even more well known when William White applied it to the short-lived Progressive Party in the USA in 1916.

All flesh is as grass. Often in Wodehouse, i.e. we are all mortal. B.1 Peter 1.24: "For all flesh is as grass, and all the glory of man as the flower of grass. The grass withereth, and the flower thereof falleth away."

All God's chillun got conferences out there. 54 p176. Lottie Blossom is paraphrasing the title of Eugene O'Neill's play *All God's Chillun Got Wings* (named from the Negro spiritual 'All God's Children Got Wings'), which caused a sensation in New York in 1924. The song 'All God's Chillun Got Rhythm' did not come out till 1937, two years after PGW's book. In his autobiography, George Grossmith Jnr (see Chap. 13), who worked in Hollywood in 1930, noticed the same phenomenon Wodehouse did. Grossmith was struck by the apparently rigid rule that nobody he wanted to speak to was ever just away somewhere, on holiday, at lunch or taking the afternoon off. They were always, always "in conference".

All he knew or cared to know. 26 p147. Keats' 'Ode on a Grecian Urn': "Beauty is truth, truth beauty,—that is all / Ye knew on earth, and all ye need to know."

All is for the best in the best of all possible worlds. 13 p175 and later. At 90 p149 PGW gives us the variation 'Everything's all right in the all-rightest of all possible worlds'. From Voltaire's *Candide*, chap. 30.

All men are brothers. 87 p130. Despite Wellbeloved's assurance, I have not found these exact words in the Bible. The French cleric François Fenelon wrote that "all men are brothers and ought to love each other". MTT Neil Midkiff for suggesting 'alle menschen warden Bruder' in the finale of Beethoven's Ninth

Symphony.

All men are created equal etc. etc. 26 p144. From the American Declaration of Independence.

All Nature smiled. 2 p211 and later. A popular phrase, probably a newspaper cliché for decent weather at cricket matches/ regattas/ tennis tournaments. I prefer the splendid line in Fielding's *Tom Thumb the Great*: "All Nature wears one universal grin."

All Quiet on the Western Front. 55 p163. Erich Marie Remarque's novel of the First World War led to a magnificent, if noisy, film in 1930.

All quiet (once more) along the Potomac. 27 p279 and later. This well-known American song comes from that period in the American Civil War (Nov 1861–Nov 1862) when George McClellan commanded the (Northern) Army of the Potomac. A cautious general, he was content to guard Washington rather than go on the offensive. His daily reports that "all was quiet along the Potomac" became famous and led Ethel Beers (1827–79) to write the words of this sad song.

All that's beautiful drifts away like the waters. 58 p146. From Yeats' 'Old Men Admiring Themselves in the Water'.

All the air a solemn stillness holds. 7 p183 and later. The second verse of Gray's 'Elegy in a Country Churchyard' begins: "Now fades the glimmering landscape on the sight, / And all the air a solemn stillness holds."

All the ills the flesh is heir to. 3 p196. S. *Hamlet* 3.1: "and the thousand natural shocks That flesh is heir to, 'tis a consummation devoutly to be wished."

All the world loves a lover. 63 p177. 1912 song or Emerson's 'All mankind love a lover'.

All the world to me, because he's. 42 p315. Sue Brown says this is how she regards Ronnie Fish and adds: "It's like something out of a song, isn't it?" She and PGW clearly had in mind Stephen Foster's 'She Was All the World to Me'.

All things to all men, (a barmaid has to be). 62 p86. B. 1 Corinthians 9.22: "I am made all things to all men, that I might by all means save some."

All things work together for good. 22 p194 and later. B. Romans 8.28: "All things work together for good to them that love God"; and T. 'Sea Dreams': "All things work together for the good of those …"

All today the slow, sleek ripples bear up shoreward, etc. etc. 37 p238. From Swinburne's 'A Word with the Wind'.

All wool and a yard wide. 26 p27. A general expression of approval. Nineteenth-century advertisement of woollen mills, i.e. their material was real wool and they gave good measure.

Allan, Maud. See SALOME DANCE.

All-down-set-'em-up-in-the-other-alley. 27 p273. In Britain, skittles are free-standing. After a player has had his three goes, someone has to go and set the skittles up again. On a fairground, this is what the barker would shout.

Allegorical pictures. If a Glasgow millionaire mayn't buy Sellers' allegorical pictures, whose allegorical pictures may he buy? 18 p19. G&S *Ruddigore* Act II: "[I]f a man can't forge his own will, whose will can forge? … if I can't disinherit my own unborn son, whose unborn son can I disinherit?" MTT Neil Midkiff.

Allez-oop/Allay-oop. 42 p235; 65 p224. I do not know if the phrase is used in America, but in circuses and variety acts in the UK, acrobats and trapeze artistes were often foreign and shouted their instructions to each other in French. MTT Agathe Muzerelle for the information that the terms are 'Allez Hop!' or 'Et hop!' with the 'hop!' being the executive word of command. The comic strip of this name came much later.

All-hands-to-the-pumps panics. 52 p279. A term that goes back to the old sailing ship days. If water got into the lower decks and the ship started to lose its stability, it was a case of all hands to man the pumps.

All's right with the world. 19 p23; 22 p25 and later. See GOD'S IN HIS HEAVEN.

All's well, Jeeves. 31 p51. See TEN O'CLOCK.

All's well that ends well. 8 p37; 52 p311. S. *All's Well That Ends Well.*

Ally Pally. Doing anything at Ally Pally? 45 p235. There was until 1970 a racecourse at the Alexandra Palace ('Ally Pally'), a Victorian landmark in north London.

Alone at last. Young Thos. being watched by Bingo 43 p26. Take your choice from G&S's *Patience*, the 1915 musical comedy *Alone at Last,* the song 'Alone at Last' from the show, a 1925 song by Gus Kahn, or maybe the song Jerome Kern wrote in 1913 for *Oh, I Say!*. Do not confuse with the once-popular American song 'There Are Moments When One Wants to Be Alone', which I am sure PGW used somewhere but cannot find. The examples given in the song included the aftermath of smoking one's first cigar, returning home after losing the housekeeping money at poker, and attending an elegant dance at which your new dress trousers split up the back.

Alpha separators (and Holstein butter-churner attachment). 40 p139; 47 p147. I have no definite source, but I am prepared to bet that PGW found them in an agricultural machinery catalogue belonging to his friend Charles le Strange, an enthusiastic dairy farmer. See Chap. 40.

Alphonse. After you, my dear A. 18 p60. See AFTER YOU.

Alphonso. 25 p130; A. who for cool assurance licks (4 lines) 29 p72; 79 p111. From Gilbert's 'The Modest Couple' in *More Bab Ballads*. The Alphonso references may be obscure to us, but PGW and his generation knew Gilbert & Sullivan and Gilbert's *Bab Ballads* by heart. People quote Homer Simpson just as readily today and expect the reference to be recognised.

Alpine hat. The blue alpine hat with a pink feather in it 85 p16. See Chap. 18.

Always Listen to Mother, Girls. 31 p201. Probably from the popular US song 'Always Take Mother's Advice' by Jenny Lindsay (1885). Two lines give a flavour of it: "Always take mother's advice, she knows what is best for your good; Let her kind words then suffice, and always take mother's advice."

Always Look on the Bright Side. 21 p90. 1855 song 'Look on the Bright Side of Life' by J. Simmonds. The song with the same title by J. Gallatly was not written till 1929.

Always merry and bright. 18 p219 and later. Lugubrious song sung by a character in the 1909 musical *The Arcadians*: "I've got a motter, Always merry and bright."

Amalekite (and a Jebusite). Janet Yorke is one 53 p43. B. 1 Samuel 15.7 & Exodus 33.2 make it clear these peoples were enemies of the godly and suffered accordingly.

Amaryllis. Sporting with A. in the shade 18 p25 and later. Milton's 'Lycidas', line 69: "Were it not better done, as others use, / To sport with Amaryllis in the shade."

Amateur Cracksman, Hornung's. 4 p30. In contrast to his brother-in-law Conan Doyle, who created the most popular fictional detective-hero of the day, E.W. Hornung (1866–1921) created the criminal-hero Raffles in *The Amateur Cracksman* in 1899. He started a craze for 'Raffles-type' plays/books. See first page of *A Gentleman of Leisure*.

Amber drawing room. 25 p8. Belpher Castle has one as well as Blandings later. I do not know enough about interior design to say when these became the fashion. Many English Stately Homes were re-designed in the early 19th century, following George IV's enthusiastic patronage of the arts (Brighton Pavilion, Windsor Castle etc.), and I suggest the owners of Belpher and Blandings may have wanted to emulate the famous Amber Room in Tsarskoe Selo, Catherine the Great's palace at St Petersburg. MTT Jean Archibald.

Amen, sound of a great. See SOUND OF A GREAT AMEN.

***America, I Like You*.** Book title. As Wodehouse said, he got the idea from the song 'America, I Love You' (1915) by Kalmar and Ruby.

American youth was emigrating to Paris, the flower of. 77 p28. While many in the 1920s came to study art, many more came to escape Prohibition.

Amok. Malays run amok, Vikings go berserk 34 p104; 42 p123. The Malayan word 'amok' came into the English language late (late 19th-century British Empire), and the Viking term 'berserk' was also new (see BERSERK below). I assume that is why PGW used both since one on its own would be too obscure. See also TURPIN, DICK and JAMES, JESSE.

Among those present. 14 p120 and often later. Bertie Wooster and others use the phrase 'merely among those present' when describing scenes when they are just spectators or ignored by everybody else. This once-universal cliché, which PGW used so well, stems from English newspaper reports of social events and the distinction they made between the important personages attending and those of less consequence. "His Royal Highness was greeted by the President, the Duke of X , Lord A, Lady B and Alderman Y. Also among those present were officers of the institution and their ladies, representatives of local organisations and …"

Amuse, elevate and instruct. 13 p21 and later. After 10 years, by pure accident, I found an old press cutting which said that "to elevate, instruct and amuse" was the motto of *Tit-Bits* magazine, launched in 1881. *Tit-Bits* was the foundation of the Newnes publishing empire and PGW wrote two pieces for it in 1900 and 1902. See Chap. 7.

Amused, we are not. See WE ARE NOT AMUSED.

Amy, once you're kissed by. See ONCE YOU'RE KISSED.

Anaconda (mine). 44 p176. By 1927 the Anaconda Copper Mining Co. of Butte, Montana, had become the world's largest non-ferrous metals company.

Ananias & Sapphira. 66 p162. B. Acts 5.1–5.10. Ananias and his wife Sapphira died because they told a lie.

Anatole. See Chap. 37.

Anaximander held the infinite as primary cause of all things. 9 p15. Greek philosopher, died 547 B.C.

Ancient Mariner — "held me with a glittering eye". 6 p247 and often up to 84. In Samuel Taylor Coleridge's *The Rime of the Ancient Mariner*, the Ancient Mariner accosts a wedding guest and, holding him with a glittering eye, tells him the very long sad story of his punishment for shooting an albatross. Similar to the Oldest Member or Mr Mulliner, he is not to be stopped. The best-known line in Coleridge's poem is: "Water, water everywhere. Nor any drop to drink."

And soon you will find that the sun and the wind … (four lines). 7 p176. See CAMEELIOUS HUMP.

And when they buried him, the little port had seldom seen a costlier funeral. 69 p89. It is easy to see why these last two lines of TENNYSON's 'Enoch Arden' stuck in PGW's mind. The metre is wrong, the length is wrong, and they don't rhyme.

Anderson's (detective agency). 21 p224. Up to 1914, the more reputable London inquiry agencies were run by retired policemen. I was not a bit surprised to find that Robert Anderson had been the head of criminal investigation at Scotland Yard in the 1890s.

Andromeda (& Perseus). 13 p188 and later. In Greek mythology, Perseus killed the sea monster about to devour Andromeda, whom he won as his wife.

Angel, ministering. 18 p96 and later. See WOMAN IN OUR HOURS.

Angel with the flaming sword stood between them. 24 p73; 64 p177. B. Genesis 3.24: "So he drove out the man; and he placed at the east of the garden of Eden cherubims, and a flaming sword which turned every way, to keep the way of the tree of life."

Angela, swept off her feet by a sheikh. 37 p214. See SHEIKH.

Angels and ministers of grace defend us. 86 p132; 96 p103. S. *Hamlet* 1.4.

Anger, more in sorrow than in. See MORE IN SORROW.

Angry Cheese, the. 36 p29. A nightclub in Panton Street, London. See Chap. 21.

Angry passions. Never let your a. p. rise 3 p22. See PASSIONS.

Angry young man was all the go nowadays, the. 81 p149; 88 p11. Although the term has been traced to Leslie Paul's 1951 autobiography, John Osborne acquired the soubriquet of 'Angry Young Man' when he brought out his 'kitchen-sink' play *Look Back in Anger* in 1956. Somerset Maugham had no time for such writers: "Charity, kindness, generosity are qualities they hold in contempt." Kingsley Amis, who had been one of them, wrote, years later, how useful the term had been for publicity purposes and added: "One morning the whole shooting match just softly and silently vanished away and there we all were, reduced to being judged on our merits again."

Anne, Sister. Scan the horizon like Sister Anne 50 p177. "Anne, sister Anne, do you see anybody coming?" Spoken by Fatima, one of Bluebeard's many wives. See Bluebeard.

Annie Doesn't Live Here Anymore. 91 p101. Popular song (1933) by Young, Burke and Spina.

Annie Laurie. 29 p92 and elsewhere. This song, words by William Douglas (1672–1748), was set to music by Lady John Scott in 1838.

Annie Oakley. 80 p10. This sharpshooter (1860–1926), one of the stars of the famous Buffalo Bill's *Wild West Show*, entranced America and Europe with her remarkable skill. The name was later used for free theatre passes which had holes punched in them to show how often they were used. This stemmed from her trick of putting half a dozen holes in a playing card as it fell to the ground.

Annoy. Only does it to a. because he/it knows it teases 5 p38 and elsewhere. See Only does it to annoy.

Another one along in a minute, There'll be (poet/ wife/ fiancée/ scriptwriter). 32 p109; 37 p56; 57 p104 and later. In London, bus conductors or drivers whose bus is full *always* reassure those left behind with "There'll be another one along in a minute".

Anschluss. Two buns forming a solid a. 62 p157. Although the term is usually used for the German takeover of Austria in March 1938, PGW was using it in the strict dictionary sense, a joining together of two things, a coagulation.

Anstey, F. 8 p113. This popular author (real name Thomas Anstey Guthrie [1856–1934]) wrote *Vice Versa* and the letters of Mr. Jabberjee.

Answer, soft. Frequent. B. Proverbs 15.1. A soft answer turneth away wrath (but grievous words stir up anger). See Soft word.

***Antelope*, S.S.** 48 p206. Steam Packet to St Rocque. See Chap. 17.

Ante-post betting (no good, always stick to S.P). 31 p153. Horse-racing phrase. Best to wait to put a bet on a horse at S.P. (starting price), i.e. when it is about to run. Betting before then (ante-post betting) has the risk the horse can be withdrawn.

Anthropophagi, and men whose heads do grow beneath their shoulders. 29 p266. S. *Othello* 1.3: "It was my hint to speak … of the Cannibals that each other eat, The Anthopophagi, and men whose heads Do grow beneath their shoulders. This to hear Would Desdemona seriously incline." PGW quoted from this play often, either as in this sense, to have someone impressing a girl with his stories of adventure, or to express the jealousy of a lover for a rival, who was often the blameless Bertie Wooster.

Antic hay. How those large flat feet would spurn the antic hay 63 p115; 72 p14. From Marlowe's *Edward II* 1.1.59: "Shall with their goat feet dance an antic hay."

Antique shop in the Brompton Road, just past the Oratory (where antique silver cow-creamers can be bought or sneered at). 59 p12. See COW CREAMER.

Antony, Marc. See ORATOR.

Ants in the pants. 82 p135. From the 1934 song 'I Can't Dance, I Got Ants in My Pants'. MTT Murray Hedgcock.

Anything Goes was her motto. 60 p184; 65 p44. A reference to the famous song 'Anything Goes' in the 1934 Cole Porter show of the same name for which PGW and Bolton wrote the original book. For those who do not know it, the tenor of the song is that, nowadays, the old restrictions on bad behaviour no longer apply; people do whatever they want.

Apes, ivory and peacocks, laden with. 65 p179; 82 p123. B. 1 Kings 10.22; also 'Cargoes' by John Masefield. The former has Solomon's ships bringing him "gold and silver, ivory, and apes, and peacocks." See also CAMELS.

Apollo (i.e. handsome chap). 27 p22. Handsome Greek deity renowned for his amorous adventures.

Apollonius Rhodus. 3 p252. A poet, 3rd century B.C., third librarian of the great library at Alexandria.

Apollyon straddling right across the way. 13 p198 and frequent later. From Bunyan's *Pilgrim's Progress*. A monster clothed in scales like a fish, wings like a dragon, feet like a bear "and out of his belly came fire and smoke".

Aposiopesis. 9 p130; 30 p304. A sudden breaking off in the middle of a sentence; Virgil used it often in the *Aeneid.* See also SYLLEPSIS.

Appetite grows by what it feeds on. 66 p 113; 67 p231. Choose from either Rabelais' *Gargantua* — "The appetite grows by eating" — or S. *Hamlet* 1.2 — "Why, she would hang on him, As if increase of appetite had grown By what it fed on …"

Apple of his eye, the. Frequent. B. Deuteronomy 32.10: "he led him about, he instructed him, he kept him as the apple of his eye."

Apples. Chaps who shoot a. off their son's heads 57 p47. The William Tell legend. See PGW's *William Tell Told Again*.

Aquitania, S.S. 74 p192. See Chap. 17.

Arab steed, his. 40 p281 and later. Caroline Norton's (1808–77) poem 'The Arab's Farewell to His Steed' was set to music and became a popular song in 1890.

Arab tent. Folded up like an Arab tent 44 p307; folded its tents like the Arabs and silently stolen away 76 p138. Longfellow's 'The Day Is Done': "And the cares, that infest the day / Shall fold their tents, like the Arabs, / And as silently steal away."

Arabian Night adventure, New. 9 p61. See NEW ARABIAN NIGHT.

Arabs, who paused to fold their tents before silently stealing away. 60 p241. See ARAB TENT.

Aram, Eugene. 6 p234 and later. Thomas Hood's poem 'The Dream of Eugene Aram' was based on a teacher and noted philologist of that name who was hanged for murder in 1759. At 35 p23, Bertie Wooster quotes the line: "I slew him, tum-tum tum!" I regret I cannot find the words 'I slew' or anything like them in the poem. At 64 p61, Bertie gives us 'Ti-tum-ti-tum ti-tumty tum, ti-tumty tumty mist (I think it's mist), and Eugene Aram walked between, with gyves upon his wrist.' The last verse of Hood's poem reads:

> Two stern-faced men set out from Lynn,
> Through the cold and heavy mist:
> And Eugene Aram walked between,
> With gyves upon his wrist.

Arbiter elegantiarum. 34 p10 and later. A judge of good taste. Roman historian Tacitus so described Petronius in his *Annals* 16.18.

Arbuckle. 25 p32; as good as A. 27 p237. A fat chap. Roscoe 'Fatty' Arbuckle (1887–1933) was a popular rotund silent screen comedian.

Arcadia/Arcady, had once dwelt in. 19 p180 and later. The phrase 'Et in Arcadia ego', which comes from an inscription on a tomb in a painting by Guercino c.1623, became popular in the 19th century. Its English translation — "I too, have dwelt in Arcady" — came to mean the speaker had had a happy youth and once enjoyed life to the full. Arcady, a region of ancient Greece, was renowned for the general contentment of its inhabitants.

Archibald the All Right. 7 p135. G&S. *Patience*, Act 1: "Yes, I am the Apostle of Simplicity. I am called 'Archibald the All-Right' — for I am infallible."

Archilochus. 29 p127. As PGW said, Archilochus is credited with devising the iambic metre about 685 B.C.

Archimedes (and "Eureka"). 48 p31 and elsewhere, including the repetition of references at 59 p116, p122, p234 and p279 which, as Kristin Thompson has pointed out, add to the humour. (See also CHILDE ROLAND.) Mathematician and inventor, Archimedes discovered the principle of displacement in his bath and shouted "Eureka!" (roughly, "I've got it!"). As PGW tells us, he was killed by a common soldier in 212 B.C.

Architecture/Art, didn't know much about. See DIDN'T KNOW MUCH ABOUT.

Arden, Elizabeth (face cream). 94 p51. This lady (1878–1966) revolutionised the American cosmetics industry, introducing mascara and lipstick matched to clothing. Born Florence Nightingale Graham, she came from a small Canadian homestead where toothbrushes were rare and deodorants didn't exist. She believed the success of her business came from the desire of women for glamour, aroused by nickelodeons and romantic novels. She and Helena Rubinstein were rivals in the cosmetics business until Rubinstein died in 1965. It was said it was the only time Arden didn't mind Rubinstein getting ahead of her.

Are there any more at home like you? 95 p167. See FLORODORA.

Are we not beasts that perish, and is not our little life rounded by sleep. 1 p106. I could be wrong, but the first half seems to be from the Bible, Psalm 49: "like the beasts that perish"; the second from Shakespeare's *Tempest* 4.1: "We are such stuff As dreams are made on, and our little life Is rounded with a sleep."

"Are you with me, Mr Beamish?" "I precede you, Mr Garroway". 38 last line. From F.B. Opper's cartoon strip 'Alphonse and Gaston'. See AFTER YOU.

Argentines and the Portuguese and the Greeks, The. 36 p106; chap who looked like 77 p39, p114 & p143. Song title. In the 1920s the big spenders in Europe were Argentinian, Portuguese and Greek millionaires who had made fortunes in the War; their lavish spending was commemorated in the song sung by the Duncan Sisters. Wodehouse's friend Charles Graves wrote of their arrival on the Society scene in *And the Greeks* (1930), to which PGW wrote the Introduction. The three references in *French Leave* are there because PGW clearly had Deauville (France) in mind. Deauville is 'Roville' in the book (see Chap. 20), and as Charles Graves makes clear, it was at Deauville and other French resorts that the Argentine, Portuguese and Greek millionaires first appeared on the social scene.

Argo, the Dexter A. See DEXTER ARGO.

Argos. Reunion of Ulysses and hound Argos 12 p244; 21 p192. See ULYSSES AT ITHACA.

Argumentum ad hominem. 78 (UK) p10. A term in logic used to describe an argument calculated to appeal to the person addressed. There is also argumentum ad baculum/ crumenam/ ignorantiam/ populum and verecundiam. (Appealing to force/ to one's pocket/ to the listener's ignorance/ to popular opinion/ to the listener's modesty.)

Ariadne (and Theseus). 41 p211; Ariadne in Naxos 24 p16. Ariadne was the girl who saved Theseus from the Minotaur. He married her as he promised, but then abandoned her, pregnant, on the island of Naxos. Ariadne in Naxos was a very popular subject of paintings in the late Victorian period; probably the best known is that by G.F. Watts c.1895.

Aristides of Smyrna. 34 p98. Famous Greek orator and poet c.180 A.D.

Aristophanes. 9 p55. Brilliant satirical Greek playwright (448–388 B.C.) whom PGW admired. See Introduction to this volume.

Aristotle. 9 p54;18 p142 and often later. Celebrated Greek philosopher and tutor to Alexander the Great, died 322 B.C. In his *Poetica* he said the ideal of Greek tragedy was to purge the emotions of the audience with pity and terror. See PITY AND TERROR.

Arlen, Michael. 52 p115 ("Oh! Look"). Arlen (1895–1956) wrote sophisticated, brittle 'Society' novels, the best-known of which is *The Green Hat*. Wodehouse knew him and was slightly shocked when Arlen said he had stopped writing because he had made enough money. Arlen specialised in coining 'smart slang' terms; 'too sick-making' is one of his. See also ARMENIAN ORPHANS.

Arliss, George. 54 p178. Arliss (1868–1946) was a distinguished British actor who went to Hollywood late in life and became famous playing such roles as Wellington, Lincoln, Rothschild and Richelieu.

Armed at (all) points. 54 p172; 97 p89. S. *Hamlet* 1.2: "A figure like your father, Armed at point exactly, cap-a-pe."

Armed so strong in honesty, it passed me by as the idle wind. 63 p72; 64 p235; 65 p214*; and later. S. *Julius Caesar*. 4.3: "There is no terror, Cassius, in your threats; For I am armed so strong in honesty That they pass me by as the idle wind Which I respect not."

[* I noted several instances where PGW got a quotation 'fixed' in his head and used it in successive books.]

Armenian orphans, in aid of the. 26 p165. The uprisings of the Armenian provinces in Turkey in the late 19th–early 20th century were met by ferocious Turkish reprisals which led to worldwide indignation. Noel Coward used to introduce Michael Arlen (see above) as the only Armenian who wasn't massacred.

Armour, Tommy. 88 p59. Golfer who won both the Open and US Open in the 1920s.

Army, a way they have in the. 7 p225. See WAY THEY HAVE.

Army & Navy Stores. 76 p116. Now a normal London department store, the Stores were once *the* shop of the British Empire. Whatever you wanted, wherever you were in the world, they would get it to you. Its catalogue was enormous (twice as big as Sears Roebuck's), and I am fortunate to have the last (1939) edition, a fascinating historical record of middle-class life of the time. Even more useful is the 1907 catalogue, which someone had the sense to reprint a few years ago. Many of the books, pictures, songs and sheet-music titles listed there will be familiar to Wodehouseans. See Chap. 36.

Army game. The old army game 63 p15; 66 p193. This American term comes from the 1890s and referred originally to a rigged gambling game. It later came to signify general deception/ cheating.

Arno, Peter. His drawings in the *New Yorker* 89 p65. Arno (1904–68) helped the *New Yorker* to establish its image with his sophisticated, satirical cartoons.

Arnold, Benedict. 72 p 106; 92 p110; "if he had sold any good forts recently?" 95 p154 & p189. In the US, a synonym for a traitor. Arnold (1741–1801) was an American officer who changed sides during the Revolutionary War and negotiated with the British to surrender West Point. He then joined the British Army, became a brigadier, and fought gallantly at Guadaloupe.

Arpege scent. 83 p17. In the 1950s, Arpege scent was the only serious rival to Chanel.

Arrant, beggarly lousy knave ... worsted stocking. 73 p 85. It is rare for PGW to join two quotations from Shakespeare together like this. The first line is from *Henry V* 4.8. The second is mostly from *King Lear* 2.2, but "beetle-headed" and "flap-eared" seem to be PGW's additions.

'Arry. See HENRY, NOT AN 'ARRY.

Arsenal. 14 p136. A famous London football team, still going strong.

Arsenic & Old Lace. 70 p227. This splendid play by Joseph Kesselring has been performed regularly since 1941. I was lucky enough to see Sybil Thorndike and Athene Seyler in it.

Art, didn't know much about. See DIDN'T KNOW MUCH ABOUT.

Artbashikeff. 37 p125; 46 p262. I suggest this is PGW's version of Artzybashev, who was not so much a Great Russian as a Rude Russian; his 1907 novel *Sanin* caused a sensation with its frank discussion of sex. See also BRUSILOFF.

Arthur. 3 p277. A young schoolboy whom Tom Brown took under his wing in *Tom Brown's Schooldays*, the archetypal school story written by Thomas Hughes. Like *Uncle Tom's Cabin*, everybody knows it but nowadays very few have actually read it.

Arthur would have grovelled before Guinevere. 18 p 145. If you know your TENNYSON, you will recall that Guinevere had reason to grovel before him (getting too close to Lancelot). King Arthur, his sword Excalibur, wife Guinevere and knights are mentioned often till PGW's 95th book and are nearly all based on Tennyson's *Idylls of the King*.

Articulo mortis, In. See IN ARTICULO.

Arundell St. 19 p1; Arundel St 33 p115 & 61 p203. The correct spelling is Arundell. See Chap. 25.

As cooks go. See COOK.

As worn. 37 p250; as now worn 31 p115. A common phrase in clothing advertisements till at least 1930. "As worn by the Royal Family/ by members of the nobility/ by the aristocracy …" When the clothing industry wanted to popularise a new fashion, its adoption by someone of note was a godsend. The phrase became so popular that PGW was able simply to write "trousers as worn", knowing his readers would pick up the allusion. The "as now worn" (31 p115) signified that the frock coat and top hat, formal dress of the days before 1914 (First World War), had been superseded by the more informal post-War 'morning dress' (black/grey tail-coat, sponge-bag trousers and top hat).

Ashburton. 12 p106; 14 p111. The Ashburton Shield. The national shooting championships are held at Bisley, 30 miles southwest of London, and schools shoot for the Ashburton Shield. Dulwich won this in PGW's time, and the school had a half-holiday to celebrate.

Ashby Hall looked partly like the Prince Regent's establishment at Brighton and partly like a mediaeval fortress. 89 p37. The description of Ashby Hall matches exactly that of Tong Castle, an extraordinary High-Gothic-Moorish-Chinese building that stood between Weston Park, Shropshire, and PGW's home at Stableford. Because it has now been demolished (c.1957), I have not included this reference in Chap. 35 (Shropshire).

Ashes to ashes, dust to dust. 78 p140. BCP. Burial of the Dead: "We therefore commit his body to the ground; earth to earth, ashes to ashes, dust to dust."

Ashley, Lady Sylvia. 70 p189. Clark Gable has "a moustache, ten million dollars and Lady Sylvia Ashley." This London girl (1904–77) did very well for herself, marrying in turn Lord Ashley (1927), Douglas Fairbanks Snr (1936), Lord Stanley of Alderley (1944), Clark Gable (1949) and Prince Dmitri Djordjadze (1954).

Ask Dad (show). 31 p92. From PGW's lyric 'Ask Dad' for the show *Oh, My Dear* (1918). 'Ask Dad' was the original title for the show before its New York opening.

Ask Mr Halleran. See HALLERAN.

Asking Papa. 7 p200 (Chapter title). Popular Victorian song 'Go and Ask Papa' (1868).

Asleep in the Deep. 36 p197; 83 p76. Sad Victorian song (1897) beloved by basses.

Aspens. Pongo quivered like an aspen 60 287; 84 p32; 85 p11 and later. In 'Jeeves and the Greasy Bird', Bertie remembers aspens as trembling rather than quivering. At 93 p80, he wonders if aspens are those things that sway. TENNYSON had no doubts: "Willows whiten, aspens quiver" in his 'Lady of Shalott'. Walter Scott thought so too; see WOMAN IN OUR HOURS.

Aspinalls of Bond Street. 64 p37; 65 p33 and later. Asprey's, not Aspinall's, are still famous jewellers in Bond Street.

Asquith, Mr. 10 often and Dedicatee of 39. Herbert Asquith (1852–1928) was prime minister 1908–16. He let it be known how much he liked *Jill the Reckless*, and Wodehouse repaid the compliment in his dedication of 39. See also DRUNKENNESS.

Assyrian comes down like a wolf on the fold. 59 pp276 & p280 and elsewhere. BYRON's 'Destruction of Sennacherib'. "The Assyrian came down like the wolf on the fold, And his cohorts were gleaming in purple and gold." Note especially 85 p120, one of the best pages Wodehouse ever wrote. There are at least a dozen half-quotes and clichés in three paragraphs, each one apposite, each adding to the humour.

Assyrians. In 'The Great Sermon Handicap', Mr Heppenstall's sermon includes a rather exhaustive excursus on the home life of the early Assyrians. I wondered what happened to the Assyrians since one doesn't hear much about them nowadays. It is a sad story. After the First World War, Britain was asked by the League of Nations to govern Iraq, one of the provinces of the recently defeated Ottoman empire. Britain did so mainly by air power but needed ground troops, the Assyrian Levies, to defend its airfields. In 1932 the British handed over control to the new independent Iraqi government, which immediately turned on the minority groups who had supported the British forces, particularly the Christian Assyrians. The Iraqi army massacred many Assyrians, but a few remained around the RAF bases still in the country. In 1941, confident that Britain was going to lose the war, an Iraqi general staged an anti-British coup and attacked the Habbaniyah airfield near Baghdad. The Assyrians defended it bravely until a British relief force arrived. After the war, the Assyrians realised they had no one left to protect them, so they dispersed to other parts of the Middle East, while a large number went to the American Midwest and California.

Afternote. The American Assyrians are still very conscious of their history. *The Daily Telegraph* of 14 Mar 2001 reported that the US Census Bureau found itself involved in a dispute going back 1,500 years. The Bureau wanted to group the American Assyrians with the American Chaldeans, who also came from Mesopotamia. Both groups refused vehemently since they had gone their different ways after the Nestorian heresy of 431 A.D., when the Assyrians backed the Patriarch of Antioch while the Chaldeans supported the Patriarch of Babylon.

Astaire, Fred. 49 p22 and later; the Astaire pom-pom dance 54 p241. Fred Astaire (1899–1987) and his sister Adele danced the Pom-Pom dance in the last show at the legendary Empire, Leicester Square, *Lady, Be Good!* (1926), book by Guy Bolton and Fred Thompson, music by Gershwin. Note also the reference to Astaire in a film at 90 p97. This is PGW's memory of *A Damsel in Distress*, in which Astaire starred in 1937.

Asthore. 18 pp167 & p169. This popular sentimental ballad was written by Henry Trotere in 1878.

Astonish it. Show Wall Street some high finance that would a. i. 24 p19. G&S. *Iolanthe*. "I am an intellectual chap, And think of things that would astonish you." (Note. After *The Sorcerer*, Gilbert had intended that his series of operettas with Arthur Sullivan should all begin with the letter P. Hence *Pinafore*, *Pirates of Penzance* and *Patience*. To his fury, the news got out, so *The Peer and the Peri* was hurriedly changed to *Iolanthe*.) MTT Jim Linwood for the information that the code name used for *Iolanthe* in rehearsals was *Perola*.

Astor (hotel). 15A p21, p75, p82; 38 p178. The Astor Hotel on Times Square, built in 1904, became New York's premier hotel, and PGW and Ethel spent their two-day honeymoon there. It has now gone; do not confuse with the present Waldorf-Astoria.

Astor, Lady. 69 p85. A forceful, energetic American (1879–1964), she was the first woman Member of Parliament to take her seat (1919). PGW met her at least once and was not impressed.

Astorbilt hotel. 21 p298; Astorbilt houses on the other side of the park 24 p50. PGW twist on the Astor Hotel, where he spent his honeymoon, and the New York houses built by such rich Americans as the Astors and Vanderbilts.

Astorgould, Rockerbilt. 13 p22. A combination of the names of the four richest men in America: Rockefeller, Vanderbilt, Astor and Gould.

Astounded at my moderation. 91 p53. See MODERATION, ASTOUNDED.

Atalanta (athlete). 44 p124. In Greek legend, a runner of such speed that she could only be beaten by trickery.

Athenaeum, the. 25 p171; 39 p94 and later up to 97 p22. See Chap. 21.

Athenaeus. 9 p18. Greek grammarian who wrote the DEIPNOSOPHISTS; he died 194 A.D.

Athenian expedition to Syracuse — Nikias' speech. 8 p20. See NIKIAS.

***Atlantic*, SS.** Frequent. See Chap. 17.

Atmosphere of utmost cordiality that statesmen hold meetings in. 89 p19; 94 p26. See CONFERENCES.

Attenborough's. 9 p245. A favourite source of money-raising among Pink 'Uns and Pelicans, it was London's most famous pawnbroker from 1880 to 1920. Its premises are still to be seen on a corner site on the Strand, a building with a splendid Victorian frontage.

Attila the Hun. 39 p202 and later. This Hun warlord (c. 406–453 A.D.) conquered much of Asia and eastern Europe with a ferocity that has kept his name alive ever since.

Au revoir, my little Hyacinth. 12 p141. Song from *The Beauty of Bath* (1906) sung by Ellaline Terriss. MTT Tony Ring

Auction, play a lot of. 22 p23. See BRIDGE.

Audace — De l'audace, et encore de l'audace et toujours de l'audace. 67 p178; 86 p20. "Boldness, and again boldness, and always boldness." Danton, the French revolutionary, coined the phrase in his speech of 2 September 1792.

Audit ale at Oxford colleges. 89 p166. The legend is that colleges brewed this extremely strong beer to celebrate or mourn the annual audit of their accounts. I think the habit may have died out by now, but after 50 years I still remember the audit ale brewed for Queen's College. It fully justified all the claims made for it.

Auge davonkommen . "Jolly well out of it". 48 p277. It should be 'Auge davongekommen'. MTT Gwendolin Goldbloom.

Augean stables. 87 p185. In Greek legend, this was an immense stable for oxen and goats that had never been cleaned until Hercules did so as the fifth of his twelve labours.

Auld lang syne. 65 p92. With words by Robert Burns, this song is sung raucously around the world every New Year's Eve.

'Aunt and the Sluggard, The'. B Proverbs 6.6: "Go to the ant, thou sluggard …" MTT Charles Gould and Fr Rob Bovendeaard.

Aunt, the whole aunt and nothing but the aunt. 65 p192. See GAME.

Aunts will be aunts. 82 p9. See BOYS WILL BE BOYS.

Australian crawl. 64 p199. This swimming style, now called simply the crawl or freestyle, arrived in England in the 1920s from Australia. My mother always called it 'the Australian crawl' and she continued to use the old 'trudgeon', which had the arm movement of the crawl but the leg movement of the breast stroke.

Authentics, the. 2 p23; 12 p74. To get your Blue at Oxford or Cambridge (equivalent to the Varsity letter in America), you must play in the annual match against the other university. No matter how good you are, missing the match means you cannot get your Blue. Those who miss their Blue and are of a high enough standard are given another distinction. They will be elected to the Authentics (cricket) club, Greyhounds (Rugger) club, Centipedes (athletics) club etc. Up to 1939, when the two universities dominated amateur sport, the colours of these clubs were well known.

Automat. 26 p207. A chain of self-service cafés, which first opened in Philadelphia in 1902 and came to New York in 1912. The last New York Automat, in 42nd Street, closed in 1991. Extemely popular, they were similar to the J.J. Lyons cafés in London.

Avilion, island valley of, where falls not hail or rain, etc. 37 p232 and often later. T. 'Passing of Arthur', six verses from the end: "To the island-valley of Avilion; / where falls not hail, or rain, or any snow, / Nor ever wind blows loudly …"

Awake, for morning in the bowl of night … etc. 32 p262. See opening lines of Edward Fitzgerald's *Omar Khayyam*. See also OMAR KHAYYAM.

Away with melancholy. 1 p99. The duet by Mozart, or perhaps the two popular songs came out with this title in 1876 and 1888.

A-weary of this great world, her little body was. 92 p 99. S. *Merchant of Venice* 1.2: "By my troth, Nerissa, my little body is aweary of this great world."

'Awful Gladness of the Mater, The'. PGW's gloss on "the gladness of the May" from Wordsworth's 'Intimations of Immortality', v. 10. "Ye that through your hearts today / Feel the gladness of the May."

Ay tank I go home, Tilbury. 50 p234. "Ay tank I go home" is attributed to the film star Greta Garbo, who caused consternation among the Hollywood moguls by her apparent indifference as to whether she appeared in films or not. Allegedly, her threat of returning home to Sweden was sufficient to get what she wanted. Her Swedish accent was always emphasised in the re-telling.

B

(MTT = My thanks to)

Baal, priests of. 21 p121 and often later. B. 1 Kings 18.28: "And they cried aloud, and cut themselves after their manner with knives and lancets, till the blood gushed out of them."

Bab Ballads (and *More Bab Ballads*). 3 p252 and frequent later. These satirical verses by W.S. Gilbert caused quite a stir when they came out (1869 & 1873). PGW admired Gilbert and quoted from them often. See also GILBERT, W.S.

Babes and sucklings. See OUT OF THE MOUTHS.

Babes in eternity. See BASSETT, MADELINE.

Bablockhythe, Lady. 35 p234. A scandalous autobiographer. This is clearly an allusion to Lady Cardigan (1825–1915), widow of the Crimea general who led the charge of the immortal Light Brigade at Balaclava. In 1905 PGW recorded that he was offered the chance to meet her, but had declined. She was an outspoken, eccentric lady whose 1909 autobiography shocked Society (I am fortunate enough to have a copy). Queen Victoria refused to receive her at Court after the scandal of her early life (she lived openly with Cardigan while his first wife was still alive). In revenge, so it is said, Lady Cardigan married a Portuguese count as her second husband. This meant that she was able to call herself the Comtesse de Lancastre, which everybody knew was the style Queen Victoria used when travelling incognito. In her later years, Lady Cardigan used to promenade in Hyde Park, wearing a curly blonde wig and three-cornered hat, and trailing a leopard skin behind her. A footman walked behind her, carrying her dog on a silk cushion. She delighted in embarrassing young men at her dinner parties by insisting they inspect the *very* décollettée bust done of her and asking if their fiancées were similarly well-endowed. See also CARNABY and WENSLEYDALE.

Baby Blobbs, Adventures of. 23 p39. The short story 'Leave It to Jeeves' came out in 1916. MTT Stu Shiffman for the information that a likely source for Baby Blobbs is George McManus' famous cartoon baby 'Snookums', which had begun in 1909. Another candidate is Milt Gross' 'Nize Baby' of 1913.

Baby Boy (film). 53 p221. I suggest this is PGW's reference to *The Kid*, the tear-jerker film of 1921 starring Charlie Chaplin with Jackie Coogan as the tousle-haired child who stirred the hearts of audiences around the world. See Chap. 28.

Baby Leroy (child film star). 54 p172. Baby Leroy (LeRoy Overacker) was born in 1931 and appeared in films from the age of six months. It was his orange juice that W.C. Fields allegedly laced with gin in one of the four films in which they starred together.

Babylon, king in. See KING IN BABYLON.

Babylon, the Scarlet Woman of. 35 p127 and frequent thereafter. See SCARLET WOMAN.

Baby's Sock Is Now a Blue Bag. 15A p200. I have been unable to trace this. US variety? English music hall?

'Baby's Vengeance, The'. 45 p94 & p256. A most immoral tale from W.S. Gilbert's *Bab Ballads.*

Bachelors as wild asses of the desert, Who was it described. 95 p133. It took me hours to work this one out, but the source is — PGW himself at chap. 20 of *Uneasy Money*. I believe that since *Bachelors Anonymous* involved so many characters arguing for and against matrimony, Wodehouse wanted some telling images and remembered Dudley Pickering's similar changes of mind 56 years before. The 'wild asses' reference is B. Job 24.5: "Behold, as wild asses of the desert, go they forth to their work; rising betimes for a prey …"

Bachelors' Club. 18 p249 and elsewhere. See Chap. 21.

Back to the army again, sergeant, back to the army again. 71 p172. See KIPLING's touching poem 'Back to the Army Again'.

Back to the bench. See BENCH.

Back to the Land. 42 p78. Political slogan. In 1905 the UK government grew concerned at the over-population of cities and encouraged training courses in a bid to get people 'Back to the Land'. This led to the phenomenon PGW describes of many educated young men trying their hand, usually unsuccessfully, at chicken-farming and other agricultural ventures. Bicky Bickersteth wanted to try it in 'Jeeves and the Hard-Boiled Egg', and Ukridge's chicken farm was an example later followed by Claude Winnington-Bates (36 p16). PGW received £1.25 from *Pearson's Magazine* for his 'Back to the Land' article in August 1905.

Back was against the wall, his. 41 p317. On 12 April 1918, when the British troops were under pressure from a fierce German offensive, General Haig issued his famous order: "With our backs to the wall, and believing in the justice of our cause, each one of us must fight on to the end."

Backing and filling. 19 p146 and later. I am told this is a sailing term for conditions when the tide is with you but the wind is against you. You back the boat to try and fill the sails; lots of movement and activity, but the boat tends to remain where it is.

Bacon, Lord. She thinks B. wrote Shakespeare 41 p15; 64 p192; and later, including "Look at Lord Bacon. Went about calling himself Shakespeare" 87 p136. There are still many Baconian enthusiasts around who contend that Shakespeare's plays were written by Francis Bacon (1561–1626). The American orator, novelist and politician Ignatius Donnelly (1831–1901) was a fanatical

Baconian and published *The Great Cryptogram* (1888) and *The Cypher in the Plays* (1899). He went on to 'prove' that Bacon also wrote Marlowe's plays and the essays of Montaigne as well as Burton's *Anatomy of Melancholy*. I think PGW's theory (*Louder and Funnier*) that Shakespeare was a theatrical fixer is just as likely and far funnier: "'Says you!' said Bacon. 'Yes, says me!' retorted Shakespeare."

In 1928 Father Ronald Knox (academic, theologian and Wodehouse admirer) used the technique described at 41 p24 to 'prove' that Queen Victoria wrote Alfred TENNYSON's 'In Memoriam'. The result he got was: "VRI the poetess. Alf T has no duties."

Bad Fairy not invited to the christening. 62 p64. See legend of the Sleeping Beauty.

Bad form. See FORM, BAD.

Bad Lands. In the middle of the B.L. 17 p103; some dismal swamp in the B.L. 39 p203. Name given to the inhospitable terrain around the White River in South Dakota.

Badgwick (place). 1 p73; 3 p136; 31 p139. See Chap. 35.

Baer, Bugs. 69p 174. Arthur (Bugs) Baer (1897–1969), witty American columnist and cartoonist.

Bailey, Bill. 7 p165 and later, including: "If a fellow's name is Bailey, you've more or less got to call him Bill", 84 p23. Bill is still a common nickname in the UK for anybody named Bailey. It stems from the enduring popularity of 'Bill Bailey', the song written by Hugh Cannon ("Won't you come home, Bill Bailey?"). For those who do not know it, the song is a wife's reproach to her husband for drinking in a bar when he should be coming home. The origin of the song was forgotten until 1970. In 1902 Bill Bailey, a teacher in Jackson, Michigan, used to call in at the local bar after work. Everybody knew his wife reproached him for this, and the piano player in the bar, Hugh Cannon, was inspired to write the song that became wildly popular. Outraged by the notoriety it brought her, Mrs Bailey secured a divorce. It was not until her 100th birthday, 68 years later, that she revealed what she still considered her shame to the world.

Note. In early editions of *Something Fresh*, the expression 'Sunny Jim' is used, since 'Bill Bailey' had not yet become popular in the UK. See SUNNY JIM.

Baked a cake. 79 p48. See IF I'D KNOWN.

Baker, Home-Run. 21 p41. In 1911 Frank Baker hit eleven home runs for the Philadephia Athletics and won his soubriquet when he hit two home runs in the winning game of the 1911 World Series. His hitting was a record in the days of the old 'soft' baseball then used. See THUD.

Balaam's ass. Digging his feet in … like B.a. 68 p91 and often later. B. Numbers 22.23. The ass that Balaam was riding saw the angel of the Lord in front of him and, as any sensible ass would do, stopped dead. Balaam, to whom the angel was invisible, beat him to get him going again. Only after the ass had stopped three times did the angel reveal himself to Balaam.

Balbus murum aedificavit. 3 p252. "Balbus built a wall" was a sentence in a popular school textbook when PGW began doing Latin at Malvern House, Dover. See Chap. 3.

Baldwin (Stanley). 52 p286. UK Prime Minister three times between 1923 and 1937.

Balin, Sir. 18 p235. One of Arthur's knights in T. *Idylls of the King*.

Balkans, friction threatening in the. 31 p7 and later. A common topic of discussion at the time. The Balkan Wars began in 1912, involving Serbia, Bulgaria, Greece and Rumania. The 'Balkan problem', a hangover from the centuries-long occupation by the Turks and the dissolution of the Austro-Hungarian Empire in 1919 is still unresolved.

Ball had fallen into the pit which my niblick had digged, my. See PIT WHICH MY NIBLICK HAS DIGGED.

Ball rolls/bounces, that's the way. See THAT'S THE WAY.

Ballet Russe. 33 p17. Ballet was a pretty staid affair in Europe until the emergence of the energetic and electrifying Ballets Russes, founded in Paris by Diaghilev in 1909.

Balliol, got a. 12 p180. Benjamin Jowett, Master of Balliol College, Oxford (1870–93), raised the intellectual level of the college to the extent that 'getting a Balliol', i.e. winning a scholarship there, meant you were very bright indeed. See also JOWETT.

Balm in Gilead. 96 p107. B. Jeremiah 8.22: "Is there no balm in Gilead; is there no physician there?"

Balmoral, Mafeking Road. 96 p117 and elsewhere. See CHATSWORTH and MAFEKING ROAD.

Baloney. Slice her where you like, she's still b. 56 p60. In the 1920s an American manufacturer of Bologna sausage wanted to advertise on radio, and various actors came to audition. They all tried to say 'Bologne/Bologna' in a French or Italian accent, but the last man simply called it 'baloney'. The manufacturer gave him the job because: "It may not be right, but that's what my customers call it." Ring Lardner, a writer PGW admired, used the term in the 1920s to describe a bad boxer, but it entered the language in 1930 when the politician Al Smith described the policy of his political opponents on radio with the words: "No matter how thin you slice it, it's still baloney." See also Chimp Twist's description of Soapy Molloy in chap. 2 of *Money in the Bank*.

Banana oil. 38 p52. A slang term of the 1920s coined by the American cartoonist Milt Gross. MTT Stu Shiffman.

Bancroft, George. 49 p273. Tough-guy film actor (1882–1956).

Bandolero. I am the. 29 p73 and later. 'The Bandolero'(1894), written by Leslie Stuart, has been rendered by Sam Marlowe, Bertie Wooster and Monty Bodkin as well as Albert Peasemarch.

Bandolero Restaurant, Shaftesbury Avenue. 20 p1. From the information given, this restaurant is unmistakeably the Trocadero, which still stands in Shaftesbury Avenue, though it is now an entertainment centre rather than a restaurant.

Banjolele. 51 p7. Bertie Wooster was forced to leave his London flat because of his banjolele, but there is disagreement as to what it was. The banjo came into the UK with the American blackface minstrel troupes in the mid-19th century. The Bohee Brothers were particularly highly regarded in the 1880s, and James Bohee gave lessons to the Prince of Wales (later Edward VII). I have been told a banjolele was a combination of banjo and ukelele, but I believe Bertie's instrument was, in effect, a miniature banjo. About 12 inches long, it had the same number of strings as a banjo, but the different skin across the smaller body produced a high-pitched 'plink-plink' rather than a banjo's 'plunk-plunk'. In Prohibition days, college boys went for a night out in their Cord auto, dressed in a raccoon-skin coat, a bottle of gin in one pocket and a banjolele stuffed in the other. I do not know whether this was the name used in America, but I have had it confirmed by an English musician who knows about such arcane instruments.

'Bank, Bank, Bank', like a bus conductor. 63 p251. Conductors of London buses call this out to indicate the bus has arrived at the Bank of England in Threadneedle Street.

Bank, New Asiatic. See NEW ASIATIC BANK.

Bank of England, Grenadier Guards song. 97 p92. See GRENADIER GUARDS.

Bank whereon the wild thyme grows, I know a. 12 p307. S. *Midsummmer Night's Dream* 2.1.

Banker of Bhong. See BHONG, BANKER OF.

Bankhead, Tallulah. 52 p18 and elsewhere. This actress (1902–68) appeared in *Her Cardboard Lover* in London in 1928. As one film historian wrote, Bankhead "frittered away her considerable talents by living too dangerously". She drank and took drugs, and her lovers could not be counted. It is said the only man she ever respected was her father, a sometime Speaker of the House of Representatives.

Banks, Rosie M. See Chap. 37.

Banned in Boston. 80 p28; 88 p60 and elsewhere. A popular phrase up to the 1930s, stemming from the rigorous, often over-rigorous, activities of the Watch and Ward (morality) Society of that city. In 1926 H.L. Mencken challenged them by selling a copy of *American Mercury*, the magazine he edited that was banned in Boston, to a leading light of the Committee, the Rev. J.F. Chase. Mencken made sure reporters were present when he handed over the magazine, took a coin in exchange and then allowed himself be arrested. In court, the judge dismissed the case and the Watch and Ward Society lost most of its influence. The intellectual level of censorship in Boston at the time can be judged from the fact that the theatrical censor got the job, firstly, because he was the mayor's cousin and, secondly, because he had lost an arm and could no longer follow his calling as a drummer in a band in a burlesque house.

Banner with a strange device, Excelsior. See EXCELSIOR.

Bannister's mile, Roger. 78 p65; 79 p161. His record mile run. I am proud to say that I was on the pavilion balcony at Iffley Road on that wet, cold evening in May 1954 when Bannister became the first man to run a mile in less than four minutes.

Bannockburn. Like a nervous English infantryman at the battle of B. 53 p160. In 1314 the army of Edward II was decisively beaten by a smaller Scots army under Robert the Bruce.

Banquet. Gentlemen, will you allow us to offer you a magnificent b.? 99 p267. G&S *The Gondoliers* Act 2.

Banquets are always pleasant things. 99 p272. From Kenneth Grahame's *The Reluctant Dragon.*

Banquo's ghost. 17 p116 and often later, including a description of the big scene at 96 p91. Induced much alarm and despondency in Macbeth, despite having "no speculation in his eye" S. *Macbeth* 3.4. See also SPECULATION.

Banzai. 12 p115; 42 p41. This Japanese greeting/exclamation ("May you live 10,000 years") became popular in England during the Russo-Japanese war of 1904–5. On their way round the world from Murmansk to fight the Japanese in the Pacific, a Russian fleet sank some British fishing boats in the North Sea, thinking they were Japanese submarines. The incident confirmed British popular support for the Japanese and brought the greeting into common use.

Barabbas, I thought it might be. 44 p172. A reference clearly known to those unlikely Biblical scholars, Mr Frisby and J.B. Hoke, when the former accused the latter of being a robber. When Pontius Pilate asked the people which prisoner they wanted him to release, Jesus or Barabbas: "Then cried they all again, saying, Not this man but Barabbas. Now Barabbas was a robber." B. John 18.40.

Barbizon school (of art). 62 p66. French school of painting whose adherents included Corot and Millet.

Bard, Wilkie. 14 p23. A lugubrious British comedian (1874–1944).

Bardell, Mr, death of. 7 p172. He was hit over the head with a quart tankard. D. *The Pickwick Papers*, chap. 34.

Bardot, Brigitte. 86 p11. Was this French beauty the last of PGW's references to good-looking actresses, which began with Edna May of *The Belle of New York* at the turn of the century?

Barmaid, British. The British b. stands alone in the matter of poise. 72 p73 and elsewhere. It has been a very long time since I saw one of the real old-fashioned barmaids, and PGW described them accurately. They were stately, full-figured ladies of immense dignity. They made it clear that they 'stood no nonsense' in their bar, though a well-turned compliment on their new hairstyle or dress might invoke a dignified smile. Like Miss Postlethwaite, they were ladies with whom one definitely 'did not take liberties'.

Barmecide meal. 19 p185. An imaginary meal — empty plates, glasses and dishes. From *Tales of Arabian Nights* ('The Barber's Sixth Brother').

Barmy in Wonderland. PGW's twist on *Alice in Wonderland* reflects his view of Barmy's immersion in the world of musical comedy. Thirty years earlier, in *Jill the Reckless*, Wally Mason had said: "There isn't anything that can't happen in musical comedy. 'Alice in Wonderland' is nothing to it."

Barney Google, the song. 94 p85. This US cartoon character was created by Billy de Beck in 1919. Barney was one of Life's unfortunates; one whom everybody picked on. The 1923 song was written by Billy Rose and Con Conrad.

Barnum. As the late B. used to say about there being one born every minute 76 p76. Phineas Barnum (1810–91) was one of the greatest showmen the world has known. 'The first American master of ballyhoo', he made the dwarf Tom Thumb (and Barnum) famous around the world. Although the phrase 'There's a sucker born every minute' is attributed to him, it was originally said by a friend of George Hull. Hull had a stone giant made, buried it, 'discovered' it, and made a fortune from the people who flocked to see it. When Hull rejected an offer from Barnum for the giant, Barnum had another one made and claimed Hull's was a fake. In the ensuing court case, Hull was able to show both were fakes, and the hoax came to an end, with Hull's friend summing up the whole business with the now-immortal phrase. 'The Cardiff Giant' (Hull's version) can be seen today in the Cooperstown Farmers Museum, Cooperstown, New York. There is still a charge to see it.

Barnum and Bailey's (Circus). 22 p183. In 1881 Barnum joined his famous circus with that of his biggest rival, James Bailey. Later it joined Ringling Brothers to become 'The Greatest Show On Earth' (still going strong).

Barnum's what-is-it. 13 p74. Barnum loved having new freaks in his shows. This was probably an orangutang, then new to America.

Barolini's Restaurant, Beak Street, 4 courses and coffee for 9 pence (20 cents). 33 p33. Up to 1939, there were dozens of small, cheap Italian/French/German restaurants like this in London's Soho district. See Chap. 25.

Baronets are proverbially bad. 42 p154. PGW also gave us: "If he had a moustache he would have looked like a baronet," as well as: "He was fingering his moustache nervously, like a foiled baronet in an olde-time melodrama." See G&S *Ruddigore* Act 1. "All baronets are bad; but was he worse than other baronets?" Gilbert (and PGW) were satirising English 19th-century melodramas which always cast a baronet as the villain. Why this order of the aristocracy was chosen for such indignity rather than dukes or earls or viscounts, I have no idea. But in barns, fit-up shows, halls and small provincial theatres up and down England, it was always the moustachioed bold, bad baronet who foreclosed the mortgage, sought to have his evil way with the (very) blonde heroine and was heartily hissed throughout by the audience. See also TIME WILL COME; TRANSPONTINE MELODRAMA; and TODD, SIR JASPER.

Baronets, baffled. 58 p182; 97 p48. See BARONETS ARE.

Baronet's sister. Would she go in (to dinner) before or after the daughter of the younger son of a peer? 41 p132. I know the world is dying to know, so I consulted my 1911 Burke's *Peerage* and Whitaker's *Almanack* of 1972. They both state that a daughter of the younger son of a peer takes precedence over a baronet's sister.

Barratry. 55 p211. This is either fraudulent action by a ship's master or crew to defraud the owners or vexatious litigation wrongly promoted by lawyers for their profit (as if they would ever do such a thing).

Barrel Club, the. 9 p26 & p98. See Chap. 21.

Barribault's. 65 p36–37 and later. See Chap. 25.

Barricades. See SEE YOU ON THE BARRICADES.

Barrymore, John & Lionel. 44 p 81. The Barrymores — John (1882–1942), his brother Lionel (1878–1954) and sister Ethel (1879–1959) — dominated the American stage for the first half of the 20th century. See also Mervyn Potter in Chap. 28.

Bartlett's Familiar Quotations. 3 p250 and later. Bartlett (1820–1905), a bookseller famous in Boston for his knowledge of literary quotations, was persuaded by his friends to produce *Familiar Quotations*, his master work, in 1855. Wodehouse found it very useful and mentioned it frequently. See Chap. 38.

Basius Secundus, attribute sentiments to. 34 p98. There was no such person as Basius Secundus, but Janus Secundus (1511–36) wrote a series of poems in different metres, some of which followed the style of Catullus. The poems dealt with kisses and kissing, and the collection was known as the Basia (Latin for kisses) — commonly called the Secundus Basia.

Bassett, Fred. 95 p11. This is PGW's compliment to the British cartoonist Alex Graham, who died in 1991. Graham's famous creation was a basset hound, Fred Basset, who appeared in newspapers around the world. When the strip was dropped from his regular American newspaper, Wodehouse campaigned for it to be reinstated. Graham was thrilled when Wodehouse wrote to tell him of his success, and they corresponded regularly thereafter.

Bassett, Madeline, obiter dicta of. I have not found an original for this lady, who first appeared in 1934. Perhaps she was a product of the sudden interest in fairies and creatures like them in the 1920s; see FAIRIES AT THE BOTTOM. And we should not forget Blake's 'Auguries of Innocence', which contains the lines: "Every tear in every eye / Becomes a babe in Eternity." MTT Barry Phelps for quoting from a poem by PGW's aunt, Miss Mary Deane:

> Tread softly where the flowers grow
> So primitive and wild
> For if you crush a single bud
> You kill a fairy child.

Persuasive, but the strong-minded Miss Deane was *very* different from Miss

Bassett. See Chap. 2.

Bastard. The pie-faced young b. 68 p98. *The Mating Season*, written in Paris in 1946, is the few instances where Wodehouse used coarse language. At p29 Corky Pirbright says bluntly that Esmond Haddock's aunts are "all bitches". I surmise this was a hangover from PGW's days in the internment camp. I regret to say that, in such all-male institutions, bad language is used so often it becomes habitual, losing all significance or meaning. MTT Fr Rob Bovendeaard for the information that 'barstard'(*sic*) also appears in chap. 2 of *Spring Fever*.

Bates, Claude and Tressider. 36 pp17, 28 & 138. Attended Wrykyn with Sam Shotter. There is a minor mystery here. See Chap. 3.

Battle axes and bishops. See Chap. 11.

Battle Creek, for the cure. 46 p212. Dr Kellogg founded this famous health farm in Michigan in 1866 and instituted a strict regime which included the now-famous flakes of corn for breakfast. It was Kellogg's brother who saw their commercial potential and marketed them in 1898. See also POST-TOASTIES.

Bauer, Miss. "Would Match Miss Bauer Against Men Swimmers" 34 p214. Sybil Bauer (1903–27) was US backstroke swimming champion. She did indeed once beat the men's record for the 200 metres, but this was not officially acknowledged.

Baxter, Prudence. The winner of the Open Girls' Egg and Spoon Race. 'The Purity of the Turf'. *(See photo, page 52.)*

Baxter, Warner. 56 p259; 60 p112. Baxter (1889–1951) was a handsome leading man who appeared in films from 1914 to 1950.

Bay trees. Going to prosper like a couple of bay trees 50 p261; 66 p139 and later. BCP. Psalms 37.36: "I myself have seen the ungodly in great power, and flourishing like a green bay tree."

Bayard (the Chevalier). See CHEVALIER BAYARD.

Bayly, Thomas Haynes. 38 p125. Bayly's (1797–1839) songs included 'The Isle of Beauty' with the line "Absence makes the heart grow fonder". See also HURRY ME.

Bazooka. Dislocated the radius bone of his bazooka. 14 p186. PGW uses it here as a comic name for some part of the body. At 60 p127 and 65 p43, he gives us "Try that on your bazooka", which is clearly a twist on "Try that on your pianola" (see TRY THAT). The *Oxford English Dictionary* confirms that a bazooka was a musical instrument made from two lengths of gas tubing and a whisky funnel which an American comedian, Bob Burns (1890-1956), invented and named in 1910 to use in his act. The OED then goes on to identify it with the kazoo (comb-and-paper) and mentions that some UK miners began a band of this sort in 1926, using what they called 'bazoukas', a variation of the kazoo. Why the name was given to the anti-tank rocket launcher later, I do not know. Presumably someone remembered Burns's two lengths of gas tubing which he had made popular in radio appearances and on film.

BBC Children's Hour. 54 p154. This excellent programme (5–6 P.M. on

Prudence Baxter, winner of the Girls' Egg and Spoon Race

The official prize was a handsome work-bag presented by Lady Wickhammersley. The proud winner is firmly clutching the enormous tray of bonbons presented to her by Mr Richard Little, Mr Bertram Wooster and other gentlemen, once the judge's decision had been confirmed. She has entrusted to her elder sister the custody of Lady Wickhammersley's work-bag, as well as the box of chocolates presented to her by Mr Reginald Jeeves in appreciation of her upholding the integrity of amateur sportsmanship, unsullied by gross commercialism.

weekdays) ran from 1922 to 1964. It had stories, plays, music, dramatisations of books, and the unforgettable Larry the Lamb.

Be it ever so humble (poky/smoky/whatever). Frequent. A typical PGW twist is at 34 p72: "Be it never so merely rented furnished, a man's little home is his little home." Just one of PGW's variations on the song the whole world knew — 'Home, Sweet Home' by John Howard Payne. See Home, Sweet Home and Chap. 36.

Be off with the old love now she was on with the new. 20 p87. *Songs of England & Scotland* (1835) and other folk references have: "It is best to be off with the old love before you are on with the new."

Beachcomber in a Somerset Maugham novel. 86 p132. See Maugham.

Beaded bubbles winking at the brim. 77 p81. See Hippocrene.

Beak. Frequent. UK slang term for someone with the authority to punish you — a magistrate, a judge and later, by extension, a schoolmaster. *Brewer's Phrase and Fable* attributes it to the beag, a gold collar worn by Anglo-Saxon judges. See also Nibs.

Beale. 7 p51. Wodehouse would have met few ex-NCOs by 1906. One he certainly knew was Sergeant-Major Beale, who trained the Dulwich College Army cadets till 1901.

Beale Street Blues. 32 p180. Popular song by W.C. Handy, 1916.

Beam. Why beholdest thou the mote that is in thy brother's eye, but considerest not the beam that is in thine own eye, Wooster? 93 p86. B. Matthew 7.5: "Thou hypocrite, first cast out the beam out of thine own eye; and then shalt thou see clearly to cast out the mote out of thy brother' eye."

Beamish boy. Bertie, my beamish boy 76 p 221 and elsewhere. Lewis Carroll's 'Jabberwocky' in *Alice Through the Looking-Glass*. "And hast thou slain the Jabberwock? Come to my arms, my beamish boy!"

Bean. Frequent. US slang for the head. See also OLD BEAN.

Bean, old (as a friendly greeting). See OLD BEAN.

Beano. Frequent. A shortened form of bean-feast, a festive occasion/party. From the custom of London firms giving their workers an annual party at a time of year when beans were in plentiful supply. An industrial equivalent of the agricultural harvest supper.

Beans. Frequent in Wodehouse, but with variations of meaning. 'Give him beans' is encouraging someone fighting. 'Full of buck and beans' in *The Mating Season* refers to the traditional belief in racing circles that giving a horse beans before a race would liven him up. *Brewer's Phrase & Fable* attributes the usage denoting money to the French 'biens' meaning property. Brewer also refers to a French proverb: "If he gives me peas, I'll give him beans" (i.e. tit for tat; I'll hit him back).

Bear him company. 17 p123. Longfellow's 'The WRECK OF THE HESPERUS': 'the skipper had taken his little daughter / To bear him company'.

Beard from Clarkson. See CLARKSON.

Bearded like a pard. The soldier bearded like … full of strange oaths 81 p85; 83 p50. S. *As You Like It* 2.7: "Then a soldier Full of strange oaths and bearded like the pard." ('The seven ages of man' speech.) See also FRECKLED.

Beards. 31 p118. Beards had been unfashionable in England for about 200 years until the soldiers coming back from the Crimean War re-introduced them in 1856. By the 1870s the rough shaggy Crimean style had been refined to the Peaked, the Spade and the Square. The play *Our American Cousin* made the Dundreary (long mutton-chop side-whiskers) fashionable in 1872–73, but by 1911 the only popular beard was the York, the naval officers' beard 'as worn' by George V. See also BEAVER and MOUSTACHE, but note also McAllister in Chap. 15.

Bears, eaten by. 42 Preface; 45 p125. Elisha was mocked and jeered at by children who promptly got their just deserts in B. 2 Kings 2.24: "And there came forth two she bears out of the wood, and tare forty and two children of them." See also WATTS.

Beasts of the field/beasts that perish. See MAN ABOVE.

Beating of its wings, I hear the. Indicating the imminence of money 26 p174 & 33 p134; very nearly getting the bird at a concert 43 p111; getting the sack 50 p127. The phrase became popular after the politician John Bright made a powerful speech in the House of Commons in 1855 in which he said: "The angel of death has been abroad throughout the land; you may almost hear the beating of its wings." Do not confuse with 'floating in the air' — see RAT, SMELT A.

Beatle, Beatle and Beatle of Liverpool. 88 p208. We all know this refers to the four Liverpudlean pop stars of the '60s and early '70s, but will our grandchildren know? See MAISIE.

Beau Brummel. 64 p54. See BEAU DAWLISH and WHO IS YOUR STUFFED FRIEND?.

Beau Dawlish. 20 p12 and other Beaux later. PGW writes often of owners of large country houses whose great-grandfathers had gambled away the family money. By using the prefix 'Beau' he places these spendthrift ancestors firmly in the period 1780–1820, when Beau Brummel ruled London fashion and every gentleman worth the name looked forward to losing his money with grace and style at Watier's, Almack's and other gaming establishments. At least one bet involved thousands of pounds (hundreds of thousands today) on which raindrop would reach the bottom of a window first. My favourite bet of that period occurred when a man collapsed in the doorway of a club (White's, I think it was). The members gathered round him and a book was opened on whether the unfortunate would live or die. After all bets had been recorded, there was silence for a while till one member suggested diffidently that a doctor be called. This caused outrage: "What! Call a doctor? We'll have no foul play here! Let him take his chance!"

Beaux and Bucks were the dandies/fops of the time, though the Bucks tended to be more energetic in their activities. Mad Jack Mytton, a Buck rather than a Beau, jumped his horse over the Mess dining table at a regimental dinner and used to drive his gig straight across country, taking it over or through all the hedges, ditches and rivers that he came to. For a modern equivalent, see BLOOD.

Beau sabreur of Romano's. 42 p25. PGW is classifying Gally Threepwood as a leading light of the raffish society that gathered in Romano's restaurant (see Chap. 5). A similar term was applied to Dumas' Musketeers, D'Artagnan, Athos, Porthos, etc.

Beau Widgeon. 55 p177. See FOREIGN LEGION.

Beaumont & Fletcher. 50 p122. Elizabethan/Jacobean playwrights, rivals of Shakespeare.

Beautiful bountiful Bertie, my. See BERTIE.

Beautiful Eyes. 15A p75. Song from the 1909 Broadway musical *Mr Hamlet.*

Beautiful, the Book/Word/Film Beautiful. See BOOK BEAUTIFUL.

Beauty fades, these things remain. 81 p196. I have been unable to find this phrase. Plato? The Bible? Tennyson? In the context of PGW's story, I suggest: "Kissing don't last; cookery do!" in Meredith's *Ordeal of Richard Feverel.*

Beauty is in the eye of the beholder. 19 p72 and later. The phrase occurs in

Margaret Hungerford's *Molly Bawn* and in Lew Wallace's *The Prince of India* (1893).

Beaver. People shouting Beaver at you 31 p118, 44 p90 and later. In 1919 beards enjoyed a short return to fashion among Bohemians and the 'Arty-Crafty lot', and spotting beards in the street became a popular game. If you saw a beard before your friend did, you shouted 'Beaver!' and scored a point. Certain types of beard (white, very long, red etc.) scored extra points. Spotting King George V himself (Royal Beaver) won the game at once. See *Laughing Gas* where Joey Cooley/Lord Havershot finds himself "among a band of criminals who were not wilful beavers, but had merely assumed the fungus for the purpose of disguise".

Beaverbrook, Lord. 34 p5. An energetic newspaper magnate and politician (1879–1964). Similar in many ways to Lord Northcliffe (see Chap. 7).

Became him/her well, or well became her. With a dignity/ intrepidity/ womanly warmth/ womanly sympathy that became him/her well. 28 p41 and often later. In a talk he gave on Wodehouse in 1982, Richard Usborne (1910–2006) wondered where this came from, and I brooded on the problem for weeks. I concentrated on the sound and rhythm and came to the conclusion that it was post-Dickens but pre-1914. On this basis, I decided to have a look at the works of Ouida and Marie Corelli. I found it at the end of Marie Corelli's 1896 best-seller *The Mighty Atom* when a lowly-born — but oh, how noble — peasant speaks with a simple dignity which became him well. Just the sort of phrasing PGW would have picked up. I have subsequently learned it also appears in Mrs Gaskell's *Cranford* (MTT John Fletcher), in Trollope and in Hardy, but I'm still proud of tracking it down in Marie Corelli.

Becher's Brook. 59 p170; 72 p67; and the Canal Turn 91 p155. The Grand National is England's premier and longest steeplechase. Its most notorious jump is Becher's Brook, where the high bank and fence conceal a stream immediately behind them. See also Chap. 2 (son-in-law).

Becket, Thomas à, and King Henry II. 63 p229; 84 p112. In 1170 Henry said either "Will no one rid me of this turbulent priest" or "Who will free me of this turbulent priest?" The result was the murder of Becket in Canterbury Cathedral.

Bedivere, Sir. 79 p143; 91 p123. He was the chap reluctant ("dividing the swift mind") to throw Excalibur away in T. 'The Passing of Arthur'.

Bedouin's Love Song. 25 p93. Popular American song written 1888.

Beef Trust. 81 p179. ('Freddie, Oofy and the Beef Trust') When Teddy Roosevelt attacked the monopolies controlling vast sectors of American commerce (the trusts) at the start of the 20th century, one of the groups who resisted him fiercely were the financiers controlling the meat-packing industry centred on Chicago. They were known as the Beef Trust. See also KINGS.

Been and gone and done it, you've. 2 p75; 3 p216 and later. A Cockney phrase, generally expressing shock/horror/alarm at some act just done. Breaking someone's window with a football, hitting a policeman by accident would be typical incidents to invoke the phrase from one's companions. Gilbert used the phrase in his 'Gentle Alice Brown' (*Bab Ballads*).

Beer with a drop of gin in it. 50 p135. PGW mentions this drink a few times. It was commonly known as a Dog's Nose.

Beery, Wallace. 49 pp251, 256 & 273; 68 p47. US film actor (1880–1949). Played 'heavy' and tough-guy parts and won an Oscar in 1931 in *The Champ.* MTT Neil Midkiff for the information that Beery played a hefty Swedish housemaid in drag in short silent films (1914–16). The references to Dame Daphne Winkworth in *The Mating Season* and Lady Bassett in 'Strychnine in the Soup' are therefore even more appropriate.

Bee's roller-skates. "Aurelia, old girl, you are the bee's roller-skates" 41 p38. Along with such phrases as the elephant's instep, the sardine's whiskers, the canary's tusk, this nonsensical American term of approbation was coined in the early 1920s.

Beetle crushers. 64 p57 and elsewhere. UK slang for large boots 1869 onwards. In PGW the term usually refers to policemen's boots, which always seem larger and more impressive than those of lesser mortals.

Beevor Castle, Kent. See Chap. 29.

Beezley, Miss Florence. 3 p88. See Chap. 2.

'Before taking' pictures in the adverts (Haddock's Headache Hokies etc). 68 p96; 69 p29; 82 p100. Among the advertisements in every popular British or American magazine from 1900 to 1939, there was always a picture of a man/woman tormented with pain 'before taking'. The second picture shows him/her radiant with relief from headaches/arthritis/rheumatism/whatever 'after taking' the product advertised.

Beggar maid. See Cophetua, King.

Beginning, not an end as the blighters say in books. 25 p241. The nearest I can find is "the arrest was not a beginning but an end" from chap. 4 of Victor Hugo's *Les Miserables*. Alternatively, there is S. *Midsummer Night's Dream* 5.1: "That is the true beginning of our end."

Behrman, Sam. 77 p196. American playwright (1897–1973).

Belasco, David. 23 p243. New York playwright and theatrical impresario (1853–1931), whose habit of wearing a clerical collar disconcerted many.

Belfast. One of its livelier nights 31 p204. The civil disorder in Northern Ireland did not begin in 1969. The sad 20th-century pattern of violence there began in 1912 when Asquith brought in his Home Rule for Ireland Bill. A quarter of a million Unionists came out on to the streets in Belfast to express their strong and emphatic disapproval.

Belial. See Sons of Belial.

Believe It or Not. 51 p19. See Ripley's.

Bell, rung the. See Rung.

Belle Dame Sans Merci, La. 70 p31 & p152; 97 p29. Keats' poem of the same name.

Belle of Boulogne. 13 p10. See Chap. 24.

Belle of Wells. 9 p239. See Chap. 24.

Bellman. Said the B., "What I tell you three times is true" 54 p293. From the Bellman's speech in Lewis Carroll's long nonsense poem *The Hunting of the Snark.*

Bells, sweet. 30 p278. See SWEET BELLS JANGLED.

Bells, The. Sir Henry Irving in *The Bells* 36 p99. See IRVING.

Belpher. 25 p7. Village and castle. See Chap. 16.

Belshazzar's feast. 54 p83 and later. B. Daniel 5. Belshazzar was a Babylonian king who gave "a great feast to a thousand of his lords". An event at the feast provides an excellent example of a phrase sinking into the national consciousness. People who have never read the Bible in their lives, and would scorn to do so, will mutter darkly in times of crisis that "the writing is on the wall". See WRITING ON THE WALL.

Belus. 28 p235. A pagan god. Worshipped by the ancient Assyrians, his magnificent temple, the Biblical tower of Babel, was destroyed by Xerxes.

Ben Adhem's name led all the rest. 25 p77. See ABOU BEN ADHEM.

Ben Battle. 68 p188. The central character of Thomas Hood's poem 'Faithless Nellie Gray' (1826), which comprises seventeen verses, each with an appalling pun. PGW gives us a flavour of it with the first verse.

Ben Bolt. 60 p212 and often later. T.D. English wrote this song in 1848. Its prominent featuring in Du Maurier's play *Trilby* in 1895 (art students in Paris, golden-hearted midinettes etc.) ensured its popularity, and it was sung at village concerts in England for the next 30 years. See also SWEET ALICE.

Bench. Back to the bench 18 p261. An American football term. A player is taken off the field and sits on the reserves' bench.

Bend. Catch him on the b./ catch him bending 14 p85 & p163 and later. In general terms, to catch someone at a disadvantage. Comic songs sung in music halls (variety) about rivals in love etc., often referred to the desire of the singer to catch his rival bending so he could be given a good kick in the pants.

Bender. Introduction to *A Century of Humour*. The tanner, a small British sixpenny coin, was also called a bender because old, solid silver ones wore away in time and bent easily. Victorian silver coins were still in circulation in the 1950s. Do not confuse with the US bender, which means a drinking spree.

Beneath my ban, that mystic man shall suffer, *coute qui coute*, Matilda. 3 p109. From 'A Sailor Boy to His Lass' in W.S. Gilbert's *Bab Ballads*.

Benedict. 20 p10. A married man; a character in S. *Much Ado About Nothing*.

Benham, George. 27 p121. A playwright. See Chap. 24.

Bennett, Arnold. 37 p188. PGW knew this famous English author (1867–1931) and was slightly startled by his approach to writing. It is reported that Bennett died of typhoid after drinking a carafe of water in Paris to show that it was safe to do so. See also COPIOUS NOTES.

Bennett, Constance. 48 p65. Glamorous American film star (1904–65).

Bensonburg. 77 p7. See Chap. 23.

Bentley, Owen. 18 p163. Whom else do we know who spent his boyhood in Shropshire, was good at cricket, wanted to write and was forced to go into a bank?

Bergerac, Cyrano de. See CYRANO.

Berkeley Square/Street/Mansions. See Chap. 25. Note 66 p212, where PGW makes a rare comment on the changing appearance of London. Terry pauses to survey Berkeley Square and regret how it had been spoilt with "their beastly Air Ministries and blocks of flats". There were many protests in 1924 when the 250-year-old covenant which forbade building on the south side of the square was overturned and an enormous block erected into which the Air Ministry later moved. The western side remains as it was and retains the beautiful buildings that surrounded the square when PGW knew it.

Berlin, Irving. 45 p205 and often later. I shall not bother to describe this musical genius (1888–1989) whose songs the whole world still sings. PGW worked with him, admired him and quoted his songs often. In 1944, when the noted British philosopher Isaiah Berlin was in the Embassy in Washington, sending back erudite weekly reports to Churchill, Mrs Churchill told her husband that Irving Berlin was visiting London. Churchill, mistaking the name, invited Berlin to lunch, which both found a disconcerting experience. When Churchill asked Berlin what he was currently working on, Berlin's reply that 'White Christmas' was still doing very well completely confused him. Conversely, Churchill's insistence that Berlin give him his considered views on how long the war would last had Berlin at a loss. Both left the table with a much lower opinion of the other. It is rumoured that Mrs Churchill knew exactly what had happened and teased her husband about it for years.

Bernhardt, Sarah. 30 p165 and later. This French actress (1844–1923), who was also an excellent sculptress and painter, entranced audiences around the world. See also HOME LIFE.

Berserk. Berserk blood of the MacGinnisses 17 p172; berserk mood vanishing 22 p148; berserk spirit was upon her 26 p143. This is one of the words for which PGW originally used a capital initial letter, since the term to describe the blood-lust of the Vikings was then new. He used the capital letter as late as *The Small Bachelor* (38 p66). See also HOOLIGAN.

Bertie. My beautiful, bountiful Bertie 76 p7; my bounding B. 93 p83; my beautiful bounding B. 93 p161. George Grossmith Jnr wrote the words to the song 'Beautiful Bountiful Bertie' for the Gaiety show *The Shop Girl*, the first British musical comedy (1894), in which he played Bertie Boyd. See Chap. 13. (PGW also gave us the racehorse Bounding Bertie at 65 p64 and 72 p143. See Chap. 31.)

Bertillon. 14 p92. French criminologist (1853–1914) who established the fingerprint system of criminal identification. PGW got slightly confused here. Bertillon did not do fingerprints; he identified criminals by taking exact measurements of certain physical characteristics such as ears. His system broke down when too many measurements were discovered to be similar and it was realised fingerprints were unique. MTT Richard Vine.

Bessborough, Duke of. 17 p156. See Chap. 16.

Best and brightest. 76 p14. 'Brightest and Best of the Sons of the Morning', a hymn by Bishop Heber (1783–1826).

Best friend, boy's/girl's/man's. See BOY'S BEST FRIEND and GIRL'S BEST FRIEND.

Best friend and severest critic. 67 p102; 89 p74. Like 'Among those present', 'Strike a new note' and 'Success has not spoiled him', this cliché seems to have died at long last. From c.1910 till c.1970, in interviews with playwrights/authors/artists, it seemed to be mandatory for him/her to say that his/her wife/husband was his/her best friend and severest critic.

Best laid plans/schemes of mice and men gang aft agley. Frequent. See MICE AND MEN.

Best of all possible worlds. See ALL IS FOR THE BEST.

Best seats. See YOU WANT THE BEST SEATS.

Bestriding his narrow world like a Colossus. See COLOSSUS.

Better a dinner of 'erbs where love is than a stalled ox and 'atred therewith. 26 p35 and later, including: "As the fellow said, better a dinner of herbs when you're all buddies together than a regular blow-out when you're not." B. Proverbs. 15.17: "Better is a dinner of herbs where love is, than a stalled ox and hatred therewith."

Better the day, better the deed. 59 p23. From Thos. Middleton's (1580–1627) play *Michaelmas Term* (1607).

Between the acting of a dreadful thing ... nature of an insurrection. 96 p141. S. *Julius Caesar* 2.1.

Betwixt the stirrup and the ground, Mercy I asked and mercy I found. 19 p107. 'Epitaph for a Man Killed by Falling from his Horse' by Camden (1551–1623). It is now believed Camden was giving a free rendering of St Augustine's "Misericordia Domini inter pontem et fontem" ("The mercy of God between the bridge and the flood").

Bet-You-A-Franc-Wodehouse. 46 p260. Early readers would have picked up the allusion to John W. 'Bet-You-A-Million' Gates'. Gates (1855–1911) was a predatory American financier whose wealth, acquired initially from barbed-wire and later steel, rivalled that of Pierrepoint Morgan. Gates's recreation was to bet vast amounts on sporting events, and he acquired the soubriquet when he bet his partner a million dollars on a horse race. The partner wisely turned down the bet, but the news got out and the nickname stuck to Gates for the rest of his life. See also KINGS.

Bevan, Aneurin. 79 p100. British left-wing politician (1897–1960). His famous remark about Conservative voters being lower than vermin was made on 4 July 1948.

Bevan, George. 25 p26; 26 p57 & p150. See Chap. 24.

Bevan, Joe. 8 p48. See Chap. 4.

Bevin, Ernie. 68 p82. A left-wing politician (1881–1951) who, as Foreign Secretary, earned the admiration of many for his realistic policy during the Cold War.

Bevo. Fed on B. as a child 60 p119. The only Bevo I have found is an American non-alcoholic 'near-beer' of 1916–23. I doubt if this is what PGW had in mind and I suggest it was some form of 'strengthening' beverage like Oxo (see OXO). There were hundreds of trade names like this from 1890 onwards. Silvo, Brasso and Rinso are still going strong — for cleaning silver, brass, and clothes, respectively.

Beware! Beware! ... Drunk the milk of Paradise, etc. 62 p33. See HONEY-DEW.

Beware of entrance to a quarrel. 8 p49 and at 8 p63 & p66. S. *Hamlet* 1.3 (Polonius's speech to Laertes): "Beware of entrance to a quarrel; but, being in, Bear't that th'opposed may beware of thee." See also POLONIUS'S SPEECH (2).

Bewitched, bothered and bewildered, I was. 76 p172. Rodgers & Hart song 'Bewitched, Bothered and Bewildered' from the 1940 show *Pal Joey*.

Beyond these voices there was peace. 7 p239; 32 p264 and later. T. *Idylls of the King* (last lines of 'Guinevere').

Bhong, Banker of. 14 p219. One of PGW's many references to the London musical comedies of the 1900s. All the early readers of the book would know what he was talking about. The Sultan of Bhong appeared in *The Country Girl*, a show at Daly's Theatre in 1902. With music by Lionel Monckton, it featured an Englishman who had been elected rajah of an exotic Eastern island: "In me you see the Sultan of Bhong, renowned in story and song." The character was based on the remarkable Sir James Brooke (1803–68), who became Rajah of Sarawak and whose family held the title for nearly a century.

Bickersdyke, John. 14 p1. Manager, New Asiatic Bank. See Chap. 21.

Bicycles. See Chap. 19.

Biding my time, I'm. That's the sort of man I'm. 67 p183; 94 p53. 'Biding My Time', a song from *Girl Crazy*, book by Bolton & McGowan, music by George Gershwin, lyrics by Ira Gershwin. The first night (14 October 1930) was a sensation. Ethel Merman (1909–84) made her Broadway debut and stunned the audience with the range and power of her voice, making the orchestra sound weak and thin. In one song she held the top note at full volume for sixteen bars while the orchestra played beneath her. A girl called Ginger ROGERS (1911–95), also making her first Broadway appearance, was in the chorus, while the orchestra included Glenn Miller, Benny Goodman and Red Nichols. I wish I had been there.

Biffen. All the Biffens in PGW (six by my count) take their name, I believe, from an apple, the Norfolk biffin, the basis of Norfolk biffin pudding. I have to add, however, that Harry Graham, the Army officer who became a brilliant librettist and whom PGW admired, wrote comedies about Reginald Biffen, best described as an unscrupulous Bertie Wooster.

Big, bad wolf. Will you not be afraid of the b.b.w? 51 p270. The 1933 Walt Disney cartoon *Three Little Pigs* had everyone singing the song 'Who's Afraid of the Big Bad Wolf?'

Big Four at Scotland Yard. 49 p1; 64 p59; 67 p61 and later. This once-common phrase was used for the four senior officers of the Metropolitan police. They were the Commissioner, the two Assistant Commissioners and the Receiver (civil and legal staff). In the 1930s another officer joined the group and the term changed to the Big Five.

Big pot. Someone of importance, a slang term used originally by Oxford undergraduates in the 1850s for 'potentates', i.e. heads of colleges and professors.

Big stick. 15A p154. Psmith comments: "I and Roosevelt." This phrase became popular in America when Teddy Roosevelt said (2 September 1901) America's foreign policy should be: "Speak softly and carry a big stick."

Bigger they are, the harder they fall. 34 p250 and later. This was said by the boxer Robert Fitzsimmons, but there is disagreement on when he said it. Some claim it was on the night before he fought James J. Jeffries in 1899. Jeffries, much the bigger (and fitter) man, won in the 11th round. Others maintain Fitzsimmons coined the phase after knocking out Ed 'The Human Freight Train' Dunkhorst, who weighed nearly 300 lbs.

Bikini, atom bomb at. 71 p21. The name of the Pacific atoll where the USA carried out atom-bomb tests in 1946 was adopted by the designers of the shocking new two-piece bathing costume for women.

Bildad the Shuhite. 26 p239; 33 p17. A friend who comes to sympathise and makes things worse. B. Job 2.11, 8.1. and 25.1. When Job was afflicted with boils and other painful ailments, Bildad and two others came to comfort him. This mainly consisted of saying that his ills were only to be expected in this cruel world.

Bill the Conqueror. So obvious that many miss it, the title is derived from one of the most famous characters in English history, William the Conqueror, who came over from France in 1066 and defeated Harold at the Battle of Hastings.

Bill the Lizard. 80 p76. See Lewis Carroll's *Alice in Wonderland.*

Billiken. 18 (3 times) and later. A small, gnome-like doll/charm. The doll version had a weighted base so that, when pushed over, it always bobbed up again. There was a craze for Billikens and Billiken charms from 1900 to 1914. After 1918, Cornish piskies and 'Joan the wad' (a female equivalent) were equally popular as good-luck charms. They are now derided as childish superstition by today's glitterati, including those who wear a crystal round their neck, convinced its 'aura' will improve their life-style/enrich their inner selves/ enable them to find themselves, etc. etc.

Billson, Battling. See Chap. 4.

Billy boil, does the? 4 p64. A billy, short for billy-can, is a small outdoor camping kettle. The Australian song 'Waltzing Matilda' (1894) made the word popular across the UK.

Billy Taylor. 4 p45. *Billee Taylor*, a musical comedy of 1880, was written by Pot Stephens and Teddy Solomon, both members of the Pelican Club.

Bimbo. Frequent in PGW, always meaning a man; see 64 p110. In the early 1900s, when PGW would have heard it in New York, it meant a tough guy, synonymous with bozo. It came to mean a young woman in the late 1920s–early 1930s. The current meaning of a beautiful, if dumb, woman came in c.1960.

Bi-metallism. 7 p72; 28 p127. From 1880 to 1914, the economic theory of basing money supply on silver as well as gold had many adherents.

Bingham, Beefy. 43 p97. See Chap. 11.

Bingley (ex Brinkley), the villainous valet. See Chap. 3.

Bingley-on-Sea. 29 p126 and later. Another example of PGW giving us a clue when he first used a place name. At 29 p126, we are told Bingley-on-Sea is in Sussex; it is the only time we are given any indication of its location. See Chap. 16.

Bingo. See Chap. 30.

Bird, get the. Frequent. To receive a poor reception from an audience, to be hissed; from the hissing noise of disapproval a goose makes. The term has been traced back to 1576. See also EGG, TO LAY AN.

Bird in a gilded cage, a. 48 p27; 54 p152 and elsewhere. At the Academy Exhibition in 1898, Frederick Goodall showed a picture, 'A Gilded Cage', depicting a beautiful girl in a harem. The sub-title was: "How can a bird that was born for joy, sit in a cage and sing?" A.J. Lamb and Harry von Tilzer wrote a wildly popular song based on it in 1900: "Her beauty was sold, For an old man's gold. She's a bi-i-ird in a gi-i-i-i-ilded cage." In 1990 I had a drink in the Birdcage Theatre at Tombstone, where a notice on the wall claimed that the theatre had inspired the song. The establishment opened in 1881 as a combined saloon, theatre and dance hall and was proud of its reputation as 'the bawdiest house in the West'.

Bird of the Difficult Eye, The. 26 p57; 91 p118. A book by Lord Dunsany (1878–1957), poet, novelist, playwright, sculptor and big-game hunter. PGW knew him and admired his imaginative writing.

Birmingham. See LADY WHO WANTED TO GO.

'Birth of a Salesman'. 69 short story title. PGW wrote this in 1950, an obvious gloss on Arthur Miller's *Death of a Salesman*, which had come out the previous year. In a letter of 1949, PGW wrote what a smash hit Miller's play was: "only the morbid stuff seems to go nowadays."

Biscuit, take the. Frequent. You sneak the biscuit every time 14 p49. Something that beats everything, an occurrence that supersedes everything else. A suggested origin is the custom among the ancient Greeks for presenting a sweetened biscuit to the most vigilant sentry on a night watch. A seemingly unlikely origin today, but not to PGW and his fellows who had studied Greek and Latin from the age of twelve or thirteen. See also CAKEWALK and GARIBALDI.

Biscuits. Stealing b. from the housemaster's/headmaster's study 12 p29 and later.

I have no evidence whatsoever that PGW indulged in this practice in his youth, but I would be surprised if he had not. I taught in two prep schools and, in both cases, the headmaster kept a tin of biscuits in his study to accompany his coffee after dinner.

Bishop. As a nickname 2 p12. See Chap. 30.

Bishop and phantom curate. 6 p174. See 'The Phantom Curate' in Gilbert's *Bab Ballads*.

Bishop of Rumtifoo. 6 p55. See 'The Bishop of Rum-ti-foo' in Gilbert's *Bab Ballads*.

Bishops and their speeches. See 44, chap. 7. A Shropshire newspaper of 1899 had an account of a school prize-giving which included the full text of the speech given by a bishop, the main speaker. It lasted an hour and a quarter and covered two complete pages of the paper. The headmaster thanked him for his 'interesting and very comprehensive address'. See also GRAVE TO THE GAY.

Bisley. 12 p106. See ASHBURTON.

Bisque, knee deep in the. 43 p23. PGW variation of being in trouble, in the soup, in the bouillon etc. See also GUMBO, MULLIGATAWNY, and OXO. Note: PGW also uses 'bisque' in the golf sense where it means a free stroke.

Bit the hand that fed it. 7 p61; bite the hand that was going to feed them 33 p17 and often later. Common misquote from Burke's 'Thoughts and Detail on Scarcity' (1800): "And having looked to government for bread, on the very first scarcity they will turn and bite the hand that fed them." In a superb seven-line sentence at 59 p184, PGW stigmatises Stiffy Byng as "a young squirt who went about biting the hand that fed her at luncheon at its flat by causing it the utmost alarm and despondency ..." (See also ALARM AND DESPONDENCY.)

Bitches, they're all. 68 p29. See BASTARD.

Bite like serpents and sting like adders. See ADDERS.

Bitter cup. 2 p33 and often later; the bitter cup was full, drained the bitter cup etc. To suffer deep anguish, bitterness, remorse etc. This was clearly a reference PGW assumed every reader would understand, but the nearest I have got is Pope's *Iliad* 22, "the bitter dregs of fortune's cup to drain". Burke followed this in his *On the Sublime and Beautiful* (1757), where he speaks of "a cup of bitterness" and "to drain the bitter cup of fortune". Nietzsche used it later. Further investigation produced many references to Psalm 73.10 ("Therefore his people return hither: and waters of a full cup are wrung out to them"), but only from various theologians explaining the verse. Perhaps PGW sat through so many sermons in which the phrase was used to emphasise mankind's unhappy lot that it stayed with him and those of his generation. Equally likely, however, is that it is PGW's memory of his time at Dulwich when he read of many Greeks, Socrates among them, committing suicide by drinking hemlock.

Bitter when it was brown. See LOOKED ON THE BITTER.

Bitter will be blended with the sweet, always the. 67 p65. Same meaning as Lucretius' crack 'Surgit amari aliquid'. See SURGIT.

Black Africa. 53 p198. MGM's *Trader Horn* was released in February 1931, during PGW's first stay in Hollywood. Publicity claimed cameras had gone to Africa for the first time and, although most of the dialogue-shots were unusable, the non-dialogue scenes provided many stock shots in Tarzan films later. MTT Neil Midkiff. See also Chap. 28.

Black as Egypt's night. 4 p195; 50 p128. See the once universally-known student song 'Riding Down from Bangor', which adapted the wording from B. Exodus 10.21: "darkness over the land of Egypt".

Black as the pit from pole to pole. 37 p19 and later. See Night that covers me.

Black beetle. If I had been a b.b. she could not have looked at me with a more scornful superiority 17 p208. See My learned friend's manner.

Black Bottom. 39 p163; Cleopatra dances it 41 p35. The Black Bottom dance of 1926 stemmed, so its proponents said, from the sluggish movements of walking through the thick mud of the Swanee River. See Swanee and also Chap 18.

Black but comely. 22 p149. B. Song of Solomon 1.5. MTT Fr Rob Bovendeaard.

Black cap, putting on the. 31 'The Purity of the Turf'. Before the capital punishment was abolished in England, a judge pronouncing the sentence of death would place a small square of black material ('the cap') on his head. MTT Neil Midkiff for reminding me.

Black Death. 52 p260; 67 p149 and later. This virulent plague killed a quarter of Europe's population in the 14th century.

Black Hand. 11 p57 and often later. See particularly 54 p104–5. I had always thought this was a PGW-created fictional gang and was surprised to find it was a feared terrorist group. A Serbian secret society, intent on reuniting all Serbs in a Greater Serbia, its activities culminated in the murder of the Archduke Ferdinand in 1914, which led directly to the First World War. The movement faded after the execution of its leaders in 1917. There was also a criminal organisation of the same name in New York from 1900 to 1920 which had strong links to the Camorra. Perhaps this was the one PGW had in mind.

Black Hole of Calcutta. 83 p22 and elsewhere. The Nawab of Bengal imprisoned 146 British prisoners in a small cell in Fort William, Calcutta, on 20 June 1756. The following morning, only 23 were still alive. The phrase is still used when people find themselves stuck in a crowded Underground train or a lift.

Black Man's Burden. 63 p63 and later. PGW's splendid twist on Kipling's poem 'The White Man's Burden'. Kipling wrote this in an attempt to persuade the USA to join Britain in bringing law and order to uncivilised parts of the world, helping to put down slavery, piracy etc. The phrase 'White Man's Burden', originally intended to encourage altruistic responsibility among the white imperial powers, unfortunately soon became misunderstood by many and became a term for white superiority. That is why PGW mocked explorers, especially the bossy female ones like Mrs Cork who made their native bearers' lives such a misery, with the term the 'Black Man's Burden'.

Black Shorts, Spode's. 59 p71. Every contemporary reader recognised that Spode and his Black Shorts were a satire on Oswald Mosley and his British Fascists (Blackshirts) of the 1930s. What I found more interesting was Gussie Fink-Nottle's remark at p72 that Spode and his followers had to wear black 'footer bags', i.e. football shorts, because "there were no shirts left". This puzzled me for years till I found out that Wodehouse, as so often, was absolutely right. In the 1930s, Europe saw new political parties coming into existence whose supporters signified their allegiance by the shirts they wore. No more strange a habit, I suppose, than the coloured ribbons people wear on their lapels today indicating their support for various causes. The Fascists of Italy and the UK wore black shirts; Hitler's supporters in Germany wore brown shirts. The Young Communist League wore red shirts, while Franco's supporters in Spain wore blue. A few years ago I learned that members of the Social Credit movement wore green shirts, as did a pro-Nazi Hungarian Party. Since yellow meant plague and everybody wore white shirts anyway, Gussie was quite right; there were no more shirts left. An excellent example of a topical reference which needs explanation today.

Black spot. She handed Archie the black spot 84 p32. Notification of impending doom/punishment made famous by R.L. Stevenson's *Treasure Island*.

Blackwell, Edward. Since E.B. was in his prime 37 p67. Renowned for his big hitting, Blackwell was runner-up in the 1904 UK Amateur Golf Championship.

Blanc, M. 13 p28; 15 p13; 46 p235. Monsieur Blanc was the enterprising Frenchman who saw the potential of a casino at Monte Carlo and got it going in 1861.

Blasco What's-his-name stuff, Vicente y. 31 p35. Vicente Blasco Ibáñez, author of the best-seller *The Four Horsemen of the Apocalypse* in 1919. MTT Elin Woodger.

Blatchford *Intelligencer and Echo*. 19 p143. This newspaper's title is another PGW variation on the Shropshire town of Bridgnorth. See Chap. 35.

Bleak House, the Thing and Thing thing in. 77 p10. Dickens' novel *Bleak House* revolved around Jarndyce v. Jarndyce, a protracted lawsuit over a legacy which only came to an end when the lawyers' fees consumed the entire estate. The lawsuit Dickens had in mind, and which all his readers knew, was the Great Jennings Case, which began before Dickens was born in 1812 and was still going on when he died in 1870.

Blessed Damozel, the (who leaned out from Heaven). 32 p151 and later. Poem (1847) and painting (1876), both by Dante Gabriel Rossetti.

Blessings ever wait on virtuous deeds. 73 p131. As Jeeves says, it is from Congreve. His 'The Mourning Bride' has: "Blessings ever wait on virtuous deeds, / And though a late, a sure reward succeeds."

Blessings on the falling out that all the more endears. 63 p79; 80 p218 and later. From T. *The Princess*, Pt 2, opening song.

Bligh, Captain (of the *Bounty*). 56 p80 and later. This grossly misrepresented

Royal Navy officer (1784–1817) should be remembered not for the mutiny on his ship, but for the remarkable voyage of hundreds of miles that he made after the mutineers had cast him and his companions adrift in a small boat in the middle of the Pacific.

Blind Hooky. 49 p14. One of those complicated card games. The dealer gives every player one card, face down. If his card is higher than theirs, he wins; if theirs is higher, they win but hardly ever do.

Blinded and stiffed with a will. 64 p81. Cursing and swearing. KIPLING uses it in 'The Taking of Lungtungpen'.

Blithe spirit … near it. 87 p97. SHELLEY's 'Ode to a Nightingale'. "Hail to thee, blithe Spirit! / Bird thou never wert, / That from heaven or near it, / Pourest thy full heart …"

Bloc of friendly neutrals. 69 p114. I do not know when the word 'bloc' became common for a political group/collection/alliance. I remember it in popular usage soon after the Second World War when the USSR had its 'Soviet bloc' of nations around its borders and under its control.

Blonde. Perhaps the fact that she was a b. and he was a gentleman, seemed to draw him strangely to this intruder 44 p102. Anita Loos' 1925 *Gentlemen Prefer Blondes* was a best-seller on both sides of the Atlantic.

Blondie. 70 p27; 97 p41. The wife of Dagwood Bumstead. See BUMSTEAD.

Blondin. 40 p151. Probably the most famous tight-rope walker, Charles Blondin (1824–97) crossed Niagara Falls a dozen times or more, blindfolded, backwards, wheeling a passenger in a wheelbarrow, etc. etc.

Blood. An awful b. 8 p14; and later, as in "he's a bit of a blood","a terrific blood". Term in use in schools and universities 1880–1950 for those young men who were Head of School, Captain of the Rugger XV, President of the Union or achieved a reputation of some sort. For the distinction between a blood and a Knut, see KNUTS below.

Blood, toil, tears and sweat. 71 p112; 80 p24. From Winston Churchill's address to the House of Commons on 13 May 1940. Now mocked and parodied, his words inspired a nation in great danger.

Blood and iron. See MAN OF BLOOD.

Blood will tell. 18 p224 and later. Heredity will out. In racing circles, it is believed a horse with good breeding will outrun a horse without it.

Bloodenough, Gen Sir Hector, VC, KCIE, MVO. 39 p112. No direct connection known, but possibly PGW's vague recollection of General Sir Bindon Blood, GCB (1842–1940), a gallant soldier who served his country for 60 years.

Bloody, bold and resolute. 96 p132. S. *Macbeth* 4.1. "Be bloody, bold, and resolute; laugh to scorn / The power of man, for none of woman born Shall harm Macbeth."

Bloody but unbowed. 76 p203. From W.E. Henley's 'Invictus' (1888). "Under the bludgeonings of chance, / My head is bloody, but unbowed."

Bloomer (footballer). 18 p251. Steve Bloomer (1874–1938), pre-eminent footballer from 1895 to 1910. His record for the number of goals scored in a season stood till Dixie Dean beat it in 1937. He scored 28 goals in 22 games for England, and a statue of him now stands in the centre of Derby.

Bloomingdale. 20 p185 and often later. America's oldest lunatic asylum, established in New York 1808, was incorporated into another establishment in 1894. Columbia University now occupies the old asylum buildings. Do not confuse with Bloomingdale's, a famous New York department store.

Blore, Eric. More E.B. than Robert Taylor 66 p37. This short, stout character actor (1887–1959) could not be more unlike the tall, handsome Taylor (1911–69) who played Hollywood heroes for 30 years.

Blossom, Lottie. See Chap. 31.

Blot on the old/on her escutcheon. 24 p10 and later. An escutcheon is the shield on which is displayed a coat of arms, originally used for identification in battle. If you belonged to an ancient family, you would be reluctant to inflict a blot of dishonour on the family arms, e.g. by marrying a chorus girl or refusing a loved aunt's request to carry out a simple little robbery. Probably from Browning's play *A Blot in the 'Scutcheon* 1.3.

Blow, blow thou cold winter wind, thou art not so … unkind as man's ingratitude. 7 p187 and later. S. *As You Like It* 2.7.

Blow, winds, crack your cheeks. 60 p218; 95 p133. S. *King Lear* 3.1: "Blow, winds, and crack your cheeks! rage! blow! You cataracts and hurricanoes, spout."

Blow the gaff. 65 p213. Criminal slang for informing the police of a planned crime; to give the game away, to act as an informer.

Blucher. He had said with B., "What a city to loot!" 13 p79. Comment by the Prussian General von Blucher (1742–1819) (who helped Wellington at Waterloo) on his first visit to London.

Blue bird (of happiness). Frequent in PGW, "looking for the blue bird", "lost the blue bird", etc. "The blue bird" had become synonymous with happiness in the 1920s. See 42 p317, where Pilbeam sees 500 pounds "flutter from his grasp like a vanishing blue bird". I was surprised to find the phrase, though an old one, came into popular use in 1909, when Maeterlinck's fantasy play *The Blue Bird* (about a blue bird that brought happiness) swept Europe and America. Maurice Maeterlinck (1862–1949), philosopher, playwright and naturalist, went on to write scholarly works on bees and birds. When he went to Hollywood, Goldwyn introduced him to everybody as "the guy who told the world about the birds and the bees". Maeterlinck was unhappy in Hollywood and soon left. Goldwyn saw him off at the station, consoling him with the assurance that he, Goldwyn, knew that Maeterlinck would be successful one day. This was no doubt a great comfort to the man who had already been awarded the Nobel Prize for Literature.

Blue Boar. 8 p52 and eight times thereafter. I have been unable to find the original of this legendary hostelry or why PGW used the name so much. The Blue Boar is the badge of the extinct earldom of Oxford and, although there are several pubs by this name around the country, I have not found any in London or near Bridgnorth (See Chap. 35). One day, perhaps.

Blue heaven. Like my blue heaven 44 p21. 1927 song 'My Blue Heaven'.

Blue Train. 52 p21. This train ran from Calais to the French Riviera direct. Designed to take the wealthy across France in luxury without having to change at Paris, it made its first run in 1922. To travel on it was a sign of status and money — akin to flying on Concorde later.

Blue were her eyes as the fairy-flax. 59 p238. From Longfellow's 'The WRECK OF THE HESPERUS'.

Bluebeard. 27 p67. A man who murders his wives. The story came into England from Perrault's *Contes du Temps* (1697), which also included Sleeping Beauty, Red Riding Hood, Puss in Boots, Cinderella and other fairy tales. The original Bluebeard is said to have been the Frenchman Giles de Retz, Marquis of Laval, who was found guilty of killing six of his seven wives and was executed in 1440.

Bluemantle Pursuivant at Arms. 69 p106. The College of Arms in London has three Kings of Arms (Garter is the senior), six Heralds and four Pursuivants: Rouge Dragon, Portcullis, Bluemantle and Rouge Croix. If you want to get an idea of their splendid State dress, look at the kings and jacks in a pack of cards.

Blumenfeld, Mr. 31 p105; 43 p123. Theatrical impresario. See Chap. 24.

Blunt knife. 84 p108. See KNIFE.

Blush of shame would have mantled the cheek of a more sensitive man, the. 92 p115. The blush of shame mantling somebody's cheeks sounds very Tennysonian but will not be found there. It seems to have been in common use in the 19th century, rather like AGONY HAD/HAS ABATED or MAZZARD. In *The Tenant of Wildfell Hall*, Anne Brontë wrote of "a faint blush mantling her cheek", and as late as *The Return of Tarzan* (1915), Edgar Rice Burroughs wrote: "'Yes,' he answered with bowed head, his face mantling with the flush of shame."

Blush unseen. 22 p105; blushing unseen in the dark unfathomed caves of Mott Street, Knightsbridge 45 p274. See GEM OF PUREST.

B.O. See HER BEST FRIENDS.

Boadicea. 29 p89 and often up to 94 p106. This British warrior queen of the Iceni led a revolt against the Roman occupation in 61 A.D. She died, probably from poison, the following year.

Boardwalk. 18 p131 and elsewhere. The boardwalk is the American equivalent to the British seaside Promenade, i.e. a walkway made of planks/duckboards beside a pleasure beach with amusement stalls and seats set along it.

Bob. Frequent. Slang for a shilling, one twentieth of a pound; since 1971, five new pence. See also TANNER.

Bodegas. 30 p91 and later. A chain of wine bars in London that specialised in serving sherry and port. The Bodega at the corner of Bedford Street and the

Strand was well known as the haunt of actors looking for jobs. That is why PGW described Gussie Fink-Nottle becoming "as pronounced a ham as ever drank small ports in Bodegas" (68 p93). I still miss the Bedford Street Bodega, which closed about 1980.

Bodmin, Jno. of Vigo Street. 55 p98. I have been unable to trace any hatter named Bodmin, or any hatter in Vigo Street in the last hundred years. Based on Bodmin's Royal Warrant and its apparent supremacy in hats, I plump for Lock's of St James's, founded 1676, who have been making hats for British monarchs for nearly 200 years. The hats they made for Wellington and Nelson can still be seen in their shop.

I wish I knew where PGW bought his top hats from. If, as one supposes, Ethel made him get a new one for Leonora's wedding (December 1932), then it's a good bet he got it from Lock's. In a letter to Bill Townend in 1933, PGW said he hoped Townend had seen the picture in the Press of him in his new topper. I wonder if there was a problem about its delivery to Wodehouse? Is it just coincidence that 'The Amazing Hat Mystery' was written a few weeks after Leonora's wedding?

Body and Soul. 51 p145 and later. Song by Green and Hayman 1930.

Bogart, Humphrey. 76 p26 and later. Unlike the tough-guy image he portrayed on screen, Bogart (1899–1957) came from a wealthy and cultured background. See also TENNIS, ANYONE?.

Bogey. 18 p130. See Chap. 27 but also COLONEL BOGEY below.

Bohea. 31 p90 and elsewhere. A strong black tea from China that became popular in the UK. Before the days of mass production and supermarkets, people used to make up their own mixtures of various type of leaf. My wife Charlotte used to mix one part of a 'light China' tea (Earl Grey) with four parts of Ceylon (darker, stronger leaf). Until recently, one could go to a good tobacconist and order your own mixture of tobacco made up, e.g. one part Latakia, two parts Cavendish etc. See also OOLONG.

Bohemia/Bohemians. 9 pp30–31 and often later. This generic term for writers and artists living in an unconventional way stems from the first gypsies who arrived in France from Bohemia about 1430. The term achieved fresh popularity with Puccini's *La Boheme* and *Trilby*; see TRILBY below.

Bohn. 1 p84. H.G. Bohn (1796–1884) produced *Bohn's Library*, cheap paperback translations of classical texts. They were still available in the 1940s, for which I and many other schoolboys were very grateful.

Bohunkus. 53 p80 and later. A pejorative American term, originally denoting someone from Bohemia, Hungary or that part of Europe. The term comes from eliding BOHemian-HUNGarian.

Boiled beef and carrots. 52 p211. Two ingredients of the atmosphere in the hall at Gussie's immortal prize-giving. The two have been indissolubly linked in England since the success of the music hall song "Boiled Beef and Carrots" in the 1890s.

Boiling oil. Frequent. The expression came into popular use with *The Mikado* and PGW used the complete quote "something lingering with boiling oil in it" in *Performing Flea* p205 (Huy Day By Day). See G&S *The Mikado* Act 2: "Something lingering with boiling oil in it."

Bois de Boulong. Walk along the B. de B. with an independent air 83 p189. The line is from Fred Gilbert's still-popular 1892 song 'The Man Who Broke the Bank at Monte Carlo'. "As I walk along the Bois Boolong" — the all-too-common English pronunciation of Bois de Boulogne (Paris).

Boles, Boles, Wickett, Widgery and Boles. 58 p194. I am still puzzled why PGW inserted 'Widgery' into this cricketing pun on a solicitor's firm. Why not have Boles, Boles, Wickett, Wickett and Boles?

Bologney, Miss Julia Ukridge's stuff is. 57 p236. See BALONEY.

Bombardier (Billy) Wells. 23 p190. English heavyweight boxer 1910–20. He went on to be the chap who banged the gong in the opening sequence of Rank Studios films.

Bon Marché. 36 p15. This (real) Brixton store took its name, as did many others, from the first purpose-designed Paris department store, built by Alexandre-Gustave Eiffel in 1870.

Bones, Massa. 12 p33; Bones and Johnson 17 p118; 32 p145 and later. In the old Christy Minstrel (black-face singing group) shows, an invariable part of the routine was one man (Mr Interlocutor) asking riddles of the others. 'Mr Bones' and 'Mr Johnson' or 'Mr Tambo' were usually the ones to reply: "No. I do not know why the chicken crossed the road." 'Mr Bones' was so named because he 'played the bones', i.e. rattled small bones in time with the music. His opposite number 'Mr Tambo' played the tambourine. See also CHRISTY MINSTRELS and MINSTREL SHOW.

Bongo on the Congo. 41 p140; 96 pp150, 165 & 169. See also PGW's lyric in *Sitting Pretty*. His geography was slightly awry here; the town of Bonga is indeed on the Congo River. Bongo, however, is 50 miles away from it.

Bongos, dongos, pongos (and the like). 28 p61 and elsewhere. In 'A Mixed Threesome', the explorer Eddie Denton comes home from Central Africa, and his "wiry frame and strong jaw without which no explorer is complete" ensure that he soon wins the love of Betty Weston. Denton tells his awed audience stirring tales of bull bongos, of pongos (or native bearers), of the dongo (or undergrowth), of a kongo (or pool) as well as jongos, longos, tongos and wongos. A telephone call to the Rwandan embassy confirmed the 'ongo' suffix is as common in central Africa as PGW told us, though the majority are family names.

Bonny Babies. 67 p38; 81 p131; 85 p153. The phrase began with the Glaxo Baby Food's 1913 advertising campaign: "Glaxo Builds Bonny Babies." Their advertising and provision of prizes for every baby competition in the country made the phrase a popular one. In 1997 an English district council banned these competitions as politically incorrect. The reason given was that a baby might lose and the trauma could affect him for life! A journalist wrote a perceptive article making the point that, whereas in most competitions, the competitors accept that someone else might win, every mother *knows* her pride and joy is the most beautiful baby in the world. Having attended many of these tense contests, he reported that the result was always greeted with universal disbelief: "How could the judge possibly prefer that snub-nosed/neckless/pale/blobby/skinny/overcoiffed/warthog-look-alike creature to my darling angel?" was the invariable reaction.

At one show in Birmingham in the mid-1970s, the judge was a nutritionist of strong views who thought all the babies, except one, were much too fat and adjudicated accordingly, giving reasons for her decision. There was a stunned silence and, over the cups of tea after the nutritionist had left, the mothers agreed to fight this heresy. Startled council officials found themselves faced with such a united front of infuriated and militant matriarchs that they had to hold the competition all over again — of which the winner was a traditional chubby Winston Churchill look-alike.

It is reported that the film actor Lloyd Bridges (1913–98) knew he would never become a major star when the news leaked out that his public career had begun with President Taft awarding him a trophy as America's fattest baby. Traditionalists will be glad to know that Bonny Babies contests are still with us. In December 2005, the national champion was Jamie-Leigh Blair of Whitehaven, Cumbria.

Bonny Bonny Banks of Loch Lomond. 60 p26 and later. See HIGH ROAD.

Bonzo. 43 p200. Aunt Dahlia's pride and joy took his name from a comic white bull terrier puppy drawn by G.E. Studdy. Bonzo first appeared in *The Sketch* in 1922, and it was the magazine's editor who thought up the name. Bonzo was an instant success; in 1926 he featured in 20 silent film cartoons and was rivalled only by Felix the Cat. 'Bonzo' became a common nickname for those little boys unfortunate enough to resemble him (I was at school with one). I suggest that PGW's use of the name might be a compliment to an old schoolfellow since he and Studdy entered Dulwich on the same day.

Book Beautiful, publisher of the. 67 p174; 88 p58 and elsewhere. I thought the phrase was simply PGW's version of the 'house beautiful' in *Pilgrim's Progress* until I visited an exhibition commemorating Aubrey Beardsley, the illustrator who worked for publisher John Lane. Lane founded the Bodley Head publishing house in 1889 and set out to change the dull, heavy format of Victorian books by using clearer print, better paper, decorative covers etc. He advertised his firm heavily as 'publishers of the Book Beautiful,' and inverted usage including the Ship Beautiful, Word Beautiful, etc., came into popular use.

Book of verses beneath the bough, a. 62 p86. Fitzgerald's *Omar Khayyam* 1.11: "Here with a Loaf of Bread beneath the bough, / A Flask of Wine, a Book of Verse — and Thou, / Beside me singing in the Wilderness — / Oh, Wilderness is Paradise enow!"

Book Society's Choice of the Month. 64 p11. Bertie Wooster and, by implication, PGW did not think too much of the Book of the Month idea, which began in the US in 1926.

Bookmaker who won billiard tournaments. 36 p80. Until comparatively recently, it was illegal to take cash bets away from a racecourse, and bookmakers adopted the habit of wearing very brightly-coloured clothing so people could recognise them in the street. Adjourning to a quiet corner meant that business could be conducted out of the public gaze. 'Bookie's tweeds' was a term long used for any 'loud' clothing.

The billiard tournament reference is much more obscure. At the corner of Wellington Street and Exeter Street off the Strand is a handsome building with a horse's head over the entrance. From c.1860 till c.1970 this was the Victoria Club, famous as being the club where all the leading bookmakers were members and settled with each other after major races. The annual members' billiards tournament was famous with hundreds, even thousands, of pounds being bet on each shot, and participants used to a normal table had to learn to cope with the club table, which had been made for Queen Victoria and was famous for its small, sharp-edged pockets. Another topical reference that needs explanation today.

Boom. Chap in Bab Ballads who couldn't walk into a room without ejaculating "Boom" 34 p16. See 'The Sensation Captain' in Gilbert's *Bab Ballads*. "He couldn't walk into a room / Without ejaculating 'Boom!' / Which startled ladies greatly."

Boomps-a-daisy. See BUMPS-A-DAISY.

Boop-boop-a-doop. 47 p57; 58 p289. In the New York musical *Good Boy* (1928) Helen Kane (1904–66), a baby-voiced singer, sang 'I Wanna Be Loved By You' and at the end of each verse added a breathless "boop-boop-a-doop". The phrase inspired cartoonist Grim Natwick (1890–1990) to create Betty Boop.

Boost for Birdsburg. 23 p99. The American 'Boosting' custom started in Spokane, Washington, in 1898. Hoping to attract more people to the town, the Spokane town council persuaded all its local organisations to participate. Every letter posted from the town had the words 'Boost for Spokane' on it, as did every package and piece of luggage carried by its citizens. The idea spread across America and it became a craze. 'Cuss America, give me Oshkosh' summarises the general feeling. Tacoma, another Washington township, took up the scheme with enthusiasm. The principles it laid down for its citizens were: 1. Boost Tacoma. 2. Boost Tacoma Night and Day. 3. Boost Tacoma When You Travel. 4. Boost Tacoma In Your Letters East. 5. Put your whole soul into it — BOOST TACOMA!

All went well till the Tacoma Town Council started dishing out free red paint for its citizens to daub 'Boost Tacoma' on every flat surface they could find and one enthusiast decided to paint the slogan on some cows. Unfortunately, he chose cows belonging to a farmer who lived in Spokane, and the resultant row caused Tacoma and Spokane to scale down their efforts for a while.

Boot polish spread on bread, eating. 12 p103; 39 p117; 91 p139. This is not as unlikely as it sounds. I have a note that it is based on an Emsworth House School anecdote PGW was told.

Booth, Edwin. 71 p89. This distinguished American actor (1833–93) was famous for his Shakespearean roles. It was his brother who assassinated Lincoln in 1865.

Booth & Baxter biscuit factory. 58 p236. See WALSINGFORD-BELOW-CHIVENEY and REDBRIDGE.

Boothby, Guy. 9 p207. A popular Australian-born author (1867–1905).

Borge, Victor. 78 p173. This witty Danish pianist and comedian died in January 2001.

Borgia family, (food) prepared by the nastier-minded members of the. 31 p13 up to 93 p115. Rodrigo Borgia (1431–1503) is succinctly described in my encyclopaedia as "the most memorable of the corrupt and secular Popes of the Renaissance". A churchman with a series of mistresses, he bribed his way to the Papacy, becoming Pope Alexander VI in 1492. Of his illegitimate children, Cesare (1476–1507) and Lucrezia (1480–1519) are the most notorious. Both Pope Alexander and his son Cesare used every means to get rid of possible rivals and acquire wealth — assassination, false imprisonment and, it was commonly believed, by poisoning them at the dinner table. For further detail, see any decent history of Europe.

Borglum, Gutzon. 63 p44; 71 p11. Borglum (1871–1941) decided that what America really needed were the heads of four presidents carved on the side of a mountain and he started work in 1927. His enormous carvings of George Washington, Abraham Lincoln, Theodore Roosevelt and Thomas Jefferson are to be seen on Mount Rushmore, South Dakota.

Borotra. 46 p147. Jean Borotra (1898–1994), 'The Bounding Basque', dominated European tennis in the 1920s–30s. I watched him at Wimbledon in the early 1950s and he still went up in the air like a ballet dancer. He played till the age of 94 and in every competition between the International Clubs of Great Britain and France from 1924 to 1992.

Borstal. 36 p37 and later. First (1902) UK reformatory for young offenders.

Bosanquet. 12 p152. B.J.T. Bosanquet (1877–1936), the cricketer who devised the 'googly' delivery of a cricket ball around 1900. Roughly equivalent to the first use of the 'curveball' in baseball. See also CURVES.

Bosh. Frequent. Worthless, empty, useless. My dictionaries say it was a Turkish word that became popular in England with the publication in 1834 of James Morier's novel *Ayesha*.

Bosher Street. 35 p159 and elsewhere. PGW version of London's oldest police station and magistrate's court, Bow Street in Covent Garden, where Henry Fielding established the Bow Street Runners in 1748. The court, directly opposite the Opera House, closed in July 2006. For an explanation of Wodehouse's usage, see ER SUFFIX.

Bosom. Having cleansed his stuff'd bosom of that perilous stuff which weighs upon the heart 26 p76; and later. See 95 p89, Shakespeare should have known better than to use 'stuff' and 'stuffed' in the same sentence. S. *Macbeth* 5.3: "Cleanse the stuff'd bosom of that perilous stuff, Which weighs upon the heart."

Boss, Oh you. See KID.

Botticellian, how. 3 p260. G&S *Patience* Act 2: "How Botticellian! How Fra Angelican! Oh, Art, we thank thee for this boon." Gilbert was satirising the Aesthetic movement of the time (Oscar Wilde et al.).

Bottle Imp. Beach felt like the man who had got rid of the Bottle Imp. 50 p172. At 34 p224, PGW gives the reference, R.L. Stevenson's *The Bottle Imp*, the story of a man who buys a bottle with an imp in it, which brings misfortune to all who own it.

Bottle, one, people striking for the use of. 70 p170. PGW had clearly noted this peculiarity of British Army phraseology. In the British Army's catalogue of stores, the noun always come first, followed by the qualifying detail. I still remember the terminology of our weapons instructor when I was a recruit: "This is a Launcher, Rocket, 3 point 5 inch, enemy tanks for the destruction of, — and I don't want to hear anybody calling it a ruddy bazooka. Is that clear?"

Bottles, bottles everywhere, in case you want a drink. 70 p169. See Coleridge's *The Rime of the Ancient Mariner*: "Water, water, everywhere, Nor any drop to drink." See also ANCIENT MARINER.

Bottleton East. Frequent. Not too hard to identify Aldgate East, a tough section of London, directly east of the City.

Bottomley, Horatio. 10 (frequently); his paper *John Bull*, 11 p28. Bottomley (1860–1933) was a larger-than-life orator, journalist and financial promoter who was eventually imprisoned for fraud in 1922.

Boudin. 86 p58. A marine painter, Eugène Boudin (1824–98) was a follower of Corot.

Bouguereau. 18 p92. Popular French painter William-Adolphe Bouguereau (1825–1905), leader of the 'Pompier School', specialised in 'refined nudes': *Triumph of Venus*, *Idyll*, etc.

Bounce to the ounce, not much. 85 p9. There was a 1960s TV advertisement for dog food: "You get more bounce to the ounce with [whatever it was], the chunky, meaty dog food." But a far more likely source is a poem by Ogden Nash:

> Dr Valentine hopes to announce
> He's collecting fantastic amounts.
> He's invented a bra
> Called Peps-oo-la-la
> Which delivers more bounce to the ounce.

MTT Neil Midkiff.

Bound and helpless. 21 p43. See BYRON's 'Marino Faliero, Doge of Venice', Act 5: "Stand crowned, but bound and helpless, at the altar."

Bounding Bertie. See BERTIE.

Bovril. 1 p101. A British meat-essence drink, originally developed c.1880. See also SINKING FEELING.

Bow, Clara. 43 p121. Hollywood film star (1905–65), the original 'It' girl in the film of that name (1927). See IT.

Bow Street police station. See BOSHER STREET.

Bowels of compassion. 93 p152. B. 1 John 3.17: "shutteth up his bowels of compassion from him, …"

Bowler hats. See Chap. 6.

Bowling, Tom. Tom Bowling act, i.e. he/she has died 14 p162. 'Tom Bowling', a song on the death of a gallant sailor, was written by Charles Dibdin around 1808 and remained popular for a century, as did many of his other sea-songs.

Bowls. Drake playing b. with the Armada in sight 26 p13. The story, almost certainly apocryphal, is that Sir Francis DRAKE was so confident of victory that he insisted on finishing a game of bowls on Plymouth Hoe, although the Spanish Armada had been sighted. Perhaps he had money on the game.

Box fruit, a nice bit of. 56 p252; 64 p51 and elsewhere. Before the days of refrigerated transport containers, 'fresh fruit' was grown in the UK, 'box-fruit' meant it had come in boxes from overseas. Bananas, grapes and other perishable tropical fruit often arrived in British shops with half the contents already rotting — hence the derisive term for a messy/complicated situation. It was one of the reasons tinned fruit became so popular.

In February 2006 the *Daily Telegraph* had an article on the history of tinned and processed food which included some interesting remarks on how certain phrases entered the language. It pointed out that canned food had been common since 1870, but the image of people being crammed together 'packed like sardines' was not used till 1911 and that 'the best thing since sliced bread' came into common use in 1969 (although the American Otto Rohwedder had invented his bread-slicing-and packaging machine back in 1928). The article had a comment by Elizabeth Knowles of the *Oxford English Dictionary*: "This sort of usage marks the moment at which something ceases to be an innovation that can really affect your life and becomes something so familiar and commonplace, it can become a figure of speech."

Boy Explorers Up the Amazon. 67 p47. From either W.H. Kingston's *Boy Explorers* or W.H. Miller's (USA) series *The Boy Explorers* (five books, 1921–26).

Boy Novelist, The. 22 p164. I have not found this expression. I think it may simply be an extension of the BOY ORATOR below.

Boy Orator. 15 p44 and later. Title bestowed upon the US politician William Jennings BRYAN in 1896.

Boy Scouts. Frequent. PGW satirised the Scout movement in *The Swoop* and in the invariably disastrous acts of kindness perpetrated by young Edwin but, surprisingly, at 85 p71 we learn that Bertie Wooster had once been a member of that body.

Boy stood on the burning deck whence all but he had fled. 25 p159 & later. Despite the firmly-held views of Monty Bodkin and Albert Peasemarch in *The Luck of the Bodkins*, neither Shakespeare nor Tennyson wrote the poem. See Casabianca.

Boy, wandering. Where is my wandering boy tonight? 20 p66 and often later. 'Oh! Where is My Boy To-night?' was an 1877 temperance hymn which swept America. The song sheet cover showed a young man drinking in a bar while, at home, a mother mourned.

Boy was … the father of the man, the. 3 p55; 52 p171. Wordsworth's 'My Heart Leaps Up': "The Child is father of the Man; / And I could wish my days to be / Bound each to each by natural piety."

Boy, what will he become, the? 12 p179; 21 p126; 78 p19. The nearest I can find is Hymn 238 in the Methodist Hymn Book: "The boys and girls of England, what will they become?"

Boy Wonder, The. 22 p110. The phrase has been in common use for centuries; David (of Goliath fame) seems to have been the first. The date is too late for PGW's story but, around 1921/2, a piece entitled 'The Boy Wonder' appeared in the *Saturday Evening Post*. It was based on the young Irving Thalberg (1899–1936), who had been appointed to run Carl Laemmle's film studio and was doing so with remarkable efficiency. Since he was under age, he was unable to sign cheques and his mother had to do it for him for the first six months. He made MGM the most profitable studio in Hollywood and was perhaps the only studio mogul PGW respected.

Boy's best friend is his mother, a. 21 p150 and later. PGW used this often because it was a popular catchphrase of the time. In 1884, two Americans, J.P. Skelly & H. Miller, wrote 'A Boy's Best Friend Is His Mother', a sentiment exactly right for the period, and the song went round the world. William Randolph Hearst quoted the phrase seriously all his life. In PGW's first published lyric, 'Put Me In My Little Cell' (*Sergeant Brue* 1904), is the line: "A burglar's best friend is his mother"(which PGW quoted at 13 p116). See other PGW variations on the theme under Girl's best friend.

Boys in the back room. 92 p180; 96 40. The term was coined in the USA in the 1870s but achieved world-wide popularity from Marlene Dietrich's song in the film *Destry Rides Again* (1939). ("See what the boys in the back room will have …")

Boys of the bulldog breed. See Where are the boys.

Boys of the old brigade (shoulder to shoulder). 8 p12; 55 p217; 65 p41 and later. See 'The Old Brigade', song by Fred E. Weatherly of which the first line is: "Where are the boys of the old brigade?" Later we get: "Steadily, shoulder to shoulder, Steadily, blade by blade; Marching along, sturdy and strong, Like the boys of the old brigade."

Weatherly (1848–1929) was a barrister who wrote dozens of popular songs but is better remembered for his exploit in another field. In the 1868 Henley regatta, he was cox of the Brasenose College (Oxford) four when the rules required each four-oar boat to have a cox. The Brasenose captain looked closely at the rules and found they required a cox to be in the boat when the race began. There was nothing to state he had to stay there. When the starting gun was fired, Weatherly promptly jumped into the water and swam for the shore, allowing Brasenose to win easily with their lightened boat. The Henley stewards equally promptly disqualified Brasenose for bad sportsmanship or some similar catch-all reason — but Weatherly is still a legendary name in rowing circles, similar to TROTT in cricket.

Boys will be boys. 20 p131. 17th-century English proverb.

Braces King. 18 p219. See KINGS.

Bracing. Margate, Bramley-on-Sea and other seaside resorts are so bracing. 29 onwards. See 'BRAMLEY IS SO BRACING'.

Bradshaw's Railway Guide. 3 p67; 39 p162. This remarkable UK railway timetable, renowned for its accuracy and scope, was first published in 1838. To the outrage of many, it ceased publication in 2006, purportedly because of the grossly fallacious assumption that everybody in the United Kingdom possesses a computer.

Brady, Diamond Jim. 23 p223. Flamboyant US millionaire (1857–1917) who adorned himself with more diamonds than good taste dictated.

Brady, Kid. 13 p13 and later. See Chap. 4.

Brahe, Tycho. 38 p114 (repeated at 70 p186). I am convinced this is PGW's version of an article he had read in an encyclopaedia. Brahe (1546–1601) was a famous Danish astronomer.

Braid, James. Scottish golfer (1870–1950). See *GOLF WITHOUT TEARS* and also Chap. 27.

'Bramley Is So Bracing'. 69 p38. Another of the once-common phrases PGW misquoted so effectively, it comes from one of the most famous UK posters. In 1909 a railway company wanted to attract holidaymakers to the small Lincolnshire coastal town of Skegness. They commissioned John Hassall, who produced a brightly-coloured poster of a jolly, bearded fisherman skipping over the sands with the caption: 'Skegness Is So Bracing'. For some reason, the poster and the caption became embedded in the nation's consciousness. PGW used it for Skegness, Margate, Bramley and other seaside resorts. Skegness adopted the phrase as their town motto and, twenty years later, honoured Hassall by making him a Freeman of the town. There was some embarrassment at the ceremony when he let slip that it was the first time he had been there. See Chap. 16.

Brand from the burning, a. 90 p102. B. Zecharaiah 3.2: "The Lord rebuke thee,

O Satan; even the Lord that hath chosen Jerusalem rebuke thee; is not this a brand plucked out of the fire."

Brass rags. See PARTED BRASS RAGS.

Brave men and fair women. 15A p75 and later. See BYRON's *Childe Harold's Pilgrimage*: "The lamps shone o'er fair women and brave men." The British Press adopted it enthusiastically as a standard cliché to describe Society events. A typical example was *The Sketch* describing the 1904 Henley Regatta: "The many delightful houses and gardens lining the river, were, as a consequence, fuller than ever of brave men and fair women."

Brave new world, this. 50 p174. Originally from S. *The Tempest* 5.1: "O Brave new world, That has such people in't." But PGW probably used it because of the furore caused by the just-published (1932) satirical novel *Brave New World* by Aldous Huxley.

Brawl, a mere vulgar. 4 p129 and often later. This comes from a once-famous *Punch* cartoon of the 1880s, of which I have a copy. It shows an irate senior officer (clearly based on the then Commander-in-Chief, the Duke of Cambridge) asking an extremely tall and languid cavalry officer: "What is the role of the cavalry in modern warfare, Mr X?" The officer's reply is: "Well, I suppose it's to give tone to what would otherwise be a mere vulgar brawl." As late as the 1980s, I heard the comment repeated by a cavalry officer to squash an infantry colleague he thought was getting above himself.

I am delighted to confirm that the remark was made to the Duke of Cambridge by a well-known member of the Pelican Club, Captain Fred Russell of the 3rd Lancers (see Chap. 5). The story went round England in a week, and *Punch* had its cartoon.

Brazil nut industry. 67 p14; 84 p36. One of the staples of the UK theatre repertoire from 1892 onwards was the comedy *Charley's Aunt*, which also did well in New York. The line that became a catchphrase, and everybody remembers, was that the aunt had returned from "Brazil, where the nuts come from".

Breach. Step into the breach 56 p101; 76 p85 and later. S. *Henry V* 3.1: "Once more unto the breach, dear friends, once more, / Or close the wall up with our English dead!"

Bread and butter, had gone on cutting (like the lady in Goethe's poem). 17 p117. Goethe wrote 'The Sorrows of Werther' in 1774. Nearly a century later, Thackeray summed up the sad story in four comic verses. They tell how Werther first met Charlotte as she was cutting bread and butter. Since she was married, he was unable to tell of his love and became so distraught that he shot himself. Thackeray's last verse is:

> Charlotte, having seen his body
> Borne before her on a shutter,
> Like a well-conducted person,
> Went on cutting bread and butter.

Bread and salt. He had frequently eaten my bread and salt 43 p284. Despite the

Biblical tone of this phrase, it does not occur in the Bible nor in Shakespeare. Bread and salt, the two food staples, had a symbolic significance and offering bread and salt to a guest was a standard welcome among the ancient Greeks. Rudyard KIPLING's poem 'I Have Eaten Your Bread' begins: "I have eaten your bread and salt, I have drunk your water and wine."

Break, break, break, on your cold grey stones. 55 p74. T. 'Break, Break, Break'.

Breaking the news to mother. 24 p242. See JUST BREAK THE NEWS.

Breathes there the man with soul so dead … wandering on a foreign strand? 36 p62–63. From Sir Walter Scott's *The Lay of the Last Minstrel*, C.6.1. See also HIGH THOUGH HIS TITLES.

Bredon. Where's this Bredon that A. E. Housman writes about? 91 p185. A fascinating remark — or slip — by PGW. See HOUSMAN.

Breeze, Edmund. 71 p143. US actor, died 1936.

Brer Rabbit. Tony, like Brer Rabbit, had lain low 3 p18. Character from the *Uncle Remus* stories by Joel Chandler Harris (1848–1908). The stories were a terrific hit when they were published in the US and UK in the 1880s. PGW's memory failed him on this one, and if he looked it up in Brewer's *Phrase and Fable*, that is wrong,too. Looking through as many of the *Uncle Remus* stories as I could find, it was Brer Fox who persistently "lay low" ('The Tar Baby'), not Brer Rabbit.

Brethren of Trinity House. 92 p12. See JURY DUTY.

Brevoort café. 24 p162. The famous restaurant of the Brevoort Hotel near Washington Square was where PGW used to celebrate when he sold a story in his early New York days. The hotel, the first to be built on Fifth Avenue, has now become an apartment block.

Brewer, Bill. 7 p105. Character mentioned in the traditional English folk song 'Widdecombe Fair'.

Bricks. Thousand of bricks/ton of bricks 57 p162; 64 p24 and elsewhere. Builders in the UK estimated quantities of bricks by the thousand till the 1930s and then changed to (cubic) tons.

Brides-in-the-Bath murderer. 40 p24. A famous UK murder case. Between 1910 and 1920, George Smith married and murdered three wives by drowning them in the bath.

Bridewell. PGW ref lost. The term, often used to denote a jail in England, comes from the Bridewell Palace just off Fleet Street in London which served as a prison from 1556 until it was demolished in 1885. Two cells were left, however, to "confine unruly apprentices". These didn't vanish till 1977, when, by good luck, I was around to tell the demolition workmen what the small underground cubicles were. They enjoyed the story enough to allow me the honour of being the last person to be locked up in Bridewell, then demolished the cells as I watched.

Bridge. Played by Jeeves and other characters. This card game took over from whist in October 1894 when Lord Brougham introduced it at the Portland

Club in London. Auction Bridge was the rage (Wodehouse used to play with Mrs Bowes-Lyons and her guests on Sunday evenings in the early 1900s and set out some unusual rules of behaviour at 10 p98–99) till Contract Bridge was devised by Harold Vanderbilt in 1925. There was a tremendous battle for supremacy between British traditionalists and the American radicals, but the supremacy of the Culbertson husband-and-wife team led to Contract Bridge becoming the standard game. There have been several scandals in the Bridge world, including the trial in 1992 of the world-class player Judi Rahin, who was accused of attacking her partner, Kathie Wei, with a two-pound silver ball. It was the biggest Bridge sensation since 1931, when John Bennett of Kansas City was shot dead by his wife, exasperated by his failure to make a contract of two spades. The trial revolved around the evidence of the great Eli Culbertson himself, who demonstrated to the jury how badly Mr Bennett had played his hand. Mrs Bennett was acquitted.

Bridge. Guarding/keeping the b., 15A p152 and later. See HORATIUS.

Bridgnorth. 12 p280. Alias Bridgefield/Bridgeford/Blatchford/Brindleford/Brindleham. See Chap. 35.

Bridmouth on Sea (about six miles from Maiden Eggesford). 55 p39; 71 p41; 96 p23. See Chap. 12.

Briggs, Anthony, J.P., M.P. 62 p143; 83 p25. This gentleman's statue stood in the High Street of Loose Chippings, Sussex. Do not confuse with Sir Eustace Briggs, another politician, whose statue in the New Recreation Ground at Wrykyn was vandalised (*The Gold Bat*) and who resigned in *The White Feather*. Although, in the political excitement of the period 1900–10, many statues of politicians were defaced by political opponents, I was unable to trace any with a particular significance for PGW. Perhaps so many were vandalised, he simply incorporated the idea in his stories.

Briggs, Stanley. 9 p60. See Chap. 24.

Bright and bounding Phipps, my. 70 p228; my bright and bounding J.G., 71 p7. Probably from Bill Nye's *Comic History of the United States* (1894): "…not the bright and bounding boy, clothed in graceful garments and filled to every tingling capillary with a soul."

Brighton, walking-race to. 6 p237. The 50-mile London-to-Brighton walking race was a popular event up to the 1930s.

***Bring on the Girls*.** PGW used the title of the song he wrote for *Oh, Lady! Lady!!* in 1918 for his 1954 book of theatrical anecdotes. The song was dropped before the show opened.

Bring out your dead. 54 p130; 62 p22 and later. During the Great Plague of 1665, carts came round the streets of London to take bodies away for burial. This was the melancholy cry used by those engaged on this ghoulish task.

Brink. Hovering uncertainly on the b. 34 p63 and "linger shivering on the brink" later. From the hymn 'There Is a Land of Pure Delight' by Isaac Watts: "And, linger, shivering on the brink, And fear to launch away."

Brinkley (who became Bingley). 93 p12. See Chap. 3.

Brinkley Court. See Chap. 26.

British Constitution. 49 p67; 51 p201. Pronouncing this phrase distinctly was a common police test of someone's sobriety. See also HE STOOD AT THE DOOR.

British Empire Exhibition at Wembley. See WEMBLEY EMPIRE EXHIBITION.

Broadmoor. 60 p89. First asylum in UK for the criminally insane.

Brodie. Did a Steve Brodie 17 p214 and later. To leave in a hurry, to jump off something. Steve Brodie (1863–1901) was the young man who jumped off the Brooklyn Bridge in New York on 23 July 1886 to win a $200 bet.

Brodley & Arnold. 17 p50. Misprint for the Latin textbook by Bradley & Arnold used in England from PGW's time to mine. MTT Tony Ring, who informs me the first edition has the correct name.

Brodrick, Mr. 6 p70. William St John Brodrick, UK Secretary of State for War 1900–03.

Broken blossom. Some b.b. you have culled and left to perish by the wayside 38 p128; 44 p28. 'Broken blossom' was a Victorian euphemism for a pure girl who had been betrayed, i.e. jilted by a heartless philanderer. *Broken Blossoms* was also a Hollywood tear-jerker of 1919, starring Lilian Gish.

Broken reed. 77 p206. B. Isaiah 36.6: "Lo, thou trustest in the staff of this broken reed, on Egypt; whereon, if a man lean, it will go into his hand, and pierce it: so is Pharaoh king of Egypt to all that trust in him."

Bronx cheer. 48 p 21 and later. A rude noise of contempt; the UK term is 'blowing a raspberry'.

Bronzed and fit. Frequent in PGW. I have been unable to find the origin of this phrase, but it was a long-lasting cliché of Victorian novelists and newspaper advertisements from 1880 to 1939.

Brooklands. 10 p24. Competing at some event at B. 68 p155. First (1907) UK car racing circuit, Brooklands, southwest of London, was famous for its steep banking.

Brookport. See Chap. 23.

Brookwood. They buried him at Brookwood 6 p46. This large cemetery, south-west of London, was opened in 1851, and because of the contrast with the squalid conditions of central London cemeteries, it became the fashionable place for burials. Since it catered for non-Christian interments as well (Jews, Hindus, Muslims), it soon became popular enough to have its own railway station.

Brother Dan (alderman with a grip on the seventh Ward). See MY BROTHER DAN.

Brother Masons. 77 opening page. Play purportedly written by Edgar Trent. A farce called *Brother Masons* was produced at the Cort Theatre, Atlantic City, date unknown but probably in the 1920s. It was written by Harry Lewis and A. Seymour Brown. Brown (1885–1947) was a well-known lyric writer ('Oh, You Beautiful Doll') and did the book and lyrics for the Broadway musical *Amelia* in 1923. There is no proof that Wodehouse knew him or the play, but it is unlikely that he did not. MTT Anne-Marie Chanet.

Brother, sticketh/stuck closer than a. See STICKETH CLOSER.

Brother-can-you-spare-a-dime stuff, doing the. 68 p186; 71 p78. The 1932 song 'Brother, Can You Spare a Dime' by Yip Harburg came to symbolise the Depression.

Brothers, Dr Joyce. 92 p54. US agony aunt/ advice columnist.

Brown Derby. 53 p201; 54 p178; 95 p11. This famous Hollywood restaurant, demolished in 1994, was built in the shape of an enormous hat (derby in the US, bowler in the UK).

Brown, Tom. 1 p309; 2 p94; 3 p272; his fight with Slogger Williams 12 p309. See Thomas Hughes' *Tom Brown's Schooldays* (1857), the archetypal English school story.

Brown's Club. 20 p13. A typical Wodehouse change of name. See Chap. 21.

Bruce and the spider, the story of. 58 p254. Legend tells of the Scottish leader Robert the Bruce hiding in a cave on the island of Rathlin in 1307 after being defeated by the English. He watched a spider making repeated efforts to fix its web and at last succeeding. Encouraged by its persistence, he left the island, gathered an army, and drove the English from Scotland.

Brummel, Beau. 13 p86 and later. Leader of fashion in London (1778–1840). See also WHO IS YOUR STUFFED FRIEND?.

Brusiloff, Vladimir. 28 p19. A typically Russian-sounding name to English/ American readers, and I never imagined it had a factual origin. But, like so many of Wodehouse's references, it was a name people recognised when the book came out. Alexei Brusilov was the Russian commander-in-chief when the Revolution began in 1917.

In July 1992 the UK was honoured by a visit from someone very like PGW's Brusiloff, the artist and enamellist Leonid Efross, a tall, fierce-looking Russian with dark, piercing eyes and a sinister black beard. He had some sittings with the Queen Mother and other members of the Royal Family and told the Press that his favourite breakfast reading was Dostoevsky, whom he held in high regard. He spoke of his work: "When I make an enamel, it is through a mystical combination of work, will and fire." The interview concluded with the announcement that he was collecting English books to take to Holland, where he was to meet Queen Beatrix: "I've found a very good English author … His name is P.G. Wodehouse." See also GOTSUCHAKOFF.

Brutus. I am no orator as Brutus is 21 p203 and often later. From S. *Julius Caesar* 3.2. Most PGW Brutus quotes are from Shakespeare's play, but see BRUTUS, LUCIUS JUNIUS.

Brutus, Lucius Junius. A stern father 34 p12; Gally explains 91 p143. A staunch republican, Brutus was the first Roman consul (c.500 B.C.) elected after the Tarquins had been expelled. As consul, he not only found his sons guilty of plotting against the State but attended their execution as well.

Bryan, William J. 20 p103; 21 p158; 27 p213. American lawyer and politician

(1860–1925) who conducted the prosecution in the famous Scopes 'Monkey' Trial (evolution vs. Biblical teaching). See also BOY ORATOR.

Bryant Hall rehearsal rooms. 26 p152. Bryant Hall was on 6th Ave between 41st & 42nd St. Originally built as the Lyric Theatre, it provided rehearsal rooms for hundreds of New York shows over the years. It was knocked down about 1930.

Brynner, Yul. 80 p95. Some remember this shaven-headed stage and film actor for the film *The King and I.* I think he was best in the superb Western *The Magnificent Seven.*

Bubble blown so big and tenuous. 79 p10. See IT IS TOO LARGE.

Bucking the line. 21 p139. An American football term for breaking through the opponents' defence.

Buck's (Club). 31 p53 and later. See Chap. 21.

Buck-U-Uppo. See Chap. 11, but note the unusual mention in *Uncle Dynamite* (chap. 11).

Buffalo Bill. 5 p57. Despite his tremendous popularity among boys of Wodehouse's time, this is the only reference to Buffalo Bill Cody (William F. Cody [1846–1917] ex-Pony Express rider, Army scout, and Indian fighter) in the novels. However, the last edition of *Punch* in 1902 has a poem by PGW welcoming the *Wild West Show* back to London: 'To William (Whom We Have Missed).'

It is difficult now to appreciate the excitement in London when Cody brought his *Wild West Show* over for the first time in 1887. Nothing like it had ever been seen before, and the Prince of Wales became an enthusiastic fan — so much so that he persuaded Cody to allow him and some 'friends' to be passengers in the famous last event, the attack by Indians on the Deadwood Stage (one of the four original coaches had been brought over). Cody agreed but nearly changed his mind when he discovered that the coach was to carry four European kings who were in England to celebrate Queen Victoria's Golden Jubilee. It was said that the Indian attack was carried out particularly fiercely that night, and the driver of the coach, who had done it hundreds of times before, got down shaking because it had brought back all too vividly the days when he really did have to drive for his life across the plains.

The high point of Cody's first visit was the private performance he gave, at her request, for Queen Victoria and her Court. The show opened with four riders entering the arena at a racing gallop, firing their guns while one waved the Stars and Stripes. To everybody's astonishment, the Queen rose to her feet and bowed her head to the flag as it went by. There was a tremendous shout from every member of the watching cast, who appreciated the significance of her action: it was the first time in history that a British sovereign had paid public respect to the Stars and Stripes. Cody always said it was the proudest moment in his long and adventurous career.

For some reason, Cody left the stagecoach behind on his last tour and it was eventually bought by Bertram Mills, a well-known circus impresario. Mills became a member of the London County Council in the 1920s and used the coach to campaign for votes. It was a far cry from the Western plains to the tree-lined suburbs of south London.

Buffalo gals, won't you come out tonight? 77 p35. US song hit 1848.

Bulldog breed. 77 p110; 86 p34. See Where are the boys.

Bultitude, Mr. 4 p130. The father in *Vice Versa*. See *Vice Versa*.

Bump Suppers. 11 p68 (at Moscow University); 51 p123 and later. The rivers Thames and Cam at Oxford and Cambridge are too narrow to allow boats to race side by side. In Eights Week, the College boats line up one behind the other and attempt to bump the boat in front. If they do so, then they move up one place the next day. If a College makes four bumps, then it is the custom to have a Bump Supper, which can be *very* exuberant affairs. Taking off your clothes and riding a bicycle round the quad, singing comic songs, would be considered very sedate. I still have the scar — literally — from my college's Bump Supper. See also Chap. 33.

Bumpleigh Hall, Steeple Bumpleigh. 64 p6. On his visits to Charles le Strange at Hunstanton (see Chap. 32), PGW would have driven by Steeple Bumpstead in Essex. Nearby is my favourite English place-name: Shellow Bowells. See also Steeple Bumpstead.

Bumps-a-daisy/Boomps-a-daisy. 64 p5; 67 p77 and later. Like 'The Lambeth Walk' and 'Under the Spreading Chestnut Tree', this was a 1930s English novelty song with actions. "Hands, knees and bumps-a-daisy, Turn to your partner and bow." The bumps-a-daisy action was bending and knocking your upper thigh/butt against that of your partner. 'Boomps-a-daisy' became a term to indicate well-being/euphoria in the same way 'heeby-jeebies' had come to indicate the reverse in America.

Bumstead, Dagwood, best husband in America. 70 p27. This famous cartoon character drawn by Chic Young made his first appearance in 1930.

Bunce, a bit of. 64 p67. UK slang for a bonus since the 18th century; something welcome and unexpected.

Bunn, the poet. 44 p269; 46 p16. Alfred Bunn (1796–1860) wrote the song 'I Dreamt That I Dwelt in Marble Halls' for *The Bohemian Girl* (1843). Bunn had a very high opinion of himself and considered his lyrics were masterpieces of English literature. Because of this, the term 'the poet Bunn' was coined by sarcastic critics.

Burbage. 46 p119. Richard Burbage (1567–1619) produced many of Shakespeare's plays. His chief rival was Edward Alleyn, who founded Dulwich College in 1619.

Burger, Hamilton. 89 p141. Unlucky opponent of Perry Mason in dozens of TV detective dramas.

Burgess's Fish Sauce shop. 51 p201; 88 p23. See He stood at the door.

Burglar. When an enterprising burglar isn't burgling, he is probably memorizing the words of some popular lyric for rendition at the next big night 36 p109.

The first part is from G&S *Pirates of Penzance*: "When the enterprising burglar's not a-burgling." I suggest the second part of the sentence is a reflection of PGW's pride that *Oh, Lady! Lady!!* had been a wow when played by the inmates of Sing Sing prison.

Burglar's best friend is his mother. See BOY'S BEST FRIEND.

Burleigh, Lord. A brief nod which, like Lord Burleigh's, spoke volumes 86 p119. The taciturn Burleigh (1520–98) was chief minister to Elizabeth I. The phrase comes from Sheridan's play *The Critic* (1779), when Burleigh comes on stage, shakes his head and exits. Sneer asks what Burleigh meant and Puff gives a six-line explanation that the nod signified vital thoughts on which the safety of the country depended. Sneer is astonished: "[D]id he mean all that by shaking his head?" Puff replies, "Every word of it." The allusion was popular for over a century.

Burlington Bertie. Song by Henry Norris 1900. This was followed by 'Burlington Bertie from Bow' by Hargreaves in 1915. See Chap. 13.

Burned child fears the spilled milk, the. 76 p29. A splendid mixing of two traditional aphorisms: "The burnt child fears the fire" and "It's no good crying over spilt milk". As PGW tells us at 70 p54, the first is a corruption of "a burned child dreadeth the fire" from Lyly's *Euphues*. MTT Anne-Marie Chanet for pointing out that PGW also gave us: "You can lead a horse to the altar, but you can't make it drink" (*Thank You, Jeeves*) and "It's an ill wind that has no turning" (*Summer Lightning*).

Burned, (not) with shame or remorse. 12 p28; 48 p274; 64 p250. A variation of the line every boy of PGW's time remembered from *Eric, or Little by Little*, the moral school story written by Dean Farrar, then a master at Harrow, in 1858. The line at chapter 10 reads: "Eric burned not with remorse or regret but with shame and violent indignation." See *ERIC*.

Burned stick. Poke in the eye with a b. s. Often up to 97 p59. For lack of anything more specific, I have always assumed this is the story of Odysseus blinding Polyphemus. I imagine PGW, a classicist, assumed everybody would pick up the reference. When he first wrote it, most of his readers would.

Bush/bushes speaking. 42 first page; similar experience to Moses 55 p93. A splendid Wodehouse twist on B. Exodus 3.4: "God called to him out of the midst of the bush and said, Moses, Moses". PGW made excellent use of inanimate objects breaking into speech, including hatboxes (with a parrot inside them) and cupboards that sneezed.

Bushman, Francis X. 25 p280. Early silent film hero (1883–1966), labelled by newspapers "the most handsome man in the world".

Business had lain in deep waters. 32 p178 and later. BCP. Forms of Prayer to Be Used at Sea: "They that go down to the sea in ships; and occupy their business in great waters." (From Psalm 107.23.)

Buster. Listen, Buster 82 p192. Bobbie Wickham's opening greeting to Aubrey Upjohn is said to stem from Buster Brown, the angelic-looking but mischievous cartoon child drawn by Richard Outcault from 1902 to 1920. The series became so popular that 'Buster' came to be used as a rude/aggressive form of address.

Butler Did It, The. 76 p89 & p219; US title of 79; 88 p107; 89 p45; 90 p35; 91 p33. The popular explanation of this phrase is that it stemmed from someone explaining the plot of a 1916 silent film to his companion very loudly — and to the annoyance of the rest of the audience. Supporters of this theory point out that the famous serial *Exploits of Elaine* (1915–16) featured an evil butler named Bennett. (See also *DANGERS OF DIANA*.) It became the American title of *Something Fishy* when PGW and his American editor Peter Schwed were arguing over the title. PGW saw a cartoon with the punch line 'The butler did it', tore it out and sent it to Schwed. MTT Tony Ring.

Butler hates hearing stories over and over again, a. 55 p272. A possible origin will be found at 78 p56–57 (UK edition). I should add that PGW's *Phrases & Notes* notebooks record surprisingly frank conversations with the servants of a cousin of his on aspects of life below stairs, and he certainly quizzed his own butler years later on a butler's problems.

Butler, the whole butler and nothing but the butler. 82 p54. See GAME.

Butler, turbulent. Will no one rid me of this turbulent butler 63 p229. See BECKET, THOMAS À.

Butlers do not grow old as we grow old. 79 p14. Laurence Binyon's 'Poem for the Fallen': "They shall not grow old as we that are left grow old."

Butt. Lord Bromborough had left his butt 57 p106. Apparently this term is unfamiliar to many Americans who know a 'butt' only as a posterior/backside. In the UK, it has at least two additional meanings. On a rifle range, it denotes the bank of earth behind the targets. This stems from the days when every town had an archery ground and built an earthen bank, a butt, behind the targets so the arrows wouldn't get lost. Secondly, when you shoot grouse in the UK, you do so on an open moor. Since a standing figure with a gun would alarm the birds, small pits are dug and the soil used to build a wall in front. This means that only the shooter's head and shoulders break the line of sight. These miniature shelters, firing positions, are called butts and were what PGW had in mind.

Butt, P.C. (and other policemen who suffer immersion). 12 p49. See Chap. 16.

Butt, Sir Alfred. 49 p227. London theatrical impresario (1878–1962) who later became an MP.

Butter and Egg Man. 82 p23. *The Butter and Egg Man* was the name of the 1925 play by George Kaufman on which PGW based *Barmy in Wonderland/ Angel Cake*, with Kaufman's agreement. The phrase comes from Texas Guinan, who ran a speakeasy, The Three Hundred Club, in New York during Prohibition and whose greeting "Hallo, suckers" became famous. One night in 1924, a customer came in, bought drinks all round and lavished money on her girls. She wanted to introduce him for a round of applause, but all he would say was that he was in the dairy business. So she got up and asked for a big hand for "my butter-and-egg man". The phrase took off, and Kaufman's play about an innocent backing a New York show came out in 1925.

Texas Guinan (1883–1933) was a skilled horsewoman from Canada (another source says Texas) and appeared in a few early films, billed as 'The Female Bill Hart'. Her speakeasy was raided often, and she instituted the pleasant custom of having the band play 'The Prisoner's Song' (a wildly-popular song of the day by Robert Massey), with all the customers joining in, whenever she was lugged off to the pen. According to an English journalist, when the Prince of Wales (later Duke of Windsor) came in one night, she introduced him to the customers with the words that he was someone who "doesn't have a backyard of his own to play in" and enjoined them to "treat him right". MTT David McDonough for the information that she was the original of Missouri Martin in the Damon Runyon stories. See also FIFTY MILLION ST BERNARD DOGS.

Butter in a lordly dish. 51 p192. From B. Judges 5.25. MTT Fr Rob Bovendeaard and Leonard Goldstein. The latter has also pointed out that "if you have butter prepare to shed it now" (51 p202) is a PGW adaptation from S. *Julius Caesar* 3.2.148: "If you have tears, prepare to shed them now."

Butter slide. 51 p214. Seabury's revenge on Sir Roderick Glossop. See Chap. 14.

Buttons and Bows. 69 p189. Song made famous by Bob Hope, who sang it in the film *The Paleface* (1948). See also Chap. 36.

Buxton. 35 p216; 65 p63. A spa town in Derbyshire; never quite as popular as Bath or Harrogate.

Buzzer. He was a buzzer 63 p37 and elsewhere. PGW used the term often to describe someone with the gift of the gab. In her book *Temples and Treasures* (1936), Helen Marion Wodehouse (see Chap. 2) wrote: "Two old ladies were buzzing together in the street as I passed."

'By Advice of Counsel'. Short story title. An English legal term. A solicitor with a difficult point of law will consult a Queen's Counsel (senior barrister) for an opinion.

By James. 6 p7. Favourite oath of Captain Kettle. See CAPTAIN KETTLE.

By Jingo. 'We don't want to fight but by Jingo if we do!' 71 p52. This song changed the course of history and gave its name to a political attitude — Jingoism. In 1878 it was clear that Russia was going to attack Turkey as part of its aim of getting a port on the Mediterranean, and the UK Parliament was undecided whether to intervene. If they sent the fleet into the Dardanelles, Russia would withdraw, but there was opposition to this course. (We had fought Russia in the Crimea 20 years before.) One night, as the House of Commons debated the matter again, G.H. MacDermott strode on to the stage of the London Pavilion and launched into 'a new patriotic song'. "We don't want to fight, but by Jingo if we do, We've got the ships, we've got the men, we've got the money too", and each verse ended (fortissimo): "The Russians shall not have Constantinople." The effect was extraordinary. The audience took it up in a dozen encores, then swarmed out of the theatre singing it at the tops of their voices. The song swept across London in two hours and crowds gathered outside Parliament daily, singing it till Parliament agreed with them. The fleet was sent in and the Russians pulled back.

By Order of the Czar. 96 p70. This novel by Joseph Hatton about Nihilists and Russian oppression was a best-seller of the 1890s, going into thirteen editions in five years. My copy confirms what Bertie Wooster told us: it is full of Russian conspirators conspiring all over the place. In a couple of pages we meet Ivan Kostanzhoglo, Countess Stravensky, Losinski and the evil General Petronovitch. PGW had already mentioned that it was just the sort of book you found in old-fashioned circulating libraries in 1929 (*Performing Flea*, letter of 27 April 1929). These circulating libraries were everywhere in the period 1900–50 because public libraries tended to be in major towns and many of them did not stock fiction which was then held to be 'frivolous'. While the more famous circulating libraries (Harrod's, Smith's and Boot's) took a pride in supplying the newest books, smaller establishments stocked far older publications, just as PGW said. They were often to be found in seaside resorts to provide entertainment for visitors, and were a profitable sideline for village post offices and local tea-shops. In the 1940s the going rate was twopence per book per week, enabling me to read the adventures of Captain Kettle, Bulldog Drummond and Edgar Wallace thrillers which my local public library refused to stock.

See also MYSTERY OF THE HANSOM CAB.

By the great horn spoon. 29 p233. This expression probably came into common use in America with the success of the 1840 song with this title. Spoons were then commonly made from horn, and the very large spoons made from the Rocky Mountain big-horn sheep were greeted with amazement.

Byron/ Byronic. PGW mentions the poet Lord Byron (1788–1824) at least 14 times. For Byron's row with the Scots (91 p209), see SCOTCH REVIEWERS below. For Byronic, Bertie Wooster's description — "a gloomy sort of bird, taking things the hard way" (68 p163) — is as good a definition as one can get.

C

(MTT = My thanks to)

C3. See A1.

Cabbages and kings. 97 p101. Lewis Carroll's 'The Walrus and the Carpenter' (*Alice Through the Looking-Glass*): "The time has come, the Walrus said: To talk of many things ... Of cabbages — and kings."

Cabins. Piccadilly Cabin 9 p221; Holborn Viaduct Cabin 34 p6. These were part of a chain of Cabin teashops in London 1900–14.

Cabs. In Wodehouse's early days in London, one travelled by steam train, by the Underground railway, by horse-drawn bus or by horse-drawn 'cab' (short for cabriolet). There were two main types of cab, the two-wheeled hansom or the four-wheeled growler and, as a young man, I was very impressed by the elderly gentlemen who still shouted for a "Cab!" rather than for a "Taxi!" For the first motor taxicabs, 'taxis' for short, see POTT, MUSTARD. See also FOUR MILE RADIUS.

Cadogan Hotel. 32 p52. A highly-respectable hotel in Sloane Street; probably best known now from John Betjeman's poem 'The Arrest of Oscar Wilde at the Cadogan Hotel'.

Caesar, Julius. This Roman was quoted/referred to by PGW for 70 years from 4 p271 onwards. The references fall into three categories. First are quotations from Caesar's *Gallic Wars* — 'overcoming the Nervii' etc. (see NERVII). Every middle-class reader recognised them, since the *Gallic Wars* was the first Latin set book British schoolboys had to translate. Second are quotes from Shakespeare's *Julius Caesar* ('liking fat men' etc.), which were equally well-known. Thirdly, many general references to Caesar became imbedded in the national subconscious. His "Alea jacta est" (the die is cast) and "Veni, vidi, vici" (I came, I saw, I conquered) were phrases every schoolboy knew. For "According to Shakespeare, Julius Caesar used to go swimming with his clothes on"; see ACCOUTRED.

Caesar's wife, ready for anything. 55 p232; 76 p163. The Gin and Angostura was more in error than erudite, but it was exactly the sort of remark people like him made, a confused memory of "Caesar's wife must be above suspicion" from Plutarch's *Life of Julius Caesar.*

Cagney, James. James Cagney stuff 52 p204; 63 p119. Various Wodehouse heroes wished they were able treat their girl friends as roughly as this Hollywood actor (1899–1986) did on screen. Probably Cagney's most memorable scene was his seizing half a grapefruit and smashing it into the face of his moll (Mae Clarke) in *Public Enemy* (1931). The scene had been carefully planned by the director and Cagney, and they had made sure poor Miss Clarke had no idea what was coming. Her shocked reaction was everything they had hoped for.

Cain (and Abel). 3 p75 and later. B. Genesis 4. The first recorded case of fratricide.

Caine, Hall. 9 p207; 10 often and later. A popular novelist (1853–1931) who enjoyed pontificating on each and every topic of the moment. His fifteen novels sold 10 million copies and he made publishing history when Heinemann published *The Manxman* in 1894 in one volume and killed off the 'three-decker' (three-volume) novels that had been the norm. See also THREE-VOLUME NOVEL.

Cake-eater. 34 p200 and later. A US term of abuse for a gigolo, someone effete.

Cakewalk. 3 p46; 6 p7 and later. Although American black-face minstrel shows of the late 19th century had introduced the cakewalk to Britain, its widespread popularity probably came from *In Dahomey* (1903), the first black musical, which was a big hit in London. The Army & Navy Stores catalogue for 1907 has twenty cakewalks listed in its Music section. They were said to stem from the custom of slaves in the USA of competing in a cakewalk on festive occasions. The couple who promenaded most gracefully, probably to music, won a cake — hence 'that takes the cake'. See also BISCUIT.

Calcutta sweep. 17A p7; 44 p233; 81 p7. Since lotteries were illegal in the UK until a few years ago, people would buy tickets in the Irish or Calcutta Sweepstakes on the English Derby. (Selling these tickets was also illegal but, somehow, very few people were charged.) Millions bought tickets which were then put into a draw, and the lucky winners were allotted a horse in the Derby. If the horse won, the ticket holder became a wealthy man.

California, as you might say, here I come. 80 p75. Al Jolson made the song 'California, Here I Come' (1924) famous in the show *Bombo*, which also featured 'April Showers' and 'Toot-Toot-Tootsie'.

Caligula. 70 p174. This Roman emperor was assassinated in 41 A.D. See also GALBA and VITELLIUS.

Call Jimmy Crockers from the vasty deep. See VASTY DEEP.

Call of the wild. 61 p56 and later. *The Call of the Wild* (1903) was a famous adventure novel by Jack London.

Callao. See ON NO PETITION.

Called his shots correctly. 84 p83. I am told this term comes from the American game of pool where you nominate the pocket you want a certain ball to go in. If it does so, you have called your shot correctly.

Calling cattle home across the sands of Dee. Frequent from 31 onwards and often used to describe Aunt Dahlia's clarion tones. From the poem 'Sands of Dee' by Charles Kingsley. With music by Henry Clay, it became a staple at Victorian musical evenings. "O Mary, go and call the cattle home, / And call the cattle home, / And call the cattle home, / Across the sands of Dee."

Calling for his pipe and his bowl and his fiddlers three. 68 p68 and elsewhere. I was slightly puzzled by these references to the nursery rhyme 'Old King Cole' until I realised PGW was describing someone keeping his spirits up. See OLD

KING COLE.

Calm-browed lad. A calm-browed lad, Yet mad, at moments, like a hatter 8 p44. From C.S. CALVERLEY's *Gemini and Virgo*. See also MAD HATTER.

Calverley, Charles Stuart. 7 p212; 8 p36; 42 p68; comments on cats and tobacco juice 78 p128. Calverley (1831–84) was a brilliant parodist in Greek and Latin as well as English, and his *Gemini and Virgo* is still well worth reading. PGW admired his verses, which is why the opening lines of Calverley's 'Ode to Tobacco' may seem familiar:

Thou, who when cares attack,
Bid them avaunt, and Black
Care, at the horseman's back
Perching, unseatest.

(See PGW's 'Good Gnus' in 'Unpleasantness at Bludleigh Court'.) See also DUN.

'Came the Dawn'. Short story title; also 53 p112 and later. This was a famous sub-title caption in the old silent films to indicate the happy ending when the hero/heroine had come through some terrific storm/hurricane/danger. It was also used when the pair of them had been forced by the same storm/hurricane/danger to take shelter in a cabin and *spend the night together*. This was considered terribly daring in the 1920s. The writers producing such sub-titles were known collectively as 'Came-the-dawners'.

Cameelious Hump. Have lightened the hump, C.H. 7 p176. From 'How the Camel Got His Hump' in *Just So Stories*, though KIPLING's version is: "Have lifted the hump— / The horrible hump— / The hump that is black and blue!"

Camels laden with gold and precious stones. 55 p156; 73 p64; an amended version is at 57 p97. B. 1 Kings 10.2. The queen of Sheba came to visit Solomon with a retinue including "camels that bare spices, and very much gold, and precious stones." Compare and contrast with Solomon's wealth; see APES, IVORY AND PEACOCKS.

Campbell, Herbert. 4 p63. English comedian (1844–1904).

Campbell, Mrs Patrick. 4 p149. This actress (1865–1940) played the original Eliza Doolittle in *Pygmalion*. She and Bernard Shaw enjoyed a friendly, though sometimes irascible, correspondence for thirty years.

Camus, Albert. C. and the Aesthetic Tradition 81 p151; 84 p135. French philosopher and playwright (1913–60). I have a suspicion that the reference in 'Joy Bells for Walter' is a crack at Camus, but I have nothing to substantiate it. MTT Gwendolin Goldbloom for pointing out that Camus had just become the second-youngest winner of the Nobel Prize for Literature.

Can the leopard change his spots or the Ethiopian his what-not? See LEOPARD.

Canal Turn, the. 91 p155; 93 p27. See BECHER'S BROOK.

Canasta. 70 p173. This card game enjoyed a craze after World War II.

Candle. You have lit a c. this day which can never be blown out 12 p235. As the Protestant Bishop Hugh Latimer was being tied to the stake before being burned to death for heresy in 1555, he said to his fellow sufferer, Bishop Nicholas Ridley: "Be of good comfort Master Ridley, and play the man. We shall this day light such a candle by God's grace in England, as shall never be put out."

Caning. An English slang dictionary of 1900 lists 39 words for this punishment; beat, tan, biff, lick, tonk, cake, whop were common terms.

Cannibals that each other eat. 73 p94. See ANTHROPOPHAGI.

Cannon to left of him, cannon to right of him, volleyed and thundered. 68 p207. T. 'Charge of the Light Brigade': "Cannon to right of them, Cannon to left of them, Cannon in front of them, Volley'd and thunder'd ..."

Canopy of heaven, broad. 38 p174. A phrase of Socrates, quoted in Xenophon's *Memorabilia.* MTT Hetty Litjens.

Can't we be friends? 44 p 207. Popular 1929 song by James and Swift.

Capacity for taking pains. See INFINITE CAPACITY.

Capone, Al. 48 p134; 51 p311. American gangster and racketeer (1899–1947).

Captain Billy's Whiz Bang. 79 p9. A popular American comic book in the 1920s. It comprised jokes, funny stories, and slightly scurrilous anecdotes of stage and film stars. MTT Jean Tillson.

Captain Coe. 14 p83; his Final Selection 66 p42. Before the days of greyhound racing or football pools, newspaper racing tipsters were followed by millions. Because advising readers which racehorse to back was considered disreputable, most UK Press tipsters adopted noms de plume, which also meant the paper could employ different people under the same name. Captain Coe, the *Daily Sketch* tipster, adopted the name in 1898 and it is still in use. In 1881 the circulation of the *News of the World* jumped from 30,000 copies a week to 80,000 after 'Pegasus' (W.J. Innes) urged his readers to put their shirt on Foxhall for the Caesarewitch and the Cambridgeshire. Foxhall won the first at odds of 9 to 2 and the second at odds of 10 to 1. A peer of the realm (and a member of the UK Wodehouse Society) was for many years 'Hotspur' of the *Daily Telegraph.*

Captain Kettle. 2 p178 and later. Captain Kettle was a fictional hero created by J. Cutcliffe Hyne (1866-1944). From the 1890s onwards, the adventures of this small, pugnacious, bearded sea captain, ready to take on all comers, entranced millions of readers. At one time, he was more popular than Sherlock Holmes. See also CAPTAIN POTT and LOST LEADER.

Captain of his soul. 30 p103 and later. Henley's poem 'Invictus': "I am the master of my fate, I am the captain of my soul."

Captain Pott, a terror to the shirker and the lubber. 4 p16. A quotation every early reader would recognise — as they would also recognise the joke contained in it. The big hit at London's Gaiety Theatre in 1900 was *The Messenger Boy*, a lavish musical which narrated the adventures of a messenger boy who had to take a letter from London to Cairo. For the Cairo scene, the Gaiety delighted the audience by bringing on a series of well-known characters from fiction who introduced themselves in song. One was Captain Pott, who appeared wearing a short pointed beard and proclaimed he was a terror to the shirker and the lubber. This was an obvious reference to the pugnacious and indomitable bearded Welsh sea-captain, CAPTAIN KETTLE (Kettle–Pott). See also MAISIE.

Capulets and Montagues. 28 p157; 40 p82. S. *Romeo & Juliet*. Feuding families, like the Hatfields and the McCoys later.

Caracole into the drawing room. 38 p39. A half-turn by a horse in dressage exercises or, as here, to prance about.

Carberry, Letitia (of the Anti-Tobaco League). 95 p21. A compliment by PGW to the author Mary Roberts RINEHART. Miss Letitia Carberry, always called 'Tish', is Miss Rinehart's most memorable fictional character, a lady of energy and colossal determination. Think of Aunt Dahlia taking up car-racing and rifle-shooting and you have Miss Carberry. If you haven't read the 'Tish' stories, I strongly recommend them.

Career, watching with considerable interest. See I SHALL WATCH.

Caribees. Hunting for buried treasure in the C. 68 p122. A term once used to describe the islands of the Caribbean in general and the Antilles in particular. W.S. Gilbert employed 'the Caribees' for any tropical location.

Carioca. 54 p216; 76 p133. A Brazilian dance, an early variation of the Maxixe, popular during the dance craze 1910–30, especially after ROGERS and ASTAIRE danced it in *Flying Down to Rio*. MTT Neil Midkiff.

Carlton Hotel. 14 p60; 33 p137 and later. A popular lunch spot, this smart hotel at the bottom of the Haymarket in London was bombed in the last war. New Zealand House occupies the site today.

Carmagnole. 53 p309; 73 p159. Frenzied dance of the French revolutionaries in 1789.

***Carmantic*, S.S.** 21 p259. See Chap. 17.

Carnaby, Lady. 35 p17. Lady Carnaby's *Memories of Eighty Interesting Years* were almost certainly based on the 'scandalous' memoirs of Lady Cardigan. See BABLOCKHYTHE.

Carnegie, Andrew. 10 p136; 14 p25 and later. This Scottish-born American industrialist (1835–1910) founded the largest steel company in the USA. He spent the last fifteen years of his life endowing charitable causes, including 2,500 libraries in the UK and America.

Carnegie, Dale. 77 p55. Carnegie's (1885–1955) *How to Win Friends and Influence People* (1926) is probably the best-known self-improvement book.

Carnera, Primo. 49 p188 and later. This gigantic Italian heavyweight boxer (1906–67) won many fights through his sheer size, but Joe Louis knocked him out in 1935.

***Caronia*, S.S.** 21 p166. See Chap. 17.

Carpe diem, the Roman poet Horace advised. 93 p6. Literally 'Seize the day'. Seize the moment/ enjoy yourself while you can. Horace's *Odes* 1.11.7.

Cars in the garage, chickens in the pot. 93 p78. See TWO CARS.

Carson, Sir Edward. 7 p72. Irish politician (1854–1935) who fought the Irish Home Rule proposals for many years.

Carter, Nick. 59 p278. This fictional American detective, created by John Coryell in the *New York Weekly* in 1886, became popular in the UK in 1900, and his adventures were still selling well up to World War II. Do not confuse him, as Stiffy Byng did, with Sidney CARTON or CARTER PATERSON.

Carter Paterson. 59 p278. For many years Britain's biggest removals/freight delivery firm. MTT Richard Vine for the information that the Berlin airlift (1948–49) was codenamed 'Operation Carter Paterson' but was hurriedly changed when it was realised this might make the Russians think we were moving, i.e. pulling out of Berlin.

Carthage, Marius among the ruins of. See MARIUS.

Carton, Sidney. 48 p307 up to 90 p140. Self-sacrificing hero of D. *A Tale of Two Cities*.

Caruso. 7 p9. Enrico Caruso (1873–1921), the world's leading tenor from 1900 till his death.

Casabianca. 10 p132; 15 p234 and frequent later. The sad story of Giacomo Jocante Casabianca, the boy who stayed at his post and died with his father, a French Navy captain, in the Battle of the Nile (1798) was narrated by Mrs HEMANS in her poem 'Casabianca': "The boy stood on the burning deck, / Whence all but he had fled." The popularity of the poem meant 'Casabianca' came to be applied to anyone who stuck to his post.

Casanova. 49 p62 up to 96 p124. Giacomo Casanova de Seigalt (1725–98), adventurer and libertine, whose autobiography (*Memoires*) delighted/shocked his many readers. He spent the last years of his life as a librarian in Bohemia.

Casey, Ben. 89 p7. *Ben Casey* was a US TV medical series 1961–66. Vince Edwards played Dr Ben Casey, and the older, wiser doctor, without whom no medical series is complete, was played by Sam Jaffe.

Cashel Byron's Profession. 76 p151. George Bernard SHAW had a great respect for professional boxers. When Gene Tunney, the quiet, intellectual world heavyweight champion came to London, the only people he wanted to meet were the author Hugh WALPOLE and Shaw, with whom he had corresponded.

Casques of men. As Sir Galahad with his good sword clove the casques of men 77 p128; 81 p133. T. 'Sir Galahad', first line: "My good blade carves the casques of men."

Cassandra. 50 p256; 71 p120. Character in Greek mythology. Daughter of Priam of Troy, she was a prophet (mainly of doom) whom no one believed.

Cast him into the outer darkness, where there is wailing and gnashing of teeth. See WEEPING AND GNASHING OF TEETH.

Castle. An Irishman's croquet lawn is his castle 7 p66; a chap's bedroom — you can't get away from it — is his castle 52 p253. From the legal dictum laid down by Sir Edward Coke (1552–1634) — an Englishman's house is his castle, i.e. you cannot enter a man's home by force without specific legal authority. It comes from his *Institutes* cap. 73. This snippet of legal lore sank deep into the national consciousness but, I regret to say, is no longer true. Today dozens of officials can enter a private dwelling as of right — and need show no authority before doing so.

Cat Came Back, The. 18 p98. A music-hall song of 1893 by Henry Miller narrating a cat's narrow escapes from death by means of a boot-jack, a brick-bat, electrocution, a cyclone, a train wreck and a stick of dynamite. It eventually succumbed to the sound of a German band playing 'TA-RA-RA BOOM-DE-AY'. German bands plagued the suburbs with their noisy playing and would only move on when desperate householders paid them to do so.

Cat i' the adage, like the poor. See DARE NOT WAIT UPON I WOULD.

Cat in another poem, he knew only they made him light and salutary meals, like a. 3 p217. C.S. CALVERLEY's poem 'Sad Memories': "They call me cruel. Do I know if a mouse or songbird feels? / I only know they make me light and salutary meals." MTT Elin Woodger.

Cat in the poem, "all claws". 3 p62. Also from CALVERLEY's 'Sad Memories': "As with one complex yell he burst, all claws, upon the foe." MTT Elin Woodger.

Catbird seat, in the. 80 p114. According to *Webster's Dictionary*, this term means to be in an advantageous position. MTT David McDonough for the information that the expression was popularised by the baseball commentator Red Barber.

Catch-as-Catch-Can. 10 p58; 14 p201. A style of wrestling, different from Graeco-Roman or Cumberland wrestling styles.

Catch him on the bend/bending. See BEND.

Catch the conscience of the king. See CONSCIENCE OF THE KING.

Cato, the censor. 58 p141. Marcus Porcius Cato (234–149 B.C.), Roman consul and censor, took a poor view of extravagance. The censors were officials responsible for supervising public behaviour and morals, hence the word 'censorious'.

Cats walking through the wet woods waving their wild tails. Long Island is full of them 78 p111. See KIPLING's 'The Cat that Walked by Itself': "the Cat went back through the Wet Wild Woods waving his wild tail ..."

'Cats Will Be Cats'. Short story title. A gloss on BOYS WILL BE BOYS (see above).

Cave-Brown-Cave, Augustus. 97 p42. A well-known English surname, like Knatchbull-Huguessen, below. There was a Cave-Brown-Cave at Dulwich in Wodehouse's time, but the best-known member of the family was probably the Rev. Sir Genille Cave-Browne-Cave, Bart., who was a big-game hunter, a cowboy in the Wild West and involved in the early movie industry before entering the church and becoming a rural vicar. His *From Cowboy to Pulpit* came out in 1926. He was clearly a very different man from his ancestor Sir John Cave-Browne-Cave, who, after a very good dinner, took it into his head to fight a duel with an armchair in the Carlton Club. The armchair lost.

Caviare. One man's c. being another man's major-general 82 p71. A splendid mix of the Latin proverb "One man's meat is another man's poison" and the line in

Hamlet 2.2. 465: "Twas caviare to the general." See ONE MAN'S MEAT.

Caviare to nuts. 65 p135. The usual expression in England was 'from soup to nuts', meaning the totality of something (see SOUP TO NUTS). Since Wodehouse had been living in France for some years before he wrote this, I surmise that a French formal dinner in the 1930s began with caviare, not soup.

Cawnpore. 92 p41; 94 p69. PGW got this reference wrong, but at the age of 88 or 89, who can blame him? It was LUCKNOW which was relieved; at Cawnpore (Indian Mutiny 1857) all the British soldiers were massacred.

Cawthorne, Joe. 56 p259. US character actor (1868–1949).

CBO. 42 p311. A misprint. There is no such British decoration or award as the CBO. As a senior officer in the Guards, Major General Sir Miles Fish would probably have been awarded the CVO (Commander of the Royal Victorian Order). Indeed, his knighthood could well have been a KCVO (Knight Commander). Since PGW's father was a CMG (Companion of the Order of St Michael and St George) and many of PGW's relatives were awarded similar honours, I would attribute the error not to ignorance but the proximity of the letters V and B on PGW's typewriter. See also OBEs.

Celebrity at home. 6 p248. Between 1890 and 1914, English magazines were full of interviews with celebrities 'At Home'. I recall that at least one actress was "never happier than in her garden" while another was "happiest among my books". In 1903 the then-freelance PGW conducted four interviews like this for *V.C.* magazine.

Cerberus. C. of Messrs. Goble and Cohn 26 p144. In Greek mythology, Cerberus was the three-headed dog that guarded the infernal regions.

Ceres. 18 p27. Mythological goddess of corn and harvests who gave us the word 'cereal'.

Certain something the others had not got, that. 70 p112 and elsewhere. I suspect strongly that it is Jerome Kern's 1927 song 'That Little Something', but I have not found the lyrics.

C'est terrible mais ce n'est pas le diable. 3 p256. PGW twist on the comment of Marshal Bosquet as he watched the suicidal Charge of the Light Brigade at Balaklava: "C'est magnifique, mais c'est ne pas la guerre." ("It is magnificent, but it is not war.")

Cham of Tartary, a hair from the beard of the Great. 93 p27. S. *Much Ado About Nothing* 2.1: "I will … bring you the length of Prester John's foot; fetch you a hair off the Great Cham's beard." 'Cham' is another version of Khan (prince). The reference is probably to the English folk memory of Kubla Khan (1214–94), 'the great Khan', whose empire covered Asia from China in the east to Hungary in the west. (Prester John was a legendary figure, a European who is said to have conquered a vast empire in southern Asia in the 11th century. Another version of the legend associates him with Ethiopia in east Africa.)

Chamberlain, Joseph. As Mr. C. might say, half a loaf is better than no bread 3 p272. Joseph Chamberlain (1836–1914), a leading British politician, advocated increasing the trade and self-sufficiency of the British Empire. PGW is referring here to his famous campaign of 1902–3 to give tariff preference to wheat imported from British colonies. PGW wrote the song 'Mr Chamberlain' for Seymour Hicks' 1905 show *The Beauty of Bath* and heard them encored three nights in a row. See also PGW's 'The Parrot' in *The Parrot and Other Poems*. Chamberlain was prominent enough at the time for PGW to use 'Joseph' as a nickname for any boy called Chamberlain (see 2 p189). See also THINKING IMPERIALLY.

Chamberlain, Neville. 46 p194. Chamberlain (1869–1940), son of Joseph above, was Chancellor of the Exchequer 1923–24 and prime minister 1937–40.

Chandler, Raymond. See MARLOWE, PHILIP.

Chanel Number 5. 76 p167; 77 p7 and later. Coco Chanel created her famous scent in 1921.

Chaney, Lon. You look like L.C. made up for something 39 p262. This film actor (1883–1930) was famous for his remarkable disguises, which led to many jokes. "Don't step on that spider, it might be Lon Chaney in disguise" was one.

Change his feelings with the climate, a man cannot, as Horace said. 13 p68. See HORACE'S PHILOSOPHY.

Channing, Carol. In *Hello Dolly* 88 p179. This actress (b. 1921) was a huge hit in the 1964 Broadway musical.

Chanticleer at the sight of the sun, he flaps his wings and crows. 18 p100. This is clearly from Chaucer's 'Nun's Priest's Tale', the story of a rooster who escapes from a fox, but the wording must be from a version of Chaucer I have not found.

Chap in Bab Ballads who couldn't walk into a room without ejaculating "Boom". 34 p16. See 'BOOM'.

Chap of infinite resource, a. See RESOURCE AND SAGACITY.

Chapel folk. 93 p103. This was a term widely used for Baptists, Methodists and others who attended 'chapel' rather than 'church' and tended to disapprove of the 'laxity' of the Church of England. MTT Murray Hedgcock.

Chappie. Frequent. Colloquial version of 'chap'. Like much English slang, it began in the upper classes in the mid-19th century. The spread of music halls (vaudeville) led to many comic songs mocking their social superiors, and the term went out of Society use c.1880 to be replaced by 'Johnny'. This was common for about ten years till the music halls killed it off in the same way. However, 'Stage-door Johnnies', an Edwardian term for the young men who waited outside the stage-door to take a chorus-girl out to dinner, is still recognised today.

In 1905 PGW made a note of the actor-manager Seymour HICKS standing over a playwright to stop him using 'chappie', which Hicks knew was no longer the smart phraseology. Nevertheless, it remained in everyday currency (see 'The Sausage Chappie'), and PGW had an unerring ear for popular usage.

Charchester. 2 pp27, 54, 59, 89. PGW portmanteau name for a fictional school.

English readers would recognise the combination of two famous establishments: Charterhouse and Winchester. See also Harchester.

Charge of the Light Brigade. 45 p274 and elsewhere. T.'s poem of same name.

Chariest maid … her beauty to the moon. 54 p179. See Maid.

Charing Cross. 13 p68. The 'centre of gravity' of London has shifted now, but Charing Cross, the corner where the Strand and Whitehall run into Trafalgar Square, is the official centre of London. A small brass plate in the ground a few feet north of the statue of Charles I marks the exact spot. The plate has more than symbolic importance. If you are a government official, you receive the 'London Allowance', about 50 pence (or a dollar a day) in my time, if you work within six miles of that plate.

Charing Cross Station, the clock at. See Clock at Charing Cross Station.

Chariot, fiery. See Snatched up to heaven.

Charity towards all, with malice towards none. 41 p71. From Abraham Lincoln's second inauguration speech, 4 March 1865, though what he said was "With malice toward none; with charity for all".

Charles, his friend. 3 p153; 8 p93 and elsewhere. A theatrical term from c.1870, generically attributed to the hero's friend/companion in a melodrama. Similar theatrical terms for standard roles were 'Aged Parent', 'faithful old retainer','respectable gentleman', or the Good Old Man or bad Baronets who foreclosed mortgages. Robert Morley once said he had spent forty years playing 'respectable gentleman' parts.

Charley's Aunt. 34 p265 and later. This splendid farce of 1892 by Brandon Thomas maintained its popularity for nearly a century. See also Brazil nut.

Charm dissolves space. 74 p49. A misprint(?) for 'The charm dissolves apace'. S. *Tempest* 5.1.

Charteris. 1, 3 and 13. See Chap. 3.

Charybdis. See Scylla.

Chase my Aunt Fanny up a gum tree. 81 p190; 82 p73; 84 p9 and later. Pseudo--Cockney expression of surprise. I recollect a radio comedian (Arthur Askey?) using it as a catchphrase c.1938–50. Neil Midkiff suggests the gum tree reference connects it to the Australian soldiers who came to Britain to fight in the First World War.

Chastised with scorpions instead of with whips. 87 p53. B. 1 Kings 12.11: "My father hath chastised you with whips, but I will chastise you with scorpions."

Chasuble, too many orphreys on his. 39 p72. See Chap. 11.

Chatsworth, Mafeking Road, East Dulwich. 80 p221. PGW gave us house names and addresses like this because it was an excellent way of classifying their residents. With the growth of the suburbs round England's cities in the late 19th century, shopkeepers and clerks moving into them emphasised their step up in life by naming their houses rather than numbering them. If you had done well enough to move from a tenement in 37 Bread Street in the middle of London out to the leafy suburbs, it was a point of pride to call your new house, no matter how small, The Cedars, The Laurels, The Elms or something like it.

Another fashion was to adopt the names of famous stately homes. Hence there are still hundreds, if not thousands, of small terrace houses whose stained-glass doors bear titles of palaces like Sandringham, Blenheim or Chatsworth. Queen Victoria's affection for her Scottish castle made Balmoral a very popular choice, while Chatsworth is the enormous Stately Home of the Duke of Devonshire.

In 1904 *Punch* mocked the pretensions of the new suburbanites. It noted that houses rented at £30–£50 a year were content with such names as: Bellevue, Fairview, Bella Vista, Rosedene, Mossdene, Willowdene and The Laurels. Larger villas, costing £100 a year to rent, made their superiority clear with names like The Holme, The Hurst, The Croft and The Grange. I am informed that it was not until the 1930s that the Post Office started insisting on numbers being used. My boyhood home was Harrow House, Dagnall Park, which has its name engraved on the gate posts. The number (10) was not used till fifty years after the house had been built. See also MAFEKING ROAD.

Note. A report in *Wooster Sauce*, the journal of the PG Wodehouse Society (UK) (No. 34, June 2005) noted that when the present owners of Threepwood, Record Road, Emsworth (see Chap. 16) bought the house in 1989, the 'Threepwood' name plate I saw in 1971/2 had been replaced by 'Holyrood House'. Holyrood is the Royal palace in Edinburgh.

Chatterleyesque, so. 88 p62. The explicit sexual content of D.H. Lawrence's *Lady Chatterley's Lover* (1928) caused it to be banned in England until 1960, when a famous court case cleared it for publication. Literary modernists regard this as a critical turning point in the history of English literature, when we cast off the shackles of hypocrisy and censorship etc. etc. Others consider the decision legalized pornography.

Chatterton. 38 p250. Thomas Chatterton, an English writer who committed suicide in 1770 at the age of 17.

Chaucer, Geoffrey. 18 p82. Best remembered for his *Canterbury Tales*, Chaucer (1340–1400) was a versatile man employed at various times as courtier, spy, controller of customs and excise, and a very efficient clerk of works (materials and costing clerk) at the Palace of Westminster. The enormous oak roof beams he bought for Westminster Hall in 1399 were not replaced till the 1920s and, I have to add, by the same family firm that provided the original beams 520 years before.

Chauffeurs. Augustus Briggs, Voules, etc., gave the impression of being above the softer emotions. The 'haughty chauffeur' joke was popular in the UK for years and the sentiment was expressed often in Wodehouse. See Chap. 15 for more detail.

Check. Fifty minutes without a check 1 p115 and later (mainly from Aunt Dahlia). A fox-hunting term meaning a good run after a fox without losing the scent, hounds going astray or some other hold-up.

Cheer without inebriating (i.e. tea). 63 p37. The term has been used as a synonym for tea ever since Cowper wrote "the cups that cheer but not inebriate" in his *The Task,* Bk 4, 'The Winter Evening'.

Cheers. See THREE CHEERS and GOODBYE.

Cheeryble Brother(s). 13 p96 and often up to 92. Dickens was happy to acknowledge that this kind-hearted pair were based on the brothers William and Daniel Grant of Manchester, whom he met in 1838. At 92 p31 PGW puts them in Dickens' *Oliver Twist* when he should have said *Nicholas Nickleby.* An excusable mistake at the age of ninety.

Cheese-hound. 22 p56. Slang term for a mongrel. Probably from a Dutch breed called a keeshond, formerly used as a guard dog on Dutch barges. MTT Dr Tim Healey.

Chekhov/Tchekhov. 44 p139; 49 p231 and later. PGW's view of the depressing, if thought-provoking, plays of Anton Pavlovich Chekhov (1860–1904) was shared by many theatre-goers.

Chelsea. 9 p32; 18 p10. From c.1890 to 1939, this was the artistic quarter of London, the equivalent of New York's Greenwich Village. PGW lodged here from 1900 to 1908. See Chap. 25.

Cheltenham. 67 p10 and later. This spa town in Gloucestershire became synonymous with genteel respectability during the 19th century and, as PGW implied, was a favourite spot for retired Service officers and Colonial civil servants. PGW's parents moved there from Shropshire in 1902 and they loved it, whereas PGW loathed it. Some years later, they moved to Bexhill-on-Sea. It was the association of these names in PGW's mind that led to Bill Oakshott defying his uncle in *Uncle Dynamite* with: "Go back to Cheltenham, if you like. Or Bexhill." See Chap. 16.

Cheops of the Fourth Dynasty. 19 p47. Cheops is probably best remembered today as the man who built the Great Pyramid c.3000 B.C.

Cherubim, quiring to the young-eyed. See PATINES OF BRIGHT GOLD.

Cheshire Cat. 17 p153; 25 p100 and later. See Lewis Carroll's *Alice in Wonderland.* The origin of this creature can be seen on the wall beside the altar of St Peter's church, Croft, Darlington; Carroll's father was vicar here. A memorial tablet is supported by the stone heads of two cats, and Carroll noted the fact (which I checked myself) that, as you kneel down at the Communion rail, the upper halves of the cats' faces disappear, leaving only the widely-grinning mouths in your line of vision. By a happy coincidence, the two figures directly above the cats are wild men of the woods. The heraldic term for them is Wode'wose or Wode'ose, and they can be seen on either side of the Wodehouse family escutcheon.

Cheshire Cheese. 16 p111 and later. This splendid Fleet Street pub was built around 1670, after the Great Fire of London, although its cellars are some 200 years older, part of the monastery that once stood on the site.

Chesterfield, Lord. 1 p109; 6 p88; up to 96 p81. The 4th Earl (1694–1773), statesman and author, is now best remembered for *Letters to His Son,* in which he stressed elegance, politeness and style in all written and spoken communication.

Chesterton. 4 p215. A small hamlet, two miles from Wrykyn school. In real life, a small hamlet near Stableford, Shropshire. See Chap. 35.

Chesterton, G.K. Takes Flesho 28 p200; falling on a sheet of tin 41 p90; 46 p131. This grossly overweight (hence PGW's remarks) author (1874–1936) is now probably best remembered for his Father Brown stories, while his brilliant use of paradox is all too often overlooked. His *The Flying Inn* should be compulsory reading for politicians.

Chevalier Bayard. 48 p187. Bayard (1473–1524) was the French *chevalier sans peur et sans reproche* (knight without fear and without reproach) whose bravery and courtesy to his foes made him famous across Europe. Sir Philip SIDNEY was known as 'The English Bayard'.

Chevalier, Maurice. 53 p302; 94 p168. This French singer and actor (1888–1972) was on stage and in films for sixty years. He was seen at his mature best in the film *Gigi* (1958). The reference to "Maurice is not a Knight of the Golden Fleece" etc. at 94 p168 is from the song 'The Son of a Gun Is Nothing but a Tailor' in the 1932 Paramount musical *Love Me Tonight*, in which he starred. Rodgers & Hart wrote it for Jeanette Macdonald to sing. MTT Elin Woodger.

Chew each mouthful thirty-three times. 14 p251;19 p37; 27 p247 and later. See FLETCHERIZE.

Chewing gum. Taste lingers like a celebrated chewing gum 29 p26; 36 p137 and later. I have been unable to trace which brand PGW meant, but he commented in a letter that Billy Rose, with whom he worked in 1929, was the author of the song 'Does the Spearmint Lose Its Flavour on the Bedpost Overnight'(1924).

Chez Jimmy, Paris. 48 p18; 77 p54. A famous bar in Paris 1920–60. 'Jimmy' was James Charteris, whose memoirs of goings-on in Paris came out in 1934.

Chick nor child, he had neither. 86 p100. A 'chick' was the term for a son, a 'child' was a girl. (At 91 p188 Vanessa Polk uses the correct term because PGW's generation knew the difference.) In a rural economy, people wanted boys in their family who could help work the land. I remember old ladies in Ireland in the 1950s meeting a mother taking her newly-born daughter out for the first time and 'congratulating' her with the words: "Never mind, dear. Perhaps next time it will be a boy."

Chickadee, my little. See MY LITTLE CHICKADEE.

Chicken farms (tomato farms/duck farms). 4 p19 and later. Encouraged by the Back to the Land movement of 1905 (see above), many middle-class young men believed they could make money from these ventures. If uneducated farmers could, so could they, was the general idea. The tedious work and constant problems of croup, black spot and other diseases did not enter into their plans till it was too late.

Chickens in the pot. See TWO CARS IN THE GARAGE.

Chickens, just us. See JUST US CHICKENS.

Chiderdoss, Doss. He liked D.C's stuff in the *Sporting Times* 26 p205. This was the pen-name of A.R. Marshall, one of the many writers who gave the *Pink 'Un* its distinctive tone. See Chap. 5.

Chi-ike/Chiyike. 43 p107 and elsewhere. Frequent. To make rude noises/to jeer or deride. Appears to have come into general use in both the US and UK about 1895 from a Cockney term that began c.1860.

Child. See HEART OF A LITTLE CHILD; LITTLE CHILD COULD; LITTLE CHILD WASHED CLEAN.

Child is the father of the man, the. 51 p306; 79 p174; 82 p43. Wordsworth's 'My Heart Leaps Up': "So be it when I shall grow old, Or let me die! The Child is Father of the Man."

Childe Roland to the Dark Tower came, sir. 59 p45; 68 p44, p45, p68, p83 and p246. The writer Kristin Thompson has pointed out how effectively PGW used the repetition of the joke. While the primary reference is S. *King Lear* 3.4, it is probable that Browning's poem 'Childe Roland to the Dark Tower came' was also in PGW's mind.

Childish things. See PUT AWAY CHILDISH THINGS.

Chillicothe, Ohio. 56 p61; 73 p9. I do not know if PGW had any special reason for making this the hometown of Joey Cooley and Mrs Spottsworth. I suspect there is a private joke in here somewhere. Was PGW just contrasting the quiet life of Chillicothe to Hollywood? Similar to "Will it play in Peoria?" See also Chap. 28.

Chimes at midnight. He had heard the c. at m. 42 p25 and elsewhere. S. *2 Henry IV* 3.2: "Youth is the time … to hear the chimes at midnight; to see sunrise in town and country."

Chimney, seven days in Brixton jail for failing to abate a smoky. 50 p230; 78 p67 and later. See NUISANCE MUST NOW CEASE.

Chin chin. There has been much academic discussion on the changes in meaning of this expression. Its use now seems to be restricted to a toast, an alternative to 'Cheers'. It is one of those terms we picked up when the British Empire was at its height and the British Army was serving all over the world. When I joined my regiment in 1952, there were at least 40–50 Indian words still in common use amongst the senior N.C.O.s. Service in China brought back the Chinese greeting 't'sing t'sing', immediately anglicised to 'Chin chin'. But see also GOODBYE.

Chin prognathous. The nose was broad, the ears prominent, the chin p. 65 p28. 'Prognathous' — jutting, strong — seems an odd word for PGW to use until one recalls his letter to *The Times* of 30 November 1937. There he wrote that the fishlike Wooster face was hereditary but everything was relative. Compared with Sir Roderick Glossop, Tuppy Glossop and even Jeeves, "Bertie is definitely opisthognathous" (has a receding chin). But in the Drones, among Freddie Widgeon, Catsmeat Potter-Pirbright and particularly Augustus Fink-Nottle, Bertie's chin "will seem to stick out like the ram of a battle ship".

Chinee, Heathen. 7 p215. See HEATHEN CHINEE.

Chingachgook. 20 p140 and later. See Fenimore Cooper's *Last of the Mohicans*.

Chirgwin. 12 p292. George H. Chirgwin was popular black-face singer of minstrel songs. One night, by accident, he left a patch of skin on his face unblacked. The audience loved it and it became his trade mark. He died in 1922, aged 66.

Chi-yiking. 40 p137. See CHI-IKE.

Cholmondely. Where you call C. Marchbanks, (the sort of cockeyed thing you must expect in England) 89 p87. The English habit of eliding long names can be irritating to foreigners. We pronounce Marjoribanks as Marchbanks, Cholmondely as Chumley, Mainwaring as Mannering, Leveson-Gore as Looson-Gore, Urquhart as Erket and Wriothesley as Roxley, etc.

Chops and tomato sauce. 80 p16; 84 p172. PGW was quoting Serjeant Buzfuz's famous remark in D. *The Pickwick Papers* as an example of barristers browbeating witnesses. In the Trial chapter, Buzfuz declaimed on the sinister significance of Mr Pickwick's (completely innocent) note that he would like 'Chops and Tomata sauce' for dinner.

Chorasmian shore. 34 p222. SHELLEY's 'Alastor', line 272. See ALASTOR.

Chorus girl was a simple chorus girl to him. 27 p214. See PRIMROSE AT THE RIVER'S BRIM.

Christian, up and smite them. 72 p42. Hymn 'Christian, Doth Thou See Them' by Neale. The third to fifth lines are: "How the troops of Midian, / Prowl and prowl around. / Christian, up and smite them."

Christie, Agatha. 46 p62 and often later. PGW had a high regard for this writer (1890–1976) of detective stories, and this was reciprocated. Her *Hallowe'en Party* is dedicated to him.

Christopher Robin. 65 last words; has ten little toes 68 p200. See A.A. MILNE's poem 'Hoppity', which begins: "Christopher Robin goes, Hoppity, hoppity, hoppity, hoppity, hop." The second reference is from 'Cradle Song'. "Oh Timothy Tim, Has ten pink toes, And ten pink toes has Timothy Tim. They go with him, Wherever he goes, And wherever he goes, They go with him."

Christy Minstrels. 11 p24. Edwin Christy (1815–62) began the 19th-century black-face minstrel craze when he formed the first recognised troupe in 1849. They became so popular that within ten years every troupe claimed to be 'Christy Minstrels'. The term is still often used to describe black-face singing groups. See also MINSTREL SHOW and MOORE & BURGESS.

Chula Vista, picking lemons at. 89 p125. PGW always admired the adventures of his schoolfellow Bill Townend, who sailed across the world in tramp steamers and whose experiences had included lemon-picking at Chula Vista, California. See 'Old Bill Townend' in *Weekend Wodehouse*. See also Chap. 34.

Church Lads Brigade. 18 p252 and frequently later. A succinct, if jaundiced, description is at 92 p139. See Chap. 11.

Church Militant. 85 p117 and elsewhere. BCP. The Communion Service: "Let us pray for the whole state of Christ's Church militant here on earth." See also

Chap. 11.

Church of Abyssinia. See ABYSSINIA.

Church steeple loves the cloud above it, the. 91 p209. In 1928 PGW adapted Molnár's play *The Play's the Thing*. MTT Tony Ring for pointing out that the line appears in Act 2. Tony has evidence to indicate that PGW, rather than Molnár, wrote it, and I think he is right.

Churchill, Charles. 93 p75. A satirist (1731–64) who attacked politicians and fellow authors.

Churchill, Winston. 52 p286 and later. Churchill (1874–1965) was the last orator who grasped his lapels as he spoke. The habit stemmed from the days before 1919 when everybody wore a frock coat. See Chap. 6.

Resemblance of babies to Churchill (71 p174); Churchill was fully aware of this. He is recorded as growling to one proud mother: "Madam, all babies look like me." See also THINGS UP WITH WHICH SHE WOULD NOT PUT.

Churchyards yawn and graves give up their dead. 99 p271. Sounds Shakespearian but will be found in 'The Spectre of Tappington' (*The Ingoldsby Legends*) by Rev. Richard Barham.

Cicero. 12 p242; Cicero & Clodius 33 p43; 46 p39. This Roman statesman and orator came to a violent end in 43 B.C. His speeches against Catiline and Clodius were famous.

Cigar or cocoanut. 7 p94;14 p49 and later. The choice was the traditional prize at side-shows at English fairgrounds when you rang the bell or hit the target or got three darts on the right playing-card. It was also the title of a comic song sung by Harry Freeman in the 1890s. See also RUNG THE BELL.

Cigarettes. Frequent. Cigarettes were introduced into Britain by soldiers returning from the Crimean War in 1855. Until then we had smoked pipes or cigars. Made from Turkish, Egyptian or Russian tobacco, the new cigarettes were expensive. They were also given exotic 'Turkish' or 'Egyptian' names; Queen of the Harem and Mustapha (a real brand) are typical examples to be seen in early PGW school stories.

Cheaper American (Virginian tobacco) cigarettes, which arrived about 1880, were known as fags, gaspers, stinkers or 'toofahs'/ 'toofers' (two for a ha'penny, a phrase still in common use in the 1950s). That is why, at country houses, Bingo would pillage Bertie's cigarette box, since the local village shop would not sell the more expensive brands. The First World War cut off supplies of Turkish and Egyptian tobacco, increasing the American share of the market. Hence the common remark (which PGW quotes at 40 p32 and elsewhere) as you offered your cigarette-case: "Turkish this side; Virginian that." The habit persisted amongst first-year undergraduates at Oxford as late as 1953. A year later, most of us had grown out of it and just bought the cheaper American tobacco.

See also MURAD and UMUSTAPHAS.

Ciro's nightclub. 31 p76. See Chap. 21.

Cities of the Plain. 22 p156 and later. B. Genesis 13.12. These were Sodom and

Gomorrah, whose fate is described at Genesis 19.24. "The Lord rained upon Sodom and Gomorrah brimstone and fire from the Lord out of heaven." The punishment of Lot's wife's for being curious (being turned into a pillar of salt) is two verses on.

Citizen, fat and greasy. 26 p90. See FAT AND GREASY CITIZEN.

Civil disobedience. 60 p 84; 68 p114 and later. The term came into common use in the 1930s when Gandhi's independence movement in India employed it as an effective method of rebellion. No violence was involved, simply refusal to obey certain laws.

Claridges. 31 p13; 32 p62; 41 p245; 42 p65. This magnificent hotel is exactly where Lady Constance would have gone for tea (as Ethel Wodehouse used to). It is better known to Wodehouse enthusiasts as Barribault's. See Chap. 25.

Clarkson, beard from. 44 p56; 81 p21; 97 p38. This eccentric, diminutive wig-maker (1861–1934) provided wigs for every theatre in London for forty years. His premises at 41 Wardour Street (still there with the plaques beside the door recording Sarah Bernhardt and Henry Irving's attendance at the 1904 reopening) also provided fancy-dress costumes to Society, with clients ranging from Queen Victoria to the famous murderer Dr. Crippen. As an advertising stunt, he once had a batch of imitation cardboard sovereigns made with his head on one side. When someone suggested it was a bit of a cheek to put his head on the back of a sovereign, he was highly indignant: "On the back! Can't you see? It's on the front!"

Claudius. King Claudius in Hamlet watching The Mouse Trap 67 p163. S. *Hamlet* 3.2. Agatha Christie used the reference for her play *The Mouse Trap*, which has been running in London without a break since 1952.

Cleanse the bosom of perilous stuff. See BOSOM.

Clemenceau, looked like. 67 p14. Mugsy Bostock looks like him, as does the Duke of Dunstable. This French statesman (1841–1929) was famous for his large, white, bushy moustache.

Clement's Inn. Psmith has digs in 14 p59. See Chap. 25.

Cleopatra. 27 p125 and often (28 times) later. Nearly all the references I have found to this lady come from S. *Antony & Cleopatra*, but see HOME LIFE.

Cleopatra's pep talk. 72 p71. See ACTIUM.

Client. This, if I mistake not, Watson, is our c. now 26 p190; 42 p102 and later. A classic Sherlock Holmes line. See Conan DOYLE's 'Wisteria Lodge' or 'Thor Bridge'.

Cliff, Laddie. 49 p 227. Light-comedy UK actor (1891–1937).

Clock at Charing Cross Station. 32 p84 and later. The large, four-sided clock that hung in the middle of Charing Cross Station was a traditional London meeting place, equalled in popularity only by Swan & Edgar's on Piccadilly Circus. Some years ago the railway authorities decided to take it down, but public protest forced them to save it. It is now on the wall over the ticket offices.

Clodius. 33 p43. Roman politician. See Cicero.

Clothes Stakes. 60 p56. The original of this, the Great Hat Stakes, was related by J.B. Binstead, the most famous of the Pink 'Uns and Pelicans, in his *Pitcher in Paradise* (1903). See Chap. 5.

Clothing the palpable and familiar / With golden exhalations of the dawn. 28 p166. From Coleridge's *Death of Wallenstein*, Act 5 Scene 1.

Cloud no bigger than a man's hand. See Cloud that arose.

Cloud, swooping or descending from a. 17 p113; 42 p122; 79 p97. According to Homer, when Zeus, Athene or some other Greek god or goddess came down to earth, they usually did so in a cloud.

Cloud that arose out of the sea like a man's hand. 26 p117; a cloud no bigger than a man's hand 34 p125. B. 1 Kings 18.44. "Behold, there ariseth a little cloud out of the sea, like a man's hand."

Clouds of witnesses. 3 p194. B. Hebrews. 12.1: "we are encompassed about with so great a cloud of witnesses …"

Clovelly, Felix. 19 p14. See Chap. 16.

Clowes. 4 p5; 8 p11; 12 p37. As with Charteris, I think there is a lot of PGW in Clowes. Some of his conversations have a strong 'ring' of memory rather than imagination. See Chap. 3.

Clutch of circumstance. See Fell clutch of circumstance.

Clytemnaestra. 3 p268. Adulterous wife of King Agamemnon, whom she killed when he returned from the Trojan wars.

Coal hole. Not easy to find a good coal hole nowadays 88 p127. A minor comment but it needs some explanation. When the residential estates of London, Mayfair, Kensington, Belgravia and the like were being built in the early 19th century, the standard heating fuel was coal. If you walk through these areas today, the houses are normally set back some ten feet from the pavement with railings to stop the pedestrian falling down into the sunken space between the pavement and the basement of the house. This space is known as 'the area'. To save carrying sacks of coal through the house, a coal cellar was constructed on the street side of the area, underneath the pavement. Small round coal-hole covers were set along the pavement through which the coal was delivered. A careless coal man would often leave the cover off, allowing people like Freddie Widgeon to claim they had fallen into the hole.

Coal holes went out of use in the 1950s when the severe London 'smog' forced Parliament to pass the Clean Air Acts and ban the use of coal in London and other major cities. As pavements were repaired and replaced, many of the covers vanished, exactly as Freddie said. Another example of PGW noting social changes in a London he had left thirty years before.

Coal Hole, The. 33 p56. Beside the Savoy in the Strand. With The Cheshire Cheese, The Shakespeare at Victoria Station (9 p35) and The White Hart at Barnes (33 p59), The Coal Hole is one of the four London pubs mentioned in PGW still on the same site under the same name. The unnamed pub opposite

Julian Eversleigh's rooms in Rupert Street (*Not George Washington*) is still there (The Blue Posts). See Chaps 25 & 34.

Coast, stern and rock-bound. 60 p189 and elsewhere. See STERN AND ROCK-BOUND COAST.

Cobb, Constable. 18 p30. Second policeman in PGW's novels to be ducked, or threatened with a ducking. See Chap. 16.

Cobo Bay. 9 p14. A bay in Guernsey, Channel Islands. PGW went to school in the Channel Islands for a time, but this reference is clearly to his holiday there in 1905.

Cochran, C.B. 46 p271; his revue 49 p227. Cochran (1872–1951) can best be described as the UK equivalent of Florenz Ziegfeld. He managed sideshows, boxers, wrestlers, escapologists (Houdini) and later produced successful plays and musicals. See also HACKENSCHMIDT.

Cockburn, Charlie. 66 p104. A clear reference to C.B. Cochran, above.

Cocktails (general). I am not going to attempt to identify the weird and wonderful cocktails drunk by PGW's young men. I suggest that some were his own invention, inspired by the hundreds of different concoctions popular in the 1920s and 1930s. I wonder how many readers can identify the drinks listed at page 221 of my *Esquire Drink Book* (1957): Homestead, Honolulu, Hula-Hula, Hurricane, Imperial, Java Cooler, Journalist and Knockout? For Green Swizzles, See Chap. 38.

Cocoa Tree. 13 p61. This St James's Street club, once famous for its gambling along with White's and Watier's, is now defunct. See BEAU DAWLISH and Chap. 21.

Cohan, Mr George. His poetry is not punk 18 p125; 23 p223. Cohan (1878–1942) is a legend in the American theatre. On the stage before he was ten, he danced, composed and sang his own songs, wrote his own shows, produced and directed. His unabashed sentimentality and patriotism kept his audiences happy for fifty years. His songs 'Mary's a Grand Old Name' and 'Give My Regards to Broadway' are enduring reminders of why New Yorkers loved him.

Cohen and Corcoran, a beautiful friendship. 62 p86. I found this completely by chance when my wife asked me to chase up a reference in a book she was editing on F.D. Roosevelt. Ben Cohen (1894–1983) and Thomas Corcoran (1900–81) were two young lawyers who acted as legal advisors to F.D. Roosevelt during his twelve-year presidency. Their efficiency and teamwork became legendary. The pair of them drafted the Securities Exchange Act of 1934 and went on to introduce such ground-breaking New Deal legislation as the Federal Housing Administration, the Tennessee Valley Authority, the Public Utility Holding Company Act and the Fair Labor Standards Act as well as the initial charter for the United Nations. Cohen drafted the legislation and Corcoran sold it to politicians using his remarkable legal skill, wit and personal charm. They were among the young men brought into Roosevelt's administration by the lawyer Felix Frankfurter who became known collectively as the 'Happy Hotdogs'.

(*Felix* is Latin for happy.)

Cohen Bros of Covent Garden. 37 p156; 41 p79; 64 p39; 86 p152 and elsewhere. An obvious reference to the famous clothing and dress-hire firm of Moss Bros in London's Covent Garden. The firm still flourishes, though their present site is across the road from the establishment PGW knew. The old building, which they left in 1989, had the slowest, creakiest lift in London, but I always made a point of walking through all the floors to admire the extraordinary range of hire-clothing and uniforms available. If you wanted the right clothing for a function anywhere in the world, Moss Bros would provide it. If you needed, like Lords Emsworth and Ickenham, to hire an earl's ceremonial robes (see 84 p33), Moss Bros had them in stock. If you were appointed a deputy judge in Hong Kong or Third Secretary to the embassy in Ulan Bator, Moss Bros would see you right. They are still the main providers of hired morning dress (topper and tail coat) for weddings, Royal Ascot and similar festivities. When an elderly viscount met the chairman of the firm in the grandstand looking out over the course one Derby Day, he greeted him with the words: "Morning, Moss. Stocktaking?" See MOSS BROTHERS.

Cohort of the Damned (in which broken men may toil and die and, dying, forget). 55 p177; 71 p129. KIPLING's 'Gentlemen-Rankers' is the origin of 'Cohort of the damned' but for the rest of it, see FOREIGN LEGION.

Cohorts all gleaming with purple and gold. 72 p155. See ASSYRIAN.

Collar. A three-collar man. See THREE-COLLAR MAN.

College yells. 18 p223; 70 p82; 88 p154. PGW learned of these calls to spur on your college football team during his short visit to America in 1904. In March 1905 he wrote an article on the subject for the Old Alleynians' (Dulwich Old Boys) magazine. He listed some of the American yells, including Dartmouth's "Wah hoo wah, wah hoo wah, da-da-da Dartmouth, wah hoo wah T-i-g-e-r!" He recommended that the Old Alleynians introduce the custom for their Rugger matches and suggested a possible version. It began: "Yah, yah, OAs!!"

Afternote. Since the original 1878 Dartmouth "Wah hoo wah" was purportedly based on an American-Indian expression, Dartmouth banned its use in 1977 as being politically incorrect.

Collier, Mr William. 15A p220; 23 p223. American comedy character actor (1866–1944).

Collins, Lottie. 46 p96; 79 p180. English music hall singer and dancer (1866–1910).

Collins, Wilkie. 81 p22. Heavily bearded English novelist (1824–89), author of *The Woman in White*, one of the earliest detective mystery novels, now transformed into a spectacular musical.

Colman, Ronald. 44 p18, p135; 46 p149 & p 271 and later. This handsome actor (1891–1958) thrilled two generations of filmgoers. He played Beau Geste, Bulldog Drummond, Sidney Carton and other heroes.

Colney Hatch. 3 p191 and frequent later. This area in north London was the home of England's largest lunatic asylum, built in 1851. Eventually the local residents, worried that the asylum brought the area into disrepute, managed to get the locality renamed New Southgate (where I live at present). The asylum closed in 1993 and the buildings have now been turned into expensive luxury flats. The sales brochure makes no mention of their previous use. See also EARLSWOOD.

Colonel (a golf ball). 7 p220. Because of the once-universal use by golfers of the term 'Colonel Bogey' (see below), the word 'colonel' was often used for a golf ball.

Colonel Bogey. 18 p130. In Chapter 27 I explain that 'bogey' was once the term for the score a scratch golfer would make. This meant that a player could go out and play by himself 'against bogey'. Around 1890, when golf became wildly popular in the UK, cartoons and humorous verses appeared about the mythical figure 'Colonel Bogey'. He was portrayed as a tall, thin, fierce, elderly gentleman, dressed in Norfolk jacket and plus-fours who never hit a bad shot. The 'Colonel Bogey' march (*The Bridge on the River Kwai*) is named after him.

Colosseum. Could Mitchell carry it with a full brassie shot? 28 p92; lions and Christians 67 p243. This enormous stadium in Rome is where gladiatorial fights were staged and Christians were allegedly devoured by lions. Its ruins are still awe-inspiring and, having viewed them, I am pretty certain not even Abe Mitchell (1887–1947), 'the best golfer never to win the Open', would have attempted the shot. It might be possible with a baffy, but certainly not with a brassie (see Chap. 27). Even then, the ball would have fallen into the centre of the arena.

Mortimer Sturgis was not alone in viewing things from a sporting point of view. The Rev. Edward Lyttelton, cleric, county cricketer and headmaster of Eton, once said that he could never walk down the carpeted aisle of a church or cathedral without wondering if it would take spin. (See Chap. 3.)

Colossus, bestriding his narrow world like a. 63 p132; 67 p8 and elsewhere. S. *Julius Caesar* 1.2: "Why, man, he doth bestride the narrow world / Like a Colossus; and we petty men / Walk under his huge legs, and peep about …" Despite the Colossus being an enormous single upright statue, it was later widely believed that it straddled the harbour entrance at Rhodes. This mistake was 'confirmed' by the many paintings showing this version of it.

Colossus (of Rhodes). 19 p125 and later. One of the Seven Ancient Wonders of the World, this was an enormous bronze statue at the entrance to the harbour at Rhodes from 280 to 220 B.C.

Combe Regis. 7 p22. In the first edition of *Love Among the Chickens*, PGW used the real name, Lyme Regis. In the 1921 re-write, he changed it to Combe Regis. See Chap. 12.

Come and they cometh, say. See GO AND HE COMETH.

Come back victorious or on the shields of your soldiers. 1 p175. I remember having to translate this a very long time ago, but I have been unable to trace the reference. I had thought it was the valediction of a Roman mother to her son, but I was wrong. MTT Richard Vine and Dr Tim Healey for pointing me to Plutarch's *Moralia*, where a Spartan mother says it to her son.

Come in like a lion/lioness, go out like a lamb. See LION/LIONESS.

Come into the garden, Maud. See MAUD.

Come, let me clutch thee. See IS THAT A BOTTLE.

Come on, Steve. 78 p99 and later. Steve Donoghue was the leading British jockey between the two World Wars, and 'Come On, Steve' became a catchphrase, a universal expression of encouragement.

Come one, come all, this rock shall fly from its firm base as soon as I. 49 p183; 65 p232. From Scott's 'Lady of the Lake' c5.10.

Come the three corners of the world and we shall shock them. 72 p94. S. *King John* 5.7.

Come unto these yellow sands. 68 p194. From S. *Tempest* 1. 2, set to music later by Purcell.

Come up and see his etchings. See ETCHINGS.

Come up and see (sue) me some time. 54 p161; 64 p70; 72 p101 and later. This phrase has joined 'Play it again, Sam' and 'Elementary, my dear Watson' as a misquotation that has become part of the language. In the film *She Done Him Wrong* (1933), Mae West said, "Come up some time and see me." One film historian believes that the audience automatically paraphrased it in their minds and came out of the cinema quoting the more rhythmic version which they were convinced they had heard. A possibility, but another authority states Mae West realised the misquotation had become a trademark and used it in her later films.

Cometh in the morning, it. 52 p129. See JOY IN THE MORNING.

Cometh not, he/she. See MARIANA OF THE MOATED GRANGE.

Comforted, refused to be. See REFUSED TO BE COMFORTED.

Coming events do not always cast their shadows before them. 66 p30. Thomas Campbell's poem 'Lochiel's Warning'.

Coming in or going out, chap in Dickens who is always. PGW ref lost. D. *Martin Chuzzlewit*, Chap. 49 (Mr Sweedlepipes).

Commination Service. 29 p122 and later up to 97 p84. BCP. The Commination Service, or 'Denouncing of God's Anger and Judgements Against Sinners'. The opening words have a vigour and robustness rarely heard in ecclesiastical circles today:

"Brethren, in the primitive church there was a godly discipline, that, at the beginning of Lent, such persons as stood convicted of notorious sin were put to open penance and punished in this world, that their souls might be saved in the day of the Lord; and that others, admonished by their example, might be the more afraid to offend.

"Instead whereof, until the said discipline may be restored again, (which is much to be wished) ..."

On this splendid note, the minister then calls down curses upon various types of evil-doer. (I love the phrase "which is much to be wished".)

Committee of Public Safety signing a death warrant during the Reign of Terror. 54 p171. This body presided over the worst excesses of the French Revolution.

Company's own water, both H & C? 44 p98 and later. PGW had already used the phrase in *Summer Lightning* but this reference is more appropriate. It was to be seen in just about every British housing advertisement from 1900 to 1930. As new estates grew up around London and other major cities, buyers wanted reassurance on the purity of the water supply. The 'companies' were the municipal water companies created around 1890 and were subject to medical and legal regulation. See also GRAVEL SOIL.

Compleat Slacker. 3 p239. See *The Compleat Angler* by Izaak Walton.

Complexion, schoolgirl. See SCHOOLGIRL COMPLEXION.

'Comrades'. 33 p65. Popular song by Felix McGlennon (1890).

Concatenation of circumstances. 64 p89 and elsewhere. Sounds typical Shakespeare but my dictionaries say it is from Daniel Webster's (1782–1852) 'Argument on the Murder of Captain Joseph White' (1830).

Concealment, like ... like what, Jeeves? Like a worm i' the bud, sir. 51 p58 and later. See SHE NEVER SAID A WORD ABOUT HER LOVE.

Condemned man made an excellent breakfast, the. 26 p13. For some reason, this phrase was always used by UK newspapers when they reported someone's hanging.

Coney Island. 22 p89. This amusement park at the southwest corner of Long Island, New York, still exists but is a shadow of its former self. PGW thoroughly enjoyed his visit there in 1915 and wrote about it for *Vanity Fair.* He must have written 'Crowned Heads' immediately afterwards.

Conferences between statesmen which are conducted thoughout in a spirit of the utmost cordiality, one of those. 67 p177; 82 pp95 & 170; 84 p10 and later. PGW picked up this cliché in the 1950s when politicians realised the Cold War needed new diplomatic methods. I had forgotten how common the phrase 'utmost cordiality' had become until he reminded me. Previously we had had 'diplomatic exchanges'. Now we had the United Nations and everybody started having summit conferences which were always conducted in an atmosphere/spirit of ...

Confessions of Alphonse, The. 84 p167. "Instantly as a man wish to borrow money of me, I dislike him. It is in the blood. It is more strong than me." Wodehouse was quoting directly from the second page of chapter 4 of *The Confessions of Alphonse* (a French waiter) by Barry Pain (1864–1928). See Anatole in Chap. 37.

Confessions of those who had behaved as they ought not to have behaved. 42 p198. BCP. General Confession (Morning Prayer): "And we have done those things which we ought not to have done." MTT Jim Linwood for reminding me of this one.

Confused noise without, a. 8 p32 ("As Shakespeare put it") and later. S. *Tempest* 1.1 has "*A confused noise within*: 'Mercy on us!'"

Conscia mens recti, nec … revocare gradum. 1p164. See THUCYDIDES.

Conscience of the king, catch the. 85 p73. S. *Hamlet* 2.2: "The play's the thing / Wherein I'll catch the conscience of the king."

Conscious of his position. The wretched man seemed fully c. of his p. 59 p189. See POSITION.

Consent. Vowing he'd ne'er consent, consented. See VOWING.

Consolidated Nail File and Eyebrow Tweezer Corporation. 66 p7. Note also later: Consolidated Hamburgers/Peanuts/Pop-Corn/Rails. PGW's usage sounds a trifle odd to UK ears; America uses the word 'consolidated' for commercial conglomerates whereas the UK tends to say 'amalgamated'.

Consols. 10 p85;18 p205. Government bonds, a safe investment. The first Government Consolidated Funds, their correct name, were issued in 1757, paying one per cent interest.

Constabulary duties to be done. 70 p176. G&S *Pirates of Penzance* Act 2. MTT Charles Gould.

Constitution Club. 29 Introduction. See Chap. 21.

Consul the Almost Human. 29 p176 and often later. See Chap. 27.

Consummation devoutly to be wished, a. 3 p179 and frequent later. S. *Hamlet* 3.1 ('To be or not to be' speech). "… 'tis a consummation devoutly to be wished. To sleep; perchance to dream; ay, there's the rub …"

Contented cows, (made) from. 47 p149 and elsewhere. PGW gave us contented pigs at 68 p77 and 76 p222, contented lemons at 88 p73 and contented hens at 93 p5 & 96 p155. When Carnation, the tinned-milk firm, were working out how to sell their new product in 1906, they were anxious to find something to make it sound as homely and attractive as bottled milk. "Made from contented cows" proved a popular and successful advertisement for 40 years. MTT Herb Woodger for the information that Carnation sponsored a radio show in the 1940s with the introductory song 'Waiting for the cows to come home', which included the lines: "They're down in the dell. Mooooo! Contented you can tell. Mooooo!"

Contrite heart/spirit, meek and. See SPIRIT, HUMBLE AND CONTRITE.

Conversation, had no. 74 p189; 94 p73; 95 p60; 97 p11. PGW reminded Bolton that Brichoux says "She was a nice girl but she had no conversation" in the third act of *The Girl Behind the Gun*. Since PGW and Bolton wrote the book, I assume he was right.

Convict 99. 9 p200. This popular adventure serial began in Harmsworth's *Answers* in 1892. Written by Mr & Mrs Connor Leighton, it ran for years.

Cook. A good cook as cooks go and as cooks go, she went. From the Wodehouse/Bolton/Gershwin 1926 show *Oh, Kay*! See Chap. 24 for its origin.

Cook, Dr. 15A p153; 23 p139. The centre of a big scandal of the early 20th century. Just after the news came out in 1909 that Robert E. Peary had reached the North Pole, Dr Frederick Cook claimed to have reached it six days before Peary had. Many people believed him and he toured theatres for years, recounting his adventures. It was later proved that he was a shocking liar, and he went to prison for fraud in 1923.

Cook, looking like a. Lady Hermine Wedge was short and dumpy and looked like a cook 65 p12. It is difficult to explain this image today since these ladies have become very rare. In the Victorian days of big households with many servants, the cook bore a heavy physical load. She chopped, stirred, mixed and cooked for twenty, thirty, even fifty people. Handling all those two/five-gallon saucepans and pots developed muscles and shoulders like a prizefighter. If you saw Ruth Mott in the splendid UK TV series *The Victorian Kitchen*, you will know what I mean. In very general terms, up to 1940, if you saw a middle-aged lady, clearly strong, broad of build, with arms and shoulders to match, you were probably looking at a cook. It wasn't the food they ate that gave them their impressive build; it was the hard work that went into cooking it.

Cookie crumbles, that's the way the. See THAT'S THE WAY THE COOKIE CRUMBLES.

Cooley, Joey. 56 p8. See Chap. 28.

Coon Band Contest, The. 6 p8. The 1907 Army & Navy Stores catalogue lists this as a cakewalk by Pryor.

Coon Drum Major, The. 2 p57. This 1899 cakewalk by Leslie Stuart was made popular by Eugene Stratton, who sang it in music halls up and down the country.

Coon songs, refined. 40 p134. The CHRISTY MINSTRELS and numerous other black-face singing groups made songs from the Old South fashionable in late Victorian England. The 1907 Army & Navy Stores catalogue advertised Coon Song Albums. If the Stores sold them, you can be sure they were perfectly respectable.

Cooper, Alfred Duff. 68 p35. One of the two jokes PGW made about the man who did him so much harm (see also TALLEYRAND). It was Duff Cooper, Minister of Information, who forced the BBC to let William Connor make his infamous broadcast attacking PGW on 15 July 1941. The BBC told him it was "clearly libellous" but Cooper (1890–1954) insisted on its being broadcast. His authorised biographer (John Charnley) says: "It was a scurrilous, vulgar, cheap and nasty piece of character assassination …" See also PULBROOK, MISS EUSTACIA.

Cooper, Fenimore. 20 p139 and often later. Cooper's (1789–1851) *The Last of the Mohicans* (1826), sometimes called the first Western, is full of Indians, including Chingachgook, moving noiselessly through forests "without letting a single twig crack beneath their feet". PGW clearly meant this book but I could not find this line in it. MTT Neil Midkiff, who found it in Cooper's *The Deerslayer*.

Cooper, Gary. 70 p224. American film star (1901–61).

Cooper, Gladys. Mother was no Gladys Cooper 22 p56. This beautiful actress (1888–1971) joined the Gaiety in 1906 and was on the stage for over sixty years. In 1908 she married Herbert Buckmaster, later founder of Buck's Club, a major source of the Drones (see Chap. 21).

Coopers Hill. 8 p97. Cramming/coaching establishment designed to get boys through the exams for Sandhurst (the UK equivalent of West Point).

Cootes, Eddie. 32 p174. I wonder if this gentleman's name is one of PGW's private compliments. I note that Fred Coots (1897–1985) was a prolific American composer who had at least one song in *Sally* (1920). Eddie Cootes appeared two years later.

Cophetua, King, and the beggar maid. 17 p30 and later. T. 'The Beggar Maid', last line. Shakespeare had it in *Romeo & Juliet* 2.1, but TENNYSON's is the line people remembered. "Cophetua sware a royal oath: 'This beggar maid shall be my queen!'"

Copious notes. Often. At 74 p208, PGW remembered Arnold Bennett saying he had taken them as he watched his father die. From what I have learned of Bennett, this is very likely. See BENNETT, ARNOLD.

Corbett. If Mr Corbett had any worries that day in Carson City 17 p73; 23 p243; 33 p60. The heavyweight championship fight between Robert Fitzsimmons and Jim Corbett on 17 March 1897 marked the beginning of modern boxing. It was the first fight to be staged in a specially-built open-air arena and the first to be recorded on film. Fitzsimmons, widely held to have no chance, won in the fourteenth round. See also MCVEY, CONNIE.

Corcoran. The narrator of the Ukridge stories got his name, as several of PGW's characters did, from W.S. Gilbert. See G&S *Pinafore* and *Utopia Ltd.*

Cordiality, in an atmosphere of the utmost. See CONFERENCES BETWEEN STATESMEN.

Corelli, Marie. 9 p151; 10 p137; 18 p169. This lady (1855–1924) wrote very popular sensational novels. See BECAME HIM/HER WELL.

Corfby Hall, near Much Middlefold. 32 p324. See Chap. 35.

Corn (chaff) before the red-haired bloke's sickle. 57 p220; 76 p156 and later. See Wordsworth's 'The Excursion': "ripe corn before his sickle fell."

Cornelia, mother of the Gracchi. 72 p73. See GRACCHI.

Cornish Express on way to Penzance, could have stopped the. 28 p112 and later. At 73 p120, this becomes the US Twentieth Century Limited, but at 76 p60 it is back to the (British) Cornish Express going through a tunnel. In the 1920s, the Cornish Riviera Express was famous for the record speeds the train achieved.

Corot. 21 p230. French painter (1796–1875).

Corps, school. 3 p110; 6 p57. From c.1870 onwards, most British public (private) schools had an Army cadet corps. See ALDERSHOT.

Corpse at an Egyptian banquet. 21 p199. MTT Elin Woodger for finding the source of this very obscure reference. According to Herodotus, it was the custom for Egyptian banquets to finish with a corpse, or a model of a corpse, being brought into the dining room. The object was to remind guests that, no matter how enjoyable the banquet, we would all die one day. Nowadays I suppose the equivalent would be dimming the lights in a restaurant or telling people their taxi is waiting.

Corpus (Christi). Plays Wrykyn at Rugger 8 p95. Corpus Christi is the Oxford college Armine Wodehouse attended. See Chap. 33.

Corruptio optimi pessima. 28 p108. The alleged source of this Latin tag, which translates as 'the corruption of the best is worst of all', is Pope Gregory I. MTT Hetty Litjens.

Cortez. Stout C. and all his men 9 p33 and later up to 94 p145. See NEW PLANET HAD SWUM INTO HIS KEN.

Corybantes, the Phrygian, danced. 42 p114. The Corybantes were the priests of Cybele in Phrygia who went into a delirium of frenzied dancing during her festival. She was a Greek earth-mother goddess.

'Cottar's Saturday Night, The'. 46 p240. Painting by Sir David Wilkie (1785–1841) of the scene described in Burns' poem of the same name. Wilkie's painting of scenes of rural life were very popular.

Cotton, Henry. 57 p147; 81 p149. Englishman who revived British golf with four victories in the Open 1930s–40s.

Cough drop, what a. 93 p110. Because a cough drop was thought to be so beneficial, the term became Cockney slang for someone of whom you had a high opinion, someone you were glad to see. The usage goes back to at least 1870 and was certainly still common in the 1960s.

Could these things be? 8 p106. See THINGS.

Counted his blessings one by one. 66 p7; 68 p160. 'Count Your Blessings', originally written by the Rev. J Oatman in 1897 as a childen's hymn, soon became popular as a sentimental song. MTT Elin Woodger.

Courage, patience and perseverance will always find a way. 70 p56. Both Thomas Jefferson and John Quincy Adams expressed sentiments like this. The nearest I have found is Jefferson writing to William Short in 1792: "Persuasion, perseverance and patience are the best advocates on questions depending on the will of others."

Courage we bring to them. See IT IS NOT —S THAT MATTER.

Court. The present C. is extraordinarily strict in its views 21 p48. Mrs Crocker was right. In contrast to the raffish New Money that had characterised the Court of Edward VII (1901–10), the Court of George V and Queen Mary (1910–36) was an extremely sober and austere institution which disapproved strongly of late nights and abhorred gambling of any sort.

Court Theatre. 9 p99. This London theatre, now the Royal Court, specialised in 'advanced' plays. In 1907 PGW summed up its clientele in a poem. The first verse reads:

> They're the Pioneers of Progress, they're the Devotees of Art,
> They're the men with bulging foreheads, they're a race of souls apart;
> No ordinary drama can rely on their support —
> It is Culture — yes, sir, Culture that they ask for at the Court.

Courtneidge. 22 p17. Robert Courtneidge (1859–1939) produced and directed successful London musical comedies from 1900 to 1930.

'Courtship of Miles Standish'. 40 p59. Poem by Longfellow in which a man asks another to plead his cause with a girl. Despite the pleader's best efforts, the girl falls in love with him, not the man he is pleading for. The kind-hearted Bertie Wooster found himself in similar embarrassing imbroglios.

Covent Garden Balls. 7 p10; 9 p81 & p85 and later. In the days when there were no public dance halls (see Chap. 18), the Covent Garden Balls were lively events in London's night life. Beginning in 1892 and held in the Royal Opera House every three weeks or so, they were Bohemian evenings which anybody who had a guinea (a week's pay for a workman) could attend. Noisy, rowdy fancy-dress affairs, their habitués included young Army officers, girls from the stage, from the oldest profession and, very occasionally, young ladies. These last, however, would always be masked and accompanied by a brother or some other respectable gentlemen since attendance was considered very daring and shocking.

As PGW tells us, the balls finished about 5 A.M. when the crowd would surge round to the Hummums Hotel seeking breakfast. Fights did indeed occur with the Covent Garden market porters, and the rule was that if he beat you, you gave him half a crown. If you beat him, you gave him two half crowns. The balls flourished till 1910, and there is evidence that PGW attended one of them himself around 1905. Years later an elderly Army officer remembered them fondly as: "Fancy dress, pretty girls, then later — a black eye — a cut lip — and the milk train to Aldershot."

Cow creamer. Uncle Tom's cow creamer, like Toby jugs and horse brasses, was one of those useless decorative objects that people in Britain have collected for over 200 years. As far as I can ascertain, the first were made by John Schuppe, a Huguenot silversmith, who came to England and began to make them about 1750. The habit of having tea in the afternoon had only recently begun and since tea and coffee were then expensive, only the wealthy possessed complete tea equipages. I think it was the Duchess of Bedford, a leader of fashion, who decided to make a feature of her tea set. Society followed her lead, elaborate tea equipment became fashionable, and Mr Schuppe's cow creamers became the thing to have. They are completely impractical and unhygienic since the interior is rough, jagged and full of inaccessible corners where milk will collect and go bad.

A few years ago I consulted Bentley's, a famous London shop specialising in antique silver. They told me that cow creamers are still being made, that a modern version could cost £500 upwards but a Schuppe would cost £15,000 or more. They agreed that nobody actually used them for pouring milk; they were just something people liked to collect. As I was leaving the shop, I remembered the other thing Aunt Dahlia said. What was the point of her remark about modern Dutch? The Bentley's man looked puzzled until I remembered she had made the remark back in 1938. He said that, in 1938, you would indeed check the hallmark to make sure it wasn't modern Dutch. Around 1890–1900, Dutch silversmiths had done very well making copies of Schuppe's model and selling them in England as originals. PGW took great care over this sort of technical detail.

Note. The antique shop PGW referred to "in the Brompton Road — it's just past the Oratory" bears an astonishing resemblance to James Hardy & Co, 235 Brompton Road (their letterhead says 'Opposite the Oratory'), who are still flourishing on the site. I do not claim that it is Hardy's but would point out it was the only jeweller and silversmith within a quarter of a mile when PGW wrote about it. I couldn't afford to buy a cow creamer there, so I just bought a small silver pig instead. It seemed appropriate.

Cow, purple. See PURPLE COW.

Coward rage that dares to burn but does not dare to blaze. 53 p143. Fifth verse of 'Peter the Wag' in Gilbert's *Bab Ballads.* MTT Mr & Mrs Alan Follett.

Coward, the poet, stressed advisibility of avoiding its ultry-violet rays. 87 p72. See ULTRY-VIOLET RAYS.

Cox's Bank. 42 p77. This English bank, founded 1758, became Cox & King's in 1922 and is now part of Lloyd's Bank group.

CQD. 18 p238; 24 p221. The universal distress call before SOS replaced it by international agreement in 1906. CQ meant all stations were signalled, the D meant distress. It became known as 'Come Quick — Distress/Danger'.

Cracked from side to side. 97 p96. See CURSE HAS COME UPON ME.

Crackling of thorns under a pot, (His laughter is as the). 28 p107; 44 p139 and later. B. Ecclesiastes 7.6: "As the crackling of thorns under a pot, so is the laughter of a fool."

Cramped your style. 30 p149. George Grossmith Jnr (see Chap. 13) said in his autobiography that the phrase came into use in the 1880s when a man and girl took a hansom cab. Though it was considered a romantic form of transport, you were so tightly squeezed together that there was no room for any hanky-panky. It literally cramped your style.

Crawford, Joan. 52 p58. I am not sure why PGW said Gussie Fink-Nottle resembled this American film star (1906–77). Perhaps it was simply that she 'registered' shock/horror on screen more realistically than her peers?

'Crawshaw and Francis Thompson, a Comparison and a Contrast'. 34 p63. PGW described exactly the sort of scholarly article people like Mr Hammond wrote. Crawshaw was a 17th-century poet; Thompson (1859–1907) wrote 'The Hound of Heaven' before dying of consumption.

Craye, Florence. See Chap. 2.

Cream in her coffee, salt in her stew, You're the. 70 p150. 'You're the Cream In My Coffee', US song by De Sylva, Brown and Henderson 1928.

Creature, wild. Some wild c. caught in a trap who sees the trapper coming through the woods 17 p53 and later. PGW's recollection of the lines in T. 'Geraint and Enid': "a sudden sharp and bitter cry, / As of a wild thing taken in the trap, /

Which sees the trapper coming thro' the wood." PGW used 'some wild creature trapped' often, including the variation at 45 p167.

Crecy, Battle of. B. Wooster's ancestors did dashed well at it 51 p20. In 1346 Edward III's army routed the French with his archers, as Henry V was to do later at Agincourt. Crécy was the battle where the Prince of Wales killed the King of Bohema and adopted his crest of three feathers and motto 'Ich Dien', the badge and motto of Princes of Wales ever since.

Creosote, rich as (as the saying is). 81 p70. The Cockney version of the phrase 'as rich as Croesus'. Croesus, king of Lydia c.550 B.C., was reputedly the richest man in the ancient world.

Cribb. 6 p153. Tom Cribb (1781–1848) was champion prizefighter of his time.

Crichton Mansions, Berkeley Street. See Chap. 25.

Cricket. In an address to the New York Dutch Treat Club in the 1960s, the diplomat Lord Bancroft said: "Cricket is a game the British, not being a spiritual people, had to invent in order to have some concept of eternity."

Crime doesn't pay ... (enough). 72 p23. I am told the phrase 'crime does not pay' was first popularized by the Dick Tracy comic strip (1927) drawn by Chester Gould. I have also read that the 'enough' suffix came into use as a sarcastic comment on corrupt policemen who always wanted a larger bribe.

Crippen, Dr. 36 p166. Probably best remembered now as the first murderer to be caught by radio. Crippen (1861–1910) murdered his wife, then escaped to Canada by ship. A description of him was sent to London by radio from the ship and he was arrested on landing.

Cripps, Sir Stafford. 54 p252 and later. Labour politician (1889–1952), remembered now for his austerity measures as Chancellor of the Exchequer after the Second World War.

Crispian. The mention of C. to a veteran of Agincourt 60 p149. S. *Henry V* 4.3: "And hold their manhoods cheap while any speaks That fought with us upon Saint Crispin's day."

Crispin's day, had fought shoulder to shoulder on. 82 p7. See CRISPIAN.

Criterion. Come over to the C. for a drink 33 p83; 43 p263. The famous Criterion bar on Piccadilly Circus, built in 1874, has been restored to much of its appearance in its Victorian heyday, but is now an expensive restaurant. Until recently there was still a wooden eagle on the wall reflecting its original role as what was claimed to be the first 'American Bar' in London. In contrast to English pubs where the clientele could choose from three or more rooms (bars) to drink in, the Criterion had, and still has, one long bar running the entire length of the room.

Croesus. 70 p47. See CREOSOTE, RICH AS.

Crofton, Salop. 12 p177. See Chap. 35.

Cromer, Lord. 46 p271. British film and play censor 1922–36.

Crosby. Letting it go like a Crosby 57 p198. Although Bing Crosby (1905–77) is probably best known now from the films he made, the 1937 reference by

PGW reflects his pre-eminence in the world of light music before the war. The recording studios loved him because he would listen to the orchestra play the melody once, walk on, sing the song, and walk off. There was never any need for another session. He and Bob Hope were keen golfers, and I have a photograph showing my father with Hope and Crosby when they played at Walton Heath (see Chap. 27). My father said later: "I don't know about his singing but he's got a lovely swing."

Crosse to Blackwell. What attracted C. to B. or Swan to Edgar? 28 p33. Over the years the 'dual' names of some businesses became so well known, it was difficult to think of one without the other. Crosse and Blackwell were England's best-known manufacturers of jam and preserves. Swan and Edgar founded the once-famous shop on Piccadilly Circus. The American equivalent would be Sears & Roebuck or Barnum & Bailey.

Crossroads, dirty work at the. See DIRTY WORK.

Crossword puzzles. 39 p10 and often up to 93 p101. As PGW says, the first crosswords were simple affairs in which a sun god (two letters) was always Ra and a three-letter prophet was Eli. They began in the *New York World* newspaper in 1913, the only paper to print them till 1924. In that year, a collection of them were published by two Harvard graduates and sold over 400,000 copies — and that is how Simon and Schuster got their start. Crossword mania swept America, and a man shot his wife because she refused to help him with one. The first English crossword appeared in November 1924 (*Sunday Express*).

Crowded hour/second. One crowded second of glorious life 3 p272; one crowded hour of glorious life is worth … 15A p32; a few crowded hours of Bailey's dashing imbecility 24 p250. Thomas Mordaunt's (1730–1802) poem 'The Bee': "One crowded hour of glorious life / Is worth an age without a name."

Crown. I don't care if he wears a c., he can't keep kicking my dawg around. 17 p65. See I DON'T CARE IF HE WEARS.

Cruft's Dog Show. 36 p122. Britain's premier dog show. Charles Cruft (1852–1938) was a brilliant dog-food salesman who realised every dog owner believed his dog was the finest in the world and would willingly pay show-entrance fees to prove it.

Crumpet, old. 26 p298 and later. Warm greeting to a friend. Crumpet had a general meaning of the head, similar to 'bean' or 'egg'. I used all three terms — 'old bean', 'old egg' and 'old crumpet' — up to the 1960s. 'Crumpet' for attractive women is a more recent usage. See also EGG and OLD BEAN.

Crushed to earth, it/they will rise again. Moustaches 36 p159; Bingo Little 61 p65; butlers 66 p117; pig men 72 p97; waxed moustaches 94 p47. See William Cullen Bryant's poem 'The Battlefield': "Truth, crushed to earth, shall rise again."

Cry of some strong smoker in his agony. 32 p98. See STRONG SMOKER IN HIS AGONY.

Crystal Palace. 18 p252; 43 p193. Built for the 1851 Great Exhibition in London, this was the largest glass structure in the world. After the exhibition, it was re-erected on Sydenham Hill in south London and became a rough equivalent to New York's Madison Square Gardens. The grounds were used for major sporting events till Wembley was opened in 1923. I remember my parents taking me up to the attic of our house to watch the Palace burn down in 1936.

'Cuddle Up' revue at the Palladium. 31 p195. I have not found a show by this name, but Irving Berlin wrote a song with this title in 1911, as did eighteen other composers later.

Cup of coffee, let's have another. See LET'S HAVE ANOTHER.

Cup runneth over, my. 83 p197; 85 p55; 93 p177. B. Psalms 23.5. "Thou anointest my head with oil; my cup runneth over."

Cup that clears today of past regrets and future fears, the. 72 p97. Fitzgerald's *Omar Khayyam*: "Ah, my Beloved, fill the Cup that clears Today of past Regrets and Future Fears." MTT Kris Fowler.

Cupboard. Top of the cupboard, every woman's favourite hiding place 59 p171 and elsewhere. Bertie quotes from the book he is reading: "Amateurs, Postlethwaite, rank amateurs. They never thought of the top of the cupboard, the thing any experienced crook thinks of at once, because — note carefully what follows — 'because he knows it is every woman's favourite hiding place.'" MTT William Sarjeant for the information that it is pretty clear that Bertie (and PGW) had read E.R. Punshon's *Mystery of Mr. Jessop*, which had come out the year before. Punshon wrote: "Amateurs though — complete amateurs; never thought of the top of the cupboard any experienced crook thinks of at once, because he knows it's every woman's favourite hiding place." PGW frequently had his characters looking for diaries, cow creamers, etc., on tops of cupboards/wardrobes and was probably as pleased as Bertie was to find support for his theory.

Curate, pale young. I was a pale young c. then 39 p68. G&S *The Sorcerer* Act 1: "Ah me, I was a pale young curate then."

Curfew had tolled the knell of parting day … o'er the lea. 67 p120. Gray's 'Elegy in a Country Churchyard'. The opening lines are: "The curfew tolls the knell of parting day, / The lowing herd wind slowly o'er the lea."

Curfew shall not ring tonight. 18 p141 and later. 'Curfew Must Not Ring Tonight', poem (1882) by Rose H. Thorpe.

Current will not turn awry and lose the name of action. 93 p120. See ENTERPRISES.

Curry day at the Savoy/Drones. 17A p42; 85 p55. I believe the custom has nearly died now, but 'curry days', i.e. when a club or restaurant served a special curry lunch, used to be a popular event. Soldiers and civil servants brought the habit back from India in the late 19th century and curry became a popular dish in London clubs. The custom lasted even longer in British Army officers' messes; catering officers would vie to produce the most splendid repasts.

Curse has come upon me. 20 p54 and frequent later. T. 'The Lady of Shalott':

"Out flew the web and floated wide; / The mirror cracked from side to side; / 'The curse has come upon me,' cried / The Lady of Shalott."

Curse of an aching heart. 61 p17. 1913 song by Fink and Piantodosi; republished in 1949 as 'You Made Me What I Am Today' (the best-known line of the song).

Curse of marriage, that we can call these delicate creatures ours. 62 p86; 74 p151. S. *Othello* 3.3.

Curves. On to all de/his curves 13 p43 & p149 and later. Baseball term, i.e. when a batter can see the curve of the ball in the air. It was the Brooklyn pitcher Arthur "Candy" Cummings (1848–1924) who developed the curveball. See also BOSANQUET.

Custer's Last Stand. 50 p22; 71 p219. See Battle of the Little Big Horn, 25 June 1876.

Custom, at the receipt of. 2 p29; 17 p170 and later. B. Matthew 9.9: "He saw a man, named Matthew, sitting at the receipt of custom: and he said unto him, Follow me."

Custom reconciles us to everything. 86 p185; 93 p73. As Jeeves said, it is from Burke's *On the Sublime and Beautiful*, part 4.

Cut. The most unkindest c. of all. See UNKINDEST CUT OF ALL.

Cut direct, the. 8 p110. To cut somebody was to refuse to acknowledge him, to ignore him completely; a tremendous insult. There were four types of cut:

the cut direct — to stare him in the face and pretend not to know him

the cut indirect — to look the other way, pretending not to see him

the cut sublime — to admire the top of some building across the street till he has gone by

the cut infernal — to stoop and tie your shoelace till he has gone by

Cyrano de Bergerac. 52 p271; 60 p97 and later. Bergerac (1619–55), a French author who was also a skilled duellist, was reputed to have fought a thousand times, and did indeed have an unusually long nose. The 1897 play by Rostand made his self-sacrifice — and his nose — famous around the world.

D

(MTT = My thanks to)

D. than the m. Kipling was right. 59 p204. See FEMALE OF THE SPECIES.

Dachshund's nose. Their feet get as cold as a d's n. 88 p17; 88 p222; 90 p16; 93 p102. Not too difficult to trace these references, as well as Poppet, the dachshund in *Jeeves in the Offing*, to Jed, the PGW dachshund in residence at the time of writing.

Daddi. My heart belongs to D. 79 p50. See MY HEART BELONGS TO DADDY.

Daddy knows best. 82 p45. A phrase from one of the many moral Victorian songs on Mother (or Father) knowing best. See also ASK DAD.

Dagonet. 18 p233. Jester at the court of King Arthur. T. *Idylls of the King*. Also the pen name of George R. Sims (1847–1922), a popular novelist, playwright and journalist. MTT Dr Tim Healey.

Daily Dozen. 48 p48 and later. Along with many other young men in the 1890s, PGW was an enthusiast for callisthenics or 'physical jerks'. Unlike most, he kept the habit up to the end of his life and was able to touch his toes when he was 90. He began with the Continental exercises popular in the UK from 1890 to 1914. Around 1918, these were superseded by the legendary 'Daily Dozen' developed by the American trainer Walter Camp (1855–1925), and I assume PGW changed with everybody else. In a letter of 20 January 1971, he said he had done them without missing a day since 1919. I think they worked. When he was nearly 90, he commented in a letter (20 June 1971) that he now weighed only seven pounds more than the 12 stone 6 pounds (174 lbs) he weighed when he left school. See also LARSEN AND SWEDISH EXERCISES.

Daily Express. Reporter from the D.E. 85 p84. This is PGW recalling the occasion when the *Daily Express* of London sent a 'personality' (Nancy Spain) to interview Evelyn Waugh. Waugh had rejected a request for an interview, and when she turned up anyway, he simply refused to open the door. The *Daily Express* were shocked and outraged, unable to believe anybody could reject a newspaper as important as they thought they were. PGW was delighted and leaped into verse on the subject. See 'Lives of the Hunted' in *Over Seventy*.

Damask cheek. 2 p242. See SHE NEVER SAID A WORD.

Dame of the British Empire. 77 p56. See OBEs.

Damned disinheriting countenance, a. 50 p127. Sheridan's *School for Scandal* 4.1.

Damocles. See SWORD OF DAMOCLES.

Damon and Pythias. 28 p33 and often later. About 350 B.C., Damon was condemned to death by Dionysius the Younger but asked to go home and settle his affairs. His friend Pythias volunteered to take his place in prison and be executed if Damon failed to return. Damon did come back and Dionysius was so impressed by this demonstration of friendship that both were freed. See also THINGUMMY.

Damozel, the Blessed. See BLESSED DAMOZEL.

Dan unto Beersheba, from. 1 p14. B. Judges 20.1. The phrase came to denote places far apart since these two cities stood at either end of the Holy Land.

Dance before him, no doubt. 60 p11 and later. B. 2 Samuel 6.14: "And David danced before the Lord with all his might."

Dance of Psyche. 20 p59. See PSYCHE.

Dance of the seven veils. 87 p 213; 91 p150. See SALOME.

Danced with the Prince of Wales. Cora once did so 69 p98. Herbert Farjeon first played his song 'I've danced with a man who's danced with a girl who's danced with the Prince of Wales' at a private party in 1928. A year later it was sung across the UK and USA. 'Danced with the Prince of Wales' became a cliché.

Dances. See SUBSCRIPTION DANCE AT CAMBERWELL; SUBSCRIPTION DANCES AT THE EMPRESS ROOMS.

Dangerous Dan McGrew. 32 p297 and later up to 97 p30. 'The Shooting of Dan McGrew' is Robert W. Service's best-known poem.

Dangers of Diana, The. 29 p207. From the early silent film serials that thrilled audiences in England and America 1914–25. *The Perils of Pauline* and *The Exploits of Elaine* featured Pearl White undergoing trials, tribulations and narrow escapes from death week after week. Other serials were *The Hazards of Helen* and *The Mysteries of Myra*. Each episode finished with the heroine in some mortal danger — about to be swept over a waterfall, be run down by a railway engine or clinging desperately to a crumbling cliff-top — hence the term 'cliffhanger'. They were wildly popular and Pearl White became world famous. She had been a circus bareback rider and did many of her own stunts, though clever camera-work made them seem more dangerous than they really were. One commentator said Hollywood would have done more if they could have got the alliteration right. PGW did and gave us the *The Vicissitudes of Vera* (39 p39).

Dangers she had passed. 29 p266. S. *Othello* 1.3: "She loved me for the dangers I had passed, And I loved her that she did pity them." See also DESDEMONA.

Daniel come to judgement. 86 p208 and elsewhere. S. *Merchant of Venice* 4.1: "A Daniel come to judgment! Yea, a Daniel! O wise young judge, how I do honour thee!"

Daniel in the lions den. 15A p45 and later. B. Daniel 6.16–23. Darius locked Daniel in with a den of lions but found him unharmed in the morning.

Danny Deever. For they're hanging D.D. in the morning 73 p151; 95 p155. KIPLING's poem 'Danny Deever' set to music by Walter Damrosch became a popular song in 1897.

Dante. Frequent. At 48 p161, PGW gives us: "The secretary smirked, as Virgil might have done had Dante essayed a mild pleasantry while he was conducting him through the Inferno." Dante Alighieri (1265–1321) finished his epic poem, the *Divine Comedy,* in 1321. Part I described Virgil conducting Dante downward through the nine levels of Hell.

Dante and Beatrice. 37 p199 and later. Note PGW's description at 41 p12. DANTE saw Beatrice (Beatrice Portinari) when he was aged nine and again when he was eighteen. He loved her desperately but never told her of his passion.

Dante Gabriel Quintin. 81 p104. I am sure there is a private joke in here somewhere, but I have been unable to find it. The Dante Gabriel (Rossetti) and the address lead me to think there is some artistic friend of PGW's involved, but I have no further information. Perhaps it was simply that St. John's Wood was, like Chelsea, an area of London favoured by artists.

Dare not wait upon I would, letting I (Like the poor cat i' the adage). 3 p155 and later. S. *Macbeth* 1.7. The adage referred to was the quandary of the cat who loved fish but did not want to get her paws wet by scooping them out of the water.

Daredevil Bertie. 59 p124. From Daredevil Desmond below or the 1938 song 'Daredevil Basil'.

Daredevil Desmond. 46p 101. A typical name for trapeze/ lion-taming/ high-diving artistes. I have not found a specific origin, but there were dozens like it. Perhaps it was simply PGW's twist on the 'Desperate Desmond' comic strip. See DAUNTLESS DESMOND and DESPERATE DESMOND.

Daredevil Esmeralda, used to dive off roofs into tanks of water. 97 p20. See HIPPODROME.

Darien, silent upon a peak in. 81 p76. See NEW PLANET.

Daring young man on the flying trapeze. 91 p144; 94 p103. The trapeze-artist Leotard was a tremendous hit in London in the 1860s, and the 1868 song about him remained popular for nearly a century. "He flies through the air with the greatest of ease, The daring young man on the flying trapeze." The costume worn by ballet dancers takes its name from him.

Dark and stormy night, It was a. 42 p103. For some reason, the opening words of Bulwer-Lytton's 1830 novel *Paul Clifford* became the standard opening for shaggy dog stories. I haven't heard them for years but they were common in my youth. (Now I think of it, I haven't heard the phrase 'shaggy dog story' for years either.) MTT Murray Hedgcock for reminding me that immortal Snoopy in the *Peanuts* cartoon always began his novels with these words.

Darkest before the dawn. 23 p39. This cliché's most likely origin is Thomas Fuller's *Pisgah Sight*, Bk 2, Chap. 11. "It is always darkest just before the day dawneth."

Darkness. Leaving the world to darkness (and to him) 94 p68. Gray's 'Elegy in a Country Churchyard': "And leaves the world to darkness and to me."

Dartmoor. 35 p193; 49 p21. England's most famous prison, on the moors in the West Country, was originally built for French prisoners in the Napoleonic wars.

Datchet, Lord. 21 p48; 31 p74; 50 p87; 55 p281. I have no idea why PGW named four peers after this small town, two miles east of Windsor. Lord Staines and Lord Runnymede take their names from the same stretch of the River Thames.

Daughter of a hundred earls. 41 p13 and often later. Note the superb twelve-line sentence PGW gave us at p187 (chap 8) of *Full Moon*. T. 'Lady Clara Vere de Vere': "The daughter of a hundred Earls, / You are not one to be desired."

Daughter of the gods, divinely tall and most divinely fair. 24 p20. From T. 'A Dream of Fair Women'.

Dauntless Desmond. 81 p129 & p144. Almost certainly PGW's recollection of two US comic strips: 'Desperate Desmond' and 'Dauntless Durham'. MTT Stu Shiffman. See also Desperate Desmond.

David. D., having his unpleasantness with Goliath, could not have made better target practice 56 p178; dancing before Saul 49 p285; 73 p154. The story of David — his harp playing, dancing and victory over Goliath — is too long to recount here. See B. 1 Samuel and 2 Samuel.

David and Jonathan. 12 p98 and later. Jonathan, the son of Saul the king, and David, the shepherd boy, swore eternal friendship, and Jonathan disobeyed Saul's order to kill David. B. 1 Samuel 18.1–4.

David Copperfield. 8 p20. See Dickens' novel.

Dawg. I don't care if he wears a crown, he can't keep kicking my d. around. 17 p65. See I don't care if he wears.

Dawn of Better Things, The. 24 p8–9. Eugenics was a popular subject from 1900 to 1930. Breeding healthy children for the brave new world was considered a good thing by many well-meaning people till Hitler took it to extremes.

Day by day, in every way. See Every day, in every way.

Day of retribution is at hand,the. 66 p18. B. Jeremiah 46.10.

Day, sufficient unto the (is the evil thereof). See Sufficient unto the day was his motto.

Daylight Saving Act. 32 p126; 52 p113. This Act (putting clocks forward one hour in summertime) was very unpopular when it was passed in 1916. Many thought they had lost an hour out of their lives.

Days of chivalry are dead, of which in stories I have read … (and four more verses) 49 p106. See 'Sir Galahad' song from *Leave It to Jane* (1917), music by Kern, lyrics by PGW.

Days of Peace and Slumberous calm have fled. 8 p40. Keats' *Hyperion*, Bk 2, l.335.

Day's work. His day's work was done 33 p67; 56 p27. 1903 song by T. Connor: 'His Day's Work Was Done'.

de Falaise de la Foudraye, Marquis. 46 p 171. The name is de Falaise de la Coudraye, not Foudraye. Henri de la Falaise, Marquis de la Coudraye (1998–1972), arrived in the USA in 1925 as the third husband of Gloria Swanson. She was the first film star to marry into the aristocracy and brought her husband back to Hollywood, having wired the studio: "Am arriving Monday with the Marquis. Arrange ovation." He went on to marry Constance Bennett in 1931 and Emma Rodriguez Restrepo in 1940.

De Gaulle, General. 88 p166. French soldier and president (1890–1970), noted for his aloof manner.

De Mille, Cecil B. 70 p176. Hollywood pioneer and autocrat (1881–1959).

De Pester, Lester. 68 p86. Gussie Fink-Nottle looks like him. Described as having a parakeet nose, bulging eyes and shrimpish appearance, Lester De Pester appeared in the strip-cartoon 'Betty', (1920–43) created by Charles A. Voight. MTT Stu Shiffman.

Dead. I wish that I was dead. See Mariana of the moated grange.

Dead body with nothing on but pince-nez and a pair of spats. 67 p18. A clear reference to Dorothy L. Sayers' *Whose Body*. "A dead man, dear, with nothing on but a pair of pince-nez." Presumably PGW added the spats as a Wodehouse touch.

Dead End Kids. 69 p149; 72 p194; 85 p102. Dead End Kids/ East Side Kids/ Bowery Boys. Term given to New York urchins of the Depression era who congregated in 'dead ends' (cul-de-sacs) on the East Side. They would swim in the river, steal from the docks and cause trouble.

The original 1935 play was a stark, realistic account of a street gang in New York, and the 1937 film *Dead End* with Humphrey Bogart made them famous. Huntz Hall (1920–99) was a success as Dippy in the film and went on to play in many Dead End Kid films. For copyright reasons, the name was later changed from Dead End Kids to East Side Kids and, later, to Bowery Boys. Hall and Leo Gorcey starred in most of the twenty-five Dead End films, which became comedies, a long way from the original concept. There were some forty-eight Bowery Boys films made that had a tremendous following across small-town America and were given local billing above MGM's biggest hits.

Dead March. 44 p261. See the oratorio *Saul* by Handel.

Dead past. Let the dead past bury its dead. See Let the dead.

Dead Sea fruit. 50 p67. From Thomas Moore's 'The Fire-Worshippers': "Like Dead Sea fruits, that tempt the eye, / But turn to ashes on the lips."

Deadeye, Dick. 67 p118. Character in G&S *Pinafore.*

Deadlier than the male. 59 p117 and elsewhere. See Female of the species.

Deadwood Dick. 9 p207. Between 1875 and 1920, there were hundreds of boys' stories written about this Western hero. Like those of his counterpart, Buffalo Bill, they had some, though minimal, basis of fact. The original, Richard Clarke, a Pony Express rider in his youth, thoroughly enjoyed the fame they brought him and rode in a Deadwood pageant attended by President Coolidge in 1927.

Deaf adder. See Adder.

Deal. Square Deal; New Deal, Fair Deal. A popular slogan of American presidents.

For Teddy Roosevelt's Square Deal (1901), see 40 p43; for F.D. Roosevelt's New Deal (1932), see 53 p32 and later. Lord Emsworth feared McAllister would bring in some sort of sweet pea New Deal at 57 p11. President Truman continued the tradition by pledging a Fair Deal in 1949.

Deal table. 12 p182. Included here since the term is, I am told, not used in America. 'Deal' is the English term for ordinary pine softwood. A deal table is a cheap, ordinary table for use in the kitchen as opposed to the oak or mahogany tables seen in dining-rooms.

Dear Abby. See ABBY.

Dear dead days beyond recall. 3 p234; 18 p50 and later. From the 1884 song 'Love's Old Sweet Song'.

Dear fellow, my. 81 p155 and frequent use at end of 90. A comedian's catchphrase c.1930. However, around 1948 PGW told Guy Bolton in a letter that the phrase had been a favourite of Reggie Fortune, the detective created by H.C. Bailey.

Death knocking. Like D., it knocked at the doors of the highest and lowest alike ... palace of the prefect and the hovel of the fag 3 p210. Horace's *Odes* 1.4: "Death with impartial foot knocks at the doors of poor men's hovels and of kings' palaces."

Death rays. Eyes go through you like a couple of death rays 35 p144. Death rays had featured in comic strips for years, but they came to public attention in England in 1924 when Mr F.T. Wall claimed he had produced a ray that would set fire to anything inflammable. In the 1930s, Mr Grindall-Matthews claimed the same thing. When the Second World War started, many people on the east coast of England felt they were safely guarded by the Grindall-Matthews invention. These were simply early radar stations but were built in such secrecy that many locals were convinced they were death-ray machines.

Death, where is thy sting, O. 14 p155 and often later. B. 1 Corinthians 15.54: "O death, where is thy sting? O grave, where is thy victory?"

Deathless Author. 2 p120. I am convinced this is PGW's compliment to Arthur Conan DOYLE, an author whom he held in high regard and with whom he later became friends. PGW played cricket with Doyle 1904–5 (Actors v Authors matches and at Doyle's cricket weekends). This reference was written, I believe, before their first meeting (probably June/July 1903), when PGW interviewed Doyle for *V.C.* magazine.

Decline and Fall of the Roman Empire, The. 41 p51 and later. See GIBBON.

Deeds must win the prize, 'tis. See 'TIS DEEDS MUST WIN THE PRIZE.

Deep. Not so deep as a well, nor so wide as a church door. See 'TIS NOT SO DEEP AS A WELL.

Deep calling unto deep. 20 p113 and often later; butler to butler 79 p19. B. Psalms 42.7: "Deep calleth unto deep at the noise of thy waterspouts; all thy waves and thy billows are gone over me."

Deeper and warmer than that of ordinary friendship. 51 p56. See SENTIMENTS DEEPER AND WARMER.

Deeper than the depth of waters stilled at even. 38 p69. This line comes immediately after "The blessed damozel leaned out from the gold bar of Heaven" in Dante Gabriel Rossetti's 'The Blessed Damozel'. See also BLESSED DAMOZEL.

Deerfoot, disciples of. 1 p47. Not Fenimore Cooper's *Deerslayer* but a well-known 19th-century runner. An American Indian, Deerfoot (c.1864–97) was famous for his long-distance running, covering remarkable distances in an hour, three hours etc. He made a great impression when he visited the UK around 1890.

Deerstalker hat. 82 p132. The term never appears in the Sherlock Holmes stories, though he is often pictured wearing one in the original illustrations. The explanation is that, in those days, it was called a travelling cap, not a deerstalker. I have one, and it is invaluable whether you are driving across Dartmoor in an open gig or are walking the Cumbrian fells in winter today. The peaks, fore and aft, keep the rain out of your neck and the side flaps can be pulled down over your ears. I do not know when the name was changed, probably when its use came to be restricted to people stalking deer in the Highlands.

Defarge, Mme. 41 p258; 93 p77. PGW had a slight problem with this lady. At 41 p258 she is Madame Lafarge. At 93 p77 she is Madame Whoever-it-was, but in both cases PGW clearly meant the evil Madame Defarge of D. *A Tale of Two Cities*. MTT Tony Ring who tells me PGW used the correct name in the first publication in the *Saturday Evening Post*. It looks as though the book publishers were the ones at fault.

Deipnosophists written by Athenaeus. 9 p18. This work by Athenaeus (d.194 A.D.) comprised fifteen books of anecdotes and history.

Delilah. 65 p154 and often later. B. Judges 16.4 onwards. Her betrayal of Samson should need no explanation.

Dell, Ethel M. 34 p267. Her virile heroes 37 p302; 67 p191–2. Dell (1881–1939) wrote *The Way of an Eagle* in 1912; see Chap. 37 for further detail.

Delmonico's. 21 p125. New York's oldest (1827) restaurant, it was the first to offer customers a choice of dishes from a menu. The original restaurant stood on Beaver Street and was patronised by Charles Dickens and Mark Twain. See also LOBSTER NEWBURG.

Delphic oracle, a little less of the. 60 p235. See ORACLE.

Dementia praecox. 51 p14. I am advised this is commonly called schizophrenia.

Demon lover. 51 p96 and later; for whom women might wail through the woods 67 p123. Coleridge's *Kubla Khan*: "As e'er beneath a waning moon was haunted / By woman wailing for her demon lover!"

Demon Rum. 48 p176. A pejorative term that became popular from the strong temperance movement in the 19th century.

Demosthenes. 3 p240 and later; chewed pebbles 93 p127, p171 & p181. The greatest of Greek orators; he practised speaking with pebbles in his mouth to cure a stammer. He died 322 B.C.

Dempsey. 27 p168 and later; the Dempsey-Carpentier fight 29 p277. Georges

Carpentier (1894–1975), a good-looking French boxer, carried Europe's hopes with him in the 1921 heavyweight championship fight which Jack Dempsey (1895–1983) won easily in the fourth round. See Chap. 4 and also FORGOT TO DUCK.

Derby hat. Threw him out with his baggage and d.h. 89 p102. See Chap. 6.

Descending from a cloud, like some god. 42 p122. See CLOUD, SWOOPING OR DESCENDING FROM.

Desdemona. 29 p266; loved him for the dangers he had passed 39 p177. S. *Othello*. See also DANGERS SHE HAD PASSED.

Desiderium or pothos. 24 p127; 34 p127; 48 p42. The first word is Latin, the second Greek. Roughly, fond memories of one's past.

Desire of a moth for a star. Frequent. See MOTH.

Desist. You pain me. 10 p61; 13 p107. A favourite phrase of English comedian George ROBEY. He greeted applause with a raised hand of mild rebuke and the phrase: "Desist. You pain me." See also TEMPER YOUR HILARITY.

Desperate. Things were desperate now and needed remedies to match 6 p187. Latin proverb: Desperate problems/diseases need desperate remedies.

Desperate Desmond. 17 p162. This American cartoon character was created in 1910 by Harry Hershfield (1885–1974).

Despondency and alarm, causing me. 51 p227. Why on earth PGW reversed the words is beyond me. It's like saying Clark & Lewis or Mason & Fortnum's. See ALARM AND DESPONDENCY.

Detail. Omitting no d. however slight. See OMITTING NO DETAIL.

Detective stories. 46 p68–70; 78 p125. PGW's classification of English detective stories in *Over Seventy*, (the Dry, the Dull, the Effervescent) neatly covered three best-selling popular detectives of the time: Edgar Wallace's Mr J.G. Reeder, R. Austin Freeman's Dr Thorndyke, and H.C. Bailey's Reggie Fortune. The sometimes tedious explanations as to how the criminal could have got from A to B (see 78 p125) will be recognised by all right-minded people as Lord Peter Wimsey's clarification of the problem in Dorothy Sayers' *Five Red Herrings*. See also MURDER AT BILBURY.

PGW enjoyed detective stories and thrillers all his life. He dedicated books to authors he particularly admired, quoted from them often, especially Conan DOYLE, and learned from their disciplined construction. He later became a fan of Rex Stout's Nero WOLFE stories.

Deus ex machina. See GOD FROM THE MACHINE.

Devastated area. 50 p258 and later. During the First World War, certain areas of France and Belgium were so destroyed, with every tree and building flattened in a sea of mud, that they were marked on maps simply as 'Devastated area'.

Devil's Island. 48 p112 and frequent up to 84 p35. A notorious French prison colony off French Guiana.

Devours her young (Aunt Agatha). 76 p7. She followed the example of Saturn, the god who devoured his children so they would not supplant him. MTT Tim

Murphy.

Dewy eve. From early morn … to dewy eve. 27 p30. Milton's *Paradise Lost.*

Dexter Argo, the. 8 p57. The *Argo* was the ship which, in Greek legend, carried Jason and the Argonauts in their search for the Golden Fleece. Dexter's was the name of the boarding house at Wrykyn to which the boys belonged.

Diabolo. 11 p12; 12 p175 & p275. I shall not attempt to describe this game in which two sticks joined by a piece of string are used to throw a double inverted cone into the air and catch it again. It was a craze in England in 1906 and was revived in 1997.

Diamond, Diamond, you/thou little know/knowest what you/ thou have/hast done. 59 p205; stringing along with the late Diamond, she little knew what she had done 59 p262; 96 p143. This was the remark of Isaac Newton to his dog who had overturned a candle, burning the notes of many years' work. "O Diamond! Diamond! Thou little knowest the mischief done."

Diamond Horseshoe. 71 p54. This name, now to be seen on bars and gambling joints around the world, has its origin in the horseshoe-shaped Dress Circle of the old Metropolitan Opera House in New York (demolished 1967). At an opening night in the 1890s, a journalist was so struck by the amount of jewellery on display in the front row, he described it as 'The Diamond Horseshoe'. The phrase took off.

Diamond, the late Legs. 49 p73. This notorious American gang leader was shot on 18 December 1931.

Dick, Where Art Thou? 80 p30. An unusual newspaper headline till one remembers the popular Victorian song 'Alice, Where Art Thou?'

Dickey. A clean dickey 81 p74. Until soft-fronted evening shirts came into use, the normal model had a stiff, and I mean stiff, heavily starched front. Laundering and starching these was expensive, and people who had to wear evening dress constantly (waiters) began to wear a 'dickey'. This was a single, oval-shaped, detachable stiff front which could be worn over a normal shirt, held in position at the neck and waist, and was much cheaper and easier to clean. Bertie Wooster would never have worn one, but the waiters and attendants in the clubs and restaurants he used would all have done so. The term is not extinct; a black bow tie is still often called a 'dickey bow'.

Dickson, Dorothy. 74 p146. See Chap. 24.

Dictating their stuff to a stenographer. Authors who turn out five thousand words a day by d. their s. to a s. 33 p129. I am sure PGW was thinking of Edgar Wallace (1875–1932) whose rate of output was legendary.

Did he sleep? Did he dream? Or were visions about? 1 p53. Bret Harte's *Further Language from Truthful James* begins with the lines: "Do I sleep? Do I dream? / Do I wonder and doubt? / Are things as they seem? / Or is visions about?"

Didn't know much about architecture, but knew what he liked. 68 p184. At 91 p41 Lady Constance doesn't know much about Art but liked more clothes on the subject. The cliché "I don't know much about music/art/poetry/whatever, but I know what I like" is still common. Max Beerbohm made it famous in *Zuleika Dobson*, his splendid 1911 satire on Oxford, and Gelet Burgess used it in *Are You a Bromide?*

Didn't mind death but couldn't stand pinching, like the lady in the Ingoldsby Legends. See INGOLDSBY LEGENDS.

Dido. Claude and Eustace playing dido. 31 opposite the title page. This has no connection with Virgil's 'Aeneas and Dido'. It was a term for playing the fool.

Dido, Death of. 2 p56 & p150. In Virgil's *Aeneid*, Aeneas and his Trojans were shipwrecked at Carthage, and Dido, the queen, fell in love with Aeneas. He returned her affection but was told by the gods he must leave and fulfil his destiny by founding a nation (Rome) in Italy. He reluctantly sailed from Carthage and looked back to see the huge funeral pyre of Dido, who had killed herself in her grief at his going.

Die in the last ditch. See DITCH.

Die is cast, the. 26 p305; 85 p76 and elsewhere. When a Roman general returned to Italy after his tour of duty, he had to leave his army at the Rubicon river in Northern Italy. To bring them across into Roman territory was a threat to the government. When Julius Caesar returned from Gaul with his legions, he 'crossed the Rubicon', i.e. brought his soldiers over, thereby signifying his intention to take control in Rome. He is credited with the remark: "Alea jacta est" (the die is cast), i.e. an irrevocable step has been taken.

Die Zeitbestimmung Vermittelst Des Tragbaren Durchgangsinstruments Im Verticale Des Polarsterns. 70 p187. Astronomical work by Wilhelm Dollen, published 1863.

Died for his country. CAPTAIN KETTLE came at last reluctantly, died for his country in record time and flashed back again to the saucer 3 p215. Dying for your country is a trick many dogs and cats are taught by their proud owners. On the command, the animal will either collapse on the ground or, for better dramatic effect, collapse on his back with his paws waving pathetically in the air. I include the reference since I am told the phrase is not used in America; the command there is a simple "Play dead".

Dig you. I don't dig you 85 p187. I don't know why PGW wrote this. He always liked using contemporary vernacular, but this slang term of the 1940s/50s does not sound right coming from Bertie. Its use by Lord Emsworth's grandson George in the previous book, *Service with a Smile*, was perfectly appropriate.

Dignity that became him/her well. See BECAME HIM/HER WELL.

Digs/digging. Where are you are digging/ where are your digs? 14 p59 and later. 'Digs' was/is a common term in UK for lodgings where your landlady would 'do for you', i.e. provide breakfast and dinner. It is alleged to stem from the 'diggings' of the gold and diamond rushes of America and South Africa and the subsequent sudden demand for accommodation.

Diligent Apprentice ... and the Idle Apprentice. 54 p25. Around 1750, the painter Hogarth published a series of engravings in aid of the Foundling Hospital of which he was a Governor. Entitled 'Idleness' and 'Industriousness', the series contrasted the lives of two orphans. The Idle Apprentice who drank, smoked and gambled was eventually hanged, while the complementary picture of the Industrious Apprentice showed him riding in glory as Lord Mayor of London.

Ding-basted as a stig tossed full of doodle-gammon. 21 p77. My comments on this line from *Piccadilly Jim* are tenuous at best, and I await clarification.

Firstly, the word 'stig' does not appear in the *Oxford English Dictionary*. (The story 'Stig of the Dump' does not count.) It is, however, common in Scandinavia and means 'sty', in the sense of pigsty. If we accept this origin, then where would PGW have read it or heard it? I believe the answer must be New York rather than London.

Secondly, although, in his later years, PGW avoided writing dialect or attempting to write in a local accent, he did it very well in his early stories. Bat Jarvis and Spike Mullins may sound like caricatures today, but Wodehouse was one of the few Englishman who could write every-day American speech accurately. He took a lot of trouble over this and a typical example from his notebook of September 1905 records his transcription of the speech of a little Cockney girl:

> Overheard near Clapham on Sunday afternoon.
> 1st small girl (hurrying): It's gorn three.
> 2nd ditto: 'Ow do you knaow?
> 1st girl: 'Cos the pubs are shut.

Two lines further down, he has the note: "G'wan artvit' = Go on out of it."

Since 'stig' means a pig-sty, and gammon — in Britain anyway — is a cut of pork, continuing the pig connection, I was pleased to find Webster's dictionary confirmed my view that the word 'doodley-squat' means 'excrement'. I therefore suggest that, in the same way PGW misheard the word 'rannygazoo', he heard the colourful expression 'doodle-gammon' in a street or restaurant in New York from a first- or second- generation Scandinavian American. (See also RANNYGAZOO.)

Jimmy Crocker was expressing, in a complicated way, that he was deep in a pile of muck in a pigsty. Today we would say: "He was up to his neck in it."

Ding Dong, Ding Dong. See YEOMAN'S WEDDING SONG.

Dinner from any host would smell as sweet. 13 p17. S. *Romeo & Juliet* 2.2: "What's in a name? that which we call a rose By any other name would smell as sweet."

Dinner of herbs. See BETTER A DINNER OF 'ERBS.

Diogenes Laertius. 9 p15. The quotation mentioned is from Diogenes Laertius' book on Theophrastus, who died about 278 B.C. Diogenes Laertius fl. 200 A.D. (do not confuse with the Diogenes who lived in a tub).

Dior. 77 p 63. Christian Dior, well-known French dressmaker (1905–57).

Dirty work at the crossroads. 18 p238 and later, a term covering general skullduggery. It has been claimed PGW was the first to use the term, but it appears in the melodrama *The Girl Who Took the Wrong Turning* by Walter Melville (1906). The Melville brothers were famous for re-using old scripts on which they did not have to pay copyright. This was another of those phrases from Victorian melodrama that stayed in the public consciousness for a century. See TODD, SIR JASPER and TRANSPONTINE MELODRAMA.

Discobolus. 7 p42. The Discus Thrower is a famous statue by Myron, Greek sculptor 5th century B.C. Copies of it were and are to be seen in art classrooms across the world.

Discretion is the better part of valour. PGW used this popular misquotation often. It is from S. *1 Henry* IV. 5.4: "The better part of valour is discretion."

Dishpot. An overbearing dishpot; that's what you are 67 p141; 93 p23 & p124. At the end of the 19th century, the Shah of Persia made two State visits to London. The newspapers were full of stories of the power he wielded as supreme despot, and 'dishpot' was the Cockney version of the term. For the Foreign Office's problems during his visits, see SHAH OF PERSIA.

Disobedience, civil. See CIVIL DISOBEDIENCE.

Disposition. A happy d. and a wild desire to succeed 36 p228. I have been unable to trace the song to which PGW refers.

Dissipated saw. Looking far less like a hatchet than a dissipated saw 84 p108. See KNIFE, BLUNT.

Distance lends enchantment to the view. 13 p157. From the poem 'Pleasures of Hope' by Thomas Campbell (1777–1844).

Distinction that made all the difference. 32 p268. From Fielding's *Tom Jones* Bk 6, Chap. 13.

Distinguish between the unusual and the impossible. 12 p185 & p264 and later. Used often in the Sherlock Holmes stories. See *The Sign of Four* (chap. 6), 'The Blanched Soldier' and 'The Beryl Coronet'.

Distressed Daughters of the Clergy. 52 p119. See PAGEANT IN AID OF DISTRESSED DAUGHTERS OF THE CLERGY.

District Messenger. 32 p53; 67 p24; 83 p17. Before the days of motorcycle couriers, London and other cities had dozens of District Messenger offices where uniformed boys were available to run errands, deliver urgent documents, collect things from a shop etc. The 1903 hit musical *The Messenger Boy* was a dramatic version of the sort of tasks a boy could be given. See also CAPTAIN POTT.

District visiting stuff. 53 p148. Before Britain became a welfare state in 1945, District Visitors were social workers who visited poor households who had applied for medical help or financial assistance. Their report on the merits of the case depended to a large extent on the cleanliness and respectability of the household. Their visits therefore came to be regarded as a form of inspection.

Ditch. Die in the last d. 18 p84. Attributed to William III ("I will die in the last ditch"). See 38 p32 for Sigsbee H. Waddington's struggle to avoid dressing for dinner with a bunch of Eastern stiff-shirts. "At six fifty-seven he was fighting in the last ditch."

Dividend. 52 p34. Bertie broods over a telegram with the help of "two dry martinis and a dividend". The 'dividend' is the small amount left in the bottom of the cocktail shaker. No matter how accurately cocktails are measured, the melting of the crushed ice or ice cubes involved will result in a small residue. Though this will not have the authority of the first drink poured, it is a welcome dividend/bonus.

Dividing the swift mind, this way and that. Often in PGW. T 'The Passing of Arthur' (Sir Bedivere's reluctance to throw Excalibur into the lake): "He gazed so long / That both his eyes were dazzled as he stood, / This way and that dividing the swift mind."

Divinity. By adroit use of the d. which hedges a detective 1 p265. S. *Hamlet* 4.4: "There's such divinity doth hedge a king, / That treason can but peep to what it would."

Divinity that shapes our ends, rough hew them how we may. 7 p171 and later. S. *Hamlet* 5.2.

Dix, Dorothy. 63 p15; 70 p63 and later. Pen name of Elizabeth Gilmer (1870–1951), whose advice to the lovelorn and worried was syndicated across the USA from 1917 to 1939. On three days a week, she dished out a homely sermon. On the other three days, she answered readers' letters. In 1939 she published *How to Win and Hold a Husband.*

Do It Now. 12 p305; 29 p182 and often later. This slogan appears to have begun in the USA around 1860. Both Lord Northcliffe and William Randolph Hearst made sure their employees got the message by putting it in every office. See Chap. 7.

Do you know? Frequent. The irritating "do you know" and its alternative "don't you know" at the end of every sentence became fashionable around 1885. A nervous young clergyman in the East End of London used them constantly from the pulpit and somebody told the actor-manager Beerbohm Tree, who introduced the phrase into his hit play *The Private Secretary* (1884). There was a 'Do You Know' polka in 1887 and at least two comic songs with the title. See 'A Letter of Introduction' where Bertie says: "Oh, I don't know, you know, don't you know." See also What?

Doctor Livingstone, I presume. 54 p102 and later. This quotation remained in common use in the UK until the 1970s. David Livingstone (1817–73), a Scottish doctor and missionary, spent years exploring Africa and was thought to be lost in 1871. As a publicity stunt, H.M. Stanley was sent out by the *New York Herald* to find him. Having tracked him across hundreds of miles of jungle, Stanley walked up to him in a small clearing and uttered the words that became famous around the world.

Dodger, Artful. 45 p224. Leading member of Fagin's gang in D. *Oliver Twist.*

Dog with a collecting box on its back … in aid of the Railwaymen's Orphanage. 54 p23. I have a very faint memory of these pre-1939 and I recall one, after its death, was stuffed and stood in a glass case on Wimbledon Station for many years. A porter who had known the dog in life told me it had raised thousands, especially after it learned to target adults with children whom it would approach before sitting up and begging in a manner designed to soften the hardest of hearts.

Dog-races, what happened that day at the? See 73 p181 for a possible explanation. Many country people feared the introduction of greyhound racing in the 1920s; they were sure it would kill the sport of coursing in which live hares are used. Incidents of live hares or rabbits on greyhound tracks are not unknown. The question is — how did they get there? Did Lord Ickenham introduce some similar distraction to see what the effect would be? Others have certainly done so. On 2 March 1991, the Press reported:

> *Teenage Teddy Bear Thrower Wrecked Greyhound Derby*
> Six greyhound puppies streaking towards the finishing line at a racing track stopped chasing the electric hare and dived on a teddy bear thrown by a teenage spectator, a court was told yesterday.

PC Philip Gilroy described how 18-year-old Colin Eastick had been arrested for his own protection: "Had we not escorted him from the premises, his physical wellbeing and possibly his life may have been endangered… . If the police had not been on hand, we could well have had a riot." Eastick was fined £100 and £82 costs after being found guilty of causing harassment, alarm or distress. All bets were cancelled and stakes refunded after the race was declared void. "The magistrates also ordered the teddy bear should be confiscated."

Dogs of war are now loose, the. 12 p194. S. *Julius Caesar* 3.1: "Cry,'Havoc!' and let slip the dogs of war."

Dog-stealing. 43 p133; 88 p84. Jeeves' knowledge of aniseed being extensively used in the dog-stealing industry ('Jeeves and the Dog McIntosh') may seem anachronistic, but dog-stealing was common in London till well into the 1920s. (I am told this crime has again become popular in the UK.) The changes in fashionable breeds mentioned in 'The Inferiority Complex of Old Sippy' were reflected in the prices dog-owners were prepared to pay. In 1919 Alsatians were the dogs everybody wanted; they became so expensive that, in 1920, the *Times* pointed out reprovingly that it cost as much to buy a pedigree Alsatian puppy as it did to buy a house.

Doing business at the old stand. 34 p197. See STAND.

Doing things that he ought not to have done. See WE HAVE DONE.

Dolce far niente. 3 p6. Italian proverb; it is pleasant to do nothing. See also Pliny the Younger: "That indolent but agreeable condition of doing nothing."

Dolly Varden. 28 p85. See D. *Barnaby Rudge*. The straw bonnet with curled-up sides still worn today is named after her — 'as worn' by Jennifer Ehle in the TV version of *Pride and Prejudice*.

Dolores. 'Oh, My Dolores, Queen of the Eastern Sea'. 67 p185. 1941 song by

Louis Alter.

Dome of many coloured glass, Stains the white radiance of Eternity. 57 p157. The golfing giants of the early 20th century, James Braid and J.H. Taylor, were clearly familiar with Stanza 52 of SHELLEY's 'Adonais': "Life, like a dome of many-coloured glass, Stains the white radiance of Eternity."

Don Juan. 45 p135 and frequently later. The Don Juan legend was common all over Europe from the 17th century. BYRON's poem is just one of many accounts of his amorous adventures.

Done. If 'twere done, 'twere better 'twere done quickly. See IF 'TWERE DONE.

Done the state some service, You have. 15 p160. S. *Othello* 5.2: "I have done the state some service."

Donnybrook. There's going to be a sort of D. before it's done with 4 p77. Donnybrook, outside Dublin, was famous for its annual fair that lasted fifteen days. It was so notorious for the riots and fights that took place that 'a Donnybrook' became a common term for a free-for-all fight.

Don't fire until you see the whites of their eyes. 38 p241 and later. Often attributed to Israel Putnam at the Battle of Bunker Hill in 1775, it is now believed that it was William Prescott who issued the order. Whichever it was, he was following the example of Frederick the Great, who so instructed his soldiers in 1757.

'Don't go down the coal-mine, Daddy'. 43 p51. This song was written by an itinerant songsheet seller after the pit disaster at Whitehaven, Cumbria, in 1910. Lawrence Wright bought the copyright for £5 and sold a million copies in three weeks. He set up an office in Denmark Street and made it the centre of London music publishing, similar to New York's Tin Pan Alley.

Don't slam the lid. 73 p189. Attributed to W.C. Fields when asking for an aspirin to ease his hangover. See 74 p233.

Don't take any wooden nickels. See WOODEN NICKELS.

Don't you know? See DO YOU KNOW?

Doodle-gammon. See DING-BASTED AS A STIG.

Doolin of Mayence, his sword Merveilleuse. 57 p82. This mediaeval hero of Saxony was a contemporary of Roland and Oliver. See also FLAMBERGE and JOYEUSE.

Doom had come upon me, the. 52 p265. T. 'Lady of Shalott'. See CURSE HAS COME UPON ME.

Doom, impending. See IMPENDING DOOM.

Dostoevsky. 26 p120 and later. The Russian author Fyodor Dostoevsky (1821–81) wrote of crime, guilt and redemption.

Dotheboys Hall. 52p44; 82 p123. The appalling scholastic establishment in D. *Nicholas Nickleby*.

Doughnut Family, the. 21 p119. A Wodehouse creation. In the short story 'Concealed Art' (*Strand* 1915), Reggie Pepper has a pal whose wife thinks he is a great artist, and he is frightened to admit to her that he is the creator of the Doughnut family comic strip. All ends well. See also Percy Gorringe's dilemma in *Jeeves and the Feudal Spirit*, 37 years later.

Dove in Genesis who found no rest. 21 p2. B. Genesis 8.9: "But the dove found no rest for the sole of her foot, and she returned unto him in the ark ..."

Dovey, Alice. 74 p16 and p197. This lady played the second lead in the musical hit *The Pink Lady* (New York 1911, London 1912) which was so successful that pink became the fashionable colour of the year. PGW once entertained towards her feelings deeper and warmer than those of ordinary friendship. See Chap. 38.

Down among the wines and spirits. 57 p207; 61 p124 and elsewhere. I originally thought this simply likened someone's low spirits to being down in the cellar, but it comes from music hall (variety) stage bills in the UK. At the bottom of each poster were advertisements for the wines and spirits available at the bar. The bills showed the acts in order of importance, one below the other, and if you were unknown or unimportant, you were put 'down among the wines and spirits'. By transference, the term came to mean you were gloomy and 'down' as well.

Down in the forest, something stirred. 28 p23; 64 p171 and elsewhere. The first line of Harold Simpson's poem 'Down in the Forest' (1906), which became a popular romantic song. PGW made good use of the phrase, men with beards eating/about to speak etc. In *Ring for Jeeves* p178, there is the splendid: "Down in the forest of pimples on the butler's face, something stirred. It was a look of guilt."

Down South. 2 p47. A cakewalk by Myddleton (1901); listed in Army & Navy 1907 catalogue.

Doyle, Sir Arthur Conan. PGW had a tremendous admiration for Doyle (1859–1930) and quoted him from his first book, *The Pothunters*, to his ninety-sixth, *Aunts Aren't Gentlemen*. They played cricket together and got on well enough for Doyle to invite Wodehouse down to play in his cricket weeks at Hindhead in 1905 and 1906 (see Chap. 10). PGW's notebooks record a dozen or more of Doyle's remarks on those occasions, including what Doyle reckoned was the lowest point in his literary career. A publisher gave him a picture — two girls in a boat, as I recall — and told him to write a story to fit it.

Wodehouse and Doyle were members of the same club, the Constitutional (see Chap. 21) and lunched together as late as April 1925, when PGW reported that Doyle spoke as impressively as he wrote. Doyle, a keen cricketer, once played against the legendary W.G. Grace and bowled him. He was so delighted at dismissing the most famous cricketer in the world, he wrote:

Out — out beyond question or wrangle!
Homeward he lurched to his lunch!
His bat was tucked up in an angle,
His great shoulders curved to a hunch.

Doyle's house, Undershaw in Hindhead, Surrey, became a hotel with Doyle memorabilia on the walls and the heraldic stained glass windows he designed. In 2012, a developer wanted to turn it into flats but enthusiasts managed to overturn the proposal. See also Robinson, Fletcher.

Dracula, Count. 88 p58. This story of werewolves and vampires by Bram Stoker (Henry Irving's business manager) was a sensation when it came out in 1897.

Drags its slow length along like a languid snake. 12 p267. See Snake, languid.

Drake, Sir Francis. 26 p13 and later. English sailor and adventurer (1540–96) who plundered Spanish treasure fleets, sailed round the world and helped destroy the Armada in 1588. See also Bowls.

'Drake's Drum'. Peasemarch sang it often 80 p75 & p189. A stirring song, words by Newbolt (1897), music by Hedgecock and Stanford.

Draw water and to hew wood, you have got to. 20 p42. B. Joshua 9.21: "Let them be hewers of wood and drawers of water unto all the congregation."

Dream at daylight. Slip away from him like a d. at d. 44 p136. From Isaac Watts' hymn 'O God, our help in ages past'. "They fly forgotten, as a dream / Dies at the opening day."

Dream of joy. Oh Harold, my d. of j. 59 p86. Coleridge's *The Rime of the Ancient Mariner*, part 6, has: "Oh! Dream of joy! is this indeed / The lighthouse top I see?"

Dreams of avarice. See Wealth beyond the dreams of avarice.

Dreever Castle ghost story. 13 p69. This is almost certainly the Glamis Castle Horror story. The legend is that a deformed monster was the first-born child of an 18th-century Earl of Strathmore. Because of its hideous appearance, it was hidden in a secret room in the castle and lived there for seventy or eighty years. PGW knew some of the Bowes-Lyons family but, as he said, the legend was well known. I offer no comment on its veracity, though I have read several accounts of it from remarkably authoritative sources.

Dreiser, Theodore. 86 p149. Dreiser (1871–1945), American writer best known for his intellectual novels, unbent to help his brother Paul write the popular song 'On the Banks of the Wabash' in 1899.

Dressy men you meet up West, a specimen of the (as a songwriter earlier in the century had described). 92 p19. This could be any one of hundreds of music hall songs, but I suggest a good candidate is 'Burlington Bertie from Bow'. Written in 1915, it was one of the many Cockney music hall songs mocking the upper classes. The singer describes his poverty but enjoys behaving 'like a toff'. "I walk down the Strand with my gloves on my hand, Then I walk back again with them off." See Chap. 13 for the popularity of 'Bertie' songs.

Drew, John. Wears a Longacre hat 23 p42. This handsome US actor (1853–1927), the grandfather of John and the other Barrymores, had a house in East Hampton from 1902 to his death in 1927. MTT David McDonough.

Dried seaweed. See Seaweed, dried.

Drinkwater, John. 32 p108. Actor, playwright and poet (1882–1937) whose plays included *Abraham Lincoln* (1918).

Droitgate. 'Romance at Droitgate Spa'. Droitgate is PGW's combination of two famous English spa towns, Droitwich and Harrogate. At Droitwich you float in the heavily-salinated brine baths; at Harrogate you drink the waters. PGW and Ethel visited both of them in the 1920s and, as the *Daily Mail* of 26 March 1926 reported, PGW used to work in the baths with his manuscript on a tray in front of him. The baths staff tell me this was quite normal; tea-trays were often served to people as they spent their specified hour or so in the water.

The main source of 'Droitgate Spa', though, is HARROGATE, which had the Pump Room and Rotunda where a band belted out operatic overtures.

Droitwich (and its brine baths). 17 p12 and later. See DROITGATE and Chap. 26.

Drones. Wodehouse first used the term in *Mike* and bestowed it on his immortal young men's club later (see Chap. 21). The origin of the term lies in a speech made by Joseph Chamberlain in the 1880s. Chamberlain was a renowned orator, equalled at the time only by Gladstone and Asquith. Attacking the House of Lords, he declared them to be "drones of the hive". The phrase stuck in the public (and Wodehouse's) consciousness along with Chamberlain's 'Think Imperially'. See THINKING IMPERIALLY.

Drop the pilot now. 72 p119. 'Dropping the pilot' was the caption of the legendary cartoon in *Punch* of 29 March 1890. Tenniel depicted the Kaiser's dismissal of Bismarck (who had unified Germany) and shows Bismarck walking down the pilot's gangplank with the Kaiser watching from above. The theme has been repeated by British cartoonists ever since, especially when prime ministers retire. Lloyd George, Baldwin and Churchill are three examples I remember.

Dropping like the gentle dew upon the place beneath, then swishing down in a steady flood. 29 p166; ex-secretaries upon the lobelias beneath 42 p183; and elsewhere. S. *Merchant of Venice* 4.1: "The quality of mercy is not strain'd, / It droppeth as the gentle rain from heaven / Upon the place beneath …"

Drowsy numbness pained his sense. 53 p234 and elsewhere. See HEAD ACHED.

Drunkenness. Upper-class synonyms included: scrooched, fried, boiled, squiffy, paralytic, whiffled, blotto, under the influence, pie-eyed, soused, submerged, high as a kite, woozled, ossified, plastered, stewed, stinko, stoned, two sheets in the wind, pixillated (ex USA 1930), over the Plimsoll line.

All classes used the term 'tight'.

Lower-class terms were: tiddley, canned, got a little bit on, came over so bad, a bit tuppenny, a little bit all-overish, had a skinful, tanked, one over the eight. The last term stems from the advice given to the recruits who flocked to join the army in 1914. Eight pints of beer was 'acceptable', but nine was considered excessive.

At the immortal prize-giving at Market Snodsbury, Bertie Wooster muses: "It just shows, what any member of Parliament will tell you, that if you want real oratory, the preliminary noggin is essential. Unless pie-eyed, you cannot hope to grip." Wodehouse dedicated *Meet Mr Mulliner* to the Earl of Oxford and Asquith who, when he was Prime Minister, "was unanimously judged able to make a better speech drunk than anyone else sober". See ASQUITH, MR.

Dry the starting tear, Nay. 3 p167. See NAY, DRY THE STARTING TEAR.

Du Barry. That modern Du Barry, wrecker of homes 49 p61. Madame du Barry (1741–93) was the mistress of Louis XV.

Du Maurier's Punch cartoons. 41 p10. George Du Maurier's (1834–96) cartoons and illustrations enlivened *Punch* from 1864 to 1896. His girls were depicted as haughty goddesses six feet tall, similar to the Gibson Girl. His novel *Trilby* (1894) was dramatised with great success. Do not confuse with his son Gerald, famous actor-manager (1873–1934), or with Gerald's daughter Daphne Du Maurier, the writer (1907–89). See also GIBSON GIRL and TRILBY.

Duff & Trotter. 62 p11 & p20; 89 p10; 97 p38. Despite its being described as being on an island site in Regent Street, I and many others feel this prestigious establishment can only be Fortnum & MASON in Piccadilly. See Chap. 31.

Dug-out. The old dug-out 69 p12. This derogatory term was used often in the Second World War to describe elderly officers who had served in World War One.

Duke of Plaza Toro, the. 2 p87. G&S *The Gondoliers* Act 1. "He led his regiment from behind. He found it less exciting."

Dulac, Edmond. 46 p267. In 1930, RMS *Empress of Britain* was launched to travel between UK and Canada. Built to rival the liners on the UK–New York run, a tremendous effort was made to make it special, which included calling in famous artists to design and decorate the interior. Sir John Lavery was one, and Dulac decorated the Cathay Lounge. From what I read, it was the most luxurious liner in the world with an astonishing 38 (cubic) shipping tons of space per passeneger. See also GREIFFENHAGEN.

Dumb Brothers League of Mercy, Our. 41 p147. See DUMB CHUMS LEAGUE.

Dumb Chums League, Our. 49 p189. With the Dumb Brothers League of Mercy, this is clearly PGW's version of Our Dumb Friends League, the charity who set up the Blue Cross organisation for treating sick animals.

Dun. Under every hat a dun 7 p212. PGW twist on the line "Under every hat a don" from Charles Stuart CALVERLEY's poem 'Hic Vir, Hic Est'. A 'dun' is a UK term for a debt collector. Calverley wrote the lines about his first day at Cambridge when he assumed every man he saw was a senior member (don) of the university.

Duncan, George. 28 p111 & p201 and later. Winner of the 1920 Open, Duncan (1883–1964) was noted for his fast play. He took his club, addressed the ball once and hit it without delay, waggles or practice swings.

Dunsinane. 32 p83; 62 p103. S. *Macbeth* Act 5, Scenes 4–6. Malcolm's army disguised themselves with branches from the forest as they advanced on Dunsinane.

Dunstable, Duke of. 60 p8 and later. Another name PGW took from G&S (*Patience*). See Chap. 41.

Durance vile, in. 51 p82; 76 p53. Burns' poem 'Fragment — Epistle from Esopus to Maria' (1799) in *Posthumous Pieces*: "In durance vile here must I wake and weep." The poem purports to have been written from prison and 'in durance vile' soon came to be a common term for being in the jug.

Durand, Alan. Dedicatee of *Mike.* See Chap. 10.

Durante, Jimmy (Schnozzola). 52 p271; 54 p226. Gravel-voiced American comedian (1893–1980) with a very prominent nose.

Durbar, the (Delhi). 23 p44; 67 p14. The ceremony with which India acknowledged George V as Emperor of India at Delhi in 1911 was the most elaborate coronation the world has seen. It lasted four days and a million people took part, from 200 or so princes, rajahs and rulers, each with their own retinues and bodyguards, down to the soldiers and attendants who swept the four-square-mile arena each night.

Dust beneath his chariot/taxi wheels, less than the. 37 p121 and later. From Laurence Hope's (real name Adela Hopkinson [1865–1904]) 'Indian Love Lyrics', which were sung in every Edwardian drawing room. "Less than the dust beneath thy chariot wheel …"

Dusty answer. 84 p68. As Lavender Briggs says, it is from George Meredith's *Modern Love*.

Duty. Done his duty as expected to by England 7 p70. See ENGLAND EXPECTS THAT EVERY MAN WILL DO HIS DUTY.

Duty of man, whole (to be a sportsman). 1 p15. B. Ecclesiastes 12.13: "Fear God, and keep his commandments; for this is the whole duty of man."

Duty, stern daughter of the voice of God. 67 p137 and elsewhere. Wordsworth's 'Ode to Duty': "Stern daughter of the voice of God! O Duty! if that name thou love …"

Dwelt in marble halls with vassals and serfs at my side, I. 62 p74; 77 p18. Song from *The Bohemian Girl* (1843) by Alfred Bunn: "I dreamt that I dwelt in marble halls / With vassals and serfs at my side."

Dwornitzchek, Princess Heloise von und zu. 58. See Chap. 37.

Dying Rooster. Sounded like the final effort of a D.R. 20 p9&11; 68 p72. A pedlar's licence allowed the bearer to walk the roads selling goods off a tray to passers-by. In London, I recall, it was often used by beggars who would sell things like matches, bootlaces, etc., and rely on the charity of the buyer not to ask for any change. The Dying Rooster PGW referred to was a sort of Whoopie cushion. A rubber container was inflated like a balloon and the outrushing air produced a noise purportedly similar to a dying rooster.

E

(MTT = My thanks to)

Eagels, Jeanne. 71 p143. This US actress (1890–1929) made her name as Sadie Thompson in Somerset Maugham's *Rain* (1922). She starred in PGW's *Her Cardboard Lover* in New York in 1927.

Eagle, Solomon. 2 p43. In *Journal of the Plague* (1665), Daniel Defoe wrote of Solomon Eagle, who ran around London stark naked, exhorting all and sundry to repent because "The end of world is nigh".

Earl. Bill Bailey would be an earl if he murdered about 57 uncles and cousins. 84 p26. I suggest this is a private Wodehouse joke. If PGW had murdered about this number of uncles and cousins, he would have become Earl of Kimberley.

Earl Piccadilly/Earl of Piccadilly. 78 p50–51. The style Earl of Somewhere (Ickenham, Emsworth etc.) dates back to the Norman Conquest, when William the Conqueror dished out bits of England to his supporters and gave them a title to go with it. Thus, the Earl of Surrey would own a large chunk of the county of Surrey. The 'of' originally implied ownership of land; hence, in Wodehouse's example, Earl Piccadilly (presumably with no land) would be sneered at by the Earl of Elsewhere. However, Earl Piccadilly is the older form of address. The titles of duke, marquess, viscount and baron were all introduced by the Normans. Earl was the only noble title used among the Anglo-Saxons before the Normans arrived, and they were styled simply Earl Something. Thus, Earl Piccadilly could retort that his title followed the old English style and was not a later Norman-French adaptation. William the Conqueror allowed the Anglo-Saxon earls to keep their style of address as an exercise in public relations, instead of converting their titles to count, the French equivalent. And, since their wives had no pre-Norman title, that is why an earl's wife is a countess. Many modern earls preferred the older style when the honour was bestowed on them, including Earls Haig and Attlee.

Earl who keeps his carriage, a first-class. 67 p13. Lord Ickenham says that he has risen to this exalted rank. G&S *Patience* Act 2: "And when she grew up she was given in marriage / To a first-class earl who keeps his carriage." In the 19th century, 'to keep a carriage' was a measure of wealth. You had to pay a coachman (and groom?); buy a horse/horses, which cost as much to keep as the coachman did; buy the coach and all the harness; and then build a coach-house for your carriage, stables for the horses and accommodation for the coachman and groom.

Earliest pipe of half-awakened birds. See PIPE OF HALF-AWAKENED BIRDS.

Earls Court sideshowman. 18 p79. Earls Court, a London fairground/ exhibition centre was opened in 1887. It was famous for its Great Wheel (Ferris Wheel) and Buffalo Bill's Wild West Show. Originally similar to Coney Island, it is now a trade and exhibition centre.

Earlswood. 41 p33. This famous lunatic asylum, thirty miles south of London, closed in 1996. The north London equivalent was COLNEY HATCH.

Early or American period. 79 p15 & 16. PGW twist on the earnest talk among the artistic coterie of Picasso's 'early' or 'blue' period (c.1901–5).

Early to bed and early to rise (makes a man healthy and wealthy and wise). 91 p5. 16th-century English proverb.

Earth has not anything to show more fair. 95 p87. From Wordsworth's sonnet 'Composed upon Westminster Bridge'. Wordsworth was admiring the view from the bridge towards the City of London, which then had no fewer than fifty-three Wren churches whose elegant spires were in perfect harmony with the magnificent dome of St Paul's Cathedral (365 ft) rising above them. The view changed little until about 1960 when, for the first time, buildings over 120 feet in height were allowed in London. I still remember my outrage when I saw the first skyscraper rear above St Paul's.

Eased his stuff'd bosom. See BOSOM.

East. 3 p275. Friend of Tom Brown in *Tom Brown's Schooldays*.

East Bampton. 69 p80. See Chap. 23.

East Wibley. 64 p37. See WEOBLEY.

East Wobsley. 12 p8; 39 p15. See WEOBLEY.

Eastman, Monk. 15A p124. See Chap. 23.

Eastnor. Where the Little Nugget was staying 17 p12. Eastnor Castle, Herefordshire, is the impressive 19th-century Gothic revival seat of Lord Somers. It is about thirteen miles west of Hanley Castle, Worcs, and I visited it as a possible source of Blandings. It isn't. I think PGW used such a real name the same way he used WYMONDHAM. An aunt of his married the Rev. Bromley Somers Cocks, a relative of Lord Somers, and PGW would certainly have known of the relationship.

Ebionites. 69 p62. A second-century heretical Christian sect who believed Jesus was only a man.

Ebury Street, London. 18 p22 and later. From 1890 to 1939, this street was well known for the number of houses offering inexpensive lodgings and was popular among young writers, dramatists and the like. As PGW implied, many of the houses were owned by ex-butlers who had served in the nearby palatial establishments of Belgravia. There are still many small private hotels in the street. MTT Murray Hedgcock for the information that the 1911 census (2/3 April) has PGW living at 99/101 Ebury Street. The owner was John Holborn, lodging-house keeper.

Eckleton. 6 p8. Another example of PGW using a local Shropshire name for his fictional schools. He took Ackleton, just along the road from Stableford, and altered the name slightly as he did to Beckbury, which became Beckford. See Chaps 3 and 35.

Eclipse first, the rest nowhere. 2 p223. Eclipse was the supreme English race-horse in the 18th century, unbeaten in eighteen races. The quotation, in common use for nearly 200 years, comes from racing terminology where other horses more than a certain distance behind the winner (six lengths today) are said to be 'nowhere'. MTT Dr Tim Healey.

Economic Royalist. You had got another E.R. on your hands 61 p110; 66 p7 and elsewhere. Term used by F.D. Roosevelt for the American 'big business men' who opposed his New Deal welfare measures. See also KINGS.

Eden, voice that breathed o'er. See VOICE THAT BREATHED O'ER EDEN.

Edge of Night, The. During the last years of his life, Wodehouse never missed an episode of this American TV soap, and his admiration of it was well-known. In *The Spectator* (24 March 2001) Robert McCrum wrote that Wodehouse's "death was remarkable in the history of soaps … when a real event made it into the script." When his death was announced, the script was hurriedly altered so the next episode opened with a character sadly reading Wodehouse's obituary and saying "a man has died who gave so much pleasure to so many". A pleasant tribute.

***Edinburgh Castle*, S.S.** 31 p209. The Castle Line ran a regular UK–South Africa steamer service for over 100 years till 1970. The *Edinburgh Castle* PGW mentions was the second ship by that name. It was launched in 1910, served as a troop carrier in the First World War, resumed passenger duties in 1919, and was commandeered again as a Navy accommodation ship moored off Freetown in 1939. She was eventually sunk in 1945 when it proved too expensive to bring her back to Britain.

Edith searching for the body of King Harold after the Battle of Hastings. 58 p248; 67 p232. This was Edith of the Swan's Neck, Harold's mistress, who loved him dearly. See Bulwer-Lytton's *Harold, The Last of the Saxon Kings* (1848). MTT Dr Tim Healey.

Edwardes, George. 10 often; 11 p30. Edwardes (1852–1915) took over the Gaiety Theatre and made it London's most glamorous theatre. Some of his Gaiety Girls, forerunners of the Ziegfeld Follies Girls, married into the aristocracy. See Chap. 24.

Edwin and Angelina in real life. 9 p150. The plaintiff and defendant in G&S *Trial by Jury*.

Eels, jellied. See 'Uncle Fred Flits By'. Along with cockles and winkles, eels have always been popular in the East End of London. Jellied eels, a down-market version of quails in aspic, are still available from most fish shops. The brothers Fred and Charles Cooke sold their shop, the last to sell live eels across the counter, just a few years ago. It was their father who first sold jellied eels in London around 1900.

Ee-yah! Ee-yah! 48 p95. This college yell is used by Ohio State, Mississippi State, Texas A & M and Oklahoma State amongst others. See COLLEGE YELLS.

Egeria and Numa Pompilius. 34 p5. Numa Pompilius, King of Rome, died 672 B.C. Egeria was the nymph who inspired him and in whose name he introduced legislation.

Egg. Good egg, bad egg, old egg. Frequent. Common 19th-century US and UK terms for a man. 'Egg', 'BEAN' and 'CRUMPET' were all slang terms for the head and, by transference, to the man as well. See also OLD BEAN.

Egg, picnic. See HARD AS A PICNIC EGG.

Egg, to lay an (a flop). Often in PGW. Three of my dictionaries state that it comes from a duck in cricket, i.e. getting no runs since the O on the scoreboard is held to resemble a duck's egg. But see BIRD, GET THE.

Egg, virtually from the. 64 p47. Bertie is quoting from Horace's *Ars Poetica* Bk 3, l.147 'ab ovo'. Helen of Troy sprang from an egg 'engendered' by Leda and the swan (Zeus in one of his disguises). Don't ask!

Eggs, Beans and Crumpets. PGW just took the slang forms of address common among the young men of the day and used them as collective terms. See CRUMPET, EGG and OLD BEAN. If he had written it thirty years before, he would probably have called it 'Chappies and Johnnies'; see CHAPPIE.

Egypt, recent excavations in. 28 p123. PGW's topical reference to the finding of Tutenkhamun's tomb the year before the book came out.

Egypt, thinking it was a town in Illinois. 33 p140. There is no town in Illinois called Egypt, but the southern section of the state has been known colloquially as Egypt since the early 19th century. One theory is that this stems from the excellent corn grown there when the rest of the Illinois crop failed ('corn in Egypt'). Another theory is that Cairo, the southernmost town of the region, stands on a major river confluence, resembling the Nile delta, and the 'Egypt' term reflects this.

Eight-ball, we are behind the. 63 p120. US pool term for being in a disadvantageous position. The UK equivalent is to be snookered behind the black.

Eighteen-day diet. 49 p238. Dieting fads changed as frequently then as they do today. This one was popular at the time PGW wrote. See also 'JUICE OF AN ORANGE'.

Einstein, Albert. 85 p13; 87 p23. This physicist (1879–1955) should need no explanation.

Einstein's Theory of Relativity. 49 p34. Einstein's 1916 theory was confirmed by the 1919 solar eclipse and became a tremendous talking-point in the 1920s. The FOURTH DIMENSION became a common phrase, as in 'The Great Hat Mystery'.

Eisenhower. 69 p198 (a Pekinese). General, later president, Dwight D. Eisenhower (1890–1969) is quoted at 73 p41 as "having recourse" to a "strategic retreat". I was startled by the phrase since, in the British Army at least, we never use the term 'strategic retreat'. We occasionally have to conduct 'a tactical withdrawal', but that is a very different matter.

Eked out a precarious livelihood by taking in one another's washing. That story of the people on the island 18 p21. MTT Neil Midkiff and others who traced this back to 1876, when the *Saturday Review* (November 11), had a comment by Froude, the historian, on "an account of the doings of the late Mr Augustus Smith in the Scilly Islands. The natives of that group, before Mr Smith's time, are popularly said to have eked out a precarious living by taking in each's washing." The same comment has apparently been made of the Isle of Man and Orkney. It sounds very much like a joke from *Punch* c.1850–60, but I have been unable to find it.

Elastic Stocking King. 21 p128. See KINGS.

Elba (could not imprison Napoleon permanently). 33 p13. Napoleon was exiled to the isle of Elba in the Mediterranean in 1814 but escaped, resumed power, and was only finally defeated at Waterloo in 1815. We then sent him off to St. Helena in the South Atlantic, much further away and safer.

Elementary, my dear fellow. 14 p70; my dear Watson 15A p140 and up to 97 p11. MTT Catherine Cooke for enabling me to study the London archive of Holmeseana. Like 'Play it again, Sam' or 'Come up and see me some time', 'Elementary, my dear Watson' is commonly misattributed. It appears nowhere in Conan DOYLE but was popularised by William Gillette, the American actor who made his name as Holmes in a play Doyle allowed him to adapt. It received a new lease of life in the first Holmes talking film *Return of Sherlock Holmes* (1929). Clive Brook spoke it as the last line and confirmed the opinion of millions that, if Doyle didn't write it, he should have. In passing, the magisterial *Oxford English Dictionary* quotes the reference in *Psmith Journalist* as the first (English) written usage.

Elephant who never forgot. 53 p209. Phrase popularised by 'An Elephant Never Forgets', a British music hall vaudeville song of the 1880s, revived in the 1930s.

Elijah and the ravens. 44 p52 and later. See RAVENS.

Eliot, George. 67 p28. This lady, real name Mary Ann Evans (1819–80), wrote of social and moral problems.

Eliot, T.S. 76 p125. One of my reference books says this poet (1888–1965) had become established among the avant-garde by 1922 and refers to his use of objective correlation and dissociation of sensibility. I doubt if Bertie would have enjoyed him.

Elisha and the bears who ate the children who mocked him. 21 p114 and frequent later. See BEARS, EATEN BY.

Eliza. Meet the bloodhounds 45 p172; crossing the ice 58 p283. From Harriet Beecher Stowe's *Uncle Tom's Cabin* — like *Pilgrim's Progress*, a book everybody knows but which, nowadays, very few have read. See *UNCLE TOM'S CABIN*.

Elizabeth, Queen. 42 p273 and often later. Aunt Agatha resembled her. Queen of England from 1558 to 1603, Elizabeth was a very strong-minded woman. She had good reason to be: until the age of 25, her life was constantly in danger and there were plots against her throughout her reign.

Elks. 73 p71. An American benevolent brotherhood, founded 1868.

Elmer. Often. PGW realised early on that all he had to do was to name a man Elmer and a girl Sadie to make them unmistakeably American to English readers. There are few British people with these names. The popularity of Elmer stems from Ebenezer and Jonathan Elmer, two brothers, doctors and patriots who fought in the American Revolution. In the years immediately after that conflict, the name Elmer was even more popular than Washington.

Elsie books, the. 30 p55. This series of twenty-eight books about Elsie Dinsmore was written by Martha Finley between 1867 and 1905. It covered Elsie's adventures from girlhood to motherhood and grandmotherhood, "shedding an incredible quantity of tears along the way." The same review of American literature notes: "Children suddenly stopped reading them about 1905."

Elsmore, welcome to. 9 p269. Misprint for Elsinore. S. *Hamlet*.

Embassy (night club). 31 p76 & p192. See Chap. 21.

Embury Hill, a Roman camp two miles from Sedleigh school. 12 p188. An excellent example of PGW's altering real place names for his novels. This is Elmley Castle, near Sedgeberrow. See Chap. 3.

Emeriti. 2 p54. A cricket club of Old Boys from Catholic private schools.

Emerson, George. 19 p49. See Chap. 2.

Emerson the philosopher. Quoted at 35 p240. The American Ralph Waldo Emerson (1803–82). "A friend … masterpiece of nature" is from his essay 'Friendship'.

Emperor of Germany. 3 p33 & p43. See KAISER.

Emperor to a black-beetle (my learned friend's manner). 18 p16. See MY LEARNED FRIEND'S MANNER.

Empire, the (music hall/theatre). 17A p39; 21 p48; now a theatre, not a music hall 30 p192. This music hall (later a theatre), on the north side of Leicester Square, London, was the centre of London's nightlife 1880–1914. Fred & Adele Astaire starred in the last show before it was demolished in 1927 and replaced by the present cinema. See Chap. 5.

Empire Boys, The. 9 p188. Patriotic song by A.C. Hamby (1903).

Empress of Stormy Emotion. 70 p177. See Chap. 28.

Empress Rooms, West Kensington. 36 p116. See SUBSCRIPTION DANCES AT THE EMPRESS ROOMS.

Empyrean of pure cheek. It passes out of the realm of the merely impudent and soars into the boundless e. of p. c. 1 p272. From Ambrose Bierce's *Cobwebs from an Empty Skull* (1874): "…transcends the limit of the merely impudent, and passes into the boundless empyrean of pure cheek!" MTT Chris Paul.

Emsworth. 12 p16. See Chap. 16.

Emsworth, 8th Earl of. We know little of the 8th Earl except that his sons Clarence and Galahad and his many daughters were terrified of him. *(See page 148.)*

Emu. A large Australian bird, three letters 49 p113. See CROSSWORDS.

The 8th Earl of Emsworth

Father of the 9th Earl, the 8th Earl was not remembered kindly by his family. In *A Pelican at Blandings* , chap 7, we learn that his wife was terrified of him, while, in chap 8, Gally says his father could open an oyster at sixty paces with a single glance. In chap 3 of *Sunset At Blandings*, Gally agrees with Vicky Underwood that he was terrifying: "That voice, those bushy eyebrows." A few pages on, even Lady Florence admits that "Father was a bully and a tyrant ..."

This rare photograph shows the 8th Earl about to give hell to a tenant farmer behind with his rent. He is accompanied by his eldest daughter, Lady Ann Threepwood.

End man at a minstrel show. See MINSTREL SHOW.

End of a perfect day. 33 p125. "When you come to the end of a perfect day", from the song 'A Perfect Day' by Carrie Jacobs-Bond (1910).

End of all things. 17 p160 and later. B. 1st Epistle of Peter 4.7: "But the end of all things is at hand: be ye therefore sober, and watch unto prayer."

End shall justify the means, the. 9 p148. The only written source I can find for this timeless moral argument is Matthew Prior's *Hans Carvel* (1701): "The Ends must justify the Means."

Enemy hath done this, an. 8 p80. B. Matthew 13.28: "An enemy hath done this" (in this case, mixing weed seeds with the corn seed).

England. A savage country, where ice, central heating and corn on the cob are unobtainable. 29 p148–9. I am glad to say things have improved. I shall refrain from commenting on the difficulty of finding marmalade, sausage rolls, decent toast (or toast-racks) or Marmite in the USA.

England expects that every man will do his duty. 7 p70; 80 p155. Nelson's famous signal to his fleet before the Battle of Trafalgar (1805).

England is En-ger-land still, For (patriotic song)**.** 46 p98; 78 p48. Method of emphasis all too often used by singers in rendering 'England Is England Still', 1886 song by J.B. Geoghegan.

England, my England. 11 pp9 &11. From W.E. Henley's poem 'For England's Sake'.

Englishman's shortest prayer, Barry Pain says. 1 p105. In 1902, school stories avoided terms like words 'My God!'. See also PAIN, BARRY.

Entente Cordiale. 4 p276 and later. At the end of the 19th century, we were arguing with the French over bits of Africa we thought belonged to us and they thought belonged to them. Edward VII worked very hard to ease matters and, with his encouragement, Britain and France signed the Entente Cordiale in 1904.

Enterprises of great pith and moment. 93 p120; something of far greater 76 p94. S. *Hamlet* 3.1 ("To be or not to be" speech): "And thus the native hue of resolution / Is sicklied o'er with the pale cast of thought, / And enterprises of great pith and moment / With this regard their currents turn awry, / And lose the name of action."

Enterprising burglar. See BURGLAR.

Envy, malice, hatred and all uncharitableness. 20 p77. BCP. The Litany.

Epictetus. 18 p252. The writings of this Stoic philosopher (55–135 A.D.) were full of cracks like the one in 'The Goal-Keeper and Plutocrat'. PGW's version is a free translation of Epictetus' view that very little is certain in this world.

Epipsychidion, Shelley's. 18 p160. I imagine Barstowe quoted the section: "An isle under Ionian skies, / Beautiful as a wreck of Paradise." The hungry Elsa Keith would probably have preferred line 591: "I pant, I sink, I tremble, I expire!"

Epstein's Genesis. 46 p273. This was the 'shocking', 'outrageous', 'modern' 1930 sculpture of a heavily-pregnant woman (now on display in Manchester) done by Jacob Epstein (1880–1959), who was 'influenced by vorticism and African art'.

ER suffix. Throughout PGW. This form of slang began at Harrow School in the 1850s and became common at Oxford and Cambridge soon afterwards. Association football (round ball) is still Soccer; Rugby football (oval ball) is Rugger. The Dean of your College was the Deaner, and Lord Bodsham (55 p11 &12) was 'the Bodders'. The habit seems to have been most popular at Oxford and reached extraordinary lengths in the 1920s. The Rev. Talbot Rice, rector of St Peter Le Bailey, was known as the Tagger Ragger of St Pragger LeBagger. When I went up to Oxford in 1953, the suffix was still in use, though modified, among public (private) schoolboys. So, your prep school was your 'prepper', Broad Street was 'the Broader', the High Street was 'the Higher' and a waste-paper basket was still, for some, a 'wagger pagger bagger'.

Perhaps the last person to use this slang habitually was Brian Johnston, the cricket commentator who died in 1994. He and his fellow broadcasters used to refer to each other on air in this way. So Johnston was 'Johnners', Henry Blofeld was (and is) Blowers, and so on. Godfrey Evans said his abiding memory was the time he entered the commentary box with news of the latest betting odds from the bookmakers Ladbroke's on the Test match they were broadcasting. Johnston announced to listeners across the nation: "Ah! Here comes Godders with the odders from Ladders". (See also Chap 30.)

And now you know how the Bow Street police court, opposite the Royal Opera House, became PGW's legendary police court at BOSHER STREET.

Era of universal happiness will set in. 68 p158. An early philosophical ideal propounded by SOCRATES and his followers.

Erastianism. 56 p98. State supremacy in church government. Named after Erastus (Thomas Lieber, 1524–83). The Church of England is, strictly speaking, Erastian.

Eric. 12 p28 & p222; 39 p205. *Eric, or Little by Little*, the most famous 'moral' school story for boys and universally mocked by them, was written in 1858 by Dean Farrar (1831–1903); he wrote *St Winifred's* five years later. It was because of the strong contrast with books like these that boys enjoyed PGW's realistic school stories. PGW referred to it simply as *Eric*, knowing all his readers would pick up the reference. See also JEAMES, OUR.

Ernle-Plunkett-Drax-Plunkett. 72 p84. I suggest PGW chose this name since it was popularly believed to be the longest English surname. From memory, this was a shortened version. I recall the correct name is something like Plunkett-Ernle-Erle-Drax-Plunkett. Further research reveals the longest UK surname was that of Major L.S.D.O.F Tollemache-Tollemache-de Orellana-Plantaganet-Tollemache-Tollemache, killed in France in 1917. Until her death in 1946, we were proud to have amongst us Lady Caroline Jemima Temple-Nugent-Chandos-Brydges-Grenville.

Err is human, to. 93 p125. Pope's 'Essay on Criticism': "To err is human, to forgive divine."

Error, mortal. See MORTAL ERROR.

Escoffier, cooks like. 90 p143. Escoffier (1847–1935), undoubtedly the greatest chef of his time, created bombe Nero, pêche Melba and toast Melba at the Savoy Hotel. Originally the toast was named in honour of Madame Ritz, but, as a good hotel manager's wife should, she made Escoffier change the name to flatter the Savoy's guest, Dame Nellie Melba.

Escutcheon, a blot on the old/on her. See BLOT.

Espionage. Oh, cruel, cruel e. 18 p73. I regret I have been unable to find the melodrama Bailey refers to.

Essop, J. 3 p236. The equivalent PGW twist in American terms would be a reference to the baseball player B.R. Uth. See JESSOP.

Etchings. Come up and see his e. 93 p99. Stanford White, the brilliant architect who designed, amongst other things the arch at Washington Square, was shot at Madison Square Gardens (which he had also designed) by Harry Thaw in 1906. In private life, White was the leading member of a group of New York roués who called themselves the 'Sewer Club'. At least two reference books credit Stanford White with coining the phrase: "Come up and see my etchings." Nowadays "Care to come up for a coffee?" fulfils the same purpose.

Eternal City, The. 14 p67. Book by Hall CAINE 1901.

Eternal verse, married to. 80 p101. See MARRIED TO ENTERNAL VERSE.

Ethics of Suicide. See SCHOPENHAUER.

Etna. The kettle was hissing on the Etna 2 p243 and later. This small camping stove used methylated spirits to boil the kettle for the tea in your school study that was so welcome after a hard game of Rugby. While later models were pressurised, I believe the original Etnas just burned a simple wick.

Eton and Harrow cricket match. 80 p9 & p18. This is the oldest cricket fixture in the world and takes place every year at Lord's. In PGW's newspaper *The Globe* of 4 July 1904, there was a report that it was "now well recognised that more young ladies" attended the Eton/Harrow and Oxford/Cambridges matches at Lords than all the other games there put together.

Until 1939 the Eton-Harrow match was a full-dress affair attracting up to 10,000 spectators attired in top hats and morning dress for the men and hats and Ascot dresses for the ladies. Eton boys wore tail coat and top hat and carried a tasselled cane. That is why, in *Company for Henry* (p139), PGW speaks of something standing out as plainly as a Palm Beach suit at the Eton and Harrow match. The tradition of the family driving onto the ground in the horse-drawn family coach to cheer on young Charles/John/Peter lasted a surprisingly long time. There were coaches on the Lords' grass for the match up to about 1950. This once important occasion in the social calendar now attracts little interest.

Eton Boating Song. 9 p250; 56 p227. This superb song (the second-best waltz in the world) was written by Algernon Drummond with words by W.J. Cory. The piano arrangement now commonly used was written by Evelyn Wodehouse, a cousin of PGW's.

Eton or 'Arrer fellers, broken-down. 18 p70. Eton and Harrow are England's best-known public (private) schools. When their fictional alumni go wrong, they really go wrong. The shame of such tales is equalled only by the agony of reading of a crashed Balliol man. In the late 19th–early 20th century, Balliol acquired the reputation for turning out Oxford's cleverest young men. Richard Usborne, in his witty, ground-breaking review of popular English literature, *Clubland Heroes*, summed it up in two superb sentences (which Captain Brabazon Biggar would wholeheartedly endorse). Out East, where you are on your own and British fair play does not apply: "you might find a Balliol man drinking himself to death and being jeered at by dagoes. There are some things it is not good for a white man to look upon."

Wodehouse visited Eton in the 1930s and told me in a letter that it was highly unfair that headmasters were so awe-inspiring. I had written to him of Dr Birley, headmaster of Eton, a very tall, impressive man, while PGW had in mind a predecessor at Eton, Dr Alington (though he never forgot his equally tall and impressive headmaster at Dulwich, A.H. Gilkes). See also GUTENBERG BIBLE.

Euclid. Was absurd, as E. would say 2 p172; E.'s definition of a straight line 20 p41. Horace Davenport illustrates his definition of a straight line — length without breadth — at 60 p10. This Greek mathematician, fl. 300 B.C., formulated many of the rules we learned in our geometry lessons. See also ABSURD.

Eugene. The world champion is called E. 40 p39. This was Gene Tunney, an unusual world heavyweight champion (1926–28) who knew what he wanted and how he could get it. He refused to talk platitudes to sportswriters, stopped boxing as soon as he had made enough money, married a socialite and went on to lecture on Shakespeare at Yale. When he came to London as world champion, he infuriated the Press by refusing to give any interviews. The only person he spent time with was the playwright George Bernard Shaw, with whom he had had a long correspondence.

Eureka! 34 p131 and often thereafter. See ARCHIMEDES.

Euripides. 2 p97 and later. Greek tragic poet, died 407 B.C.

Evans, P.C. 53 p61; 87 p176. The guardian of the peace in Market Blandings who arrested George Cyril Wellbeloved. In the second reference, his partner is P.C. Morgan. It is a subtle point, but British readers will note that both these members of the Shropshire County Constabulary have Welsh names. When PGW lived in Shropshire, his local policeman was P.C. Lloyd (another Welsh name). No surprise, really, since it was long the prudent habit of county police forces to recruit from outside their borders. This prevented policemen being embarrassed by having to apprehend their brothers or cousins for poaching, moving pigs without a licence, or failing to abate their smoky chimneys.

Even Homer used to nod at times. See HOMER USED TO NOD.

Even tenor of her life had been interrupted, the. 63 p228. The phrase 'even tenor of his way' seems to have been a favourite 19th-century phrase for anybody who led a peaceful life or followed one occupation all his life. The nearest source I can find is Gray's 'Elegy Written in a Country Church-yard': "They kept the noiseless tenor of their way."

Even unto half of my kingdom. See HALF MY KINGDOM.

Evening dress, faultless. 13 p10 and later. In Victorian novels, the handsome hero always appeared in "faultless evening dress". In 14 p76, PGW wrote "faultless evening dress so beloved of female novelists" because he knew his readers appreciated the phrase had already become a well-worn cliché. I have worn this on only a few occasions and I have to say that the rigid white starched shirt front, the white bow tie that had to be tied correctly first time and the coat-tails that always seemed an inch too long, meant that 'faultless' evening dress was not as common as novelists would have us believe. Purists argue that Fred

ASTAIRE broke the rules when he persuaded his London tailor to shorten the white waistcoat so it did not show below the coat, but I would cite him as one man whose evening dress really was faultless. See also SOUP-AND-FISH.

Every day, in every way, I ... grow more and more like a fish 32 p77; am getting better and better 53 p182; know less and less about more and more 42 p164; get pottier and pottier 84 p18 etc. Emil Coué (1857–1926), a French doctor, convinced millions that constant repetition of the words "Every day in every way I am getting better and better" (37 p155) would keep them in good health. In the 1920s, the whole world seemed to be saying it to itself. PGW's variations of the phrase would be recognised by every contemporary reader.

Every day is a fresh beginning, Every morn is the world made anew ... 79 p75. 'New Every Morning', poem by Susan Coolidge (1835–1905), best known for *What Katy Did*. MTT Elin Woodger.

Every little bit added to what you've got, makes just that little bit more. 65 p24 and elsewhere. It was in this spirit that the most dignified of butlers accepted a humble shilling pressed into their hand. Title of a popular song by the Dillon brothers (1907).

Every Nice Girl Loves a Sailor. 96 p88. Ella Retford popularised the music hall song 'All the Nice Girls Love a Sailor' (1900) by A.J. Mills.

Every prospect pleases and only man is vile. 30 p199 and later. 'From Greenland's Icy Mountains' by Bishop Heber (1783–1826). When the hymn was published, the British Colonial Office was furious. The second verse begins:

What though the spicy breezes
Blow soft o'er Ceylon's isle,
Though every prospect pleases
And only man is vile.

They sent him a strong protest, pointing out these words were inappropriate to a British colony and insisting he replace the word 'Ceylon's' with 'Java's' (Java was a Dutch colony). He must have stood firm because it is still 'Ceylon's' in my First World War (Army Service edition) hymn book.

At 18 p7, PGW gives us the gloss: "But what is a pleasant voice if the soul be vile?"

Everybody wants the key to my cellar. 29 p70. Song (1919) by Rose, Baskett & Pollock. A Prohibition reference, I assume.

Everybody who was anybody. Phrase describing smart social gatherings, coined by the music hall comedian George ROBEY. The phrase is still in common use.

Everybody Works But Father. 21 p171 and later. Popular 1891 UK music hall comic song. A US version came out in 1905, written by Jean Havez.

Everywhere. See OUT OF THE EVERYWHERE.

Evil Eye Fleagle of Brooklyn. See FLEAGLE, EVIL EYE.

Evil that men do lives after them, the. 3 p219. S. *Julius Caesar* 3.2: "The evil that men do lives after them, / The good is oft interred with their bones."

Excavation. If you know a superior excavation. 28 p245. PGW gloss on 'If you know a better hole ...' See HOLE.

Excellent, as an English poet will say in a few hundred years, to have a giant's strength, but it is tyrannous to use it like a giant. 5 p75. See S. *Measure for Measure* 2.2: "O! it is excellent to have a giant's strength, but it is tyrannous, To use it like a giant." MTT John Graham.

Excelsior. A young man with a banner marked E. 36 p13 and often later; short story title 69; at 77 p43 it was a pair of trousers. Longfellow's poem 'Excelsior'.

Excuse it, please. Often. An American phrase that PGW picked up early. Used by receptionists and telephone operators, it was equivalent to the "Ay beg your poddon" of their British counterparts.

Exercises, Larsen. 19 p7. See LARSEN and SWEDISH EXERCISES.

Exeter Hall (where bishops gather in gangs). 25 p171. A large hall built in the Strand, London, in 1829 for meetings of religious organisations and committees. The Strand Palace Hotel stands on the site now.

Exhibition. British Empire E. at Wembley 35 p146. See WEMBLEY EMPIRE EXHIBITION.

Exile from home splendour dazzles in vain, An. 21 p44. It took me a long time to find this one. Everybody I asked had a vague recollection of it, but no more. It is from the *second* verse of HOME, SWEET HOME.

Exit, cautious through gap in hedge. 22 p15. PGW states this was a familiar stage direction of melodrama. I fear it was not familiar to me and I have been unable to find it.

Exit hurriedly, pursued by a bear. 43 p282; 78 p64. S. *Winter's Tale* 3.3. The *Over Seventy* piece is one of the rare occasions when PGW matched himself against Shakespeare. I think the PGW version is much funnier and, quoting Alan Bennett's best monologue, "has more idiomatic force".

Expeditionary force, the other members of the. 70 p119. I include this because I am told the term is no longer familiar. The British Army units sent to France in 1914 and 1939 to fight Germany were named the British Expeditionary Force (B.E.F.). When the US came into the First World War, the troops sent to Europe were known as the American Expeditionary Force (A.E.F.).

Express, Cornish/Scotch. See CORNISH and SCOTCH EXPRESS.

Extricated from her sea of troubles. 76 p116. S. *Hamlet* 3.1 ('To be or not to be' speech): "Or to take arms against a sea of troubles."

Exuberance of his own verbosity, intoxicated with the. See INTOXICATED WITH THE EXUBERANCE.

Eye, held me with a glittering. See HELD ME WITH A GLITTERING EYE.

Eye, jaundiced. See JAUNDICED EYE.

Eye like Mars to threaten and command, an. 17 p208 ; and 'an eye like Mother's' later. S. *Hamlet* 3.4: "An eye like Mars to threaten and command. A station like the herald Mercury."

Eye of a needle. It is easier for a rich man to pass through the e. of a n. than for a gold tooth to win its way across the gangplank of the Aquitania. 46 p273. B.

Matthew 19.24: "It is easier for a camel to go through the eye of a needle, than for a rich man to enter into the kingdom of God."

Eye sublime. See FRONT, FAIR.

Eye, the poet's (in a fine frenzy rolling). See POET'S EYE.

Eye was not dimmed nor his natural force abated, his. 42 p27; 65 p63 and later. B. Deuteronomy 34.7. Description of Moses in his old age.

Eyes like stars, started from their spheres. 59 p121. S. *Hamlet* 1. 5: "Make thy two eyes, like stars, start from their spheres".

Eyes, subdu'd. 87 p115. See SUBDU'D EYES.

F

(MTT = My thanks to)

Face is a book where men may read strange matters. PGW ref lost. S. *Macbeth* 1.5: "Your face, my thane, is a book where men may read strange matters."

Faceless Fiend. 49 p278 and later. Faceless Fiends and Master Criminals featured in thrillers and the distinction between thrillers and detective stories (Agatha Christie, Dorothy L. Sayers etc.) cannot be emphasised too strongly. In thrillers, the baddie was known from the start and the novel portrayed the struggle of the hero to defeat him. Edgar WALLACE and Sidney Horler wrote thrillers, not DETECTIVE STORIES.

Faces that launch a thousand ships. 54 p130 and later; stopped a thousand clocks 76 p77. A description of Helen of Troy, whose beauty brought about the Trojan War. It is from Marlowe's *Dr Faustus*, line 1328: "Was this the face that launched a thousand ships, And burnt the topless towers of Ilium." The second remark is PGW's mix of Marlowe and a popular Cockney insult still in use in the 1960s: "You've got a face that would stop a clock."

Faces well calculated to stop any clock. 77 p80; 84 p31. See FACES THAT LAUNCH A THOUSAND SHIPS.

Fades, now, the glimmering landscape on the sight. See ALL THE AIR A SOLEMN STILLNESS HOLDS.

Faery lands. 79 p85. From Keats' 'Ode to a Nightingale'. "Charm'd magic casements, opening on the foam / Of perilous seas, in faery lands forlorn."

Fagged for him at Winchester. 26 p12. In England, the word 'fag' has three meanings. Firstly, it is the term for a cheap cigarette: "Got a fag on you?" Secondly, it was the custom in boarding schools for junior boys to carry out jobs (fagging) for senior boys: cleaning his cricket boots, making tea in his study, running messages, tasks of that sort. So, in Wodehouse's school stories, a row in the passage would be "just a crowd of noisy fags" (juniors). Finally, by extension, it came to mean, as it still does, some laborious task. A five-mile run, writing 500 lines etc. is "an awful fag".

Failing to abate a smoky chimney. 50 p230; 64 p59; 90 p152. See NUISANCE MUST NOW CEASE.

Failures, This was one of our. 3 Preface. See Chap. 6 (Evening Dress). The story is that Beau Brummel's valet was met on stairs with a load of discarded neck cloths. "These, sir, are some of our failures." The equivalent in those Regency days of today's neck ties, tying a cravat correctly was quite an art and Beau

Brummel excelled in it, even giving lessons to the Prince of Wales. But apparently, no one ever equalled the elegance of Brummel's, which he tied himself.

Faint yet pursuing. 13 p205; but perservering 73 p83. B. Judges 8.4: "And Gideon came to Jordan, and passed over, he, and the three hundred men that were with him, faint, yet pursuing them."

Fair Deal. See DEAL.

Fair women and brave men. See BRAVE MEN AND FAIR WOMEN.

Fairbanks, Douglas. 23 p223 and later. This famous actor (1883–1939) played Jimmy in PGW's *A Gentleman of Leisure* in 1911 (Playhouse Theatre, New York), which is why the 1921 UK edition is dedicated to him. He also recommended PGW to the Algonquin Hotel in New York, and PGW said this made him a favoured guest. When Fairbanks played in the 1921 film *The Three Musketeers*, it was the most expensive film yet made. Since the studio had spent all that money, Fairbanks thought the least he could do was to grow a period moustache. It was one of the most influential fashion statements of the decade. His wife, Mary Pickford, and everybody advised against it since, in the USA of that time, such moustaches were worn only by comics, elderly gentlemen and gigolos. He went ahead anyway, and the moustache came back into fashion. If it had not been for him, Ronald Colman, Errol Flynn and David Niven would probably have been barefaced.

Fairies at the bottom of our garden, There are. Inserted to show there were ladies like Madeline Bassett. I do not know when the modern fashion for fairies began; I suspect it stemmed from Barrie's *Peter Pan* (1904). It certainly received a boost when the poem 'There Are Fairies at the Bottom of Our Garden' by Rose Fyleman (1877–1957) appeared in *Punch* (23 May 1917). For some reason, the phrase entered the language, although it was only one of a score of poems she wrote on the subject. She was serious in her belief in fairies, published a book on them and pestered A.A. Milne to write fairy stories for the children's magazine she edited.

Fairies, I do believe in. 72 p109; 73 p220 and later. J.M. Barrie's *Peter Pan*. "Do you believe in fairies? ... If you believe, clap your hands!"

Fairies shedding tears. Every time a fairy sheds a tear, a wee bit star is born in the Milky Way 52 p115. See TEAR.

Fairy bugles, blowing of. 40 p182; among the rushes 91 p119. Possibly a faint memory of T. *The Princess*, Pt 4, or perhaps W.M. Call's 'The Bird and the Bower': "I hear no more the fairy bugles blow."

Faith alone. It appeared to have no legs but to move by faith alone (a small woolly dog) 53 p47. See B. 2 Corinthians 5.7: "For we walk by faith, not by sight." MTT Adrian Smith for the suggestion that another possible source is Martin Luther's famous theological doctrine 'sola fide', justification 'by faith alone'.

Faithful old retainer. 12 p5. See CHARLES, HIS FRIEND.

Falernian wine, sat up too late over the. 70 p95; 76 p22. The most highly-regarded wine in ancient Rome.

Fall of the House of Usher. 28 p93. Short story by Edgar Allan POE.

Fall on each other's necks. 35 p201. MTT Adrian Vincent for reminding me of this one. This occurs in the Bible frequently when people greet each other joyfully. See two examples at Genesis 33:4 and Acts 20:37.

Falleth like the gentle rain from heaven upon the place/lobelias beneath. See DROPPING LIKE THE GENTLE DEW.

Falls to earth, you know not where. 59 p86 and elsewhere, usually "he fell to earth, he knew not where". Longfellow's 'The Arrow and the Song': "I shot an arrow into the air, It fell to earth I knew not where."

Famine. Seven years of f. we read of in Scripture 97 p72. B. Genesis 41.27: "And there shall arise after them seven years of famine; and all the plenty shall be forgotten in the land of Egypt."

Famous Players Co, everybody is sick of. 38 p101. This Hollywood company filmed PGW's *A Gentleman of Leisure* in 1923. Founded by Adolph Zukor in 1912, it was later absorbed into Paramount.

Famous victory. Why it was I cannot tell, said he, but 'twas a famous victory 21 p82. Southey's 'Battle of Blenheim'.

Far, far better thing I do than I have ever done. 42 p235; 50 p268 and later. See end of D. *Tale of Two Cities*.

Farewell, a long. See LONG FAREWELL.

'Farewell to Legs'. Short story title 57. In January 1930 *Cosmopolitan* magazine published 'Jeeves and the Kid Clementina'. MTT Nick Townend for the information that another article in the same edition, entitled 'Farewell to Legs', dealt with the sudden lengthening of women's skirts. It was one of the many occasions when Wodehouse got a plot, a title or a useful twist from articles in magazines to which he had contributed (see VAN TUYL).

MTT Charles Gould for pointing out that Hemingway's *A Farewell to Arms* had come out the year before. The soubriquet 'Legs' may or may not have been common, but it was certainly well known in America from Al Capone's equivalent in New York, the hoodlum and racketeer Legs Diamond (shot dead 18 December 1931).

Far-flung and held dominion over palm and pine, she was. 63 p21. KIPLING'S 'Recessional': "God of our fathers, known of old, / Lord of our far-flung battle-line, / Beneath whose awful Hand we hold / Dominion over palm and pine."

Fascist salute. Raising his hand in a sort of F.s. 48 p192. Mussolini had introduced this salute when he seized power in Italy in 1922 and Hitler adopted it later, as Oswald Mosley did in Britain. The Fascist salute was performed by sticking the right arm up in the air at 45 degrees with the hand outstretched. In December 2005 there was uproar in Italy when a footballer used the same gesture (now illegal in Italy) to celebrate scoring a a goal.

Fashionable crowd. Among the f.c. we noticed … PGW ref lost. PGW was quoting a newspaper cliché of reports of smart social events from c.1920 to c.1960. See also AMONG THOSE PRESENT.

Fasting for a good man's love. 70 p131; 94 p95. See THANKING HEAVEN.

Fat and greasy citizen. 26 p90 S. *As You Like It* 2.1: "Sweep on, you fat and greasy citizens!"

Fat Boy in Pickwick. 87 p208. Joe, employed by Mr Wardle in D. *The Pickwick Papers*. See also FLESH CREEP.

Fat men — and pigs — whom Julius Caesar liked to have about him. 91 p90; 95 p24 and elsewhere. S. *Julius Caesar* 1.2: "Let me have men about me that are fat; sleek-headed men and such as sleep o' nights." See also CAESAR, JULIUS.

'Fat of the Land, The'. Short story title 81. B. Genesis 45.18:

"... and ye shall eat the fat of the land."

Fate, a heart for any. 64 p7. See LET US BE UP AND DOING.

Fate bearing gifts, look askance at. 19 p150. See TIMEO DANAOS.

Fate cannot touch you. Wear Galloway's Tried and Proven (suspenders) and fate cannot touch you. 18 p89. In 1910, when this was written, upmarket American magazines were advertising Paris Garters (sock suspenders) with the slogan 'No Metal Can Touch You'. MTT Neil Midkiff.

Fate, feared his. See MONTROSE.

Fate sneaks up with the bit of lead piping/ waiting in the wings/ about to administer a sandbag. 23 p41 and later. From the ancient Greeks' belief that hubris will always be overtaken by Nemesis. When life is going really well, something always comes along to spoil it. See also NEMESIS.

Fate that is worse than death, the. 51 p176 and elsewhere. Bertie Wooster, a confirmed bachelor, uses the phrase to describe marriage. PGW borrowed it from Victorian melodrama where the term was always used when the pure heroine was threatened with the loss of her purity. A phrase rarely heard today.

Fate/He moves in a mysterious way (His wonders to perform). 24 p208 and later (of Jeeves). Cowper's *Olney Hymns* 33: "God moves in a mysterious way / His wonders to perform; / He plants his footsteps in the sea, / And rides upon the storm."

Fath, Jacques. Sports costume 73 p9. In the 1950s, Jacques Fath (1912–54) rivalled Dior in haute couture.

Father Abraham. I'm for 'em, Father Abraham 26 p248. See I'M FOR 'EM.

Father, Let me be your. See LET ME BE YOUR BANKER.

Father's in the pigstye, you can tell him by his hat. 26 p311 and up to 87 p171. I chased this reference for years without success and was then fortunate enough to meet Mr Max Tyler of the Music Hall Society, who knew it at once. It is the last verse of 'Seven and Sixpence', a comic song written and sung by Sam Mayo about 1900. Each verse has four lines setting the scene, then three lines of a repetitive chorus, followed by the punch line. The last verse tells of a salesman calling at a farm and asking the farmer's daughter where the farmer was:

Father's in the pigstye,
Father's in the pigstye,

Father's i-i-i-i-i-i-in the pigstye.
You can tell him by his hat!

Faultless evening dress. See EVENING DRESS.

Faults. With all her f. I love her still. See LOVED HER STILL.

Fauntleroy, Little Lord. 20 p85 and often up to 87 p126. The story of this angelic child by Frances Hodgson Burnett (1849–1924) first appeared in the *St Nicholas Magazine* in 1885. It was an instant success, as was the play of 1888. Every mother in the UK and USA who could afford it immediately forced their sons into the famous velvet suit with lace collar and let their hair grow long enough to have ringlets. The touching belief was that the costume would transform the little brutes into angels on earth. It was only equalled in popularity by the sailor suits made fashionable by the four little princes (later Edward VIII, George VI and the Dukes of Gloucester and Kent).

Bertie Wooster (as well as the Duke of Dunstable [see 84 p14]) was forced into both costumes in his childhood — perhaps PGW was, too. A photograph of him aged five shows him in a sailor suit, but at least this was not worn with long ringlets. These boys' sailor suits were still on sale in London in the 1950s.

On a visit to London, Mrs Burnett was presented with a diamond bracelet by English writers because she had won the law case when, for the first time, it was decided that the rights of the play of her book belonged to her as author. After her death, her son, Vivian, on whom L.L.F. was based, wrote her biography. For information, she got the idea of the velvet suit and lace collar from Oscar Wilde, who wore them when he visited her in 1882.

Faust Up To Date. 25 p200. 1888 London musical comedy hit by George R. Sims.

FBI. 85 p78 and elsewhere. Federal Bureau of Investigation. Founded in the presidency of Theodore Roosevelt, its first head was Charles Bonaparte, great-nephew of Napoleon. According to a recent UK Press report, one can now buy a kilt in Edinburgh of an approved FBI tartan. Has it a motif of red, white and blue? Or is it one of those 'quiet' tartans that fade into the background?

Fear, nameless. Frequent. See NAMELESS FEAR.

Fear no/any foe/Goble in shining armour. See FOE.

Feared his Fate too much to put it to the touch/test (to win or lose it all). See MONTROSE.

Feast of Belshazzar. See BELSHAZZAR'S FEAST.

Feast of reason and flow of soul. 21 p151 and frequent later. Pope's 'Epistles & Satires Imitated. To Mr Fortescue': "There St. John mingles with my friendly bowl / The feast of reason and the flow of soul."

Features, finely chiselled. See FINELY CHISELLED FEATURES.

Features of interest. …a problem which… seemed to present several f. of i. 58 p229. Again from Conan DOYLE; see 'The Blanched Soldier'.

Feelings deeper and warmer than those of ordinary friendship. See SENTIMENTS DEEPER AND WARMER.

Feet. Standing with reluctant feet where the brook and river meet/ eggs and bacon meet. See STANDING WITH RELUCTANT FEET.

'Feet of Clay'. Short story 69. B. Daniel 2.42: "And as the toes of the feet were part of iron, and part of clay, so the kingdom shall be partly strong and partly broken."

Felix the cat. 41 p184; 88 p260. Famous early film cartoon animal created by Pat Sullivan. Micky Mouse came later.

Fell clutch of circumstance. That do not wince at the … unbowed 76 p141; 96 p153. As Jeeves says, it is from Henley's 'Invictus'.

Fell out. See WE FELL OUT.

Fell to earth, he knew not where. 76 p175. See FALLS TO EARTH.

Fellow, my dear. 90 pp143–144, p179, p189. See DEAR FELLOW.

Fellow of infinite jest, of most excellent fancy. 3 p243; 17 p5 and later. S. *Hamlet* 5.1: "Alas! Poor Yorick. I knew him, Horatio; a fellow of infinite jest, of most excellent fancy."

Fellow travellers. 79 p62. Phrase for Communist sympathisers that came into popular use in 1950s–60s. I have subsequently learned it was used in Comunist pamphlets as early as 1908. MTT Daniel Love Glazer.

Felt it here, I. 73 p148. PGW was satirising the then-new system of Method acting, where 'empathy' for the role is considered all-important.

Female of the species so much deadlier than any male. 21 p229 and often later. At 52 p247, we read "the f. of the s. being more d. than the m." At 59 p204, PGW simply says "D. than the m." The first four verses of KIPLING's 'The Female of the Species' each end: "For the female of the species is more deadly than the male."

Fermain Bay, Guernsey. 9 p1. PGW had holidayed at Guernsey the year before he published *Not George Washington*.

Fermin, on the *Orb* staff. 9 p57. See Chap. 7.

Ferraro, headwaiter of the Berkeley Hotel, Piccadilly. 44 p79; 55 p250. Ferraro was indeed headwaiter at the Berkeley in the 1920s–30s. He ran a tight ship, and to ensure the Berkeley remained the popular lunch spot for the younger set, he kept a close eye on his clients' behaviour. Anxious upper-class mothers were reassured when the news got out that, when a young man sent a note to a young lady across the restaurant, Ferraro took personal charge of the matter and would only pass on the note if he approved of the sender.

Few in the pod. See YELLOW AND FEW.

Fezziwig, Mrs., one vast substantial smile. 4 p57; 15 p163 (US version). In the American version of *The Prince & Betty*, PGW gives the full attribution of Mrs Fezziwig to D. *A Christmas Carol*. He did not do so in *The Gold Bat* because he assumed his English schoolboy readers would know the reference. "In came Mrs Fezziwig, one vast substantial smile."

ffinch-ffarrowmere, Sir Jasper. 39 p44. See below.

ffrench-ffarmiloes of Dorset, not the Kent lot. 41 p83. See below.

ffrench-ffrench , a co-respondent. 80 p25. The ff spelling of names normally means that the family is an old one and received an honour or a grant of land from a grateful sovereign. Spelling was very different in those days. The name 'Wodehouse' has nowadays been modernised by most bearers of it to Woodhouse. But when John Wodehouse was given his knighthood for valour on the field of Agincourt (1415), the clerk who drew up the official document lengthened the 'o' in the middle by inserting an 'e' after the 'd'. In those days, that was the way 'god' was lengthened to 'good'. And if your royal grant said your name was spelt a certain way, you were stuck with it.

The double ff was used by clerks of the time to indicate a capital *F* because the capital was very similar to the lower case, and the habit remained in use till the 18th century. The change may have coincided with the decision of a Fleet Street publisher, Mr Bell, to get rid of the irritating lower case *f* that was also used as a secondary *s*. It is thanks to him that we no longer wish succefs, long life and happinefs to young princefsefs.

MTT Gwendolin Goldbloom for a detailed exposition on this 'preliminary ess', known in German as a 'Scharfes S' or 'Eszett'. In Gothic type there were several forms of the letter *s*, one of which resembled a lower-case *f* without the crossbar. This was developed in various ways including a form of *fz*, which in turn became used in Germany for double esses, using a character very like the Greek beta, i.e. a capital *B* with a tail continuing the left-hand stroke downwards.

Fiat justitia, ruat coelum. 92 p14. Let justice be done though the heavens fall; Latin proverb popularised by Ferdinand I (1503–64).

Fiddling while Rome burns. 60 p169. Legend says the Emperor Nero (54–68 A.D.) set Rome on fire to emulate the destruction of Troy and played his lyre to celebrate the nine-day conflagration that nearly destroyed the city.

Field, Mr Godfrey. 12 p30. Music hall singer, died 1921 at 72.

Fields. Fresh fields and pastures new. See Fresh fields.

Fields are white with daisies. When the f. are white with daisies, he'll return 14 p45 and later. From either the 1904 song 'The Fields Are White With Daisies' by William Pratt or the poem 'Deirdre' by R.D. Joyce (1830–83).

Fields, W.C. Looked like W.C. Fields 77 p189. This American actor (1879–1946) had an unusually large nose. Originally a juggler, Field claimed to have done his act at Buckingham Palace. See also My little chickadee.

Fiend, faceless. See Faceless fiend.

Fiend, frightful. See Frightful fiend.

Fiend in butler's shape. 56 p187; in human shape 43 p72; 46 p75 and later. A "fiend in human form" seems to have been a common usage from Chaucer onwards.

Fiend that slept. Wake the fiend that slept in Ronald Fish 50 p34; 82 p182. Watson used this term for Sherlock Holmes' drug habit, but I suggest PGW is referring to the blood lust that civilisation suppresses but which can be roused in all of us. Herman Melville's "fighting man is but a fiend" sums up the idea.

Fierce light that beats upon the throne. 71 p177. T. *Idylls of the King*, Dedication: "In that fierce light that beats upon a throne, And blackens every blot."

Fiery furnace. 26 p66 and frequent later. B. Daniel 3.20. The emergence from the fiery furnace unharmed of the holy men, Shadrach, Meshach and Abednego, convinced Nebuchadnezzar that their God was more powerful than his. Being cast into a fiery furnace was a punishment threatened by many Old Testament prophets.

Fifty million St Bernard dogs can't be wrong. 64 p126. PGW twist on a popular 1920s song 'Fifty Million Frenchmen Can't Be Wrong', a phrase brought back by US servicemen in 1918. Cole Porter (1891–1964) wrote a show by that name in 1929. When Texas Guinan (see BUTTER AND EGG MAN) and her troupe of girls were refused entry to France in 1931, she told the American Press: "It just shows fifty million Frenchmen can be wrong" and toured her show round the USA with the title 'Too Hot for Paris'.

Fifty minutes without a check. 1 p115 and later. See CHECK.

Fifty-three, There's never a law of God or man runs north of. See LAW OF GOD OR MAN.

Fifty-two today, I'm. 66 p63. See TWENTY-ONE TODAY.

Figaro. Like Figaro, I laugh that I may not weep 28 Preface. From Beaumarchais' script for *The Barber of Seville* Act 1, Sc 2.

Fight. You have fought the good fight 14 p255 and later. B. 2 Timothy. 4.7: "I have fought a good fight, I have finished my course, I have kept the faith." 'Fight the Good Fight' is the motto of the Church Lad's Brigade (see Chap. 11).

Fight it out on these lines if it took all summer, prepared to. 19 p116 and frequent up to 91 p112. Dispatch sent by General U.S. Grant to President Lincoln on 11 May 1864. "I purpose to fight it out on this line, if it takes all summer." PGW gave the attribution to Grant at 91 p112; in his last books, he gave the origins of many of the quotations he used.

Fighting became general again all along the Front. 43 p305. Phrase constantly in the papers during the First World War. A patrol would go out, be spotted, sentries began firing, then the machine-guns and artillery opened up and "fighting became general ..."

Fighting in the last ditch. 38 p32. See DITCH.

Fighting words. These, unfortunately, proved to be f.w. 79 p99. For a long time, the nearest I could get was "them's fighting words" by Yosemite Sam in the Bugs Bunny cartoons. I have since learned the phrase appears in *Gullible's Travels* (1917) by Ring Lardner, whom PGW admired for his splendid use of the vernacular. MTT Richard Vine.

Figure as full of curves as a scenic railway, a. 76 p168. From the splendid Fred ASTAIRE and Jack Buchanan film *The Band Wagon* (1953). MTT Kristin Thompson.

Filmer, Rt Hon A.B. (Cabinet Minister). 43 p18; 93 p24. See Chap. 2.

Filthy. Trying to make a bit of the filthy. 45 p27. The Biblical phrase 'filthy lucre' was so well known, Wodehouse saw no need to amplify it. B. I Peter 5.2 includes the words "not for filthy lucre".

Findeth a wife. Whoso findeth a wife, findeth a good thing 60 p301; 72 p205; findeth a butler 80 p122. B. Proverbs 18.22: "Whoso findeth a wife findeth a good thing, and obtaineth favour of the Lord."

Fine frenzy. Frequent. The quotation "poet's eye in a fine frenzy rolling" sank into the popular consciousness and 'a fine frenzy' became a long-lived cliché. See POET'S EYE ROLLING.

Finely chiselled features. 12 p166 (of Mike Jackson's three-year-old sister) and frequently thereafter, including the abbreviated form of 'f.c.f.'. PGW used the phrase often and usually satirically, mocking the popular clichés introduced by Victorian novelists like Ouida and Marie Corelli. Up to 1939, heroes in romantic novels always wore 'faultless evening dress', looked 'bronzed and fit' and had 'finely chiselled features' (as well as a title, a good income and a Stately Home). Aquiline, bony, Aunt Agatha–like looks were thought to indicate good breeding while the lower classes were depicted as having round, pudding-like features. Such was the assumption in popular fiction.

The last occasion I saw the term used seriously was in the obituary of Princess Ileana of Romania (23 January 1991). The daughter of King Ferdinand and the Queen Marie who made such an impression in the USA (see PGW musical *Rosalie*), the young Princess Ileana was renowned for "her finely chiselled features". On her marriage her official title was Her Imperial and Royal Highness the Most Illustrious Archduchess and Lady … etc. etc. At the end of her life, as Mother Superior of a convent near Pittsburgh, she answered the telephone with a curt "Hapsburg here".

Fines, trousering the. 85 p40. See TROUSERING THE FINES.

Finest hour. This was his 83 p197; my finest hour 97 p42. From Churchill's immortal speech of 18 June 1940 which still stirs the blood. If you don't believe me, consult a history book on Britain's isolation and desperation at that time, then read the speech again. An American historian said it took him twenty years to appreciate how close Britain was to defeat and how important to our survival Churchill's speeches were. "Let us therefore brace ourselves to our duties, and so bear ourselves that, if the British Empire and its Commonwealth last for a thousand years, men will still say: 'This was their finest hour.'"

Fire in his bosom. Can a man take fire in his bosom and his clothes not be burned 61 p143. B. Proverbs 6.27.

Fire into the brown. 12 p198; 57 p111. If there was no definite target to be picked out from the horde charging at you, you told your soldiers to "fire into the brown". In the days before combatants learned to advance in dispersed formation, you were bound to hit somebody. I think the Chinese in the Korean War were the last to launch mass-formation attacks. A young French officer countered this by reverting to similar archaic methods, getting his regiment to fire by volleys, which worked astonishingly well. I remember this because I was severely ticked off by my superiors for practising volley-firing with my platoon. I still think I was right; it was strongly rumoured we were to be sent to Korea.

Fire that glows with heat intense she had turned the hose of common sense, on. 72 p59. G &S. *Iolanthe* Act 2. "On fire that glows / With heat intense, / I turn the hose / Of common sense."

Fire when ready, Gridley. 25 p104. Admiral Dewey's famous order at the battle of Manila Bay 1898 (Spanish-American War).

Firm flesh. Lots of firm flesh 63 p53. Until the slimming craze began c.1924, many UK magazines advertised products to put on weight. One such was Sargol:

Are You Too Thin?
SARGOL will make you nice and plump.
Would a little more flesh make you more stylish and attractive?
If so, you should try SARGOL.
This Coupon entitles any thin person to one 2/6d package of SARGOL.

First-class earl who keeps his carriage. See EARL WHO KEEPS.

First fine careless rapture. See RAPTURE.

First in war, first in peace, first in the hearts … 40 p92. Henry Lee speaking of George Washington in 1799.

First, last and all the time, Bertram Wooster. 51 p273; and yours to command Ickenham 84 p37. Possibly PGW's recollection of Milton's *Paradise Lost* Bk 5, l.165. "Him first, him last, him midst and without end."

First Murderer. Instead of looking like a First Murderer, he looked like a rather kindlier Second Murderer 71 p196. I thought this was just a PGW humorous crack, but he was right. See S. *Richard III* 1.4. The scene ends with the Second Murderer repenting of his actions and the First Murderer calling him a coward.

First that ever burst. PGW ref lost. Coleridge's *The Rime of the Ancient Mariner*: "We were the first that ever burst / Into that silent sea."

Fish. Does eating fish help the brain? Bertie Wooster attributes Jeeves' intelligence to his consumption of fish. In 1995, Dr Sanders, professor of nutrition at King's College, London, confirmed that the fatty acid (DHA) in salmon, trout, mackerel ('oily' fish) improves one's powers of reasoning. He agreed with Bertie Wooster's theory and suggested that Wodehouse had heard it as one of the 'old wives' tales' which scientists mock till twenty years of expensive research reveal the silly old women were right after all. There are so many instances of this that someone has suggested doctors should have such traditional aphorisms included in their training courses. It would save billions of pounds.

Fish, fellow named. A man who … mistook the coal scuttle for a mad dog and tried to shoot it with the fire-tongs. Fellow named Fish 90 p131. This very late reference to Major General Fish, brother-in-law of Lord Emsworth, puzzled me. Maybe PGW simply liked the anecdote which originally appeared in

Heavy Weather at page 206 (chapter 10).

Fish gotta swim, birds gotta fly … 70 p24. Song 'Can't Help Lovin' Dat Man of Mine' from Jerome Kern's *Show Boat.*

Fish slice. Along with toast racks, the fish slice became a traditional British wedding present in the late 19th century. Resembling a spatula, it is a knife with a very broad blade used to serve 'slices' of fish which would fall off a normal knife. I am told it is uncommon in the USA. See WEDDING PRESENTS.

Fisher (Lord). 11 p32. Strong-minded First Sea Lord (Royal Navy) 1904–10 and 1914–15.

Fitch, Clyde. C.F. had a play with the word 'damn' in it 88 p283. This American playwright (1865–1909) wrote thirty plays in twenty years. The one that caused the fuss was *The City* (1909), in which someone said "God damn you", purportedly the first time 'damn' had been spoken on the New York stage. George Bernard SHAW's *Pygmalion* of 1914 caused an equal fuss in London when Eliza Doolittle swept off the stage with the words: "Not bloody likely. I'm going in a taxi." My parents would not allow me to use the word 'bloody' but did not object to 'not Pygmalion likely'.

Fitch, Sir Abercrombie. 91 p169. See ABERCROMBIE & FITCH.

Fitzsimmons, (Bob). 4 p105 and later. This boxer (1863–1917) administered a left jab into Jim Corbett's solar plexus on St Patrick's Day in 1897, winning him the heavyweight championship.

Five Orange Pips (the Sherlock Holmes story). 15 p275; 'Adventure of the Five Orange Pips' 92 p132. PGW's reference at 92 p132 is correct, but I wonder why he did not say that Crispin Scrope's theory was based on Doyle's 'A Scandal in Bohemia'.

Five-Year-Planner, this bally. 51 p182. From around 1930 to its collapse in the late 1980s, the rigid U.S.S.R. State-controlled economy set out its agricultural and economic targets in a series of Five-Year Plans, and the phrase became well-known. PGW was merely confirming Brinkley's political outlook. He had been described as "this blighted Bolshevik" a few lines before.

Fives bat. Six of the best with a fives bat 41 p297; 67 p15. Fives is a game akin to handball, i.e. hitting a ball with your hand against a wall. There are three major versions: Rugby fives; Eton fives, and Winchester fives. Gloves are worn to protect the hands of players. In one of his superlative pieces on Wodehouse, Richard Usborne regretted that he had not managed to find out what a fives bat looked like. I also tried many sources, including the UK governing body, but got nowhere.

I found the answer by sheer luck when I gave a talk at Radley College and concluded by mentioning my problem. The following morning, the College Librarian showed me a fives bat and was kind enough to send a photograph of it. (*See photo opposite*.)

The use of a bat for fives seems to have died out around 1875–85 but, as can be seen, it was a perfect instrument for applying to the rear ends of boys

A fives bat

(Picture by courtesy of Radley College)

to inculcate good behaviour and respect for their elders and betters. At Radley its use was not completely arbitrary. Though difficult to see in the picture, usages were recorded, i.e. Smith got 3, Jones got 6. Robinson got 9 etc.

Compared with a walking stick or cane, which could sting like an adder, a flat-sided fives bat was a mild chastisement. At Winchester (see Chap. 3) in the 1890s, the prefects used to bend the victim over and draw a line in chalk on his rear end to aim at. The headmaster found out, was horrified at this sadism, and banned the practice. The prefects obeyed him. No chalk lines were drawn on the trousers, but the head had said nothing to stop the first prefect chalking his cane so that a line appeared after the first stroke.

Flag days. At 61 p229, Ukridge complains about the plethora of flag days: Rose Day, Pansy Day, Daisy Day etc. Flag-selling began in the first month of the Great War, August 1914. Mrs George, wife of a Great Western Railway driver, made some little flags for her children from matchsticks and scraps of red, white and blue ribbons. Her milkman saw them and suggested she sell them in aid of the Prince of Wales National Relief Fund for dependants of servicemen. Mrs George was thanked by Queen Mary, and the first national Flag Day was held in aid of the Belgian Relief Fund in October 1914. By 1918 there seemed to be flag days every week; for the blind, for orphans, the limbless, refugees, every conceivable cause. The practice continued throughout the 1920s until consumer resistance (no doubt from people like Ukridge) reduced the number of appeals. I have a note that flag-sellers were also later made to stay in one spot, where they could be evaded if necessary.

Flagpole sitter. Trying to exchange thoughts with a f.s. 55 p118. To see how long you could sit on top of a flagpole was a craze of the 1920s like the Charleston, cloche hats or marathon dancing.

Flamberge. 57 p82. Charlemagne's favourite sword. I had not appreciated the importance of swords in mediaeval Europe till I looked this one up. Brewer's invaluable *Dictionary of Phrase and Fable* lists thirty-eight famous swords and their makers. See also Lord Ickenham's great sponge Joyeuse.

Flaming sword. Across the threshold of this Eden the ginger whiskers of Angus McAllister lay like a f.s. 53 p158; whipped out a f.s., and drove you from the garden 65 p132. See Angel with the flaming sword.

Flannelled fools. 2 p72; 3 p18. Kipling's 'The Islanders' (1902): "With the flannelled fools at the wicket or the muddied oafs at the goals."

Flap his wings and crow. He wanted, as it were, to flap his wings and crow 7 p221. Chanticleer is as near as I can get.

Flashman. 3 p279. The bully in *Tom Brown's Schooldays* whose later adventures were chronicled by George Macdonald Fraser (1925–2008). If you do not know much 19th-century history, Fraser's Flashman stories are an excellent way to learn.

Flaubert, Gustave. 38 p190 up to 97 p62. Flaubert (1821–80) was noted for his highly polished style. Henry James was another who agonised for hours over the right word.

Fleagle, Evil Eye (a full whammy). 70 p100. A baddie in the 'Li'l Abner' cartoon strip by Al Capp. If E.E. Fleagle gave you one of his looks, you were in trouble. His single whammy, i.e. a piercing venomous glance, cast a spell on you. His worst, the quadruple whammy, could melt a battleship. A man not to offend.

Fleeing like the wicked man in the Psalms. 34 p177. I couldn't find it in the Psalms and I suggest a better bet is B. Proverbs 28.1: "The wicked flee when no man pursueth."

Flesh, all flesh is as grass. 25 p312 and often later. See All flesh.

Flesh creep. I wants to make your f.c. 87 p208. See D. *The Pickwick Papers*, chap 8.

Flesh, firm. 63 p53. See FIRM FLESH.

Flesh is weak. See SPIRIT WAS WILLING.

Flesh, too, too solid. Some of that too, too solid flesh is certainly going to melt 80 p206. S. *Hamlet* 1.2: "O! that this too too solid flesh would melt."

Fletcherize. 20 p186; 30 p41. This was once a common term. Horace Fletcher (1849–1919) of Lawrence, Mass., a businessman-turned-nutritionist, reckoned that he kept healthy by chewing everything thirty-three times. He made many converts including Edison, Rockefeller, and Mr Gladstone. Chewing food thirty-three times is mentioned frequently in PGW.

Fling wide the gates. See GATES.

Flint, Captain. 43 p27. A pirate in R.L. Stevenson's *Treasure Island*.

Flood. Taken at the flood leads on to fortune 33 p125. See TIDE.

Floor of heaven is thick inlaid with patines of bright gold ... 70 p111. See PATINES OF BRIGHT GOLD.

Florodora, the famous sextette in. 30 p88. The musical comedy *Florodora* (London 1899, New York 1900) had a song 'Tell Me, Pretty Maiden, Are There Any More At Home Like You?' which swept the world. Every theatrical landlady of the 1920s–30s reputedly claimed to have been in it, and I have a note that the original New York sextette all married millionaires. The show was written by Owen Hall (James Davis), a famous Pelican with whom PGW worked in 1904. See Chap. 5.

Florizel, Prince. See PRINCE FLORIZEL.

Flower, meanest. See MEANEST FLOWER.

Flower of American youth was emigrating. See AMERICAN YOUTH.

Flower pots. 32 p256. See SAY IT WITH.

Flowers at our feet. We could not see what f. were at our feet etc. 62 p123. Keats' 'Ode to a Nightingale': "I cannot see what flowers are at my feet, / Nor what soft incense hangs upon the boughs."

Flowers in May, welcome as the. The proverb "fresh as the flowers in May" goes back to 1566 and was revived in the 1901 song by Dan J. Sullivan.

Flowing bowl. 76 p22 and elsewhere. PGW needed only these two words for his contemporaries to pick up the reference. This is an old English folksong which I sang in my childish treble, and I am sure he did as well. It runs: "Come Landlord fill the flowing bowl, Until it doth run over, ... For tonight we'll merry, merry be, Tomorrow we'll be sober." An odd song to teach eight-year-olds, but I still remember it delighting our proud parents as we trilled it at the tops of our voices. Drinking songs seem to be acceptable so long as they are traditional Olde Englishe. Perhaps it's like swearing — if it's Shakespeare, it doesn't count.

Fluff in your latchkey. 55 p42. See SKIN OFF YOUR NOSE.

Flushing the brow, Like a full-blown rose. 27 p235. See THOUGHT CAME LIKE.

Fly oceans and things and cross Africa on foot and what not (Clarice Fitch used to). 57 p166. See Chap. 22.

Fly through the air with the greatest of ease. 76 p165. See DARING YOUNG MAN.

Flying like the youthful hart or roe over the hills where spices grow. 76 p100; 80 p151. Isaac WATTS' hymn 'The Strength of Christ's Love'.

Flying wedge. 63 p17. An American football term. This game was copied from Rugger and many variations were introduced over the years to make it more attractive to American fans. Around 1895, the rules allowed one side to grab the ball, form a solid block of the whole team with the ball in the middle, and just march up the field in wedge formation. Apart from making the game very dull, so many deaths resulted (broken necks and backs) that President Theodore Roosevelt intervened to get flying wedges banned.

Flynn, Errol. A dashing man 70p161; in like Flynn 87 p109. Handsome film star (1909–59). The phrase 'In like Flynn' became popular after a scandal in his 'active' social life.

Foam of perilous seas. See SILVER BELLS.

Foch, Ferdinand. A plan F. might have been proud of 43 p52. This French general (1851–1929) halted the German advance on the Marne in 1914.

Foe. I fear no f. in shining armour (though his lance be bright and keen). Frequent. Popular Victorian drawing-room ballad (1876) by Edward Oxenford, it is in the 1907 Army & Navy catalogue under 'Standard Songs'. 26 p248 has "Adjust the impression that I fear any Goble in shining armour because I don't."

Folded tent. Folded up like an arab tent 44 p307; it has folded its tents like the Arabs and silently stolen away 76 p138. See ARAB TENT.

Follies girl. A Ziegfeld Follies girl who had been left out in the rain 89 p46. See FOLLIES, PROMOTED.

Follies On The Roof. 23 p220. There was a New York nightspot by this name in 1916. It cashed in on the popularity of Flo ZIEGFELD's famous series of Follies shows which began in 1907.

Follies, promoted clothes-prop from the. 30 p102. A girl from Ziegfeld's Follies who couldn't act, sing or dance but looked gorgeous. The equivalent in London were the Gaiety Girls who played 'thinking' parts, i.e. all they had to do was to come on stage and look beautiful. See also ZIEGFELD, FLORENZ.

Follow the green line. 51 p26. Apparently it is common in American hospitals for coloured lines to be painted on the floor showing the way to different departments. In Boston, I followed the red line painted on the pavement which takes the pedestrian to historic sites around the city.

Follow through. It's all in the follow through 63 p243; and later. Vital when hitting people with pistols, kicking young Edwin, coshing Spode, beating gongs, pushing policemen into ponds or hitting drunks with your umbrella. This was a golfing mantra of the 1920s–30s. If you didn't 'follow through', you got nowhere. See 'Leave It to Algy': "In hitting men with Homburg hats over the head, the follow-through is everything."

Followed the gleam. See GLEAM.

Fons et origo. 64 p253; 68 p101 and elsewhere. Latin tag. The beginning/source of something — literally the fount and origin. 'Fons et origo mali' (malum = a bad thing) at 73 p45 is Jeeves' admission that he was the fount and origin of the current unhappy state of affairs.

Fool some of the people some of the time. 19 p3 and later. Abraham Lincoln's famous dictum of 8 September 1858: "You can fool all of the people some of the time and some of the people all of the time, but you cannot fool all of the people all of the time."

Fools-there-was. 18 p72. See KIPLING's 'The Vampire'. First words: "A fool there was." (Third line is "A rag and a bone and a hank of hair".)

Foot of the white man has not trod nor the Gospel preached, where. 44 p97. This ought to be KIPLING, but the nearest I can find is a poem by C. Mackay : "Valleys where the white man's foot, / Ne'er treads …"

Football. 43 p294. Soccer (round ball) and Rugger (oval ball) developed into their present forms in the 19th century, though there are other versions still played at various schools. PGW was a keen Rugger player at Dulwich and played for the Hong Kong and Shanghai Bank as well. In *Very Good, Jeeves*, Tuppy Glossop plays for Upper Bleaching against Hockley-cum-Meston in a match which originated in the reign of Henry VIII. Jeeves tells Bertie that the game then lasted from noon till sundown, covered several square miles and seven deaths resulted. I am delighted to state that several of these historic 'mass' football matches are still played. In the Derbyshire town of Ashbourne a match dating back 800 years is played every Shrove Tuesday; it involves hundreds of players trying to get the ball between goal posts set three miles apart. The newspapers report it is "played with few rules" though "murder, manslaughter and the use of automobiles is forbidden".

Footnotes. 78 pp 9–11. I would not have put in this note if the newspapers had not reported that an apparently well-educated British TV celebrity had failed to win a million pounds for charity by having no idea of the meaning of the words 'E pluribus unum'. To save the time of the reader in looking up dictionaries of quotations, I shall just say of PGW's footnotes in *Over Seventy*:

Page 9 Footnote 4. The *King Lear* ref. is Act 1, Sc 2, l.169.

Page 10 Footnote 1. It was Gaul, not Theodora, which was divided into three parts (see IN TRES PARTES DIVISA) and *argumentum ad hominem* is covered at ARGUMENTUM. The *usque ad hoc* means roughly 'till now/ to this point.' It is only fair to add that Theodora (500–547 A.D.) proved to be a strong-minded, sensible and politically skilful spouse of the Emperor Justinian but is still commonly remembered as having been a courtesan before she hooked the emperor.

Page 10 Footnote 4. I regret to say that a basset does not exist. The name 'basset hound' is simply a variation of the French 'basse hound' i.e. a dog with a low back.

Page 11. Footnote 1. A fardel was a heavy load you carried on your back.

Force, irresistible (and immovable object). See IRRESISTIBLE FORCE.

Ford. Called a Ford a Ford 38 p3. Written when Henry Ford had put the mass-produced car (15 million Model Ts) within the reach of all. There was no stigma attached to having one, but it was definitely considered inferior to Daimlers, Astons and the dozens of other more expensive models. It is PGW's twist on the claim of plain-speaking people that they call a spade a spade. See also Browning's 'Aristophanes' Apology': "We've still our stage where truth calls a spade a spade." The phrase was originally coined by Erasmus as a term of pity for uneducated peasants who had poor command of language. The reversal of meaning came about 200 years later in reaction to the pretentious flowery speech that had become fashionable.

Ford, Henry. Or any other confirmed peacemaker 36 p180. One of the forgotten incidents of the First World War was Ford's (1863–1947) attempt to stop it in 1915 by chartering a 'Peace Ship' and sending it to Europe full of famous philosophers, clergymen etc. whose influence would, he hoped, bring Europe to its senses.

Forde, Florrie. 79 p180. Famous UK music hall singer (1876–1940).

Forefathers, our rude. 21 p76. Gray's 'Elegy in a Country Churchyard'. "each in his narrow cell for ever laid, / The rude forefathers of the hamlet sleep."

Foreign Legion, that cohort of the damned. 55 p177 and later. P.C. Wren's 1920s novels of the Foreign Legion, in which he had served, were best-sellers in the UK. His three best-known are *Beau Geste, Beau Sabreur* and *Beau Ideal*. Ronald Colman (1926) and Gary Cooper (1939) played the Beau Geste role in popular films. Mervyn Potter (71 p129) intended to "join the Foreign Legion, that cohort of the damned where broken men toil and die and, dying, forget". See also COHORT OF THE DAMNED.

Forever Amber. 70 p182; 80 p25. This 1944 novel by Kathleen Winsor of goings-on at the Court of Charles II was considered highly scandalous when it came out, as was the later film of the same name.

Forgot to duck. 82 p110. After Jack Dempsey's sensational defeat by Gene Tunney in 1926, his comment to his wife — "Honey, I forgot to duck" — became famous. The phrase came back into popular use when President Reagan quoted it to his wife after he was shot in 1981. See also DEMPSEY and EUGENE.

Forgotten Man, the. 69 p238. On 7 April 1932, F.D. Roosevelt made his famous 'Forgotten Man' speech. Setting out his New Deal, a vast programme of public works, he spoke of "the forgotten man at the bottom of the economic pyramid". The popularity of the term was strengthened by the superb song 'Remember My Forgotten Man' in the film *Gold Diggers of 1933*. (Roosevelt had probably read *The Forgotten Man and Other Essays* (1919) by the academic and political scientist William Sumner.)

Forlorn. The word was like a knell 33 p45; 40 p62. A PGW misquote or a misprint. From Keats' 'Ode to a Nightingale'; it should be 'bell', not 'knell'.

Form, bad. Frequent. Bad manners; saying/doing things that offend the social code.

Formula, attempts to find a. 72 p47. A newspaper cliché of the 1950s. During the Cold War and labour disputes of the time, statesmen/trade union leaders etc. were constantly trying to 'find a formula'. Similar to AGONIZING REAPPRAISAL.

Forsyte, Soames. 37 p135; 46 p34. In the 1920s–30s, John Galsworthy's *Forsyte Saga* books were read by everybody. The materialistic Soames Forsyte was the main protagonist.

Fort, Charles. 86 p148. This eccentric newspaperman (1874–1932) specialised in collecting remarkable facts and stories to demonstrate the ignorance of scientists and their inability to explain many natural phenomena. His admirers founded the Fortean Society in 1931 and began a magazine in 1937 called *Doubt*, dedicated to the rebuttal of scientific dogma.

Fort Sumter. First gun fired from F.S. 15 p87. 4.30 A.M. on 12 April 1861 saw the beginning of the American Civil War when the Confederates opened fire, not from but at the Union-held Fort Sumter. Constitutionally, this was a very important point since Lincoln was able to claim that the Confederates were rebels who had attacked Union forces.

Forth, Gilbert's Policeman. 9 p61. See Gilbert's 'Peter the Wag' (*Bab Ballads*).

Fortnum & Mason. 45 p199. This very superior establishment in Piccadilly, founded nearly 300 years ago, is considered by many to be the original of DUFF & TROTTER. See Chap. 31.

Fortune, Reggie. 64 p230. One of the gentleman-detectives so popular in the 1920s, of whom Lord Peter WIMSEY is now probably the best remembered. Fortune was created by H.C. Bailey (1878–1961).

Fortune to the test, put his (to win or lose it all). 22 p3 and elsewhere. A common misquotation of MONTROSE.

Fosdyke, Captain Jack. See Chap. 28.

Fought the good fight. See FIGHT.

Four ale bar. In the days when English pubs had different bars for different classes of customer, (Private/Snug/Saloon/Public), 'four ale bar' was used for the cheapest (Public) bar where beer was fourpence a quart. The rise in price from twopence to twopence ha'penny a pint in 1912 aroused nationwide protest. The term 'four-ale bar' persisted for forty years, long after its meaning had been forgotten. Similarly, Cambridge May Balls have for decades been held in June and it had become the custom to pay 'morning calls' in the late afternoon twenty years before the young Wodehouse had to make them in his early or London period (1900–10).

Four Arts Ball in Paris. 55 p89; 65 p69. In the period 1870–1910, Paris students organised this annual event, which was notorious in the UK for the 'goings-on' that were firmly believed to, well, go on. From memory, the four arts were painting, sculpture, poetry and literature.

Four Hundred, The. 15A p114 and often later. A term that came to mean 'High Society'. When Mrs Astor was ruling New York Society with a rod of iron in the 1880s, her social secretary, Ward McAllister, said that New York Society comprised those people invited to her famous annual ball at 350 Fifth Avenue. He told the Press "there are only about four hundred people in fashionable New York Society". The term became immortal and is still used by sleazy nightclubs and gambling joints around the world. See also DIAMOND HORSESHOE and SUBMERGED TENTH.

Four mile radius, the. 14 p22; 23 p107. The famous black London taxis (Hackney carriages) have been strictly regulated since their predecessors began 300 years ago. Cab and taxi fares were fixed for travel within a four-mile radius from Charing Cross. If you wanted to travel beyond that, you had to strike a specific bargain with the driver and they could refuse to carry you. See also CABS.

Four Million, The. 24 p12. O. Henry (1862–1910) adapted the phrase 'the Four Hundred' to write a series of superb short stories about ordinary New Yorkers, under the title *The Four Million*. The term became synonymous with the population of the city. See also FOUR HUNDRED.

Four point seven. 7 p71. The 4.7-inch gun was the standard minor armament of the Royal Navy in 1900. They were the guns taken across country by train and ox-cart to save Ladysmith in the Boer War.

Four stout rogues in buckram let drive at me. 37 Preface. S. *1 Henry IV* 2.4.

Fourth Dimension. 55 p97; 56 p78. Einstein's Theory of Relativity, time, light etc. aroused heated discussion in the 1920s. *Punch* (19 Dec 1923) summed up the popular confusion:

> There was a young lady called Bright
> Whose speed was far faster than light.
> She set out one day
> In a relative way,
> And returned home the previous night.

Fourth of June, the bally rot that used to take place on. 15A p246. Psmith is referring to the festivities that occur at Eton on June 4 each year. These include a regatta, cricket matches, prize-givings and countless other activities. PGW described the influx of parents, brothers and sisters in 'The Fourth of June', part of the short-lived revue *Nuts and Wine* that he wrote with C.H. Bovill in January 1914.

Fowler's book on English usage. 94 p102. Henry Fowler (1858–1933) brought out his magisterial *Modern English Usage* in 1926.

Fox, Charles James. Caught a Rowcester cheating at cards in Watier's 73 p152. Fox (1749–1806), a brilliant Radical politician, was a gambler, statesman, drunkard and superb orator. ("Unless pie-eyed, you cannot hope to grip.")

Fox gnaw his tender young stomach, let a (Spartan boy). 25 p204 and later. Retaining your composure under the most trying of circumstances. The regime for boys in Sparta in ancient Greece was tough, to put it mildly. They were not punished for theft, they were punished for being found out. A Spartan boy stole a fox, hid it under his shirt and, rather than be found out, let it bite into his stomach and kill him. I have known the story all my life but was unable to confirm it. MTT my granddaughter Rachael Murphy for doing so. (Do not confuse with vultures gnawing at your bosom, an entirely different matter. See PROMETHEUS.)

Fra Angelican, How. 3 p260. The quotation is from G&S *Patience* Act 2. *Patience* was Gilbert's satire on the Aesthetic Movement of the time (Oscar Wilde et al.), and among the Movement's favourite painters was Fra Angelico (1387–1455).

Frank and Ernest. 29 p100. This was a famous 1920s comic duologue, similar to Pat and Mike in *The Mating Season*. For some reason, one line lingered on in the UK till my boyhood. A friend would approach you and say he had something serious to discuss, he wanted you to be frank and earnest. And you replied: "All right. I'll be Frank and you be Ernest." At the age of ten, this was terribly witty. See also TINNEY, FRANK.

Frank, forthright and fearless. 88 p11. PGW used this several times and I have been unable to trace it, although I remember it from the 1950s. I am sure it was the motto/sub-title of some newspaper or scandal magazine. See AMUSE for a similar example.

Frankenstein. 16 p129 and elsewhere. See Mary Shelley's 1818 novel. My favourite PGW Frankenstein quote illustrates the purported divide between Old Etonians and the rest of the world. In *Laughing Gas*, at p299, Eggy Mannering discusses marriage with Joey Cooley. Joey says: "Looks don't mean a thing. Didn't Frankenstein get married?"

"Did he?" said Eggy. "I don't know. I never met him. Harrow man, I expect."

Freckled like a pard. 96 p5. From Keats' 'Lamia' pt 1: "Striped like a zebra, freckled like a pard" (a leopard). Similar to BEARDED.

'Freddie, Oofy and the Beef Trust'. Short story title. See BEEF TRUST.

Frederick the Infallible, I am never wrong. 45 p33. G&S Patience Act 1: "I am called 'Archibald the All-Right!' — for I am infallible."

Free Foresters. 12 p211. This famous wandering cricket club was founded in 1856 and is still a major force in amateur cricket. MTT Bill Tyrwhitt-Drake, a Wodehousean and Free Forester.

French general who brought up the reserves to the Battle of the Marne in taxi-cabs. 57 p277. This was General Gallieni, Military Governor of Paris in September 1914.

French, Inspector. 64 p230. Famous 1920s fictional detective created by Freeman Wills Crofts (1879–1957).

French Leave. MTT Anne-Marie Chanet and Mark Hodson for pointing out the close resemblance between this novel and the plot of *The Gibson Girls*, the show Wodehouse and Bolton tried to sell to Ziegfeld. Three girls living on a farm inherit a small legacy and decided to take it in turns to pretend to be rich and find a husband etc. etc. See Chaps 8 & 20. The expression has nearly died away now, but 'to take French leave' meant to desert your post/ leave your job/ go home without permission. In fairness, I have to add that in French, the equivalent expression is 'aller à l'Anglais'.

Fresh Air London children. 53 p140; 61 p239. The Fresh Air Fund to give deprived London children fresh air, i.e. a holiday in the country, was founded by *Pearson's Weekly* in 1892. *Punch* took up the theme with a cartoon based on the notice seen in London parks, 'Do Not Walk On The Grass'. It showed a little ragamuffin looking at large, empty open fields and exclaiming in awe: "Cor, Miss! Are we reelly allowed to walk on it?"

Fresh fields (and pastures new). 24 p227. A common misquote of Milton's 'Lycidas': "fresh woods and pastures new."

Fretful midges. 63 p10. See MIDGES.

Fretful porpentine. See PORPENTINE.

Freud. 35 p137. The theories of Sigmund Freud (1856–1939) and Carl Jung (1875–1961) were greeted with a healthy sceptism by many in Britain.

Frew Dat brick, who. See GOLLY, MASSA.

Friar's Balsam. 94 p164. A well-known proprietary remedy for colds. Camphor is a major element in its curative effect.

Friend is a masterpiece of Nature, a. 35 p240. Emerson's 'Essay on Friendships': "A friend may be well reckoned the masterpiece of Nature."

Friend of all the world, the little. 58 p41 and later. No, not Pollyanna. It is Kim from KIPLING's *Kim*, chap. 1.

Friend that sticketh closer than a brother. 26 p16. B. Proverbs 18.24: "A man that hath friends must shew himself friendly; and there is a friend that sticketh closer than a brother."

Friends of my youth. 7 p10. Possibly inspired by ch.3 ("Of Two Friends of my Youth") from A.C. Doyle's *Micah Clarke* (1889).

Frietchie, Barbara. 96 p6. From Ogden Nash's 'Taboo to Boot', which begins:

One bliss for which
There is no match
Is when you itch
To up and scratch.

MTT David Lull.

Every American knows Whittier's poem 'Barbara Frietchie'. For English readers unfamiliar with it, I should explain that the poem recounts a dramatic incident during the American Civil War (1861–65). Stonewall Jackson (a Southern general) was taking his army north and marched through the enemy town of Frederick. Seeing a Union flag flying from a window, his soldiers fired at it. According to Whittier, Miss Frietchie then leaned out the window and waved the flag defiantly while uttering the immortal words: "Shoot if you must this old gray head, But spare your country's flag!" And Jackson, properly ashamed, gave the order: "Who touches a hair of yon grey head, Dies like a dog. March on!"

(American readers should look away at this point.) In fact, Miss Frietchie was a very old lady and had no idea who the soldiers were. She merely enjoyed the sight of so many young men in uniform passing under her window and thought it was some kind of parade. She grabbed a flag, waved it to show her appreciation, and Jackson's soldiers, realising the situation, politely ignored her. But, as the man said in the film *The Man Who Shot Liberty Valance,* if the facts conflict with the legend, print the legend.

If you visit the house today, you will see Winston Churchill souvenirs on sale. They commemorate an occasion of which the town is very proud. Churchill came to tour the house and, as news of his visit spread, a crowd gathered outside. When he came out, he delighted them by reciting the entire poem from the doorstep with all the dramatic intonation he could give it.

Frightful fiend doth close behind him tread, a. 17 p4 and later. From Coleridge's *The Rime of the Ancient Mariner*, pt 6. Do not confuse with the foul fiend (APOLLYON) in *Pilgrim's Progress*.

Frinton and its ozone. 94 p103. The seaside resorts on the East coast of England are, let us say, not quite as warm as those on the south or west coasts, but have a strong east wind which is meant to do one good. See 'BRAMLEY IS SO BRACING'.

Fritz. Everything's on the fritz nowadays. 34 p122. An American expression, dating from c.1902, meaning everything is in a state of disorder, of chaos.

Frock coat. 7 p239. You did *not* wear a frock coat in the country except for weddings, funerals and church on Sundays. In London, yes, but not in the country. See Chap. 6.

Frohman, Charles. 11 p24; 74 p122. Frohman (1860–1915), a highly-respected American impresario, took many English plays to New York. He died on the *Lusitania* when the Germans torpedoed her in 1915.

From ledger to ledger/sport to sport they hurry me to stifle my regret. 14 p118; 71 p126; 85 p10 and elsewhere. See HURRY ME.

From the grave to the gay, etc. See GRAVE TO THE GAY.

Front, fair. His large fair front and eye sublime declared Absolute rule 60 p252. Milton's *Paradise Lost* Bk 4, l.299.

Froth blowing at the Carmody Arms. 40 p119. Drinking beer; from the head of froth there should be on a properly-poured pint. PGW got the phrase from the Froth Blowers, a charity formed in the 1920s to collect money for good causes in pubs. Since the charity encouraged beer drinking, it did very well.

Frozen Assets (US title *Biffen's Millions*). A phrase coined by the American Press to describe the money 'frozen' when F.D. Roosevelt closed every bank for ten days in March 1933.

Fry, C.B. 10 (frequently); 11 p12; 12 p1. At the beginning of the 20th century, when amateurs were pre-eminent in sports and games, C.B. Fry (1872–1956) was the most admired amateur of all. At Oxford, he got his Blue for cricket, athletics and association football. In his last year there, he put down his cigar and set a world long-jump record that stood for years. Three years later he played in the association football Cup Final. He got his County cricket cap in 1894, played for his country when he was 27, and captained England when they defeated Australia and South Africa in 1912. He was offered the throne of Albania, but had enough sense to turn it down.

FRZS. Pilbeam was one 42 p249. FRZS stands for Fellow of the Royal Zoological Society. When the London Zoological Gardens ('the Zoo') was founded in 1828, the Society needed money to pay for it and a sizeable donation made you a member of it — a Fellow. The public paid an admission fee to enter the Zoo, but Fellows entered free and, up to 1955, were allowed in on Sundays when the public were not. To become a Fellow became a harmless sign of social respectability akin to getting a ticket to the Royal Enclosure at Ascot or joining the MCC. PGW was persuaded to become a Fellow in the 1920s. One writer records him looking at one of those apes with coloured stripes on an embarrassing part of its anatomy and remarking: "That ape is wearing his club colours in the wrong place." The story was corroborated by an Australian Wodehousean in 2004.

Fu Manchu, Dr. 80 p154; 81 p79. This fiendish arch-criminal was the creation of Sax Rohmer (1886–1959). From 1913, readers revelled in the stories of this villain whose evil plans to take over or destroy the world took suspense to its limits.

Fuel some of the people some of the time. 40 p92. See FOOL SOME.

Fugitive from a chain gang. 70 p100. *I Am a Fugitive from a Chain Gang* was Warner Brothers' 'powerful' film hit of 1932.

Full many a glorious morning have I seen (flattering the mountain tops with sovereign eye and then turn into a rather nasty afternoon). 59 p83; 65 p138 and elsewhere. This is from Shakespeare's *Sonnets* 33, which begins: "Full many a glorious morning have I seen / Flatter the mountain-tops with sovereign eye."

Full of strange oaths. 12 p70; 59 p184. See BEARDED LIKE A PARD.

Fur and whiskers. Oh! My fur and whiskers! 86 p128. See the White Rabbit in Lewis Carroll's *Alice in Wonderland.*

Furnace. I had passed through the f. 51 p16. Difficult to decide whether PGW was referring to the Biblical story (see FIERY FURNACE) or was using the analogy of steel/iron being tempered in a furnace to give it strength, hardness, etc. I suggest the Bible is more likely. See also 'TRIED IN THE FURNACE'.

Fuss and feathers. 84 p26. Needless fuss, unnecessary formality. The term stems from the fan of ostrich feathers carried by debutantes for their presentation at Court until 1939 and the long feathers on the hats worn with full diplomatic dress. US General Winfield Scott (1786–1866), an elderly but far-sighted strategist, was derided as 'Old Fuss and Feathers'.

Fussy man. He was not a f.m. 67 p152; No one can call Bertram Wooster a fussy man 68 p24; 96 p5. A.A. Milne's 'The King's Breakfast': "Nobody … could call me a fussy man."

Futurist pictures. 17 p 63. This artistic movement was highly regarded by the glitterati in the period up to 1914.

Fuzzy Wuzzy. 29 p105. KIPLING's poem 'Fuzzy-Wuzzy' paid tribute to the Sudanese warriors the British Army (including Winston Churchill) had fought in the 1890s. The name, given to them in respect, not derision, came from their tightly curled, frizzed hair styles.

G

(MTT = My thanks to)

Gable, Clark. 54 p225 and later. This handsome film actor (1901–60) once caused a panic in the American clothing industry. When he took his shirt off in *It Happened One Night* (1934) to reveal not his vest/undershirt but his manly chest, sales of undershirts dropped by 40% across America.

Gaby and a guffin. 7 p163; 18 p125 and later. Both words are still in use among Scots. A gaby is an empty-headed, talkative person while a guffin is a goop or simpleton.

Gadarene swine. The Wrecking Crew (see Chap. 27) are expected to hurl themselves into the lake on the second hole 37 p116; the Gadarene swine, rounding into the straight, must have experienced the same uneasy sensation 63 p146; 68 p49; and later. B. Mark 5.13. Jesus, having cast out devils, let them enter into a herd of swine who promptly threw themselves into the sea.

Gaff, blow the. See BLOW THE GAFF.

Gaiety Theatre. 14 p80 and later. See Chap. 24.

Gainsborough's Girl In Blue. 92 p31. I knew his 'Blue Boy' and his 'Pink Boy' but have been unable to trace his Girl in Blue. A PGW invention, but it was so plausible I tried to find it.

Galahad, Sir. 13 p43 and later. T. *Idylls of the King*. Galahad was the only knight to find the Holy Grail.

Galatea. 32 p21; 63 p87; 66 p166 and later. In Greek legend, Pygmalion made a female statue (Galatea) so beautiful that he fell in love with it and the gods made it come to life for him. See also PIG SOMETHING.

Galba. 70 p174. As PGW says, he was assassinated, as was Vitellius the same year (69 A.D.). It was a bad year for Roman emperors. Otho (another one) killed himself to save VITELLIUS doing it for him.

Gall and wormwood. 93 p62. B. Lamentations 3.19: "Remembering mine affliction and my misery, the wormwood and the gall."

Galsworthy, John. 46 p34, p40 and p83. This English author (1867–1933) is now best remembered for his series *The Forsyte Saga*. See FORSYTE, SOAMES.

Galumphing all over England. 57 p15; 92 p35. See 'Jabberwocky' in Lewis Carroll's *Alice Through the Looking-Glass*, where the Jabberwock's slayer "went galumphing back".

Game, the whole game, and nothing but the game. 3 p270; the shark and nothing but the shark 52 p132; the aunt, the whole aunt and nothing but the aunt 65 p192; the butler, the whole butler and nothing but the butler 82 p54. From the oath taken by witnesses in English courts that they will tell the truth, the whole truth and nothing but the truth.

Gamp, Sairey. 47 p85. From D. *Martin Chuzzlewit.* Mrs Gamp was a midwife who liked her alcohol and took her large baggy umbrella with her everywhere. Hence the term 'gamp', still in use for an old, battered umbrella. In France, the term for such umbrellas is 'un Robinson' after Robinson Crusoe's home-made effort.

Gandhi hasn't had a square meal for years. 52 p128. This Indian statesman's (1869–1948) habit of undergoing lengthy bouts of fasting was well-known.

Gans, Joe. 30 p214 and *America I Like You* p20. Gans (1874–1910) was light-weight champion from 1902 to 1908.

Ganymede. As in Junior Ganymede Club (see Chap. 21). It has been pointed out to me that not everyone knows that Ganymede was the cup bearer (wine waiter) of the gods in Greek mythology. An appropriate name for Jeeves's club, though details of how Ganymede got the job are not really appropriate for family reading.

Garbo, Greta. 43 p218 and often later. Beautiful, enigmatic Swedish film actress (1905–90). See also AY TANK I GO HOME.

Garden. Being shown round the garden and being told how good it looked a month ago 65 p91. This is still the curse of visiting any English garden — and it's true. Visitors always arrive when last month's flowers have faded and this month's are not yet out. Ruth Draper made this the basis of her most popular monologue.

Garden lies at the bottom of the river, the. 47 p129; 73 p23. This was a well-known joke in the 1920s. After the First World War, there were enormous numbers of new houses built in the UK and among the most popular were bungalows beside the River Thames. Their small size was glossed over by developers who introduced the term 'bijou' to make them sound fashionable (it worked well then as it does today). Advertisements trumpeted claims about "the river at the bottom of your garden". In the winter of 1924, there was severe flooding in the Thames valley and everybody who had boasted of their riverside retreat had to endure the comment that their garden was now at the bottom of the river.

Garden of the Hesperides. 56 p35. See Chap. 28.

Gardenia, the. 42 p25 and three times up to 97 p22. This late Victorian nightclub, where commissionaires fought for the honour of throwing Gally out, stood next door to the Alhambra in Leicester Square. Famously raided in 1894, it closed around 1902 after many of its habitués caught typhoid (the drains had been badly laid). See Chap. 5.

Gardner, Erle Stanley. 70 p206 and later. This American crime writer (1889–1970) is now best remembered for his Perry Mason stories. PGW had a great respect for writers like Gardner, men who worked within tight parameters yet formulated ingenious plots.

Garibaldi. It fairly sneaks the Garibaldi 8 p77; and later. PGW gloss on the English expression 'take the biscuit' ('that beats everything'). The Italian patriot Garibaldi (1807–82) got a tremendous reception when he visited London in the 1860s and a new biscuit was named after him.

MTT Dr Tim Healey for the reminder that the common term is 'squashed fly biscuit'. See also BISCUIT.

Garrulus Glandarius Rufitergum — and other birds. 40 p111. Why PGW suddenly decided to use the Latin names for birds is beyond me, though I would bet money that he got them from a bird book in Charles le Strange's library at Hunstanton (see Chap. 32). At page 109 of *Money for Nothing*, he gives the correct Latin terms for the jay, jackdaw, sparrow and Dartford Warbler, though ornithologists will know that the last-named is now called *Sylvia undata*, not *Melizophilus undata*. For those who do not have their bird book handy, the three birds he did not identify in English at page 111 of that book — the *Dryobates major anglicus*, the *Sturnus vulgaris* and the *Emberiza curlus* (misprint for *cirlus*) — are, respectively, the Great Spotted Woodpecker, the Starling and the Cirl Bunting.

Gas and gaiters, all is. 43 p233; 56 p41 and elsewhere. D. *Nicholas Nickleby* chap 49. Expression of contentment/jollity, but I have been unable to discover the origin. The common belief that it is to do with the church (bishops used to wear gaiters) disregards the fact that, when Dickens wrote, many people wore gaiters. My theory is that since *Nickleby* was published 1838–9, perhaps Dickens coined the phrase to describe dances or festivities of the time. Assembly rooms and halls in which such events were held would be proud of their then-new gas lighting, an immeasurable improvement on oil lamps and candles, and formal dress (knee breeches and gaiters) would be worn. If I am right, it puts the expression into the same category as SOUP-AND-FISH and VINE LEAVES IN HIS HAIR. 'All gas and gaiters' is still used to describe a happy occasion, though it is now uncommon.

Gas explosion occurs in London street, sir, slaying four. 54 p183 and elsewhere. In the 1920s, as new suburbs sprang up round London and other cities, there were several of these incidents. Many occurred through the gas companies not indicating clearly where their pipes were laid and their subsequent dramatic discovery by water, electricity and sewage workmen wielding pickaxes.

Gaspard the Miser. 66 p51 and four times later. MTT Jean Archibald for finding this reference, which had eluded me for years. Gaspard was the villain in the French operetta *Les Cloches de Corneville*, which was a hit in Paris in 1877. It had one season in London in 1878 under the title *The Chimes of Normandy*. Because these references appear so late in PGW, I think he may have seen the operetta in Paris during his time there in 1944–47.

Gate-crashing. An epidemic of what is technically known as g.-c. 44 p152. PGW clearly had in mind the famous Bridgewater House row of two years before

(1928), when a hostess expelled some socially-prominent gate-crashers. See Chap. 18.

Gates, fling wide the. 3 p223 and later. *HYMNS ANCIENT & MODERN*: 'Ten Thousand Times Ten Thousand' by Alford, as well as a rousing chorus in Stainer's *Crucifixion*.

Gather ye rose-buds while ye may. 43 p158; 93 p6. Herrick's 'To Virgins, to Make Much of Time'.

Gatsby. See GREAT GATSBY.

Gawd-help-us. The British G-h-u seems to flourish 67 p16; and later. Bertie Wooster so described Madeline Bassett and the abominable Brinkley/Bingley. A Gawd-help-us is a very difficult term to describe since it has changed its emphasis over the last seventy years. PGW used it to describe somebody whose manner/clothes were beyond redemption, a hopeless case. I first heard it used as an invocation of the Almighty by sergeant-majors when confronted by a soldier who could not tell his left foot from his right or from a building foreman when a workman walked across fresh cement. I suggest today's equivalent would be someone who is 'a dead loss' or 'a waste of space'.

Gaynor, Janet. 51 p48. American film star (1906–84), first actress to be awarded an Oscar (1929).

Gazebo. 13 p86 & p183 and later. New York slang for a man/guy/chap. One of PGW's rare errors, I suggest. 'Gazabo' (pronounced gazaybo) was indeed New York slang for a man, but PGW, I believe, assumed it had the same spelling as the English word for an open-sided summerhouse. He made a similar error with RANNYGAZOO. In both cases, I think he heard them spoken in a New York street, but they were probably uttered by people whom one would hesitate to stop and inquire how they spelled the expression they had just used. That master of American detective stories, Rex STOUT, used 'gazabo' in *The Rubber Band* in 1936.

Gazeka. 11 p60; 12 p11 & p15. It took me fifty years to find this one. See Chap. 30.

Gazelles, dear. 37 p55 and frequently thereafter. Subject to correction, every PGW gazelle comes from Thomas Moore's poem 'The Fire-Worshippers', part of *Lalla Rookh*. "I never nursed a dear gazelle, / To glad me with its soft black eye, / But when it came to know me well, / And love me, it was sure to die!" See also HOPES, FONDEST.

Geddington School. 12 p85; 14 p112. Another PGW method of devising fictional names for schools. Geddington is PGW's disguise for Uppingham, a public school who used to play Rugger matches against Dulwich in Wodehouse's time. If you travelled by train to Uppingham, as PGW and the Dulwich team did, the last stop before Uppingham was Geddington. See Chap. 3 and also ECKLETON and TUPPENHAM .

Geisenheimer's. 22 p103 & p203; 26 p153. See Chap. 23.

Gem of purest ray serene, Full many a. 45 p272 and later. Gray's 'Elegy in a Country Churchyard': "Full many a gem of purest ray serene, / The dark unfathom'd caves of ocean bear: / Full many a flower is born to blush unseen / And waste its sweetness on the desert air."

Genée, Adeline. 9 p219. Famous prima ballerina at the Empire Theatre, Leicester Square, London 1890–1910. See Chap. 5.

Genesis. 21 p2. First book in the Bible.

Genevieve. 21 p305. The name of the patron saint of Paris achieved widespread popularity with 'Oh, Genevieve, sweet Genevieve' etc. This raucous song has been popular since George Cooper wrote it in 1869.

Genghis Khan. Mentioned in 53; 57 p172 and later. Fearsome Mongol warlord (1162–1227) who conquered the whole of Asia and invaded southeast Europe.

Genius, (an infinite capacity for taking pains). See INFINITE CAPACITY.

Gentleman, no, but an old friend. 59 p92. See WHO WAS THAT.

Gentleman of majestic port. 36 p106. See next entry.

Gentleman of stateliest port, what Tennyson called a. 90 p27. Ten lines from the end of T. 'Morte d'Arthur': "King Arthur, like a modern gentleman, / Of stateliest port."

George. Let G. do it. 18 p87; 63 p140; 85 p153. Some reference books say this phrase originated in Louis XII, who had great confidence in his minister, Cardinal George d'Amboise (1460–1510). A far likelier origin for the PGW usage is the series of cartoons with this title drawn by the American George McManus between 1900 and 1914. MTT Dr Tim Healey, who informs me that it became a catchphrase from an early popular comedy film, *Gertie the Dinosaur*. At intervals, the phrase 'Let George do it' appeared in the screen.

Get the bird. See BIRD, GET THE.

Get thee behind me, Satan, and look slippy about it. 66 p144 and later. B. Luke 4.8: "And Jesus answered and said unto him, Get thee behind me, Satan."

Ghent to Aix, good news from. See GOOD NEWS.

Giant Squirt. See Chap. 14.

Giant's strength, It is excellent to have a. See EXCELLENT.

Gibbon, his *Decline and Fall of the Roman Empire.* 41 p51 and later. It took Edward Gibbon (1737–94) from 1776 to 1788 to write his masterpiece. See his complaint to Dr Johnson at 72 p96.

Gibbons, Stanley. 66 p31. Britain's best-known stamp dealer. Their shop in the Strand stands on the site of Romano's.

Gibbs, Wolcott. 78 p84. This writer (1902–58) was the *New Yorker's* dramatic critic from 1939 till his death. Not to be confused with another influential drama critic, Alexander Woollcott (see ALEXANDER OF THE *TIMES*).

Gibraltar among goal-keepers. 18 p251. Gibraltar's impregnability to attack was a source of great pride in Victorian England.

Gibson Girl. One of those tall beastly girls 42 p56; elderly Gibson Girl 77 p62. Charles Dana Gibson (1867–1944) was the American counterpart of George du Maurier in England. His drawings in the *New York World* depicted upper-class society, and the tall, elegant, wasp-waisted Gibson Girls he drew were the ideal of American beauty till 1914. They were based on his wife, sister to Lady Astor.

Camille Clifford, a young, unknown American actress, sprang to fame by playing the Gibson Girl on stage in New York and London (see *Plate 4*). A tall girl, her looks, 16-inch waist and superb carriage meant all she had to do was her famous gliding walk across the stage and she brought the house down. In London she did so in *The Prince of Pilsen* (1903) and then appeared in *The Catch of the Season*. She went on to marry Lord Aberdare's heir, which made her sister-in-law to the Earl of Bradford of Weston Park, Shropshire. See Chap. 24.

'The Gibson Girl'
(Camille Clifford, 1885–1971).
This American actress retired from the stage when she married the Hon. Henry Bruce in 1906. After his death in action in December 1914, she returned to the stage for one engagement in 1916, but left it permanently when she married Captain J.M.J. Evans in 1917.

Gideon Bible. 58 p161. The Gideons, whose aim is to put a Bible in every hotel bedroom across the world, was founded in 1899. A very worthy aim, but I wish they used the Authorised Version.

Gift of seeing ourselves as others see us. 25 p182. Burns' poem 'To a Louse': "O wad some Pow'r the giftie gie us / To see oursels as ithers see us!"

Gilbert, W.S. PGW, who always maintained Gilbert (1836–1911) was a genius, quoted his *Bab Ballads* and operettas dozens of times, and was delighted when a newspaper critic said PGW's lyrics had a Gilbertian quality.

Wodehouse met Gilbert at least once, when he was taken to lunch with him by his cousin Jim Deane in August 1905. Wodehouse covered five and a half foolscap pages with Gilbert's anecdotes on that occasion, one of which he used later in 'The Truth About George'. In an altercation with the ticket collector at High Street Kensington, Gilbert was grabbed by the collar. Gilbert promptly knocked the official down the steps of the station. "Before I did it the place was almost deserted, but directly I hit him porters, guards, policemen, and spectators seemed to spring from everywhere. A policeman grabbed me by the shoulder and marched me off to the p. station. On the way, of course, I met everyone I knew. It was like a Royal procession — bowing to right and left every moment."

Wodehouse's notes make no mention of the incident he recounted at least twice later in his books. He was listening to Gilbert tell an anecdote and as Gilbert paused before the punch line, the nervous young Wodehouse gave a shout of laughter, thinking it was over. He said he never forgot the look of hatred in Gilbert's eyes — nor the look of doglike devotion in those of the butler who had heard the story a hundred times (see 'The Code of the Mulliners'). The nearest Wodehouse got to it in the notes he made that day back in 1905 is a record of an exchange between Gilbert and Miss Mackintosh with whom Gilbert was playing croquet:

> Miss M. "How hot the sun is when it comes out." W.S.G. "Yes. You know, it's just as hot when it doesn't, only we don't feel it." This is said in a solemn, grim way like all his best nonsense remarks. Whenever he comes to the point of a funny story, he always looks very dour.

In an article 'On the Writing of Lyrics' in *Vanity Fair* (June 1917), PGW spoke of the difficulties of being a lyric writer and the way he had to restrict his material. He wrote: "And even a metropolitan audience likes its lyrics as much as possible in the language of everyday. That is one of the thousand reasons why new Gilberts do not arise. Gilbert had the advantage of being a genius, but he had the additional advantage of writing for a public which permitted him to use his full vocabulary, and even to drop into foreign languages, even Latin and a little Greek when he felt like it. (I allude to that song in 'The Grand Duke'.)"

Gilding the refined gold, painting the lily. 14 p157. S. *King John* 4.2.11: "To gild refined gold, to paint the lily, / To throw a perfume on the violet."

Gillette razor. 36 p105. This ingenious American (1855–1922) deserved every penny he earned by revolutionizing shaving with his safety razor.

Gimp. 39 p142. Most American slang dictionaries say that 'gimp' means someone who is lame or crippled. Here, clearly, it does not. I suggest it is another example of a slang word coming to mean the reverse of its original usage; thus, in 2006, 'wicked' from a teenager meant splendid or good. MTT Jim Linwood, who points out that in G&S *The Gondoliers*, 'jimp' is used as a compliment.

Gioconda smile. 34 p153 and elsewhere. This is the Mona Lisa portrait by da Vinci. Her correct name and style in English would have been 'Mrs Lisa del Giocondo'. In Italian this is Madonna (my lady) Lisa del Gioconda. Madonna is usually shortened to Mona — hence Mona Lisa. Why on earth it appears as the 'Monna Lisa' in 'Doing Clarence a Bit of Good' (23 p191), I do not know. An unusual misprint or maybe the usual pronunciation of the time.

Gird up your loins, Jeeves, and accompany me. 59 p172; 96 p69. B. Job 38.2: "Gird up now thy loins like a man."

Girdle round the earth in forty minutes, I'll put a. 18 p153. S. *Midsummer Night's Dream* 2.1.

Girl and the Artist, The. 20 p29. See Chap. 24.

Girl behind the gun, the. 94 p68. PGW remembering the title of the Wodehouse, Bolton and Ivan Caryll musical of 1918?

Girl behind the vase (had stepped on the tee and had begun her preliminary waggle). 48 p286. See GIRL BEHIND THE GUN.

Girl from Brighton, The. 22 p2 & p10. See Chap. 24.

Girl from Dublin, The. 19 p29. See Chap. 24.

Girl in Pink Pyjamas, The. 34 p69. There may have been a show with this title but I think this was a compliment to Alice DOVEY, who appeared on stage in pyjamas in *The Pink Lady* (1911). In view of Wodehouse's admiration for Miss Dovey, this seems very likely. MTT David Jasen. See Chapter 38.

Girl that Men Forget, You're the Sort of. 36 p 30. See YOU'RE THE SORT OF GIRL.

Girl's best friend is ... The song 'Diamonds Are a Girl's Best Friend' did not come out till 1949, and I think a more likely origin for PGW's frequent references was the wildly-popular song 'A Boy's Best Friend Is His Mother' (see BOY'S BEST FRIEND). PGW gave us several variations on the theme. At 29 p187 a girl's best friend is her elephant gun. At 63 p151 a woman in the wild's best friend is an automatic pistol. At 65 p121 a girl's best friend is her mother; at 83 p200 a blackjack occupies the same role. At 88 p201 it is diamonds followed by blackmail. (At 76 p164, Bertie says that a blackjack is the man of slender physique's best friend.)

Girls' Own Paper, The. 73 p25. Companion paper to the famous 'respectable' English boys' magazine, *The Boys' Own Paper*, which began in 1879 and lasted till the 1960s.

Girls will be girls. 28 p213 and later. Gloss on the 17th-century proverb 'boys will be boys'. Anthony Hope (1863–1933) used the phrase in his *Dolly Dialogues*.

Girton. 3 p88 and later. For some reason, this Cambridge women's college has always been regarded as more serious-minded than Newnham or its Oxford counterparts. See Chap. 2.

Gish, Lillian. (Bingo) looked like L.G. coming out of a swoon 31 p243; 42 p53; 43 p204. I am puzzled by the comment on Bingo's resemblance to this actress (1893–1993), whose career spanned from *An Unseen Enemy* (1912) to *The*

Whales of August (1987). Her wide-eyed innocence might be what PGW had in mind, though I have seen a slang dictionary entry: "'Don't Gish me' — don't entice me / persuade me to do something."

Gissing, (George). 9 p114; 83 p37. This gloomy writer (1857–1903) specialised in describing the degrading effect of poverty on character.

Give me anything but love, baby. You can't 83 p175. 1928 song 'I Can't Give You Anything But Love, Baby' by Fields & McHugh.

Give me to live with love … Love in idleness. 39 p162. From Laman Blanchard's 'Dolce far Niente'. See Love is everything.

Give them a thingummy and (they'll) take a what-do-you-call-it. 52 p288 and often in PGW in various forms. From the old English expression: "Give him an inch and he'll take an ell." An ell was the old cloth measure, about 1¼ yards.

Give Yourself a Pat on the Back. 55 p58; 68 p153. 1929 song by R Butler.

Given me the office. Had not Bill Oakshott done so 67 p95. Criminal slang for passing on information, 'tipping me the wink', that sort of thing.

Glad, I'm glad, glad, glad. 34 p246; 83 p142 and elsewhere. See Pollyanna.

Gladiators, Roman. 59 p158. Throwing a sheet over Spode is the sort of thing they did "and were rather well thought of in consequence". PGW had Bertie use the wrong term because it was the one people like Bertie remembered. Individual fights in the Colosseum were fought between a gladiator and a retiarius. Gladiators were armed with sword and shield; it was the retiarius who was armed with a trident and net which he tried to throw over his gladiator opponent. In *The Small Bachelor* we are specifically told George Finch emulated a retiarius when employing the tablecloth to prevent arrest by Officer Garroway. (Note. In some editions, the publishers got it wrong and gave us 'retarius'.)

Gladstone, Herbert, writes to The Times. 11 p29. The youngest son of William Gladstone, Herbert (1854–1930) also went into politics and was an efficient and hard-working Cabinet Minister.

Gladstone, William. What Mr Gladstone said in 1878 32 p100; you can fuel some of the people all of the time, and you can fuel all of the people some of the time etc. 40 p92; his bust is broken 66 p195; his chewing everything 33 times 19 p37; 43 p232. This Liberal statesman (1809–98) dominated British politics in the second half of the 19th century. (His first Cabinet included the head of the Wodehouse family, Lord Wodehouse, who was later made first Earl of Kimberley.) For his eating habits, see Fletcherize. The fooling some of the people all of the time is from Abraham Lincoln — see Fool some of the people.

"What did Mr Gladstone say in 1878?" was one of those seemingly meaningless phrases that entered the language, and it was still in use when I was a schoolboy in the 1940s. The standard response was: "I don't know. What did Mr Gladstone say in 1878?" And then, of course, one got some rude remark about one's personal appearance or habits.

I found the origin by sheer chance when reading through the Parliamentary reports in *The Strand* magazine of 12 March 1912. The report recalled the occasion twenty-eight years before, in 1884, when Sir Richard Cross had come into the Chamber after a dinner given by W.H. Smith (the First Lord of the Admiralty satirised in Gilbert's *HMS Pinafore*). It had been an excellent dinner and Sir Richard was, let us say, mellow. He stood up, looked round the House and waved a piece of paper on which he had noted a comment by Mr Gladstone of fourteen years before:

"He began with great dignity. 'What did the Prime Minister say in 1870?' and paused — for too long. An Opposition member laughed and Sir Richard looked at him sternly and said 'I hear an honourable gentleman smile'. This brought a roar of laughter from the whole House while Sir Richard regarded the throng with supernatural gravity." The report went on: "Time after time, following upon interjectionary remarks, he produced his scrap of paper and, about to read it, paused to inquire: 'What did the Prime Minister say in 1870?' Whereupon another burst of uncontrollable laughter again broke forth."

I am delighted to have found the origin of a catchphrase which began with a politician's post-prandial meanderings in 1884, but was still current in 1944.

Gladys, the heroic. 'Lord Emsworth and the Girl Friend'. *(See photo overleaf.)*

Glands, monkey. 33 p125. In the 1920s there was a craze for these, which many people believed would renew their youth and energy. Voronoff of Vienna had started successful treatments on this basis in 1914. See also Conan Doyle's 'The Creeping Man'.

Glass darkly, saw them as through a. 80 p29. B. 1 Corinthians 13.12: "For now we see through a glass, darkly."

Gleam. Tennyson character who followed the g. 42 p219 and later. T. 'Merlin and the Gleam'. Each stanza finishes with the words 'the Gleam' and the last line is "Follow the Gleam".

Glimmering landscape. Now fades the g.l. on the sight 76 p94 and elsewhere. See ALL THE AIR A SOLEMN STILLNESS HOLDS.

Glittering eye. See HELD ME WITH A GLITTERING EYE.

Glorious in his apparel. PGW ref lost. B. Isaiah 63.1: "Who is this that cometh from Edom, with dyed garments from Bosrah? This that is glorious in his apparel, travelling in the greatness of his strength?"

Glory. Then leg it where glory waits you 27 p254. Song by Thomas Moore (1779–1852) in *Irish Melodies*. "Go where glory waits thee."

Glow Worm, The. 3 p94 & p258. See Chap. 3.

Glyn, Elinor. 46 p149. This English writer (1864–1943) aroused comment with her 1900 book *Visits of Elizabeth* and outrage with her *Three Weeks* in 1907. It was she who coined the term 'It' for sex appeal and worked as a screenwriter in Hollywood for a time. Mrs Glyn cut quite a dash in Hollywood, especially when the news got out that four suitors for her hand had once fought in a lake, emerging to wash themselves in champagne — or so she claimed. See also IT; PRINCESS, SCANTILY-CLAD; TIGER-SKIN.

Go and he cometh, chap says. 51 p279; 66 p25 and later. B. Matthew 8.9. The

Gladys, Lord Emsworth's girl friend

"... a small girl of uncertain age ... a combination of London fogs and early cares had given her face a sort of wizened motherliness .... She was the type of girl you see in back streets carrying a baby nearly as large as herself and still retaining sufficient energy to lead one little brother by the hand and shout recriminations at another in the distance."

centurion said to Jesus, "and I say to this man Go, and he goeth; and to another, Come, and he cometh; and to my servant, Do this, and he doeth."

Go and sin no more. 80 p47. See Go, WOMAN.

Go back, I want to, I want to to go back ... 22 p103 and later. See Chap. 36.

Go life is, what a. 8 p53. A 'go' in the meaning of some unusual event was common from D. *The Pickwick Papers* to Lupin Pooter in Grossmith's *Diary of a Nobody*, though the exact wording occurs in neither of these. Perhaps it is from H.G. Wells' *Kipps* (1905): "I was thinking jest what a Rum Go everything is."

Go thee, knave, I'll have none of thee. Shakespeare. 12 p306. Psmith may have found this line in Shakespeare. I have not.

Go To It. 39 p180 and later. This exhortation became popular in Britain in the First World War. It was also the name of a musical show that flopped in New York in 1916 (see *Bring on the Girls*). See also HOLE.

Go West, young man. 26 p90; 38 p225 and later. See 53 p226 where Wilmot Mulliner would have done so if he was not out West already. Horace GREELEY popularised this famous phrase in the *New York Tribune* and used it constantly in articles and speeches. He was punctilious, however, in always attributing it to John Soule, who first coined it in an article for the *Terre Haute Express* in Indiana in 1851.

Go, woman, and sin no more. 94 p189. B. John 8.11. To the woman taken in adultery, Jesus said: "Neither do I condemn thee; go, and sin no more."

God can make a tree, Only … 50 p54. See ONLY GOD.

God from the machine. 28 p178 and later. (Deus ex machina). Theatrical device used in Greek tragedy when a god, appearing at the last moment to solve everything, was let down on the stage by a crude crane. It has come to mean a playwright's bringing in some surprise element to solve the problems of his characters. Similar to Jeeves using a cosh, a putter, the club book or some other dramatic outside factor to bring about the happy ending.

God, Homeric. Like some H. G. swooping from a cloud 17 p113. See CLOUD, SWOOPING.

God makes sech nights, All white and still. Fur'z you to look and listen. 7 p96. 'The Courtin' from James Lowell's *The Biglow Papers*, Introduction to Second Series.

God of battles, Great. 47 p104. T. 'The Revenge', stanza 9.

God's country. 24 p116. My *Oxford Dictionary of Quotations* has this under Anon but traces it back to 1865. It adds that 'God's own country' was not coined till 1921.

God's Good Man. 9 p153. Novel by Marie Corelli (1855–1924).

God's in his Heaven. Frequent from 19 on. Browning's 'Pippa Passes': "Morning's at seven; The hill-side's dew-pearled; The lark's on the wing; The snail's on the thorn; God's in his heaven — All's right with the world."

Goethals, Colonel. 22 p157. Supervised building of the Panama Canal 1907–14 and became first governor of the Canal Zone on its completion.

Goethe, anxious for more light. 50 p128. Goethe's (1749–1832) last words were "More light".

Goethe's poem, woman in, who kept on cutting bread and butter. 17 p117. See BREAD AND BUTTER.

Go-fever in Kipling's book, the man with. 13 p94. This is Dick Heldar in KIPLING's *The Light That Failed,* who had the wanderlust and could never settle anywhere.

'Go-Getter, The'. This short story title is another example of PGW's topicality. The term had just come to the UK from the US, where it had originated in 1922. It was coined by a journalist to describe an enthusiastic salesman/business man who would overcome difficulties to 'go get' what he wanted.

Going West so prompt. 42 p48. This UK phrase stems from the First World War as a euphemism developed to avoid using the word 'dead' (see GOODBYE). 'He's gone West' meant someone had been killed. In the Second World War, the Royal Air Force developed a similar term for airmen who did not return: "He's gone for a Burton." (Burton was a famous brand of beer.) General

Bernard Rogers (US Army) told me the American Army equivalent is: "He's bought the farm."

Going where money is. 77 p15. See MONEY.

Gold. Would you buy me with your g.? 30 p68; 89 p219. Popular 1898 song by Foreman & Rosenfeld: 'Gold Will Buy Most Anything but a Pure Girl's Love'.

Gold cure. I wonder if the g.c. would be any good 67 p156. In the 1930s, 'the gold cure' was a fashionable treatment to cure alcoholism. It used gold chloride, and was developed by the KEELEY CURE INSTITUTE.

Gold, gilding. See GILDING THE REFIND GOLD.

Gold in them thar tooth. 56 p164; in them thar Hokies 65 p98. Gloss on "gold in them thar hills". Revived by Yosemite Sam in the Bugs Bunny cartoons, its origin lies in George Stephenson, who made an impassioned speech to the gold miners of Dahlonega, Georgia, in 1849, in an attempt to stop them leaving for the gold rush in California. In 1828, the hills around Dahlonega had seen America's first gold rush, and Stephenson was convinced there was still gold to be mined. Mark Twain recounted the incident in his 'Golden Age' and paraphrased Stephenson's appeal to "There's gold in them thar hills". MTT Elin Woodger.

Gold Stick In Waiting. 69 p106. An officer of the Royal Household, usually a distinguished retired Guards officer. At the time of writing, the Princess Royal, Colonel of The Blues and Royals, is Gold Stick; Colonel Hamon Massey, Commander Household Cavalry, is Silver Stick. In common with other Royal Household officials, the stick is a badge of office. The Lord Chamberlain, for example, carries a white wand, and Black Rod ceremonially bangs on the door of the House of Commons each year with his black rod to summon the members to hear the Queen's speech. When Her Majesty the Queen Mother died in 2002, her Chamberlain broke his wand over her grave to show his duties were ended. The tradition of the wand/stick of office goes back to the Romans, whose officials and army officers carried them.

Golden ass. See ROSE-LEAVES.

Golden Rule, the. 26 p223. Do unto others as you would they do unto you. B. Luke 6.31. MTT Adrian Vincent.

Goldwyn, Sam. See Chap. 28.

Golf and the world golfs with you; hawk and you hawk alone. 46 p128. See "Laugh and the world laughs with you. / Weep and you weep alone." from the poem 'Solitude' (1883) by Ella Wheeler Wilcox. It became a popular song in 1896.

Golf Without Tears (US title of *The Clicking of Cuthbert*). Braid's *Golf Without Tears* 37 p40. In 1895 Lady Florence Bell published a French textbook for young children entitled *French Without Tears*. It was wildly successful, remaining in print for years, and the phrase embedded itself in the nation's subconscious. Terence Rattigan used it as the title for a successful play in the 1930s and said later that, with such a familiar phrase, he knew it couldn't fail.

I had not realised what a cliché it had become till I looked it up in the British Library, which lists 98 titles with the suffix 'Without Tears'. They range from Ballet Without Tears through Botany Without Tears, Crosswords, German, Hunting, Journalism, Latin, Motor Cycling to Onions, Poetry and Poodles Without Tears.

Golliwogs, five. 18 p247. Because political correctness has gone to the lengths it has, it is worth remembering that the small black doll was the creation of Bertha Upton, who wrote poems of Golliwog's adventures for her daughter in the 1890s. The adventures of Golliwog and his companions, the Dutch Dolls, delighted children around the world for sixty years before anyone dreamt of objecting to the cheerful, happy child's toy.

Golly, massa, who frew dat brick? 8 p31. Not traced, but I would suggest the popularity in the UK of the Brer Rabbit stories may have had something to do with it.

Gone and done it. See BEEN AND GONE.

Gone with the wind. Frequent, including 72 p125. PGW was using the phrase long before the famous book was published in 1936. The best source I can find is the 1896 poem 'Non Sum Qualis Eram' by Ernest Dowson (1867–1900). "I have forgot much, Cynara! Gone with the wind, / Flung roses, roses, riotously, with the throng."

Gone without a cry. 65 p192; 67 p106; 72 p120. I have a strong recollection of BYRON or Keats or SHELLEY using the phrase, but "Gone without a word" from S. *Two Gentlemen of Verona* 2.2. is as near as I can get.

'Good Angel, The'. 18 p149. Burton's *Anatomy of Melancholy* Pt 1, Sect 2: "Every man hath a good and a bad angel attending on him in particular all his life long."

'Good Cigar Is a Smoke, A'. Story title 88 p183. KIPLING's poem 'The Betrothed': "A woman is only a woman but a good cigar is a smoke."

Note. PGW used this quotation often, putting his own twist on it. Sometimes it is easy to miss. In 'Rallying Round Old George' (*My Man Jeeves*), for example, PGW writes that "an income, after all, is only an income, whereas a chunk of (jimmy) o'goblins is a pile." Whenever you read: "An X is only an X but a good Y is a Z", then it is from Kipling's poem which everybody knew. Like Dickens, he was popular at every level of society.

Good, he never had it so. 84 p164. See NEVER HAD IT SO GOOD.

Good in the worst of us, There is. 59 p55. The first line of the poem 'Good and Bad' by Edward Hoch: "There is so much good in the worst of us."

Good man down, You can't keep a. See YOU CAN'T KEEP.

Good man taking his rest, the. 17 p174 and later. At 60 p136 "The good man loves his pig". I have been unable to find the 'good man' reference PGW used often. It is not Shakespeare, nor Tennyson nor the Bible. Perhaps it was a general theatrical term — see CHARLES, HIS FRIEND.

Good name in man or woman etc. etc. 31 p43. S. *Othello* 2.3.

Good news from Aix to Ghent. 34 p200 and later. Browning's poem 'How They Brought the Good News from Ghent to Aix'. PGW, like everybody else, occasionally got Ghent and Aix the wrong way round. With Longfellow's 'The Wreck of the Hesperus' and TENNYSON's 'The Brook', this poem was drilled into English schoolboys for nearly a century. See 67 p200 for: "Annoyed, for no girl bringing the good news from Aix to Ghent likes to find Ghent empty when she gets there ..."

Good night, sweet Prince, and flights of angels sing thee to thy rest. 91 p104. S. *Hamlet* 5.4.

Good old man in melodrama. 21 p82 and later. A theatrical term for a type of role (see CHARLES, HIS FRIEND), a victim who was always being turned out of his cottage by the bad baronet (see BARONETS) or a faithful old retainer who accompanies his young master into exile. See faithful old Adam, "O good old man" in S. *As You Like It* 2.3 or "A good old man, sir" in S. *Much Ado About Nothing* 3.5. Their later counterpart, Old Adam Goodheart in G&S *Ruddigore*, classified himself as "I belong to that particular description of good old man ..."

Good time coming, a. There certainly is 7 p148. Probably from the US hymn 'The Good Time Coming' by Charles Mackay (c.1880), but maybe from Walter Scott's *Rob Roy*: "There's a good time coming, boys, / A good time coming."

Good woman is a wondrous creature, cleaving to the right, A. 39 p94. This has such a strong Biblical ring that it put me off the scent. It is Tennyson, but will not be found in his *Poems*. It appears in Vol. 1 of the 1897 *Life of Tennyson* written by his son. MTT Elin Woodger.

Goodbye. *Doctor Sally/ The Medicine Girl* has the most comprehensive list of ways of saying farewell. (The date in brackets shows the year the term became fashionable/ popular.) Tinkerty-tonk, Toodle-oo (1907), Pip-Pip, Chin-Chin, Teuf-Teuf, Honk-Honk, Ting-Ting, Poo-boop-a-doop and Cheerio (1910) are some of the variations PGW used. Some of these came from the period 1900–14 and arose from early motor-car horns. In a letter of the 1950s, PGW said 'Tinkerty-tonk' was Knut slang of about 1912. When you left in your motor and waved farewell, you honk-honked your horn. If you were on a bicycle, you rang your bell (ting-ting) or pip-pipped the small horn which some bicycles had till the 1950s. 'Pip! Pip!' was a catchphrase among London Cockneys c.1895 and became fashionable slang for 'Goodbye' in 1920.

Often the term changed its meaning and became an acknowledgement of a favour done, an informal way of saying 'Thank you'. So, Pip-Pip and Chin-Chin became an acknowledgement for a drink. You raised your glass to the man who'd bought it for you and said 'Cheers', 'Pip-Pip', 'Chin-Chin' or some other phrase. 'Cheers' became a toast, then came to mean a general reply to such comments as 'See you later', 'Until next time', 'Cheerio', etc. Denis Mackail and Wodehouse argued over this point in the 1950s, neither appreciating how quickly slang had changed. I believe PGW also forgot later which terms had been used for greeting or parting since *Jeeves in the Offing* (1960) opens with Bertie using 'pip-pip' as a greeting and Aunt Dahlia replying, "And a rousing toodle-oo to you."

I was brought up to say "Thank you", not "Cheers" (too new and unacceptable in my parents' view) when someone gave me a drink, but I notice that "Cheers" has now been given another use. Nowadays shop assistants put the items in a bag and give it to me, saying: "There you go". I reply "Thank you" and they say "Cheers". All part of the rich fabric of a living language, I suppose.

The reason for the popularity of such terms was the First World War. Many more Britons were killed in the First World War than in the Second, and the average survival time of a young infantry officer in the trenches was three weeks. The word 'Goodbye' quickly went out of use. It was too final, too definite to be used when you and the other person knew only too well you would probably never see each other again. A whole set of synonyms came into use, all designed to avoid using the word. In 1915, the song that swept the country finished with the words: "Bon soir, old thing! Cheerio, Chin-chin; Napoo, Toodleoo, Goodbyeeee!" ('Toodle-oo' was the Cockney version of the French 'a toute à l'heure'.) The habit stayed and the alternative terms remained in use through the 1920s and 1930s.

'Toodle-oo' and all the rest of them may seem affected upper-class slang to us today, but they are a reflection of the bloodiest war Britain ever fought.

See also CHIN CHIN.

Goodbye Boys, I'm Going to be Married Tomorrow. 20 p86. 1913 song by Harry von Tilzer.

'Goodbye to All Cats'. 55 p125. PGW twist on the title of Robert Graves' superb book *Goodbye to All That* (1929). PGW knew the GRAVES FAMILY well, shared digs with Robert's brother Perceval, and wrote introductions to at least two of Charles Graves' books (another brother). The boys' father, Alfred, best known for writing the song 'Father O'Flynn', published his autobiography the year after Robert's book came out. He called it *To Return to All That*.

Goodbye to all that. 72 p111. See GOODBYE TO ALL CATS.

Goodbye, Tosti's. See TOSTI'S GOODBYE.

Goodness me, Why what was that? Silent be, It was the cat. 6 p187. From G&S *Pinafore*, Act 2. MTT Anne-Marie Chanet and Ian Michaud.

Goodnight, Sweetheart. 51 p17. 1931 song by Ray Noble.

Goodwill and fixtures. A going concern with all the g. and f. 56 p124. A term commonly used in England when you bought a business or a shop. The price would normally include the goodwill (the right to continue using the name) and the fixtures (plant, machinery, shelving, etc).

Goodwin, Archie, in the Nero Wolfe stories. 92 p91. Goodwin was Nero WOLFE's right-hand man in the books by Rex Stout.

Google, Barney. See BARNEY GOOGLE.

Gool them. Maybe we didn't g.t. 26 p137. My US slang dictionary says this comes from the word 'goal' and means to attract a lot of applause.

Goose, a bit of. A bit of goose for you, Angela, old girl 52 p170. Origin unknown but clearly meaning a fortunate occurrence, a bonus. MTT Murray Hedgcock. See also BUNCE.

Gordian knot, cut the. Would have cut the G.k. of his difficulties 1 p179. To solve an insoluble problem. In Greek legend, Gordius, king of Phrygia, suspended the yoke of his wagon to a beam with a knot so intricate and ingenious that no one could undo it. When Alexander the Great came to see it, he was told that whoever undid it would conquer Asia. Alexander promptly drew his sword and cut through the knot.

Gordon, Max. 71 p118; 78 p170. This New York theatrical producer (1892–1978) was renowned for the lengths to which he would go to raise funds for his shows. He once perched on a high window ledge and threatened to throw himself off unless he got the money.

Gorgeous East. Holding the g. E. in fee 14 p224. From Wordsworth's 'On the Extinction of the Venetian Republic', written to mourn its surrender to Napoleon.

Gorgon. Turns people to stone 18 p133; has snakes instead of hair 67 p134; 92 p118; turned people to blocks of ice 97 p49. The three Gorgon sisters were Stheno, Euryale and Medusa (the one with snakes instead of hair), who turned to stone all those they gazed upon. PGW's error about blocks of ice at 97 p49 is attributable, I suggest, to his age.

Gorky, Maxim. 7 p97; 26 p120. This Russian writer (1868–1936) wrote depressing novels of social misery.

Gotch, wrestler. 10 p57 and later; 14 p185. See HACKENSCHMIDT.

Gotford scholarship. 8 p18. There are a couple of scholastic prizes at Dulwich College that could be what PGW had in mind, but I have found no supporting evidence.

Gotsuchakoff. 6 p48; 10 p58 and later. If foreigners insist on having names that sound funny to British ears, then it would be silly not to use them. In any event, Russians weren't popular in Britain in 1905 (see BANZAI). Prince Gortschakoff was Russian Foreign Secretary in the late 19th century and was thought by Britain to have alarmingly 'expansionist' views. PGW's early readers would have picked up the reference at once. See also BRUSILOFF.

Gould, Nat. 10 p139; 78 p99. This English writer (1857–1919) wrote countless novels, all of which seemed to culminate in the hero winning some horse-race against terrific odds.

Government by the people … 62 p221. From Lincoln's Gettysburg address.

Governor of North Carolina to South Carolina, remark of. 7 p134. See JUDICIOUS REMARK.

Gowans fine, plucked the. 5 p214; 32 p136 and later. Robert Burns' 'Auld Lang syne'.

Grable, Betty. 68 p245; 71 p98. This Hollywood film star (1916–73) with superb legs was the favourite pin-up in World War II.

Gracchi, mother of the. 70 p59. Cornelia Sempronia, mother of Tiberius and Caius Gracchus, was a woman of great dignity, virtue, piety and learning.

Gracchus, Tiberius. 3 p235. Son of Cornelia Sempronia above, was a political reformer who fought hard for the rights of the people. He was assassinated 133 B.C.

Grace of God. There but for the G. of G. goes (Bertie Wooster/ whoever). 46 p168; 52 p 211; 64 p151. Another phrase that stuck in the popular memory for hundreds of years. Watching some wretches being taken off for execution, John Bradford (1510–55) said: "But for the Grace of God, there goes John Bradford." Ten years later, he was burned at the stake for heresy.

Grafters, some policemen are born g., some achieve graft. 13 p28. See SOME ARE BORN WITH SPRAINED WRISTS.

Grahame, Kenneth. 3 p249. Grahame (1859–1932) is best remembered today for his *The Wind in the Willows.*

Grail, Holy. The Holy Grail sliding down the sunbeam 30 p41; and later. T. *Idylls of the King* ('The Holy Grail').

Grand Duke, Gilbert's. 2 p94; 3 p276. Rudolph in G&S *The Grand Duke* Act 1. "I am very young, but not as young as that."

Grand National ... he came in third once. 90 p25. See BECHER'S BROOK.

Grant, Cary. 69 p210; 94 p108. Handsome film actor (1904–86).

Grant, General, (fight it out along these lines). 91 p112. See FIGHT IT OUT.

Grapple to your soul with hoops of steel. 20 p77 and later (sometimes as hooks of steel, probably a printer's error). S. *Hamlet* 1.3: "Grapple them to thy soul with hoops of steel."

Grass, all flesh is as. See ALL FLESH IS AS GRASS.

Grateful and comforting, somebody's something is both. 1 p21; 3 p44. This was Epp's Cocoa. I noted it as a regular half-page advertisement with the headline 'Grateful — Comforting' in newspapers of 1901.

Grave to the gay, from the manly straightforward to the whimsically jocular. (Bishop's speeches) 44 p138. See Pope's 'Essay on Man', Epistle IV, l.379. "Grave to gay, from lively to severe." See also BISHOPS AND THEIR SPEECHES.

Gravel soil. "Gravel soil? Spreading views?" 68 p9. Like COMPANY'S OWN WATER, 'Gravel soil' was a phrase constantly used in advertisements for boarding schools and houses for sale. It may have stemmed from the fact that a high gravel content meant septic tanks drained more easily. Whatever the reason, gravel soil came to be accepted as 'a good thing'.

Graven on her heart would be the words 'It is with reference to the young man Weatherby, madam'. 62 p228. At 73 p43 Lord Rowcester says "Three thousand and five pounds two and six" would be found carved on his heart. Mary Tudor, Queen of England (1553–58), who lost Calais, the last English foothold in France, said that when she died the word 'Calais' would be found graven on her heart. Another of those odd quotes that stuck in the popular memory.

Graves family. During my early research into the factual background of Wodehouse's fiction, I was fortunate enough to meet Perceval Graves, who shared rooms with PGW in Walpole Street back in 1901–2 and played with him in the Actors v. Authors cricket match. It was he who told me of Wodehouse's habit (he was then still in the bank) of vanishing upstairs after the evening meal and writing in the bathroom, the only place where he would not be disturbed by the conversation of his landlady and her daughter. It was Perceval Graves who took PGW down to The Red House, Lauriston Road, Wimbledon, to meet his family, and PGW wrote introductions to books by Percival's brother Charles later. (See end of Chap. 25.) When another brother, Robert Graves (1895–1985), the poet and novelist, received the Queen's Gold Medal for Poetry from the Queen in 1968, he confided to her that they were related — each was descended from Mahomet through King Edward IV. He suggested she should announce this fact in her next Christmas Broadcast since it would delight her Muslim subjects. The report went on: "The Queen then turned the conversation." See also 'Goodbye to All Cats'.

Grayson, Victor. 10 p77–78. This Member of Parliament (b.1881) disappeared in September 1920. Conspiracy theorists believe he was murdered by 'interests' he was going to expose. Maundy Gregory, the chap who 'sold' honours, was suspected by many. See Peerages.

Great Cham of Tartary. See Cham of Tartary.

Great Gatsby, The. 71 p44. Famous novel (1925) by F. Scott Fitzgerald, whom PGW met in Great Neck.

Great horn spoon. See By the great horn spoon.

Great is truth and mighty above all things. 39 p83. MTT Tony Ring for pointing out this is from the Apocrypha, Esdras 4.51, not 4.41.

Great Lover, the. 53 p297. Casanova? Don Juan? Lothario?

Great Lovers Through the Ages. 35 p201 and later. At money-raising charity events in the 1920s–30s, one sure way to get an audience for the tableaux was to secure the services of pretty debutantes and actresses. In 1927 a constant theme was Lovers Through the Ages. In one charity show, Lady Rosse, a Society beauty, appeared as Ariadne, while Tallulah Bankhead played Cleopatra in The Great Pageant of Lovers. Lady Rosse later took up interior design, and it is reported that when she first went to visit the tenants on her Irish estate, she entered one old woman's cottage, decrepit, dirty, insanitary, looked round and gushed: "My dear! It's perfect! Don't change a thing!" See also Pageants.

Great Picnic, The. 12 p56. See Chap. 3.

Great Swifts. 87 p39. See Chap. 29.

Great Unwashed, The. 24 p106. A contemptuous term for the lower classes, used by Edmund Burke. Walter Scott used it later.

Great was his fright, So, / His waistcoat turned white. 73 p171. Lewis Carroll's 'The Hunting of the Snark'.

Great White Way, the. 15A p82 and later. This term for Broadway was popularised by a 1901 play of that name written by Albert Paine.

Greatest happiness of the greatest number. 12 p64. "That action is best, which procures the greatest happiness for the greatest numbers." See Treatise II, sec 3, para 8 of *Inquiry Into the Original of Our Ideas of Beauty and Virtue* (1725) by Francis Hutcheson (1694–1746). Or from Joseph Priestley's 'Essay on Government' (1768), or from Jeremy Bentham, who admits he got it from Priestley, who got it from Hutcheson and so on and so on.

Greatest men, so little does the world often know of its. 9 p134; 15 p128; 24 p7 and later. From *Philip Van Artfelde* (1834) Pt 1, Act 1 Sc 5. by Sir Henry Taylor (1800–86): "The world knows nothing of its greatest men."

Greatly respected, Mr Pett died again. 21 p61. PGW was using a cliché of obituary columns of the time. Unless a man was a downright villain, he was always said to have died "respected by all" or "held in great respect by all who knew him".

Grecian gifts. 13 p54. See TIMEO DANAOS.

Greek drama/tragedy/play. 20 p45 and often up to 95 p160. PGW did Latin and Greek at school and learned from the literature of both. Greek tragedy was as familiar to him as Shakespeare or Dickens is to us. A recent newspaper article pointed out that Greek tragedy occupied the same position with the ancient Greeks that soap operas do with us today. They both revolve around family relationships, murder, jealousy and misunderstanding. When action took place offstage, either too complicated to stage or too horrific to show, then the Greek chorus would intone the bad news so the audience knew what had happened. See 49 p221 and 57 p192–3, where the two Beans speak as one Bean, and PGW's later description of the Greek chorus as "as glum a lot as you could meet in a month of Sundays".

Greek Syndicate. One of those punters … who rook the G.S. out of three million francs 55 p192; 62 p23. Led by Nicolos Zographos, this group of Greek gamblers dominated the baccarat tables of European casinos in the 1920s.

Greeks, Ten Thousand, beholding the sea. 41 p298. See XENOPHON.

Greeley, Horace … Delane. 38 p225. Greeley (1811–72) was one of the great American newspaper editors of the 19th century. A man of immense influence, he founded the *New York Tribune* in 1841. Delane (1817–79) was his English equivalent, editor of *The Times* 1841–77.

Green baize cloth over that kid, somebody put a. 12 p4; 37 p280 and elsewhere. In both references above, PGW had a child repeating a phrase *ad nauseam* as a parrot does, and he was repeating the then-standard response. (See also SIT ON HIS HEAD and PUT A SOCK IN IT.) In the days when many households had a parrot, if you wanted it to stop talking, you threw a cloth over his cage and the parrot, thinking it was nighttime, would be quiet. Green baize, now usually restricted to billiard tables, was then to be seen in every household. It had many uses, including covering the doors leading to the servants' quarters and lining cutlery and plate drawers, while green baize aprons were worn by the butler and footmen when they cleaned the silver.

'Green Eye of the Little Yellow God'. 73 p104. This poem, once as popular as 'Dangerous Dan McGrew' or 'Gunga Din', recounts the tale of 'Mad' Carew, the dashing young officer who steals the jewel from the statue of the Hindoo god to give to the Colonel's daughter. It is she who finds his body after the temple priests have avenged his sacrilege. The 1911 poem by J. Milton Hayes (1884–1940) remained popular till the 1950s. The first verse give a taste of the rhythm that made it so popular for recitation:

> There's a one-eyed yellow idol to the north of Khatmandu,
> There's a little marble cross below the town;
> There's a broken-hearted woman tends the grave of Mad Carew,
> And the Yellow God forever gazes down.

As Sir Roderick Carmoyle tells us, idol's eye stories, white men stealing some fabulous jewel from an Indian/Malayan/Burmese temple and being pursued by sinister natives anxious to get their property back, were used constantly in British magazines from 1885 to 1914. PGW used the same basic idea with *The Luck Stone*, and Ashe Marson was glad of the suggestion in *Something Fresh* for his 'Wand of Death'. See also WHITEST MAN I KNOW.

Green, Hetty. 62 p158. This American lady lived in squalor but, on her death in 1916, left a hundred million dollars from shrewd investments.

Green Jackets, The. 14 p7. An English regiment, founded in 1755, former title Royal Americans. They were the first to wear a green uniform rather than the red coats which made their brave wearers such excellent targets for the French, Indians and rebel colonists.

Green line, follow the. 51 p26. See FOLLOW THE GREEN LINE.

Green, sported side by side on the. See SPORTED ON THE GREEN.

Green Swizzles. See Chap. 38.

Green you, probably trying to. 3 p49; 4 p260. To 'green' somebody was to play a joke on a newcomer, a novice, someone easy to deceive. See also Chap. 37 (Anatole).

Green-eyed monster that doth mock the meat it feeds on. 96 p13. S. *Othello* 3.3: "O! beware, my lord, of jealousy; It is the green-eyed monster which doth mock The meat it feeds on."

Greiffenhagen, Maurice. 46 p267. This painter (1867–1931) of tasteful nudes also provided an enormous picture for the top of grand staircase for RMS *Empress of Britain*, launched 1930. See also DULAC.

Grenadier Guards guarding the Bank of England. 97 p92. Lord Emsworth sings the song from a show he saw a long time ago. Richard Usborne (see Note 43 of *Sunset at Blandings*) tried many sources to identify this song but without success. I can confirm there is no song by this title in the British Library. I suggest it might be a lyric, never used, that PGW wrote himself around 1902–9, when he was employed as a lyric writer by Seymour Hicks and the Gaiety Theatre. From 1790 until 1973, a detachment of Guardsmen marched through London every evening to mount guard over the Bank of England. A Guards colleague told me the food provided by the Bank was superb, but it was a very long way to march carrying your sword.

Gretna Green or somewhere. 50 p261. Marriage in England and Wales required more formalities than were required under Scottish law. For many years couples who faced opposition to their union travelled to Gretna Green just over the Scottish border.

Grey hairs in sorrow to the grave (to bring Tuppy's). 52 p247 and later; his clipped moustache in sorrow to the grave 97 p29. B. Genesis 42.38. "Then shall ye bring down my gray hairs with sorrow to the grave."

Grey, Zane. 38 p27. This prolific writer of Westerns (1872–1939) sold 13 million copies. See also *Riders of the Purple Sage*.

Greyhound released from the slips, like a. 64 p215. S. *Henry V*. 3.1: "I see you stand like greyhounds in the slips, Straining upon the start."

Greyhounds. See DOG-RACES.

Grief, void, dark and drear which finds no natural outlet. 83 p 63. Coleridge's 'Dejection: An Ode'.

Griffith, D.W. 38 p102. This film director (1875–1948) led the way in modern film production. The reference at 39 p31 is to the remarkable crowd scenes in his *The Birth of a Nation* (1915).

Griffo, Young. 78 p17. See Chap. 4.

Grimpen Mire, the Great. 95 p12. See Conan DOYLE's *The Hound of the Baskervilles*.

Grind the faces of the poor. 77 p199. B. Isaiah 3.15: "What mean ye that ye beat my people to pieces and grind the faces of the poor? Saith the Lord God of hosts."

Grinned horrible, a ghastly smile, like Death in the poem. 38 p39. Milton's *Paradise Lost*, Bk 2, l.845: "Death / Grinned horrible a ghastly smile, to / Hear his famine should be filled."

Grip. Give you the grip 48 p239. I am told this form of handshake is a Masonic sign of recognition.

Ground, solid. O let the solid ground not fail beneath my feet etc. 29 p83; 53 p173. T. *Maud*, Pt 1, Sect 11, verse 1.

Grover, a young fellow called. 78 p 93 (*Over Seventy*). Cricket must have more 'records' than any other game in the world. Most runs in an over in a Test/county/club match, most runs in an over on a certain ground, most runs on that ground by a last wicket stand, most catches taken in one match, etc. etc. C.A. Alington satirised the whole cricket records system with this splendid limerick. He was headmaster of Eton, went on to become Dean of Durham and wrote good detective stories. For those who do not know it:

There was a young fellow called Grover

Who bowled twenty-two wides in an over.
Which had never been done
By a clergyman's son
On a Thursday in August in Dover.

Grundy, Mrs. 48 p173; 66 p194; 77 p117. This lady, who has become the symbol of moral respectability, was a character in Thomas Morton's 1798 play *Speed the Plough.*

Gruntled. He (Jeeves) was far from being gruntled 59 p9; 68 p85. PGW did not coin it. I have been told that Guy Bolton read it somewhere and passed it on to PGW. It is a perfectly good word. The 1961 *Unabridged Webster's Dictionary* (not the College edition) states firmly that it is a British dialect word, meaning to put in good humour. It gives examples of its use by W.P. Webb (Texan historian) in 1963, by Emrys Hughes and by Christopher Morley, the novelist. I have to add that the 1979 edition contradicts this and states that it means to grunt or sulk. I suspect Webster's lost the plot here. Possibly, as I know has happened with one dictionary publisher, the person responsible for words beginning with 'G' never bothered to check with the man doing 'D'. Afternote. It is now back in the *Oxford English Dictionary*.

Guardees. A pop-eyed, smirking toothbrush-moustached Guardee 49 p155; a Bart who is also a Guardee is a rival the stoutest-hearted cove might well shudder at 61 p199; wearing the tie of the Brigade of Guards 89 p103; 93 p35. Because I have been asked if the Guards are the same as the National Guard in America, I should make it clear that PGW was referring to the Brigade of Guards, five regiments who can be described as the elite of the British Army. Their smartness on parade is famous across the world and equalled only by their gallantry in action. By some mysterious process, their senior warrant officers (sergeant-majors) inspire awe and respect among all who come into contact with them, and I have seen them politely, but very firmly, 'correcting' Royalty and four-star generals. 'Guardees', i.e. officers in the Brigade, were usually from the top of the social scale, which meant that a Guards officer who was also a baronet had a clear head-start in rivalry for a young lady's affections. In 'The Man Who Disliked Cats', Captain Bassett was in the Scots Guards, as was PGW's cousin James Deane (see Psmith in Chap. 37).

Guarding the bridge. See HORATIUS.

Guelph Hotel, London. 17 p3; 19 p19; 22 p122. PGW's change of the Coburg Hotel's name to 'Guelph', the family name of Britain's Hanoverian kings, was an allusion everybody recognised when he wrote it. The Coburg was named after the German duchy where Queen Victoria's Albert came from. It changed its name to the Connaught Hotel during the First World War, probably around the same time (1917), and for the same reason, that George V changed the name of the British Royal family from Saxe-Coburg-Gotha to Windsor.

Guffin and a gaby. See GABY.

Guide, philosopher and friend. 19 p27 and later. See Pope's 'Essay on Man',

Epistle 4, l.390: "Thou wert my guide, philosopher and friend."

Guillotine, the woman who knitted at foot of the. 93 p77. See DEFARGE, MME.

Guinea stamp, rank is but the. See 'RANK IS BUT THE PENNY STAMP'.

Guinevere. 30 p305; 48 p. See T. *Idylls of the King* ('Guinevere').

Gumbo, right in the. 15A p201; 27 p37. Another twist on being in the soup, i.e. being in trouble. Similar PGW coinages are 'up to one's neck in the Bovril'. See also BISQUE and OXO.

Gunga Din. 28 p130 and often later. This KIPLING poem was popular at amateur concerts in the UK for many years. PGW gives us the last line at 68 p65 & 73 p187: "You're a better man than I am, Gunga Din."

Gutenberg Bible. In the Blandings Castle library 19 p45. Robert Birley, headmaster of Eton (1949–63), had a great admiration for Wodehouse. He told me that he regarded Wodehouse as the last of a line that began in Shakespeare's day, writers brought up on the Classics, the Bible and the Book of Common Prayer. He had learned his craft before the advent of radio, film or television, and I was right to admire him.

Sir Robert Birley, as he later became, paid Wodehouse a practical compliment. In 1970 he published a booklet on the 100 most interesting books in the Eton library and naturally included its rare Gutenberg Bible, one of 48 in the world. In the middle of the half-page description, he inserted the sentence: "To the recorded copies of the Gutenberg Bible should be added one in the library of Blandings Castle in Shropshire." In a letter to Wodehouse, he said he hoped he would be approached by some German professor "to whom I shall suggest he catches the 11:18 or 2:30 train from Paddington Station to Market Blandings". He let it be known later that he never caught a German professor, but he had caused considerable anxiety to the famous New York bookseller H.O. Kraus.

My grateful thanks to Michael Meredith, the College Librarian, for searching out and sending me the last copy of this splendid addition to bibliographical scholarship.

Guv'nor. The. 22 p17. Nickname of the UK theatrical impresario George Edwardes, who made the Gaiety Theatre famous.

Guys and dolls. 93 p128. *Guys and Dolls* is a musical comedy (1950) by Frank Loesser.

Gypsy song, singing a. 51 p241; 84 p39 and elsewhere. Probably from one of two popular songs, 'The Happy Gipsy' by Sidney Nelson (1867) or 'I'm a Merry Zingara' by Balfe.

Gyves upon his wrists, walked between with. 25 p75 and later up to 97 p25. See ARAM, EUGENE.

H

(MTT = My thanks to)

Ha!, … as the Biblical character who spoke that word among the trumpets. 58 p275. See War horse.

Habit. In his h. as he lived 58 p293. See In his habit.

Hackenschmidt. 12 p183; 22 p54; with Gotch 14 p185. At the beginning of the 20th century, there was a craze for professional wrestling in Britain. Boxing was banned in many places, so C.B. Cochran, Britain's equivalent to Florenz Ziegfeld, decided in 1900 to stage wrestling matches. His great discovery was the Estonian George Hackenschmidt (1878–1968). They made each other's fortunes; Cochran was a brilliant showman and Hackenschmidt was a superb wrestler. Within a year he and Cochran had made wrestling the biggest draw in variety.

Hackenschmidt had one problem — he could not fake a fight; he wrestled to win, always did, and people got bored. He claimed to be world champion and no one disputed this till he went to America, where his defeat by Frank Gotch, an Iowa farmer, in 1908 stunned the sporting world as much as Corbett's victory over John L. Sullivan in the boxing ring had done in 1892.

MTT Murray Hedgcock for informing me that Hackenschmidt's ashes lie in the West Norwood cemetery, London.

See also Zbysco.

Hadn't said Yes, but … she hadn't said No. 71 p119. Song 'She Didn't Say Yes, She Didn't Say No' (1931) by Harbach and Kern.

Hagen, Walter. 47 p141; 69 p72. Elegant, suave American golfer who single-handedly raised the social status of professional golfers in the 1930s.

Haggard, Rider, compared to Homer. 3 p59; 4 p196. British writer (1856–1925) best known for his 1885 novel *King Solomon's Mines*. Based on his own experiences in Africa, Haggard wrote it for a five-shilling bet that he could produce a best-seller like Stevenson's *Treasure Island* of two years before.

Hail to thee, blithe spirit (Shelley would say). 46 p38 and later. MTT Charles Gould and many others for correcting my gross error and informing me this is from Shelley's 'To a Skylark', not a certain other gentleman's 'Ode to a Nightingale'. One of those laughable misunderstandings.

Haileybury. 6 p60 and three times later. See Chap. 3.

Hailsham, Dr, runs a slimming clinic. 81 p14. One of PGW's ripostes to the people who persisted in attacking him after the war. Quinton Hogg (1907–2001), a

British politician who urged strongly that PGW should be prosecuted, became Lord Hailsham. He was rotund in build, thereby allowing PGW to get in this crack.

Hair in a braid. Often in PGW. Ready for anything; ready for the fray. I suggest this comes from PGW's Classical education and that the reference is to the Spartans who tied their hair in a braid before going into battle. Another possibility is the song 'Queenie with Her Hair in a Braid' from *The Girls of Gottenberg* (1907).

Hairs, grey. Bring Tuppy's grey h. in sorrow to the grave. See GREY HAIRS.

Hairy Ainus. See AINUS.

Hales, A.G., war correspondent. 11 p111. Hales (1860–1936) was a well-known British war correspondent, reporting on the Boer War (1900–1) and the Balkan and Russo-Japanese wars later.

Half a loaf is better than no bread. See CHAMBERLAIN, JOSEPH.

Half my kingdom, even unto half my k. 50 p132 and later. B. Esther 5.6. This is what the king offered Esther, "who obtained favour in his sight".

Half pint. Frequent. General term for any small person.

Half the world has no idea how the other half lives, one. 72 p214 and elsewhere. "Half the world knows not how the other half lives." Traditional proverb revived by *How the Other Half Lives*, a book on the appalling housing conditions of New York's slum tenements by the social reformer Jacob Riis. Its success led Theodore Roosevelt to institute much-needed reforms, similar to those urged by *Cosy Moments* in *Psmith Journalist.*

Half was not told unto me. 68 p70; 72 p82 and later. When the Queen of Sheba visited Solomon, she was very struck by both his wisdom and his wealth. B. 1 Kings 10.7: "and, behold, the half was not told unto me; thy wisdom and prosperity exceedeth the fame which I had heard."

Half-a-league, half-a-league onward blokes. 54 p160 and later. T. 'The Charge of the Light Brigade'. It begins: "Half a league, half a league, / Half a league onward, / All in the valley of death, / Rode the six hundred."

Hall & Knight. 3 p196 and later. This was the standard school algebra book from PGW's boyhood to mine.

Halleran, Ask Mr. Advertisements along roads in Long Island 34 p232. MTT Karen Shotting for the information that 'Ask Mr Halloran, the Real Estate Man' was a well-known slogan in Flushing, Long Island, for many years.

Halloa! Halloa! Halloa! What? 23 p45. I deliberately chose this reference to introduce the vexed question of Hallo — Hello — Hullo, which illustrates how quickly a language can change. (For the suffix 'What?', see WHAT.) The *Oxford English Dictionary* says 'Hallo' is/was an exclamation of surprise, used when one meets a friend unexpectedly. In this usage by PGW c.1919–20, it is clearly an exclamation rather than a salutation.

There has been much discussion as to when Hallo/Hello/Hullo became the common greeting. Stephen Fry believes it began with the growing use of the telephone in the 1890s. This certainly occurred in America, where an article in a 1904 women's magazine on 'Telephone Manners' stated firmly that "Hulloa" was now the correct form with which to open your conversation. This is supported by p317 of *A Damsel in Distress* when George Bevan says "Hello" on the telephone and then remembers he is in England and should have said "Are you there?" Further down the page, the heroine tells him not to say "Hello" because it sounds so abrupt. The OED agrees with her and says the word 'Hello' became the accepted 'telephonic' greeting in the UK in 1932. The question is — what did people say before that? They probably simply said "Good morning", or "Good afternoon".

The fall from favour of these once universal greetings is said to be due to one man, Thomas J. Barrett (1842–1914). Now regarded as the father of modern advertising, he turned Pears' Soap into the best-known product in the world (see LANGTRY). He decided the soap would sell even better if it was incorporated into a popular catchphrase. When his staff told him the most common phrase in the language was "Good Morning", he created the phrase: "Good Morning, have you used Pears' Soap?" This became the curse of the country for 20 years. Reluctant to have the phrase automatically repeated back to them, people simply stopped saying "Good morning". An intriguing theory.

'Hallo', in its various forms, certainly began as an exclamation. "Hallo, hallo, hallo! What's all this, then?" was the traditional query of an English policeman when coming upon something out of the ordinary. Perhaps the informality of the 1920s confirmed its use in reaction to the more formal "Good morning"; perhaps Mr Barrett did bring about this minor revolution. But at least we know that when *A Damsel in Distress* came out (1919), "Hallo" was not the term Lady Patricia Marsh expected to hear. See also HO!

Halls of Montezuma, From the. 91 p214. March of the US Marine Corps, written 1847.

Halsey Court. See Chap. 25.

Ham. 68 p93. This term of derision for an actor is said to come from either the word 'h'amateur', by which professionals mocked amateur actors pronouncing words badly, or from the ham fat used to take off makeup. It is believed to have originated in the US about 1912 and come to the UK after the First War.

Hamadryad. 34 p14. A wood nymph who presided over trees.

Hamlet's aunt. Which book of Dickens is it where a woman looks like H.'s a.? 89 p40. The answer is D. *David Copperfield*, chap. 25 — Mrs Henry Spiker. Dickens' characters were so well known, their characteristics entered the language. My mother often used to describe people by likening them to someone in Dickens. As a boy I asked her why she referred to people as "a real Mark Tapley" or "he's another Pecksniff" or "she's just like Rosa Dartle". She replied: "Read Dickens and you'll find out." Are Scrooge and Micawber the only two commonly referred to today?

Hammams/Hummums, Old. 9 p91; 31 p213. See Chap. 25 (Hotels).

Hammer, Mike. 79 p167; 86 p212. Fictional private eye created by Mickey SPILLANE.

Hammerhead. 82 p53. An American term for someone stupid, a blockhead.

Hand that rocks the cradle is the hand that rules the world. 85 p154. Poem by William Ross Wallace (1819–81), set to music in the US 1895 and published in the UK 1901. It was promptly parodied in the UK with 'The Hand that Rolls the Pudden' (1904).

Hand, touch of a vanished (and the sound of a voice that has gone). See TOUCH OF A VANISHED HAND.

Hands Across the Sea. 39 p170 and elsewhere. This 1899 march by John Philip Sousa was written to celebrate the amity between the USA and her allies (this was in the aftermath of the Spanish-American War). It became so popular in both the UK and the US that it came to be used to denote an American visitor to Britain and vice versa. The original words by Byron Webber seem to have vanished from people's minds. "Hands across the sea! Feet on British ground! The old blood is bold blood, the wide world round."

Hands to the plough. When we put our hands to the plough, we do not readily sheathe the sword 52 p52; and later. As far as I can work out, this is PGW's mix of two sources: B. Luke 9.62 and Mr Asquith. Luke has: "No man, having put his hand to the plough and looking back, is fit for the kingdom of God." On 9 November 1914, after the outbreak of the First World War, Mr Asquith, then Prime Minister, said: "We shall never sheathe the sword which we have not lightly drawn …"

Hangover cures. Frequent. PGW mentions various ingredients, Worcester sauce, cayenne pepper and raw eggs among them. On 24 December 1998, the *Daily Telegraph* printed a recipe for what it called the traditional Prairie Oyster. "Put into a glass the unbroken yolk of a free-range egg. Pour on top a jigger of brandy, a teaspoon each of wine vinegar and Worcester sauce, two dashes of tabasco, a dash of salt and cayenne pepper. It must be drunk in one swallow."

Every Wodehouse reader has his favourite description of the reactions of the patient having taken Jeeves' pick-me-up. Mine is the effect it has on one's eyeballs.

PGW refers three times to the chemist "at the top of the Haymarket", which my directories show was James Heppel and Sons. They have gone now, but the tradition lingers on. I read a few years ago that two of the clubs in St James's Street had had big dinners the night before and that there had been "a heavy run on Harris's hangover cure". Harris's have been in St James's Street since 1790 and created their 'Pick Me Up' in the 1850s; their remedy has since been amended slightly to render "the potion rather more acceptable to modern tastes".

I visited Harris's the following week when the conversation went roughly as follows:

"Good morning, sir. Can I help you?"

"Yes. Before you show it to me, could I ask some questions about your hang-over cure?"

"Certainly. What would you like to know about it?"

"Well, firstly, is it dark brown in colour and sinister in appearance?"

"Yes, it is."

"Oh! Well, secondly, does it taste revolting?"

"Yes, it does indeed."

"Thirdly, forgive me asking this but I do have a reason. Does it make your eyes pop out?"

"Yes."

"What! Really? How does it do that?"

"It's the ammonia we put in it!"

I have not yet needed this elixir, but clearly Harris's of St James's Street (on the left-hand side as you walk down) has the right idea.

Afternote. Christine Hewitt informs me that owing either to legislation or inability to secure the right ingredients, this panacea is no longer available. Eheu fugaces!

Hanwell. 80 p8. A well-known London lunatic asylum, founded in 1831.

Ha'penny dips. 81 p184. Gas and electricity came to some parts of rural England very late. In some places, mains supplies did not arrive till the 1970s. Gas, candles and paraffin (kerosene) were what PGW would have used for lighting during his boyhood. The ha'penny dips were cheap candles, made from dipping a wick in melted tallow. They were sold in small butcher's shops and general stores.

Happiness consists in anticipating an impossible future. 9 p166. Probably from Schopenhauer's *Emptiness of Existence*: "No man is happy. Man strives all his life through for an imaginary happiness, which he seldom attains."

Happiness, spread a little. 92 p192; 94 p64. Song from the 1929 musical *Mr Cinders*.

Happy birthday. 88 p205. This song was written by Mildred Hill and her sister Patty in 1893. There was a sensation in 1934 when the ladies reminded the broadcasting companies and Western Union that they owned the copyright of the most popular song in America and they would like some royalties, please. They got them, but Western Union promptly closed down its singing birthday message service (see *Spring Fever*).

Happy Day. See Oh, happy day.

Happy Days Are Here Again. 58 p176 and elsewhere. Song from the 1929 film *Chasing Rainbows*; it became famous as F.D. Roosevelt's campaign song in 1932.

Happy mean. 8 p63. Used by many writers but an early source is Horace's *Odes* 2.10.5: "Whoso loves well the golden mean."

Happy thought. 6 p58. A compliment by the young Wodehouse to F.C. Burnand (1836–1917), the editor of *Punch*, who accepted PGW's first contributions in

1902. Burnand's book *Happy Thoughts* was the humorous diary of a young man who, every page or so, introduces a new topic with the heading 'Happy Thought'. See also POPGOOD AND GROOLY.

Happy Warrior. 63 p234. Wordsworth's 'Character of the Happy Warrior', but the 'Happy Warrior' was also the nickname of Alfred E. Smith, Governor of New York, who lost the 1928 presidential election to Herbert Hoover.

Harborough. 49 p143. PGW's mix of two well-known English Public Schools: Harrow + Marlborough = Harborough.

Harchester. 39 p106. Ditto. Harrow + Winchester = Harchester. See also CHARCHESTER.

Harcourt, Hope, heroine of the musical *Anything Goes*. See Chap. 24.

Hard as a picnic egg. 93 p162 and elsewhere. Simile for someone tough, hard-boiled etc. Summed up well in the 'Ballad of Yukon Jake'(1921) by Edward Paramore (1895–1956), a parody of 'Dangerous Dan McGrew': "Oh, tough as a steak was Yukon Jake, Hard boiled as a picnic egg. He washed his shirt in the Yukon dirt, And drank his rum by the keg."

Hard Hearted Hannah, the vamp from Savannah. 39 p28. 1924 song by Bigelow and Bates.

Hardy, Thomas. 35 p191 and often later. A realistic — i.e. gloomy — writer (1840–1928). If things can go wrong, they will go wrong, was his general approach. The reference at 72 p142 (a couple missing their wedding through a misunderstanding) is very similar to his *Far from the Madding Crowd*.

Harlequin three-quarters of us all, makes. 18 p212; 85 p24. The Harlequins are a famous Rugby football team. Membership was originally restricted to Rugger players from Oxford and Cambridge who wanted to carry on playing, but did not want to be tied to a normal club. When PGW wrote of them, the Harlequins were famous for always playing an open, fast game as opposed to the many clubs who preferred a 'tight' (i.e. dull, defensive) game.

Harley Street. 35 p136; 65 p39 and elsewhere. Just north of Oxford Street, London, this has been the home of England's most prestigious doctors for over a century.

Harlow, Jean. 53 p285; 54 p65. This platinum blonde film actress (1911–37) was as famous for her turbulent private life as she was for her screen successes.

Harrige's. 73 p14 & p182, the first English store to have escalators. Although Harrod's (see below) had appeared under their own name in PGW's books, they objected to being named in *Ring for Jeeves*, so PGW mixed their name with that of their rival Selfridge's to create Harrige's. PGW was correct on the escalators, which Harrod's introduced in 1898. For the first month each escalator was manned by a member of staff armed with brandy and sal volatile for those customers overcome by the experience of a moving staircase. See also SQUARE ONE. For "might be able to buy a knighthood at Harrige's" (73 p218), see PEERAGES.

Harrod's. 7 p59; 33 p246; 34 p5 and later. For many years London's most prestigious department store, it was founded in 1849 and its motto 'Omnia Omnibus Ubique' (Everything for everyone everywhere) became famous. They have met some unusual challenges, including providing an elephant (ordered by Ronald Reagan, then governor of California) for a Republican Party gathering. They also enabled Guy Bolton to keep his promise to his wife Virginia that she would be buried in an English country churchyard. See Chap. 24.

Harrogate. 31 p223; 35 p216. The routine described by PGW was accurate, and you can still imbibe the waters at the Pump Room. Up to 1939, the Harrogate 'high season' was the last fortnight of July to mid-August. The London Season, which began in May, could be an exhausting affair and the wealthy and aristocratic would endure the discomfort of Harrogate to settle their livers before 'the Twelfth'. (12 August was when grouse shooting began and 'Society' travelled to Scotland to do it. As late as the 1960s, there were special trains running from St Pancras and King's Cross to transport them to the grouse moors.)

PGW described the Harrogate routine so well because he took the waters there in 1924 (and published 'Clustering Around Young Bingo' less than four months later). He and Ethel stayed at the Grand Hotel, Harrogate, from 1 September to 1 October. It is still there, though it is now an office building called Windsor House, and it is a pleasant stroll down the hill through the park to the Pump Room *(see photo opposite)* and a good healthy uphill walk to return. It was probably the insistence on the early rising and walking to the Pump Room that did people most good. I make no comment on the curative qualities of the water, though from personal experience I can assure readers it tastes foul and does indeed smell strongly of bad eggs.

The prescribed routine was:

7–7:30 A.M. Rise. Walk to and take first drink at Pump Room.
7:30–8:15 Gentle walk. Take another glass at Pump Room.
8:15–9:00 Listen to band. If advised, take third glass of water.
9:00 Walk back to hotel. Breakfast.
10:00 Morning paper or writing letters.
11:00 Sherry.
11:30 Second visit to Pump Room. Another glass of water.
12:00 Gentle walk round the gardens. Another glass of water if advised.
1:00 Walk back to hotel. Lunch.
2:00 Rest followed by walking, golf or drive in countryside.

PGW visited another spa, Droitwich, two years later, where you float in the water, not drink it. The two spas combined to make PGW's 'Droitgate Spa' (see DROITGATE), but the references to the Pump Room and the band playing (the bandstand was across the road from the Pump Room) make Harrogate the major source.

Harrow House, Dover. 18 p179. This is based on Malvern House, the prep school in Dover PGW attended before going to Dulwich. See Chap. 3.

Hart, as pants the. See PANTS THE HART.

The Pump Room at Harrogate

The motor cars in the picture show the photograph was taken around 1924, the year the Wodehouses took the waters at Harrogate. The band-stand was at the bottom right, out of picture.

Hart or roe, steady on his pins as a. 85 p24. See FLYING LIKE THE YOUTHFUL HART.

Hart, William S. 38 p21. Hart (1870–1946) was a popular star of innumerable Westerns in the old silent days.

Harvest. What would the h. be? See WHAT WOULD THE HARVEST BE?

Harvey, a big hit. 71 p93. This 1944 play (the chap with a phantom rabbit) ran for years and is still being revived.

Hat is on the side of his head, his. 68 p172 and elsewhere. In the days when every man wore a hat (see Chap. 6), the way it was worn was an indication of the wearer's mood. Clapped carelessly on the side of the head, it indicated a reckless free spirit, out for joy and jollity. If even more on one side, it indicated that the wearer was, if not inebriated, certainly mellow, 'flown with wine' etc. In the British film *Jack Ahoy!* (1933), the main character, a Bertie Woosterish young man played by Claude Hulbert, expressed his satisfaction with life by singing 'My Hat's on the Side of My Head'.

Hat was still in the ring. 38 p236. This stems from the early days of boxing when it indicated a willingness to fight on. Since fights then lasted as long as the participants could stand (bouts could go to a hundred rounds or more), it indicated determination. Theodore Roosevelt indicated his willingness to stand again for the presidency in 1912 by using the phrase.

Hatchet. Less like a h. than a dissipated saw. See KNIFE, BLUNT.

Hate becomes pity, pity forgiveness and forgiveness love. 63 p239. From Nietzsche's 'Thus Spake Zarathustra'. MTT Elin Woodger.

Havant, Duchess of. 13 p43; the Havant case 19 p137. See Chap. 16.

Having a wonderful time and wishes I was there. 93 p54. Since picture postcards came into common use at the end of the 19th century, the traditional British greeting on the card you sent home from your holiday has been: "Having a wonderful time. Wish you were here." I am informed there is a breakaway movement in the USA which uses: "The weather is beautiful. Wish you were here", but such deviation is rare in the UK. See also HELP IS A THING.

Hawk, Harry (Unce Tom Cobley etc). 7 p105. The old English country ballad 'Widdecombe Fair', recounting the adventures of Harry Hawk and six friends riding one horse, is still popular today.

Hawk-Eye. Old Hawk-Eye Wooster. 51 p38. See Chap. 30 of *The Last of the Mohicans*. Of Hawk-Eye, it says: "His sight never fails."

Hawkshaw, the detective. 40 p199; 42 p104; 43 p45. Fictional detective in UK boys' magazines from 1892 to 1940, though his adventures on stage began as early as 1863. Sexton Blake was a later, more successful rival; Dick Tracy was a US equivalent.

Hay, Ian. I.H. is a slim chap 66 p103. Hay (1876–1952), who wrote the plays *A Damsel in Distress* (1928), *Baa Baa Black Sheep* (1929), and *Leave It to Psmith* (1930) with PGW, was indeed a slim, dapper man.

Hayling Island. 18 p51. See Chap. 16.

Hayling, Lord Arthur. 16 p41. See Chap. 16.

Hays, Will. 46 p28. Alarmed by the publicity aroused by the current drugs and sex scandals of 1922, the Hollywood moguls hurriedly created an organisation that would vet all films from a moral point of view. The man chosen to head it was Will H. Hays (1879–1954).

Hazzard, Jack, actor. 74 p197. This actor married Alice DOVEY in 1916; he died 1935.

He is your man and he's doing you wrong. 63 p17. See song 'Frankie and Johnnie' purportedly based on an incident in New Orleans in the 1850s, though some say St Louis in the 1880s.

He seemed to feel a breath of life along his keel. 62 p78; 64 p241 and later. See PIG SOMETHING.

He/she cometh not. 31 p76; 71 p119 and later. See MARIANA OF THE MOATED GRANGE.

He stood at the door of Burgess's fish sauce shop, welcoming him in. 51 p201; 88 p23. The poet Lord BYRON coined the phrase 'Burgess's fish sauce shop', claiming it was the best test for sobriety. At 56 p93, PGW expanded this into the tongue-twisting "Ethelberta Oswaldthistle stood at the door of Burgess's fish-sauce shop, dismissing the Leith police with silly shibboleths." Burgess's, who advertised in the first edition of *The Times* in 1788 and whose shop was a landmark in the Strand for 150 years, are still in business.

He wanted what he wanted when he wanted it. 24 p91; 86 p45. See Want what they want.

Heacham, Lord. 53 p63. See Chap. 32.

Head ached. His h. a., and a drowsy numbness pained his sense. 53 p234; 79 p51 and elsewhere. Keats' 'Ode to a Nightingale'. "My heart aches and a drowsy numbness pains my sense, as though of hemlock I had drunk."

Head on a charger. The blighter whose head I want on a charger 27 p9. See the sad end of John the Baptist in B. Matthew 14.11.:"And his head was brought in a charger, and given to the damsel; and she brought it to her mother." A charger was a large serving dish.

Head on which all the sorrows of the world had fallen. 42 p29 and later. See Sorrows of the world.

Healthward Ho, Lowick. 40 p27. *Healthward Ho* was the name of a publication produced c.1912 by Eustace Miles, squash champion and prolific writer on many subjects including health and food.

Healthy mind in the healthy body, the. 57 p265. Translation of 'Mens sana in corpore sano' from Juvenal's *Satires* 10.356.

Hear the beating of its wings. See Beating of its wings.

Hearst, William Randolph. 73 p219; 83 p68. This newspaper magnate (1863–1951) must have had the largest collection of ancient buildings and historic furniture in the world. (When David Niven stayed at Hearst's San Simeon, he slept in Richelieu's bed.) On one occasion, Hearst admired a monastery in Spain, bought it, dismantled it, built a railway line to take the stones to the coast, and shipped them to California. He also provided a new monastery to replace the one he had bought. A biography claims that, at one time, Hearst and his mother owned 56 houses between them. As Capt Biggar said in *Ring for Jeeves* when Mrs Spottsworth listed her six houses: "Nice to have a roof over your head." (MTT Neil Midkiff for the information that Hearst brought at least three mediaeval religious buildings over from Europe. One is now at Vina, California, another is in North Miami Beach while the third was bought by Huntington Hartford and is in Nassau in the Bahamas.) See also Chap 7.

Heart belongs to Daddy, my. See My heart belongs to Daddy.

Heart bowed down (with weight of woe, To weakest hopes will cling). 32 p271 and often later. The song 'The Heart Bowed Down' was written in 1843 for the *Bohemian Girl,* words by Bunn, music by Balfe. A 'standard' song in the Army & Navy Stores 1907 catalogue.

'Heart Foam'. "A little thing of my own. I call it 'Heart Foam'. I shall not publish it" (quoting England's greatest librettist) 2 p101. From 'A little thing' to 'publish it', is from G&S *Patience* Act 1. To the end of his life, PGW maintained that W.S. Gilbert was the best librettist of all.

Heart for any fate, I'll be up and ready with a. 61 p209. See Let us be up and

DOING.

Heart has ne'er within him burned, whose. 21 p117. See BREATHES THERE THE MAN.

Heart, meek and contrite. 36 p89; 63 p12. See SPIRIT, HUMBLE AND CONTRITE.

Heart of a little child. His heart is the heart of a little child 12 p196; 21 p196; 66 p71 and later. See the touching death scene of Colonel Newcombe in Thackeray's *The Newcombes*. See also G&S *Ruddigore* Act 1.

Heart stood still, my. See MY HEART STOOD STILL.

Heart was young, when the. 42 p43. See Lehar's song 'When the Heart Is Young'.

Hearts and Flowers. Played on cinema organs 35 p201. In the days of silent movies, this piece by Tobani and Brine (1899) was *always* played on the piano or organ during the big love scene.

Heart's in the Highlands a-chasing the deer, my. See MY HEART'S IN THE HIGHLANDS.

Hearts just as pure and fair may beat in Belgrave Square. 26 p77. G&S *Iolanthe* Act 1.

Hearts that beat as one, two. 28 p105 and elsewhere. See TWO HEARTS.

Hearty, happy and healthy overpowering sort of dashed female. 23 p45. Around 1919 there was a craze for synchronised gymnastics and various women's organisations took up the habit. I seem to recall the words 'Heart, Happiness and Health' as the motto of some such society, though I have not been able to link it to the League of Health and Beauty, who achieved much publicity with a mass gymnastic display in Hyde Park.

Heat. See NOT THE HEAT.

Heathen Chinee. 7 p215. From Bret Harte's (1836–1902) once universally-known humorous poem 'Plain Language from Truthful James' (1870): "The heathen Chinee is peculiar, / Which the same I would wish to explain."

Heaven, blue. See BLUE HEAVEN.

Heaven protects the working girl. 71 p103 and later. Marie Dressler, the heavyweight comedienne (1871–1934), made her name singing 'Heaven Will Protect the Working Girl' in the 1909 show *Tillie's Nightmare*. Three lines give a flavour of it:

> You may tempt the upper classes
> With your villainous demi-tasses,
> But Heaven will prote-e-e-e-e-ct the working girl.

They don't write them like that any more.

Heavenly Waltz Company. 20 p18. PGW twist on *The Waltz Dream*, a musical of 1911.

Heavy and weary weight of this unintelligible world, the. 93 p167. See WEIGHT.

Hecuba. See WHAT'S HECUBA TO HIM.

Heeby-jeebies. 37 p260 and later. This expression of apprehension (popular enough to give its name to a short-lived dance) was coined by the cartoonist Billy de Beck in his cartoons in the early 1920s. He also gave the world

'HOTSY-TOTSY', 'Horse feathers' and the character Barney Google. See also JIM-JAMS.

Heir of the ages. 32 p263; 59 p176; 69 p207. T. 'Locksley Hall': "I the heir of all the ages, in the foremost files of time."

Held me with a glittering eye. 22 p23 and later. Coleridge's *Rime of the Ancient Mariner*: "He holds him with his glittering eye — the Wedding Guest stood still."

Hell hath no fury like a woman scorned. 40 p73; like a woman who wants her tea and can't get it 43 p241; like a woman who's come eighty miles to be made a fool of 47 p82; and elsewhere. From Congreve's *The Mourning Bride* 3.8. "Heav'n has no rage, like love to hatred turn'd, / Nor Hell a fury, like a woman scorn'd."

Scorned women are doing well nowadays. My favourite is Lady Moon, who was scorned when her husband, Sir Graham Moon, went off with another woman. On 27 May 1992, Britain read with delight how she expressed her fury on a spouse who enjoyed the finer things of life. When she saw his new, expensive BMW car outside the other woman's house, she poured ten pints of white paint over it. She followed this up by taking a sledge-hammer and breaking through the door that separated his wing of their house from hers. She cut four inches off the sleeves of each of his thirty-two Savile Row suits, then took seventy bottles of vintage wine and port from his cellar and distributed them around the village, leaving them on doorsteps like a milkman. These included Chateau Latour at £300 a bottle. His riposte was weak to say the least: "Sir Peter said it was not conduct becoming to a lady."

Hello. See HALLOA! HALLOA! HALLOA! WHAT?

Hello, huge. Give him a huge hello. See HUGE HELLO.

Hell's foundations are quivering. 35 p181 and frequent later. See hymn 'Onward Christian Soldiers'. "Hell's foundations quiver / At the shout of praise."

Help in time of trouble, a very present. 57 p281. B. Psalms 46.1: "God is our refuge and our strength, a very present help in times of trouble."

Help is a thing I am always glad to be of. 84 p136. Typical PGW skill with words. Just by inverting a common phrase, he made it funny. See also THINGS UP WITH WHICH.

Hem of whose garment I ought to be kissing. 90 p189. A vague recollection, I suggest, of B. Matthew 9.21, where a sick woman touched the hem of Jesus' garment and was cured. MTT Adrian Matthews for suggesting also B. Luke 7.38.

Hemans, Mrs. 53 p276 and later. The poetess Mrs Felicia Hemans (1793–1835) gave the world "The boy stood on the burning deck" and "The stately homes of England, How beautiful they stand". See CASABIANCA and STATELY HOMES.

Hemingway, Ernest. 64 p92; 68 p213; 73 p62. PGW sometimes spelled the name of this adventurous writer (1899–1961) with two 'mm's. Perhaps a misprint, but maybe from habit, since PGW had used the name Hemmingway in four previous stories.

Henderson, Dolly. 42 p310; 91 p21. See Chap. 38.

Hendon. Since they started that College at Hendon 64 p58; and later. After various scandals in the Metropolitan Police in the 1920s, it was decided to open a police officers training college at Hendon in London on the lines of Sandhurst/West Point. There was tremendous opposition from the police unions and the college only lasted from 1934 to 1939, although the name is still used to refer to the Peel Centre, opened in 1974 and serving the same function.

Hengist and Horsa. 63 p6. Because of their names, these two men have remained in the popular memory. They were the first Teutonic invaders of England after the Romans left, landing in Kent in 449 A.D. Jeff Miller's joke ("Horsa, keep your tail up") is from the popular 1930s song by Hirsch and Kaplan, 'Horsey, keep your tail up'.

Henley regatta. 76 p31 and later. This has been going since 1839 and is still a highlight in the social round. See also Chap 22.

Henries, pick up the. 32 p209. By implication, this is US slang for feet or shoes, but I have been unable to find the explanation. A reference to Henry Foote, the 19th-century politician perhaps? Or was Henry a popular make of shoe?

Henry II. Will no one rid me of this turbulent butler? 63 p229. See BECKET, THOMAS À.

Henry, not an 'Arry. 1 p137. When PGW wrote this, 'Arry and 'Arriet were terms for males and females of the lower classes, popularised by the *'Arry* poems by E.J. Milliken in *Punch* (1877–89) and Phil May's cartoons (1880–1900). To classify a man as a Henry meant he was definitely higher up the social scale than an 'Arry.

Henry, O. 90 p155. PGW had a great admiration for Henry (William Sydney Porter 1862–1910) and was very proud that a New York paper said one of his early stories ('At Geisenheimer's'; see Chap. 23) showed him to be a second O. Henry. Henry's whip-crack endings to his short stories were famous, and every young writer of the day tried to imitate him.

Henry of Navarre, helmet of. See NAVARRE.

Henson, Leslie. 46 p124; 49 p227; 56 p124. This popular pop-eyed actor (1891–1951) played the comic lead in PGW's *Sally* and *The Beauty Prize*.

Her best friends won't tell her, but she suffers from B.O. 91 p82. PGW's gloss on two well-known American advertisements. The 'best friends' part comes from the LISTERINE mouthwash advertisement of 1923 to prevent bad breath. The term 'B.O.' (body odour) was coined by a deodorant manufacturer in 1919 and the Lifebuoy soap firm advertised their product in the 1930s as the best counter to this dreadful affliction. In the 1950s we used to joke about how far advertising could go. I recall vividly a friend of mine claiming he had seen an advertisement in an American magazine: 'Make Your Armpit Your Charm Pit' and we refused to believe him. I owe Allan Law an apology. This was indeed the slogan of the Stopette spray deodorant company.

Herbert, A.P. On every corner 78 p87. Herbert (1890–1971) served at Gallipoli in the First World War, became a barrister and a writer for *Punch*, wrote musicals, was the last MP for Oxford University, and wrote brilliant books on fictional law cases in which Mr Albert Haddock proved the law was indeed 'a ass'. A splendid chap, Herbert endeared himself to all as a Member of Parliament by his constant badgering of the House of Commons to allow people to enjoy themselves. When Parliament decided to restrict pub opening hours while keeping their own bars open all the time, Herbert announced he would lay criminal charges against the Speaker for "keeping a disorderly house". The House of Commons backed down. It was following his example that I used to pay my Income Tax on lavatory paper (Herbert recommended an eggshell). The Income Tax people didn't like it and I had to remind them that, as Herbert had pointed out, a cheque was merely a signed authority to draw money from my account. So long as it was durable, the material was unimportant. I should add they dealt with it very well. They took it for three years and then wrote me a splendid letter admitting I was right but asking me nicely to stop. If I didn't, they would have to start charging me extra 'administrative costs'.

Hercules at the crossroads (duty or pleasure). 3 p193; spun wool for Omphale 24 p75; a labour of Hercules 25 p26. For the story of the twelve labours of Hercules, see any good edition of legends of Greece and Rome. PGW, like most schoolboys of his time, had worked his way through them in English, Latin and probably Greek.

Here today and gone tomorrow, I often say. 76 p199. A common expression which Aphra Behn (1640–89) used in her book *The Lucky Chance*.

Here's mud in your eye. See MUD IN YOUR EYE.

Hero, my. See MY HERO.

He's a bear, he's a bear. 28 p240; 36 p35 and later. I have found contradictory explanations for this. The term is American, meaning both good and bad. "He's a bear", "It will be a bear of a fight", etc., was in common use in the USA 1910–40. I also remember it as a common interpolation by the audience when listening to ragtime or jazz. I consulted many people on this, but nobody knew what I was talking about. I eventually remembered the song and looked it up. In 1911 Irving Berlin wrote the words and music to 'Everybody's Doing It Now', a ragtime song where the last line reads: "It's a bear, It's a bear, It's a bear, there!" It became a popular jazz tag-line for twenty years.

The only UK equivalent I can think of is the 1908 music hall (vaudeville) song 'Let's All Go Down the Strand' by Castling and Murphy. At the end of the line, the singer pauses and the orchestra plays six notes before he resumes. Around 1910, somebody in the audience decided to sing the words "And have a banana" to the six notes. It has been sung this way ever since.

He's all the world to me. See ALL THE WORLD.

He's in the pig sty. You can tell him by his hat. 87 p171. See FATHER'S IN THE PIGSTYE.

Hesperus, The Wreck of the. See SKIPPER and WRECK OF THE HESPERUS.

Hew to the line, my poppet, and let the chips fall where they may. 68 p26. The only source I have found is a speech (5 June 1880) by Roscoe Conkling nominating Ulysses S. Grant for a third term as president: "Hew to the line and let the chips fall where they may."

Hewn from the living rock. 21 p59 and elsewhere, especially tough 'granite-faced' policemen. The phrase seems to have become popular in the late 19th century with the discovery of the many ancient churches carved deep into the rocky hillside in Lalibela, ABYSSINIA. As an alternative, B. Isaiah 51.1 has "look unto the rock whence you are hewn."

Hey-nonny-nonny and a hot-cha-cha. 57 p99; 60 p274 and later. Both terms are well known on their own (Olde English/Jazz American), but their use together is strange. MTT Catherine Bott, who reminded me the words appear in the film *Singin' in the Rain*, but that was too late. The *Oxford English Dictionary* states that George Kaufman used the combined phrase in his Pulitzer prize-winning musical *Of Thee I Sing* (1931), and PGW borrowed them to use in 'Buried Treasure' a couple of years later.

Hicks Corners. 22 p106; 27 p274. US derisive term for small country towns. Little-Puddlebury-in-the-Marsh is an equivalent UK usage.

Hicks, Seymour. 4 p151. This famous actor-manager for whom PGW wrote lyrics in 1906–7 appears as Higgs in *The Head of Kay's* and Briggs in *Not George Washington*. Hicks (1871–1949) played the debonair man-about-town to perfection. In Edwardian London, when Fashion was all, he made a bet he could set a new fashion in a week. Appearing as a witness in a law case, he astounded everybody by wearing a pink, not white, shirt with his morning dress. Within two days, young exquisites were wearing pink shirts along Piccadilly.

Hicks Theatre in Shaftesbury Avenue. 9 p82; 10 often. Seymour HICKS (see above) built this theatre in Shaftesbury Avenue in 1906 and put his name on it. Unfortunately, the significance of the word 'hick' overcame his own popularity, and he was forced to change the name to the 'Globe'.

Hiding behind settees, sofas, desks etc. See SETTEES.

Higgs. See HICKS, SEYMOUR.

High hills, skip/leap like h.h. See HILLS.

High, middle and low justice. 53 p27 & p158; 58 p18; 68 p171. Bertie was exaggerating in the third reference but making the point that Esmond Haddock as a J.P. — Justice of the Peace (local magistrate) — was looking forward to punishing Gussie Fink-Nottle if he had the chance. I have been unable to trace the origin of the term 'high, middle and low justice', but I am pretty sure it stems from the period, roughly 1100–1300, when the English legal system was developing into its present form. The sovereign delegated his authority as judge to his senior judges (today's High Court), with lesser powers given to junior judges, and minor offences being dealt with by local justices of the peace (J.P.s). Thus, a J.P. could fine somebody or give him thirty days in jug, but crimes calling for a longer sentence had to be transferred to a higher court.

Very serious offences went straight to a King's Justice.

The theory that a High Court Justice acted in place of the sovereign meant that, until some thirty years ago or so, it was considered treason to kill a High Court Judge while he was trying a case. It is also the reason that a judge on his way to or from court is treated with such respect. Some years ago, I had occasion to visit the Courts of Justice in the Strand in London and I happened to be wearing a bowler hat, wearing a dark suit and swinging my umbrella in a sober manner. As I paused on the pavement, a policeman nearby took one look at me, stepped out on the road and stopped the traffic, assuming I was a judge on my way to try a case. I touched my bowler in acknowledgement and tried to cross the road with the appropriate judicial gravitas.

High road. Jeeves will take the h.r. and I'll take the low road 51 p25; 55 p138; 60 p26 and p167 and later. From the traditional Scottish song 'The Bonnie Bonnie Banks of Loch Lomond', words by W.M. Lawson (1845). Favourite song of Rupert Baxter, who sings the first verse, beginning: "You take the high road and I'll take the low road" at 60 p167.

High thinking, tribal dances and … vegetarianism. 63 p55. Wordsworth's 'Written in London. O Friend! I Know Not' has the line: "Plain living and high thinking are no more." This was the phrase commonly used to describe the household of the austere and abstemious philosopher Thomas Carlyle (1795–1881) in Chelsea. Philosophers, reformers and writers congregated there, even though they ate badly. Whether Wordsworth borrowed the phrase or whether he coined it to describe Carlyle's menage, I do not know. "Plain living and high thinking" is still useful shorthand to describe those households where you are given poor food and no alcohol, but can enjoy elevating and intellectual conversation.

Note. In the late 19th century in the UK, the phrase 'Higher Culture' became popular and the term 'high thinking', i.e. cultural and philosophical discussion, became a cliché.

High though his titles, proud his name. 21 p118. From Scott's *The Lay of the Last Minstrel*, ten lines after the line "Breathes there the man, with soul so dead". See also BREATHES THERE THE MAN.

Highball. 19 p61. I think this was one of the earliest uses of this term in the UK and I suggest PGW used it because *Something Fresh/Something New* first appeared in America. In the UK, Lord Emsworth would have had a whisky tumbler (a squat, wide-bottomed glass) beside him, not a highball. In the 1890s, New York barmen adopted the habit of calling glasses 'balls' — and a tall glass became known as a highball. The term was then transferred to the whisky and ice inside it and was common in New York by 1900.

Highlands, My heart's in the. See MY HEART'S IN THE HIGHLANDS.

Hill and dale. 87 p89. See OVER HILL AND OVER DALE.

Hill, Rowland, used to go to Price's. 45 p232. Hill (1795–1879) introduced prepaid postage, i.e. postage stamps, in the UK in 1840.

Hills. Skip/leap like the hills/high hills. Often in PGW. B. Psalms 114.6 has: "Ye mountains that ye skipped like rams; and ye little hills, like lambs." Psalm 68.16 has: "Why hop ye so, ye high hills?"

Hip and thigh, smiting. 6 p127; 12 p213. B. Judges 15. 8. This is Samson dealing with the Philistines: "And he smote them hip and thigh with a great slaughter."

Hipparchus of Rhodes. 38 p115; 70 p186. Hipparchus was a mathematician and made several important astronomical discoveries. He died about 125 B.C.

Hippocrene, the blushful. 12 p111 and later. Although this was originally water flowing from a sacred fountain on Mount Helicon in Greece, Keats' poem 'Ode to a Nightingale' turned it into a legendary red wine. "O for a beaker full of the warm South, / Full of the true, the blushful Hippocrene, / With beaded bubbles winking at the brim..."

Hippodrome. Three Small-Heads at the Hippodrome 12 p16; all the rest of the Hippodrome 23 p158. The Hippodrome Theatre, still in Charing Cross Road, opened in 1900 and specialised in performing animals and circus/sensation acts. Aquatic spectacles were staged using the river Cran, which runs beneath the theatre. Annette Kellerman dived from the roof into a small tank of water, and a series of mountebanks including Dr Cook (see above) appeared there. Cross-talk acts (Pat and Mike) were popular and included the Three Small Heads and the Two Macs (see Chap. 24).

Hippogriffs, Keep ye eye skinned for. 64 p6. Milton's *Paradise Regained*, Bk 2.l, l.541 introduced the term: "Without wing / Of hippogriff." Half horse, half griffin, the hippogriff should not be confused with the hippocampus, which was half horse, half dolphin.

His master's voice. 70 p158. The HMV (His Master's Voice) record company whose famous trademark came about by accident. In 1899 an English painter, Francis Barraud, borrowed a machine from the then Gramophone Company to use as a prop while he was painting his terrier, Nipper. Nipper enjoyed the sound, and the picture of him listening attentively soon became well known. The company saw its possibilities and bought it for their trademark in 1901. Nipper, now stuffed, is to be seen in the company's shop in Oxford Street, London.

His nibs. See NIBS.

His-not-to-reason-why. See REASON WHY.

Hissing and a byword. 52 p172; 93 p44. PGW mixed two Biblical phrases here, but the two words seemed to have been paired for a century or more. I have certainly heard them in sermons, as I'm sure PGW did. The hissing, as one would expect, comes from Jeremiah (a 'Jeremiah' is still a common term for a confirmed pessimist). B. Jeremiah 29.18 concludes his warning to the ungodly by foretelling famine, pestilence and that they would "be a curse, and an astonishment, and an hissing and a reproach, among all the nations whither I have driven them". Of the six 'byword' references in the Bible, the nearest seems to be 1 Kings 9.7: "and Israel shall be a proverb and a byword among all people."

Hittites and Hivites. 61 p147 and later. B. Exodus 3.8 and later. The Hittites and Hivites were numbered among the ungodly and were punished for it by having their lands taken by the Israelites.

Hivite and a Jebusite, no less, a (Lionel Green is). 63 p85. B. Exodus 33.2: "And I will send an angel before thee; and I will drive out the Canaanite, the Amorite, and the Hittite, and the Perizzite, the Hivite and the Jebusite."

Ho! 3 p122 and frequently from the lips of English policemen up to 97 p91. There is scope for an academic paper here. My suggestion that 'Hallo' (see HALLOA!) began as an exclamation rather than a greeting draws support from Webster's (American) dictionary. Webster says 'Ha!' to express surprise or joy is pre-12th century and is from Old English. 'Hey!', interrogative or exclamatory, is 13th century; 'Hi!' as a greeting is 15th century, as is 'Ho!' to draw attention to something. The question is when and why did the different sounds come to indicate such different meanings?

Ho, Jolly Jenkin. 49 p106. Popular song (1900) from Arthur Sullivan's opera *Ivanhoe*, based on the novel by Sir Walter Scott.

Hog-calling industry of western America. 84 p13 and elsewhere. See Chap. 40.

Hoggish slumber, sunk in. 20 p169 and later. Though it sounds Shakespearian, I believe it comes from 'Savonarola' Brown (*Seven Men*) by Max Beerbohm (1919).

Holborn Viaduct Cabin. 34 p6. See CABINS.

Hold, enough. 8 p49. S. *Macbeth* 5.8: "Lay on, Macduff, And damned be him that first cries 'Hold, enough!'" See also LEAD ON.

Holding the gorgeous East in fee. See GORGEOUS EAST.

Hole. If you know a better hole 27 p280; and later. At 28 p245 PGW has "if you know a superior excavation". In 1915 a British officer in the trenches in France, Bruce Bairnsfather, started drawing cartoons of 'Old Bill', a disgruntled cynical old soldier. One of them showed a young recruit querying Bill's choice of a water-filled hole to take refuge from the shells raining down on them. Bill's reply "If you know a better 'ole, go to it" entered the language.

Holmes, Sherlock. PGW quoted this famous character from his third book up to his ninety-third and had a tremendous admiration for Arthur Conan DOYLE. A few years ago a newspaper reported that Abdul the Damned, Sultan of Turkey (1876–1915), who had a harem of 1,000 women, found his greatest relaxation in having Sherlock Holmes read to him in translation by his butler.

Holy City, The. 36 p197. 1892 song by Stephen Adams, popular with male choirs.

Holy Grail. See GRAIL, HOLY.

Homburg hats. 18 p207. It was Edward VII, then Prince of Wales, who introduced the Homburg into fashion in the 1880s–90s. When PGW wrote of it here, it was still slightly dashing, and George Balmer would not have dreamt of wearing it in London. He would have stuck to his topper or bowler.

Home again. Oh to be home again, home again, home again 38 p157. From Henry

Van Dyke's poem 'America for Me'.

Home. A man's h., bedroom, croquet lawn, etc., is a man's castle; see CASTLE. Are there any more at h. like Clarence? 24 p150; see FLORODORA.

Home body. Simple little home body … never happier than among my books and flowers 56 p23. After the Fatty Arbuckle scandal (1921) and other lurid press reports of goings-on in Hollywood, the studios changed their publicity approach. They stopped retailing stories of glamorous nightclubs and parties and portrayed their stars as God-fearing, home-loving folks who eschewed the high life, especially alcohol.

Home Companion. 36 p13. See Chap. 7.

Home from the hunt. 63 p253; and Esmond Haddock at 68 p222. See R.L. Stevenson's poem 'Requiem': "Home is the sailor, home from the sea, / And the hunter home from the hill."

Home Gossip. 19 p12. See Chap. 7.

Home, James, and don't spare the horses. 86p 213. I have known this phrase all my life and assumed it came from some Victorian melodrama where the bold, bad baronet ordered his coachman to take him home. I was wrong. The British Library states it is a 1934 song by Fred Hillebrand.

Home life of the late Lord Tennyson, How different from the. 60 p71. I was delighted to see PGW using this famous anecdote. In an essay, Irvin S. Cobb wrote of the night in 1879 when Sarah Bernhardt was playing in *Antony and Cleopatra* in London. When she heard of her lover's, Antony's, defeat, she stormed, she raved all over the stage, shrieked, screamed and sobbed, wrecked some of the scenery in her frenzy and, at last, dropped to the floor in a convulsive, shuddering heap. In the spellbound hush before the applause broke out, a middle-aged matron was heard to remark to her neighbour: "How different, how very different from the home life of our own dear Queen!" (Queen Victoria)

Home, no place like. 23 p249. Line from HOME, SWEET HOME.

Home Rule for Ireland. 7 p94. Suffice to say that in the period 1900–12, the question of Home Rule for Ireland led to a lot of trouble. The Liberals wanted it, the Conservatives and Unionists resolved to resist it.

Home, Sweet Home. This song (1823), words by John Howard Payne, dug itself into the American subconscious. The home in question is still to be seen on Long Island. See Chap. 36.

Home Whispers. 29 p203. See Chap. 7.

Homer used to nod at times, Even. 2 p163. Common phrase in UK — roughly, the implication is that even the cleverest of us can make a mistake; From Horace's *Ars Poetica*, l.359: "Sometimes even good Homer nods."

Homer when he smote his blooming lyre, went and stole what he thought he might require. 2 p160. I.e. even the greatest of writers borrow from others. KIPLING's poem 'When 'Omer Smote 'Is Bloomin' Lyre': "When 'Omer smote 'is bloomin' lyre / He'd 'eard men sing by land an' sea; / An' what he thought 'e might require, / 'E went an' took — the same as me!"

Homeric god swooping from a cloud. 17 p113. See CLOUD, SWOOPING.

Homeric laughter from the bridge above. 8 p56. The schoolboys were being watched from the bridge above; PGW used the analogy of Homer, who often described the gods laughing at the antics of mortals below. Another possible explanation is that, if you had to go into the cheapest seats of a UK theatre, as high up and as far back as possible, the box office clerk, certainly up to 1970 or so, would tell you that you were "right up in the gods". The term comes from the Greek/Roman theatres where statues of gods were placed around the top of of the high back wall.

Homeric question. 3 p274. From 1860 to 1914, there was bitter argument amongst academics as to whether Homer existed. Did he write everything attributed to him or was it the work of several individuals?

Homeric warrior snatched from the thick of battle in a cloud, some. 34 p89. In the ninth year of the siege of Troy as recounted by Homer, the two sides agreed to settle the matter by single combat. Paris, the prince of Troy, who had started the whole thing by running away with Helen, the wife of Menelaeus, king of Sparta, met the wronged husband outside the walls of Troy as the two armies watched. When it became clear that Menelaeus was winning, the goddess Venus saved Paris by snatching him up to heaven in a cloud. This unsporting outside interference led to both armies falling on each other with renewed bitterness and caused the war to last another year before Troy was finally defeated.

Homes, stately, of Wimbledon/England. See STATELY HOMES.

Honest sweat. Brushing the honest sweat from the brow 43 p110 and often later. See VILLAGE BLACKSMITH.

Honey-dew hath fed, on. 15A p12; 44 p155 and later. Coleridge's *Kubla Khan*: "And all should cry, Beware! Beware! / His flashing eyes, his floating hair! / Weave a circle round him thrice, / And close your eyes with holy dread, / For he on honey-dew hath fed, / And drunk the milk of Paradise."

Hong Kong. 19 p49. See Chap. 2.

Honk-honk. See GOODBYE.

Honolulu Queen, My. 22 p13. Song by Penn and O'Dea 1889. MTT Tony Ring.

Honourable man. Oakshott was an honourable man 57 p267. S. *Julius Caesar* 3.2: "Brutus is an honourable man."

Hoodlum. 88 p176. I would include this term because of its bizarre origins. Apparently, it began in the US in 1872 and came to the UK in 1898. Muldoon was the leader of a San Francisco gang and it became known that his name was reversed in criminal circles (backslang) to protect his identity. He was known as 'Noodlum'. He was captured, the story got out and went across America but the first telegraph operator hit the wrong key and the word 'hoodlum' was born. Lexicographers still argue over the origin, but at least they agree it stemmed from San Francisco 1870–2.

Hooks of steel. 39 p19. Misprint for hoops of steel. See GRAPPLE TO YOUR SOUL.

Hooligan. 1 p65; 3 p105; 9 p32; 12 p45. On the first three occasions PGW used this, he spelled it with a capital H because it was then a new word in the language. By 12 p45 (*Mike*) it had become part of normal speech, so PGW only gave it a lower-case 'h'. One dictionary states Hooligan was the name of a rural troublemaking family circa 1888. A more probable origin is the series of 1891 UK cartoons by John Stafford featuring an Irish labourer named Hooligan. See also BERSERK.

Hooligan, the Happy. 18 p52. US cartoon character, a tramp with a mule named Maud, was first drawn by Fred Opper in 1900, probably an imitation of Stafford's UK cartoons (above).

Hope, Bob. 70 p152; 73 p155. This long-lived comedian (1903–2003) needs no explanation.

Hopes, fondest. Seen my fondest hopes decay 81 p177. Thomas Moore's 'The Fireworshippers' from *Lallah Rookh*: "Oh! Ever thus, from childhood's hour, / I've seen my fondest hopes decay, / I never lov'd a tree or flow'r, / But 'twas the first to fade away." See also GAZELLES.

Hopkins, Harry. 69 p100. Hopkins (1890–1946) was a brilliant administrator in the presidency of F.D. Roosevelt.

Hopley. Shortest fight since Hopley won the heavy-weights 8 p131. See Chap. 4.

Hopper, Hedda. 68 p112; 70 p221. This ex-film actress (1890–1966) became a remarkably influential and powerful Hollywood columnist whose work was syndicated round America for forty years. PGW did a successful radio interview with her in Hollywood in July 1937. In a letter to Leonora, he said he wrote a draft comic interview beforehand, giving her most of the good lines, and that it was a great success. Her only rival was Louella PARSONS (1880–1972).

Hoppity-hoppity-hop. 65 last line; 68 p95 & p188; note especially 'Rodney Has a Relapse' in 69; 71 p11. For the reason for PGW's satire on the Christopher Robin poems of A.A. Milne, see MILNE.

Horace's philosophy for those who travel ... with his climate. 13 p68. Horace's *Epistles* 1.11: "They change their sky, not their soul, who run across the sea." PGW quoted from this Roman poet (65–8 B.C.) often up to *Much Obliged, Jeeves*.

Horatio (I knew him). See FELLOW OF INFINITE JEST.

Horatius, his masterly handling of traffic over the bridge. 8 p113; holding the bridge 12 p150. These and other references to somebody fighting a brave rear-guard action are from Macaulay's 'Horatius' in his *Lays of Ancient Rome*. According to legend, Horatius and two comrades, Lartius and Herminius, held the narrow bridge across the Tiber to stop the Tuscan army attacking Rome. While the Romans frantically destroyed the bridge behind them, the three held off every attack till at last Horatius sent his two comrades back and as the bridge collapsed, threw himself into the river and managed to swim to the Roman bank.

Hornswoggling. 57 p30. Early 19th-century US slang for swindling.
Hornung's Amateur Cracksman. See AMATEUR CRACKSMAN.
Horny-handed toiler. 25 p10. See SONS OF TOIL.
Horror from Outer Space. 82 p21; 85 p20; 94 p36. In the 1950s, there was a plethora of Space-Horror movies. Typical titles were *It Came from Outer Space*, *The Terror from Beyond Space* etc.
Horsa! Keep your tail up. See HENGIST AND HORSA.
Horse feathers. See HEEBY-JEEBIES.
Horse, Old. See Chap. 34.
Horsewhipping. 58 p172 and later. In 73 p178, Colonel Wyvern faces a social difficulty: "Infernally awkward, calling on a fellow to horsewhip him and having to ask him for the loan of his horsewhip to do it with. Still, there it is … that's how it goes." But what exactly is a horsewhip? The only ones I knew by that name were the long, thin stick with a long lash on the end used by drivers of stage-coaches who were reputed to be such 'a fine whip' they could flick a fly off the ear of the leader horse. Then there were the whips used in fox hunting which have a short rigid handle and a long lash, designed to remind hounds of their duty. How could you grasp a man by the scruff of his neck and chastise him with either of these? Both are far too unwieldy so I took the question to London's leading horsewhip emporium. Once they had assured themselves I didn't want to do any horsewhipping myself, they were very helpful. In their view, the name has been changed, though they did not know when. If you have occasion to horsewhip somebody nowadays, you purchase a riding crop or a switch. These are flexible leather-covered sticks about three feet long which you apply to the rear end of your horse to remind him who is in charge. They are eminently suitable for chastising miscreants on the steps of their club.

I found confirmation in the report of London's last threatened horsewhipping, in 1994, when Judge Harkess was photographed with the riding crop with which he proposed to horsewhip the sometime Tory MP, Alan Clark. I think I would do the same if I had learned that Mr Clark had seduced not only my wife but my two daughters as well.

Hosea, the prophet and what he said to the children of Adullam. 61 p154. A slight error on PGW's part, I suggest. Hosea had some harsh words to say to the children of Israel (see B. Hosea 4.2) but I can find no connection between him and Adullam which, according to every Biblical reference I can find, was a cave. See 1 Samuel 3.4, 1 Chronicles 11.15, 2 Samuel 23.13, and Micah 1.15.
Hot diggedy dog. PGW ref lost. Phrase first coined by American comedian Walter Catlett (1889–1960), who played in PGW's *Sally* in 1920.
Hot dog. 38 p5 and elsewhere. Well-known today as a sausage served inside a bread roll, the term first appeared in print in the USA in 1903. It is reported to have first been served to the public at Coney Island in 1874 but, along with many other now-traditional American foodstuffs, achieved national popularity at the 1892–3 Chicago Exposition. MTT Stu Shiffman, who informed me

the term was coined by cartoonist Tad Dorgan, who couldn't spell the word 'dachshund' for the dachshund sausages he portrayed in his cartoons. So he called them hot dog sausages instead.

Hot time in the old town tonight. 6 p49 and later. Composed as a march by Theodore Metz in 1886, it had words added by Joseph Hayden ten years later. The song became well known when it was adopted by Teddy Roosevelt's Rough Riders who took part in the charge at the Battle of San Juan Hill in the Spanish-American War of 1898. Roosevelt used it in his successful presidential campaign later.

Hotel Cecil. 16 p93. Europe's biggest hotel opened on the Strand in 1886. Shell-Mex House is on the site now.

Hotel Picardy where Valerie Twistleton lunched with two f. and three m. 60 p16. PGW and Ethel stayed at the Hotel Picardy in Le Touquet in August 1934. It was while staying here that they decided to buy a house, Low Wood, in Le Touquet. See Chap. 20.

Hotfoot. Some hidden hand had given him the h. 68 p164. This practical joke seems to be unknown outside America unless one has read Damon Runyon's 'Sense of Humour'. A hotfoot is administered by sneaking up behind somebody, sticking a paper match in his shoe between the upper and the sole near the little toe, and then lighting the match. When the flame explodes the match head, the result is a nasty hole in the victim's shoe as well as causing him excruciating pain. Mervyn Potter describes a slightly different procedure at 71 p37.

Hotsy-Totsy. Rendering everything h-t 52 p80. Coined by Billy de Beck, American cartoonist (died 1942). The phrase became popular enough to ensure the success of the 1925 song 'Everything Is Hotsy-Totsy Now'. See also HEEBY-JEEBIES.

Houdini. A knot that might have perplexed H. 28 p209 and up to 87 p177. The feats of this escapologist (1874–1926) are still judged remarkable by modern exponents.

Houndsditch Wednesday. 18 p250. Typical PGW gloss on a name for a football club. See SHEFFIELD WEDNESDAY.

Hour, finest. See FINEST HOUR.

Hour produced the man, the. 48 p130 and frequent up to 95 p117. Together with its forerunner 'Cometh the hour, cometh the man', the phrase has become a well-worn cliché among sportswriters, but nobody — and I have been looking for years — seems to know where it originated. The nearest I can find is "The hour is come but not the man" from Scott's *Heart of Midlothian*, heading in chap 4. Another candidate is: "The hour was on us. / Then where the man" from 'Lincoln', a poem by J.V. Cheney.

House of Usher. See POE, EDGAR ALLAN.

House, the. Was at the H. with me 13 p235. See Chap. 33.

Houses in between. If it wasn't for the h. in b. 2 p7. PGW used the organisation of the school into 'houses' to quote a reference every contemporary reader would recognise. There was at the time (1903) a very popular music hall song by E. Bateman in which a Cockney boasted that from his top window you could see as far as Hackney Marshes (equivalent to the New Jersey marshes), "If it wasn't for the houses in between".

Housman, A.E. Where's this Bredon that A. E. Housman writes about? 91 p185. A fascinating remark; it is the only time PGW hints at the two sources of Blandings, Weston Park and Sudeley Castle. It adds nothing to the humour, the plot doesn't need it, so why did PGW write it?

There are two points to note. Firstly, Housman (1859–1936), poet, Classics scholar and academic, was, it has recently been learned, an admirer of PGW's writing. Maybe PGW was re-paying the compliment. Vanessa Polk clearly had in mind the lines from Housman's famous 1896 set of poems 'A Shropshire Lad': "In summertime on Bredon, The bells they sound so clear." Secondly, when Vanessa asks Gally Threepwood what is the hill she sees from the tower of Blandings castle, he tells her it is the Wrekin.

PGW was 89 when *A Pelican at Blandings* came out. I suggest that he forgot his normal caution over revealing real locations and this one slipped out. (See Chap. 9 where Croxted Road does not appear under its own name until 1972.) From Weston Park in Shropshire, the Wrekin is indeed 'the hill on the horizon'. From the other source of Blandings, Sudeley Castle in Gloucestershire, Bredon is even more obviously 'the hill' that stands out on the landscape. It dominates the valley just a few miles away from the castle. I was fortunate enough to be on Bredon on a beautiful summer evening when three of the several churches around its base had their bell-ringing practice as Housman described. It was an unforgettable experience. See also Chap 39.

Hovering uncertainly on the brink. 34 p63. See BRINK.

How art thou fallen, Lucifer, son of the morning. 27 p88 and later. As Parker says in the first reference, it is B. Isaiah 14.12: "How art thou fallen from Heaven, O Lucifer, son of the morning."

How different from the home life of the late Lord Tennyson. 60 p71. See HOME LIFE.

How do we go? 15A p167 and elsewhere. 1900 song by Charles Collins 'How Do We Go, Old Cockalorum'.

How dear to this/my heart are the scenes of my childhood. 72 p117; 90 p171. See OLD OAKEN BUCKET.

How goodly are thy tents, O Jacob. 49 p293. MTT Tony Ring, who found that the correct reference in the original magazine publication was B. Numbers 24.5, not the 44.5 printed in later editions. In any event, I'm sure readers don't need reminding that Numbers finishes at 36.13.

How Many Pins Does the Prime Minister's Hat Hold? See Chap. 7.

How strange are the customs of France. See LARDY, GILBERT'S LORD.

Howard, Leslie. 54 p225. Handsome Hungarian-born actor (1890–1943) who appeared in PGW's play *Her Cardboard Lover* (1927).

How's chances? 83 p61. Forgotten now, this song became popular as a method of proposing after the hero wooed and won the heroine by singing it in Irving Berlin's *As Thousands Cheer* (1933). "How's chances, say, how are the chances of making you love me the way I love you."

Hoxton or the Borough, two gentlemen of. 1 p109; 15A p187. These were two extemely rough districts of London. The Borough is the old name for Southwark, the only part of the City of London lying south of the river. It came into existence because the old London Bridge was too narrow to take carts or coaches and all goods and passengers travelling into London from the south had to disembark or be unloaded here. The result was that it became a rowdy neighborhood, full of inns and lodging houses.

Hoyle, according to. 83 p64; 96 p175. Edmond Hoyle's (1672–1769), *Short Treatise on Whist* went into many editions, as did his books on Brag, Piquet and Chess. 'According to Hoyle', i.e. the right way to play a hand, was still a common phrase in the 1960s.

Hue of resolution. The native h. of r. is sicklied o'er by the pale cast of thought 59 p44. See ENTERPRISES.

Huge hello. Give him a huge hello 67 p92; 93 p51. Clearly from Damon Runyon, whose narrator of New York gangster stories invariably greeted unsavoury characters in this manner. The more dangerous/unsavoury the character, the huger the hello.

Huguenot's Farewell. 48 p271 and later. Subject to correction, I assume PGW was referring to the famous painting 'The Huguenot' by Millais (1829–96), which shows a sad wife taking leave of her Huguenot husband and trying to persuade him to wear the white armband that will save him from Catholic attack. (This was just before the Massacre of St Bartholomew 1572.) At 83 p53, PGW refers to Millais' Huguenot.

Hullo. See HALLOA!

Hullo, girls. 68 p13. Archetypal opening words of juvenile lead or hero's friend in any English comedy/farce/musical from 1900 to 1939. Often expanded to: "Hallo, girls! Anyone for tennis?" See TENNIS.

Hullo, hullo, hullo, it's a different girl again. 66 p182. Stanwood had in mind the music hall song (c.1910) 'Who's Your Lady Friend?' The gist of the song is that the singer has just met a man with his new wife and proceeds to embarrass him by recounting the number of girls he has seen him with before. From memory, the last verse is: "Hullo, hullo, Who's your lady friend? Who's the little lady at your side? It isn't the girl I saw you with at Brighton, Who, who, who's your lady friend?"

Human Boy, The. 1 p150; 2 p147. The first of a series of excellent school stories written by Eden Philpotts in the 1890s. See also STEGGLES.

Humble and contrite spirit. 32 p179. See SPIRIT, HUMBLE AND CONTRITE.

Humble, be it never so. 32 p203. Line from the song HOME, SWEET HOME.

Hun is at the gate, the. 72 p41. KIPLING's poem 'For All We Have and Are'(1914): "For all we have and are, / For all our children's fate, / Stand up and take the war, / The Hun is at the gate."

Hundredth chance, the. 32 p178. This obscure reference comes from the best-seller *The Hundredth Chance* (1917) by Ethel M. Dell (See Chap. 37), followed by a film of the same name in 1920. MTT Elin Woodger.

Hunky Dory. 63 p207. All is well, everything is fine. Came into use in the US 1860–80. One alleged origin was US sailors' pronunciation of the name of the main street of pleasure in Yokohama.

Hunstanton, Lord. 38 p26. See Chap. 32, and also WHAT?

Hunter, a mighty. 63 p112. See MIGHTY HUNTER.

Huntin', shootin', and fishin', not to mention swimmin', tennis-playin' and golfin'. 88 p83. It is heard less now, but PGW was satirising the habit among the upper classes of droppin' the letter 'g' when usin' a present participle. I recall readin' about somebody havin' come into money and "gone terribly upper class, he's bought himself some jodhpurs and started dropping his g's." I remember meeting a fox-hunting landowner sixty years ago who abbreviated his speech so much, it was difficult to understand him. Like the Duke of Dunstable, his "How are you?" came out as "Har'yer?" and hunting was not just "huntin", it was "h'nt'n".

Hunting we will go, A-. See A-HUNTING.

Huntley, G.P. 78 p115. British actor (1868–1927) who specialised in silly ass parts in light comedies, like George Grossmith. Perfect for playing Bertie Wooster, PGW said.

Hurluberlu. 52 p258. Anatole's expression of annoyance is one of the few words of French slang with which I am familiar, if only because it is so like the English word with the same general meaning — hullabaloo. A tremendous fuss, uproar, disturbance etc. The German term is surprisingly similar. 'Welch ein Tohuwabohu' means 'What a row/ disturbance/ uproar'. See also LOUFFIER.

Hurricane, The. 61 p78. 1937 film with C. Aubrey Smith, Dorothy Lamour and Mary Astor. Samuel Goldwyn was very proud of it. See Chap. 28.

Hurry me. From ledger to ledger they hurry me to stifle my regret. / And when they win a smile from me, they think that I forget. 14 p118 and later. PGW's twist on the poem 'Oh No, We Never Mention Her' ("from sport to sport they hurry me, to stifle my regret etc.") by Thomas Haynes Bailey (1797–1839). Set to music in the late 19th century, it became popular in Victorian drawing rooms. MTT John Fletcher.

Hutton, Betty (a race horse here). 70 p195. Star of Hollywood musicals in the 1940s/50s.

Hyacinth, au revoir, my little. 12 p141. See AU REVOIR.

Hybrias the Cretan. 16 p53; 47 p74; "wealth being a burly spear and brand and a right good shield of hides untanned which on his arm … he ber-huckled" 67 p64. By Elliott and Bucalossi, it appears in the list of Standard Songs in the

1907 Army & Navy Stores catalogue. There is a private joke here. PGW sang it at a Dulwich concert in 1899, and *The Alleynian* report (probably written by him) specifically comments on his 'ber-huckled'.

Hymn for those of riper years at sea. 49 p293. PGW blend of two services in the BCP: 'The Order of Baptism for those of Riper Years' and 'Forms of Prayer to be Used at Sea'.

Hymn of Hate. 51 p224. First World War phrase. Early in the First World War, Ernst Lissauer published his 'Hymn of Hate', a poem claiming that England was Germany's only real enemy and had to be destroyed. The Kaiser awarded him an Iron Cross for it. The term was adopted by the British Army for the artillery barrage fired by the Germans every evening to disrupt units who were moving in and out of the trenches under cover of darkness.

Hymns Ancient & Modern. 49 p57; 83 p214; 93 p71. This splendid hymnal (1861) was in universal use across the Church of England for sixty years, and its hymns were known by everybody. Its successors seem to change every few years and become more and more 'modern' and 'relevant'. To people of my generation, they also seem more and more unmusical and banal. See Chap. 11.

I

(MTT = My thanks to)

I am the Bandolero. 29 p73 and later. See BANDOLERO.

I and Roosevelt. See BIG STICK.

I and Soapy. 'Nice and simple for I and Soapy' 63 p98; 'room reserved for I and my husband' p26; 'except through I and Soapy' p97. I am puzzled as to why PGW gave this affectation to Dolly Molloy. Among people unsure of correct speech, it was at one time thought that the word 'me' was not 'genteel', and they would go to great lengths to avoid using it. Barry Humphries' Dame Edna Everidge has the same habit. Did PGW know someone in Le Touquet or in the camp who spoke like this?

I cannot tell a lie, Uncle. 13 p191. See the remark attributed to George Washington: "Father, I cannot tell a lie. I did it with my little hatchet."

I did not love as others do … (four lines down to**) the belle of.** 7 p90. C.S. CALVERLEY's 'Gemini and Virgo'.

I didn't raise my boy to be a soldier. 21 p282. US song 1915 by Bryan and Piantadosi reflecting the anti-war sentiment of the time. The second line is "I brought him up to be my pride and joy".

I don't care if he wears a crown, he can't keep kicking my dawg around. 17 p65. Perhaps a version of Champ Clark's presidential campaign song 'They Gotta Quit Kicking My Dawg Aroun' (1912).

I fear no foe in shining armour. 29 p119 and later. See FOE.

I felt it here. See FELT IT.

I have heard the beat of the offshore wind … Pull out on the trail again. 26 p90. Uncle Chris was adapting KIPLING's 'The Long Trail': "You have heard the call of the offshore wind …"

I hear the beating of its wings. 33 p134. See BEATING OF ITS WINGS.

I knew him, Horatio. See FELLOW OF INFINITE JEST.

I Knew Him When club. 69 p13. Whittier wrote: "Of all sad words of tongue or pen, The saddest are these: 'It might have been.'" In 1920 Arthur Guterman parodied it: "Of all the cold words of tongue or pen, The worst are these: 'I knew him when'." See WORDS OF TONGUE.

I know your secret. 44 p9; 89 p17. Lord Biskerton was sure he could make money by telling perfect strangers he knew their secret, but was willing to be paid for his silence. Just a few years ago, an enterprising gentleman in Tokyo did just that, writing to 200 people picked at random from the telephone directory. He made a fortune before the police caught up with him.

I Lift Up My Finger and I say Tweet-Tweet. 51 p145. See Tweet-tweet.

I love a lassie, a bonny, bonny lassie. 39 p12. This 1906 song was made famous by Harry Lauder, who sang it for over 40 years.

I love little pussy, her coat is so warm. See Pussy.

I love you, that's all I can say. 43 p60. 1898 song by Dillen & Kelly.

I only know I love thee. 15A p199. Song by Howard Talbot (1896).

I shall watch your future career with some considerable interest. 25 p168 and and frequently later. PGW uses it in the sense of sacking/saying goodbye to somebody whom you hope not to see again. I have always assumed it is a cliché from one of those business training advertisements which begins with the boss getting rid of somebody. The young man takes the advertised course and, surprise, surprise, takes over the firm from which he was sacked. I hope some reader will enlighten me.

I shot a flask into the air: It fell to earth I know not where. 44 p278. Longfellow's 'The Arrow and the Song'. "I shot an arrow into the air, It fell to earth I know not where."

I slew him, tum-tum tum. See Aram, Eugene.

I Stopped and I Looked and I Listened. 93 p43. See Stopped and looked and listened.

I wandered through a world of women, seeking you. 77 p167. MTT Alekh Bhurke for finding this one. It is from Jack London's *Sea Wolf* (chap. 23), where London quotes Arthur Symons: "I wandered all these years among a world of women seeking you." (*Pall Mall Gazette* 2 September 1895). Arthur Symons (1865–1945) was a poet, translator and critic.

I was a king in Babylon. See King in Babylon.

I was a pale young curate then. See Curate.

I wish I was dead. 97 p25. Vicky's remark was all the more appropriate since it came immediately after Gally's comment that she was clearly as down among the wines and spirits as Mariana of the Moated Grange. See Mariana of the moated grange.

I Zingari. 8 p97; 12 p73. An amateur cricket club, founded in 1845, whose colours are black, red and gold and who have their own private rules and terminology. 'I Zingari' is Italian for 'the gypsies'.

Iago. Oh, Iago, the pity of it 73 p121. S. *Othello* 4.1.

***Ibex*, S.S.** (steamship on the Guernsey-Southampton run)**.** 9 p30. By chance I discovered this was indeed the name of the ship on this run. PGW would have travelled on it when he holidayed in Guernsey the year before he wrote the book.

Ichabod (Itchabod). 25 p91; 45 p150; 67 p22. B. 1 Samuel 4.21: "And she named the child I-cha-bod, saying, The glory has departed from Israel …"

***Idylls of the King*.** 29 p61 and often later. After Shakespeare and the Bible, Tennyson was PGW'S favourite source of quotations.

If butlers come, can cocktails be far behind? 42 p255. PGW used the phrase 'If

X comes, can Y be far behind?' often. Scotties and Stiffy at 59 p90 and 85 p68; Pirbright the Peke and Celia Todd at 69 p184; Sandy Callender and letters to be answered at once at 87 p102. From SHELLEY's 'Ode to the West Wind': "If Winter comes, can Spring be far behind?"

If I'd known you were coming, I'd have baked a cake. 79 p48. 1950 song popularised by Bing Crosby: 'If I Knew You Were Coming, I'd Have Baked a Cake.'

If 'twere done, then 'twere well 'twere done quickly. 13 p50 and frequent later. Slight adaptation of opening lines of S. *Macbeth* 1.7. In *Very Good, Jeeves*, "As Shakespeare says, if you're going to do a thing you might just as well pop right at it and get it over." In *Joy in the Morning*, PGW gives us the variant: "If the thing was to be smacked into, 'twere well 'twere smacked into quickly, as Shakespeare says."

If you can something something and never something something. 87 p87; 92 p165. PGW's version of KIPLING's poem 'If'. The lines misquoted are from the third verse: "If you can make one heap of all your winnings / And risk it on one turn of pitch-and-toss / And lose, and start again at the beginnings / And never breathe a word about your loss."

In 1999 some worthy institution initiated a competition to find Britain's favourite poem. There was an astonishingly strong response and, to the outrage of the intelligentsia and glitterati, Kipling's 'If' won by a mile. They denounced it as old-fashioned and morally inspiring — a dreadful thing for any poem to be. In 2000 they tried again and 'If' repeated its runaway success. They then changed the rules so it didn't qualify any more.

If you have butter prepare to shed it now. 51 p202. See BUTTER IN A LORDLY DISH.

If You Knew Susie Like I Know Susie. 39 p13. 1925 song by de Sylva, popularised by Al Jolson.

If you want to know the time, ask a policeman. 22 p169. See POLICEMAN.

If You Were the Only Girl in the World. 57 p27. Sung by George Robey in *The Bing Boys*, it was one of the most popular songs of the First World War.

Youth but knew, If. 17 p130; 83 p15. 'Si jeunesse savoit, si veillesse pouvoit' (If youth but knew, if age could). 'Les Premices', Epigramme 191 by Henri Estienne (1532–98).

Iliad, The. 3 p274; like some god in the I. 42 p122. In Homer's account of the siege of Troy, the deities were constantly intervening on one side or the other.

I'll be your sweetheart (and next four lines). 3 p144. 1900 song 'I'll Be Your Sweetheart', also entitled 'Bluebells'.

Ill wind that has no turning, it's an. 42 p93. PGW's keen ear picked up some people's habit of misquoting proverbs and put them in the mouths of Bertie and his friends. Sometimes PGW did it so skilfully, it is easy to miss them. Here, he mixed "It's an ill wind that blows nobody good" with "It is a long lane that has no turning". See also BURNED CHILD.

Illegal or immoral or fattening. 92 p46. In the 1930s, Alexander Woollcott (see

Alexander of the Times) wrote: "All the things I really like are either illegal, immoral or fattening." This then became a popular song in 1950 — 'It's Illegal, It's Immoral or It Makes You Fat'.

Ills the flesh is heir to. 3 p196. S. *Hamlet* 3.1 ('To be or not to be' speech): "The thousand natural shocks the flesh is heir to, 'tis a consummation devoutly to be wished."

I'm biding my time. See Biding my time.

I'm for 'em, Father Abraham, a hundred thousand strong. 26 p248. A misquotation of James Gibbon's Civil War song (*New York Evening Post*, 16 July 1862): "We are coming, Father Abraham, three hundred thousand more", a response to Lincoln's call for more volunteers.

I'm Leaving Monte Carlo. 46 p239. 1907 song by Lyle and Edgar.

I'm telling the birds, telling the bees, telling the flowers, telling the trees. 40 p217. 'I'm Telling the Birds,Telling the Bees', 1926 song by Bowen & Friend.

Immemorial elms. 18 p154. See Moan of doves.

Immovable mass and the irresistible force. 23 p114. See Irresistible force.

Impending doom. 43 p15; 50 p108 and later. Common translation of the Requiem chant, an important part of sung funeral Masses in the Catholic Church. 'Dies irae, dies illa' ('Day of wrath and doom impending') by Tommaso Di Celano (1185–1255).

Impney Hotel. 74 p187. Now called Chateau Impney Hotel. See Chap. 26.

Importance of Being Earnest, The. 72 p27. Oscar Wilde's 1895 comedy.

'In Alcala'. 18 p258. There are twelve towns in Spain called Alcala, but Wodehouse was quoting from *Mirette*, an 1894 opera by André Messager. It includes the song 'Long Ago in Alcala'. For the building PGW had in mind, see Chap. 23.

In and Out Club. 25 p36. Formerly occupied by the Army & Navy Club, this building on Piccadilly has two large gates on which are painted the words 'In' and 'Out', which became the popular nickname for the club. When the Army & Navy left for new premises in St James's Square a few years ago, they did so in grand manner. With a piper at their head, the oldest members and committee led them in procession along Piccadilly to their new home. In January 2005, I noticed that the pillars supporting the portico of the new club house have been painted 'In' and 'Out'. Completely inappropriate, but I was delighted the club was keeping the old nickname going.

In articulo mortis. 73 p135. A legal expression, which I would translate as 'on the point of death'. In English law, things said by a dying man. If there were witnesses to it, something said 'in articulo mortis' used to be accepted in lieu of a sworn statement.

In his habit as he lived. 58 p293. S. *Hamlet* 3.4: "My father, in his habit as he lived; Look! Where he goes, even now, out at the portal."

In his hand he bore the brand / Which none but he might smoke. 7 p30. I had known this line — or something very like it — all my life, but I was unable to find it. MTT Nigel Rees, who sought expert advice and identified it as the line describing Astur in Macaulay's *Lays of Ancient Rome*: "And in his hand he shakes the brand, / Which none but he can wield." I was furious with myself because I *had* known it — but it was 60 years since I had read it.

In like Flynn. See FLYNN, ERROL.

In spring a young man's fancy lightly turns to thoughts of love. 86 p209 and elsewhere. See LIVELIER IRIS.

In tres partes divisa. 78 (UK version) p10. Every schoolboy knew the phrase 'Gallia est omnis divisa in partes tres' ('All Gaul is divided into three parts', or 'Gaul, as a whole, is divided into three parts'). They are the opening words of Julius Caesar's *Gallic Wars*.

Incense, keeping his vicars off the. 41 p170. See Chap. 11.

Include me out. 60 p222; 64 p133; 85 p71. One of many solecisms attributed to Sam Goldwyn (1882–1974); his son said (13 November 1982) that this one was genuine. See Chap. 28.

Incogniti. 2 p22 and later. A well-known amateur cricket club. ('Incogniti' is Latin for 'the unknown'/'the unrecognised'.)

Income, after all, is only an income whereas a chunk o' goblins is a pile. 23 p155. See 'GOOD CIGAR IS A SMOKE'.

Income Tax. Many references. Like Lord Emsworth, PGW had strong views on this and had problems with the American and UK authorities. See Tony Ring's *You Simply Hit Them with an Axe*.

Indian clubs. 24 p216; 25 p175. For those who don't know them, these clubs resemble the skittles in ten-pin bowling. They were adopted by the British Army in India c.1880 to strengthen soldier's muscles and coordination, and the habit became popular in the UK. Synchronized club-swinging displays by large groups (soldiers, cadets, Boy Scouts etc) were a feature of public events from 1890 to 1930.

Indian Love Call. 68 p187. Song from Rudolf Friml's musical *Rose Marie* (1924).

Indian Love Lyrics. 49 p134; 87 p56. This series of yearning love songs — which include 'Pale Hands I Loved Beside the Shalimar', immensely popular at the begining of the 20th century — was written by 'Laurence Hope', real name Ada Nicolson (1865–1904).

Indian, poor. Poor Indian who threw away a pearl richer than all his tribe. 58 p208 and elsewhere. S. *Othello* 5.2: "of one whose hand, Like the base Indian, threw a pearl away Richer than all his tribe."

Indian sign. We have the Indian sign on him 66 p122. According to Webster's, this was an English expression indicating a hex or spell.

Infant Samuel at prayer. Broken 18 p169; intact 21 p161; intact 25 p98; broken 28 p85; broken 33 p15; broken 59 p128; broken 76 p182. This was to be seen in every middle-class Victorian household. MTT John Radford and Edward Cazalet for the information that the Victorian painter James Sant (1820–1916) (see SOUL'S AWAKENING) produced a picture of an angelic child at prayer with the title *Speak Lord for Thy Servant Heareth*. Reproduced as an engraving and renamed *The Infant Samuel,* its sales soared. Sant, however, portrays the angelic child as sitting up in bed to say his prayers. I therefore suggest the painting by Joshua Reynolds (1723–92) showing a child saying his prayers 'properly', i.e. on his knees, is the better source.

A statuette of the wide-eyed innocent child was exactly the sort of thing the Victorians loved. It is no longer made by British potteries; the only one I have managed to acquire is a Japanese copy (but see Chap. 31).

Inferno, the. Blandings is Freddie's idea of the Inferno 32 p56. It was DANTE's *Divine Comedy* that introduced the word 'Inferno' to describe Hell.

Infinite capacity for taking pains. 3 p6; 6 p5 and later. Often quoted as Carlyle's definition of genius. It comes from his *Frederick the Great*: "Genius' (which means the transcendent capacity of taking trouble, first of all).'

Infinite resource and sagacity. See RESOURCE AND SAGACITY.

Infirm of purpose. Give me the sandbag. 36 p164; airgun 41 p164; 91 p193. Appropriately, PGW gave these lines to women since it was Lady Macbeth who declared: "Infirm of purpose! Give me the daggers." S. *Macbeth* 2.2.

Inge, Dean. 46 p19; 51 p177. This famous cleric (1860–1954) was Dean of St Paul's 1911–34. He loved writing for the Press, prophesied doom and gloom interminably, and earned the nickname 'the Gloomy Dean'.

Ingersoll. Ten minutes by my I. 45 p105. Robert Ingersoll (1859–1928) made his fortune in the 1890s by manufacturing the first watch to be sold for a dollar. His advertising was superb: "The Watch That Made The Dollar Famous."

Ingersoll, Colonel Robert. 68 p71 & p204. Enthusiastic lecturer and advocate of agnosticism (1833–99).

Ingoldsby Legends. Lady who didn't mind death but couldn't stand pinching 2 p77; the silk-and-satined little treasures she had read about in 25 p113. *The Ingoldsby Legends* are a collection of stories and poems satirising contemporary life and mediaeval legend. Written by the Rev. Richard Barham in 1840, they were in every Victorian library and still read well today. The lady who couldn't stand pinching appears in 'The Tragedy'. The satined pages are from 'The Jackdaw of Rheims'.

Ingratitude, man's. 36 p40. S. *As You Like It* 2.7 ("Blow, blow thou winter wind" etc).

Inlaid with patines of bright gold. See PATINES.

Inside stand, the. 48 p22; 90 p35. PGW's 1935 play *The Inside Stand* was based on his *Hot Water* of three years before. (See also *Sitting Pretty* and *Bill the Conqueror* under KERN, JEROME.) The term is used by crooks when they can get an accomplice into the household.

Inspector Biffen Views the Body. 76 p218. See Dorothy L. Sayers' (1893–1957) *Lord Peter Views the Body.*

Instruct/ interest, elevate and amuse. 32 p150 and p275; 51p158; 65 p76 and elsewhere. See AMUSE, ELEVATE AND INSTRUCT.

Interest, I shall watch your future progress/career with. 25 p168 and often later. See I SHALL WATCH.

Interested me strangely, the man's story had. 43p 92. This sounds typical of Sherlock Holmes, but the phrase occurs in Sax Rohmer's *The Yellow Claw* (1915).

Interesting and instructive afternoon (one of Uncle Fred's). 55 p205 and elsewhere. This was a Victorian cliché for any worthy outing/ expedition. I found plenty when reading through Kent and Shropshire local papers of the 1890s. The *Shrewsbury Chronicle* (1898) had a report on an Evening Party for Old Folks: "An interesting and instructive evening was enjoyed by all." And yes, it did include a lecture by the vicar using magic lantern slides.

Interesting Bits. 33 p171 & p190; 61 p205; 69 p254. PGW gloss on the London periodical *Tit-Bits*. See Chap. 7.

Intimidate me, they can't. 31 p206; 34 p12; 41 p165; 82 p63. If, like Sir George Pyke in *Bill the Conqueror*, your son is going to be buttered all over the pavement by a racing gang, you face the prospect with a fine, fearless unconcern. The racing gang couldn't intimidate Sir George. I have not found the original quote, but a biography of William Randolph Hearst says he made the same defiant public statement when his newspaper sellers in Chicago (a thousand miles away) were meeting forceful and violent opposition. See Chap. 7.

Into each life some rain must fall. 26 p262; 37 p194 and later. Probably best remembered for the 1944 song of that name by Roberts & Fisher, it was also a 1921 song by Gershwin. These were too late for use by PGW, who, like them, was probably quoting Longfellow's 'The Rainy Day' (1842): "Into each life some rain must fall, / Some days must be dark and dreary."

Intoxicated with the exuberance of his own verbosity. 93 p142. This quotation was still in common use in the 1950s, though PGW changed it slightly. It was Disraeli (1804–81) speaking of Gladstone, 27 July 1878: "Inebriated by the exuberance of his own verbosity …"

Ippleton, Worcs. 10 p8; 39 p17; Earl of 88 p123. See Chap. 26 (Powick).

Irish members causing trouble in the House. 4 p31. Between 1890 and 1910, the Irish members of Parliament often held the balance of votes in the House of Commons. This occasionally led to their flexing their muscles and forcing the administration of the day into very awkward positions. It used to be said that the future of the British Government depended on whether or not the Irish leader, Tim Healy, had had a good dinner.

Irish Sweep, the. 69 p233 and later. Similar to CALCUTTA SWEEP.

Irishman's croquet lawn is his castle. 7 p66. See CASTLE.

Iron bands, muscles as strong as. 25 p186 and later. See VILLAGE BLACKSMITH.

Iron entered his soul. The iron neatly inserted into Gethryn's soul 2 p33; 20 p32; and often later. BCP. Psalm 105.18: "Whose feet they hurt in the stocks; the iron entered into his soul."

Iron hand, touch of the (in the velvet glove). 51 p72 and later. French proverb — iron hand in a velvet glove. First attribution is to Charles V (1500–58).

Iron Pirate, The. 12 p100. Excellent 1883 adventure story by Max Pemberton.

Irresistible force and the immovable mass/object. 23 p114 and elsewhere. This logical paradox has been attributed to Zeno, a Greek philosopher of the 5th century B.C. If a force is irresistible, then there can be no object that is immovable. If there is an object that is immovable, then there cannot be such a thing as an irresistible force. The songwriter Johnny Mercer ignored the logical contradiction, but spoke of the result if the situation should ever occur in his 1954 song 'Something's Gotta Give'.

Irving, Sir Henry, in *The Bells*. 36 p99. Irving (1838–1905) dominated the English stage for the last 30 years of his life. The first actor to be knighted, his playing of the haunted murderer in *The Bells* (1871 onwards) remains a legend.

Is it true what they say about Dixie? 62 p215. I was surprised to find this song was not written until 1936 (Caesar and Lerner).

Is that a bottle I see before me, its handle to my hand? 71 p175. PGW twist on S. *Macbeth* 2.1: "Is this a dagger which I see before me, The handle toward my hand? Come, let me clutch thee ..."

Is that a ladder I see before me, its handle to my hand. 15A p161. See entry above.

Isaiah. The prophet Isaiah had a gift for taking the dark view 60 p124; and later. He did indeed, as B. Isaiah Chaps 28–30 make clear.

Isis magazine at Oxford. 18 p179. This undergraduate magazine, against all expectations, is still going after more than a century. Every Oxford undergraduate sneers at it — and wishes he/she were writing for it.

Island of Girls show. 18 p264. Probably a reference to the famous musical *Florodora*. (Florodora was the name of the island on which the pretty girls lived.) See FLORODORA.

Island Race, the. 48 p210. The British.

Islands of the Blest. 38 p123. KIPLING's 'The Three Decker': "In endless English comfort, by county-folk caressed, I left the old three-decker at the Islands of the Blest."

Isle, sceptred. See SCEPTRED ISLE.

Israel, Kings of. 14 p151. See JUDAH, KINGS OF.

It. 48 p148. The first 'It' girl was Clara Bow (1905–65), who shocked, scandalised and delighted filmgoers in the 1920s and 30s without benefit of nudity or much of a figure. In 1927 she earned the name by starring in the film *It*. Since she was told the censors would not accept the words 'sex-appeal' in a film, Elinor GLYN, who wrote the book and film script, coined the term 'It' instead.

It ain't all lavender. 91 p82; 96 p145. Victorian music hall song of 1894, sung by Harry Kendall. It described life in a house with a factory on one side and an abattoir on the other.

It cometh in the morning. 52 p129. See JOY IN THE MORNING.

It is not —s that matter, but the courage we bring to them. Actresses' photographs 39 p234; aunts 68 p10. I have known this expression all my life, but the nearest I can find is the opening line of Hugh WALPOLE's *Fortitude* (1913):

"'Tisn't life that matters! 'Tis the courage you bring to it." MTT Elin Woodger.

It is too large, a bubble blown so big and tenuous … suds. 79 p10.*The Cream of the Jest* (1917) by influential fantasy writer James Branch Cabell: "the empire is too large, a bubble blown so big and tenuous that the first shock will disrupt it in suds."

It might have been. See WORDS OF TONGUE.

It sinks and I am ready to depart. 79 p189 and PGW's twist at p190. Landor's poem 'Finis': "I warmed both hands before the fire of life; It sinks, and I am ready to depart."

It was a dark and stormy night. 42 p103. See DARK AND STORMY.

It was Jim/ Gertrude. See JIM, IT WAS.

Italian, the modern. See MODERN ITALIAN.

Itchabod. 45 p150. See ICHABOD.

Ivy. Let's go to the Ivy. 83 p42. Smart London restaurant.

Ivy on the old garden wall, the. 55 p220; 82 p143. 1903 song by A.J. Mills. "Just like the ivy on the … I'll cling to you."

I.W.W. stuff. 25 p251. The Industrial Workers of the World, a militant labour organisation, was founded by Eugene Debs in the USA in 1905 in opposition to the more moderate Federation of Labour.

J

(MTT = My thanks to)

Jabberjee, Mr Hurry. 2p141; "a beaming simper of indescribable suavity" 3 p111; "sotto voce with gratification" 7 p17. In today's political correctness, Mr Jabberjee would never be allowed. At the end of the 19th century, hundreds of young Indians came to London to read law, which led F. Anstey (1856–1934) to write a series of essays for *Punch* in the 1890s, supposedly written by one of them. These became the rage and the whole country quoted Mr Jabberjee, a pompous young Indian law student, who wrote weekly letters to 'Hon'ble Punch', describing his experiences as a visitor to England. His style of speech was orotund 18th-century Augustan English, and ten words were used when one would do, mixed in with Shakespearean misquotations. A visit to Shakespeare's birthplace induced feelings of awe: "Here the Swan of Avon was hatched." When asked to keep quiet: "I became once more sotto voce and the silent tomb." Bertie Wooster's speech owes much to Mr Jabberjee.

When somebody complained that this was a cruel parody, hundreds wrote in saying this was exactly how many Indians spoke English, and one quoted an application for leave from his clerk on the grounds that: "Honoured Sir, Deeply regret to inform you that the hand that rocked my cradle has kicked the bucket." When 'Mr Jabberjee' announced he was no longer going to write for 'Hon'ble Punch', *Punch* was astonished to receive dozens of applications from real Indian law students, all claiming they wrote exactly as Mr Jabberjee did.

Towards the end of his life, PGW asked his old friend, Bill Townend, where the phrase 'Hon'ble So-and-So' had originated. He had forgotten Mr Jabberjee, whom he had quoted so often seventy years before.

Those familiar with Indian actors on British television will have noticed how the older ones speak a correct but slightly out-of-date English. "He is a jolly fine fellow" is a phrase one no longer hears from native English speakers but frequently from elderly Indians. It is English speech of the 1940s — and the British left India in 1947. A few years ago, a journalist reported being amazed by the English he heard in Istanbul: "We have here absolutely spiffing carpets." He thought they were joking or were all Wodehouse enthusiasts. What he was hearing was the English language the British Army spoke when they were last in Turkey (just after the First World War).

But then, so much of PGW's phraseology and terminology seems dated today. There are not many recordings of everyday British speech from the 1920s, but they confirm that people did indeed speak in the manner he described. In 2006 a newspaper published some extracts from the diary of a fighter pilot in the last war. The language he used was indistinguishable from Bertie Wooster's reported speech. Noting a weekend's leave in 1941, the 22-year-old pilot wrote: "Went along to the Ritz Rivoli Bar and had a few snifters. Beetled into the Berkeley for dinner, then staggered along to Hatchett's for a nightcap."

In case anybody thinks Bertie Wooster's speech was restricted to effete, ineffective young men, I think it worth mentioning that the officer quoted (Squadron Leader Neville Duke) shot down 27 enemy aircraft, flew 485 operational sorties and finished the war with a DSO, the DFC and two bars and the AFC (Distinguished Service Order, Distinguished Flying Cross and Air Force Cross).

Jabberwocky. Her pug dog Jabberwocky 60 p113; Barmy's uncle Theodore resembles the Jabberwock 70 p160; 80 p134. See 'Jabberwocky' in Lewis Carroll's *Alice Through the Looking-Glass*.

J'accuse. 76 p54. Zola's famous letter of 1898 on the Dreyfus case.

Jack the Ripper. 53 p253 and later. Perpetrator of a horrific series of murders in the East End of London in 1888. He was never caught and there have been (too) many books written and films made 'proving' who it was.

Jack-rabbit surprised while lunching. 25 p7. PGW twist on a nymph surprised while bathing. See SURPRISED WHILE BATHING.

Jackson, John, in the old prize-ring. 3 p156. Gentleman John Jackson was boxing champion of England 1795–1800.

Jackson, Mike. 12. See Chap. 10.

Jacob. Jacob had nothing on me. I was willing, even anxious, to sweat myself to the bone to win you 54 p59; 94 p16. B. Genesis 29.20: "And Jacob served seven years for Rachel; and they seemed unto him but a few days, for the love he had to her." At 60 p229, Jacob wrestled with an angel. B. Genesis 32.24: "And Jacob was left alone; and there wrestled a man with him until the breaking of the day."

Jacobs, W.W. 7 p97. PGW had a great admiration for Jacobs (1863–1943), who wrote humorous short stories about Bob Pretty, the Night Watchman, and Sam Small.

Jael, wife of Heber. 28 p123 and nine times thereafter. B. Judges 4.21: "Then Jael, Heber's wife took a nail of the tent, and took a hammer in her hand, and went softly unto him, and smote the nail into his temples, and fastened it to the ground; for he was fast asleep and weary. So he died."

Jamaica? No, she went of her own free will. 67 p8. This pun was a favourite in the old cross-talk acts in British music halls.

James, Henry. 3 p118 up to 83 p107. This writer (1843–1916) was reputed to spend up to half an hour choosing exactly the right word. While some made a point of chewing everything 33 times (see FLETCHERIZE), James decided everything should be chewed a hundred times, which, as one biographer said, "curtailed his social life considerably". He saw the light after two years and blamed his nervous breakdown on the time he had spent overchewing.

James, Jesse. 19 p58 and later. PGW was covering his bets here. James (1847–82) was not well known in Britain till Hollywood introduced him. To cater for both US and UK readers, Mr Peters in *Something Fresh* also mentions two British villains, Captain Kidd and Dick Turpin. I wonder how many Americans knew who they were.

James the Second, attacked tobacco. 78 p129. A misprint. It was James I (reigned 1603–25) who loathed smoking and wrote *A Counterblast to Tobacco* (1604) to publicize his disapproval.

Jamshyd … once gloried and drunk deep. 79 p117. See Lion and the lizard.

Japanese umbrellas. 59 p164; 82 p179. Gilbert & Sullivan's *Mikado* began the craze for these ornate, brightly coloured objects. Although PGW called it an umbrella, I think that today it would be termed a parasol. Until the 1920s, a sun-tan was something to be avoided, and every lady would carry a parasol at summer events such as Wimbledon, Henley and Eights Week. See Chap. 20.

Jarvis, Bat. See Chap. 23.

Jasper, Sir. See Todd, sir jasper.

Jaundiced eye. 53 p13. Freddie Threepwood is one of those who rather invite the jaundiced eye. T. 'Locksley Hall': "Left me with the palsied heart, and left me with the jaundiced eye."

Jazz Singer, The. 57 p257. Famous as first talking film (1927).

Jazz spats. 31 p211. Because of the excitement arising from the arrival of jazz music in the UK just before the First World War, the word 'jazz' was used for anything new, smart, colourful, up-to-date. The expression 'very jazzy' is still common when commenting on someone's colourful waistcoat or socks.

Jealous. Of one not easily j., but, being wrought, perplexed in the extreme. See Loved not wisely.

Jealousy is a hydra of calamities, the seven-fold death. 18 p54. Young's *The Revenge*, Act 2 Sc 1.

Jealousy, the green-eyed monster. 42 p118. S. *Othello* 3.3: "O! beware, my lord, of jealousy; it is the green-eyed monster which doth mock The meat it feeds on."

Jeames, our. 1 p163. James was the name frequently given by Victorian employers to their footmen and/or coachmen. Cockney derision turned this into Jeames, exemplified in Thackeray's *Yellowplush Papers*. Wodehouse always addressed his schoolfellow, Eric George, in letters as 'Jeames'. In the 1890s, when *Eric, or Little by Little* was the most despised school story in Britain, a boy would rather die at the stake than admit to his fellows his first name was Eric. See Chap. 30 and also *Eric*.

Jebb. 3 p117. This Cambridge academic (1841–1905) was pre-eminent in the field of Greek scholarship.

Jebusite. Janet Yorke is one 53 p43; and later. A term of dislike. See also Hivite

AND A JEBUSITE.

'Jeeves and the Impending Doom'. See IMPENDING DOOM.

'Jeeves and the Song of Songs'. See SONG OF SONGS.

Jeeves and the Tie That Binds. See TIE THAT BINDS.

Jeffreys, Judge. 59 p95; 68 p231. This judge was notorious for the severe sentences he passed in the Bloody Assize on those who took part in Monmouth's Rebellion of 1685.

Jeffries, James J. 15p176 and later. Ukridge's crouching style of dancing resembles him (see Chap. 4). Until Jeffries (1875–1953; heavyweight champion 1899–1906) came along, boxers stood straight up, head back, with their arms out in front of them. Noble but vulnerable.

Jellicoe, Tom. Poor T.J., the darling of the crew. 12 p244. One of Charles Dibdin's many patriotic sea-songs c.1790.

Jellied eels. See EELS.

Jellygraph. Our handwriting will be recognised if we j. it 1 p267. I am sure the comment at p271 that most people find one trial of jellygraphing sufficient was based on PGW's personal experience. Jellygraphing was a messy process in which the sheet of print was pressed onto a bed of jelly to leave an impression. Copies were made by pressing blank sheets onto the jelly. I have heard that PGW produced an illicit magazine, similar to *The Glow Worm*, when he was at Dulwich. See Chap. 3.

Jenny kissed me when we met. 50 p309. Leigh Hunt's poem 'Rondeau': "Say I'm growing old, but add, Jenny kissed me."

Jeremiah. The works of the prophet Jeremiah. 40 p118; 57 p187. Jeremiah took a censorious view of just about everything and regularly threatened those around him with the wrath of God.

Jerkwater little place. 15 p13. With 'tanktown', an American expression indicating a very small town. It stems from the days when trains had to take in water regularly and would stop at a watertank beside the track and jerk down the chain to put water into the engine. 'Jerkwater' towns were so small, the watertank was the only reason trains stopped there.

Jeshurun waxed fat and kicked. 66 p89. B. Deuteronomy 32.15. 'Jeshurun' was another term for Israel, and the phrase describes the growing wealth of the Israelites and their subsequent forgetting that God had provided such prosperity for them.

Jessop/ J. Essop. 2 p198; 3 p236; 6 p3. Gilbert Jessop (1874–1955) was a cricketer renowned for the ferocity with which he hit the ball and the speed of his scoring, including his Test century for England in seventy-five minutes, on 13 August 1902 ('Jessop's Match'). His performance there upset an otherwise certain Australian win and England won by one wicket in a nerve-wracking finish. It was never forgotten by the young PGW, who always mourned missing Jessop's performance because he had to leave the ground and return to work in the bank.

Jewel in the idol's eye. Chap who steals the jewel that is the idol's eye and … sinister Indian priests around the corner. 58 p123. PGW grew up on these stories. See 'GREEN EYE OF THE LITTLE YELLOW GOD'.

Jewel of gold in a swine's snout … 39 p95; 80 p66. See VERILY.

Jewels are no more good to you than a hole in the head if they are under water. 94 p45. See GEM OF PUREST RAY SERENE.

Jezebel. 18 p37 and often later. This lady married Ahab, who later became king of Israel. The term 'painted Jezebel' comes from B. 2 Kings 9.30: "And she painted her face …" She then introduced the worship of Baal into Israel, which led to her unpleasant death on the orders of Jehu. B. 2 Kings 9.33–37. describes her being thrown out of the window, trodden underfoot by horses and, allegedly, eaten by dogs.

Jim, it was. He tore off his whiskers and it was Jim 53 p91; it was Gertrude 54 p192; Aunt Dahlia intends to do the same at 76 p193. PGW gave us the source at p 134 of *Bring on the Girls*. Charlie Case (d. 1916), a black-faced US comedian, had a routine in which he parodied the sentimental songs and recitations popular at that period. His best-known sketch concluded with the line: "He tore off his false whiskers and it was Jim."

Jim-jams. UK version of the heeby-jeebies. 48 p224. G&S *The Grand Duke* Act 1. "Then you've got to a state which is known / To the medical world as 'jim-jams.'"

Jimpson weed, a human. 30 p200. I am informed this refers to the American thorn apple.

Jno. As in Jno. Robinson, the Market Blandings taxi driver. The name 'John' was abbreviated to Jno. from the 15th century onwards in tenant rolls, Court judgements and legal documents to save the clerk's time. Young Thos. acquired his spelling the same way, as did Fredk., Ed. and Wm. elsewhere. This form of spelling is still to be seen on tradesmen's vans and shop fronts.

Job, his comforters and his boils. 26 p239 and later. B. Job 2.7: "So went Satan forth from the presence of the Lord, and smote Job with sore boils from the sole of his foot unto his crown." For Job's comforters, see BILDAD THE SHUHITE.

Jocund Spring. 23 p197. The phrase comes from Milton's *Comus* but was used by many poets later, including Longfellow. PGW clearly knew it as a typical title for a Victorian painting, but I could not find it in any of the encyclopaedias I consulted. At last I had the good sense to ask a member of staff of the London Library. MTT Rebecca Russell, who informed me that 'Jocund Spring' by W.J. Hennessy was a hit at the Royal Academy show of 1881.

John, Augustus. 37 p264. John (1878–1961), for long the *enfant terrible* of British painting, was equally famous for his affaires.

John D. As rich as J.D. 18 p267 and later. When PGW wrote this, every reader knew he was referring to John D. Rockefeller (1839–1937) who made Standard Oil the biggest oil company in the world. In 1879 it controlled 90% of US stocks.

Johnnies and chappies. See CHAPPIE.

Johnson, Doctor. London may have suited Doctor J 7 p13. Dr Johnson (1709–84) said, "No, sir, when a man is tired of London, he is tired of life; for there is in London all that life can afford." (20 September 1777)

Johnson Slam, the. 7 p140. Combined with the Tilden Slosh comment (see TILDEN), PGW was clearly referring to W.M. Johnson, the American who won Wimbledon in 1923.

Johnston, Eric. 67 p224 and later. Censor of Hollywood films who took over from Will HAYS in 1945.

Johnstown flood. 30 p46; 87 p161. This Pennsylvania town suffered severe damage when the dam above the town broke in 1889 and more than 2,000 people drowned. A song commemorating the event was sung all over America for years.

Jo-Jo, the dog-faced boy. 27 p97. I found this character by pure chance. He was one of the freak shows at Coney Island around 1910. Among the other attractions were Jimmy DURANTE and the seventeen-year-old Mae WEST, already a veteran actress, playing in *Uncle Tom's Cabin*.

Jolliest of all possible worlds. 53 p140. See ALL IS FOR THE BEST.

Jolson, Al. 46 p53. This American singer (1886–1950) is now best remembered as the first to sing on film (*The Jazz Singer* 1927). His catchphrase was "You ain't heard nothing yet" (71 p88). This originated early in his career, about 1910, when he was singing in a club in competition with building operations next door. When the drills paused for a moment, he yelled at the audience, "You ain't heard nothing yet" and launched into the next song as loud as he could. The reaction was so favourable that he kept the phrase in his act thereafter, and he, Kahn and De Sylva wrote a popular song with the title in 1919. See also Chap. 38 ('Bully for Mr Bartlett').

Jonah. One of those fellows who always come up smiling 61 p65; his whale 68 p26 & p110. B. Jonah Chaps 1&2. When a storm blew up, the sailors decided Jonah was to blame and threw him overboard, whereupon he was swallowed by a great fish. Three days later the fish vomited him out on to dry land. The term 'Jonah', for someone believed to bring bad luck to a ship, has lasted a very long time.

Jones, Bobby (R.T.). 37 p52 and elsewhere. Jones (1902–71) was the only golfer to win the four (UK and US) Amateur and Open golf championships in one year (1930).

Jones, Jennifer. 68 p245. US film actress (1919–2009).

Jonson, Ben. 50 p122 and later. This poet and playwright (1572–1637) was buried in Westminster Abbey. Reluctant to put his friends to much expense, he had asked that his grave occupy as little space as possible. He was therefore buried standing up, and the stone over his grave was inscribed simply 'O rare Ben Jonson'.

Joppa, Battle of. 54 p121; 84 p84 and elsewhere. Won by Richard Lionheart in

1191 at the end of the third Crusade.

Joseph prophesying before Pharaoh. 39 p275. B. Genesis Chap 41. Pharaoh asked Joseph to explain a worrying dream. Joseph did so well that Pharaoh sent him "over all the land of Egypt".

Joshua(y), my son (went to Philadelphia(y)). 66 p11. From the 1907 US song 'Wal, I Swan!' by Benjamin Burt.

Journey's End. 55 p16. Originally from S. *Twelfth Night* 2.3, but PGW was probably using the title of R.C. Sherriff's superb and moving 1927 play about the First World War. The original cast had all served in the trenches and some wore their old uniforms. MTT Tony Ring for suggesting that it could also stem from PGW's lyric 'Journey's End' from *The Cabaret Girl.*

Journeys end in lovers meeting. 13 p108. S. *Twelfth Night* 2.3: "Trip no further, pretty sweeting; Journeys end in lovers meeting."

Jove reached for his thunderbolts. 25p 60. If you had translated as much Greek as PGW had, you would know all about Jove's method of punishing humans for their wrongdoings.

Jovean coiffure. 33 p144. I assume PGW considered Charlton Prout's haircut similar to the tight curls seen on statues of Jove.

Jowett, if I was no. 17 p49. Benjamin Jowett (1817–93), Master of Balliol College, was a man of great intellect and influence. He is now probably best remembered by the verse:

> First come I; my name is Jowett.
> There is no knowledge but I know it.
> I am the Master of this college;
> What I don't know isn't knowledge.

Joy. Bring a little joy into any life 67 p13. See RUNYON, DAMON.

'Joy Bells for Walter'. 81 story title. See PGW song lyric 'Joy Bells' from *The Beauty Prize* 1923.

Joy in heaven over one sinner that repenteth, more. 90 p92. B. Luke 15.7: "that likewise joy shall be in heaven over one sinner that repenteth, more than over ninety and nine just persons, which need no repentance."

Joy in the Morning. Joy had certainly come in the morning 36 p56; 64 title. B. Psalms 30.5: "weeping may endure for a night, but joy cometh in the morning."

Joy, jollity and song, all was. 14 p175 and later. I have not found the source, but PGW noted it in 1905; see ABBREVIATIONS.

Joy reigns supreme. 43 p233 and later. If ever a quote should come from the Bible, this one should, but doesn't. I then tried *HYMNS ANCIENT AND MODERN*, but this provided nothing either. The end of Act 1 of G&S's *Mikado* has: "For joy reigns everywhere around" and this is near as I can get. MTT Ian Michaud.

Joy will be unconfined. 42 p16; 61 p261 and later. BYRON's *Childe Harold's Pilgrimage* C.3, St.22: "On with the dance! Let joy be unconfined."

Joyce, Peggy. 46 p170. Archetypal gold-digging Ziegfeld Girl (1893–1957), this lady arrived in Hollywood with $3 million of alimony from five husbands and at once embarked on a torrid affaire with Charlie Chaplin. Having heard some of her tales of Paris, Chaplin produced his film *A Woman of Paris*.

Joyeuse. Lord Bromborough's moustache 57 p82; Lord Ickenham's sponge 60 p142; 67 p170. PGW's reference to the custom of kings and great warriors in mediaeval times giving names to their swords; Arthur's Excalibur is a familiar example. Joyeuse was one of Charlemagne's two swords; FLAMBERGE was the other.

Jubilee Watering Trough. 40 p11 and frequent later. During the 19th century, when the horse was the main form of transport, the rapid growth of towns and heavy industry meant a decrease in the number of watering-holes, ponds etc. where horses could drink. Queen Victoria's Golden (1887) and Diamond (1897) Jubilees were commemorated up and down the country by the installation of new watering troughs in towns and villages. Since most were at cross-roads or traffic junctions, thousands were destroyed when roads were widened for modern motor traffic. However, some Jubilee models survive, including an excellent example at Epping, just north of London. It is a splendid affair with water basins on opposite sides for humans and horses and another, at ground level, for cattle and dogs.

Jubilee watering trough

This magnificent specimen, with the author and his granddaughter flanking it, was erected in Epping, Essex, to commemorate Queen Victoria's Golden Jubilee in 1887.

Judah, kings of. 19 p139 and later. My knowledge of the Old Testament is abysmal, and I must confess I had assumed these were the same as the kings of Israel. They were not. After Solomon's death (975 B.C.), his kingdom was split in two. Rehoboam became first king of Judah and Jeroboam became king of Israel.

Judicious remark ... of the governor of North Carolina to the governor of South Carolina. 7 p134. By coincidence, I was in North Carolina when I found this reference. In 1857, a runaway slave from South Carolina escaped across the state line into North Carolina, where he had friends. The governor of South Carolina asked his opposite number to dinner, then made a strong speech urging the restoration of the slave to his owner. When he finished, he turned to the governor of North Carolina and asked, "What do you say?" The reply was: "It's a long time between drinks."

Judson Hotel. The yellow cross of the J.H. shines on Washington Square 22 p99 & p 155. Built as a Christian lodging-house for working girls in New York, the Judson building stands on the south side of Washington Square. I am delighted to say the large cross on the building is still lit at night.

Juggernaut. Driving an ambulance rather than a j. 58 p227. See WHEELS OF JUGGERNAUT.

'Juice of an Orange, The'. Short story. I knew dieting became fashionable in the 1920s, but I had not realised how popular 'single item' diets were. A newspaper advertisement of 6 July 1937 bears a remarkable resemblance to the advice given to Wilmot Mulliner.

The Bread and Butter Diet

Breakfast. Two slices of bread and butter and half a pint of milk.

Noon. Two slices of bread and butter.

4 P.M. Two slices of bread and butter, and as a stimulant (!), one cup of tea but only ONE lump of sugar.

7 P.M. Two slices of bread and butter with milk or pure tomato juice, as preferred.

On retiring, another slice of bread and butter may be taken.

But there is some good news: "Between meals as much cold water may be drunk as desired."

Ju-Jar. 12 p111. A well-known (at that time) ointment for easing sprains, soreness etc.

Jukes family. Lord Emsworth is like one of the less intelligent members of the J.f. 72 p10; and elsewhere. Until c.1940 this was a common term in the US for the simple-minded. It stems from an 1877 study carried out by Dr Goddard, who found that a mentally sub-normal couple had produced a vast family of mentally-handicapped descendants who were all in prison, asylums or institutions. Goddard gave the family the fictional name of Jukes, and this remained a generic term for the feeble-minded for many years. George Bernard Shaw and H.G. Wells were vocal British advocates for Eugenics and selective breeding, while Margaret Sanger led the campaign in America from about 1905. She had plenty of followers and Mrs Lora Delane Porter of *The Coming of Bill/Their Mutual Child* is an accurate portrayal of them. I was surprised to learn that the US Supreme Court (Oliver Wendell Holmes) agreed that compulsory sterilisation of the feeble-minded was justifiable and some 30,000 men and women were so dealt with up to 1940.

Junior Ganymede Club. See Chap. 21.

Jury duty. 92 p12. The list of occupations exempt from jury duty in England used to be as varied and extensive as PGW said. Roughly, it was based on the idea that the services of the juryman might be needed more urgently outside the court than in it. The Brethren of Trinity House, for example, are responsible for lighthouses, buoys and pilotage in British waters and take their name from the Guild of the Holy Trinity, who looked after Thames lighthouses back in the 16th century. It would clearly be inappropriate to swear in as juror a Brother who might have to dash off and mend a lighthouse lamp at any moment.

As a member of the Armed Forces (liable to be sent anywhere in a hurry), I was also exempt, but an official of the Central Criminal Court informs me that the rules have now changed to such an extent that he believes everybody is now liable for jury service except, maybe, the Lord Chancellor and the Prime Minister.

Just break the news to Mother. 25 p242; 57 p211. The sad 1897 song 'Break the News to Mother' by Charles Harris was wildly popular, extolling as it did both heroism and the virtues of Mother.

Just like Mother makes. 7 p51; 25 p18 and frequent later. A favourite expression of Aunt Dahlia's. It comes from an advertisement for a flour company to be seen in American magazines from 1900 to 1940 which showed a delighted family beaming as mother puts an apple pie on the table: 'Just Like Mother Makes.' This was so successful, Pet Milk produced a 1915 version with a similar picture and the claim that it produced cakes and pancakes: 'Like Mother Used To Make.' The New England Mincemeat people came in on the act later with an equally happy family and the caption: 'The Kind That Mother Used To Make'.

Just us chickens. 92 p19. 19th-century American joke. A man enters a hen-house to steal chickens. The farmer hears them squawking, grabs his gun and shouts: "Who's that in my hen-house?" The reply is as above. (It sounds better on stage.)

Justice be done and the righteous given their due. 34 p84. This should be in the Bible, but I could not find it there or in Shakespeare. B. Psalms 37.29 is as near as I could get: "The righteous shall inherit the land, and dwell therein for ever."

Justice, high, middle and low. See HIGH, MIDDLE AND LOW JUSTICE.

Justitia. Fiat justitia ruat coelum. See FIAT JUSTITIA.

Juvenal. Made J. seem like a tactful pacifist. 30 p145 and later. Juvenal (c.55–127 A.D.) wrote savage satires on politicians and on the social customs of his time.

Ian Hislop of *Private Eye* summarised this Roman satirist very well: "To modern eyes any line in Juvenal is complete drivel, but after ten minutes in the footnotes and a fortnight in the Bodleian, you will probably find it is the most corkingly audacious quip you have ever heard."

J'y suis, j'y reste. 76 p16. "Here I am; here I stay," said by General MacMahon in the Crimean War when he was warned the trenches his division had taken might have been mined by the retreating Russians.

K

(MTT = My thanks to)

Kafka. 83 p33; 87 p169. Franz Kafka (1883–1924) wrote the sort of books about which Alan Bennett said: "The Channel is a slipper bath of irony through which we pass these serious Continentals in order not to be infected by their gloom."

Kaiser, the. 3 p11 and later; as Wilhelm II p42. Although he was the nephew of Edward VII, Kaiser Wilhelm (1858–1941) became unpopular in Britain in 1899 when he supported the Boers in the Boer War. A figure of hate during the First World War, the Kaiser abdicated in 1918 and lived in Holland till his death in 1941. In his last years, his favourite author was P.G. Wodehouse.

Kansas. One of those high winds which … blow through the state of Kansas 84 p90. The world outside the United States knew little of these until the film *The Wizard of Oz* (1939).

Kant. 9 p6. German philosopher Immanuel Kant (1724–1804).

Kaplan, Hyman. 86 p141. PGW was very taken with this immortal character created by Leo Rosten. The reference here is a compliment to Rosten, who came to lunch at Remsenburg while Wodehouse was working on the book.

Karloff, Boris. 68 p24 and often later. This actor (1887–1969) made his name playing 'horror' parts, Frankenstein's monster, etc. It was one of Hollywood's ironies that the tall, threatening man with the Russian-sounding name was in reality William Henry Pratt, a gentle, courteous Englishman, born in Dulwich, educated at Uppingham, who had intended to join the diplomatic service. MTT David McDonough for the information that Karloff appeared in the 1919 film *The Prince and Betty*.

Katie, bar the door. 15 p296. It is remarkable how long this phrase has lasted. It commemorates Catherine Douglas, who, in 1437, tried to defend James I of Scotland by putting her arm through the security slots in the door to his chamber to stop assassins coming in. The swine simply axed through her arm and killed the king anyway.

'Kay Day by Day', I'd like to write a book on. 6 p12. See 'Huy Day by Day' in *Performing Flea* forty years later.

Kaye, Danny. 78 p135. A gifted comic film actor (1908–87).

Kean. 9 p100. Edmund Kean (1789–1833) was the leading classical actor of his day.

Keaton, Buster (whom the fourth Countess [of Emsworth] closely resembled). 50 p226. A superb comedy film actor (1895–1966).

Keel, stir of life along her. 52 p107 and later. Bertie got this one slightly wrong. See PIG SOMETHING.

Keeley Cure Institute. 48 p13. A famous American clinic for drying out alcoholics.

Keep the home fires burning. 27 p217. The popular British song of World War I, 'Keep the Home Fires Burning', made its composer, the 21-year-old Ivor Novello, famous.

Keeping the bridge. See HORATIUS.

Keith circuit. 26 p137. In 1900, Benjamin Keith controlled more than 100 theatres across the USA; by 1914, he controlled 400.

Kennecott (copper) mine. 44 p176. A famous ore strike in America. See also ANACONDA.

Kennedy, Bart (of the Daily Mail). 11 p91. Kennedy (1861–1930) had sailed round the world, fought Indians in America, looked for gold in the Klondyke, and sung in opera. He finished up as the *Daily Mail*'s war correspondent.

Kern, Jerome. His song hits 34 p231. Wodehouse was paying an apposite compliment to his friend Kern (1885–1945). *Bill the Conqueror* first appeared as a magazine serial in May 1924 and was based on the plot of the Bolton-Wodehouse-Kern show *Sitting Pretty*, which had opened just a month before. Wodehouse must have worked on the show and book simultaneously. See also INSIDE STAND.

Kerr, Jean, and her snake. 92 p6. A book by Jean Kerr (1923–2003), *The Snake Has All the Lines*, hit the headlines in 1960. She was a witty author while her husband was a playwright and dramatic critic who won a Pulitzer Prize. I had thought the title of the book came from a review of a poor performance of *Antony and Cleopatra.* However, MTT Neil Midkiff for the information that it stems from the occasion when the Kerrs' son came home and announced he was to be Adam in the school play, but he was unhappy because "the snake has all the lines".

Kettle, Captain. See CAPTAIN KETTLE.

Keystone Kops. Men's chorus dancing like 26 p198; 64 p212. This was the troupe of comic actors formed and directed by Mack Sennett (1880–1960), who made audiences roar with laughter with their antics in comic chases in the early silent film days.

Kid, Oh you. See OH YOU KID.

Kidd, Captain. 13 p29 and frequent up to 94 p93. A famous pirate (1645–1701) who, reputedly, left a treasure for which many people are still looking. R.L. Stevenson's *Treasure Island* is probably the best-known story of such searches. Authorised to attack French ships as a privateer, Kidd found piracy more profitable. Despite helping to build Trinity Church in New York City, he was hanged as a pirate in London.

Kilkenny cats. Consumed each other after the fashion of K. c. 18 p108. The legend is that two cats fought each other so fiercely that all that was left were the two tails. The phrase stems from the bitter rivalry between two towns in

County Kilkenny who spent so much money on lawsuits disputing the boundary between them, they were both left bankrupt.

Kind hearts are more than coronets (And simple faith more than Norman blood). 26 p36 and frequent later. T. 'Lady Clara Vere de Vere'.

King Henry and the White Ship. 19 p7. One of the scraps of historical information once known by every British schoolboy was that, after his son William had died on the White Ship in 1120, Henry I never smiled again.

King in Babylon. I was a king in Babylon and you were a Christian slave. Frequent. The lines are from W.E. Henley's 'To W.A.', number 37 in his *Echoes of Life and Death* (1899). The first PGW reference is at 13 p242, the impossible-to-index phrase: "when you were a tiddley-om-pom and I was a thingummajig."

King Kong. 54 p109 and later. The monster gorilla of the 1933 film remarkable for its then-revolutionary special effects.

King who … would never smile again. 71 p131. See KING HENRY.

Kings. Because we are sensible enough to have a monarchy in Britain, we do not use the 'King' nickname as often as Americans do. I have only found three British 'kings': George Hudson the Railway King, Barney Barnato the Kaffir King, and Richard Oastler the Factory King. In 19th-century America, several men gained control of complete industries. Known as 'robber barons' or 'economic Royalists', men like Vanderbilt, Rockefeller and Carnegie made incredible fortunes. PGW adopted the custom for characters in his stories who had gained a monopoly in some field.

In real life, I have found references to the Artichoke King (Ciro Terranova), Barbed Wire King ('Bet-You-A-Million' Gates), Borax King (Francis Smith), Chocolate King (Milton Hershey), Grapefruit King (J.A. Harris), Gunpowder King (DuPont), Oil King (Leo Koretz), Peanut King (Pembroke Gwaltney), Pineapple King (James Dole), Railway King (Jay Gould and EH Harriman), and Steel King (Andrew Carnegie). There were certainly enough of them to inspire PGW to give us ten fictional 'Kings': Braces, Cheese, Dog, Elastic Stocking, Ham, Newspaper and Tobacco Shop, Night Club, Onion Soup, Sardine and Suspender as well as his Mackerel Monarch and Sardine Sultan.

Kipling, Rudyard. PGW quoted from Kipling (1865–1936) often and respected him as a man who wrote outstanding short stories and poems that everybody, from soldiers and costermongers to peers and princes, knew. (See IF YOU CAN SOMETHING.) He was critical of some of Kipling's later stories, but applauded his view on "raking slag out of a fire", i.e. going through a draft and taking out anything superfluous. He met Kipling at least four times, maybe more, because they both belonged to the Beefsteak Club, and he was proud that Kipling once asked him for advice on how to end a short story. He was delighted when Ian Hay told him that Kipling had said 'Lord Emsworth and the Girl Friend' was the best short story Kipling had ever read.

They certainly corresponded for a time, and I have a note that PGW sent Kipling's letters to Bill Townend. In a letter I saw at a London auction,

Wodehouse wrote that the only letter from Kipling he could remember was one written when PGW was writing *Thank You, Jeeves*. He must have sent Kipling a draft chapter because Kipling asked him to make Bertie Wooster 'blacked out', not 'blacked up'. Wodehouse wrote that he did so, but only because Kipling asked him to. And that is why my edition has 'blacked up' at page 212 but 'blacked out' at page 232.

Kiss again with tears, as Alfred Tennyson puts it. 87 p74. See WE FELL OUT.

Kiss the place and make it well (and would some little story tell). 54 p106 and elsewhere. See MY MOTHER.

Kissed by goddesses. Like men kissed by goddesses in dreams 50 p125; 84 p120. The legend of Artemis and Endymion is the nearest source I can find.

Kissing Time. 74 p130. UK title for PGW's US show *The Girl Behind the Gun*. As PGW said, the title worked for the UK since 'Any Time Is Kissing Time' was a song hit from *Chu Chin Chow*, the wildly-popular UK show of three years before.

Kitchener, Lord. 3 p115. An extremely efficient and successful British general (1850–1916).

Knatchbull-Huguessen. 67 p99; 76 p48; 88 p95. Along with ERNLE-PLUNKETT-DRAX-PLUNKETT and CAVE-BROWN-CAVE, a perfectly good English name. I wonder if PGW's choice of it had any connection with the family of that name who were neighbours of Leonora's in Kent.

Knavish tricks of enemies. 95 p134. The second verse of the British National Anthem runs:

> O Lord our God, arise,
> Scatter our enemies,
> And make them fall;
> Confound their politics
> Frustrate their knavish tricks
> On thee our hopes we'll fix;
> God save us all.

These robust sentiments are very rarely heard today.

Knell, the word was like a. 33 p45. See FORLORN.

Knew not Spiller, a people that. 12 p185. B. Exodus 1.8: "Now there arose up a new king over Egypt, which knew not Joseph."

Knew or cared to know. That was all he knew, or cared to know 26 p147. Keats' 'Ode on a Grecian Urn': "Beauty is truth, truth beauty — that is all / Ye know on earth, and all ye need to know."

Knife, blunt. Not a blunt k. but some such instrument as … described by the poet Gilbert as looking far less like a hatchet than a dissipated saw 84 p108. In 'Annie Protheroe' in Gilbert's *Bab Ballads*, Gilbert Clay so mistreated his executioner's axe, it "Was far less like a hatchet than a dissipated saw".

Knight, parfit gentil. Bertie Wooster aims to be one 43 p145 and later. Description of the Knight in the Prologue to Chaucer's *Canterbury Tales*: "He was a verray parfit gentil knight."

Knitting up the ravelled sleave of care, Beach was. 72 p16. See SLEEP WHICH KNITS.

Knobs on, with. Often in PGW. An expression of emphasis, similar to 'with bells on' or 'in spades'. Thus, an insult or rude remark would be met with the reply: "Same to you — with knobs on." Origin uncertain but perhaps from houses, pieces of furniture, which were highly decorated to emphasise their owner's wealth. Thus, while one landowner might have an old manor house and simple columns at the gates at the end of his drive, his 'new-money' neighbour would surmount each column with a decorative stone ball and put them at various points along his roofline as well. The 'fussy' Victorian style of architecture favoured such decorations.

Knole. 44 p279; 74 p178. A beautiful and ancient stately home in Kent. Bigger than Blandings (see 91 p103), it is one of the great 'calendar' houses with 365 rooms, 52 staircases and 7 courtyards.

Knotted and combined locks from parting ... porpentine. See PORPENTINE.

Know all is to forgive all, to. (C'est tout comprendre, c'est tout pardonner.) Often in PGW and a phrase I have known all my life, but the nearest source I can find is Madame de Stael's *Corinne* (1807): "To know all makes one tolerant." Perhaps it is one of those remarks that have been so quoted/misquoted over the years, the original has been lost.

Know, Do you/ Don't you. See DO YOU KNOW.

Know, you don't. As the song hath it, you don't know, they don't know 1 p181. See YOU DON'T KNOW.

Knowledge. What he didn't know about Woman wasn't k. 18 p71. PGW's gloss on the Benjamin JOWETT rhyme.

Knowledge comes, but Wisdom lingers. 80 p102. T. 'Locksley Hall': "Knowledge comes, but wisdom lingers and I linger on the shore."

Knowledge, peculiar and extensive. 6 p60. See PECULIAR.

Knox, John. 63 p12; would have disapproved of Dolly Molloy 94 p52. Strong-minded Scottish divine (1505–72) who took a very dim view of women in general and the then queens of England, Scotland and France in particular. His 'Trumpet Blast Against the Monstrous Regiment of Women' made the point.

Knox, N.A. 12 p23. PGW played in the Dulwich First XI for two years. In Wodehouse's last year, N.A Knox (1884–1935), his junior by three years, joined him in the school team. Knox went on to play for England against South Africa and for the Gentlemen v. Players (best of the amateurs against best of the professionals). In 1907, bowling for the Gentlemen, he produced the remarkable figures of 5 for 73 and 7 for 110 (MTT Murray Hedgcock). PGW was proud of having played on the same team as Knox and ghost-wrote an article for him. See Chap. 3.

Knubble of Knopp, Lord. 41 p78 and later. PGW used this name four times and I ransacked *Burke's Peerage* to find a name like it. I was unsuccessful, but see

Lord SLYTHE AND SALE.

Knuts. In *Vanity Fair* (Sept 1914), Wodehouse told Americans about 'The Knuts of London'. He pointed out that the Knuts were the descendants of the Beaux, Macaronis, Johnnies, Swells, Dudes and Bloods. He credited George Grossmith Jnr (see Chap. 13) as the first to emphasise the difference between a BLOOD and a Knut. A Blood was a young man who drew attention to himself, got himself thrown out of restaurants, that sort of thing. The Knut was far too listless to do anything so energetic. He was bored to tears by most things but did them because they were the thing to do — attending Church Parade in Hyde Park, going to the Eton & Harrow match and the like. His chief relaxation was dancing or bread-throwing. He and his fellows had their own slang, which constantly changed. Pleasant occurrences 'brace him awf'ly' and a friend was 'a stout fellow' whereas an enemy was 'a tick'.

In the foreword to *Joy in the Morning* (1974 edn), PGW wrote that the world of the Knuts had gone and that George Grossmith Jnr and G.P. Huntley had played them perfectly on stage.

Kreisler. The sort of look K. or somebody like that beholds in the eyes of the front row 41 p38. Charismatic violinist (1875–1962).

Kruscheff. 86 p160. Nikita Khrushchev (1894–1971) was leader of the Soviet Union 1958–64.

Kruschen feeling, that. 40 p35. A feeling of well-being, of cheerfulness, from the 1920s–50s advertisement for Kruschen liver salts, which claimed to produce such a sense of euphoria.

Kubelik. 6 p50. Jan Kubelik (1880–1940) was a violin virtuoso who gave his first recital at the age of eighteen.

Kubla Khan. What K.K. would have called a stately pleasure dome 86 p33 and later. Coleridge's *Kubla Khan*: "In Xanadu did Kubla Khan / A stately pleasure-dome decree." Kubla Khan (1216–94) was a Mongol emperor, grandson of Genghis Khan.

K.V.O. 61 p18. Major-General Sir Everard Slurk, KVO, is among those arriving at Nice. KVO is clearly a misprint for KCVO (Knight Commander of the Royal Victorian Order). MTT Tamaki Morimura for picking this one up. See also CBO.

L

(MTT = My thanks to)

Labour Government (won't let you take any money out of England)**.** 70 p207. For some years after the Second World War, the maximum amount of money you could take out of the UK was, from memory, £25. This severely restricted holidays abroad. MTT Jim Linwood, who remembers being allowed to take only £5 when he went to France in 1947.

Labourer in the vineyard. 90 p96. B. Matthew 20 1–16. Parable of the man who hired labourers to work in his vineyard and paid them all the same, even though some had worked for only one hour while others had worked throughout the day.

Labourer worthy of his hire. 91 p129. B. Luke 10.7: "And in the same house remain, eating and drinking such things as they give; for the labourer is worthy of his hire."

Labourer's task. Now the labourer's task is o'er 68 p214; 94 p145. 1870 hymn by Ellerton & Dykes.

Lacking in repose. Bottle's manner was noticeably l. in r. 53 p129. See REPOSE.

Lad, calm-browed. 8 p44. See CALM-BROWED LAD.

Laddie. In another half-jiffie ... he would be addressing me as 'laddie'. 68 p93 and elsewhere. The habit of British actors addressing each other this way goes back to the mid-19th century.

Lads. The lads. Often. A term covering race-gangs, 'heavies' and bookmaker's 'minders'. Do not confuse with LADS OF THE VILLAGE.

Lads of the village. 12 p235 and later. A term used from 1885 to 1914, covering KNUTS, BLOODS, mashers, toffs — the young men about town who sought amusement in London's West End. The 'village' was reckoned to be that section of London between Hyde Park Corner and St Paul's. See Chap. 5.

Lady in Ingoldsby Legends who didn't mind death but couldn't stand pinching. 2 p77. See INGOLDSBY LEGENDS.

Lady of Shalott. Like a male Lady of Shalott. 41 p246 and later. In T. 'The Lady of Shalott', the lady in question cried: "The curse is come upon me." In view of Dudley Finch's exasperation at Bobbie Wickham's being forty minutes late for lunch, I would have thought a more appropriate reference would have been Tennyson's 'Mariana' who cried "He (She) cometh not". See MARIANA.

Lady of the Lake. 32 p157. Walter Scott's lengthy poem.

Lady who wanted to go to Birmingham and they were taking her on to Crewe.

67 p16. From the UK music hall song 'Oh, Mr Porter', sung by Nellie Wallace c.1900–20.

Lafarge, Madame. 41 p258. An error or a misprint. See Defarge.

Lafayette. The late L. 16 p84; Lafayette, we are here 48 p96. The Marquis de Lafayette (1757–1834) was a French aristocrat who fought with the Americans in the American Revolution. When the US came into the First World War in 1917, General Pershing laid a wreath on Lafayette's tomb in Paris and his aide Colonel Stanton spoke the words (often attributed to Pershing): "Lafayette, we are here."

Lamarr, Hedy. 68 p24; 70 p152. Gorgeous film star (1913–2000).

Lambeth Walk. Mr Steptoe sings it at 62 p85. I was slightly surprised that an American would know this popular Cockney song and novelty dance, but apparently it did well in the US as well. Lupino Lane introduced it in the 1937 show *Me and My Girl.*

Lamour, Dorothy. 68 p121; 69 p115. This actress (1914–96) was famous for the *Road* films with Bob Hope and Bing Crosby.

Lancelot. 18 p52. Bravest of Arthur's knights, who got a bit too close to Queen Guinevere. T. *Idylls of the King.*

Land fit for heroes. 28 p122; 93 p45 & p78. In November 1918, Lloyd George exhorted voters to reward the returning soldiers by making England 'a land fit for heroes'. The subsequent unemployment and social misery soon made the term ironic.

Land flowing with milk and honey. 19 p105 and later. B. Exodus 3.8: "unto a land flowing with milk and honey …"

Land of Hope and Glory. 9 p276. Best-known of Elgar's then-new Pomp and Circumstance marches.

Land of the free and home of the brave. 94 p182. Last line of the first verse of 'The Star-Spangled Banner' by Francis Scott Key.

Landscape, glimmering. Now fades the glimmering l. on the sight. 76 p94 and elsewhere. See All the air.

Landseer. 58 p121; 65 p136. Best-known animal painter (1802–73) of the 19th century. He was also the reluctant sculptor of the lions in Trafalgar Square, allegedly at Queen Victoria's insistence, which he modelled from a dead lion from London Zoo. The corpse lay in his studio long enough for his family to move out, the servants to leave and the health authorities to be called. See also Stag at bay.

Langley End. 45 p9. See Chap. 26.

Langtry, Mrs. 70 p152. A very late reference by PGW to Lily Langtry (1853–1929). Best known as the Jersey Lily, she was a 'favourite' of Edward VII and, later, a successful actress. She was the first 'lady in Society' to make money by endorsing a commercial product, Pears' Soap (see Halloa!), and she was very proud that Langtry, Texas, was named after her. Her first London address was 17 Norfolk Street, where PGW lived later.

Language. Every man should know at least one l. besides his own 48 p79. I have been unable to find the origin of Packy Franklyn's remark. I suspect he was merely repeating a popular cliché of the time. See also AMERICAN YOUTH.

Languid snake (drags its length along like). See SNAKE, LANGUID.

Lardy, Gilbert's Lord ('How strange are the customs of France'). 77 p42. See Gilbert's Lorenzo de Lardy in *Bab Ballads.* "And Lord Lardy would smile and observe, 'How strange are the customs of France.'"

Large fair front. See FRONT.

Larger Life. 19 p6; 38 p75. The Larger Life purported to make you more aware/ think beyond the mundane/ widen your horizons etc. This phrase to describe self-improvement was popular in the early 1900s; the British Library has eight books entitled *The Larger Life* published between 1891 and 1902. PGW tended to emphasise the 'widen your horizons' aspect, i.e. living it up. In *Barmy in Wonderland* (p29), Barmy Phipps reckons Mervyn Potter "when it came to leading the larger life, had few equals".

Lark on the wing, the snail on the thorn and all that? 68 p74. See GOD'S IN HIS HEAVEN.

Larsen exercises. 19 p7. At the beginning of the 20th century, keep-fit manuals were all the rage. For the original of Ashe Marson's mentor, I nominate Lieutenant Muller, late of the Danish Army and Inspector of Danish Sanatoria. An article in the *Strand* (1912) said his exercises, "can be performed in the home in 15 minutes, which time includes taking a bath (not necessarily a cold one) in the normal way. Endorsed by ex-President Roosevelt, Lord Alverstone, Lord Nunburnholme and Sir Robert Baden-Powell." See also DAILY DOZEN.

Lasky, film mogul. 46 p21. Jesse Lasky (1880–1958) made *The Squaw Man* in 1913; he later became head of Paramount.

Last Days of Pompeii, The. A survivor of/ looking like something left over from 69 p78; 71 p74. This Roman city was destroyed by a volcanic eruption in 79 A.D. PGW's reference is to the historical novel *The Last Days of Pompeii* (1834) by Edward Bulwer-Lytton.

Last of the Romantics. 77 p90; 79 p45. If this is a quotation, I have not found it. I suggest it is probably PGW's twist on the line in S. *Julius Caesar* 5.3. "The last of all the Romans, fare thee well. / It is impossible that ever Rome / Should breed thy fellow."

Laszlo portrait. 48 p36. The portrait painter Philip de László (1869–1937) was second only to SARGENT in popularity in Britain.

Latimer, Bishop (and Hebrews 13.4). 46 p184. Latimer was burned for heresy in 1555. I am not going to quote Hebrews 13.4 in a book for family reading. See also CANDLE.

Lauder, Sir Harry. 10 p54 and often later. This Scottish comedian and singer (1870–1950) was top of the bill for over fifty years. His 'Keep Right on to the End of the Road' touched the heartstrings of every audience, especially those who remembered how he sang it at a charity concert during the First World

War two hours after he had heard his son had been killed in France. See also RABBUT.

Laugh that I may not weep, I. 21 p173. Song from *I Pagliacci.*

Launched a thousand ships, face that. See FACES THAT LAUNCH.

Laurels in the quiet evenfall. Came shimmering through them 42 p115; 52 p189. See SHIMMERING THROUGH THE LAURELS.

Law is a hass, the. 83 p111. See Mr Bumble, Chap. 51 of D. *Oliver Twist.*

Law of God or man. There's never a law of God or man runs north of fifty-three. 26 p223. KIPLING's 'The Rhyme of the Three Sealers'.

Law, there ought to be/ have been a. See THERE OUGHT TO BE.

Law, Unwritten. 23 p195. See UNWRITTEN LAW.

Lawful occasions, go freely and without fear about his. 44 p79. BCP. Form of Prayer to Be Used at Sea: "security for such as pass on the seas upon their lawful occasions ..."

Lawrence, Gertrude. 54 p136; 68 p24. This brilliant comedy actress (1898–1952) appeared in PGW's musical comedies. He held her in high regard. See also *MIDNIGHT FROLIC.*

Lawrence. T.E. (of Arabia). 44 p18. Heroic, charismatic Englishman (1888–1935) who led the Arab revolt against the Turks in the First World War.

Lay an egg. Theatrical term for a flop/a failure. See EGG, TO LAY AN.

Lay of the Last Minstrel. 32 p157. Another long (48 pages) poem by Walter Scott, roughly on the same lines as *Romeo & Juliet*, about two lovers from feuding families.

Lazarus. In person 44 p8; Kid L., the man without a bean 51 p60. Lazarus was the chap who fed on "the crumbs which fell from the rich man's table". B. Luke 16.21.

Lazlo. Misprint for LASZLO.

Le Touquet. 35 p210 and later. See Chap. 20.

Leacock, Stephen. 7 p97. This economist and academic (1869–1944), with whom PGW once had lunch, is now best remembered for his witty and satirical essays.

Lead, Kindly Light. 51 p195. Hymn by Newman.

Lead on, Macduff. 1 p249. In popular use till c.1960 to indicate your willingness to join a friend in a fight with somebody, the phrase is a misquotation of S. *Macbeth* 5.7. "Lay on, Macduff; And damn'd be him that first cries, 'Hold, enough!'"

Lean and hungry men are most dangerous. 19 p26; 54 p142. S. *Julius Caesar* 1.2: "Yond' Cassius has a lean and hungry look; / He thinks too much: such men are dangerous."

Leander. 76 p31. A prestigious rowing club founded in 1818, originally restricted to Oxford and Cambridge oarsmen. Their 'Leander pink' scarves and socks are a feature of Henley.

Leaping from crag to crag, untamed chamois of the Alps. 15A p162 and later;

from blonde to blonde (Mr Chinnery) 58 p27. A popular phrase, but the nearest I could find was Wordsworth's *The Prelude* (Book Eight): "His staff protending like a hunter's spear, / Or by its aid leaping from crag to crag."

Lear, King. Frequent. His family problems 66 p29. S. *King Lear*.

Learn in suffering. Every poet, Garroway, has to learn in suffering before he can teach in song 38 p250; 63 p204. SHELLEY's 'Julian and Maddalo': "They learn in suffering what they teach in song."

Learn, O thou of the unshuffled features and agreeable disposition. 59 p24. Unusual phraseology for Bertie Wooster to use unless one remembers the tremendous popularity of the Kai Lung stories by Ernest Bramah (1867–1942). He popularised this ornate form of speech, much as F. Anstey had made Mr Hurry JABBERJEE's orotund language famous.

Learned friend's manner, My (intolerable in an emperor to a black-beetle). 18 p16. See MY LEARNED FRIEND'S MANNER.

'Leave It to Algy'. 81 short story title. Perhaps because of the happy memories of his successful 1917 show *Leave It to Jane*, PGW went on to use the titles 'Leave It to Jeeves' and *Leave It to Psmith* later. Did 'Leave It to Algy' (August 1959) come from the successful revival of *Leave It to Jane* four months before?

Leave our country for our country's good, we. 31 p212. See WE LEAVE OUR COUNTRY.

Leaving not a rack behind. But he had gone, leaving not a rack behind 59 p137 and elsewhere. PGW used this often, but it eluded me till its repetition in 59 made me determined to find it. S. *The Tempest* 4.1: "And, like this insubstantial pageant faded, / Leave not a rack behind."

Leaving the world to darkness (and to him). See DARKNESS.

Legion of Frontiersmen. 11 p28. Founded by Roger Pocock in 1906, the volunteers of this unofficial organisation act as messengers and scouts in wartime. They wear a uniform like the Canadian Mounties but with a blue, not red, jacket.

Legree, Simon. 25 p17 and frequent up to 95 p32. Evil overseer in Harriet Beecher Stowe's *UNCLE TOM'S CABIN*.

Lely, Sir Peter. 25 p103; 62 p10. Famous portrait painter 1618–80.

Lend me your ear. 18 p43. S. *Julius Caesar* 3.2: "Friends, Romans, countrymen, lend me your ears; I come to bury Caesar, not to praise him."

Leno, Dan. 4 p63; 46 p96. Leading British music hall comic dancer and comedian (1860–1904).

Leopard. Can the l. change his spots or the Ethiopian his what-not? 43 p223; 46 p248; and later. B. Jeremiah 13.23: "Can the Ethiopian change his skin, or the leopard his spots?"

LeRoy, Mervyn. 69 p86. LeRoy (1900–87) was a famous director and producer whose films included *The Wizard of Oz*.

Lesser breeds, ignoring the. 69 p225. KIPLING's 'Recessional': "Such boasting as the Gentiles use, / Or lesser breeds without the Law—".

Lestrade, Inspector. 90 p163. A Scotland Yard officer in the Sherlock Holmes stories.

Let 'em all come! PGW ref lost. "Are we downhearted? No! let 'em all come" are the last two lines of the chorus of the 1898 song 'Here We Are! Here We Are Again!!' by Charles Knight. They became wildly popular when it became known that the Kaiser had sent a telegram encouraging our enemies, the Boers, in South Africa and when the French were being equally rude to us.

Let 'em eat cake. 70 p201 and elsewhere. Commonly but wrongly attributed to Marie Antoinette (1755–93) as an expression of callous disregard for the problems of others. PGW would also have known it as the title of a short-lived 1933 musical by his friends George and Ira Gershwin.

Let George do it. See George.

Let me be your banker. 92 p169. PGW's variation of 'Let me be your father', a term that became a cliché in the UK. The first successful 'Teach Yourself' correspondence courses in the UK were started in 1876 by James Henry Bennet. They were very popular, and when a widowed mother wrote asking advice on what to do with her two sons, Bennet introduced the phrase in his advertisements, which ran till the 1950s. The photograph in the advertisement depicted him as a kind and paternal man whom any parent or student would trust implicitly.

Let the dead past bury its dead. 47 p27; 50 p131 and later. Longfellow's 'A Psalm of Life': "Trust no Future, how'er pleasant! / Let the dead past bury its dead." The poet probably remembered B. Matthew. 8.22: "Follow me: and let the dead bury their dead."

Let there be no moaning at the bar. See Moaning at the bar.

Let us be up and doing. 32 p235; 67 p21 and elsewhere. Longfellow's 'A Psalm of Life': "Let us then be up and doing, With a heart for any fate."

Let your light so shine that eventually you would … put the bite on him. 72 p88. B. Matthew 5.16: "Let your light so shine before men, that they may see your good works."

Let your Yea be Yea and your Nay be Nay. 38 p43; 66 p19 and later. B. Epistle of James 5.12: "Let your yea be yea; and your nay, nay; lest ye fall into condemnation."

Lethe, waters of. 18 p209. One of the rivers of Hell in Greek mythology. The souls of the dead drank from it and forgot whatever they had seen, done or heard.

Let's all go down the Strand. 22 p34. Title of a popular song of 1908 by Harry Castling. The Strand and Leicester Square were then the centre of London's night life, full of bars, restaurants and theatres. See also He's a bear.

Let's all go round to Maud's. 76 p126. 1904 song 'Let's All Go Up to Maud's' by Mills and Farrell.

Let's have another cup of coffee; let's have another slice of pie. Often in PGW. 'Let's Have Another Cup o' Coffee', a song from Irving Berlin's *Face the Music* (1932), one of the 'cheer up' songs written during the Depression.

Letting 'I dare not' wait upon 'I would', like the poor cat i' th'adage. See DARE NOT.

Levels of the lake. What Tennyson described as the shining levels of the lake. 80 p146. T. 'Morte D'Arthur'. "He, stepping down / By zig-zag paths, and juts of pointed rock,/ Came on the shining levels of the lake."

Leverhulme. 34 p5. This soap manufacturer and philanthropist (1851–1925) was made a baron in 1917 and viscount in 1922.

Lewis, Sinclair. 54 p132; 67 p188 and later; a good husband for Corky Pirbright 68 p223. Why Bertie would have associated Corky with this American author (1885–1951) puzzled me. MTT Charles Gould, who points out that, at 68 p213, Gussie says Corky needs someone like Ernest HEMINGWAY and Bertie simply confused one well-known American writer with another.

Liberty and the pursuit of happiness. 21 p79 and later. Some British readers may have forgotten "Life, liberty and the pursuit of happiness" from the American Declaration of Independence.

Liberty Hall. 24 p27 and later. From Goldsmith's *She Stoops to Conquer*: "This is Liberty Hall, gentlemen. You may do just as you please here."

Liberty of the tree'd possum. 18 p137. See POSSUM.

Librettist, England's greatest. 2 p101. An early tribute by PGW to W.S. Gilbert. See 'HEART FOAM'.

Liddle & Scott. 4 p231. Misprint for Liddell and Scott. This is still the standard Greek lexicon, first published in 1843. Henry George Liddell, the co-author, was Dean of Christ Church, Oxford, and father of Alice Liddell, the original of Lewis Carroll's Alice. MTT Tony Ring for confirming that the correct names were used in the original *Captain* magazine publication.

Lie deliberate. 20 p108. See LIE DIRECT.

Lie direct. 25 p83. S. *As You Like It* 5.4: "The retort courteous … the quip modest … the reply churlish … the reproof valiant … the countercheck quarrelsome … the lie circumstantial … the lie direct."

Life. (1) Into each l. some rain must fall. See INTO EACH LIFE.

(2) While there is L. there is hope 68 p206. From the Latin proverb 'Aegroto, dum anima est, spes est' (I am sick but while there is life, there is hope).

Life and soul of the party. 32 p145. From the 1890–1930 magazine advertisements for confidence-building courses. One in front of me reads: "Are you shy? I was but now I am the life and soul of every gathering. Women cluster round me …"

Life had been just one damned feminine voice after another. 62 p154. Maybe from 'One damn thing after another', the song by Noel Coward (1925) or Elbert Hubbard's *A Thousand and One Epigrams*: "Life is just one damn thing after another." A common phrase, but I think it became famous when Standard Oil received the 1911 Supreme Court ruling that reduced its market position (90% of US oil stocks). Rockefeller's deputy John Archbold announced the Court's decision to the other directors with the words: "Well, gentlemen, life's just one damn thing after another." Or, maybe, the 1926 London revue *One Dam Thing After Another*.

Life is gentle and the elements mixed in him just right. 96 p152; Life was gentle and the elements so mixed in him … was a man 44 p294. S. *Julius Caesar* 5.5.

Life is real, life is earnest (and the grave is not its goal). 2 p2 and frequent up to 93 p8, where PGW couples it with 'LIFE WAS ONE GRAND SWEET SONG'. Longfellow's 'A Psalm to Life': "Life is real! Life is earnest! And the grave is not its goal." At p215 of *Thank You, Jeeves*, Bertie gives us: "life was stern and earnest and that time was passing." PGW knew the poem well enough to have Bertie combine the line with the first line of the following verse: "Art is long and Time is fleeting."

Life is short and time is flying. 27 p222. PGW was either putting a twist on Longfellow's "Art is long but Time is fleeting", see directly above, or going back to the quote Longfellow had in mind: "Ars longa, vita brevis." ("Art is long, life is short" from Hippocrates' *Aphorisms*.)

Life, liberty and the pursuit of happiness, obtain our full helping of. 63 p72; 67 p149; 95 p61 and elsewhere. See LIBERTY AND THE PURSUIT OF HAPPINESS.

Life of Riley. See RILEY.

Life was one grand sweet song. 23 p65 and later. Charles Kingsley's 'A Farewell (To C.E.G.)': "And so make Life and Death, and that For Ever, / One grand sweet song."

'Life with Freddie'. 88 story title. PGW gloss on the 1936 book and 1939 play *Life with Father* by Clarence Day. The play set a record for the New York stage; it ran till 1947.

Life's fitful fever. After life's fitful fever, it slept well 55 p148. S. *Macbeth* 3.2: "Duncan is in his grave; After life's fitful fever he sleeps well."

Light. As if a sudden bright l. had shone upon him 63 p38. See SAUL OF TARSUS.

Light and salutory meals. See CAT IN ANOTHER POEM.

Light Brigade fellows, I'm like those. 81 p73. See T. 'Charge of the Light Brigade'.

Light had shone upon his darkness, a. 72 p98. B. John 1.5: "In the beginning was the Word and the Word was with God … And the light shineth in darkness; and the darkness comprehended it not."

Light in thy bower, there's a. Beach sings it 42 p236. Either Thomas Moore's 1835 song 'A Lady Sat in Her Bower' or the 1882 song 'Shall I?' by Gilbert and Amy Cochran.

Light of her husband's life and the moon of his delight. 65 p200. Light of my/his/her life seems to be a common expression, but the second phrase is from Fitzgerald's *Omar Khayyam*: "Ah, Moon of my Delight who knows't no wane, / The Moon of Heaven is rising once again."

Light that beats upon a throne, the fierce. See FIERCE LIGHT.

Light that never was on land or sea, a. 38 p251 and later. Wordsworth's

'Suggested by a Picture of Peele Castle in a Storm'.

Lightened my darkness. 33 p112 and later. BCP. Order for Evening Prayer: "Lighten our darkness".

Like a lingering tune ... that night in June with you-oo. 53 p133. The 1927 song 'A Night in June' seems a good source.

Like one that on a lonesome road ... behind him tread. 33 p22. See FRIGHTFUL FIEND.

Lilies of the field (they toil not neither do they spin). Frequent. B. Matthew 6.28: "Consider the lilies of the field, how they grow; they toil not, neither do they spin."

Lillie, Beatrice. 59 p62; 70 p81. Brilliant actress and comedienne (1894–1989) who specialised in revue, played in *Oh, Joy!* (1919).

Limehouse. Comparing its blues with mine 68 p32. Gertrude LAWRENCE made the 1922 song 'Limehouse Blues' famous.

Limehouse Nights. 84 p42. This early 20th-century book dealt with the evils of London's docklands, Chinese opium dens, crimpers and thieves etc.

Lincoln Hotel, Curzon Street. 40 p22. I do not know why PGW changed the name of the real Washington Hotel in Curzon Street, where he once stayed, to the Lincoln, but the origin is obvious.

Lincolnshire Poacher, The. 1 p124. Trad. English song. "Oh, it's my delight on a moonlit night, In the season of the year."

Lindbergh. 44 p18. John Alcock and Arthur Whitten Brown flew the Atlantic first in 1919, and 88 others did so before Charles Lindbergh (1902–74) caught the attention of the world by flying it solo in 1927.

Lindsay & Crouse. 71 p64. Among other shows, Howard Lindsay and Russel Crouse re-wrote *Anything Goes* (1934), for which the original book was written by Bolton and PGW.

Lines are cast in pleasant places, His ... goodly heritage. 71 p8. B. Psalms 16.6: "The lines are fallen unto me in pleasant places; yea, I have a goodly heritage."

Linger shivering on the brink. See BRINK.

Lingering look behind, one last long. See ONE LAST LONG.

Linnet, song of. The song of the linnet is 'Tolic-gow-gow, tolic-joey-fair ...' 58 p193. One of the odder references in PGW. *Summer Moonshine* has a writ-server/debt collector as a major character and, if you are writing of writ-servers and their methods, the Pink 'Un and Pelican books are an obvious source. PGW knew these books well (I provided him with one to complete his set), and he told me in a letter that Arthur Binstead, 'The Pitcher', was a master writer. At page 23 of Binstead's *Pitcher in Paradise*, which I know PGW possessed, a man demonstrates his knowledge of the song of a linnet: 'Tolic-gow-gow, tolic-joey-fair ...' and all the rest of it, syllable by syllable.

Lion and the lizard keep the Courts where Jamshyd gloried and drank deep. 42 p105. Fitzgerald's *Omar Khayyam*.

Lion/lioness. In danger, after having come in like a lioness, of going out like a lamb 63 p178; Come in like a lion, take your snootful, and go out like a lamb 76 p64. English and American weather proverb: March comes in like a lion but goes out like a lamb. But, the important thing is the word 'If' at the beginning. In other words, if March comes in like the one, it will go out like the other and vice versa.

Lip, long upper l. was stiff once more. See STIFF UPPER LIP.

Lipton, Sir Thomas. 10 p52 and later; how he got his start 60 p113. This Scottish millionaire grocer (1850–1931) (Lipton's Teas) started from the bottom and worked his way up by dealing fairly with his customers. He was knighted, competed for the America's Cup, and the KAISER was furious that his uncle, King Edward VII, "could go yachting with his grocer".

Listerine. This mouthwash took its name from Lord Lister (1827–1912), the Victorian doctor who developed antiseptics. Lord Lister fought hard to stop his name being used commercially, but a firm in the USA used it anyway and had great success. Presumably that is why Listerine is better known there than it is in the UK. See also OFTEN A BRIDESMAID and HER BEST FRIENDS WON'T TELL HER.

Little acts of kindness. 18 p123. When Ebenezer Brewer (1810–97) was not gathering material for his *Dictionary of Phrase and Fable* (1874) and his other (thirty!) compilations, he worked as a schoolmaster. Among the poems he wrote for children was one entitled 'Little Drops of Water'. The fourth verse is: " Little acts of kindness, / Little deeds of love, / Make this earth an Eden / Like the heaven above." MTT Charles Gould for pointing out Wordsworth's 'Lines composed a few miles above Tintern Abbey' had included: "That best portion of a good man's life, / His little nameless unremembered acts, / Of kindness and of love."

Little body was a-weary. See A-WEARY.

Little child could have led it, a. 42 p84. See the hymn 'A Little Child Shall Lead Them' by Colegrave & Brooke (1893), based on B. Isaiah 11.6: "The wolf also shall dwell with the lamb, and the leopard shall lie down with the kid; and the calf and the young lion and the fatling together; and a little child shall lead them." See also 1906 song by Charles Harris.

Little child washed clean of sin. 33 p174. From 'Child's Prayer' by Fowles (1877).

Little Church Around the Corner. See Chap. 23.

Little deeds of kindness, little acts of love. 15A p179. See LITTLE ACTS.

Little Englander. 18 p179. See THINKING IMPERIALLY.

Little Eva. 25 p30. Lovable child in *UNCLE TOM'S CABIN*. Do not confuse with Eliza in same book.

Little folding of the hands in sleep will do him good. 70 p149. See REST, A LITTLE.

Little Gooch Street, runs up to Shaftesbury Avenue. 25 p25. Almost certainly Monmouth Street. I wonder why PGW used a false name? Perhaps he was thinking of nearby Goodge Street.

Little Lord Fauntleroy. See FAUNTLEROY.

Little more and how much it is, that. 14 p41; 71 p56 and elsewhere. Robert Browning's 'By the Fireside' (1855): "Oh, the little more, and how much it is!"

Little Mother. Frequent. Usually a Threepwood niece, sent to Blandings to get over a love affair, who decides to make Lord Emsworth's life hell by becoming a Little Mother and performing unrelenting acts of kindness all day long. I suggest the term stems from L.T. Meade (1854–1914), whose remarkably popular girls' stories included *Little Mother to the Others* (1896).

Little port had seldom seen a costlier funeral, the. See AND WHEN THEY BURIED HIM.

Little rest, a. A little rest, a little folding of the hands in sleep 19 p157 and elsewhere. B. Proverbs 6.10 and 24.33: "Yet a little sleep, a little slumber, a little folding of the hands to sleep ..."

Little, Richard - 'Bingo'. In the original 1926 script of Bolton and Wodehouse's *Oh, Kay*!, the heroine addresses her brother the Duke of Datchet as 'Bingo'. See Chap. 30 for a possible origin.

Little Tich. See TICH.

Little victims play (regardless of their fate). See REGARDLESS.

Little Willie. See WILLIE.

Littlewood's Pools. 73 p31; 81 p32. Football pools were the first lottery-type big money prizes allowed in Britain since lotteries based on pure chance were illegal till very recently. Football pools, in which you forecast the results of some sixty-plus football matches on a form, were held to be a 'test of skill' and were therefore legal. In the early days, one poor woman, who had got them all right, lost the money because she admitted in court that she had put crosses where her cat had placed its paws on the list.

Lived and had their being. 12 p148; 66p27. B. Acts 17.28: "For in him we live, and move, and have our being ..."

Livelier iris. A l. i. gleams upon the burnished dove 31 p9; and later. T. 'Locksley Hall': "In the Spring a livelier iris changes on the burnish'd dove; / In the Spring a young man's fancy lightly turns to thoughts of love."

Liver pill. What you want is a l. p. 8 p14. In the 19th century, various firms convinced the public that a good liver was the most important element of their health. Mr Beecham (1820–1907), father of Sir Thomas, spent a lot of money advertising his liver pills as being 'worth a guinea a box' and made a fortune.

Living. Plain living and high thinking 32 p277. See HIGH THINKING.

Livy. 3 p1; 8 p53. This Roman historian (59 B.C.–17 A.D.) was liked by British schoolboys because he narrated events in a straightforward manner, without too many eloquent diversions or commentaries as to what the gods thought about them.

Lloyd George. 13 p45 up to 96 p97. The Welsh politician David Lloyd George (1863–1945) still arouses adverse or enthusiastic comment. He introduced Old Age Pensions in 1908 but stripped the House of Lords of their power in 1911.

Prime Minister in the First World War, he lost influence thereafter. See also PEERAGES.

Lloyd, Marie. 31 p185 and later. This Cockney queen of the English music hall (1870– 1922) was no beauty, but she could belt out a song that made you laugh and cry at the same time. Among her best-known are 'Oh, Mr Porter' and 'My Old Man Said Follow the Van', which elderly Britons will still sing raucously whenever the opportunity offers.

Lo! Psmith's name led all the rest. 32 p205. See ABOU BEN ADHEM.

Loaded. A man who didn't know it was loaded. See MAN WHO DIDN'T KNOW.

Loaf, standard. See STANDARD LOAF.

Loamshire. 30 p193. There is nowhere in England by this name, but for some reason it became a popular term for a fictional county. See also SOUTHMOLTONSHIRE.

Lobb, shoes by. 81 p181. Lobb's of St James's Street are London's oldest and most prestigious boot and shoemakers.

Lobster. This mad professor who gets this girl into his toils and tries to turn her into a l. 39 p39. Miss Postlethwaite's account of the *Vicissitudes of Vera* showing at the Bijou Dream has strong echoes of H.G. Wells' 1896 novel *The Island of Dr Moreau.*

Lobster Newburg. 89 p67. Delmonico's, New York's oldest restaurant, were the first to serve this dish after Mr Wenburg, a shipping magnate, gave Delmonico the recipe. It was a tremendous success, and Delmonico named it Lobster Wenburg, a fact of which Mr Wenburg was inordinately proud. One night Mr Wenburg came in drunk and started a fight. He was thrown out and Delmonico changed the name of the dish to Lobster Newburg, by which it has been known ever since. See also DELMONICO'S.

Local Boy Makes Good. 48 p69; 86 p92. This cliché, once universal in small-town newspapers, seems to have died at last.

Loch Lomond (taking the high road and low road). See HIGH ROAD.

Lochinvar, Young. 13 p148 and later up to 96 p57. Synonym in the UK for an impetuous young lover. See Scott's *Marmion*, Chap 5.12: "So faithful in love, and so dauntless in war, / There never was knight like the young Lochinvar."

Locks, gory. Never shake thy gory locks at me. See NEVER SHAKE.

Locks to part and each particular hair to stand on end, knotted and combined. 63 p158. See PORPENTINE.

Locust. The years that the locust has eaten 91 p84. B. Joel 2.25: "I shall restore to you the years that the locust hath eaten, the canker-worm, and the caterpiller, and the palmerworm, my great army which I sent among you."

Logomachy that marked him out as a future labour member. 7 p31. When PGW wrote this, there were very few Labour Members of Parliament, but they were already causing concern with their radical ideas.

Lollobrigida, Gina. 80 p86. A beautiful and shapely Italian actress (1927–).

Lombard, Carole. 61 p112. A film actress (1908–42).

London and Oriental Bank. See NEW ASIATIC BANK.

London School of Economics. 84 p92. A college of London University, popularly believed in the 1930s–50s to be a hotbed of radical Left Wing teaching.

Long farewell to all your greatness … nips his roots … 57 p74; 73 p126–7. S. *Henry VIII* 3.2.

Long John Silver, changed sides like. 72 p106. See R.L. Stevenson's *Treasure Island.*

Long, long trail, the. 34 p180 and later. 1913 song 'There's a Long, Long Trail A-winding' by King and Elliott.

Long Otto. 15A p24. See Otto the Ox.

Longacre Square/hat. 18 p189; 23 p42. I have not discovered whether there was ever a Longacre hat, but Longacre Square was the original name of today's Times Square in New York. The Square was renamed on 8 April 1904 after the *New York Times* had built its new office block there.

Look for the silver lining. 34 p30; 67 p20 and later. PGW quoting the song from his musical *Sally*. See also Chap 24.

Look here upon this picture, and on that. 22 p16; and on this 64 p142. S. *Hamlet* 3.4: "Look here upon this picture, and on this."

Look, look, lookie, here comes cookie. 66 p61. Song 'Here Comes Cookie' by Mack Gordon from the film *Love in Bloom.*

Look upon his like again, we shall not. 90 p68. S. Hamlet 1.2: "I shall not look upon his like again."

Looked on the bitter when it was brown. 7 p167. PGW twist on 'Look not thou upon the wine when it is red' (bitter is a type of English draught beer); see Adders.

Looking far less like a hatchet than a dissipated saw. 84 p108. See Knife, blunt.

Loose Chippings. 62 p28 and later. PGW realised this sounded like a typical English place name to Americans. When roads in Britain are re-surfaced, wet tar is put down followed by a layer of gravel-chippings which are then rolled into the tar. Since some of the chippings always lie loose on the top, notices are put up warning motorists of 'loose chippings'.

Lord have mercy on his soul. 88 p87. See May the Lord.

Lord High Executioner. 5 p2. This is Koko in G&S *The Mikado.*

Lorelei. 60 p268. The Lorelei were sirens who sat on a rock on the banks of the Rhine and sang to lure sailors to their doom. They were the creation of Heinrich Heine (1797–1856), who wrote 'Die Lorelei' while staying at No 32 Craven Street, London in 1828.

Loretto. 63 p174. A well-known Scottish public (private) school, where they play very good Rugby.

Lost in London, like the heroine in a melodrama. 34 p178. The 1874 melodrama called *Lost in London* ran for years.

Lost Leader, The. 13 p79 and later. Title of a poem by Browning, reproaching Wordsworth for accepting the post of Poet Laureate in 1843. The phrase was well-enough known for *Punch* (4 March 1903) to publish a half-page poem by PGW under this title mourning the retirement of the fictional hero, Captain Kettle, into private life.

Lost Patrol, The. 56 p260. Tough 1934 war film in which just about everybody gets killed.

Lost Weekend, The. 68 p81. 1945 film, based on the book by Charles Jackson, about a drunk who goes on five-day bender.

Lot. His disapproval of the Cities of the Plain 22 p156; 23 p217. B. Genesis 19.13: "For we will destroy this place because the cry of them is waxen great before the face of the Lord; and the Lord has sent us to destroy it."

Lot has been cast in pleasant places, his. 15A p91 and later. B. Psalms 16.6: "The lines are fallen unto me in pleasant places; yea, I have a goodly heritage."

Lot's wife and the pillar of salt. 49 p286 and often later, including B. Wooster's account at 76 p173. B. Genesis 19.26: "But his wife looked back from behind him, and she became a pillar of salt."

Lothario. 42 p122; 67 p126. Odd how this synonym for a philanderer has lasted though its origin is forgotten. He was a character in the 1703 play *The Fair Penitent* by Nicholas Rowe.

Lotos Club. Cyril Waddesley-Davenport's New York club 53 p217–8. PGW was a member of the Lotos. See Chap. 21.

Loud and clear. Both had come through loud and clear 93 p94. This phrase to signify good radio reception originated in the Second World War. "Hallo Alfa Bravo. How do you hear me? Over." "Hallo Alfa Bravo. Loud and clear. Over."

Louffier. "Allez-vous-en, louffier" 52 p255. When Anatole woke up to find Gussie Fink-Nottle making faces at him through the skylight, he was understandably perturbed and made his perturbation clear. MTT Anne-Marie Chanet for explaining that 'louffier' was a general slang term of contempt for someone dirty, or stupid. PGW's next sentence says just about the same thing. "Get out of here, you no-good (louffier)" is followed by "Tell the boob to go away". *Right Ho, Jeeves* came out in October 1934. PGW lived in France from March 1932 to March 1933 and no doubt picked up a few phrases appropriate to such an occasion. See also Marmiton de domange and Chap. 37 (Anatole).

Louis, Joe. 62 p102 and later. Highly-respected world heavyweight boxing champion 1937–49.

Love. (1) He could not give her anything but l. 95 p100. See Give me anything. (2) I never told my l. but let concealment like a worm in the bud 26 p55 and elsewhere. S. *Twelfth Night*. 2.4. See She never said.

Love a lassie, I. See I love a lassie.

Love as others do, I do not (plus 3 lines of verse). 7 p90. From 'Gemini and Virgo' by C.S. Calverley.

Love, be off with the old love. See Be off with.

Love conquers all. 41 p302 and frequent elsewhere. From Latin tag 'Omnia vincit amor'. Virgil's *Eclogues* Bk 10.

Love had come to Bill Hardy that summer day. 89 p43. PGW version of typical sub-title from the old silent movies.

Love in Idleness. 57 p82. Common name for a purple flower of the daisy family.

Love in springtime. 94 p191 and elsewhere. Three songs were written with this title in the 1930s.

Love is blind. 83 p172. 14th-century proverb; also S. *Merchant of Venice* 2.6.

Love is everything. Yes, love indeed is light from heaven, a spark … how love exalts the mind. 39 p161–162. I suppose Lancelot Mulliner's being a poet should have forewarned me of the complications of these eight lines. "Yes, love indeed" down to "from earth our low desire" is from Bryron's 'The Giaour' line 1134. The next section Lancelot intones, "Give me to live with love" down to "'Tis Love in idleness", is from 'Dolce Far Niente' by Laman Blanchard. "When beauty fires the blood, how love exalts the mind" is from Dryden's 'Cymon and Iphigenia'. I was glad to see the back of this one.

Love is indestructible. Its holy flame burneth for ever. 64 p128. Southey's 'Curse of Kehama'.

Love is like a glowing tulip … See MY LOVE IS LIKE A GLOWING TULIP.

Love is Nature's second sun, Garroway (and 8 more lines). 38 p121. From the play *All Fools* 1.1, by George Chapman (1559–1634).

Love laughs at locksmiths. 13 p204 and later. English proverb.

Love me and the world is mine. 15A p199 and elsewhere. Lord Emsworth sings it at 53 p107 and Ivor Llewellyn does so at 94 p85. 'I Know I Love Thee' by Ball and Reed (1906).

Love of the moth for the star. See MOTH.

Love Parade, My. See MY LOVE PARADE.

Love passing the love of women. See PASSING THE LOVE.

Love that makes the world go round, it's. 33 p162 and later. Maybe from the French proverb, maybe from G & S *Iolanthe*, but probably from the popular song (1896) by Clyde Fitch, music by William Furst.

Love the Cracksman (play). 13 p12. Maybe based on the 1907 New York play *The Thief*, but far more likely from the 1906 play *Raffles*, the famous gentleman thief created by E.W. Hornung in 1899 in the best-seller *The Amateur Cracksman*. See RAFFLES.

Love the highest. We must needs love the highest when we see it. PGW ref lost. T. 'Guinevere'.

Love tunes the shepherd's reed … love is heaven and heaven is love. 38 p120 and again at p139. Scott's *The Lay of the Last Minstrel*, C3.2.

Love was like a red, red rose, his. 61 p171. Burns's poem 'My Love Is Like a Red Red Rose.'

Love will find a way. 59 p16; 71 p17. 16th-century English proverb and popular song in the 1919 show *A Southern Maid*.

Loved and lost. 32 p178 and elsewhere. T. 'In Memoriam' 27: "Tis better to have loved and lost / Than never to have loved at all."

Loved her still, he. 58 p9. 1888 song 'With all her faults, I love her still' by Rosenfeld and Hitchcock.

Loved not wisely but too well. 58 p201; 62 p100. S. *Othello* 5.2: "then, must you speak / Of one that lov'd not wisely but too well; / Of one not easily jealous, but, being wrought, / Perplexed in the extreme."

Note. At 73 p195, PGW gives us the quotation down to 'but too well', omits the next four lines about the base Indian throwing away the pearl, and resumes the speech with: "of one whose subdued eyes albeit unused to the melting mood, / drop tears as fast as the Arabian trees their medicinal gum."

Loved ones far away of whom the hymnal speaks. 63 p47. See PEACE, PERFECT PEACE.

Lovers meeting, his pilgrimage was to end in. 97 p62. See JOURNEYS END IN LOVERS MEETING.

Love's Young Dream. 18 p73; 20 p97 and later. Poem by Thomas Moore.

Love-sick maidens in Patience. 85 p20. The love-sick maidens sing the opening chorus in G & S's *Patience*. It was around his 85th book that PGW began to insert the sources of his quotations when, as he said, he realised his readers no longer knew the Bible, Shakespeare, Tennyson or Gilbert & Sullivan as well as he did and needed help in picking up his allusions.

Lower Barnatoland. 67 p33; 86 p126. An allusion from PGW's youth. Barney Barnato (1852–97) was one of the adventurers who went out from England and made a fortune in the South African diamond mines in the 1880s. Their lavish and tasteless expenditure (and lower-class origins) when they came back to England meant that London Society treated them with reserve. Lower Barnatoland clearly refers to Lower Basutoland, which adjoins the area where Barnato and others made their fortunes. (The centre of the diamond-rush area, Kimberley, is named after the head of the Wodehouse family, the Earl of Kimberley.)

Lowest of the low. Now a term of abuse, this was once an official classification of a social class. In Victorian England, Government studies into poverty classified the poor as: poor, very poor, poorest of the poor, and the lowest of the low.

Lowick, station at. 40 p251. See Chap. 26.

Loy, Myrna. 58 p186. American film actress (1905–93).

Lucifer, fallen like. See HOW ART THOU FALLEN.

Lucknow. Marched on beleaguered L. 12 p66; 38 p242 and later. The 87-day siege of Lucknow (Indian Mutiny 1857) and its relief by Havelock's Highlanders was commemorated by TENNYSON in the poem 'The Defence of Lucknow'. See also CAWNPORE.

Lucretius. 9 p44; 93 p191. Jeeves' translation of Lucretius (93 p191) is as good as you would expect from someone with PGW's mastery of the Classics. See also SURGIT AMARI ALIQUID.

Lucullus. A banquet of L. 46 p188; 71 p15. This successful Roman military leader (115–47 B.C.) was renowned for his fondness for luxury and the extravagance of his meals. Do not confuse with VITELLIUS, who took things further.

Lugger. Once aboard the l. 21 p164. Like 'Sir Jasper' (see TODD, SIR JASPER), the line "Once aboard the lugger, and the maiden's mine!" from Victorian melodrama stayed in the British subconscious for over a century. If the hero wasn't stopping the bold, bad baronet from foreclosing the mortgage, he was rescuing the heroine from the b.b.b's minions who had seized her to satisfy his evil desires. (A lugger was a small sailing vessel.) The phrase came originally from *The Gipsy Farmer* (1846) and was revived in *My Jack and Dorothy* at the Elephant & Castle Theatre in 1889. See BARONETS and TRANSPONTINE MELODRAMA.

Luigi. The great L. of the Embassy. 74 p154. Luigi Naintre was as important in London's nightlife as PGW said. He came to prominence at the end of the 19th century as head-waiter, then manager, at Romano's (see Chap. 5) and later made the Embassy the smartest nightclub in London in the 1930s. See Chap. 21.

Lungs were willing but the memory was weak, the. 36 p22. See SPIRIT WAS WILLING.

Lunts, the. 71 p167. Alfred (1892–1977) and his wife Lynn Fontanne (1887–1983) were the pre-eminent acting team of their time. Their reputation was equalled only by the Barrymore family.

Luny bin. 12 p260. English slang for a lunatic asylum.

Lupin, Arsene, in disguise. 13 p18. Famous fictional French criminal created by Maurice Leblanc (1864–1941), akin to Raffles.

Lupino, Ida. 68 p103. Actress (1914–95), daughter of Stanley Lupino (next entry).

Lupino, Stanley. 49 p227. English actor, dancer and writer (1894–1942), one of the many Lupinos, a theatrical family who have been on the stage since 1620 or so.

***Lusitania*, S.S.** 14 p 56. See Chap. 17.

Lusus naturae. 58 p100. Latin for 'a wonder of nature'.

Lutz, Meyer. 25 p200. German composer and conductor, 1823–1903. Musical director at the Gaiety Theatre 1873–1903.

Luxuries so much more necessary than necessities. 6 p211; 61p105 and later. Attributed to John L. Motley (1814–77): "Give us the luxuries of life, and we will dispense with its necessities."

Lycidas, Milton's. 78 pp120–121. A *jeu d'esprit* (I think that's the right phrase) reflecting PGW's lifelong reading and respect for the classic poets. The last two lines:

> With this he rose and puffed, as such men do,
> Tomorrow to fresh foods and dainties new.

are familiar if you know your Milton, who gave us, in 'Lycidas':

> At last he rose and twitch'd his mantle blue;
> Tomorrow to fresh woods and pastures new.

Lyfe so short, the craft so long to lerne. 18 p82. From Geoffrey CHAUCER'S *Parliament of Fowles.*

Lyly's *Euphues.* 70 p54 & p106. John Lyly (1554–1606) sought to raise the standard of literature by using an elegant, artificial style to write this book, but the effect was very short-lived. 'Euphuism'/ 'euphuistic' is still a term for a tedious, pedantic writing style.

Lyons Popular Café. 9 p35 and later. UK café chain 1920–1960s.

'Lyrics from a Padded Cell' by Xenophades. 3 p251. See XENOPHADES.

M

(MTT = My thanks to)

Mabel. That's me all over, Mabel 28 p232; 30 p148. Edward Streeter (1891–1976) wrote four 'Dere Mable' books (1918–20), the humorous adventures of a young American soldier in France in 1918, recounted in letters to his girlfriend back home. The expression came up in every letter and became a catchphrase. MTT David McDonagh and Louise Collins. PGW knew Streeter; see Chap. 14 of *Bring on the Girls*.

McAllister, Ward. 74 p64. McAllister (1827–95) was aide-de-camp to Mrs Astor, queen of New York Society. See FOUR HUNDRED.

McArthur, General. 71 p137. When forced out of the Philippines by the Japanese in March 1942, McArthur (1880–1964) said, "I shall return" — and did so in October 1944.

Macbeth. PGW quoted from or referred to Shakespeare's play frequently and gives the gist of it at 69 p31. My favourite reference is at 64 p187, where Bertie Wooster says Nobby Hopwood "came leaping towards me, like Lady Macbeth coming to get first-hand news from the guest-room".

McCoy, Kid. 6 p156; 79 p43. See Chap. 4.

Macdonald, Philip. 46 p62. Detective story writer (1895–1980).

Macdonald, Ramsey. 55 p219. Labour Prime Minister (1924).

MacDuff. Lead on, MacDuff. See LEAD ON.

McFadden, Clarence. His inability to dance 22 p197. 'Teaching McFadden to Dance', song by M.F. Carey. Carey wrote several comic songs in the 1890s. For some reason, renewal of copyright perhaps, the British Library dates this song to 1954.

McGarry, the chappie behind the bar. See Chap. 21.

McGraw, Mr. Napoleonic gifts of Mr M. 21 p12. Manager of the New York Giants 1902–32, nicknamed 'Little Napoleon'. His team won ten National League pennants and three World Series.

Machiavelli. 13 p121; 25 p140 and often later. This far-sighted Italian writer and statesman (1467–1527) achieved his reputation for cunning and scheming with his book *The Prince*.

Mackerel Monarch, Sardine Sultan. 32 p76. See KINGS.

McLaglen, Victor. 49 p256. This rough, tough film actor (1883–1959), perhaps best remembered now as John Wayne's sergeant major in John Ford Westerns, served in the Boer War and the First World War and won a well-deserved Oscar for *The Informer*. His father was a bishop who taught his five sons to box to professional standard.

Maclean, Kaid. 10 occasional; 11 p43; 13 p67. A brilliant exponent of the bagpipes, Sir Harry Maclean (1848–1920), a British Army officer, became chief instructor (kaid) to the Sultan of Morocco's army 1877–1909. His capture by the rebel Raisuli in 1907 was headline news around the world.

McTodd, Ralston. 32 p12. See Chap. 37.

McVey, Connie. Jumped into the ring same as Connie McVey did when Corbett fought Sharkey 24 p239. On 22 November 1898, Jim Corbett was well ahead of Tom Sharkey on points when, in the ninth round, his second, Connie McVey, jumped into the ring. The referee had no choice but to disqualify Corbett.

Macy's department store. 88 p139. A large department store in New York, as famous over there as Harrod's is in Britain.

Mad Hatter, the. 42 p294. See *Alice in Wonderland*. The name stems from the mercury then used in the manufacture of hats, which led to insanity among hatters. See also March Hare.

Mad Mullah, the. 11 p21. Nickname of Mohammed bin Abdullah who led anti-British revolts in Somaliland from 1899 to 1920.

Madame Whoever-it-was who used to … guillotine. 93 p77. See Defarge.

Maddest, merriest day of all the glad New Year. 15A p182 and frequent later. T. 'The May Queen'.

Madding crowd, far from the. 3 p68; 12 p293 and later. Gray's 'Elegy in a Country Churchyard': "Far from the madding crowd's ignoble strife, / Their sober wishes never learn'd to stray."

Made it so, they. 12 p36. An odd response by Mike and Wyatt to Mr Wain's orders, but Royal Navy terminology was well-known in Victorian England, and "Make it so" was the way an order was issued in the Navy. When the officer on watch wanted to change course, he would send a sailor to the captain to ask permission. The captain would reply "Make it so" and the sailor would go back and report "Make it so, sir". The phrase in TV's *Star Trek* continues this tradition.

Madeira, overland to. 31 p230. Marion Wardour could not have travelled overland to Madeira since it lies in the Atlantic Ocean. It was one of the few factual mistakes PGW made, and he never forgot it. He was remarkably sensitive to letters from readers pointing out errors like this and made a point thereafter of checking technical details thoroughly. When he was in his late eighties, he took a taxi fifty miles to discuss with a jeweller how Jeeves would recognise a fake necklace. His anxiety to be factually accurate was extremely useful when identifying his locations. When he said fictional X was so many miles from real Y, all I had to do is get out a pair of compasses and describe a circle round Y. See Droitwich in Chap. 26 for one example.

Madrid. A scrap like New Year's Eve in M. 61 p59. When Wodehouse wrote this, the Spanish Civil War had just come to an end, a conflict that had shocked

Europe with the ferocity with which it was fought. The attack on Madrid, December 1936–January 1937, had seen particularly bitter fighting.

Maecenas. 46 p188. This wealthy Roman (d. 8 B.C.) supported and sponsored writers including Horace and Virgil.

Maenad. 9 p23; 37 p239. A distraught woman. From the priestesses of Bacchus whose dancing at his festivals were so frenzied, they seemed more like mad women.

Maeterlinck, Maurice. 9 p6 and later. This Belgian philosopher, dramatist and natural historian (1862–1949) won the Nobel Prize for literature in 1911. See BLUE BIRD.

Mafeking Road. In Balham, Bramley-on-Sea, Cheltenham, West Dulwich and Maiden Eggesford) 9 p270; 69 p56; 86 p126; 96 p117 and elsewhere. When new housing estates are built in Britain, the roads tend to be named after a politician of the day, some local feature (Church Avenue, Church Court, Church Close) or some recent national event. The 19th century saw a vast amount of building in Britain and many streets can be dated by the name they were given. Thus, one can be pretty certain that the fifteen Waterloo Roads, Avenues and Terraces in London were built by speculators soon after the battle of 1815, while the myriad Jubilee Streets commemorate Victoria's Golden and Diamond Jubilees of 1887 and 1897. Mafeking Roads/Avenues commemorate the Relief of Mafeking (Boer War 1900), while Churchill Roads, Ways and Avenues came after the Second World War.

PGW, always an acute observer of social change, noticed this trend as early as 1907 (*Not George Washington*). His parents' address in Bexhill was Ewart Lodge, Jameson Road. William Ewart Gladstone was a famous Prime Minister and the Jameson Raid (South Africa) was in 1895. I have seen Ewart Lodge and 1895–1900 would fit it perfectly. See also CHATSWORTH.

Maharajah's ruby. Affair of the theft of the marajah's ruby 36 p87. See 'GREEN EYE OF THE LITTLE YELLOW GOD'.

Mahomet. What M. did when the mountain would not go unto him 15A p236; 50 p300. See Bacon's *Essays* 12 ('Boldness'): "If the hill will not come to Mahomet, Mahomet will go to the hill." See also MOHAMMED'S COFFIN.

Maid, the chariest. The chariest maid, he felt, is prodigal enough if she unmask her beauty to the moon 54 p179. S. *Hamlet* 1.3.

Maiden Eggesford, Somerset. 55 p39 and later. See Chap. 12.

Maiden's Prayer. 15 p45; 38 p50 and later. A popular sentimental song (1858) by Badarzeweke and Ullman.

Maisie. The celebrated Maisie manages to get right there in time 3 p23. 'Maisie' was a song in *The Messenger Boy*, the Gaiety show of 1900, and each verse ended: "Maisie gets right there." It was sung by Rosie Boote, who became Marchioness of Headfort the following year, one of the legendary Gaiety Girls who married into the aristocracy. See also CAPTAIN POTT and Chap. 24.

Make a note. See Note.

Malays run amok. 34 p104. See AMOK.

Malemute saloon. 53 p278; 63 p105; whooping it up like a bunch of the boys in the Malemute saloon 76 p156; and later. See Robert Service's 'The Shooting of Dan McGrew'.

Malice towards none. 41 p71. See CHARITY TOWARDS ALL.

Malmsey. A butt of M. would have been more in your line I fancy 50 p204. S. *Richard III* 1.4. "Take that, and that; [Stabs him] If all this will not do, I'll drown you in the malmsey-butt within." Malmsey was a strong sweet wine. See also MALVOISIE.

Malone, theatrical producer. 22 p17. PGW wrote this reference to J.A.E. Malone (1860–1929), a London theatrical producer, years before he worked with him.

Malvern House School. See Chap. 3.

Malvern School. 2 p80. See Chaps 3 and 10.

Malvoisie, a stoup of. 26 p11; 85 p22. From Anthony Trollope's 1866 story, "The Gentle Euphemia": "Ho! there, butler! another stoup of Malvoisie, and let it be that with the yellow seal." Malvoisie was another name for MALMSEY. MTT Chris Paul.

Mammoth Publishing Company. 19 p3. See Chap. 7.

Man above the level of the beasts of the field, raises. 27 p121; above the level of beasts that perish 63 p190; 91 p39. 'Beasts of the field' is a common term in the Bible. Exodus 23.11 has "that the poor of thy people may eat: and what they leave the beasts of the field may eat." At 63 p190, PGW gives us "these little acts of kindness … that raised Man, the Boy Scout, above the beasts that perish." See B. Psalms 49.12: "Nevertheless man being in honour abideth not: he is like the beasts that perish."

The crack about Man being raised above the level of the beasts does not appear in the Bible. The nearest I found was Genesis 1.29: "And God said, Let us make man in our image, after our likeness; and let them have dominion over the fish of the sea, and over the fowl of the air, and over the cattle, and over all the earth, and over every creeping thing that creepeth upon the earth."

Man and beast, good for etc. 2 p72 and frequent thereafter. See ACCOMMODATION FOR MAN AND BEAST.

Man from Mexico, The. 15A p220. This New York comedy (1897 & 1909), starring William Collier, revolved around a man arrested in a nightclub and given thirty days in jug. He managed to persuade his wife he was on a business trip to Mexico for that period. Even though she visited the prison he was in, she did not spot him and he returned home in due course with a strong Spanish accent, and got away with it.

Man, he is your. 63 p17. See HE IS YOUR MAN.

Man in England sent to prison for things done by a man who looked like him. 21 p132. This is the famous Adolph Beck case, where Beck was sentenced to seven years for fraud in 1896. In 1901 there was sufficient new evidence to secure his release. He was soon arrested again on a similar charge, and it was only at this point that the real criminal was caught and Beck's innocence proved. The case caused such a stir, especially when Conan DOYLE supported Beck, that the Criminal Appeal Court was created.

Man in the Iron Mask. 58 p273; 60 p262 and later. Dumas' novel made this character famous. The story was based on fact, an unfortunate imprisoned by Louis XIV for forty years, and historians argue over who it was. The favourite is Count Girolamo Mattioli.

Man is born to sorrow as the sparks fly upwards. 26 p38. B. Job 5.7: "Yet man is born unto trouble, as the sparks fly upward."

Man of blood and iron. 13 p172 and later. This was Bismarck (1815–98), the strong man who unified Germany (under Prussian control). The term was applied to him after he made a powerful speech to the Prussian House of Deputies on 28 January 1886 in which he stressed that Prussia's future would be won by "blood and iron".

Man of wrath. 7 p14; 8 p119; 36 p236 and later. The best source I can find is B. Proverbs 19.19: "A man of great wrath shall suffer punishment; for if thou deliver him, yet thou must do it again."

Man or mouse, Are you? 65 p203 and later. 16th-century proverb: Today a man, tomorrow a mouse.

Man so faint, so spiritless, so dead, so dull in look … 54 p186; 72 p50. S. *2 Henry IV* 1.1.

Man that is born of woman is of few days and full of trouble … Ashes to ashes, dust to dust. 78 p140. BCP. Order for the Burial of the Dead.

Man Who Came Back, The. 49 p77. This play about a drunk who reformed had a two-year run in New York 1916–17.

Man who didn't know it was loaded. 43 p60. The popular song of 1949 ('I Didn't Know the Gun Was Loaded' by Fort & Leighton) is far too late to be the origin. Was there an earlier version or was it simply (as it still is) a common cause of firearms accidents?

Man who never sleeps, the. 94 p148. I'm sure PGW liked having Chimp Twist quote the motto of the Pinkerton Detective Agency: "We never sleep".

Man who smothered the two princes in the tower, looking like the. 53 p15. S. *Richard III* 4.3. For centuries Richard III has been vilified as the usurper who killed the two little princes in the Tower of London. I adhere to the opposing view, that it was Henry VII, as argued in Josephine Tey's superb *The Daughter of Time*.

Man who's square. His chances are always best, the man who's square. No circumstance can shoot a scare into the contents of his vest. 15 p32. Not found. Bret Harte maybe? The Biglow Papers? Robert W. Service? A parody of Robert W. Service?

Man With A Hoe. See Chap. 27.

Man, young, who flew through the air with the greatest of ease. 65 p224. See DARING YOUNG MAN.

Mananas. 54 p223. See Yes … he had no mananas.

Manchester thinks tomorrow what mother thinks today. 58 p11. PGW twist on a popular phrase of late 19th century when Manchester was the centre of British industry: "What Manchester thinks today, London thinks tomorrow." The relationship between the two cities was akin to that of Chicago and New York.

Mandalay. 49 p106. 'On the Road to Mandalay', popular song by Oley Speaks from the poem by Kipling. Hear it sung by a good strong baritone and you can see why Kipling was appreciated by everybody from music hall audiences to Edward VII.

Manna in the wilderness. Often. See 85 p134 for a description of the incident by B. Wooster. B. Exodus 16.35: "They did eat manna, until they came unto the borders of the land of Canaan."

Manners Makyth Man. 78 p36. Well-known motto of Winchester, a public school founded by William of Wykeham in 1382. PGW had a cousin there. See Chap. 3.

Manoeuvres of Arthur. 7 p32. This appears in the first edition of *Love Among the Chickens* so cannot come from Saki's well-known *Chronicles of Clovis* (1912), and presumably comes from the 1898 four-act comedy *The Manoeuvres of Jane*. MTT Tony Ring.

Manresa Road, Chelsea. 9 p32. See Chap. 25.

Mant, Colonel. 19 p129. See Chap. 16.

Many Cargoes. 3 p247. Book of humorous short stories by W.W. Jacobs (1863–1943). See 74 p142.

Many waters cannot quench love. 49 p288. As Augustine said, from the Song of Solomon 8.7: "Many waters cannot quench love neither can the floods drown it."

Many-headed, the. 25 p46; 33 p194 and later. From Horace's Epistles Bk 1: "The people are a many-headed beast" and later in Massinger's *The Unnatural Combat* 3.1 (c.1630): "The fury of the many-headed monster, the giddy multitude."

Marbury, Bessie. 74 p14. This theatrical agent (1856–1933) was the first to secure a percentage of box-office takings for her clients, who included PGW. She also produced several Princess shows.

Marcel-wave. Up to her M-w in proof sheets 59 p12. I was surprised to learn Marcel Grateau created his Marcel wave as early as 1872. I know ladies who still favour it.

March from Aldermaston. See Aldermaston.

March Hare, the. 42 p294. See *Alice in Wonderland*. 'Mad as a March Hare' is an old English expression. It comes from the antics of male hares in March who, in their search for a mate, fight each other standing upright on their hind legs and generally behave in an eccentric manner. See also Mad Hatter.

Marciano, Rocky. 78 p85; 79 p90. World heavyweight champion (1952–56), who won a record 49 fights in a row.

Marconi. Biggest thing since Marconi invented the victrola 38 p102. Just in case anybody thinks Marconi did so, I should point out that PGW was emphasising Sigsbee Waddington's ignorance. Guglielmo Marconi (1874–1937) developed radio and sent the first messages across the Atlantic in 1901. See also VICTROLA.

Marconi shares (scandal). 17A p39. The Marconi Scandal of 1913 centred around the purchase of Marconi shares by members of the British Government who, many believed, had been given inside information.

Marcus Aurelius. 9 p23 and frequent later. This Roman emperor (121–180 A.D.) was a leading philosopher of the Stoic school, besides being "a sort of primitive Bob Hope or Groucho Marx" (73 p155). It is from his *Meditations* Bk 9, Chap. 18, that PGW quoted: "Nothing happens to any man that he is not fitted by Nature to bear."

Margate (too bracing). 29 p135. See 'BRAMLEY IS SO BRACING'.

Mariana, Father George. Said the saraband did more harm than the Plague 42 p114. This strict Spanish Jesuit (1536–1624) would certainly have considered the saraband, Spain's exuberant popular dance of the time, as decadence of the worst order.

Mariana of the moated grange. 25 p91 and later, including two lines of the poem at 73 p93. PGW read Tennyson all his life, and when the Germans interned him, he took his Tennyson with him as well as his Shakespeare. Although Tennyson entitled his poem simply 'Mariana', he explained the background by adding a sub-title: 'Mariana in the Moated Grange (*Measure for Measure*)'. That is the phrase that PGW and many others subsequently used.

In S. *Measure for Measure*, Mariana had been betrothed to Angelo, but when she lost her money, he ignored her. She got him back later on, but Tennyson's poem stresses her misery as she waited for him in her sad moated grange. It is the sadness and waiting that PGW emphasised. Six of the seven verses end with the lines: "'He cometh not,' she said; She said, 'I am aweary, aweary, I would that I were dead.'"

***Marie Celeste*, the case of the.** *Marie Celeste* 60 p262, 81 p20 and 87 p178; *Mary Celeste* 84 p87. This maritime mystery was still a topic for heated discussion in my youth. In 1872 the ship *Mary Celeste* (its proper name) was found drifting in the Atlantic. Food was set out on the table, nothing appeared to have been disturbed or stolen, but the captain, his family and the crew had completely disappeared. Conan DOYLE wrote a popular short story about it: 'J. Habbakuk Jephson's Statement'.

Marines, U.S. 64 p214 and later, especially in *Cocktail Time*, where PGW refers to them six times. I suggest PGW's usage stems from the plethora of Marine films after World War II.

Mario's. See Chap. 21.

Marinus of Tyre. 38 p114; 70 p186. Geographer and mathematician, 2nd century A.D.

Marius among the ruins of Carthage. 7 p255 and later. Plutarch's *Lives* described Marius (155–86 B.C.) taking refuge in Africa and looking at the ruins of Carthage which had, like him, been brought down by treachery.

Mark over! Bird to the right! 7 p65. A term used when shooting grouse, pheasants etc., to warn that a bird is coming over.

Market Bumpstead. 18 p218. I wonder why PGW didn't use the real names of two places he certainly knew: Helion Bumpstead or STEEPLE BUMPSTEAD?

Markham Square, a dismal backwater. See Chap. 25.

Marlowe, Philip. 79 p167; 86 p212. Private eye created by Raymond Chandler (1888–1959), who arrived at Dulwich the term after PGW had left. When complimented later on his mastery of gangster's argot, he attributed it to the Latin and Greek he had done at Dulwich. He said such a training enabled one to distinguish between slang that was real and mere imitation or parody.

Chandler and Wodehouse never met but had a friend in common in Bill Townend, who met Chandler in Hollywood when he recognised the school ribbon on the other's straw hat. Chandler always held his old school in high regard and named Philip Marlowe after his old House there. Reviewing a biography of Chandler, Charles Spencer pointed out that though Chandler and Wodehouse wrote on very different fields, they shared many attributes. These were a brilliant gift for similes, a mistrust of intellectuals, superb readability and heroes who never lose their innate decency no matter what kind of trouble they are in.

Marmiton de domange. 52 p258. MTT Anne-Marie Chanet for the information that this was a slang term for — how do I put this — the man who collected your household 'night soil', i.e. the contents of your cess-pit or outside lavatory. See also LOUFFIER.

Marne, Battle of the. 57 p277. See FRENCH GENERAL.

Marquis de Falaise de la Foudraye. 46 p171. See DE FALAISE.

Married to eternal verse. He said you were m. to e.v. 80 p101. Wordsworth's 'The Excursion' Bk 7: "Wisdom married to immortal verse."

Marsh, Richard, author of 'A Spoiler of Men'. 8 p53. This writer of light novels died in 1915.

Marshall & Snelgrove. 14 p117. A London department store, now closed.

Marshall Field. The Marshall Field of Rudge 40 p17. Marshall Field was a pre-eminent Chicago department store. Gordon SELFRIDGE became a partner in Marshall Field at 28 and left to start Selfridge's in London in 1909.

Martial, translations of. 9 p44. Martial's (40–104 A.D.) main work comprised fourteen books of epigrams, many of which still read well today.

Martin. Can't do nothing till Martin gets here. See WE CAN'T DO.

Martinis, twenty-six. 85 p127. "I once read about a man who used to drink twenty-six martinis before dinner, and the conviction was beginning to steal over me that he had had the right idea." I may have got the wrong reference but I think this is PGW's recollection of the lines by the American humorist George

ADE (1866–1944), whom PGW admired. In his 'R-E-M-O-R-S-E', Ade wrote:

When you've had one, you call for two,
And then you don't care what you do.
Last night I hoisted twenty-three
Of these arrangements into me.
My wealth increased, I swelled with pride,
I was pickled, primed and ossified.

The second verse has the lines: "Last night at twelve I felt immense; / Today I feel like thirty cents." See also THIRTY CENTS.

Marvis Bay. 20 p33. See Chap. 23.

Marx Brothers. Like being on a desert island with the M.B. 65 p15; More like Groucho Marx than anything human 68 p14; like being on a desert island with Groucho Marx 70 p135; 76 p53. It is reported that when the Marx Brothers joined MGM, they had a contract but nobody had any ideas for them. Everything had to go through Irving Thalberg, and he was always too busy to see them. At last they decided to grab his attention. They broke into his office, lit a splendid fire, put on bathing costumes, ordered food and drinks from the cafeteria in Thalberg's name, and made themselves comfortable till he eventually arrived. It worked.

Mary (and her little lamb). 53 p100 and later. 'Mary Had a Little Lamb' from *Poems For Our Children* by Sarah Hale (1830).

***Mary Celeste*, the case of the.** 84 p87. See *MARIE CELESTE*.

Masefield's *Reynard The Fox*. 65 p152. Inserted as a compliment to a poet PGW knew and admired. When John Masefield (Poet Laureate 1930–67) was awarded the Order of Merit, he received many congratulatory telegrams. The first was from the Archbishop of Canterbury, the second from PGW. Masefield said the juxtaposition delighted him since he felt PGW's clerical stories had done much for the Anglican church.

In a letter, PGW wrote that he and Ethel had met the Masefields at Droitwich (see DROITGATE SPA) and had got on well with them till Ethel got a bad cold. She announced she was going to bed and would take take a little whisky to help her sleep. Masefield's wife was a rigid teetotaller and, after some minutes, decided to take Ethel a remedy of her own. She was shocked to find Ethel in bed with not a small tot but a bottle of whisky on the bedside table.

Mason, Perry. 85 p60 and later. This defending counsel's adventures, written by Erle Stanley Gardner (1889–1970), were made into films in the 1930s onwards and were a staple of TV in the 1960s.

Massacre of the innocents. 18 p12. B. Matthew 2.16, Herod's infanticide campaign: "Then Herod, when he saw that he was mocked of the wise men, was exceeding wroth, and sent forth, and slew all the children that were in Bethlehem, and in all the coasts thereof, from two years old and under …"

Master of his fate. See CAPTAIN OF HIS SOUL.

Masters, Edgar Lee. His influence on modern literature 21 p199. This American lawyer (1868–1950) leapt to fame with his *Spoon River Anthology* (1915), a volume of free-verse poems revealing the secret lives of people buried in a Midwestern cemetery. I suspect that PGW did not hold free-verse poets in high esteem.

Matter. Ranks of things that matter 27 p85 and elsewhere. Attributed to both Lloyd George and A.J. Balfour. Balfour (1848–1930) went on to add: "Very few things matter at all."

Matters not how straight the gate … captain of my soul. See CAPTAIN OF HIS SOUL.

Matthews, Jessie. 59 p44. Vivacious English actress (1907–81).

Maud. 3 p260 and later. T. *Maud.* The best-known line today is: "Come into the garden, Maud." Tennyson had in mind the gardens of Harrington Hall, near Horncastle. He was in love with the daughter of the house, Rosa Baring, but her parents rejected him and he wrote the poem later in her memory.

Maugham, Somerset. 55 p266; 70 p206; and later, including 73 p141. This English writer (1874–1965) visited islands around the Pacific and met beach-combers, missionaries with doubts and drink problems, and pillars of society who had 'let themselves go'. His *Notebook* includes a fascinating account of the people he encountered, and his famous short story 'Rain' (Sadie Thompson) was based on a woman he met out there. As Captain Biggar told us in *Ring for Jeeves*, "Drink, women and unpaid gambling debts" brought many a chap to degradation in those hot exotic places.

Maundrell, last of the old Bohemians. 9 p100. From Wodehouse's *Phrases and Notes* notebooks, it is clear he was writing of Old Odell, who commented to Wodehouse of someone at a Yorick smoker: "I would describe him as an inveterate entertainer. He doesn't mind how he entertains and there is no stopping him." See Chap. 21.

Mauvais quart d'heure. 3 p137. A French term adopted for the period when guests just stood around and chatted politely until dinner was announced. Drinks were not served, hence the term. One social historian says the interlude was so awful that, around 1880, a daring hostess served sherry and things improved greatly. See *Diary of a Nobody*, where Mr Pooter was surprised, and slightly shocked, to be offered a drink by the Poshes before dinner. I think it probable that PGW never saw his aunts or clerical uncles offer drinks before dinner. Wine with dinner, certainly, but …

Maxton doesn't dance. 55 p238. A dour Scottish socialist politician, James Maxton (1885–1946) represented a Glasgow constituency from 1922 till his death.

May all their troubles be little ones. 45 p67. This awful pun has been a staple of speeches at English weddings for over a century.

May, Edna. 4 p150 and later. When the female lead of the hit show *The Belle of New York* (1897) was unable to play one night, this seventeen-year-old chorus girl stepped in and made the part her own. She came to London with it and was such a success that she stayed over till her marriage in 1911.

May good digestion wait on appetite. 79 p57. S. *Macbeth* 3.4.

May, Phil. Phil May's lady ejected by a barman 2 p170. The sketch by Phil May (1864–1903), the finest cartoonist of his day, appeared in *Punch* in 1893. It depicts a bedraggled shrew indignantly telling the barman that next time she'll patronise a respectable establishment. It can be seen at p55 of *Life in London* in the *Punch Library of Humour* series.

May the Lord have mercy on your soul, And. 38 p22; 47 p82. When Britain still had the death penalty, these were the words with which a judge concluded his sentence of death. See also PLACE WHENCE HE HAD COME.

Mayer, Louis B. 70 p178; 71 p48. This Hollywood mogul (1885–1957) began as a scrap merchant, then a cinema manager, studio head, and founded MGM in 1924. See Chap. 28.

Mayfair Men. 62 p100 and later. 'Mayfair men' was a phrase coined by the newspapers in 1937 when some upper-class young men, led by Charles Hardy, carried out a violent jewel robbery in London. They were sentenced to long terms of imprisonment and Hardy received twenty strokes of the cat o'nine tails as well.

Mazzard. Were accustomed to describe as the m. 21 p76; 31 p12; and later. As PGW says, this term for the head had nearly disappeared from popular use when he wrote it, though he would have heard it as a boy. A newspaper of 9 July 1887 reported the trial of a Belgian, appearing on music halls as 'the tallest soldier in the world', who had got drunk and started throwing his weight about. The magistrates took a stern view: "These colossal creatures must be made to feel that they cannot with impunity run riot in the streets of London and knock Her Majesty's subjects over the mazzard with big sticks."

MCC. 14 p214 and later. The Marylebone Cricket Club occupies in cricket a position akin to that of St Andrews in golf.

Mean, the happy. 8 p63. See HAPPY MEAN.

Meanest flower that blows. 16 p16. Wordsworth's 'Intimations of Immortality': "To me the meanest flower that blows can give / Thoughts that do often lie too deep for tears."

Meaning of the act, within the. 7 p57 and later. A legal term commonly seen on public notices governing drinking, betting, car-parking and the like where the regulation states under such-and such Act of Parliament these are permitted in certain places or under certain conditions "within the meaning of the Act".

Means of support. No visible m. of s. 95 p43. Until the 1950s, a policeman in the UK could stop a tramp and check that he had some visible means of support, i.e. had some money on him. If he had none, then he could be taken into custody under the Vagrancy Act as a Suspicious Person or Itinerant Vagrant. For this reason, tramps would always ensure they had at least a shilling on them to avoid the charge. See also SPIV.

Mecca, peculiar aroma of a. 14 p186. The Meccas were a London chain of tea/

coffee shops from c.1890 to c.1925. I have been unable to identify the aroma in question, but older UK readers will recall the smells that seemed to be peculiar to hospitals (ether and disinfectant), school dining halls over which the smell of over-cooked cabbage hung like a pall and the combination of steam, oil and smoke that pervaded railway stations. *Kelly's Directory* for London (1907) shows there were at least two Meccas within 200 yards of the bank where Wodehouse worked. I think it very probable that the young clerks sneaked off there for a quick break.

Mechlin lace. Irreproachable Mechlin lace at his wrists 52 p78 and p96; 59 p195; 96p161. See SCARLET PIMPERNEL.

Medias res, without delay into. 76 p44. "In medias res" from Horace's *Ars Poetica*. To get to the nub, get down to business — 'into the middle of things'.

Medicine ball. 8 p63; 24 p43; 64 p172. Are these still used? They were large, soft leather balls stuffed with some material that made them very heavy and were used in a variety of gymnasium exercises. Since PGW implies they were new to Sheen, I think they may have been introduced in the 1890s along with Indian clubs, as part of the Keep Fit craze that swept the country. They were invented and popularised by William MULDOON.

Medulla oblongata. You mean a sublunary m. o. diathesis 60 p141; obscure ailments of the m. o. 61 p169. The medulla oblongata is the part of the brain that tapers off into the spinal chord. The reference in 60 is perhaps from Cole Porter's excellent medical patter song 'He never said he loved me', but Gilbert had used it in the 'Story of Prince Agib' in his *Bab Ballads* fifty years before.

Medusa. 45 p64 and later. See GORGON.

Meek and contrite heart. See SPIRIT, HUMBLE AND CONTRITE.

Meek shall inherit the earth, the. 39 p77. B. Psalms 37.11: "But the meek shall inherit the earth; and shall delight themselves in the abundance of peace." Also Matthew 5.5: "Blessed are the meek: for they shall inherit the earth."

Meet it is I set it down that one may smile and smile and be a villain. 84 p108. S. *Hamlet* 1.5.

Melancholy had marked him for her own. 48 p130 and elsewhere. Gray's poem 'The Epitaph': "Fair Science frown'd not on his humble birth, / And Melancholy mark'd him for her own."

Mellingham Hall. 92 p9; 94 p32. The second reference gives the address as Mellingham Hall, Mellingham, Sussex. This could be PGW's memory of Wellingham, Sussex, just north of Lewes, but I have a strong suspicion that the house and estate are based on his recollections of Hunstanton. See Chap. 32.

Melodrama, transpontine. See TRANSPONTINE MELODRAMA.

Memory returning to her throne. 44 p278. See REASON RETURNS.

Men, all. See ALL MEN ARE BROTHERS and ALL MEN ARE CREATED EQUAL.

Men are men, where. 32 p138; 43 p282. There was a silent film of this name made in 1921. MTT Nigel Rees.

Men are suspicious, prone to discontent. 96 p7. Herrick's 'Present Government

Grievous'.

Men in the Bab Ballads who both knew Robinson. 74 p14; 78 p185. See GILBERT's 'Etiquette' in his *Bab Ballads*. Gray and Somers were shipwrecked on an island but, because they had never been formally introduced, they had to ignore each other. One day Gray heard Somers wondering out loud about his old friends, including Robinson. Since he also knew Robinson, Gray, apologizing profusely for his intrusion, was at last able to introduce himself.

Men might come and men might go, but John went on for ever. 40 p82; 73 p136. T. 'The Brook': "For men may come and men may go, / But I go on for ever."

Men Who Did and Women Who Shouldn't Have But Had a Pop At It. 49 p226. PGW knew his readers in 1933 would pick up the reference to the scandalous 1895 novel *The Woman Who Did* by Grant Allen. The heroine, a 'free-thinker', a 'New Woman' and all the rest of it, lived with a man because she wanted his child out of wedlock. She had the child, but the man died and she was left alone with her shame.

'Men Who Missed Their Own Weddings' (and 'Single Day Marriages'). 9 p45. See Chap. 7.

Mencken knows everything. 70 p154. H.L. Mencken (1880–1956) was a prominent literary figure of his day — essayist and forthright critic of literature and institutions. His masterpiece was the lengthy and magisterial work *The American Language*. PGW certainly held him in high regard. I wonder if the compliment was a response to Mencken's statement in *The American Language*, Supplement 1, p507: "The only latter-day English novelist who can speak American is P.G. Wodehouse." (Mencken was quoting D.B.Whitman's letter on 'American Slang in England' of 4 May 1937.) MTT David Landman.

Menjou, Adolphe. 62 p106. Suave film star (1890–1963).

Mens sana in corpore what-not. 59 p29. See HEALTHY MIND.

Mentioned in dispatches. 91 p160. Gallantry medals are issued sparingly in Britain. Someone whose conduct does not qualify for a medal, but is of sufficient merit to be noted in the official record, is entitled to wear a small oak leaf on the campaign medal ribbon.

Mere vulgar brawl. See BRAWL.

Meredith and his 'Modern Love'. 41 p10; 84 p68. George Meredith's (1828–1909) *Modern Love* comprises a series of poems about a husband and wife growing more and more unhappy with each other.

Meredith (Chimp Twist's fictional employee). 83 p134. A compliment to PGW's US agent Scott Meredith. See also SCHWED.

Meredith (football player). 14 p74; 18 p251. Billy Meredith was a leading player for Manchester United in the 1900s.

Merrie England. 12 p334. A term revived by Edward German's splendid 1902 musical of the same name.

Merry. 3 p237. The classical scholar William Merry (1835–1918) published a new translation of the *Odyssey*.

Merry and bright, always. See Always merry.

Merry heart doeth good like a medicine, a. 49 p312. B. Proverbs 17.22: "A merry heart doeth good like a medicine but a broken spirit drieth the bones."

Merry Widow, The (and the Merry Widow Waltz). 13 p242 and later. Franz Lehár's (1870–1948) still enchanting 1905 musical.

Mess of porridge. Selling your birthright for a mess of porridge 45 p61. PGW's variation (following Mrs Gamp in Dicken's *Martin Chuzzlewit*) of "a mess of pottage". B. Genesis 26. 30–34 recounts how Esau was so hungry, Jacob forced him to trade his birthright for "bread and pottage of lentils". The "mess of pottage" phrase, which stuck in people's memory for centuries, comes from the summary of the chapter in the Geneva Bible version.

Messenger in a Greek play bringing bad news. 89 p92. See Greek drama.

Messmore Kendall. 74 p121. One of those names that PGW realised sounded American to UK ears, like Ike, Spike, Sadie and Mamie. Hence Messmore Breamworthy 65 p67 and later. See also Names.

Methusaleh. 39 p288 and later. He lived 969 years according to the Bible; he did not eat grass. As Uncle Fred pointed out (67 p242), that was Nebuchadnezzar.

Metropole (hotel). 74 p168. See *Midnight Frolic*.

Mewling and puking. In my nurse's arms 76 p107; babies in the Drones 81 p90. S. *As You Like It*. 2.7: "Mewling and puking in the nurse's arms."

Mexico, war in. 20 p102. In 1914–16, when the book was written, there was a civil war in Mexico and Pancho Villa led a raid into New Mexico. The American Army sent a force 300 miles into Mexico to try and capture him, attracting far more publicity than the war then going on in Europe.

'Mgoopi 'Mgwumpi, chief of the Lesser 'Mgowpi. 57 p169. I think PGW was slipping in another joke here, similar to his use of Gotsuchakoff. It was only when I pronounced the words out loud that I picked it up. A goop is a fatuous person, while in UK dictionaries a mugwump is a derisive term for someone of importance or one who disassociates himself from political parties. In America it has a specific meaning: the reforming Republicans who left the Party in 1884 rather than support James Blaine.

Micawber, Mr. 4 p72 & p231 and later. A charming but ineffectual paterfamilias in Dickens' *David Copperfield*, always in financial difficulties but always optimistic that something would turn up. It was Mrs Micawber's constantly reiterated statement that she would *never* desert Mr Micawber.

Mice and men whose best-laid schemes (have gone away). 18 p101 and frequent later. PGW's gloss on Robert Burns's 'To a Mouse': "The best laid schemes o' mice and men gang aft a-gley."

Michigan. 22 p103. Famous 1914 "I want to go back" song by Irving Berlin. See Chap. 36.

Middlewick, Earl of. In the 1930 play *Leave It to Psmith*, the seigneur of Blandings is not the Earl of Emsworth, but the Earl of Middlewick. See Chap.

39 for an explanation.

Midford, Hampshire. 23 p191. We know it as Midhurst, Sussex.

Midges, fretful. 63 p10. Rossetti's 'Blessed Damozel'. "As low as where this earth / Spins like a fretful midge."

Midian, the hosts/troops of. 19 p145 and later. See CHRISTIAN.

***Midnight Frolic* at the Hotel Metropole.** 74 p168. Soon after the PGW and Grossmith show *The Cabaret Girl* had opened in London in 1922, George Grossmith decided to introduce cabaret to London. He did so in the Metropole Hotel in Northumberland Avenue. It was the first cabaret in England, 'The Midnight Follies', and people flocked to enjoy this new entertainment with their dinner. The London County Council took a different view and tried to close it down on the grounds that the hotel did not have a licence for it. The hotel replied that since cabaret was so new, there was no appropriate licence to be applied for and they would carry on. The LCC brought more pressure to bear, but Grossmith and the hotel defied them. Only when the Prince of Wales made it clear how much he enjoyed his evenings there did the LCC back off. The hotel was taken over by the War Office in 1940, but the black-and-white 1923 'Midnight Follies' sign was still in the hall when the building was sold in November 2003.

Gertrude LAWRENCE made her name in Grossmith's cabaret and it was where PGW first saw her, although he later wrote that cabaret was an irritating interruption of a decent meal.

Midshipmite, The. 49 p106. Popular 1875 song by Fred Weatherly.

Might be for years or it might be for ever, It. 25 p45 and later. Song 'Kathleen Mavourneen' by Crawford and Crouch (1837).

Mighty, hunter, a. 63 p112. B. Genesis 10.9: "Even as Nimrod the mighty hunter before the Lord."

Mighty rushing wind. See WIND.

Mighty things from small beginings grow, Dryden said. 84 p83. He did so in *Annus Mirabilis*. "By viewing nature, nature's hand-maid art, Makes mighty things from small beginnings grow ..."

Mile, four-minute. 80 p104. See BANNISTER.

Milestones on the Dover Road. The lady in Dickens who spoke of them 63 p48. Mr Finching's aunt at Chap. 23 of *Little Dorrit.*

Militant churchmen ancestors, the blood of a hundred. See CHURCH MILITANT.

Milk and honey, a land flowing with. See LAND FLOWING.

Milk of human kindness. Overflowing with the m. of h. k. 50 p174; 72 p15; the milk chocolate of h. k. 89 p159. S. *Macbeth* 1.5: "Yet do I fear thy nature; / It is too full of the milk of human kindness."

Milk of Paradise. See HONEY-DEW HATH FED.

Millay, Edna St Vincent. 69 p174. US poetess (1892–1950). After Vassar, she went to live in Greenwich Village with other artistic rebels of the 1920s. She gave dramatic public readings of her poems, which brought her increased sales if not critical approval. Her most quoted quatrain is: "My candle burns at both ends. / It will not last the night; / But, oh, my foes, and, oh, my friends — / It gives a lovely light."

Millbourne Bay. 18 p23. See Chap. 16.

Miller, Johnson, deaf choreographer. 26 p138. See Chap. 24.

Miller, Marilynn (who became Marilyn Miller). See Chap. 24.

Mills bomb. 41 p111; 48 p131. A hand grenade (36 Grenade in UK parlance).

Mills of God grind slowly but grind exceeding small. 85 p120. Longfellow's 'Retribution', a translation of a poem by Friedrich von Logau: "Though the mills of God grind slowly, yet they grind exceedingly small; / Though with patience he stands waiting, with exactness grinds he all."

Mill-Stewart. 3 p236. PGW satire on John Stuart Mill (1806–73), philosopher and social reformer who read Greek and Latin by the age of eight and began studying the Greek philosphers and their teachings at twelve.

Milne, A.A. (creator of Christopher Robin). 65 p252 and later, especially *The Mating Season* (1949). Milne (1882–1956) and PGW had very similar careers. Both were successful writers of light, humorous stories, both wrote for *Punch* in their early days, and they collaborated on theatrical projects. PGW admired some of Milne's plays but grew to dislike Milne even before Milne attacked him over the Berlin broadcasts. Several contemporaries have written that Milne was jealous of PGW in the 1930s, especially of the critical acclaim which Milne never achieved.

Mind, noble. See NOBLE MIND.

Mind over matter. See TRIUMPH OF MIND OVER MATTER.

Minds with but a single thought, two. 41 p146 and later. See TWO HEARTS THAT BEAT AS ONE.

Miner's dream of home. 21 p38. This popular song by Leo Dryden, about a miner in Australia who longs to return home to England, was published in the 1890s.

Minerva. Springing fully armed like M. from the brow of Jove 58 p176. The details of this Greek legend are not suitable for family reading.

Ministering angel. See WOMAN IN OUR HOURS OF EASE.

Minor prophet of the Old Testament. See PROPHET OF THE OLD TESTAMENT.

Minorities, oppressed. See OPPRESSED MINORITIES.

Minstrel show. End man at a m.s. 21 p140. Minstrel (blackface) shows began with Edwin Christy in 1849 (see CHRISTY MINSTRELS) and the format soon became stereotyped. In the first part, the 'olio', the minstrels sat on chairs with Mr Interlocutor (the straight man) in the middle who exchanged cross-talk with 'Mr Tambo', player of the tambourine, at one end and 'Mr Bones', player of the bones, at the other. In the second part, individual minstrels sang, danced and did monologues, finishing with a burlesque performed by the whole troupe. The innumerable minstrel troupes were popular in both the US and UK till the early 20th century. Amos 'n Andy and Al Jolson's success were based on the minstrel tradition. See also MOORE & BURGESS.

Minstrel tuning his harp now prepares to sing, the. 72 p96; 89 p44 and elsewhere. I am sure I remembered this from struggling through Virgil's *Aeneid* at school, but was unable to trace it. MTT Classicist Dan Garrison for confirming (within minutes of being asked!) that it is from the first Book of the *Aeneid*, lines 740–741 ('cithara personat aurata').

Minute. There'll be another one (poet/wife) along in a m. See ANOTHER ONE.

Minute-gun, a snort like a. 59 p265. In sailing races, the competitors take up their positions and manoeuvre against wind and tide till the starting gun goes off. A gun is fired one minute before the start to warn them how much time there is to go.

Miracles, age of. 12 p297. S. *All's Well That Ends Well* 2.3: "They say miracles are past."

Mirror of Tennyson's Lady of Shalott, cracked from side to side like the. 97 p96. See CURSE HAS COME.

'Miserable sinner' bits in the Litany. 96 p97. BCP. The Litany 'or General Supplication, to be sung or said after Morning Prayer, upon Sundays, Wednesdays, and Fridays, and at other times when it shall be commanded by the Ordinary'. The first four four verses and responses all conclude with the words "have mercy upon us miserable sinners".

Miss America. 72 p41 and later. This beauty contest began as a publicity stunt by Atlantic City, New Jersey, famous for its four-mile boardwalk (promenade in the UK). They started it in 1921 in an effort to keep visitors coming to the resort after Labour Day, the normal end to American summer holidays. The first winner was Miss Margaret Gorman, 5 ft 1 in, 30-25-32, whose victory made the form-fitting one-piece bathing suit the standard swimming wear for women across America and Europe.

Miss Dolby, I presume. 95 p59. See DOCTOR LIVINGSTONE.

Miss in baulk. 7 p199 and later. A billiards term. Since a player has to play his first stroke up the table from the baulk line, if the other two object balls are behind his ball — in baulk — he might misjudge his rebound off the top cushion, come back and miss them. He incurs a two-point penalty for doing so, having committed 'a foul', but his opponent does not have the option of having the other two balls repositioned ('re-spotted') on the table, as he would for other foul strokes. A player may often deliberately play this shot for various reasons i.e. deliberately 'giving a miss in baulk'.

Miss Otis. Like Miss Otis, he would be unable to lunch today 86 p139. One of Cole Porter's funniest songs (1934), it is said it was written for a bet. At a lunch party, someone challenged Porter to write a song based on the next words to be spoken in the room. In the natural hush that followed, the butler entered and announced to the hostess: "Miss Otis regrets she's unable to lunch today, Madam."

The obvious question is — who was this lady? In the smart circles Porter moved in, it should be easy to identify her. Was she one of the famous engineering 'Elevator' Otises, or perhaps one of the New York legal family or the equally well-known medical Otises? Has nobody followed this up?

Mission in Kennington. 2 p90. See Chap. 3.

Missouri. I'm from M., I want to be shown 15 p85; men from Missouri 18 p120. This American expression of cynical disbelief became popular in 1899. Willard D. Vandiver, a Missouri politician, used it constantly at a banquet in New York that year and the phrase stuck. The 'official' nickname for Missouri is 'The Show Me State'.

Mr and Mrs Fitch. 95 p130. Song by Cole Porter, 'Mister and Missus Fitch', in Porter's *Gay Divorce* (1932).

Mister Black Man. 7 p176. One of the many CAKEWALK songs popular at the time, written 1904 by Arthur Pryor. MTT David Jasen.

Mister Moon, old. 25 p34; 32 p203. PGW satirised the songwriting industry often with song titles like this, but his satire tended to become reality later. In 1939 the world bought thousands of records of 'Old Mister Moon' by David Carlyle.

Mitching Hill. There has been much discussion of the location of the setting for 'Uncle Fred Flits By'. I suggest the argument for Dulwich has strong support from Lord Ickenham's comment at page 108 of *Uncle Fred in the Springtime*, when he recalled fondly "that day down in Valley Fields". See Chap. 9.

Mitford, Nancy. 78 p50; 79 p87. This writer (1904–73) was slightly chagrined when her *Noblesse Oblige* (1956), a series of light-hearted essays on upper-class speech ('U and Non-U') written with Alan Ross, achieved far greater sales than her excellent biographies or novels had.

Mix, Tom. 38 p21. This leading cowboy hero (1880–1940) of early Westerns was, a British newspaper claimed, the man who started the habit of the good guys wearing white hats to distinguish them from the sinister black-hatted baddies.

Mixture is too rich, the. 20 p84; 82 p17; 91 p27; 94 p76. Up to c.1960s, when you started your car on a cold morning, you pulled out the 'choke' to mix more petrol with the air in the carburettor. If you pulled out the choke too far, the mixture became 'too rich' and the car would come to a stop. See also PLUGS.

Mizner, Addison. 74 p116. This con man (1876–1933) set himself up as architect to the wealthy, though he had no training or qualifications. With his brother Wilson, a miner, prizefighter and gambler, he initiated the Miami development boom of 1924–26 in which they both made millions. The first house he built there was for Kid McCoy. See also SUCKER.

Moab is my washpot and over what's-its-name he has cast his shoe. 67 p8; 83 p12. B. Psalms 60.8: "Moab is my washpot; over Edom will I cast out my shoe."

Moan of doves in immemorial elms, the. 18 p154. T. *The Princess* Pt 7.

Moaning at the bar. Let there be no moaning at the bar 31 p212 and later. T. 'Crossing the Bar': "And may there be no moaning of the bar, When I put out to sea."

Moderation, astounded at my (own). 91 p53. Famous reply of Clive of India in 1773 when accused of corruption. "By God, Mr. Chairman, at this moment I stand astonished at my own moderation."

Moderation in all things. 93 p107. Greek proverb and also Plautus' *Poenulus* 1.2. "Modus omnibus in rebus optimum est habitu." (Moderation in all things is the best rule.)

Modern Italian. If this was what the m. I. was like, no wonder the country had had to have a dictatorship 38 p206. Mussolini's march on Rome and his assumption of power in 1922 as dictator had caught the attention of the world. His example was followed by Hitler and Franco in the 1930s.

Mohammed's coffin, suspended between heaven and earth. 27 p116. It was long believed that this coffin at Medina was suspended in mid-air. Burckhardt, the explorer, found the belief was false. See also MAHOMET.

Mojave Desert. 30 p182; 44 p10; 46 p24; 77 p126. PGW was always fascinated by the adventures of his old friend Bill Townend, who, apart from picking lemons in California, also went prospecting in the Mojave Desert c.1913. See Chap. 34.

Molotov (said No all the time). 70 p28. USSR Foreign Secretary (1890–1986), his 'Nyet' (No) to all proposals of the Western Powers in the 1940s–50s was famous.

Moment, work of a. See WORK OF A MOMENT.

Moments when a fellow needs a friend. 52 p14; 72 p120; 80 p47. Line from the song 'But Not For Me' from the 1930 show *Girl Crazy* by George and Ira Gershwin. Or maybe from the 1919 comic strip 'When a Feller Needs a Friend'. MTT David Jasen.

Mona Lisa. 23 p191 and often later. See GIOCONDA SMILE.

Monaco, Prince of (and his fish). 15 p18. Prince Albert I of Monaco (r. 1889–1922), a highly-respected marine biologist, created the famous aquarium at Monaco around 1900.

Money. Going where money is 77 p15. T. 'The Northern Farmer, New Style': "Don't thou marry for money, but go where money is."

Monkey Brand, Old. 40 p265. An appropriate description of 'Chimp' Twist and a term readily understood by PGW's contemporaries. Monkey Brand was the name of a soap which, so the advertisements said, would clean floors, windows, carpets, walls, brassware, everything except clothes. The advertisement, surmounted by a picture of a monkey's head, appeared on the back cover of hundreds of magazines c.1890–c.1930.

Monkey glands. See GLANDS.

Monks of Rheims. As heedless of grammar as the monks of Rheims 4 p240. Barham's *Ingoldsby Legends* ('The Jackdaw of Rheims'). "Heedless of grammar, they all cried 'That's him!'" See INGOLDSBY LEGENDS.

Monocle. Did Bertie Wooster wear one or not? His picture on the posters in 'Jeeves and the Spot of Art' implies that he did, but there is no mention of it in the canon. I suggest the answer lies in the fact that, in every story featuring Bertie that I have found in the *Strand* magazine between 1926 and 1930, the artist Charles Crombie always depicted him with a monocle. Many modern illustrators do the same, no doubt to reinforce the silly-ass image.

Montgomery, Robert. 54 p75. Was this a private compliment to Montgomery (1904–81), who starred in the film *Piccadilly Jim*?

Montreal. Oh God! Oh, Montreal 79 p8. See Oh God!

Montrose. 40 p77 and later. At 80 p118, from his 'My Dear and Only Love':

He either fears his fate too much,
Or his deserts are small,
That puts it not unto the touch,
To win or lose it all.

James Graham, Marquis of Montrose (1612–50), a brave soldier and brilliant tactician, won some remarkable battles for Charles I but was betrayed and executed in 1650.

Monument, leap off the. 22 p187. This 202-foot-high column in London, commemorating the Great Fire of 1666, was a popular spot for suicides until the upper balcony was caged in.

Moodiness had claimed him for her own. 27 p248. See Melancholy had marked him.

Moon and blood. Turn the moon red with blood 71 p111; turn the moon to blood 82 p75; and later. The nearest I have found is B. Revelation 6.12: " and the sun became black as sackcloth of hair, and the moon became as blood."

Moon Assurance Co. 9 p108. A thin disguise for England's then largest insurance company, the Sun Assurance Co. See also Planet Insurance.

Moon of his delight, the. 76 p30. Fitzgerald's *Omar Khayyam* St.74.

Moonlight Sonata, played by Fenn. 6 p51. PGW's brother Armine played this Beethoven piano sonata at a Dulwich College concert. See Chap. 3.

Moore & Burgess Nigger Minstrels. 11 p24. Around 1880, this black-face troupe took over from the Christy Minstrels as the leading minstrel show in Britain. See also Christy Minstrels and Minstrel show.

Moore, Dinty. 71 p40. Miss Moore got her name from the famous New York restaurant owned by Dinty Moore. It was extremely popular with showbiz people; it was here that lyricist Irving Caesar (1895–1996) urged Gershwin to write 'Swanee' in 1919.

Moore, Thomas. This poet (1779–1852) was popular and successful in his lifetime, and his poems were set to music and achieved equal success at the end of the Victorian period, during PGW's boyhood. Moore was the man who wrote poems about the Minstrel Boy, of losing dear gazelles, of love locked out, of the Peri at the gates of Paradise, and of going where glory waits thee.

Moping owl in Gray's 'Elegy'. 50 p153. "The moping owl does to the moon complain."

Moral. He points the moral and adorns a tale 76 p49. Dr Johnson's poem 'Vanity of Human Wishes': "He left the name, at which the world grew pale, To point a moral, or adorn a tale."

Morality clauses (in Hollywood). See Chap. 28.

More blessed to give than to receive. 1 p30 (a right cross to the jaw). From B. Acts 20.35.

More in sorrow than in anger. Often. S. *Hamlet* 1.2. "A countenance more in sorrow than in anger."

More sinned against than sinning. 21 p175 and later. S. *King Lear* 3.2. "I am a man, More sinned against than sinning."

More, that little (and how much it is). See LITTLE MORE.

More things in Heaven and earth etc. 56 p78. See THERE ARE MORE THINGS.

More to be pitied than censured. 21 p39 and frequent thereafter. If you have the misfortune to be a Frenchman who can't speak English, or a relative of the Duke of Dunstable, or you are forced into doing something because Aunt Dahlia stood over you making hunting noises, you are more to be pitied than censured.

I am very proud of this one. I could not find it in any of twenty or more American and English dictionaries of quotations, and I only got it when I started saying the words in various rhythms. When I tried a solemn Victorian monologue style, I was sure I was on the right track.

In 1891 W.B. Gray of New York noticed some yobs making rude remarks to a tired old slattern, a woman of the streets no less. He went home and produced the song that fitted the sentiment of the times perfectly.

She Is More to Be Pitied than Censured

She is more to be pitied than censured,
She is more to be helped than despised.
She is only a lassie who ventured,
On Life's stormy path, ill-advised.
Do not scorn her with words fierce and bitter,
Do not laugh at her shame and downfall;
For a moment, just stop and consider
That a man was the cause of it all!

Try this with all the sonorous emphasis you can give it and you can see why there wasn't a dry eye in the house. No wonder PGW never forgot it.

Morgan, Pierpoint. 30 p237 and later. It was commonly believed that this financier (1837–1913) controlled nearly half the heavy industry of the United States.

Moriarty, Professor. A juvenile Prof. M. 2 p16 & p41; and later. This Napoleon of crime, created by Conan Doyle, became so well known that the term came to apply to any evil-doer.

Morituri te salutant. 26 p302. When gladiators entered the Coliseum to fight to the death before the Emperor, Petronius quoted them in his *Life of Claudius*: 'morituri te salutant' (those about to die, salute you).

Morn to dewy eve, from early. 27 p30. PGW's recollection of "From morn to noon, he fell; from noon to dewy eve". Milton's *Paradise Lost* 1.742.

Morn was at seven and the hillside dew-pearled. 89 p26 and elsewhere. See GOD'S IN HIS HEAVEN.

Morning, full many a glorious. See FULL MANY.

***Morning Globe* (newspaper).** 32 p34. PGW's tribute to *The Globe*, the London paper where he learned so much. See Chap. 7.

Morning stars, went to reside with. See RESIDE WITH.

Morris, Old Tom and Young Tom. 28 p84 & p255. Old Tom (1821–1908) and his son dominated golf in Scotland during the 1860s and 70s. Young Tom, having won the Open four times, died in 1875 at the age of twenty-four. His memorial, which shows him addressing a golf ball, stands against a wall in St Andrew's churchyard. The ball is kept sparkling white by the St Andrew's undergraduates, who apply a coat of paint to it each year.

Morrison, Alex. 69 p178. His book *A New Way to Better Golf* was very popular in the 1930s. My father had a copy, and I recall doing the exercises Morrison recommended.

Mortal Error. 41 p102. For Christian Scientists, mortal error is a synonym for sickness and suffering. MTT Bennett Quillen.

Mortals (to command success). See NOT IN MORTALS.

Moses and bushes speaking. See BUSH/ BUSHES SPEAKING.

Moses and Mt. Pisgah. 18 p119; 25 p94 and frequent later; PGW uses it in the joyful sense of seeing the Promised Land. B. Deuteronomy 34. Mount Pisgah is where Moses saw the Promised Land which he knew he could not enter, where he took his leave of the Israelites and where he died.

Moses Bros of Covent Garden. 33 p34. See MOSS BROTHERS.

Moss Brothers. 84 p33 and elsewhere. Moss Brothers, always pronounced as 'Moss Bross', are England's best-known dress hire firm. It was only recently that I realised that PGW used the real name, Moss Bros., when he wanted to mention them seriously but called them Cohen Bros when he was making fun of them. For more detail, see COHEN BROS.

Mote that is in thy brother's eye. 93 p86. See BEAM.

Moth. Desire of a moth for a star 28 p211 and later. A favourite crack of Madeline Bassett's. SHELLEY's 'To — One Word Is Too Often Profaned': "The desire of the moth for the star, / Of the night for the morrow."

Mother. There's always room for another song boosting M. 27 p270. See Chap. 36.

Mother. (1) Always Listen to M. See ALWAYS LISTEN. (2) Just like M. makes. See JUST LIKE. (3) My M. See MY MOTHER. (4) Somebody's M. See SOMEBODY'S.

Mother knows best. Frequent. This traditional aphorism was the title of a book by Edna Ferber (1927) and a comedy of the same name.

Mother, She's Pinching My Leg. 33 p191. There is no such song listed in the British Library, but 'Ma, She's Making Eyes At Me' was very popular the year before PGW wrote this.

Mothers-in-law elect. 18 p125. PGW's memory of G&S *Mikado.* Katisha is described thoughout as "his daughter-in-law elect".

Mother's Knee. 27 p268. See Chap. 36.

Mother's pride and joy, his/a. Frequent. A common phrase but, if a single source is needed, there is "a mother's pride, a father's joy" from Scott's poem 'Rokeby' (1813). Jennie Hill ('The Vital Spark') used to reduce her music hall audiences to tears in the 1890s with her rendering of a song of a mother's grief at her son's death: "For he was her only son, Her hope, her pride, her joy."

Motor mascot. Bertie Wooster has a face like a m.m. 31 p116. In the days when cars had proper bonnets/ hoods, the front end was surmounted by a radiator cap. When your car overheated, you undid this to pour water in. When mass production of cars produced thousands looking exactly the same, the fashion sprang up of replacing the standard cap with one with a mascot on it. If your car was expensive, however, you kept the mascot provided by the manufacturer. The lordly Hispano-Suiza had a flying stork, while Dolphin cars displayed a dolphin. The most famous radiator cap of all, the Spirit of Ecstasy still seen on Rolls-Royces, was introduced in 1910. It was modelled by Miss Eleanor Thornton, born 1880, who worked for the first secretary of the Royal Automobile Club before becoming secretary to the chairman of Rolls-Royce, the 2nd Lord Montagu. She died when her ship was torpedoed in the First World War; there is a monument to her in Beaulieu parish church beside the Montagu family pew.

There were hundreds of mascots to choose from: Indian chiefs, Old Bill, Billikens, comic policemen, every sort of animal. Which particular model Bertie was meant to resemble, I don't know, but I suggest one good candidate is the mascot Ruston-Hornby put on their vehicles. It was the beaky-nosed Lincoln Imp, modelled on a grotesque gargoyle on Lincoln cathedral.

Mount Anville, Lord. 19 p137. See Chap. 16.

Mount Pelée. 44 p221. This volcano in the West Indies had a violent eruption in 1902.

Mountain girl. You're doing all right for a mountain girl, as the song says. 83 p113. None of my six music reference books were of any help in tracing this song, and even the vast resources of the Internet failed. I finally found the answer at 86 p141 (*Frozen Assets*) when I read that Lord Tilbury's brother was very fond of the 'Mountain Girl' song sung by Dorothy Shay. Shay (1921–78) was a well-known singer of hillbilly songs, and 'Mountain Girl' was one of her hits.

Mountain Greenery. 86 p146. Song from *Garrick Gaieties* by Rodgers & Hart 1926.

Mourned like Niobe (and would not be comforted). 24 p203 and later. Niobe lost her ten children in one of Greek mythology's more savage stories and was turned to stone herself. S. *Hamlet* 1.2 has "Like Niobe all tears; why she, even she … Would have mourned longer." But perhaps PGW confused her with Rachel, who also mourned and would not be comforted. B. Matthew 2.18: "Rachel weeping for her children, and would not be comforted, because they are not."

Mouse Trap, The. See CLAUDIUS.

Moustache. Chimp Twist has to shave his to act as valet to Ivor Llewellyn 94 p32. Chimp has had this forced on him before, but not specifically as a valet. PGW went back a long time on this one. There was a period, roughly 1890–1930, when moustaches and beards were a mark of class or occupation (see BEARDS). For example, it was commonly understood at that time that any well-dressed, clean-shaven man in London's West End was either a barrister, an actor or a manservant since moustaches were severely discouraged in these occupations. Conversely, young Army officers would be told to grow a moustache, whether they wanted to or not. I have to add that, among the very few occasions when I was met at the front door of a Stately Home by a butler, I was extremely startled to be greeted by one wearing a moustache. I have no idea why. Perhaps reading so many books on the period had sunk into my subconscious.

Mouth (that which goeth into). See NOT THAT WHICH GOETH.

Move in a mysterious way, your wonders to perform. See FATE/HE MOVES.

Moved by faith alone. See FAITH ALONE.

Moving accidents by flood and field. See ACCIDENTS.

Moving finger writes, and having writ etc., The. 51 p221; 58 p33. Fitzgerald's *Omar Khayam.*

Moykoff, boots made to order by. 33 p34. This bootmaker is now part of Lobb's of St James's St. See LOBB.

Much Middlefold on the Hill and Lesser M. in the Vale. 2 p126 and later. See Chap. 35.

Mucus. Has the mucus of a good story. 53 p292. See Chap. 28.

Mud. Name will be mud 42 p262 and later. One source claims that the term comes from Dr Mudd, the man who set John Wilkes Booth's leg after he shot Lincoln. Another says it is from the 1916 song 'The Sentimental Bloke' ('My name is Mudd').

Mud in your eye, Here's. A toast that came into popular use in the UK during the trench warfare of the First World War. It was better to get mud in your eye than shrapnel or a bullet. The idea was later extended further with the toast 'SKIN OFF YOUR NOSE'.

Muggs, J. Fred. 75 (US version); the dedication to Peter SCHWED mentions him. MTT Barry Phelps and Ella Palmer for revealing that Muggs was a star of breakfast TV in America (1953–57). He received a huge amount of fan mail which was dealt with by his staff since Muggs was unable to write himself, being a chimpanzee.

Mulberry bush. See ROUND AND ROUND.

Muldoon. Runs health cure establishments 19 p143; and later. William Muldoon

(1852–1933) was a well-known figure of his time. At various stages of his career he was a policeman, a highly-respected professional wrestling champion and a superb trainer. He took John L. Sullivan in hand and made him world champion, after which Sullivan decided he need not train any more. Muldoon later ran energetic keep-fit courses for wealthy business men in White Plains as PGW told us, and became a New York Boxing Commissioner. When he died in 1933, he was chairman of the New York Athletic Commission.

Mulligatawny. Deep in the mulligatawny and no hope of striking for the shore 85 p93. PGW twist on the expression to be in the soup (to be in trouble) plus the hymn by P.P. Bliss (1838–76) 'Pull for the shore': "Pull for the shore, brothers, pull for the shore." See also BISQUE, GUMBO, and OXO.

Mulliner, Sacheverell. At his best on Proust, Russian Ballet, Japanese prints and James Joyce 49 p146. By giving this young man the name Sacheverell, PGW immediately 'classified' him for British readers. In the 1920s–30s, the three Sitwells — Edith (1887–1964), Osbert (1892–1969) and Sacheverell (1897–1988) — seemed to be involved in every avant-garde artistic movement.

Mumbling Mose. 7 p172; 8 p20. Popular 1905 cakewalk by Thurban. See CAKEWALK.

Mumbo-Jumbo. The curate has gone over to the worship of Mumbo-Jumbo 25 p78. A popular poem of 1914 was 'The Congo' by Vachel Lindsay. It included the lines: "Mumbo-Jumbo, god of the Congo … And of all the other gods of the Congo, Mumbo-Jumbo will hoo-doo you."

Munday, Jimmy. 23 p216; 35 p105 (repeat). Billy Sunday (1862–1935), a baseball player, became a popular preacher. He had tremendous success and was perhaps the last of the barn-storming preachers who fulminated about the imminence of hell fire rather than Christian charity. His influence waned after 1919 when Prohibition came in and he had fewer evils to fulminate against.

Murad. He would have been nonchalant and lit a Murad 49 p120. Murad was an expensive Turkish cigarette. See CIGARETTES.

***Murder at Bilbury Manor* … Hilbury … Milbury … Silbury.** 58 p190. PGW was clearly struck by Dorothy L. Sayers' *Five Red Herrings*, in which the solution depends on breaking a similar highly complex alibi. He wrote a long letter to the humorist Will Cuppy in 1933 complaining how this form of detection had become so tedious.

Murder of Roger Ackroyd, The. 46 p67. Agatha Christie's 1926 mystery. I was shocked by PGW's strong hint to the solution.

Murderer, First, in Shakespeare. 54 p127. See FIRST MURDERER.

Murders, stratagems and spoils. 2 p88. I think PGW slipped slightly here when he changed Shakespeare's 'treasons' to 'murders'. My favourite PGW version of this quote is in *The Small Bachelor* when he combined American slang and Shakespeare to describe Sigsbee Waddington, the synthetic Westerner, as "grim and squiggle-eyed and ripe for murders, stratagems and spoils". See also MUSIC.

Murray, Arthur. 80 p37 and later. This well-known American teacher of ballroom dancing, a protegé of Vernon Castle, was the equivalent of the UK's Victor Sylvester. He opened his first dance studio in 1913 and had over 400 by 1950. He endeared himself to millions of Americans by devising five basic steps for those who wanted to learn to dance quickly. He died in 1991, age 95.

Music. Percy had no music in his soul and was fit for murders, stratagems and spoils 49 p81; man that hath no music in himself 51 p15; and elsewhere. S. *Merchant of Venice* 5.1. "Since nought so stockish, hard, and full of rage, / But music for the time doth change his nature. / The man that hath no music in himself, / Nor is not mov'd with concord of sweet sounds, / Is fit for treasons, stratagems and spoils."

Mussolini. 41 p77 and frequent later. This Fascist dictator governed Italy 1922–43.

Mustn't. Tell them they mustn't 2 p174; directions from a bishop to a vicar wanting to use incense 39 p104. From a famous cartoon in *Punch* (1872, Vol 63 p202) where a harried mother tells the housemaid to find her daughter: "See what she's doing and tell her she mustn't."

Mutt and Jeff. 43 p82 and later. This long-lasting American cartoon strip by Henry Fisher began in 1907, probably in imitation of the successful UK cartoon pair Weary Willie and Tired Tim (1896 onwards). It featured two friends, one tall, one short (the classic combination: Abbott & Costello, Flanagan & Allen etc.). Mutt was the tall one and Fisher named the short one after James J. Jeffries, the heavyweight boxer. The strip was highly successful, and there were seven New York musicals based on it. When the 1917 show *Mutt and Jeff Get Divorced* opened, the New York riot police squad was called in as 2,000 people fought for tickets. I believe the success of Mutt & Jeff and the many tall man/ short man comedy acts stem from the American duo of Weber (short and fat) and Fields (tall and thin), who began their long and successful career in the 1870s; see WHO WAS THAT LADY.

Mutual Friend, the. 1 p67. The unpopular Plunkett's nickname was an ironic twist on Dickens's *Our Mutual Friend*.

My beautiful bountiful Bertie. 93 p161. See BERTIE.

My bride, my wife, my life, O we will walk this world etc. 28 p105. T. *The Princess*, last eight lines before the Conclusion. "My wife, my life. O we will walk this world, Yoked in all exercise of noble end."

My brother Dan is an alderman with a grip on the Seventh Ward. 13 p256. I have not found this quotation. Perhaps from the 1895 US song 'Since My Brother Got A Job in Union Square' or from *Mr Dooley's Opinions* by Finley Dunne (1867–1936)?

My Country, 'tis of thee, Sweet land of liberty, (Of thee I sing). 53 p227. First two lines of 'America' (1831) by Samuel Smith (1808–95). Do not confuse with the 1931 political satire musical *Of Thee I Sing* by George & Ira Gershwin.

My cup runneth over. See CUP RUNNETH OVER.

My dear fellow, oh my dear fellow. 90 last line. See DEAR FELLOW.

My Heart and I. 26 p197. This is probably Hubbel's song in the 1920 show *Honours Are Even* since Richard Tauber's hit song was years later.

My heart belongs to Daddy. 72 p163; belongs to Daddi 79 p50. PGW couldn't resist the pun on the 14th-century painter and Cole Porter's 1938 song 'My Heart Belongs to Daddy'.

My heart stood still. 47 p93 and elsewhere; stood stiller 85 p96. 1927 song by Rodgers & Hart in *A Connecticut Yankee'*, popularised in the UK by Jessie Matthews. "I took one look at you, 'Twas all I had to do, And then my heart stood still." MTT Barry Day for pointing out that PGW had written "You simply made my heart stand still" in the song 'I Found You and You Found Me' in *Oh, Lady! Lady!!* in 1918.

My Heart's in the Highlands a-chasing the deer. 23 p214; 48 p10. Title of poem by Burns. The phrase was a popular one, and thirteen songs with this title were published between 1890 and 1920. One was written by Arthur Wimperis for *The Gay Gordons* (1907), for which PGW also wrote two lyrics.

My hero. 18 p135 and often later. While the phrase undoubtedly comes easily to the lips of women addressing the man they love, it achieved prominence with the heroine's hit song 'My Hero' in Oscar Strauss's successful *The Chocolate Soldier* (1908). The song was popular at amateur concerts for thirty years, allowing the lady concerned to sing at full volume, display tremendous emotion and finish off with a note like a steam whistle. See Muriel Kegley-Bassington's performance in *The Mating Season*.

My learned friend's manner would be intolerable in an emperor to a black-beetle. 18 p16. Although this has a very strong ring of G&S *The Mikado*, the comment was made by Lord Justice Coleridge (1820–94). He was quoting the remark made in court by a barrister named Maule about the superior attitude of the opposing counsel, a man named Cresswell. "My learned friend's manner would be intolerable in Almighty God to a black beetle." The phrase stuck in people's minds and was later used to describe Lord Curzon's mannner when addressing the House of Lords. (In his early stories, PGW avoided using the word 'God' since many magazines felt it offended their readers. See ENGLISHMAN'S SHORTEST PRAYER.)

My little chickadee. 59 p14; 93 p143. Endearment used by the hard-drinking, misogynistic American comedian W.C. FIELDS and the title of his 1940 film.

My Little Grey Home in the West. 21 p92 and later. As popular in the US as 'My Hero' was in the UK (see MY HERO), this 1911 song by Lohr and Eardley-Wilmot was the favourite among contraltos at amateur concerts for a very long time. See Chap. 36.

My love is like a glowing tulip that in an old world garden grows. 29 p87. 1896 song by William Forest.

My Love Parade. 51 p16. Song from the 1929 show *The Love Parade,* script by Guy Bolton. The film made the following year established him in Hollywood.

My Mother. Frequent in PGW. The poem by Anne (1782–1866) and Jane Taylor

(1783–1824) ran: "Who ran to help me when I fell, / And would some pretty story tell / Or kiss the place to make it well? / My mother." See also PUSSY.

'My son Joshuay'. See JOSHUA.

'My Sweetie Is A Wow'. 40 p60. 1917 song by Irving Berlin.

Mynn, Alfred. 3 p272. Famous cricketer (1807–61), first fast round-arm bowler.

Mysterious way, moving in a. See FATE/HE MOVES.

Mystery of the Hansom Cab, The. 96 p70. PGW was making the point about small local circulating libraries not bothering to keep up to date. Bertie Wooster, looking for some holiday reading, hesitated between *The Mystery of the Hansom Cab* and *BY ORDER OF THE CZAR* (1890). *The Mystery of the Hansom Cab* was a runaway 1886 best-seller by Fergus Hume (1858–1932). A syndicate bought his rights to it for £50 and set themselves up as the Hansom Cab Murder Company. They made a fortune.

N

(MTT = My thanks to)

Naboth and his vineyard. 85 p73. B. 1 Kings 21. A sad story. Naboth had a vineyard King Ahab wanted and Ahab's wife Jezebel secured it for him by having Naboth falsely accused of blasphemy. For her comeuppance, see JEZEBEL.

Naked without a penny has the actor become. 79 p72. Answer: Kean. Take away a penny ('d' before metrication came in) — you are left with Nake. Scramble the letters = Kean.

Name led all the rest, his. See ABOU BEN ADHEM.

Name of Englishman. Sullies the grand old name of Englishman 55 p279. See T. 'In Memoriam': "The grand old name of gentleman, / Defamed by every charlatan, / And soiled with all ignoble use."

Name will be mud. See MUD.

Nameless fear. A n.f. shot through me 52 last page and later. T. *Maud* Pt 2.6. "Back from the Breton coast, / Sick of a nameless fear."

Names. PGW took trouble over his names. Good honest heroes have good honest names — Bill, Joe or Mike. Dudes, Drones and those like them have names that end in y or ie — Freddie, Reggie, Bertie, Motty etc. Americans are immediately recognisable, to British readers anyway, by being called Ike, Spike, Mamie, Sadie (Sadie Rockmeteller features as early as 1908; see 10 p15), Messmore, Sigsbee and Dwight.

On titles, PGW was equally accurate and, in *Big Money*, makes the point that Lady Surname is merely the wife of a baronet or knight. An earl's daughter/sister is Lady First Name Surname. I was slightly shocked that Lord Emsworth's sister Dora in *Pigs Have Wings* (1952) is referred to twice as Lady Garland, not Lady Dora Garland. Maybe his editors got it wrong. Or maybe he absorbed the atmosphere of where he was living and slipped into local forms of speech, forgetting different terms were used on the other side of the Atlantic. Thus, the colour grey became gray (US spelling) in his later books. See also HIGHBALL and TITLES.

Napoleon. I found nearly 100 references to Napoleon (1769–1821) in PGW's books, and the sunken road at Waterloo which British troops used so effectively is mentioned three times (see SUNKEN ROAD). Napoleon had died sixty years before PGW was born, but the embedded memory of his domination of Europe, his threat to Britain, and his final defeat at Waterloo was very strong in Victorian England. To put it in context, bullies in England are still called 'little

Hitlers', and he died sixty years ago. See also Elba.

Napoleon of Crime. 50 p134. See Conan Doyle's 'Final Solution' and Moriarty.

Napoo. 26 p302; 27 p26 & 130. This emphatic negative was brought back by British soldiers from France after the First World War. *Il n'y en a plus* (there is no more).

Narcissus. 49 p88. This young man in Greek legend was so beautiful, he fell in love with his own reflection.

Nash, Ogden. 96 p5. Ogden Nash (1902–71) married a very rich Baltimore woman who felt Baltimore Society was the only thing that mattered and disapproved strongly of his work. He loved writing for the theatre, but she was so ashamed of this that he stopped. His verses, the more strained the better, were much admired by his fellow writers. One book on the period says: "In the 1930s and 1940s, ingenious word play was very highly regarded… . It was the ingenuity, the skill with words that was exemplified by Gilbert, Browning (*sic*) and Ogden Nash. The more contrived, the more stretched the rhyme, the funnier it was thought to be." Nash said his inspiration was the Sweet Singer of Michigan (see Chap. 37).

Natchez, young lady from. 70 p176. The full version of this Ogden Nash limerick is:

There was a young belle from old Natchez,
Whose garments were always in patchez.
When comment arose
On the state of her clothes,
She drawled, "Where Ah itchez, Ah scratchez!"

Nation, Carrie. 4 p69 and later. Mrs Nation (1846–1911) was a vigorous American advocate of temperance who believed in direct action against the Demon Drink. Six feet tall, she became famous for storming into bars and smashing the bottles with an axe. It is recorded that when she visited the bar run by John L. Sullivan, late heavyweight champion, he hid in the cellar.

National Liberal Club. Guest Night at 55 p241; 61 p13. I presume PGW specified the National Liberal because it was one of London's largest clubs. I mention it because, by happy coincidence, it was in the Savage Club, who lease rooms from the National Liberal Club, that The P G Wodehouse Society (UK) held their first meetings. These were as much "a perfect maelstrom of gaiety" as anything Bottleton East can produce.

National Sporting Club — 'NSC'. Frequent in PGW. See Chap. 4.

Native hue of resolution was sicklied o'er etc. etc. 48 p124 and later. See Enterprises.

Natives seemed friendly so I decided to stay the night, the. 28 p63 and later. I read this phrase often when looking through the memoirs of explorers and big-game hunters. See Chap. 22.

Nature abhors a vacuum. 29 p29. Appears in both Rabelais' *Gargantua*, chap. 5 (1534) and Spinoza's *Ethics* of 1677.

Nature, expelling. Expelling Nature with a pitchfork 18 p224; you may drive out Nature with a pitchfork but it will always return 43 p223. The latter quote is an accurate translation of Horace's *Epistles* 1.10.24: "Naturam expellas furca, tamen usque recurret."

Nature hath framed strange fellows in her time. 60 p64; 65 p104. S. *Merchant of Venice* 1.1.

Nature might stand up and say to all the world: This was a man. 44 p294. S. *Julius Caesar* 5.4.

Nature smiled. See ALL NATURE.

Nature's final word, Man is. 53 p148; 55 p187. Probably from Milton, but I have not found it.

Nature's sweet restorer, tired. 43 p51 and later. Not Shakespeare but the first line of 'Night Thoughts' by Edward Young (1683–1765). Why Jeeves should erroneously attribute it to Shakespeare, I do not know. Perhaps he was simply taking the easy way out and agreeing with the young master. See also NIGHT, SABLE.

Naval Treaty. If I had been a N.T. 56 p89; and later. See Conan DOYLE's 'The Naval Treaty'.

Navarre, white plumes of. 18 p43 and later. This refers to Henry IV of Navarre in Macaulay's poem 'Ivry': "Press where ye see my white plume shine, amidst the ranks of war, / And be your oriflamme to-day the helmet of Navarre."

Nay, dry the starting tear. 3 p167. MTT Neil Midkiff for pointing out this is from 'Etiquette' in Gilbert's *Bab Ballads*: "Down went the owners — greedy men whom hope of gain allured: Oh, dry the starting tear, for they were heavily insured."

Nay, Sire, a revolution. 12 p59; 34 p253. Rochefoucauld to Louis XVI when the news arrived of the storming of the Bastille (1789): "Is it a revolt?" "Nay, Sire, it is a revolution."

Nazimova. 30 p115; 71 p143. Russian-born film actress Alla Nazimova (1879–1945) was well-known for her irregular private life.

Ne quid nimis. 73 p46. Do not take things to excess. From Terence (190–159 B.C.).

Ne sutor ultra whatever it is. 43 p44. Ne sutor ultra crepidam judicaret. Latin proverb. Lit: Let the cobbler not judge on matters beyond his own shoe, i.e. people should restrain from criticising/ interfering in things not of their concern.

Near thing. A very n. t. 73 p113. See WATERLOO, BATTLE OF.

Nebuchadnezzar. In search of better pasture, with the air of a N. 58 p223; she was a female N. (Veronica Wedge with a rose in her mouth) 65 p139; and elsewhere. One of the Biblical references PGW and his fellows remembered from Sunday School was that Nebuchadnezzar ate grass. B. Daniel 4.33: "and he was driven from men, and did eat grass as an oxen."

Need is greater than mine, Thy. See SIDNEY, SIR PHILIP.

Neither a borrower nor a lender be. 83 p199. See POLONIUS'S SPEECH (2).

Nell. Means to do right by our Nell 42 p45; 68 p27; 88 p255. Possibly from Victorian melodrama involving a wicked Sir Jasper (see TODD, SIR JASPER). But more likely from the well-known remark attributed to Charles II (1630–85), who, on his deathbed, urged his brother to look after Nell Gwynne. The usual version is: "Let not poor Nelly starve."

Nellie, the Beautiful Cloak Model. 15 p247;15A p142. This New York play by Owen Davis opened in December 1906 and ran for years.

Nelson touch, the. 90 p63. A phrase still in use, commemorating Nelson's bold and unorthodox tactics in sea battles.

Nemesis. 3 p23 and later, especially 59 p89, when Constable Oates is riding his bicycle no hands. In Greek and Latin mythology, hubris (overweening pride/conceit) was always overtaken by Nemesis, a fierce deity intent on punishing evil deeds or people who get above themselves. See FATE SNEAKS UP.

Nemo me impune lacessit. 7 p86. Motto of the Most Ancient and Most Noble Order of the Thistle: No one hurts me with impunity.

Neo-Vorticist. 49 p48; 70 p27. The adherents to this movement sought to 'purify' the ideals of Percy Wyndham-Lewis (1882–1957). In 1908 he returned from a stay in Europe and, with a reputation as a daring artistic genius, made himself leader of the Vorticists, British counterparts of the Cubists and Futurists on the Continent. His Vorticist magazine *Blast* caused a stir, and Lewis was a social lion till 1914, when the World War made such things unimportant. An art critic has pointed out that the UK received infusions of artistic and avant-garde ideas from the Continent on an annual basis between 1890 and 1914. For their general reception in Britain, see Chap. 18 (1910).

On a technical note, the Vorticist school of painting was based on Cubism and Futurism, which followed the rhythm and forms of the machine. I am informed that Vorticism has "flat geometric lines and arcs radiating from one salient point, the vortex, giving the effect of rotary and often vertiginous motion".

Nervii. The day I overcame the Nervii 43 p172; 52 p126; 67 p97; Intro to *A Century of Humour*. PGW probably read this in the original (Caesar's *Gallic Wars* 2.15) before he read it in Shakespeare's *Julius Caesar* 3.2. I know I did.

Never give a sucker an even break. See SUCKER.

Never had it so good. 84 p164. On 20 July 1957, Harold Macmillan (1894–1986), British Prime Minister, made a speech in which he said that Britain "had never had it so good" but went on to query how long this would last. His fears for the future are now forgotten. His political opponents made sure that "never had it so good" is still quoted as a term of derision.

Never let your angry passions rise. See PASSIONS.

Never shake thy gory locks at me. 96 p95. S. *Macbeth* 3.4: "Thou canst not say I did it; never shake Thy gory locks at me."

Nevermore (quoth the Raven). See RAVEN.

New Arabian Night adventure. 9 p61. R.L. Stevenson wrote *The New Arabian Nights* in 1876. They comprised a series of adventure stories set in contemporary

London with 'Prince Florizel' playing a leading part. See also PRINCE FLORIZEL.

New Asiatic Bank; London and Oriental Bank; etc. This institution appears in eight books from *Psmith in the City* onwards and is clearly based on the Hong Kong and Shanghai Bank, 31 Lombard Street, where Wodehouse worked from September 1900 to September 1902. He described it accurately in *Psmith in the City* as a training ground for young men before they were appointed to branches in the Far East. It had a thriving Rugger team, of which the Bank was kind enough years ago to send me a photograph, with Wodehouse in the front row. As Mike Jackson (and Wodehouse) discovered, most of the young men were also public schoolboys starting their careers. PGW remembered it kindly and kept an account there for the rest of his life. See also Wyatt in Chap. 3 and Mr Bickersdyke in Chap. 21.

'The New Asiatic Bank'
(Hong Kong & Shanghai Bank)

Since no photographs exist of the Lombard Street building in which Wodehouse worked, HSBC have been kind enough to provide this picture of its successor in Gracechurch Street, opened in 1913.

(Courtesy of HSBC Group Archives)

New Deal. See DEAL and ROOSEVELT, F.D.

New planet had swum into his ken, as if a. 60 p199. Keats' 'On First Looking into Chapman's Homer': "Then felt I like some watcher of the skies / When a new planet swims into his ken; / Or like stout Cortez when with eagle eyes / He star'd at the Pacific — and all his men / Look'd at each other with a wild surmise — Silent, upon a peak in Darien."

New York police force ... known as the Finest. 87 p18 and elsewhere. 'New York's Finest', the term commonly used to describe the New York Police, goes back to 1874. For information, 'New York's Bravest', the term for the firemen, began around 1900, while 'New York's Strongest', the Sanitation Department (dustmen), is a more recent coinage.

Newgate Calendar. 14 p5. A popular publication, describing murders, crimes and villains published c.1700–c.1850. It took its name from the Newgate Prison in London; its modern counterparts are publications like *True Crime Stories* etc.

News of the World. 62 p100. This British Sunday newpaper still leads in unearthing sexual and criminal scandals.

Nibs. His Nibs 7 p143 and later. Cockney slang 1820 onwards for any superior person. "He's a proper Nib" etc. See also BEAK.

Nice bit of box fruit. See BOX FRUIT.

Nice girl but she had no conversation, She was a. See CONVERSATION.

Nickels, wooden. See WOODEN NICKELS.

Nicklaus, Jack. 88 p64. This superb golfer (b. 1940) delayed his retirement till 2005 so he could finish by playing in the Open at St. Andrew's.

Nicknames. See Chap. 30.

Nietzsche. Fundamentally unsound 35 p33 and later. The German philosopher Friedrich Nietzsche (1844–1900) called for a new race of supermen to replace outworn Christianity. Hitler admired him. 'Nuff said.

Night (had a thousand eyes). Nanny Byles, like the night, had a thousand eyes 69 p25. Francis Bourdillon's poem 'Light': "The night has a thousand eyes, / And the heart but one."

Night, sable goddess from her ebon throne ... 48 p179. Poem 'Night Thoughts' by Edward Young (1683–1765): "Night, sable goddess! From her ebon throne, In rayless majesty, now stretches forth Her leaden sceptre o'er a slumbering world."

Night that covers me. Out of the night that covers me, black as the pit from pole to pole 37 p190 and later. W.E. Henley's poem 'Invictus'.

Nightingale. A nightingale sang, conscious of a rave notice from the poet Keats and a star spot in a BBC programme 73 p107. Keats' 'Ode to a Nightingale' is well-known but the second reference needs some explanation. In 1924 the BBC did a live broadcast from a wood in Surrey. Miss Beatrice Harrison had found that if she played her cello in the wood at night, a nightingale would come and sing to the music. The BBC set up their equipment, Miss Harrison began to play, and the nightingale duly turned up and joined in. The broadcast was a sensation.

Nihil humanum alienum. 15 p10. From Terence (190–159 B.C.). Roughly — I am interested in whatever people do.

Nijinsky. 49 p302 and later up to 94 p104. This dancer (1890–1950) revolutionised ballet with his extraordinary athleticism. When asked how he stayed in the air so long, he replied that he just jumped as high as he could and hung around for a while.

Nikias. 8 p20. An unlucky general who led the Greek fleet against the Sicilians in 414 B.C. and was executed for his inefficiency a year later. See your Thucydides for a contemporary account.

Nil Admirari. 40 p148; 60 p290. From Horace's *Epistles* 1.6.1. Literally, let nothing surprise you. Keep cool, don't get excited.

Nimshi the son of Bimshi. 49 p285. Nimshi will be found at B. 1 Kings 19.16: "Jehu the son of Nimshi"; and 2 Kings 9.2: "Jehu the son of Jehoshaphat the son of Nimshi …" I have not found Bimshi.

Ninety-Seven Soups, Waddington's. See WADDINGTON'S.

Nineveh and Tyre, gone with. Frequent up to 97 p90. A general comment on past glories now gone for ever, like the Pelican Club, Romano's and the Empire Theatre in Leicester Square. See KIPLING's 'Recessional': "Lo, all our pomp of yesterday / Is one with Nineveh and Tyre." These once-great cities had fallen into ruins by the second century B.C.

Niobe mourning for the loss of her children. 34 p292 and later. See MOURNED LIKE NIOBE.

Niven, David. His moustache is very becoming 76 p15; 82 p31. Perhaps PGW had Jeeves say so because Niven (1910–83) had played Bertie Wooster in the 1936 film *Thank You, Jeeves*.

No home should be without one. 94 p73. This phrase is still to be seen advertising every form of household equipment, but its origins go back to 1900 or earlier. I have a strong recollection of seeing it in early *Strand* magazines. The Bissell carpet sweeper? A vacuum cleaner? A refrigerator?

No human being has done this horrid thing. 3 p208. I have been informed by many people that this is from Conan DOYLE's *The Sign of Four*, chap. 6: "a child has done this horrid thing".

No love where there is not perfect trust, There can be. 64 p46. The nearest source I can find for this aphorism is the hymn 'O Perfect Love'. The first line is "O perfect love, all human thought transcending". The second verse finishes: "With childlike trust that fears nor pain nor death."

No Man's Land. 25 p206. The term came into use in the First World War for the piece of land separating the trenches of the opposing armies, sometimes only a hundred yards apart. It was strewn with mines and booby-traps, and any movement seen in No Man's Land led to artillery and machine-guns opening fire.

No more worlds to conquer. See ALEXANDER.

No Nudes Is Good Nudes. This title for *A Pelican at Blandings* is PGW's American publisher's twist on the wartime phrase used by relatives of servicemen. "No news is good news" meant a soldier had not been killed, wounded or captured, since any of these events would have led to the dreaded official telegram arriving to inform his next of kin.

No others need apply. 1 p115; 37 p252 and elsewhere. A notice commonly seen in the UK, 1890–1939, outside factories and offices when a job vacancy had been filled.

No place like home, what? 23 p249. From the song HOME, SWEET HOME.

No taxation without representation. 46 p83. A popular phrase in America around 1775, coined by James Otis (1725–83).

No vice in X. See VICE IN SPILLER.

No wedding bells for —. For her 18 p242; for Plummer 25 p156; for him, 33 short story title; and later. The song 'No Wedding Bells for Him' was in the London show *The Girl Who Took the Wrong Turning or No Wedding Bells for Him* (1906), put on by the Melville Brothers at the Lyceum. E.P. Moran and Will Heelan made the song 'No Wedding Bells for Me' popular across America.

Noble mind. What a n. m. is here o'erthrown 78 p188 and later. S. *Hamlet* 3.1.

Noblesse oblige. 14 p147 and later; 55 short story title. *Maxims and Reflections* (1808) by Gaston, Duc de Levis: "Nobility has its obligations."

Nod which, like Lord Burleigh's, spoke volumes. 86 p119. See BURLEIGH.

Nolle prosequi. 52 p165 and later. Latin tag; to be unwilling to do something. 'Nolo' is Latin for 'I am not willing'; 'volo' means 'I am willing'.

None but the brave deserve the fair. PGW ref lost. From either John Dryden's poem 'Alexander's Feast' and/or G&S *Iolanthe* Act 2. MTT Jim Linwood.

None like her. There is none like her, none 36 p163; and later. T. *Maud* Chap 18: "I have led her home, my love, my only friend, / There is none like her, none."

Nordstrom, Minna. 53 p266. Presumably this is PGW's comment on the way fashions for names changed in Hollywood. The name Minna Nordstrom reflected the ballyhoo of Greta Garbo's sensational success the same year. See Chap. 28.

Norman blood. Simple faith is more than Norman blood 7 p123 and often later. T. 'Lady Clara Vere de Vere': "Kind hearts are more than coronets, and simple faith more than Norman blood."

North Atlantic. 70 p187. Purportedly based on a German treatise on the measurement of time and written by Rodgers and Hammerstein, this sounds very similar to their 1949 hit show *South Pacific* mentioned at page 227.

Norworth Court. 16 p100. See Chap. 16.

Nose, got it up his. 23 p58. Bertie was likening Lord Pershore's living it up in New York to the experience of most people when they first drink champagne — the bubbles go up your nose.

Noses. Things for altering the shape of noses 21 p154, 58 p288. *The Strand* magazine advertised these for at least thirty years. Page 68 of the February 1906 edition has C. Lees Ray of 10E Central Chambers, Liverpool, stating that he purveys: "The only patent Nose Machines in the world. Improves ugly noses of all kinds. Scientific yet simple. Can be worn during sleep." He would also "remedy ugly outstanding ears with my Rubber Ear Caps. Hundreds of successful cases. 7/6d post free". By 1926 he had done well enough to proclaim that his office was no longer in Liverpool but at "Criterion Buildings, Piccadilly Circus, London".

Nosey Parker. 19 p132 and often later. Someone who sticks his nose into other people's business. The term goes back over 400 years to Matthew Parker (1504–75), Archbishop of Canterbury appointed in the reign of Elizabeth I. In the previous twenty-five years, the church in England had been Catholic, Protestant, Catholic and Protestant again, and Parker wanted to ensure that clergymen were observing the latest change. His searching investigations into their lives led to the nickname Nosey Parker.

Not an end but a beginning (as they say in the stories). 56 p30; 63 p137. Possibly Winston Churchill's speech of 10 November 1942: "This is not the end. It is not even the beginning of the end. But it is, perhaps, the end of the beginning." Or from S. *Midsummer Night's Dream* 5.1. "That is the true beginning of our end."

Not as other men. 3 p42. B. Luke 18.11: "God, I thank thee that I am not as other men are."

Not in mortals to command success. 82 p117. Addison's *Cato* 1.2.

Not Really a Coward. 7 p106. A typical title for a boy's school story from 1880 onwards. Unfortunately, the copyright libraries do not keep as many juvenile books as they should, and there is nothing by this name in the British Library.

Not Really a Duffer. 12 p 226. This title is not in the British Library catalogue. A possible origin is *The Duffer* (1906) by Warren Bell, editor of *The Captain*. PGW paying a compliment to the man who had first taken his school stories perhaps?

Not so but far otherwise (like the mariner of infinite resource and sagacity). 3 p133; 12 p197. See RESOURCE AND SAGACITY.

Not so deep as a well, nor so wide as a church door. See 'TIS NOT SO DEEP AS A WELL.

Not that which goeth into the mouth defileth a man. 90 p92–93. B. Matthew 15.11. The verse continues: "but that which cometh out of the mouth, this defileth a man."

Not the heat, but the humidity. 36 p1; 84 p124–5. This cliché apparently began in New York and was said in a play in 1906.

Note, make a. When found, make a note of. 31 p106. Axiom of Captain Cuttle in D. *Dombey & Son*.

Nothing, airy. 72 p27. See AIRY NOTHING.

Nothing but the game/ shark/ aunt/ butler. See GAME.

Nothing here for tears, nothing to wail or knock the breast. 76 p51. Milton's *Samson Agonistes*. "Nothing is here for tears, nothing to wail / Or knock the breast; no weakness, no contempt."

Nothing like a dame. See THERE IS NOTHING.

Novel of the middle west, hero of (a gloomy lot). 37 p89. Did PGW have the novels of Willa Cather or Sinclair Lewis in mind?

Now fades the glimmering landscape. See ALL THE AIR.

Now is the time for all good men to come to the aid of the party. 4 p 273 and later. Cicero coined a political slogan very like this, but the current usage comes from Charles Weller, a court reporter who was asked by his friend, the inventor Charles Scholes (1816–67), to try out Scholes' new typewriter in 1867. Weller picked out the sentence used in typing lessons for decades afterwards.

Now is the winter of my discontent made glorious summer by this J.B. Butterwick. 94 p84. See WINTER OF MY DISCONTENT.

Now slept the crimson petal and the white. 50 p236; 67 p120 and later. T. *The Princess* Intro: "Now sleeps the crimon petal, now the white." Set to music by Roger Quilter in 1904, it became popular with young men who wanted to hint delicately at their feelings for a young lady, often the one who played the accompaniment on the piano for them, blushing prettily the while.

Nuisance must now cease, This. 31 p196 and elsewhere. As more and more people moved into cities in the 19th century, many local by-laws were introduced to cope with urban crowding. Wisely, the legislators left certain matters undefined under the general heading of 'nuisance'. This could be making too much noise or failing to abate a smoky chimney, i.e. not having it swept which meant your neighbours would find their houses filled with soot. Council officials would come along and, if appropriate, a Nuisance Abatement Order would be issued stating that the particular nuisance 'must now cease'.

Number three omnibus. 33 p154. This was a London bus PGW knew well. In addition to nearly running over Mr Grindlay in 'No Wedding Bells for Him' (see NO WEDDING BELLS), it was the bus used by Kay Derrick in *Sam the Sudden* to travel from Central London to Valley Fields. The No. 3 bus still stops at the corner of Croxted Road, Dulwich, a few yards from where PGW lived. See Chap. 9.

Number Five, Wooster. 82 p156. PGW twist on Chanel No. 5. See CHANEL.

Numbness seemed to be paining his senses. 65 p12. Keats' 'Ode to a Nightingale': "My heart aches, and a drowsy numbness pains My sense."

Nunc dimittis. 13 p245. A general dismissal: "Lord, now lettest thou thy servant depart in peace; according to thy word." BCP. Evening Prayer & B. Luke 2.29.

Nuts in May. 56 p188. Corruption of an ancient nursery rhyme: "Here we go gathering knots in May", i.e. posies of flowers. But also a song by PGW in *The Golden Moth* (1921).

Nymph in 'L'Allegro'(bringing with him quips and cranks and wreathed smiles), like the. 78 p133. Twelve pages after giving us a twist on Milton's 'LYCIDAS', PGW is quoting from Milton's 'L'Allegro': "Haste thee Nymph, and bring with thee, Jest and youthful jollity, Quips and cranks and wanton wiles, Nods and becks, and wreathed smiles."

Nymph surprised while bathing. See SURPRISED WHILE BATHING.

O

(MTT = My thanks to)

O for the wings of a dove. See WINGS OF A DOVE.

O Perfect Love. 50 p69 and often later. This hymn was so popular at weddings that PGW was able to use the one as a synonym for the other. It was written by Mrs Dorothy Gurney in 1883.

Oaths, full of strange. 12 p70 and 59 p184. See BEARDED LIKE A PARD.

OBEs want watching too. 49 p2. I have been asked about OBEs so often by American Wodehouseans that I felt an explanation was required. I apologise for its length.

While awards for bravery in battle are common to all nations, the Orders of Chivalry in Britain are usually civil awards given for service to the nation. Some are of great antiquity (Order of the Garter) and some are now defunct. While their value in the scheme of things is debatable, it is arguable that if a man has spent years working without reward for a political party, giving him an MBE is better than rewarding him with a job as a judge or ambassador, for which his only qualification is his political allegiance.

The newest Order is the Order of the British Empire (1917), created when the First World War made the government of the time realise a more flexible form of awarding honours was needed. The Order of the Bath (1725) and Order of St Michael and St George (1818) only had the grades of Knights Grand Cross, Knight Commander and Companion. These were all awards for 'senior' people — senior diplomats, generals, admirals and the like. The Order of the British Empire was deliberately structured to reward people far further down the chain. Unfortunately, because the Order was introduced by then Prime Minister Lloyd George (see PEERAGES), it was, for some time, regarded with some suspicion and even derision, as in PGW's usage.

For convenience of recognition, I shall use military examples, with civilian equivalents when I can. If you were a corporal or sergeant who had leapt into a river to save a drowning child or were a postman who had never missed a day's duty in forty years and kept an eye on the well-being of the old ladies along your route, then you would receive the BEM (British Empire Medal). If you were a senior sergeant major who had trained young officers at Sandhurst for ten years, a captain or major who had coped with some emergency (flooding, a plane crash), or a junior civil servant whose expertise in some field had been invaluable, you were made an MBE (Member of the Order of the British

Empire).

Next up is the OBE (Officer of the Order). This was given to majors/lieutenant colonels whose jobs as planners or logisticians made them ineligible for gallantry awards but without whom the success of an operation would have been impossible. A civil equivalent would be a senior police officer who said he would reduce crime in his area — and did so. The OBEs PGW satirised were the financiers who had provided some service, albeit a minor one, to the government in office.

Next is the CBE (Commander of the Order). This was awarded to one-star/two-star generals who had performed well in an operation or crisis, to scientists who made some medical discovery or to government civil servants who had served their country loyally but would not be promoted any further. It used to be said in the Army that a CBE was the kiss of death — it was a consolation prize for not making three stars. (Sir Watkyn Bassett was a CBE, which was the appropriate award for a senior stipendiary magistrate.)

Next up is the KBE (Knight of the Order), which meant you were now known as 'Sir John Smith'. Awarded to three/four-star generals, senior civil servants and leading manufacturers (Bill Gates would have qualified over here) and fund-raising entertainers like Bob Geldof. A lady becomes a Dame of the Order (DBE).

The top rank, GBE (Knight Grand Cross of the Order), was awarded to people like the Chief of the General Staff (head of the British Army) and Permanent Under Secretaries of State (the permanent civil servant head of a Government department).

PGW's father was created CMG (Commander of the Most Distinguished Order of St Michael and St George) for his services as an official in Hong Kong. It gave him immediate status when he retired back to Britain. It was not a knighthood, but very near it, an honour usually awarded to Foreign Office and Diplomatic Service officials. I should repeat here the Whitehall joke I heard often and which was recounted in that superb TV series *Yes, Minister*. Speaking of the eagerness of civil servants to receive such an honour, a secretary tells his Minister how much it means to Foreign Office officials. Rather than transcribe the entire speech (copyright!), I will give the gist.

"What's this CMG?"

"That stands for Call Me God. The next one up is KCMG. That means Kindly Call Me God."

"Oh, I see. What's the top one? GCMG?"

"Yes. That stands for God Calls Me God!"

Obiter dicts. 64 p233. Clearly a misprint/ typo. 'Obiter dicta' is the term used in England for legal remarks made by a judge which are not critical to the case. They are supplementary comments of legal interest but not judicially binding. See 66 p187 for the correct singular form — obiter dictum.

O'Brien, Philadelphia Jack. 58 p239. World light-heavyweight champion

(1878–1942), retired 1912. See also Chap 4.

Occasions, lawful. See LAWFUL OCCASIONS.

Octopus of Crime. 88 p37. A 1934 thriller by Brant House.

Oddenino's (also called Oddy's). 18 p221 and later. A London restaurant. The check girl who put descriptions of customers in their hats is at 91 p122. See Chap. 18 (the Savoy Scandal).

Oddfellows' Hall. 25 p8. The Oddfellows (Odd Fellows in USA) are a British fraternal society akin to the Elks and Shriners in the USA.

Ode to the College. 3 p222. See Chap. 3.

Ode to Tobacco. 42 p68. By C.S. CALVERLEY.

Odo, Bishop. 49 p303. Half-brother of William the Conqueror, this cleric (1036–97) fought at Hastings in 1066. See Chap. 11.

Of course. She is, of course, the sister-in-law of the Duchess of Peebles 43 p 61; see also chap. 2 of *Hot Water*. The phrase 'of course' was — and still is — a cliché among gossip columnists from about 1920 onwards. It made the readers feel that, like the writer, they were 'in Society' and would, of course, already be well aware of this snippet of smart gossip. With 'as worn', 'atmosphere of utmost cordiality' (see CORDIALITY) and countless others, it is another example of PGW's skill at recognizing clichés and jargon of the day and making fun of them. Many I recognised because they were the clichés of my day, too; others I found only when I read the newspapers and magazines of the 1890s and 1920s that he was parodying. The more over-used clichés became, the sooner they went out of use, which is why some need explanation today. See also AMONG THOSE PRESENT and STRIKES A NEW NOTE.

Offence was rank and smelled to Heaven, as Hamlet would have put it. 84 p65. S. *Hamlet* 3.3.

Office, given me the. See GIVEN ME.

Officer and a gentleman, like an. 46 p253; 52 p98; like a Widgeon and a gentleman 83 p84. As well as being subject to the normal criminal law of Britain, the British Army has its own penal code, set out in the Army Act. One section covered the offence of 'conduct unbecoming an officer and a gentleman'. This may seem anachronistic, but it was eminently sensible. If, for example, an officer gets drunk at an international gathering and gooses an ambassador's wife, there should be some sanction. He has done nothing actually criminal, but his action is clearly reprehensible.

Because so many men served in the Armed Forces, extracts from the Act like this came into everyday use. In 1994 Parliament deleted the words 'and a gentleman' as 'old-fashioned' and 'inappropriate'. A commentator pointed out that they had thereby expunged the word 'gentleman' from any aspect of English law, a term still accepted and respected around the world but not, apparently, in its own country. The same commentator pointed out that, despite what egalitarian politicians would have us believe, everybody in Britain knew how a gentleman should behave, but few knew how an officer should behave.

See also ALARM AND DESPONDENCY.

Often a bridesmaid, but never a bride. 70 p132. US 1923 advert for Listerine mouthwash. In the UK there was a music hall song made popular by Lily Morris c.1910–40: "Always the blushing bridesmaid, Never the blooming bride." See also LISTERINE.

OGPU. 59 p222. Initials of the Russian secret police before they became the NKVD.

Oh, ever thus from childhood's hour I've seen my fondest hopes decay. See HOPES, FONDEST.

Oh God! Oh, Montreal. 79 p8. This once popular artistic expression of disgust at Philistinism comes from Samuel Butler's 'A Psalm of Montreal'. Butler (1835–1902) was expressing the outrage he and many others felt when the news came out that the authorities in Montreal had put a copy of the DISCOBOLUS statue in a storeroom because they didn't like it.

Oh, God, put back Thy universe and give me yesterday. 78 p158. A line from the 1882 melodrama *The Silver King* by Arthur Jones, made famous by the actor Wilson Barrett (1846–1904).

Oh, happy day. 31 p61. Hymn by Doddridge and Rimbault which swept America in 1891.

Oh, Kay! See Chap. 24.

Oh, Lady! Lady!! As PGW tells us in *Bring on the Girls* (p83), the phrase was one Bert WILLIAMS had made popular.

Oh, let the solid ground Not fail beneath my feet etc. etc. See GROUND, SOLID.

Oh, Mr Porter, what shall I do? 78 p189. Favourite song of Marie Lloyd (1870–1927), 'queen of the music hall'.

Oh, say can you see by dawn's early light. 36 p106 and later. See STAR SPANGLED BANNER.

Oh, What a Beautiful Morning! 83 p82. Rousing song from Rodgers & Hammerstein's *Oklahoma* (1943).

Oh you boss! (Peggy/kid). 13 p108; 18 p262 and elsewhere. See next entry.

Oh you kid/ Oh you boss. 15A p101 and later. 'Oh, you kid' was a term of endearment in America from about 1890 to the 1960s. It never caught on in the UK, though three songs with this title were published over here in 1908, 1913 and 1914.

Oil, boiling. See BOILING OIL.

Oklahoma! 70 p227; 83 p83. The Rodgers & Hammerstein hit show (1943).

Ol' Man River. 41 p51 and frequent later. The 1927 show *Show Boat* gave an entirely new form to the American musical. It sounded the death-knell of the musical comedies of the previous fifty years, which Bolton and Wodehouse and Kern had revolutionised with the Princess shows. I think PGW realised this. *Show Boat* was so revolutionary that the London *Times* critic was not sure how to describe it. Among other comments, he wrote: "Mr Paul Robeson's song about the 'old river' is one of the two hits of the show … a rather heavyweight entertainment."

Old Adam. See ADAM.

Old bean. Often. To my surprise, my dictionaries say this term was in general use in America in the 1920s. It then came to the UK and an American dictionary of 1994 states that "it is now regarded as an affected Britishism". See also CRUMPET and EGG.

Old Brigade lent a hand, the. 51 p79. See BOYS OF THE OLD BRIGADE.

Old crumpet. See CRUMPET.

Old Faithful, the geyser. 50 p163; 80 p116 and elsewhere. So called because it erupts regularly every sixty-five minutes in Yellowstone National Park.

Old Folk. Is the old folk at home? 80 p75. Stephen Foster's 1851 song 'Old Folks At Home'.

Old Guard. Had made their charge up the hill 24 p247; dies but does not surrender 50 p50. Napoleon's final desperate tactic at Waterloo was to send his Old Guard, his crack infantry, up the hill in an attempt to break the British position. It failed. In the British advance afterwards, when the Old Guard were surrounded, they made the defiant remark about dying but never surrendering.

Old King Cole. 42 p256. English nursery rhyme: "Old King Cole was a merry old soul, And a merry old soul was he." I shall not enter into the argument as to whether he was or was not based on Coel, a third-century king of East Anglia.

Old Monkey Brand. See MONKEY BRAND.

Old Oaken Bucket, The. 22 p114; 23 p59. For over a century, this 1826 song by Samuel Woodworth epitomised Americans yearning for the simple life. The opening words are: "How dear to my heart are the scenes of my childhood."

Old order. The o.o. is in the habit of changing and yielding place to the new 3 p195; 8 p152. T. 'The Passing of Arthur': "The old order changeth, yielding place to new."

Old Reliable, The. MTT Hilary Bruce for demonstrating that 'The Old Reliable' seems to have been a common phrase in America in the 1930s. A 1936 photograph of a building in Birmingham, Alabama, shows the proprietor was:

F.M. Pointer
The Old Reliable
House Mover

One likely origin is that the phrase was used to advertise the 10th edition of *Bartlett's Familiar Quotations*, which came out in 1919. PGW had a high opinion of Bartlett; see pp39–41 of *Over Seventy*. MTT Charles Gould, who gets in on the act by pointing out that 'Old Reliable' was the soubriquet of the famous NY Yankees right-fielder Tommy Heinrich, who was given the name by radio announcer Mel Allen c. 1949.

Ollendorf. 1 p254; 2 p128. The school textbooks of Heinrich Ollendorff (1803–65) seem to have been the first to teach French or German through normal conversation. Before that, schoolchildren were drilled in vocabulary, grammar and syntax but never used 'real' (i.e. conversational) French or German at all.

***Olympic*, S.S.** 30 p85. See Chap. 17.

Omar Khayyam. 9 p207 and often later. See also PGW's lyric for *Sitting Pretty* at 74 p171. Omar Khayyam was a Persian astronomer and poet (1050–1123). But it is now thought that his epic poem, translated by Edward Fitzgerald in 1859, was very largely Fitzgerald's ideas of what Khayyam should have written. For some reason, *The Rubáiyát of Omar Khayyam* became a craze in America in 1910 and was the one volume, apart from the Bible, you could be sure of seeing in every middle-class American home.

Omar the Tentmaker. Tweed suit which might have been built by 56 p205; 79 p177; 90 p8. If you take a very large size in suits or they are too baggy, PGW says they were made by Omar the Tentmaker. He was clearly repeating a contemporary joke, but it took me years to find out what it was, and then only by chance. Flipping through the pages of an 1890s novel in a bookshop in Guildford, I came across an advert for what was claimed to be a best-seller of the time: *Omar the Tentmaker*. Completely forgotten today, like *BY ORDER OF THE CZAR*, it was hugely popular in its time. Because of the phenomenal success of Fitzgerald's *Rubáiyát of Omar Khayyam* (see entry above), other writers decided to cash in. When it became known that Omar was the son of a tentmaker and that the word 'Khayyam' means 'tentmaker', Nathan Haskell Dole (1852–1935) saw his chance. His book *Omar the Tentmaker* (1899) was a successful romantic novel describing how the humble tentmaker became a famous poet etc. etc. PGW could equally well have picked up the phrase from the New York dramatisation of 1914, which he may have reviewed for *Vanity Fair*, or from the 1922 film starring Wallace Beery.

Omitting no detail, however slight. 58 p297 and frequent elsewhere. Another of those lines that Conan Doyle should have written but didn't. It may have appeared in the play *Sherlock Holmes* written by William Gillette or maybe Wodehouse simply coined it himself in imitation of Holmes's distinctive turns of phrase.

Omphale. Spun wool for O. 24 p75. Omphale was queen of Lydia, and Hercules took time off from his twelve labours to settle down to domestic life and spin wool for her for a time.

On no petition / Is extradition / Allowed in Callao. 4 p80. I chased this quotation for over ten years; it was not until 2006 that I found the answer in an exchange on the Internet. I have no idea who 'Anonymous' is, but my thanks to him or her for the information that Robert Louis Stevenson's *The Wrecker* (1892) has: "On no condition is extradition Allowed in Callao." 'Anonymous' adds that W.B. Churchward's *Blackbirding in the South Pacific* (1888) has: "I did not know then the Callao hymn, of which the chorus is — 'On no condition is extradition allowed in Callao'." It is more than probable that PGW read the Stevenson book, but Callao's reputation was clearly well known. Hence Sir Jasper Addleton's wish to retire there in 'The Smile That Wins'.

On to all his curves. 13 p43 & p149 and later. See CURVES.

Once a footballer, always a potential footballer, even unto the grave. 22 p147.

PGW twist on "Once a gentleman, always a gentleman". D. *Little Dorrit*, chap 28, though some authorities attribute it to a comment made at the trial of Horne Tooke in 1794: "Once a clergyman, always a clergyman."

Once more into the breach. See BREACH.

Once seen, never forgotten. 94 p133. Probably from Scott's *Count Robert of Paris* (1832): "It was probably this creature, seldom seen, but when once seen never forgotten, which occasioned the ancient belief in the god Pan..."

Once you're kissed by Amy, tear up the list, it's Amy. 77 p167. From 'Once in Love with Amy', a song by Frank Loesser in the show *Where's Charley?* (1948).

One born every minute, There's. 23 p129; 44 p34. See BARNUM.

One crowded hour/second. See CROWDED HOUR.

One damned thing after another. See LIFE HAD BEEN.

One for all and all for one at Harrige's, It's. 73 p31. 'One for all and all for one' was the motto of Dumas' THREE MUSKETEERS.

One last long lingering look behind. 32 p105 and later. Gray's 'Elegy in a Country Churchyard' l.88: "Nor cast one longing ling'ring look behind."

One man's meat is another man's poison (and several variations)**.** 27 p227 and later. From the Latin proverb: Quod cibus est aliis, aliis est atre venenum. (What is food for some is black poison to others.)

One touch of nature makes the whole world kin. 'One Touch of Nature', short story title in 22; 70 p56; 95 p26. S. *Troilus and Cressida* 3.3.

One-armed paper-hanger with hives. 63 p70; 67 p156; 80 p63 and later. The origin of this phrase is usually attributed to O. Henry's short story 'The Ethics of Pig'. As is only to be expected, Mr 'Believe It Or Not' Ripley announced in 1942 that there was an Albert J.Smith of Dedham, Mass., who not only was a one-armed paper-hanger but also suffered from hives.

O'Neill, Eugene. 46 p116. "'That's all right about Eugene O'Neill,' said Shakespeare. 'These Yanks will do anything.'" An American playwright, O'Neill (1888–1953), wrote realistic, thought-provoking plays.

Only does it to annoy. 5 p38; 87 p24. 92 p125 has the full version from *Alice in Wonderland*, chap. 6:

> Speak roughly to your little boy
> And beat him when he sneezes;
> He only does it to annoy
> Because he knows it teases.

Only God can make a tree. 50 p54; 57 p172 and later. Joyce Kilmer (1888–1918) wrote the poem 'Trees' in 1913. In 1922 Oscar Rasbach set it to music and the song, beloved by tenors, swept the country. One authority says Kilmer was inspired to write it by the trees along Ryder's Lane, Route 1, New Brunswick, New Jersey. Another claims it was inspired by the ancient white oak in the grounds of Rutgers University, New Brunswick.

Onwards and upwards with the arts. 83 p113. A column with this title in *The*

New Yorker appeared regularly from 1927, and many famous writers contributed to it, including Garrison Keiller in 1975. MTT Charles Gould.

Oofy. Oofy Prosser is one of those clever PGW names. I suggest he realised that when Oofy first appeared (1931 in USA), few people would still remember that 'oofy' was 1890s Cockney/ Yiddish slang for someone with money. The word 'prosser' was of the same period and meant someone mean with money or someone always on the cadge. Oofy was therefore perfectly delineated as a wealthy but mean man.

Note. In US slang, 'oofy' apparently means a man with well-developed muscles. Perhaps from the same Yiddish origin, a man with assets.

Oojah-cum-spiff. 32 p113 and elsewhere. This phrase became popular during the First World War when conscripts were instructed by Regular N.C.Os. The most plausible explanation I have read is that it came from India, where just about every regiment in the British Army had served. 'Oojah' was a general term meaning 'anything'/'something I've forgotten the name of'. The 'cum' is good Latin and means 'with', while 'spiff' is short for 'spiffing'. Thus, it came to mean something enjoyable/pleasant/a good thing.

Oolong. 31 p110; 52 p41. Tea; one of the types of leaf grown for it. See also BOHEA.

O.P. side, the. 23 p45 and later. 'Opposite Prompt'. This stage term needed no explanation in the days when every town had a theatre rather than a cinema. In the English theatre, the Prompter is on Stage Left, i.e. on the right as the audience looks at the stage. O.P. meant the left side of the stage, as the audience looks at it. European theatres (and, I am told, US theatres) have their prompter's box in the centre of the stage by the footlights.

Ophelia. Her precedent in drowning herself 65 p199; looking like O. 72 p104. See S. *Hamlet*.

Oppenheim, E. Phillips. 33 p110; 46 p62; 69 p46; his *The Great Impersonation* 88 p128; and later. A writer of popular novels and thrillers whom PGW met and became friends with in the South of France. Oppenheim (1866–1946) claimed he gave PGW the idea of describing customers in Mr Mulliner's Anglers' Rest by the drinks they consumed. He played golf with Wodehouse at Worplesdon and recounted how PGW drove his ball so far it was lost, but was delighted when the caddie later returned to say it had been found over 300 yards from the tee. (A remarkable shot or a very tactful caddie?) Oppenheim's *The Great Impersonation* (1920) is still exciting to read. Roughly, everybody thought this chap was the real chap, but he was really the real chap pretending to be the other chap who the reader thinks is pretending to be the real chap — just about sums it up.

Oppressed minorities. 62 p134. This phrase became popular in the 1930s as a result, so I have read, of President Woodrow Wilson's concern for minority groups in various Eastern European countries.

Oracle, Delphic. 60 p235. The oracle's cave is to be still to be seen at Delphi, where you can sit on the seats of the 3,000-year-old arena and run and throw the discus as the ancient Greeks did. The oracle answered all questions put to her but, as Uncle Fred said, her answers were always double-edged, in the form of riddles. Whichever way you interpreted them, the oracle could always say later you chose the wrong meaning.

Orator. I am, like Mark Antony, no orator 30 p14. S. *Julius Caesar* 3.2: "I am no orator, as Brutus is; But, as you know me all, a plain, blunt man."

Orb, not the smallest (which you beholdest ... quiring to the young-eyed cherubim. 70 p112. See PATINES.

Orb, The. 9 p56. See Chap. 7.

Orchestrion. 29 p176. Mr Imhoff invented this device for producing the sound of a full-scale orchestra in 1850.

Orczy, Baroness. See SCARLET PIMPERNEL.

'Ordeal by Golf'. This short story title is another PGW adaptation of a phrase everybody recognised. In the Middle Ages, criminal trials were often decided by Ordeals. In Ordeal by Battle, you fought your accuser; if he killed you, you were clearly guilty. In Ordeal by Fire, the accused had to hold a piece of red-hot iron in his hand; if he was uninjured, he was innocent, but if burned, he was judged guilty. There were several variations, of which the best-known, used for witches, was Ordeal by Water. The accused had her hands and feet securely bound together before she was thrown into deep water. If she floated she was clearly a witch. If she sank, she was judged innocent, which must have been a great comfort to her grieving relatives.

Order, old. See OLD ORDER.

O'Reilly, are you the? See RILEY.

Orlando/Orlo. Frequent. See Chap. 39.

Orme. Betted on Orme that year he got poisoned 1 p40. This was a big racing scandal of 1892. After the Duke of Westminster's Derby entrant, Orme, went down with some mysterious ailment, Kennedy Jones, an enterprising journalist, convinced the duke, a suspicious chap anyway, that Orme had been poisoned. It turned out to be only a bad tooth infection, but Jones made his reputation out of the false poisoning story.

Orphreys on your chasuble. See Chap. 11.

Orrery & Cork, Lord. 91 p15. I wonder why PGW got the Earl of Cork & Orrery's name the wrong way round? A typo maybe?

O'Sullivan, Bridget. Dedicatee of *William Tell Told Again*. See Chap. 37.

Othello. Mr Carmody, like Othello, was perplexed in the extreme 40 p155; 44 p85; and later. S. *Othello* 5.2. "Of one not easily jealous, but, being wrought, / Perplex'd in the extreme; of one whose hand, / Like the base Indian, threw a pearl away."

Others abide our —. Pleasure 41 p17; question 46 p107; and later. Matthew Arnold's sonnet 'Shakespeare': "Others abide our question, thou art free."

Otis, Miss, unable to dine today. 86 p139. See MISS OTIS.

Otto, Long. 15A p24. See OTTO THE OX.

Otto of Roses, motto of. 91 p44. 'Otto of Roses' was written and sung by George Grossmith Jnr (see Chap. 13) at the Gaiety Theatre in 1907 in *The Girls of Gottenburg*. The title was a pun on both a well-known scent called attar of roses and 'Otto of Rose', described as "a pink sweet against the doubtful breath of smokers". Grossmith's song cashed in on the popularity of both. The refrain after the first verse is:

> Oh, girls all call me Otto,
> What oh! They know that my heart never closes,
> If you don't like what you've got, oh!
> Pick another from the grotto,
> Is the motto of Otto of Roses!

PGW remembered it because, in December 1907, when the show opened, he had just become 'extra lyric writer' at the Gaiety, then the most famous musical comedy theatre in the world.

Otto the Ox. 72 p58; 90 p9; Long Otto in 15A p24. Otto the Ox was a real and very nasty New York criminal in the Prohibition period.

Otway, Thomas, and his views on Woman. 29 p37 and later. This playwright (1652–85) expressed his views so strongly, I felt it worth looking him up. He was desperately enamoured of an actress, Elizabeth Barry, but she spurned his suit. In her defence, it should be said that she 'enjoyed the patronage' of Lord Rochester, who was someone people did not offend. Ask Dryden or anybody.

Ought to be/ have been a law. See THERE OUGHT TO BE.

Ouida Guardsman. 9 p96; 22 p45. Ouida was the pen-name of Marie Louise de la Ramée (1839–1908), who wrote wildly popular novels about life in high society; *Under Two Flags* is probably the best-known today. The hero is really a hero, the heroine is a lady to her fingertips, and the villain is not only evil but foreign to boot. There are good grounds for considering it a source of *Mervyn Keene, Clubman*.

Ouimet, Francis. 37 p49. It was this twenty-year-old student's victory over Vardon and Ray in the 1913 US Open that led to the explosion of golf across America.

Ouled Naïl stomach dancers. 65 p93 and frequent later up to 96. These exotic dancers of the Middle East were renowned for the flexibility of their body movements (belly-dancing type of thing). In the late 19th century, when half the British upper classes were in Africa or out East administering the Empire, their journeys took them through the Suez Canal. A display by Berber Ouled Naïl dancing girls at Alexandria was often their introduction to the temptations of the sultry Tropics. MTT David Landman for the information that they became famous in America when Sol Bloom introduced them at the 1893 Chicago World Fair.

Our eyes, like stars, do not start from their spheres … fretful porpentine. 48 p231. See PORPENTINE.

Our Man In America. 86 p52. Easy to miss, but PGW was delighted when *Punch* asked him to write for it again in 1953, which he saw as meaning the Berlin broadcasts were at last forgotten. He wrote a fortnightly column entitled 'America Day By Day' from 1956 to January 1960. It was called 'Our Man In America' from April 1960 till June 1963, when *Punch* stopped the series. PGW's comment in *Frozen Assets* was written just after the series had finished.

Our only Reece. 2 p11. Music hall reference. Arthur Roberts (1852–1933), a well-known comedian (and Pelican) of the time, was billed as 'Our Only Arthur'.

Ours not to reason why. 19 p163 and elsewhere. See REASON WHY.

Out, damned spot. 91 p68. S. *Macbeth* 5.1: "Out, damned spot! Out, I say!"

Out of evil cometh good. 26 p37; 42 p93; 85 p61. B. Romans 3.8: "(… and as some affirm that we say,) Let us do evil, that good may come?"

Out of the depths that covered him; black as the pit from pole to pole. See NIGHT THAT COVERS ME.

Out of the everywhere into here. 92 p38. From the song in George Macdonald's *At the Back of the North Wind* (1871). "Where did you come from, baby dear? Out of the everywhere into the here."

Out of the mouths of babes and sucklings. 27 p238 and later. B. Psalms 8.2: "Out of the mouth of babes and sucklings hast thou ordained strength because of thine enemies, that thou mightest still the enemy and the avenger." And B. and Matthew 21.16: "And Jesus saith unto them, Yea; have ye never read, out of the mouth of babes and sucklings thou hast perfected praise?"

Out of the night that covers me. See NIGHT THAT COVERS ME.

Out where the vest begins. In *America, I Like You*, the US version of *Over Seventy* (though the two books are very different), PGW has a splendid poem on 'Whiskers' at page 100. This is his twist on the 1912 poem by Arthur Chapman, 'Where the West Begins', which was set to music in 1917. Dependent on one's mood, Mr Chapman's verses arouse either nausea or patriotism:

> Out where the handclasp is a little stronger,
> Out where the smile lasts a little longer,
> That's where the West begins.

Outer darkness, weeping and gnashing of teeth. See WEEPING AND GNASHING.

Outsider, The. A play at 6 p163; a novel at 7 p15; a play again at 13 p10 and 18 p272. There was a real play by this name, but not till 1923. I have a strong suspicion this was a story title that PGW never used, possibly an alternative title for *The White Feather*.

Over hill and over dale. 87 p89. S. *Midsummer Night's Dream* 2.1.

Over the Rainbow. 88 p185. The song for ever associated with Judy Garland, who sang it in the 1939 film *The Wizard of Oz*.

Over the top. 25 p281; 26 p303; 82 p189. Another phrase that has changed its meaning. PGW used it in the original sense from the First World War. When an attack was launched, it meant climbing up a ladder out of your trench, 'going over the top', and walking into the machine-gun fire and shelling that killed hundreds of thousands. Nowadays, the phrase has come to mean any excessive behaviour — buying two Rolls-Royce cars, drinking vintage champagne when everybody else is on beer, that sort of thing.

Owens, Jesse. 58 p275; the Empress moves as swiftly as 60 p291. This athlete (1913–80) won four golds in the 1936 Olympics.

Ox in the teacup. 2 p234. Around 1900, advertisements for OXO showed an ox happily squashed into a teacup to provide the drinker with the condensed natural goodness of beef. PGW used it here to express the 'condensed' emotion of Lorimer's comment.

Ox nor ass. Nor your ox nor your ass nor anything that is within … 40 p176. B. Exodus 20.17, the Ten Commandments, of which the last is: "Thou shalt not covet thy neighbour's house … nor his ox, nor his ass, nor anything that is thy neighbour's."

Oxo. In the centre of the Oxo. 14 p187. Another PGW gloss for being in the soup/ in trouble. Oxo was and is a beef stock cube for making hot drinks, soups, stews, etc. It has been sold under the name since 1899, but was in existence at least fifty years before that. Florence Nightingale (1820–1910) approved of its strengthening qualities and said so in print. See also BISQUE, BOVRIL, GUMBO, and MULLIGATAWNY.

Oysters. Not oysters because the month was June 83 p159. Until some twenty years ago, one could not buy oysters in Britain in a month without a 'R' in it. The breeding season was May to the end of August, and oysters were not available during this period.

Oysters … were eager for the treat. 3 p10. From 'The Walrus and the Carpenter' in Carroll's *Alice Through the Looking-Glass*. See Wodehouse's parody of it (Chap. 16).

P

(MTT = My thanks to)

P's and Q's. See Ps and Qs below.

Pack, Jeeves. Pack with care. Pack in the presence of the passenjare. 43 p283. PGW's gloss on "Punch, boys, punch with care. Punch in the presence of the passenjare." The lines by Isaac Hill Bromley, published 27 September 1875, were inspired by the notice to conductors he had seen in New York street-cars. They became famous when Mark Twain wrote an article (*Atlantic Monthly* February 1876) saying how infuriating the rhyme was since he found it impossible to get out of his head.

Paddington Station. 3 p242 and later; a big plug for it at 91 p29. It was built as the London terminus of the GWR (Great Western Railway), which served the west of England. But, in competition with the LMS (London, Midland and Scottish), the GWR built their lines further and further north till they covered Shropshire (northwest of London) as well. Paddington was certainly the station for Blandings (see Chap. 39) whether you were going to the Shropshire Blandings (Weston Park) or the Gloucestershire Blandings (Sudeley Castle).

I believe PGW liked Paddington because, from 1896 to 1902, this was the station from which he regularly travelled home from Dulwich (and from the Bank later) to Stableford in Shropshire. The route was: train from Dulwich to Victoria — Underground to Paddington — Paddington to Shifnal (Market Blandings) in Shropshire. When his parents moved to Cheltenham, Paddington was still the station he would use. See also Waterloo.

Paderewski. 6 p50. This pianist (1860–1941), premier of Poland in 1919, was president of Poland's government in exile in 1940.

Pageant in Aid of Distressed Daughters of the Clergy. 41 p194; 52 p119; plus other pageants mentioned elsewhere. Pageants have gone out of fashion but, for a time, it was impossible to escape them. They began in 1905 when a Sherborne music teacher, Louis Parker, who had become a playwright, was asked to devise some form of outdoor entertainment to celebrate the 1200th anniversary of the foundation of the town of Sherborne. He came up with an enormous outdoor theatrical entertainment involving hundreds of locals playing Saxons, Normans, Roundheads, Cavaliers, Cromwell, Nelson, kings and queens and every historical character with whom the town could claim the slightest connection.

It was such a success that other English towns and cities decided they wanted a pageant as well, and Mr Parker did very well out of it. Oxford, St Albans, Warwick, Coventry and Liverpool were just some of the many localities who had, as one historian wrote, "residents with leisure enough to enjoy the mild fuss of committee work and organisation". 1908 saw the great Pageant Summer with hundreds of thousands of people up and down the country dressing up, many of them, like Bertie Wooster, forced into it against their will. By all accounts, some of the re-enactments had minimal connection with the town involved, but certain personages were *always* dragged in. No pageant was complete without King Alfred, Good Queen Bess, Admiral Nelson and, if English historical personalities were lacking, then Great Lovers Through the Ages would take their place (Romeo and Juliet, Pyramus and Thisbe, Antony and Cleopatra, Napoleon and Josephine etc.)

By 1910 the craze had begun to fade although it continued on a smaller scale for another 10–15 years. Another of the forgotten aspects of Edwardian England that PGW noted for us.

Pages, mediaeval, from the Ingoldsby Legends. 25 p113. See INGOLDSBY LEGENDS.

Pagliacci. 58 p269. I think Sir Buckstone should have put in Paisiello (1740–1816).

Pain, Barry. 1 p105; intro to *A Century of Humour*. PGW had a great admiration for Pain (1867–1928), who wrote a series of humorous novels of lower and middle-class life. The *Eliza* books are the best-known today. See Anatole in Chap. 37.

Pal. I was looking for a pal like you 66 p228. In the song 'A Pal like You' from *Oh, Boy!*, the last line in the refrain is "I was looking for a pal like you". MTT Tony Ring & David Jasen.

Palace of Sleep. 13 p99; 32 p169. From T. 'The Sleeping Palace', a version of the Sleeping Beauty fairy tale and a popular subject for Victorian painters.

Palairet. 2 p211. L.C.H. Palairet (1870–1933) played cricket for England against Australia in 1902.

Palais de Danse at Hammersmith. 36 p242. Opened in 1919, this was Britain's first purpose-built dance hall. See Chap. 18.

Pale Hands I Loved Beside the Shalimar. 48 p24 and frequent later. From INDIAN LOVE LYRICS. This was immensely popular in drawing rooms and can still be heard on old-time song programmes. Its 'yearning' quality made it as popular with male singers as MY HERO was with female singers. It was the only song recorded by Rudolph Valentino.

Pale parabola of joy. See ACROSS THE PALE PARABOLA.

Pale young curate. See CURATE.

Palely loitering. His niece Prudence p. l. in the drive 65 p170. I nearly missed this one. See WHAT CAN AIL THEE.

Palmer, Arnold. 88 p64. Pre-eminent golfer (b. 1929) of the 1960s and 1970s.

Palmer the poisoner. 74 p95; 82 p19. To PGW and Guy Bolton's generation, an obvious reference to one of the most famous murders of the Victorian era. Dr

Palmer, the Rugeley poisoner, was hanged in 1856 after a trial the whole country followed breathlessly. See also BRIDES-IN-THE-BATH MURDERER.

Palooka of the first water. 62 p10. From the cartoon character Joe Palooka (1928), a likeable, golden-hearted but stupid hero.

Pan-Anglican Synod, forthcoming. 49 p292; 55 p12; 81 p53. This is the conference of bishops from around the world of the Anglican (Episcopal in USA) Church held in England every ten years; today it is usually called the Lambeth Conference. One day I walked to work down Whitehall with bishops as far as the eye could see. As I passed one, I asked him what was going on. He explained and as we walked on chatting, I said: "Forgive me, sir. How should I address you?" He replied: "Oh, I am Cyprus and the Gulf (Persian Gulf) — but call me Cyprus for short!"

Pankhurst, Mrs. 10 p58; 17A p39 and later. Emmeline Pankhurst (1857–1928), respected leader of British Suffragette movement.

Pantaloon. Baxter would grow into an old white-haired, bespectacled pantaloon 57 p53. S. *As You Like It* 2.7: "The sixth age shifts Into the lean and slipper'd pantaloon, With spectacles on nose and pouch on side ..." Pantaloon, from Italian comedy and later in British pantomime, was depicted as an old man, a dotard.

Panther Woman. 54 p16; 94 frequently. "Grayce Llewellyn ... one of the best-known panther-women on the silent screen ... female Apache in *When Paris Sleeps* ..." Maybe Olga Petrova (1884–1977), who played *The Tigress* in 1914, *The Scarlet Woman* in 1916

A Panther Woman

Theda Bara, 'the Vamp' and first film sex-symbol (real name Theodosia Goodman, 1885–1955), played torrid man-hungry 'Panther Woman' film roles so well, she put the word 'vamp' (short for vampire) into dictionaries.

and *The Panther Woman* in 1918. Her real name was Muriel Harding, but who would pay to see a vamp called Muriel? Alternatively, there was Theda Bara, 'the Vamp' (1885–1955), who also played imperious man-hungry villainesses. Her films included *Tiger Woman, Darling of Paris, When a Woman Sins* — and *While* (not When) *Paris Sleeps* (1923).

For the origin of the term Panther Woman, see Chap. 28.

Pants the hart for cooling streams, as. 38 p26 and often later. The first time he used it, in *The Small Bachelor* chap 2, PGW misquoted the version in B. Psalms 42.1: "As the hart panteth after the water brooks." Thereafter he used the better-known opening line from the hymn by Tate and Brady: "As pants the hart for cooling streams, When heated in the chase." It was a popular quotation. The *Times* of 5 October 1959 reported a Rugger match played on a hot day: "the sprinkling gear was in action on the neighbouring tennis courts and many a hot Rugby hart panted for the cooling streams that jerked around …"

Panzer, Saul. 93 p141. One of Nero WOLFE's assistants in the novels of Rex STOUT that PGW admired.

Paper fastener. 50 p92; 91 p7. Lord Emsworth wore one in his dress shirt until Lady Constance made him change it. They have nearly disappeared now, but the brass paper fastener with its small round 'gold' head and two 'legs' which can be bent outwards to hold paper — or a starched dress-shirt front in place — is an excellent substitute for a stud. I have used them when I could not find my studs, and I imagine PGW did so as well. See Chap. 6.

Paper-hanger, one-armed. See ONE-ARMED.

Parable of the Talents. 93 p74. B. Matthew 25.15. I have never understood the moral lesson of this parable.

Parabola of joy, pale. See ACROSS THE PALE PARABOLA.

Paradise enow. It would be Paradise enow 42 p185; 50 p157. Fitzgerald's *Omar Khayyam*. After listing the picnic accessories — the loaf of bread, the flask of wine and book of verse — he gets to the nub: " … and Thou / Beside me singing in the Wilderness — And Wilderness is Paradise enow."

Parasangs. 34 p27 and at least five times later. Odd how a word can stick in one's mind over the years. As soon as I read this, I realised PGW (plus Bertie and Bingo) had worked his way through Xenophon's *Anabasis* as I had. As Xenophon and his Ten Thousand made their perilous way back home across Asia Minor (401–399 B.C.), they measured their progress by the Persian parasang, a distance of approximately 3½ miles. See also XENOPHON'S TEN THOUSAND.

Pard. See BEARDED LIKE A PARD and FRECKLED LIKE A PARD.

Parents signing cheques. See WE LEFT THE LOVERS LOVING.

Parfit gentil knight. See KNIGHT.

Paris, Passion in. See *PASSION IN PARIS.*

Parrots. 18 p100 and six times later. PGW liked parrots and certainly owned two in the 1920s and another in the late 1930s. The last was named Co-Co. See

Chap. 40.

Parsloe-Parsloe, Sir Gregory. MTT to John Parsloe, who has reported that his great-uncle, Ernest Alfred Parsloe, met Wodehouse, probably around 1923, who said: "Parsloe, you say, that's an unusual name. I may use it in one of my books" — and did so. Luckily, Mr Parsloe (1863–1943), a successful banker, expressed no objection to Wodehouse's idea. PGW probably gave Sir Gregory his double-barreled name to distinguish him from such commoners as Raymond Parsloe Devine (28 p14), George Parsloe (37 p27), and the putative old schoolfellow Parsloe (55 p190).

Parsons, Louella. 53 p244 and later. Longtime Hollywood gossip columnist (1880–1972). One reason for her success was that she was married to Dr Henry Watson Martin, a specialist in venereal disease and urology as well as being head of 20th Century Fox's medical department. By this means, it is said, she often heard the results of pregnancy tests before the mother did. See also HOPPER.

Parted brass rags. 58 p16; 59 p139 and elsewhere. Popular phrase that originated in the Royal Navy. In scrubbing the decks, polishing the brass and so on, it was the custom for sailors to work in pairs. Oppos (chums, mates, friends) found it quicker if one put the polish on and the other took it off. They would have their own supply of rags for the job; if they had a row and decided to work with someone else, they parted brass rags.

Parthian shaft/shot. 2 p143 and later. A telling last retort. The Parthians of Asia Minor were archers who fought on horseback. Their specialist technique was to charge at an enemy, then wheel round and ride away. It was the arrows they fired as they withdrew that caused the most damage.

Partington, Mrs. Like Mrs P. sweeping back the Atlantic with her broom 24 p157. In 1824 a Mrs Partington, who lived on the coast of Devonshire, found the Atlantic Ocean had flooded her house, upon which she grabbed a brush and started on the brave, if futile, task of brushing it out again. The story got out and Sidney Smith (1771–1845) made her famous when he likened her action to that of the politicians who resisted the Reform Bill of 1832. An American journalist, B.P. Shillaber, heard the story and wrote a series of magazine sketches based on her, full of wry, common-sense comments on every topic of the day. Mark Twain based Aunt Polly in *Tom Sawyer* on Shillaber's creation.

Pass, they shall not. See THEY SHALL NOT PASS.

Pass this way only once/through this world but once. 70 p65; 84 p163 and elsewhere. My dictionaries of quotations attribute this variously to Marcus Aurelius, Stephen Grellet, Emerson, Rowland Hill, Addison and Carlyle.

***Passers-By*, Haddon Chambers' play.** 38 p132. This play did well in both New York and London in 1911. Chambers died in 1921, age 60.

Passfield, Lord. He doesn't dance 55 p238. The social reformer Sidney Webb (1859–1947) became Lord Passfield in 1929.

Passing rich. 2 p39. Goldsmith's 'The Deserted Village': "And passing rich with forty pounds a year ...”

Passing the love of women. Loved his scarabs with that love passing the love of women 19 p43; loved baseball with a love 22 p138. “Passing the love of women” is the penultimate line in Kipling’s ‘Follow Me ’Ome’, which he borrowed from B. 2 Samuel 1.26: “I am distressed for thee, my brother Jonathan, very pleasant hast thou been unto me, thy love to me was wonderful, passing the love of women.”

Passion in Paris. 94 p136; 95 p79. At 54 p16 we read of *When Paris Sleeps*, PGW’s recollection of the real film *While Paris Sleeps* (1923); see Panther Woman. Forty books later, he had forgotten the title of Grayce’s film, so he gave us *Passion in Paris*. There were thirty-seven years between *The Luck of the Bodkins* and *Pearls, Girls and Monty Bodkin*. See also Chap 28.

Passions, angry. Never let your angry passions rise 3 p22 and often later. This is one of the many maxims of Dr Watts that PGW and every other Victorian child had drilled into them.

Past bury its dead, let the. See Let the dead.

Pasteur treatment. 61 p62. In general terms, the process of sterilising germs, named after the famous scientist (1822–95).

Pat and Mike. Two headhunters — call them Pat and Mike 49 p269; and later. Pat and Mike knockabout cross-talk acts were enormously popular in the USA and UK from c.1870 to the 1930s. They were a staple of the vaudeville/music hall scene, and audiences revelled in the appalling puns and jokes. They relied heavily on mocking national characteristics, and jokes about Cockneys, Scots and Irishmen were always well received in the UK. In American cities like New York, Dutch, German and Jewish audiences enjoyed Dutch, German and Jewish jokes. The present climate of political correctness has nearly destroyed this tradition, though it continues in a modified form. I have heard at least three comedians say they owe their success to being so clearly Scotch/Irish/Jewish themselves, they are therefore able to tell Scotch/Irish/Jewish jokes. I have to add that a Jewish comedian recently faced a legal charge from a non-Jewish member of the audience who felt his jokes brought Jews into disrepute!

Patent medicines. PGW referred to these often, reflecting the advertisements to be seen in every magazine and newspaper of the time. As late as 93 p5, PGW wrote of “one of those patent medicines which tone the system and impart a gentle glow”. Until the Drugs Licensing Acts (1910), there was no regulation in the UK or US whatever of patent medicines or ‘health tonics’ which gave you a ‘cheerful glow’ or ‘relaxed’ you. Most were pure alcohol with flavouring added; the remainder were based on opium or some other drug. There was a tremendous row when a coroner found that the death of a respected American temperance reformer was due to the half pint of a ‘teetotal health drink’ which he had unsuspectingly drunk for years. It was pure alcohol with cherry flavouring. See Soothing syrup, and Buck-U-Uppo in Chap. 11.

Pater, Walter. 34 p7 and later. Pater (1839–94), critic and aesthete, was the man who described the Mona Lisa as “the head on which all the ends of the world are come”. He advocated “cultural hedonism” and was just the sort of writer to be published in limp purple leather. See SORROWS OF THE WORLD.

Path of true love. Do you suppose the path of true love is going to run smooth? 26 p36. S. *Midsummer Night's Dream* 1.1: “The course of true love never did run smooth.”

Path straight. I've made your p. s. 83 p157 and later. B. Hebrews 12.13: “And make straight paths for your feet, lest that which is lame be turned out of the way.”

Patience. Love-sick maidens in P. 85 p20. See LOVE-SICK MAIDENS.

Patience on a monument. 1 p69; 32 p88; 43 p103 and later. S. *Twelfth Night* 2.4: “She sat like Patience on a monument, Smiling at grief …”

Patines of bright gold, all inlaid with … 34 p166 and later. S. *Merchant of Venice* 5.1: “Sit, Jessica; look, how the floor of heaven / Is thick inlaid with patines of bright gold: / There's not the smallest orb which thou behold's't / But in his motion like an angel sings, / Still quiring to the young-eyed cherubins.”

Patterne, Sir Willoughby. 37 p135. Sir Willoughby, an arrogant, self-centred man, is the central character of Meredith's *The Egoist* (1879). George Meredith (1828–1909) was a novelist highly regarded by many of PGW's generation.

Patzel, Fred. 53 p76. Perceptive readers will notice this name does not have the right Wodehouse rhythm and is probably real — as it is. See Chap. 40 and also Fred Thompson in Chap 21.

Pavlov, Dr. 87 p81. This Russian psychologist (1849–1936) is famous for his studies into conditioned reflexes. If you whistle a certain tune every day and feed dogs immediately afterwards, then they will start to bark for food every time they hear the tune.

Payn, James. 3 p118. This novelist (1830–98) was also editor of *Chambers Journal* and the *Cornhill Magazine*. His skit on Thomas Moore's lost gazelle (see GAZELLES) was:

I never had a piece of toast
Particularly long and wide,
But fell upon the sanded floor
And always on the buttered side.
(*Chambers Journal*, 2 Feb 1884)

Payne, John Howard. 88 p9 and elsewhere. The Home, Sweet Home that this songwriter (1791–1852) wrote about can still be seen on Long Island. See Chap. 36.

Paynim. 55 p79; 68 p246 and elsewhere. A general term for the pagans/ Mahommedans etc. against whom the Crusaders fought from the 11th to 13th centuries.

Pea-and-thimble man. (Now you see it, now you don't.) 59 p43 and later. Those carrying out this traditional con trick in the UK and the USA collect a crowd, put a pea under a thimble, put two other thimbles beside it, shuffle them around, and let the audience bet on which thimble contains the pea. An accomplice 'guesses' correctly twice, takes his money and walks away. But, surprisingly, no one else ever seems to win. The 'Find the Lady'/ 'Three Card Trick' works on the same basis.

Peace be on thy walls, Catsmeat, and prosperity within thy palaces … Proverbs cxxi. 6. 39 p118. PGW had enough respect for the Anglican clergy to ensure that when they quoted a Biblical reference, they usually got it right. I originally thought PGW was being subtle here and showing how a bishop, under the influence of Buck-U-Uppo, would get his references mixed up. MTT Tony Ring for showing that it was the subeditors and proofreaders of Messrs Herbert Jenkins and Doubleday Doran who were under the influence. The correct reference is Psalms 122.7. See Chap. 11.

Peace, be still, like Kipling's soldier. 92 p117. KIPLING's 'Back to the Army Again': "An' I sez to my flutterin' 'eart-strings, I sez to 'em, 'Peace, be still!'"

Peace beyond understanding (when you stop playing golf). 28 p128. B. Philippians 4.7: "And the peace of God, which passeth all understanding, shall keep your hearts and minds through Christ Jesus."

Peace, Charles. 1 p167; 13 p14 and later. This inventive and famous Victorian burglar killed a policeman and was hanged in 1879. His name was legendary in the underworld.

Peace in our time. He was all for peace in our time 71 p53. The phrase 'Peace in our time' hit the headlines when Neville Chamberlain, then prime minister, used it upon his return from meeting Hitler in Munich in 1938. Hitler had persuaded him that Germany had no more warlike intentions, and Chamberlain announced the glad news on his return by quoting a phrase everybody knew. It is from the services of Morning Prayer and Evening Prayer in the Book of Common Prayer and comes just before the first Collect.

Priest: Give peace in our time, O Lord.

Response: Because there is none other that fighteth for us, but only thou, O Lord.

Peace, perfect peace and loved ones far away. 29 p273; 53 p98 and later. A famous hymn by E.H.Bickersteth beginning: "Peace, perfect peace in this dark world of sin." The fourth verse begins: "Peace, perfect peace with loved ones far away."

Pearce and Plenty. 14 p117. I originally thought this was a Biblical quotation on peace and plenty, but Pearce and Plenty was a chain of refreshment establishments in London c.1900–10.

Pearl, orient, of purest ray serene. 45 p82. See GEM OF PUREST.

Pearl richer than all his tribe, the base Indian who threw away. 85 p164 and elsewhere. See INDIAN, POOR.

Pearl Street, New York, is darn crooked. 15A p57; 18 p197. I do not know enough American history to comment, but I note Pearl Street is curved and several financiers had their offices there.

Pearls before swine, casting. 36 p64. B. Matthew 7.6: "Give not that which is holy unto the dogs, neither cast ye your pearls before swine, lest they trample you under their feet, and turn again and rend you."

Peary, Commander. 63 p207. This American explorer (1856–1920) was the first to reach the North Pole in 1909. He deserves the credit for reaching the top of the world, though it turned out that he had missed the Pole by a few miles. Based on later, more accurate navigational instruments, it is now believed that it was not until 1990 that a UK party hit the right spot.

Peasemarch, Albert Eustace. 54 p77; 74 p95; 80 p13. I looked very hard for a source for this splendid steward but found nothing. At 74 p95, PGW says the name came from the engineer in Colonel Savage's hell-ship *Dorinda*, but I have a strong feeling that J.B. Midgeley (see *The Girl on the Boat*, p33) was a real steward and perhaps an inspiration for the Peasemarch we know so well. I have nothing other than instinct to support this view, but I am sure that on one of his many Atlantic crossings, PGW had a steward just like Peasemarch. (Note. PGW had used the name earlier in *If I Were You* [chap. 13] when Syd Price warned Sir Gregory Peasemarch about his baldness.)

Pebbles, chap who chewed. 93 p127. See DEMOSTHENES.

Peck, Gregory. 67 p123 and later. US film star (1916–2003).

Peculiar and extensive knowledge. 6 p60. D. *The Pickwick Papers* chap. 20 (Sam Weller's peculiar and extensive knowledge of London).

Peep with security into futurity. 6 p185. G&S *The Sorcerer* Act 1: " Peep with security / Into futurity, / Sum up your history, / Clear up a mystery …"

Peerages. 23 p38; 31 p120; might be able to buy a knighthood at Harrige's 73 p218. While, of course, one cannot buy a peerage, there is no doubt that prime ministers are 'grateful' for 'services to the Party', i.e. donations to Party funds. (See Lord Bridgnorth in 'Leave It to Jeeves'.) Lloyd George and his alleged agent Maundy Gregory caused a scandal by being too open about it, and the phrase 'a Lloyd George peer' was for a long time a term of derision. It was generally believed that £50,000 'to Party funds' would get you a barony (the lowest grade to get you into the House of Lords). In 1922 the arrangement became public when it leaked out that King George V had refused to accept four names Lloyd George had put forward — a tax evader, a wartime profiteer, a man who traded with the enemy, and a swindling company director. In his retirement, Lloyd George justified the system, claiming it was preferable to the American method. In the UK, once the man had made his donation to Party funds and got his title, you owed him nothing. In America, the man who paid the money would want a government position or would try to influence government policy in his favour. An interesting argument.

Pekinese dog. 35 p226 and later. See Chap. 40.

Pelissier. 11 p29. Brilliant pianist, satirist and revue artist (1874–1913) who could produce a 'potted' version of a London stage hit within forty-eight hours of its opening, satirising both the play and its music. See also PIERROTS.

Pen and Ink Club. 33 p82 & p138 and later. I suggest this is PGW's twist on PEN, which was founded by Mrs C.A. Dawson Scott in 1921, with John Galsworthy as president, to promote understanding and co-operation among men and women of letters around the world. The letters are an acronym for poets, playwrights, essayists, editors and novelists, and I suspect PGW did not regard the organisation with the respect they felt they deserved. I do not say he thought they were pretentious, but he certainly regarded with some reserve those writers who claimed to be 'men of letters'. He was a member of, and on the council of, the Society of Authors, but that comprised writers he respected.

Pen is mightier than the sword, the. PGW ref lost. From Bulwer-Lytton's *Richelieu* 2.2.

Pence. A breezy disregard for the preservation of the p. 20 p13. English proverb: "Look after the pence and the pounds will look after themselves."

Pennefather goes in fear of his life. 63 p9. From F.C. Burnand's *Happy Thoughts* of 1890, in which Pennefather, a railway porter, claims to go in fear of his life. Burnand was the *Punch* editor who accepted PGW's first pieces. An odd phrase to stick in one's mind, but I remembered it from *Happy Thoughts* as soon as I read it. See HAPPY THOUGHT.

Pennies from Heaven. 58 p270 and later. 1936 popular song from the Bing Crosby film of the same name.

People on the island who eked out a precarious livelihood by taking in each other's washing, the. 18 p21. See EKED OUT.

Perfect Love, O. See O PERFECT LOVE.

Perfumed that the winds were love-sick with him, so. 32 p223; 74 p96. S. *Antony and Cleopatra* 2.2: "Purple the sails, and so perfumed, that The winds were love-sick with them, the oars were silver …"

Peri at the gates of Paradise. 6 p210 and later up to 89 p169. Thomas MOORE's poem 'Paradise and the Peri'. "One Morn a Peri at the gate / Of Eden stood disconsolate." The poem's popularity was enhanced by many Victorian paintings depicting her sorrow ('Love Locked Out', 'The Peri at the Gate' etc.)

Peril on the deep (the hymn for those in). 28 p224. See THOSE IN PERIL.

Perilous stuff that weighs upon the heart. 33 p87. See BOSOM.

Perils of Pauline. See *DANGERS OF DIANA*.

Perplexed in the extreme. See OTHELLO.

Persecute their vocations, as Mr Kipling has it. 8 p91. I was sure this was from KIPLING's *Stalky and Co* but could not find it. MTT Nigel Rees, who found it in Kipling's *A Fleet in Being: Notes of Two Trips with the Channel Squadron* (1898), chap. 3: "With the Navigating Lieutenant on the 'igh an' lofty bridge persecuting his vocation."

Perseus. See ANDROMEDA.

Pershore, Lord. 23 p43; the Honourable Aubrey Pershore 25 p266. See Chap. 26.

Pester, Lester de. 68 p86. See DE PESTER.

Peter Pan. Girl goes to ball dressed as P.P. 9 p248. As the narrative makes clear, this was most unladylike at the time. *Peter Pan* had been first performed only three years before, and wearing such a costume (tights!), even at a fancy-dress dance, was *very* daring. Peter Pan's house in the tree-tops is mentioned at 26 p178.

Pfui. 96 p163. As PGW says, it was a favourite expression of scorn by Rex Stout's Nero Wolfe, usually just before he called somebody a witling.

P.G.W. (the other one). Philip Gordon Wylie (1902–71) was a writer and frequent contributor to the *New Yorker* magazine. He often signed his verses and articles with his initials, which still leads to confusion as to the author — Wodehouse or Wylie. (James Thurber mentions the problem in chap. 2 of his *The Years with Ross*.) McIlvaine's *Wodehouse Bibliography* traces only two Wodehouse contributions to the *New Yorker*. The first was on 30 April 1927, the second appeared on 29 October the same year.

Pharaoh. Like Pharaoh in the Good Book when all those plagues of frogs came along 66 p174; 68 p176. B. Exodus 8.6. Egypt suffered a series of unpleasant plagues until Pharaoh got the message and allowed the Israelites to leave.

Philippic. 3 p29; 34 p146. A warlike, pugnacious speech. From Demosthenes' orations against Philip of Macedon.

Philistines, we have smitten the. 8 p37. See Hip and thigh.

Photographers never, never, never shall be slaves. 39 p239. PGW twist on "Britons never, never, never shall be slaves" — from 'Rule Britannia', the patriotic song written by James Thomson (1740), sung often till thirty years ago, but now rarely heard. Its sentiments are severely discouraged by most UK politicians today who believe it is good to be proud of one's country, but not if you are British. To do so is chauvinism of the worst sort. As Keith Alsop has pointed out, it is usually sung nowadays at the Last Night of the Proms in London. (And next day, every member of the *gliterati* sneers at its inclusion. It is NOT politically correct.)

Photographically lined in the tablets of my mind when a yesterday has faded from its page. 74 p209; 80 p116. As Guy Bolton said, it is from Gilbert's *Bab Ballads* 'The Story of Prince Agib'. The poem concludes: "Photographically lined / On the tablet of my mind, / When a yesterday has faded from its page!"

Piano, put a chap's body inside a. 20 p138. See R.L. Stevenson's *The Wrong Box*.

Pianola, try that on your. See Try that.

Piccadilly Cabin. 9 p221. See Cabins.

Piccadilly Magazine (correspondence course coupon in the). 49 p148. PGW had written for this magazine two years before. It may be just pure coincidence but, reading through copies of the time, I noted it had many advertisements for such courses.

Piccadilly weepers. 69 p120. Long mutton-chop side whiskers which were high fashion in the 1860s. They took their name from the black ribbons or mourning bands (weepers) tied round a top hat for funerals. These dangled down like side-whiskers.

Pickford, Mary. 20 p189. The first internationally-famous film star (1893–1979), she was billed as 'The World's Sweetheart'. See WORLD'S SWEETHEART.

Pickwickian sense, in a purely. 50 p227. That is, it doesn't mean anything. See the first chapter of D. *The Pickwick Papers*.

Picnic egg, hard as a. See HARD AS A PICNIC EGG.

Picture, look here upon this. 22 p16; 64 p142. See LOOK HERE.

Picture, What is wrong with this? He felt like the man in the advertisement 'What is wrong with this picture?' 37 p145; 67 p153. Emily Post (see POST) published her famous book on etiquette in 1922 and sold nearly 750,000 copies over the next 25 years. Lillian Eichler's *The Book of Etiquette*, which came out before Miss Post's, is now forgotten but sold over a million. It was widely advertised across America with an illustration of some social error and the caption 'What Is Wrong With This Picture?', written by Miss Eichler, who had been a copywriter herself.

Pie. 37 p289 and later. In the 1890s, this became common American slang for anything easy, a pushover. Presumably from the analogy of eating apple pie?

Pied Piper of Hamelin. 3 p91. See Browning's poem.

Pie-eyed. See DRUNKENNESS.

Pierian fount. 62 p123. From Pope's *Essay on Criticism*: "A little learning is a dangerous thing; Drink deep, or taste not the Pierian spring." The ancient Greeks believed the Pierian stream flowing down Mount Olympus bestowed fluency on those who drank from it, similar to kissing the Blarney Stone in Ireland. I drank from the Pierian fount in 1963; my family says it made very little difference.

Pierrots, troupe of. 18 p55; 52 p24; 64 p196. From 1860 to c.1905, black-faced minstrel shows were the standard popular entertainment at UK seaside resorts. Between 1900 and 1910, they were replaced by pierrot concert troupes, who wore the baggy clothes of a clown surmounted by the conical cap. Probably because of the remarkable success of PELISSIER and his group, a pierrot troupe who took a London theatre and satirised every fashion and habit of the day, pierrot costume became the 'standard' for fancy-dress parties. In 'The Awful Gladness of the Mater'(41 p260), a Drone maintained that "the prudent man played for safety and went as a Pierrot." That is why Bertie Wooster was so shocked when Gussie Fink-Nottle wore a Mephistopheles costume: "And why not as a Pierrot? … Why this break with a grand old tradition?" (*Right Ho, Jeeves*). But by *Joy in the Morning*, Bertie took a different view, presumably because PGW had realised pierrots were now old-fashioned. See 64 p196 & p203.

Pig at eve had drunk its fill. 87 p131. See STAG AT EVE.

Piggott, Lester. 73 p182. Leading UK jockey from 1955 to 1985, who won the Derby nine times.

Pigott, Mrs. Mary Jane, cook at Rowcester Abbey 73 p179 & p210; Mrs P.B.

Pigott, Jeeves' aunt, 96 p117. See Chap. 37.

Pigs Have Wings. Book title and 1 p164. See Lewis Carroll's 'The Walrus and the Carpenter' (*Alice Through the Looking-Glass*).

Pigs in Clover. 7 p53. This was a fiddly game featuring a small box with glass on one side. Inside were small metal balls which had to be so manoeuvred that they all came to rest in certain holes in the base. Invented by C.M. Crandall in 1899 in the USA, it was introduced into the UK by Alfred Harmsworth (see Chap. 7) as an advertising gimmick for his first magazine *Answers*. It was a vast success, and *Answers'* sales soared.

Pigs, moving without a licence. At least four time including 85 p144. This is a criminal offence in the UK. See also EVANS.

Pig something, a chap called ... she starts. She moves ... 52 p107. Another of Bertie's splendid misquotations combining the Pygmalion legend (chap who made a statue which came to life, see GALATEA) and Longfellow's 'Building The Ship': "She starts, she moves, she seems to feel the thrill of life along her keel."

Pigstye. See FATHER'S IN THE PIGSTYE.

Pilch, Fuller. 3 p272; 12 p303. Famous cricketer (1804–70).

Pilgrimage was to end in lovers meeting, his. 97 p62. See JOURNEYS END IN LOVERS MEETING.

Pillar of fire that went before the Israelites. 38 p9. B. Exodus 13.21: "And the Lord went before them by day in a pillar of a cloud, to lead them the way; and by night in a pillar of fire, to give them light."

Pillar of salt, turned me into a. 64 p149. See LOT'S WIFE.

Pilot, drop the. See DROP THE PILOT.

Pilot on whom they were counting to weather the storm. 70 p119. George Canning's remark about Pitt in 1802 during the Napoleonic Wars at the inauguration of the Pitt Club: "No, — here's to the pilot that weathered the storm."

Pince-nez, dead body with. 67 p18. See DEAD BODY.

Pinch hit. 67 p186. A baseball term when one player bats in place of another.

Pink Lady, The. Alice Bulpitt came over from America with this show 58 p114; 74 p16 & p197. *The Pink Lady* opened in New York in 1911 and London in 1912. See DOVEY, ALICE and Chap. 38.

Pink Pills (for Pale People). 40 p15. In the 1900s, UK newspapers had regular advertisements for 'Dr Williams' Pink Pills for Pale People'. They comprised lengthy, heart-rending accounts of sailors who had nearly drowned, Army officers who could not find employment, clerks who had lost their job, violinists who could no longer play etc. etc. But one course of the Pink Pills changed all that. "Within hours, I felt a new confidence surging through me and now I am back in my old job with a higher salary and I have been promised promotion." "My touch on the strings has improved out of all recognition and I have secured a post in a leading theatre orchestra."

Till surprisingly late, 1930 or so, advertisers, especially of patent medicines, could make extraordinary claims for their products. I remember a full-page advertisement for 'Phospherine — the greatest of all nerve tonics, used by the Royal Family and …' The list includes a dozen European sovereigns, starting with the Emperor of All the Russias. See also PATENT MEDICINES.

Pink 'Un, The. 31 p238 and elsewhere. See Chap. 5.

Pinkerton's. 17 p68. This famous American private detective agency was founded in 1852 and came to prominence when Pinkerton foiled an assassination attempt on Lincoln in February 1861. The firm's symbol was a large eye — hence the term 'private eye' in America for private detectives.

Pip emma. Frequent. See ACK EMMA.

Pip Pip! See GOODBYE.

Pip, some (a most charming, refined, cultured, and vivacious girl). 26 p150. I would bet money this exchange between Mr Trevis and Mr Pilkington is not fiction. As happened occasionally in his school stories, the tone/rhythm of PGW's writing suddenly changed; it was recollection rather than invention. I am sure he was recalling a conversation with Guy Bolton, probably during auditions for a Princess show. Another private joke which he knew only Bolton would pick up?

Pipe of half-awakened birds, earliest. 76 p207. T. *The Princess* 4. Intro: "Ah, sad and strange as in dark summer dawns / The earliest pipe of half-awaken'd birds."

Pipe opener. 64 p15. In Wodehouse's time, this meant opening remarks on some subject. The initial approach would be punctuated by puffs on your pipe, allowing you to introduce the topic in a tactful, man-to-man manner. Thus, discussion of your son's engagement to the wrong girl or your partner's lack of wisdom in investing the firm's money in Yamahama Gold Mines would commence with some innocuous opening comment as you lit your pipe and puffed away to get it going.

Pippa Passes. 3 p90; 66 p105; 67 p238. See GOD'S IN HIS HEAVEN.

Pistol-packing mama. 94 p177. Song written by Al Dexter (1943).

Pit which my niblick has digged. It was as if my ball had fallen into the … 28 p134. B. Psalms 57.6: "They have digged a pit before me, into the midst whereof they have fallen themselves." Or Ecclesiastes 10.8: "He that diggeth a pit shall fall into it."

Pith and moment, great/ greater. 76 p94; 93 p120. See ENTERPRISES.

Pity and terror, excite with (as Aristotle recommends). 28 p18 and elsewhere. Aristotle's *Poetics* 6.1449: "With incidents arousing pity and fear wherewith to accomplish its purgation of such emotions."

Place in frosty weather still, I can feel the. 82 p108. The third verse from the end of Gilbert's 'The Story of Prince Agib' has the line "I can feel the place in frosty weather still". MTT Neil Midkiff.

Place to lay our heads, no. 88 p10. B. Matthew 8.20: "but the Son of man hath not where to lay his head."

Place whence he had come, return anon to the. 20 p66. Nutty Boyd is sunk in gloom, so PGW quoted the words of the death sentence then used in English Courts. From memory, it ran: "You will return to the place from whence you came and from there you will be taken to a place of execution, where you will be hanged by the neck until you are dead." See also MAY THE LORD.

Placed me in the hands of his solicitor, He. 83 p27. Another example of PGW's skill in making a commonplace cliché funny. If you are having problems with a neighbour whose barking dog disturbs your sleep or whose hedge is pushing your fence over, then, when all diplomatic approaches have failed, you warn him solemnly that you will have to place matters in the hands of your solicitor.

Plain living and high thinking. 32 p277. See HIGH THINKING.

Planet Insurance Company. 18 p203. Not too difficult to work out the reference to a big UK insurance companies — the Sun Insurance Company. See also MOON ASSURANCE.

Planet, new (had swum into his ken). 60 p199. See NEW PLANET.

Planks of his platform. 66 p247. Apparently this stems from political life in America, where a candidate would address open-air meetings from platforms made of planks. By transference, it came to mean the major points he wanted to emphasise.

Plans of mice and men, best laid. See MICE AND MEN.

Plants his footsteps on the deep and rides upon the storm. 72 p197. See FATE/HE MOVES.

Plate. Coming over the plate a bit too fast. 34 p191. When the sorrows of the world were coming over the plate ... 59 p224. The second reference is a splendid PGW combination of Walter PATER (see SORROWS OF THE WORLD) and baseball terminology. I am told that this is the term used when the pitcher is pitching too fast for the batter to do much about it.

Platers, selling. See SELLING PLATERS.

Platform, planks of his. See PLANKS.

Plautus. 2 p229. This Roman playwright (d. 184 B.C.) wrote twenty-five comedies which, according to the reference books, were popular in Rome for the next 500 years!

Play the game, the whole game and nothing but the game. 3 p270. See GAME.

Played many parts, had. 48 p165; 60 p15 and elsewhere. S. *As You Like It* 2.7 ('Seven ages of man' speech): "And one man in his time plays many parts, His acts being seven ages."

Player, Gary. 88 p64. An outstanding golfer (b. 1935) who played in his 46th Open championship in 2001.

Playfair, Nigel. 49 p227. UK actor-manager (1874–1934).

Plaything of an idle hour. 60 p181; 67 p131. May be from James Fenimore Cooper's *The Deerslayer* (1841): "...she was regarded as the play thing of an idle hour..."

Pleasure nor profit, neither. 57 p301; 64 p157. This phrase comes from the many newspaper advertisements, 1890–1939, urging people to take up chicken-farming, tomato growing, rabbit breeding, typing lessons etc. etc. 'for pleasure and profit'. Another of the contemporary clichés PGW used so well.

Plimsoll Law/ Line. 21 p106; 50 p147 and later. In 1876 Samuel Plimsoll (1824–98), UK politician and philanthropist, steered an Act through Parliament to ensure the safe loading of ships. Before that, owners would overload a ship in the hope it would sink and they could claim insurance. His Act introduced markings on a ship's hull giving the safe load level for various conditions; for example, the line marked WNA stands for Winter North Atlantic. The term was adopted by drinkers: when their friends had had too much, they were said to be "over the Plimsoll Line".

Pliny the Elder. 46 p39; 92 p79. Roman historian and administrator. He died in 79 A.D. when he decided to observe an eruption of Vesuvius at close quarters — too close.

Pliny the Younger. 73 p48. Nephew (62–114 A.D.) of Pliny the Elder, noted for his elegant letter-writing style.

Plomer, Rev. William P. 52 p214. This reference to the well-known writer William Plomer is puzzling. Plomer (1903–73) worked with Roy Campbell, came to London, and joined the Bloomsbury set, working as reader for publisher Jonathan Cape. Wodehouse is making some private crack about him here, but I don't know why. PGW certainly did not like him; see letter to Bill Townend of 25 January 1935 in chapter 6 of *Yours, Plum*.

Plough, put our hands to the. See HANDS TO THE PLOUGH.

Plough the fields and scatter the good seed o'er the land, We. 57 p302 and later. Popular 1860 hymn by Schulz & Campbell.

Ploughman homeward plods his weary way, the. 58 p104. Gray's 'Elegy in a Country Churchyard'.

Pluck out the Pom which is in her own eye. 51 p16. See BEAM.

Plucked the gowans fine, We two have. 59 p214 and elsewhere. Robert Burns' 'Auld Lang Syne'.

Plugs decarbonized. He wants his p. d. 52 p55. Older motorists will recall that, until about 1970–80, the petrol/air mixture in your car was controlled by the driver. To start a car, you had to 'pull out the choke' and produce a rich mixture. This meant that the sparking plugs became 'oiled-up' and cleaning them was a regular task. See also MIXTURE IS TOO RICH.

Plume of Navarre, white. See NAVARRE.

P.M.G. Pyke. 43 p235. Some editions include a dash between "P.M.G." and "Pyke must go". Most likely the abbreviation P.M.G. = Pyke Must Go, and a typographical error has obscured the meaning.

Poe, Edgar Allan. 28 p92 and frequent later. This American writer (1809–49) became famous for two types of story, tales of horror and excellent detective stories solved by intelligence rather than chance. His 'The Fall of the House of Usher' symbolises the former, while 'The Purloined Letter' exemplifies the latter. PGW quoted both.

Poet and Peasant, overture to. 61 p180. An excellent, if noisy, piece written by Franz von Suppé in 1859.

Poet's eye rolling in a fine frenzy from heaven to earth. 6 p79 and later. S. *Midsummer Night's Dream* 5.1: "The poet's eye, in a fine frenzy rolling, Doth glance from heaven to earth, from earth to heaven."

Poirot, Hercule. 59 p46 and later. Famous fictional detective created by Agatha CHRISTIE.

Poke in the eye with a burned stick. See BURNED STICK.

Policeman. If you want to know the time, ask a policeman 22 p169. The song 'If You Want to Know the Time, Ask a Policeman', by E.W. Rogers (1900), remained popular for fifty years. I still recall some lines: "Every member of the Force, Has a watch and chain of course. If you want to know the time, Ask a p'liceman." Wristwatches did not come into common use till after 1918 and policemen, who were issued with watches, were indeed constantly being asked the time. When I was a small boy walking around London, my mother always told me to ask a policeman the time so I knew when to come home.

Policemen being ducked in ponds, streams etc. See Chap. 16.

Policeman-poet, another. 67 p138. One of the minor literary events of the 1930s was the publication of a book of poems by a policeman who had been encouraged to do so by the London literati of the time. I have been unable to confirm his name. Was it PC Henry Daley or PC Robert Buckingham, both pals of E.M. Forster's? Or maybe PGW simply used 'another' because he remembered he had written a short poem about a policeman poet 40 years before. See *Daily Chronicle* of 24 November 1902.

Polish gentleman who sang 'Ding Dong Ding Dong'. 95 p173. See YEOMAN'S WEDDING SONG.

Polk ... peculiar name. 91 p15. James Polk (1795–1849) was 11th president of the United States (1845–49).

Polk, Vanessa. 91 p10. See Chap. 37.

Polkinghorne, a legal-sounding name. 49 p86. A minor reference, but it bothered me. Possibly PGW's faint memory of the lawyer in Dickens' *Bleak House* — Mr Tulkinghorn?

Pollyanna. 26 p248 and five times up to 92 p72. This 'glad child', who always looked on the bright side of things in books written by Eleanor Porter (1868–1920), spread sweetness and light with sickening enthusiasm. I have a suspicion that, like Little Lord Fauntleroy, she was more popular with parents than with children.

Polonius's speech to Laertes (1). 8 p63 (*The White Feather*). S. *Hamlet* 3.1. See BEWARE OF ENTRANCE TO A QUARREL.

Polonius's speech to Laertes (2). 60 p82 (*Uncle Fred in the Springtime*). Also from S. *Hamlet* 3.1, but nine lines down from "BEWARE OF ENTRANCE TO A QUARREL". It is Mustard Pott's reaction to a request for a loan from Pongo Twistleton. "Neither a borrower, nor a lender be; / For loan oft loses both itself and friend,

/ And borrowing dulls the edge of husbandry."

Pomp and Circumstance. 61 p186. Edward Elgar's famous suite of marches.

Pompilius Numa. 34 p5. Second king of Rome, d. 672 B.C. See also EGERIA.

Pons, Lily, I mistook you for. 60 p266. Beautiful opera singer (1904–76) who starred in Hollywood films.

Ponto. 9 p2 and later. A common name for hunting dogs in England in the 19th century, purportedly from the Spanish word for a pointer (a dog that freezes and 'points' when he sees a bird). The name appears in D. *The Pickwick Papers*.

Poo-boop-a-doop. 47 p57. A variation of BOOP-BOOP-A-DOOP.

Pooh Bah. 2 p247; they do it but it revolts them 14 p23; 19 p132; and later. G&S *Mikado* Act 1 (Pooh Bah is a pompous official): "It revolts me, but I do it!" See also the description of Baxter at 19 p132.

Poor but honest parents, I was born of. 3 p166. See RICH BUT HONEST.

Poor heart that never rejoices, It's a. 55 p169 and later. 16th-century proverb. See also G&S *The Grand Duke*.

Poor John, poor John. 26 p33 and later. A popular song of 1906 by Fred Leigh and Henry Pether in which a mother looks at her future daughter-in-law and sighs: "Poor John, poor John."

Poor thing, but mine own. PGW ref lost. S. *As You Like It* 5.4: "An ill-favoured thing, sir, but mine own."

Poor Tom Jellicoe. 12 p244. See JELLICOE.

Popeye the sailor. 69 p167; 89 p149. This spinach-loving cartoon character first appeared in a comic strip, 'Thimble Theatre', in 1929. The first of the 264 animated cartoons came out in 1933. He is credited with raising the consumption of spinach in the USA by 33% in five years, and Crystal City, Texas, home of spinach growing, put up a statue to him in 1937. When the BBC did a re-run of his cartoons in England in 1966, sales of spinach doubled.

Popgood and Grooly. Popgood, Crooly & Co. 25 p142; 59 p32; 66 p149 and later. These fictional publishers come from F.C. Burnand's *More Happy Thoughts*, though he called them Popgood & Groolly. See also HAPPY THOUGHT.

Poppy nor mandragora nor all the drowsy syrups ... 3 p255; 19 p154. S. *Othello* 3.3.

Population explosion, a sort of. 93 p53. See Chap. 37 (Lord Uffenham).

Porpentine, fretful. Knotted and combined locks ... 54 p90; 59 p162; and later, with five lines at 82 p116. S. *Hamlet* 1.5: "Make thy two eyes, like stars, start from their spheres, / Thy knotted and combined locks to part, / And each particular hair to stand an end, / Like quills upon the fretful porpentine."

Porridge, mess of. 45 p61. See MESS OF PORRIDGE.

Port. And never had the little p. seen a costlier funeral. 69 p89. See AND WHEN THEY BURIED HIM.

Portarlington. (Thomas P. Travers) 76 p106. The Earl of Portarlington stayed at Weston Park when PGW was living at nearby Stableford, but I think a more likely source of the name is to be found in Le Touquet. See Chap. 20.

Portuguese ash cans, knock you for a row of. 38 p22. I assume this was a derogatory expression of some sort that PGW picked up in New York, but I have been unable to trace its meaning.

Portuguese, the Argentines and the Greeks. 40 p49 and later. This slightly bitter song reflected the changes in European smart social circles after 1918. See ARGENTINES.

Posh. 3 p37. See PUSH THING.

Position, feeling his/ conscious of his. The prisoner who seemed to feel his p. deeply 30 p114; wretched man seemed deeply conscious of his p. 52 p256; wretched man was fully conscious of his p. 57 p23; and elsewhere. The cliché 'feeling his position'/ 'conscious of his position', i.e. the ignominy of appearing in court, comes from its constant use in newspaper reports 1880–c.1930. The shame and publicity of a criminal trial was much more feared by respectable people than the punishment awarded. I read a 1903 newspaper report of a butcher — a pillar of his community, local councillor and churchwarden — found guilty of selling bad meat and being fined five pounds. Not only was he "fully conscious of his position", he was described as "the wretched miscreant" as well. In those days, the public disgrace would certainly have put an end to his councilling and churchwardening.

Possibles v Probables. 87 p197. These were the names commonly given to the final England Rugger trials. The best thirty men in the country would play in the Possibles v Probables match, after which the selectors would choose 15 for the England team.

Possum. The liberty of the tree'd p. 18 p137. At liberty to wander but only within the confines of the tree; one move away and it is a goner. This seems to be an American hunting reference. The phrase became popular in the UK after the *Trent* incident of November 1861 when *Punch* published a cartoon reflecting the British attitude. It showed Farmer John Bull pointing a shotgun at 'possum' Abraham Lincoln up in a tree, making it clear he has to 'climb down' some time and apologise. (In the early months of the American Civil War, a Union warship had stopped a British vessel carrying two Confederate representatives to Europe and took them off. There was a tremendous Anglo-American fuss which nearly led to war, but Lincoln apologised and the matter blew over.)

Post, Emily. 58 p57 and later. Post (1873–1960), a wealthy socialite, wrote novels on upper-class Americans in Europe and was horrified when her publisher asked her to write a book on etiquette. He sent her one to look at anyway, and she was even more horrified by what she read. Her *Etiquette*, published in 1922, enjoyed a sensational success as socially-conscious Americans learned what to do and how to do it. Her column on good manners was syndicated in nearly 200 newspapers. See also PICTURE.

Postcard, picture. 93 p54. See HAVING A WONDERFUL TIME.

Post-Toasties. 15A p164. Mr Post began to sell this breakfast cereal after he was introduced to it at the Kellogg Cure clinic at Battle Creek. A relative of Dr

Kellogg's had also seen the commercial possibilities, hence the long-lasting rivalry between Post-Toasties and Kellogg's Cornflakes. See also BATTLE CREEK.

Potato chips. One cannot stop eating them 91 p16. The first were reputedly made for Cornelius Vanderbilt (1794–1877) at Saratoga Springs in 1853. He decided he wanted thin-sliced fried potatoes and sent them back repeatedly to the chef George Crum to get them cut even thinner. Eventually the right thinness was achieved and the crisp potato wafers became wildly popular. Lord Emsworth's apparent unfamiliarity with them is understandable; they first appeared in the UK in 1913 but did not become popular till the 1930s. I remember my parents being unsure what attitude to take when I bought them with my pocket money. Sweet rationing in the UK (1940–51: four ounces per week) meant potato crisps (the British term) soon became the natural alternative.

Note. We couldn't call them chips, since we had those already (fish and chips). British visitors to the US should note our chips are called French fries over there.

Pothos. See DESIDERIUM.

Pothunters, The. I include the title of PGW's first book because I am told the term is not common in America. PGW was using the common phrase for someone who likes collecting trophies. An example is a skilled racing driver who enters small competitions which he knows he will win, rather than competing in more serious races. His aim is to collect an impressive array of cups and trophies. See also p21 of *William Tell Told Again.*

Pott, Captain. See CAPTAIN POTT.

Pott, Mustard. This character got his name from two sources. First, a man who would cheat a widow or orphan at cards, as he would, was commonly described then as being "as hot as mustard". Second, when the first motor taxis appeared in London in 1907, they were French Renaults and were painted deep yellow to make them stand out as vehicles available for hire. The horse-driving cabbies they were driving out of business immediately stigmatised them as mustard pots. They were so successful, however, that an American visitor ordered a dozen and established the first Yellow Cab service in New York.

Potter-Pirbright, Catsmeat. See Chap. 24.

Pound of flesh, he wants his. 73 p128. This phrase, still common in the UK, is from S. *The Merchant of Venice* 4.1: "And lawfully by this the Jew may claim / A pound of flesh, to be by him cut off."

Pourbous. 45 p268. French painter. Either Pourbous the Elder (1545–81) or Pourbous the Younger (1570–1622).

Powell, William. 55 p17; 56 p259. This debonair actor (1892–1984) was brilliant in the *Thin Man* series of films.

Powick, Earl of. 70 p54. See Chap. 26.

Praise from Sir Hubert Stanley. See STANLEY, SIR HUBERT.

Prattler, The. 42 p44. Clearly *The Tatler*, an English magazine famous for reporting Society events.

Praxiteles. Love is a greater sculptor than P. 18 p245. The most famous of Greek sculptors, Praxiteles died about 330 B.C.

Prayeth best who loveth best all things both great and small. 69 p125. Coleridge's *The Rime of the Ancient Mariner*.

Previtali's in Oxford Street. 86 p134. PGW's memory let him down on this one, but it had been fifty years since he had written, quite correctly, that the Hotel Previtali stood in Arundell Street (*Something Fresh*). I think he confused it with Pagani's, a famous Italian café (Telegraphic address 'Soufflé') off Oxford Street.

Priam's curtain ... half his Troy was burnt. 54 p186 and later. S. *2 Henry IV* 1.1: "Even such a man, so faint, so spiritless, / So dull, so dead in look, so woe-begone, /Drew Priam's curtain in the dead of night, / And would have told him, half his Troy was burned."

Price. Every man has his p. 43 p58; all men have their p. 95 p118. Robert Walpole (1676–1745), first British Prime Minister, worked on this basis to keep his supporters in Parliament in line. His opinion of his colleagues was: "All those men have their price."

Price of the papers, the. Play at the Adelphi before you were born 42 p316; 59 p109; 81 p77; and later. I am sure PGW was quoting the title of a real play, but I have been unable to find it in the British Library. It sounds just the sort of melodrama the Adelphi was famous for in the 1890s. See also TIME WILL COME.

Price's, the barbers shop of *If I Were You.* See TRUEFITT'S.

Pride and joy, a mother's. See MOTHER'S PRIDE.

Pride of Piccadilly, the. B Wooster is at 76 p84. From the song 'Gilbert the Filbert': "the pride of Piccadilly, the blasé roué." It was sung by Basil Hallam in *The Passing Show* (1914).

Priestley, J.B. 81 p118. I do not know why PGW classified this writer (*The Good Companions* etc.) as gloomy. He enjoyed Priestley's writing, but perhaps he remembered the poor reviews Priestley (1894–1984) had given his books in the 1930s.

Prig, Betsey, Sairey Gamp and her friend Mrs Harris. 47 p85. Three ladies in D. *Martin Chuzzlewit*, though Mrs Gamp's friend, Mrs Harris, never actually appears. See also GAMP, SAIREY.

Primrose at the river's brim a simple primrose was to him. 3 p217; 15 p9; a chorus girl was a simple chorus girl to him 27 p214; and later. Wordsworth's *Peter Bell* Pt 1: "A primrose by a river's brim / A yellow primrose was to him, / And it was nothing more."

Primrose path. P. p. of their happiness 49 p281–2; to give the p. p. a solid miss 68 p171. The primrose path, to people of PGW's generation, seems to have had two very different meanings. One was the path to damnation as quoted in S. *Macbeth* 2.3.: "The primrose way to the everlasting bonfire." But S. *Hamlet* 1.3. has another meaning, signifying a love affair. "like a puff'd and reckless libertine, / Himself the primrose path of dalliance treads."

Prince and Betty, The. I wondered for years where Wodehouse got the idea for the story. *Psmith Journalist* (Psmith taking over a New York magazine and attacking a slum landlord) came out in *The Captain* magazine in 1909, stemming from PGW's time as a freelance in New York. A revised version with a love interest, *The Prince and Betty*, came out in the US in February 1912. Another version, the love story with no mention of the New York magazine or slum conditions there, came out in the UK in May 1912. Maybe he got the idea from the Seymour Hicks show of 1907, *The Gay Gordons*, for which PGW wrote two lyrics. Very similar to another theatrical hit, *The Dollar Princess,* the plot revolves around a wealthy American who wants his daughter to marry into the aristocracy but she does not want be married for her money alone. She meets a young man who does not know who she is, they fall in love, he suddenly inherits a title, but all is well because she realises he loves her for herself alone etc. etc.

Prince, Arthur. 49 p306. A UK comic ventriloquist (1881–1948).

Prince Florizel. Ended his days in a tobacco shop in Rupert Street 9 p61. See R.L. Stevenson's *The New Arabian Nights*. Stevenson based the book on the rumoured adventures of the Prince of Wales (later Edward VII). In the 1860s–70s, the Prince used to explore London incognito and accompany Captain Shaw and the London Fire Brigade on their call-outs, using a small tobacconist's shop in Rupert Street to change his clothes. Stevenson found the tobacconist's and wrote of it, and James Bone identified it in his superb *London Perambulator* of 1925. See also Chap 25.

Prince of Wales. Cora once danced with the P. of W. See DANCED.

Princess and the Swineherd, The. 29 p86. Story by Hans Andersen.

Princess, scantily-clad, lying on a tiger-skin. 48 p237; 92 p14. PGW's *Palettes of Passion* film at 49 p37 is clearly his twist on the 1924 film *Three Weeks*, based on the novel of the same name by Elinor GLYN. *Three Weeks*, which shocked the world in 1907 (and sold two million copies), featured a handsome young Englishman seduced by a Balkan princess lying on a tiger skin. A verse was immediately coined:

Would you rather sin
With Elinor Glyn
On a tiger skin?
Or would you prefer
To err with her
On some other fur?

The princess on a tiger-skin became a lasting erotic image. From 1907 onwards, man-hungry vamps in books or films were immediately recognisable by their habit of reclining languorously on tiger skins whenever the opportunity offered.

Princess, The. 18 p151 and later. Long poem by TENNYSON, popular with young ladies in summer time.

Prison. Sent to prison for things done by a man who looked like him. See MAN IN ENGLAND.

Prisoner of Chillon. 66 p107 and later. See BYRON's poem 'The Prisoner of Chillon'. The man he had in mind was François de Bonnivard, who spent twenty years imprisoned there in the 16th century.

Prisons oft, in. 13 p106. B. 2 Corinthians 11.23 is the nearest I can find: "In labours more abundant, in stripes above measure, in prisons more frequent, in deaths oft."

Private eye. A private detective. See PINKERTON'S.

'Prize Poem, The'. See Chap. 3.

Prodigal Son. 20 p123; 50 p245. The line (50 p245) saying the Prodigal Son "mixed with pigs on a clubby basis" comes from B. Luke 15.16: "And he would fain have filled his belly with the husks that the swine did eat; and no man gave unto him."

Progress, future. Watch it with considerable interest 26 p288. See I SHALL WATCH.

Prometheus. 24 p40; watching his vulture drop in for lunch 26 p62; and later references to vultures gnawing at his liver. This character in Greek legend made fun of the gods and outwitted Zeus. As a punishment, Zeus ordered him tied to a rock for 30,000 years where, each day, a vulture came to eat his liver, which miraculously grew back overnight. He was rescued by Hercules after thirty years of this ordeal. Not to be confused with the fox that gnawed at the Spartan boy (see FOX GNAW).

Prompt in the hour of peril (to stimulate and encourage). 67 p92. I looked this one up only because of the alliteration. It is from William Lloyd Garrison's protest at the U.S. Supreme Court decision in the 1858 Dred Scott case (famous slavery case).

Prophet of the Old Testament, minor (rebuking the sins of the people). 67 p141 and often later. To see how gloomy some were, have a look at Nahum and Habakkuk. MTT Fr Rob Bovendeaard, who reminded me that 'Minor Prophet' is the term used for the prophets of the last twelve books in the Old Testament since the books are so short; the ones before these who wrote longer books are known as the Major Prophets.

Propinquity that did it, it was. 86 p71; might do the work it was meant to do 94 p13. From Ogden Nash's immortal phrase: "Nothing propinqs like propinquity."

Prospect pleases, where every. See EVERY PROSPECT PLEASES.

Prosperity is just around the corner. 56 p103 and elsewhere. There is something unusual here. In 1931/32, the US was in the grip of the Depression and Herbert Hoover was hoping to be re-elected president. He adopted the slogan 'Prosperity is just around the corner', which Joey Cooley echoed in *Laughing Gas*. Elsewhere, including *Bring on the Girls* (chap. 14), Wodehouse gives us: "Let's sing to every citizen and for'ner, Prosperity is just around the corner." In the same *Bring on the Girls* reference, PGW expressed his admiration for

Ira Gershwin's lyrics and says that Ira wrote the couplet. But when I checked the show, *Of Thee I Sing*, the song title is given as 'Posterity Is Just Around the Corner' and the lyric has the line about singing "to every citizen and forn'ner" followed by "Posterity is just around the corner". It looks as though PGW did forget the show quote but remembered the political slogan.

Prosser, Oofy. See OOFY.

Prudence, Baxter. See BAXTER, PRUDENCE.

Prudent man looks well to his going, the. 49 p288. B. Proverbs 14.15: "The prudent man looketh well to his going."

Pryzsky. "Yascha Pryzsky is giving a recital at Queen's Hall tomorrow." "Atta Yascha." 48 p45. Impossible not to think of the violin maestro Jascha Heifetz (1901–87).

Ps and Qs (have to be minded). 94 p59. Some believe it comes from q and p being the first and last letters on the top row of a typewriter keyboard. Some say it comes from teaching children to write and the difficulty they have in writing a lower-case *p* with the tail on the left and the *q* with the tail on the right (the most likely in my view). A third group nominate the slate in pubs which listed drinks bought on credit. Drinkers would keep a sharp eye on whether their beer was put under the P (pints) column or the Q (quarts) column. Hence the phrase "Put it on the slate" or "Just chalk it up". A fourth theory is that compositors using hand-set type had to be careful of the mirror images of these letters.

Psalmist and the wicked man, surname unknown. 2 p68. Although the wicked feature often in the Psalms, I prefer Proverbs, specifically B. Proverbs 13.5: "A wicked man is loathsome, and cometh to shame."

Psmith, Rupert/Ronald Eustace. See Chap. 37.

Psyche, Dance of. 20 p59. PGW's analogy of Lady Wetherby's dancing to boxing is one of the funniest things he wrote, as well as being an excellent description of the high-faluting nonsense often forced on an unsuspecting public. The early readers of *Uneasy Money* knew exactly what he was mocking. Psyche, the girl who loved Cupid, was a popular subject for Victorian painters. Although nearly always depicted in the nude, she was 'classical', which excused her nudity in Victorian eyes.

Wodehouse's readers would also have recognised Lady Wetherby. She was PGW's version of Lady Constance Mackenzie, who had shocked London by doing 'classical' dances exactly like Lady Wetherby's. She was the granddaughter of a duke and daughter of an earl. Whereas Lady Wetherby danced to pay off the mortgage on the (fictional) ancestral castle, Lady Constance danced to raise funds for a school for poor children. *Vanity Fair* (April 1916) had a piece complaining about the number of such ladies then infesting New York:

> Reader, have you ever heard of any of the following ladies? Think well, now! Look back! Try to remember! Isadora Duncan, Maud Allan, Rada, Lady Constance Mackenzie, Ruth St. Denis, Terpsichore, Salome, Gertrude Hoffman and Heaven only knows what other barefoot ladies

besides?

You haven't? Well, they all seem to be in New York. This very minute! And they are barefoot DANCING every hour of the livelong day …"

See also SALOME.

Public Enemy. 56 p102 & p258 (Number 13); wants to be promoted to Number 12 74 p237. The phrase will be familiar to anybody who has read about American gangsters or seen the show *Anything Goes*. The term 'Public Enemy' appeared in 1933 but, despite popular belief, the FBI never had a list of 'Public Enemies'. They did have a list of Ten Most Wanted Men, but the 'Public Enemy' business was a newspaper stunt, and it was the newspapers who named John Dillinger as Public Enemy Number One. It may have been his death in 1934 that gave PGW and Guy Bolton their sub-plot in *Anything Goes*, about a Public Enemy No. 13 whose ambition was to be promoted to No. 12.

Publius Syrius. See SYRIUS.

Pulbrook, Miss Eustacia. 68 p186. Probably the most overlooked of PGW's private jokes, it was one of his responses to those who attacked him because of the Berlin broadcasts. Sir Eustace Pulbrook (1881–1953), chairman of Lloyd's of London, was president of the Dulwich Old Boys Association (Old Alleynians) immediately after the war and objected to Wodehouse being re-admitted to membership of the OAs. See also COOPER, TALLEYRAND, HAILSHAM and MILNE.

Pull for the shore. 43 p113. Hymn by P.P. Bliss. The refrain is "Pull for the shore, brothers, pull for the shore."

Pullman Porters. "Just see them Pullman Porters" at 26 p179 is from 'Pullman Porters on Parade', 1913 song by Abrahams and Irving Berlin. These train attendants were very popular and were the subject of a dozen songs from 1880 onward, including 'The Porter in a Pullman Car' (1880), 'The Pullman Porters' Ball' (1900) and 'The Pullman Porter Blues' (1921). There was much public sympathy for their attempts, from 1880 onwards, to be allowed to form a union, a right not granted till 1926.

Pump Room, at Droitgate Spa. 61 p163. The Pump Room in Harrogate is where you went, and still can go, to drink the waters. See DROITGATE and HARROGATE.

Punch. PGW contributed to Britain's best-known humorous magazine from 1902 to 1974. *Punch* was a pillar of English literature and humorous writing, and the news that it was to close in 1992 after 151 years was a shock to the nation. Its cartoons had reflected the events and the popular feelings of the country from the Crimean War up to the end of the 20th century. When I had the honour of writing an article for it, I delivered it by hand and met the then-editor, Stanley Reynolds. He was courteous and, I think, sensed why I had come. When I said I had hoped to be allowed a look at the famous Punch Table, he was happy to indulge me. He took me along to see it and allowed me to run my hand over the worn wood, and admire the initials carved over the years by such writers as Mark Lemon, Thackeray and Mark Twain. The magazine was subsequently bought by a businessman who re-published it for a short time, but it closed again, forever, in May 2002. See Chap. 1 for its importance to social historians.

Punctuality, the politeness of princes. 3 p45; 12 p57. Attributed to Louis XVIII.

Pure as the driven snow. 85 p109. Take your choice between S. *Hamlet* 3.1 ("as pure as snow") and S. *Winter's Tale* 4.4 ("white as driven snow").

Purloined Letter trick. 59 p264; 72 p197. Edgar Allen Poe wrote a short story that revolved around a letter which would bring the government crashing down. The villain had 'hidden' it by putting it openly on his mantlepiece, where everybody overlooked it.

Purple cow. 19 p44. This quatrain by Gelett Burgess (1866–1951) is rarely heard today. Written in 1895, it runs:

I never saw a Purple Cow,
I never hope to see one;
But I can tell you, anyhow.
I'd rather see than be one!

The fame the verse brought him became annoying, so he produced:

Ah, yes! I wrote the Purple Cow –
I'm sorry, now, I wrote it!
But I can tell you anyhow,
I'll kill you if you quote it!

'Rather see than be one' became a catchphrase for years. As late as 1942 in *Money in the Bank*, when Dolly Molloy told Chimp Twist about the loony butler (Lord Uffenham), he replied that he had never seen a loony butler but would rather see than be one.

Purple Fan, The. 37 p253. This best-seller by Rodney Spelvin (1923) sounds awfully like *The Purple Fan*, a book of 1920 written by Adrian Head. *Note.* Although my wife and I both remember our surprise and delight in finding this information, I have to admit neither of us has any idea where we got it from. Neither the British Library nor Library of Congress catalogue mentions it. But we didn't just imagine it.

Purse. He who steals his lordship's p. steals trash 73 p124; who steals my p. steals trash 93 p49. S. *Othello*. 3.3: "Who steals my purse steals trash; 'tis something, nothing; 'Twas mine, 'tis his, and has been slave to thousands; But he that filches from me my good name Robs me of that which not enriches him, And makes me poor indeed."

Pursuivants, the four. 84 p22. See BLUEMANTLE.

Push thing, the. 3 p37. The 'posh' in some modern editions is a bad mistake. 'Push' was a perfectly good word. It meant smart or up-to-date; it also had the wider meaning of a group of people. "He was in my push" was still common in the 1960s, meaning a man who was in one's regiment or set of friends. In *The Gentle Grafter*, O. Henry says: "The whole push loves a lover."

Pussy. I love little pussy, her coat is so warm 30 p115; 96 p32. Children's poem by Anne Taylor (1782–1866) and Janet Taylor (1783–1823), who also gave us "Twinkle, twinkle, little star", and "Who ran to help me when I fell, / And would some little story tell".

Pussyfoot. 45 p234. A derogatory term applied to someone who moves silently. Whether it definitely comes from Pussyfoot Johnston (1862–1945), I am not certain. He was an American temperance reformer who, allegedly, used to slide quietly into bars and saloons before launching into his denunciation. Around 1920, he was encouraged to come to Britain to persuade people to follow the USA in adopting Prohibition. He was not well received and lost an eye at one rowdy meeting. In the UK, 'Pussyfoot' was applied generally to social reformers and temperance enthusiasts.

Put a sock in it. 82 p16 and elsewhere. This term, still in common use to tell someone to stop talking, goes back to the early wind-up horn gramophones. The usual method of reducing the volume of sound was to stuff a sock down the horn; it was very effective.

Put all your troubles in a great big box and sit on the lid and grin. 34 p30. The Bolton-Wodehouse-Kern musical *Sitting Pretty* came out early in 1924, and PGW used the plot and some of the characters to write *Bill the Conqueror*, which came out later that year. It was only natural for him to include quotes from the song 'Worries' he wrote for the show. 'Worries' advised the audience to "Shove all your worries in a great big box etc etc." The paragraph at 34 p30 mentions three 'cheer up' songs: silver linings, Blue Birds and troubles in a box. The first and third were by PGW.

Put away childish things. 26 p16; put off childish things 29 p15. B. I Corinthians 13.11: "When I was a child, I spake as a child, I understood as a child, I thought as a child; but when I became a man, I put away childish things."

Put me among the G's. 25 p32; 'Put Me Among the Pigs', banned in Boston 87 p103. UK 1890s song 'Put Me Among the Girls' by Murphy and Lipton. See also BANNED IN BOSTON.

Put me somewhere east of Suez ... a small bristly moustache. 73 p12. From KIPLING's still-popular poem/song 'Mandalay'. The last verse begins: "Ship me somewheres east of Suez, where the best is like the worst, Where there aren't no Ten Commandments an' a man can raise a thirst."

Put up the wrong bird. 4 p94. A shooting term. Game birds (pheasant, partridge, grouse etc) are 'put up' by dogs or beaters who drive them towards the guns.

Putting fortune to the test, to win or lose it all. 37 p17 and later. A common misquotation of MONTROSE's 'My Dear and Only Love'.

Pygmalion and Galatea. 32 p21. As PGW says, this reversed the normal procedure whereby the marble statue (GALATEA) Pygmalion had made, came to life. See also PIG SOMETHING.

Pyramus and Thisbe did talk through a chink in the wall. 13 p23 and later. The Greek legend of Pyramus, who could only talk to his lover Thisbe through a hole in the wall, has become, for some reason, embedded in the British subconscious. For every hundred people who know they spoke through a wall, only twenty will know it comes from Shakespeare's *Midsummer Night's Dream*, and only five will know he grabbed it from Ovid, who in turned grabbed it from Hyginus, who in turn …

Q

(MTT = My thanks to)

Qem, Mr. The fellow who owns this place 15 p249. I cannot understand why PGW gave us this extraordinary name. Gooch could just have said "the fellow who owns this place". Instead PGW used a misspelt form of the Latin accusative for 'who'. He had problems with the name in the earlier UK version, so perhaps this was the reason. See Chap. 23.

Quackenbush, some Americans are called. 77 p29; 78p189. For one example, see Chap. 23 (Long Island).

Quaglino's restaurant. Veronica goes to it 65 p19. A famous London restaurant in the 1920s and 30s, Quaglino's has recently been relaunched. MTT Jeffrey Preston for proof that PGW knew Quaglino's since Mr Preston possesses a book signed by him for Betty Ross: "Best wishes at Quaglino's 8 March 1934."

Quaint Old Bird. 12 p30. This 1904 song by Morse and Madden featured in Seymour Hicks' 1905 show *The Catch of the Season*, which PGW almost certainly saw. He began working with Hicks a few months later.

Quality of mercy. Was not strained but dropped like something or other on something I didn't catch 60 p238; 60 p280; 67 p244; and elsewhere. See DROPPING LIKE.

Quarrels. Should not seek q. but being in them … 8 p66. See BEWARE OF ENTRANCE.

Queen could do no wrong, the. 48 p282 and elsewhere. English legal maxim ("the King can do no wrong") summarising the legal sovereignty of the Crown. Government departments had legal immunity from criminal prosecution till around 1950.

Queen of Sheba. 65 p56; 68 p70 and elsewhere. B. 1 Kings 10.7. She tried to impress Solomon with her wealth and splendour but found he was cleverer and richer. See HALF WAS NOT TOLD.

Queen of the Harem cigarettes. 9 p195. See CIGARETTES.

Queen of the May. Are you under the delusion that I'm to be Q. of the M.? You've called me early all right 23 p157; and later. T. 'The May Queen'. "You must wake and call me early, call me early, mother dear … For I'm to be Queen o' the May, mother, I'm to be Queen o' the May."

Queen's Club. 19 p2 and later. This London club, founded in 1886 by the energetic Lord Desborough, the man who also founded the Bath Club, furnished its members with a choice of physical recreation. Some 23 types of games have been played there. Its running track and football pitches hosted University matches, and it is still the senior English tennis venue after Wimbledon.

Queensberry rules (for boxing). 6 p153. The Marquess of Queensberry drew up rules for boxing in 1867 which were later adopted around the world. He introduced three-minute rounds, one-minute intervals, a 20-feet-square ring, and no seconds or supporters allowed in the ring while boxing was in progress.

Quenching something. Something I had read somewhere about something not quenching something 68 p18. I found the clue to this mysterious reference in PGW's next book, at 69 p65: "Of course it didn't quench my love. A love like mine doesn't go around getting itself quenched." G&S *Iolanthe* Act 2: "Oh, Captain Shaw! / Type of true love kept under! / Could thy Brigade / With cold cascade / Quench my great love, I wonder!" (Captain Shaw was the famous leader of the London Fire Brigade.)

Querouaille, Louise de. 70 p57 & p85. One of Charles II's mistresses. Their son was the first Duke of Richmond and Gordon.

Querulousness and self-pity had marked him for their own. 48 p130. See MELANCHOLY.

Question, others abide our. See OTHERS ABIDE.

Quick Service. Title of 62; 69 p83; 83 p101 and elsewhere. Once a common advertisement outside cafés/restaurants to persuade you they were not one of those establishments where you spent half an hour waiting for a waitress to ask you what you wanted and another half an hour waiting for the pot of tea you ordered. I recall this infuriating habit was particularly prevalent in seaside hotels.

Quickness of the hand almost deceived the eye. Doris Jimpson's marriages 65 p83. The traditional patter of a Three Card Trick man was: "Now you see it, now you don't. The quickness of the hand deceives the eye." See PEA-AND-THIMBLE MAN.

Quintin, Dante Gabriel. See DANTE GABRIEL QUINTIN.

Quiring to the young-eyed cherubim. 68 p200 and p205. See PATINES.

Quis custodiet ipsos custodes. 59 p209. Juvenal's *Satires* 6. Who will guard the guardians themselves?

Quiver like an aspen. 60 p287. See ASPEN.

Quorn. 52 p82. A senior (founded circa 1690) and highly respected English hunt.

R

(MTT = My thanks to)

Rabbit, Brer. See Brer Rabbit.

Rabbit, white. 80 p188. See White rabbit.

Rabbut. "This is her-r-r. No, it's a rabbut." 31 p186. In 'The Metropolitan Touch', Bingo insists Bertie accompanies him on a walk to admire Bingo's latest love, Mary Burgess. Bertie tells us the phrase is from a song of Harry Lauder's. I thought I knew most of Lauder's songs, but this was a new one on me. What I had forgotten was that Wodehouse would have seen Lauder on stage, where he interpolated patter between verses of his songs. I have known 'I Love a Lassie' as a song all my life, but a 1907 recording of his stage act has the interpolation after the second verse, when he tells the audience to keep quiet because his love is coming — she's coming — she's coming — and then the line. MTT Helen Murphy. See also I love a lassie.

Rabelais. 36 p117 and later. The writer Barbara Bowen suggests a strong similarity between Rabelais (1494–1553) and Wodehouse in their wit and use of satire. I would not disagree in theory, though much of Rabelais' appeal rested on what one reference book calls his 'coarsely boisterous and licentious language'. PGW made people laugh for 75 years without recourse to sexual innuendo.

RAC club. 39 p31. The Royal Automobile Club in Pall Mall is reputedly London's largest club.

Race is degenerating, the. 12 p128. A popular phrase of the time. Eugenics exercised the minds of many scientists and politicians in the early 20th century. See Jukes family.

Race is not always to the swift (nor the battle to the strong). 52 p192. PGW was right. I have read this in at least two accounts of school prize-givings. B. Ecclesiastes 9.11: "I returned and saw under the sun, that the race is not to the swift, nor the battle to the strong, neither yet bread to the wise, nor yet riches to men of understanding …"

Radium, Professor. 12 p181. Eccentric scientist in *Puck*, an English child's comic (1910–41).

Raffles. *The Amateur Cracksman* 4 p30; 12 p31; and later. It is said that E.W. Hornung (1866–1921) created Raffles, the gentleman crook, as a counter to Sherlock Holmes, created by his brother-in-law Arthur Conan Doyle. *The Amateur Cracksman* caused a sensation in 1899, and at least seven 'Raffles' films were made later. In 1906 Gerald Du Maurier played the part on stage in London, and the New York version was clearly the play that started all the misunderstanding in *A Gentleman of Leisure/The Intrusion of Jimmy*. PGW played cricket with both Doyle and Hornung in the Authors v Actors matches.

Raft, George. 90 p123. Smooth, slightly sinister Hollywood actor (1895–1980); a former professional athlete, gambler and associate of gangsters. When he tried to open a nightclub in London, he was refused entry to the UK because of his 'connections'.

Rag, a bone and a hank of hair, a. 29 p122; 68 p21. KIPLING's poem 'The Vampire'.

Rainbow in the sky. He felt his heart leap up … when he beheld a etc. 50 p40 and later. Wordsworth's 'My Heart Leaps Up': "My heart leaps up when I behold a rainbow in the sky."

Rainbow round his shoulder. 79 p49; 83 p11 and elsewhere. 'There's a Rainbow Round My Shoulder', sung by Al Jolson in 1928 film *The Singing Fool*.

Raining violets, It's. 32 p258. From the song 'April Showers', which Al Jolson sang in the 1921 show *Bombo*. He got thirty-six curtain calls for it on the first night. Probably an adaptation of the 1901 poem by Robert Loveman 'April Rain': "It's not raining rain to me, it's raining daffodils."

Raisuli. 10 p14; 11 p23; 13 p67. A leader of the Arab revolt against the French in North Africa in the early 20th century, he caused them trouble for 20 years. See also MACLEAN.

***Rajputana*, S.S.** 41 p126. This P&O ship was launched in 1925 for the Far East run, then was commandeered in 1939 and converted into an armed cruiser equipped with forty-year-old six-inch guns, all that were available. She was torpedoed and sunk in April 1941 while escorting an Atlantic convoy.

Raleigh, Sir Walter. 32 p68 and later. This brave sailor and author (1552–1618), who introduced tobacco and the potato into England, is remembered today for whipping off his new cloak and laying it in a puddle so Queen Elizabeth would not get her shoes dirty.

Ranjitsinhji. 2 p211. Indian prince (1872–1933) who came to England and became one of the finest batsmen the world has seen.

"Rank is but the penny stamp." "Guinea stamp, sir." 43 p260 and later. Burns' poem 'For A' That and A' That'. "The rank is but the guinea's stamp; The man's the gowd for a' that."

Ranks of things that matter. 27 p85. See MATTER.

Rannygazoo. 32 p275 and often later. I believe PGW got this one wrong. The magisterial *Oxford English Dictionary* attributes it to him and says it stems from the American word 'ranikaboo'.

PGW had a superb ear. In his early notebooks (1902–5), he used to transcribe Cockney speech and did it very well. He also noted new phrases and 'Americanisms' coming into the language. He developed the ability to mix normal speech and slang with appropriate quotations and made his readers laugh just with the way he used words.

'Reinikaboo' was noted in the USA in 1901 as a fake news-paper story. In 1907 it was described as: 'no bluff; no reinikaboo round here'. In 1947 it meant a prank. In my remarkable 1950 Swan's Anglo-American Dictionary, 'ranikaboo' is slang for a spree, a lark, a practical joke.

In a letter to Richard Usborne in the 1950s, PGW said that "Rannygazoo is a well-known American expression", but I believe he had simply misheard 'reinakaboo' or 'ranikaboo' in a restaurant or in the street in New York. Wodehouse was certainly not the man to accost a stranger and ask him to repeat something he probably wasn't intended to hear. It's a splendid word, but I am certain he would have used the correct term if he had heard it clearly or seen it written down. If, on the other hand, he deliberately changed it to his more euphonious version, then it would be the first time he had done so.

One of the reasons so many words in the *Oxford Dictionary* have their first usage attributed to PGW is that he was the first British author to put them in print. I have yet to find one that was not already in common speech in either Britain or America. But such common speech rarely appeared in print in those days. See also GAZEBO, DING-BASTED AS A STIG, and SKEESICKS.

Rapture, that first, fine careless. 19 p188 and later. Browning's 'Home Thoughts from Abroad': "Lest you should think he never could recapture / The first fine careless rapture."

Rash youth. 64 p212. "For know, rash youth … that in this star crost world … what we would." Bernard Shaw's *The Admirable Bashville* Act 3. See also ADMIRABLE BASHVILLE.

Rassendyl, Rudolph. 9 p61. Hero of Anthony Hope's 1894 *Prisoner of Zenda*, which gave rise to a new genre of novels set in Eastern Europe. The common feature was a brave English hero battling against sinister foreigners and saving the life/honour of a beautiful princess. Dornford Yates specialised in these later; see Richard Usborne's ground-breaking *Clubland Heroes*.

Rat, smelt a (and saw it floating in the air). 13 p110; 54 p151. I do not know if it is still taught in schools but I remember clearly our amusement in class when we learned of this splendid example of a mixed metaphor. It is attributed to a Member of Parliament, Sir Boyle Roche (1743–1807), an Irishman famous for his verbal slips, a sort of 18th-century Sam Goldwyn. Seeking to impress on Parliament the gravity of something, he produced the line still quoted in English textbooks today: "Mr Speaker, I smell a rat! I see him forming in the air and darkening the sky; but I'll nip him in the bud." For his 'bird' see ROCHE.

Rattigan, Terence. Is as slim as Ian Hay 66 p103. This playwright (1911–77) wrote a series of successes including *French Without Tears* and *The Winslow Boy*. See also HAY, IAN.

Ravelled sleave of care. Beach was knitting up 72 p16. See SLEEP WHICH.

Raven. Quoth the Raven, 'Nevermore' 89 p123; the one who said "Nevermore" 95 p64. Edgar Allan Poe's 'The Raven'. The phrase 'Nevermore' was popular enough for PGW to parody it in a series of Parrot poems about Tariff reform in the *Daily Express* (1903). Each verse ended with the words: "Your food will cost you more."

Ravens. Whom the ravens feed 44 p52; ravens do not feed the Ambroses of this world 54 p162; and later. Of Elijah, the Bible tells us at 1 Kings 17.6: "And the ravens brought him bread and flesh in the morning, and bread and flesh in the evening …"

***Raymond*, overture to.** 61 p181. A fine rousing piece of music written by Ambroise Thomas in 1851. MTT Tamaki Morimura.

Razed to its foundations and sown with salt. 58 p48; 73 p165. The nearest I can get is B. Judges 9.45: "…he took the city, and slew the people that was therein, and beat down the city, and sowed it with salt."

Real sense. Yes, yes, in a very real sense he understood 92 p144. The vicar's response to Chippendale's heart-rending story as to why he wanted the miniature of *The Girl in Blue*. A minor reference, but it illustrates PGW's remarkable memory. I do not know when PGW last sat through a sermon, but I am sure I have never heard 'in a very real sense' in my life except from clerical lips. Is it something they teach in theological colleges, along with controlling Village Mothers and Church Lads?

Realm of the merely impudent and soars into the boundless empyrean of pure cheek, It passes out of the. See EMPYREAN.

Realm. This realm, this England. 83 p114. See THIS REALM.

Reason returns to her throne. 13 p20 and frequent later, including such PGW variations as "limping back to her throne" and "tottering on her throne". Farquhar's *The Recruiting Officer*. 3.2. "Reason still keeps its throne, but it nods a little, that's all."

Reason why, not to. Ours not to r. w. 19 p163; His-not-to-reason-why 56 p41; and later. T. 'Charge of the Light Brigade': "Theirs not to reason why, / Theirs but to do and die …"

Rebel yell. 38 p20. Morris' *Dictionary of Words and Phrases* states it is impossible to reproduce the sound, but says it was based on Tally-ho, a hunting cry which the Southern planation owners had brought over from England.

Recamier, Madame (her salon). 55 p245; 65 p77. This lady (1777–1849) attracted to her salon all the finest minds in Paris.

Receipt of custom, at the. See CUSTOM, AT THE RECEIPT.

Redbridge. 33 p194 and later. With the mention of Biscuit Row and Fitch & Weyman's biscuit factory, it is not difficult to identify Redbridge as Reading in Berkshire, the home of Huntley & Palmer's biscuit factory. But see WALSINGFORD-BELOW-CHIVENEY.

Reed, broken. See BROKEN REED.

Reeled and would have fallen. 42 p263. See STAGGERED.

Refused to be comforted. 21 p169 and elsewhere. B. Matthew 2.18: "Rachel weeping for her children, and would not be comforted …" See also MOURNED LIKE NIOBE.

Regardless of their fate, the little victims play, Alas. 64 p30. Gray's 'Ode on a Distant Prospect of Eton College': "Alas, regardless of their doom, / The little victims play."

Regiment leaves at dawn, My. 86 p79. From the Marx Brothers film *Monkey Business* (1931), script by S.J. Perelman, who said the line came from *The Merry Widow*. MTT Nigel Rees. Also in the later film *The Secret Life of Walter Mitty*.

Reigelheimer's. 20 p51. Similar to Geisenheimer's. See Chap. 23.

Rejoice in thy youth, young man. 23 p55. B. Ecclesiastes 11.9: "Rejoice, O young man, in thy youth, and let thy heart cheer thee in the days of thy youth …"

Rejoice with me for I have found the sheep which was lost. 85 p41. B. Luke 15.6.

Rejoicing in my youth. 96 p171; 97 p8. See REJOICE IN THY.

Rejoicing in spirit. 59 p296. B. Luke 10.21 is as near as I can get: "In that hour Jesus rejoiced in spirit …"

Reluctant feet. See STANDING WITH RELUCTANT FEET.

Rem acu tetigisti. 41 p137 and elsewhere. Plautus' *Rudens* 5.2. Literally, you have touched the matter with a needle.

'Remember.' 57 p70. Because of the way PGW used this, I am sure he was thinking of 'Remember', the last word spoken by Charles I before his execution in Whitehall in January 1649.

Remembrancer, the King's. 59 p53. A very ancient office. The title is appropriate since the official concerned has to remember things; how ceremonies were conducted 100 years ago, what a judge said 300 years ago, things like that. In England, such matters are very important. Every year, amongst other ancient ceremonies, the City of London pays a rent of horseshoes and horseshoe nails to the Crown for a smithy that vanished 600 years ago. The Queen's Remembrancer attends to ensure the rent is properly paid.

Remorse like a worm i' the bud … damask cheek. 2 p242. See SHE NEVER SAID.

Rend garments and scatter ashes on his head. PGW ref lost. B. Job 2.12: "and they rent everyone his mantle, and sprinkled dust upon their heads towards heaven …"

Rent roll that ran into thousands. 53 p72. On large estates in England, the details of rent due from tenants were kept on rolls of parchment, hence 'rent rolls'. In the 1980s, I visited the office of a very old estate and asked about the deep wooden frame with small openings in it on one wall. I was told by the clerk that his predecessor had kept the old rent rolls in them till the 1920s, just in case there was a query.

Re-paints, battered. 28 p16; 92 p188. See Chap. 27.

Repent ye for the Kingdom of Heaven is at hand. God shall smite thee, thou whited wall. Abstain from fleshly lusts that war upon the soul. 95 p115. Miss Priestley was delivering a triple broadside here. The first sentence is B.

Matthew 3.2, the second is B. Acts 23.3, and the third is B. I Peter 2.11.

Repose. No longer had the r. which stamps the caste of Vere de Vere 13 p234 and later. T. 'Lady Clara Vere de Vere': "Her manners had not that repose / Which stamps the caste of Vere de Vere."

Reside with the morning stars, went to. 86 p49 and elsewhere. PGW used this as a synonym for dying, but I have not found the source. It is not Biblical or in Shakespeare. The nearest I have found is William Blake's 'Land of Dreams'. This poem, mourning a mother who has died, has: "Above the light of the morning star."

Resorted. To which the school most resorted 8 p31. An unusual choice of words unless you know Tennyson's poem about The Cock Tavern in Fleet Street (still there, thank Heaven). T. 'Will Waterproof's Lyrical Monologue': "O plump headwaiter at the Cock, / To which I most resort."

Resource and sagacity, men of infinite. 3 p133; 4 p22; Dolly Molloy is a woman of r. and s. at 94 p55; and frequent later. The Mariner in 'How the Whale Got His Throat' in KIPLING's *Just So Stories* was "a man of infinite-resource-and-sagacity". MTT Tim Murphy.

Rest, a little. A little rest, a little folding of the hands in sleep. See LITTLE REST, A.

Rest is silence, the. 63 p179. S. *Hamlet* 5.2. Hamlet's last words.

Resting. He was so good at resting, he would have made a splendid actor 4 p17. I do not know if the term is still used but, in PGW's day, an actor out of work always said he was "resting".

Retainer, faithful old. See CHARLES, HIS FRIEND.

Retiarius (net and trident). 38 p207; 73 p131; 84 p92. See GLADIATORS.

Retort courteous. 84 p66. See LIE DIRECT.

Retreating from Moscow. It was Ukridge, retreating from Moscow 33 p80. Napoleon's mistake, like Hitler's, was to underestimate the Russian winter and the difficulties of maintaining lines of supply across the vast expanse of the Russian steppes.

Revelation, Book of. 34 p32 and elsewhere. I was shocked to see PGW sometimes using 'Revelations', rather than 'Revelation'. But maybe it was his publishers who got it wrong, as they did many of his Biblical references.

Revere, Paul. 76 p140. A famous American silversmith (1735–1818) who carried a message that English troops were on the march. Longfellow wrote about it in 'Paul Revere's Ride' (1861).

Revolution. Nay, Sire, a revolution. See NAY, SIRE.

Reynard the Fox. 65 p152. See MASEFIELD.

Reynolds, Sir Joshua. 62 p10. This painter (1723–92) became the first president of the Royal Academy in 1768.

Rheims, monks of, regardless of grammar. 4 p240. See MONKS.

Rhodes. 12 p151. Wilfred Rhodes (1877–1953), a professional cricketer, was called back to play for the England team in 1930 at the age of 52.

Rialto. What news on the Rialto? 52 p11; 96 p102. S. *Merchant of Venice* 1.3.

The Rialto is the famous bridge that spans the Grand Canal in Venice. Built in 1591, it became the favourite spot for Venetians to meet and exchange gossip.

Ribstons. Right among the R. 8 p80; wedged tightly in among the R. 15A (UK) p36. A Ribston was a well-known English apple. Since apples were then packed in barrels, Psmith was implying in the second reference that *Cosy Moments* had been confined, restrained. MTT Marilyn MacGregor for raising this query, emphasising how metaphors differ between England and America.

Rice pudding. As though Sir James Piper had refused to eat his r. p. 97 p13. I wonder how many other readers remembered Mary Jane in A.A. Milne's 'Rice Pudding'? "And she won't eat her dinner — rice pudding again — What *is* the matter with Mary Jane?"

Rich as Creosote. See CREOSOTE.

Rich beyond the dreams of avarice. 77 p49. See WEALTH BEYOND.

Rich but honest parents. 8 p21. From *Ben Thirlwall's Schooldays* by Fitz Hugh Ludlow (1836–1870): "My name is Ben Thirlwall and I am the son of rich but honest parents." MTT Nigel Rees.

Rich, passing. 2 p39. See PASSING RICH.

Richard Coeur de Lion. 67 p98. Richard I, a brave but inefficient King of England, 1189–99.

Richards, Gordon. 73 p209. Britain's leading jockey for twenty years, Richards (1904–1986) was unsuccessful in the Derby till Coronation Year (1953), when, to everybody's delight, he won it at last.

Richelieu. 13 p121. A subtle, scheming statesman cardinal (1585–1642), chief minister to Louis XIII.

Rider Haggard. See HAGGARD.

Riders of the Purple Sage. 38 p34. This 1912 Western was the most popular book written by Zane GREY.

Riffs. Tramping through the hot sand without a pub in sight, with Riffs or whatever they're called potting at him from all directions 76 p48. The films *Beau Geste* and *The Desert Song* made the Riff tribesmen of North Africa familiar to all.

Rift in the lute. There has been a r. In the l. 76 p92; 80 p124; and elsewhere. T. 'Merlin and Vivien': "It is the little rift within the lute, / That by and by will make the music mute."

Right good shield of hides untanned. 47 p74; 67 p64. See HYBRIAS.

Right triumphing over Wrong. See STATUE OF RIGHT.

Riley, living the life of. 58 p310 and later. The popular song 'Is That Mr Reilly?' by Pat Rooney (1882) was soon misquoted as Riley or O'Reilly. Rooney based it on a real Mr O'Reilly, who inherited a large hotel, sat back and did nothing the rest of his life.

Rinehart, Mary Roberts. 78 p45. This American writer (1876–1958) was the creator of Tish (Miss Letitia Carberry), a lady whom Aunt Dahlia would be proud to call a friend. PGW paid her the compliment of using the name

CARBERRY, and Mary Rinehart's children say Tish bore a strong resemblance to her creator.

Rin-Tin-Tin. 46 p22; 78 p165. This ex-German Army dog (1916–32) became a superstar in the 1920s, and made a lot of money for Warner Brothers up to 1930.

Rio. Oh I'd like to roll down to Rio 44 p10. KIPLING's *Just So Stories* 'Beginning of the Armadilloes'. "And I'd like to roll to Rio / Some day before I'm old!"

Ripley's *Believe It or Not.* 51 p19; 61 p20. Robert R.Ripley (1893–1949) was a cartoonist who liked collecting odd bits of information. He began his series of unusual facts in 1918 and published his first book in 1928. The series is still running. My personal favourite is his account of the popularity of the name Johnson in Minnesota. A man put himself forward as a political candidate with the simple slogan 'My name is Johnson' and did no other campaigning. He got 44,000 out of a possible 150,000 votes.

Ripples, soft sleek. See SOFT SLEEK RIPPLES.

Ripton. 4 p9 and later. A very thin disguise of the real Repton School.

River … lies at the bottom of the garden. 47 p129; 73 p23. See GARDEN LIES.

River, weariest. See WEARIEST RIVER.

Riverhead, Lord. 94 p35. Unique, I believe, in being the only member of the PGW peerage with an American title. Riverhead, Suffolk County, New York is where Wodehouse swore his US citizenship oath.

Roast beef, compared to sunsets. See SUNSETS.

Roast beef of old England. 3 p238. A common misquote from Fielding's *The Grub Street Opera*. "Oh! The roast beef of England, / And old England's roast beef."

Robbing Peter to pay Paul. 90 p73. In 1550, Edward VI raised Westminster Abbey to the dignity of a cathedral, which meant that it received funds from the churches and parishes within its area of jurisdiction. In 1560, Elizabeth I reversed the decision and St Paul's regained its position as London's cathedral. To ensure its primacy and authority, Elizabeth also ordered that some of the estates and property of St Peter's (Westminster Abbey) were transferred back to St Paul's. At a time of religious turmoil, this aroused much controversy, and the phrase entered the language.

Roberts, Arthur. 4 p151; 10 often. Arthur Roberts (1853–1933) was a leading music hall comedian and a prominent member of the Pelican Club, where his nickname was 'The Gasper'.

Roberts, John. 2 p163. UK billiards champion c.1900–10.

Roberts, Lord. 18 p93. This superb soldier (1832–1914) was one of only two men to be awarded both the Victoria Cross (the highest award for bravery) and the Order of the Garter (the senior Order of Chivalry). For information, the other was Lord De L'Isle and Dudley (1909–91), whose ancestor was Sir Philip Sidney. Lord De L'Isle aroused adverse comment when he showed the same spirit of generosity as his forbear by raising funds in 1945 to defend General von Manstein, who was charged with war crimes. He said he would cheerfully have tried to kill Manstein if they had met during the war, but he felt he deserved a proper trial and an English barrister to defend him.

Robey, George. 10 often; 11 p71; bore a close resemblance to Lord Emsworth's maternal grandmother 19 p194. A music hall comedian, Robey (1869–1954) did his act in vaguely clerical dress, telling funny stories in a lugubrious tone rather like the American George Burns. See also DESIST and TEMPER YOUR HILARITY.

Robinson, Edward G. 61 p103 and later. 'Tough guy' actor (1893–1973), friend of the Wodehouses in Hollywood.

Robinson, Fletcher. I mention Fletcher Robinson (1871–1907) because of his collaboration with both Arthur Conan DOYLE and PGW. From 1903 till his death, Robinson edited *Vanity Fair*, a London weekly for which PGW wrote sixty-three pieces between October 1903 and October 1906. He and PGW were joint authors of several articles, including two Christmas features, but PGW clearly believed Robinson paid too little. In the *Phrases and Notes* notebooks for 1905 is an entry: "I suggest to Miss Pope that she and I call on Fletcher Robinson together & bully him for more payment. She says 'Will it do any good?' I say 'It won't do him any good.'"

Robinson is probably better known as the young journalist who met Conan Doyle in a hotel in Norfolk and told him about the legendary fierce hound that was reputed to haunt the area near Robinson's home at Dartmoor. Intrigued, Doyle accepted his invitation to visit him, and they were guided to the relevant Dartmoor landmarks by the Robinson coachman, Harry Baskerville. As a token of gratitude, Baskerville's name was used for the cursed landowning family. I have read that Doyle insisted on Robinson's name appearing with his on the first edition of *The Hound of the Baskervilles*. I have also read, however, that a book was published a few years ago, accusing Doyle of poisoning Robinson to secure all the royalties!

Robinson, Jno., Market Blandings taxi driver. Edward in *Uncle Fred in the Springtime* but reverted to Jno. later. See JNO.

Roche, Sir Boyle. His bird was sedentary compared with this elusive man 9 p269. The Irish politician Sir Boyle Roche (1743–1807) famously said in Parliament that he regretted he was not a bird and therefore could not be in two places at once. His 'bird' was quoted for nearly 150 years, while his 'rat' is still quoted for school children (see RAT, SMELT A).

Rock, hewn from the living. See HEWN.

Rock of ages. 20 p26 and later. Toplady's famous hymn (1775).

Rock shall fly etc. See COME ONE, COME ALL.

Rockefeller. 13 p29 and later. See JOHN D.

Rodgers and Hammerstein. 70 p187 and later. Richard Rodgers (composer) and Oscar Hammerstein (lyric writer) wrote superb musicals. They held PGW in high regard, as he did them.

Rodin's Thinker. 42 p279 and later. Rodin (1840–1917) produced this magnificent sculpture of a man deep in thought in 1904.

Rodney Stone. 3 p247. Adventure story by Conan DOYLE. Years later, PGW wrote to Bill Townend and recollected going down to the kiosk (still there) at West Dulwich station each month to buy the *Strand* magazine to read the latest instalment.

Roedean. 63 p111; 72 p14; 73 p105. One of England's leading girls' schools. In *Pigs Have Wings*, Monica Simmons "looked like what in fact she was, one of the six daughters of a Rural Vicar all of whom had played hockey for Roedean". MTT Kenneth Neave for correcting a PGW error. His daughter, who went to Roedean, states firmly that "Roedean never played hockey — lacrosse only".

Roegate, Bertie. 57 p27. It should be no surprise by now to learn that PGW lived at Rogate Lodge, Rogate, Sussex in 1929.

Rogers, Ginger. 58 p186. As well as being a superb partner of Fred ASTAIRE's, this lady (1911–95) was an excellent comedienne.

Roget (and his thesaurus). 58 p87; 86 p9; 89 p35. Roget's *Thesaurus* (of synonyms and antonyms) has been an invaluable aid to writers since its publication in 1852. An eminent academic, he saw it go into twenty-eight editions before he died seventeen years later.

Rogues Gallery of repulsive small boys. 51 p33. It used to be the custom in English police stations to have pictures of notorious criminals on the walls so policemen would know if they came into their area.

Rogue's March, The. 4 p70. As well as being the march played when a soldier was flogged in public, it is also the title of a book (1900) by E.W. Hornung. See also RAFFLES.

Roi Pausole. 60 p159. A very obscure reference. This book by Pierre Louÿs was published in 1901. In 1930 it was staged as an operetta, *Les Aventures du Roi Pausole*, with music by Honegger. MTT Laura Loehr.

Roland gripping his great sword at Roncevalles. 45 p167. In 778 A.D., Roland, one of Charlemagne's paladins, fought a gallant rearguard action at Roncevalles in the Pyrenees and died, having slain hundreds with his great sword Durandal. See also JOYEUSE.

Roll, bowl or pitch! Ladies halfway and all bad nuts returned! 60 p207; 73 p16. If you have ever seen a coconut shy, this needs no explanation. If you have not, you should know that a traditional, but now vanishing, feature of British fairgrounds is to put coconuts into cups on tall sticks and let people pay money to throw wooden balls and try and knock them out of the cups. If they knock them out, they win the nut. The PGW wording was the traditional spiel of the stall-holder — and I was lucky enough to hear it as recently as 1999.

Roll Out the Barrel. 76 p9. An exuberant song written by Lew Brown (1939), very popular during the Second World War. MTT David Jasen, who informs me it was originally called 'Beer Barrel Polka' (1934) by Czechoslovakians Jarimir

Vejvoda and Wladimir Timm. Lew Brown did the later English translation.

Rolling in a fine frenzy from heaven to earth. See POET'S EYE.

Rolls-Royce doesn't make any noise, a. 47 p82. The superb engineering of this car fully justified PGW's tribute. He owned one in the 1920s, and the remark was a common one for many years. In the 1950s, there was a famous Rolls-Royce advertisement which, from memory, was: "At sixty miles an hour, all you can hear is the ticking of the clock." The sequel was even more famous. In an interview, a Rolls-Royce executive apologised for the advertisement with some such words as: "We are working hard on that blasted clock."

Roman father gave his son when handing him sword and shield, the sort of look a. 64 p165. See COME BACK VICTORIOUS.

Romanoff's, Mike. 70 p80. Mike Romanoff (né Harry Gerguson, 1893–1971), a famous con man and Hollywood restaurateur, amazed David Niven with the stories he told. He claimed to be on friendly terms with many of the British aristocracy and, when challenged by the son of one peer, produced supporting evidence that astonished his questioner with its accuracy.

Romano's. 18 p223 and later; especially see 42 p149. In real life it was Stephen 'Fatty' Coleman, not Gregory Parsloe nor Gally (see 97 p76), who walked round Romano's c.1892 with a soup tureen on his head and a stick of celery in his hand, saying he was a trooper on guard at Buckingham Palace. See Chap. 5.

Rome was not built in a day. 13 p47. A Latin proverb.

Romero, Caesar. 66 p128. Cesar Romero was a handsome Latin American film star (1907–94).

Roof tree, under one's own. 12 p189 and often later. A common phrase — if you knew your Classics. Homer used the phrase often in the *Iliad* and *Odyssey*.

Room to swing a cat. See SWING A CAT.

Roosevelt, F.D. And his New Deal 53 p32 and later. Franklin Delano Roosevelt (1882–1945), 32nd US president, first used the phrase 'New Deal' in his speech at the Chicago Democratic convention of 1932. In effect, he sought to pull the USA out of the Depression by a vast programme of public works. See also DEAL.

Roosevelt, Theodore. This energetic, big-game-hunting president (1858–1919) of the USA was keen on spelling reform (see 18 p82), collected many new animal specimens on a trip through the African jungles (see 19 p50), broke the Trusts that monopolised American industry, said that America's foreign policy should be "to speak softly but carry a big stick" (see 15A p154) and popularised such phrases as 'muckraking', 'mollycoddle' and 'weasel words'. See also BIG STICK and TEDDY BEARS.

Root of the matter in him. 8 p65 and later. B. Job 19.28: "Why persecute we him, seeing the root of the matter is found in me?"

Rosary, The. 23 p133 and later. This 1898 song by Rogers & Nevin swept the world (6 million copies sold). "The hours I spent with thee, dear heart, Are as a string of pearls to me, I count them over, every one apart, My rosary, my rosary." The name was then used for a best-seller novel which someone turned it into a popular melodrama. The last scene has the heroine about to become a nun and fondling her rosary when the hero, who the villain had persuaded everybody was dead, dashes on stage just in time. It toured for years. The natural reaction to the craze came in 1911 with the song 'When Ragtime Rosy Ragged the Rosary'.

Roscius. The stage awaits R. 13 p236. Pre-eminent Roman actor, died 60 B.C.

Rose of America. 26 p146. This fictional show in *Jill the Reckless* (1920) comes from *The Rose of China*, the Bolton & Wodehouse musical that had failed just before PGW wrote the book.

Rose of Stamboul, the Sinister Affair of the. 30 Dedication. Very mysterious. *The Rose of Stamboul*, a New York show with music by Romberg, had opened a few months before PGW wrote the dedication to George Grossmith. What happened here? Had PGW and Grossmith tried to organise a London production and been thwarted by some New York producer? Had Romberg agreed a deal and then gone back on it? Will we ever know? See Chap. 17

Rose of summer. Looking like the last r. of s. 23 p131 and later. "Tis the last rose of summer / Left blooming alone ..." 'The Last Rose of Summer' (1813) by Thomas Moore was revived, with many other Moore songs, in the 1890s; the 1907 Army & Navy Stores catalogue has it under 'Standard Songs'. In *The Cabaret Girl*, PGW gave it a new twist with 'The First Rose of Summer'.

Rose, redder than the. Oofy had always been this 83 p110. Probably from Scott's "Jellon Grame": "What's paler than the prymrose wan? / What's redder than the rose?"

Rosebud. Tennyson's a little English rosebud 36 p10. T. *The Princess*, Prologue: "A rosebud set with little wilful thorns, / And sweet as English air could make her ..."

Rose-leaves and am no more a golden ass, I have eaten. 26 p56. In the second century A.D., Lucius Apuleius wrote *The Golden Ass*, the story of a young man who was turned into an ass. He underwent many ordeals and adventures before returning to human form by eating a wreath of rose leaves.

Rosenbach, Dr. Picture gets knocked down to Dr R. 38 p36. This New York dealer (1876–1952) revolutionised book collecting. It is due to him that the first authentic texts of *Hamlet* are in America, as are the Boswell Papers, the Battle Abbey cartularies, and a presentation copy of the *Faerie Queen*. It was said that the silence of the Day of Judgement will be broken by a voice as regular as that of the Recording Angel. It will be that of Dr. Rosenbach bidding for the Doomsday Book as every page is turned.

Rosenbloom, Maxie. 62 p 82. This heavyweight boxer (1906–76) — known as 'Slapsie Maxie' because of his flat, slapping blows — went into films around 1933 and played comic/tough guy parts.

Roses, a song of. 53 p128. I am unable to identify this song from the dozens that have Roses in their title, though I would suggest the first choice for a tenor would be 'Roses of Picardy' (1916).

Roses, roses, all the way. 67 p84 and elsewhere. First line of Browning's 'The Patriot': "It was roses, roses, all the way."

Rosherville. Just the place to spend a happy day. Like R. 1 p142. Rosherville is part of Northfleet on the south side of the Thames estuary. In the 19th century, it was a popular pleasure resort for Londoners who travelled down to it by paddle steamer.

Rossetti, Dante Gabriel. 85 p101. Along with many others, I suspect, the thing I remember best about this painter and poet (1828–82) is that he buried some poems with his wife but, six years later, decided he wanted them back and had them dug up.

Rouge Croix. 84 p23. See Bluemantle.

'Rough-Hew Them How We Will'. 18 p79. S. *Hamlet* 5.2: "There's a divinity that shapes our ends, Rough-hew them how we will."

Round and round the mulberry bush. 52 p180; 76 p165. A small point, but in every source I found, English and American, the words are "Here we go round the mulberry bush", which would have fitted just as well. But at 86 p10 PGW reverts to the traditional form. MTT Dr Tim Healey, who believes the original mulberry bush stood in middle of exercise yard of Wakefield Prison and women would walk their children around it.

Round the Red Lamp. 2 p91. Subtitled 'Facts and fancies of medical life', it was written by Arthur Conan Doyle (1894).

Roville. 18 p105 and later. See Chap. 20.

Royal Academy. See Academy.

Royalist. More royalist than the king 90 p188. According to the French politician and writer Chateaubriand (1768–1848), the phrase which became popular during the reign of Louis XVI was: "One must not be more royalist than the king."

Rubicon, cross the. 1 p59; 9 p33; 14 p22 and later. See Die is cast.

Ruddier than the cherry. Frequent. Lips ruddier at 63 p12 and 94 p52; cheeks ruddier at 86 p22. From John Gay's *Acis and Galatea*: "O ruddier than the cherry, O sweeter than the berry." With music by Handel, we were still singing it in prep schools in the 1940s.

Rude forefathers, our. 21 p76. See Forefathers.

Rudel and the Lady of Tripoli. 59 p59. Madeline Bassett's account covers the main points of the sad story of Rudel, Lord of Blaye, who heard so much about the beauty of Countess Hodierna of Tripoli that he decided to join the Second Crusade (1147) in the hope of seeing her. On the journey he became ill and was carried ashore at Tripoli. The countess came down from her castle to see him, and he died in her arms. Browning's 'Rudel to the Lady of Tripoli' is his idea of the poems Rudel might have written to her. (If I ever had to teach English, I would quote Bertie's comments as the best example of bathos I have ever read. After Madeline described how his servants had carried the dying Rudel on shore, PGW gives us Bertie's reaction: "'Not feeling so good?' I said, groping. 'Rough crossing?'")

Rudge Hall. 40 p12; 42 p282. See Chaps 32 and 35.

Rudge must be looked upon as a whole. See WHOLE.

Ruins of his shattered hopes. Sat among them 58 p124. Whenever a PGW character sits among the ruins of anything, PGW was quoting Plutarch. See MARIUS.

Ruins that Cromwell knocked about a bit, one of the. 56 p23. One of the popular self-mocking songs of Marie Lloyd, music hall singer, was "I'm one of the ruins that Cromwell knocked about a bit".

Rule's. 30 p91. London's oldest restaurant, founded in 1798. The separate entrance door on the right was especially installed for Edward VII to enjoy private dinners with his lady friends upstairs.

Rumplemayer's. 25 p299. This fashionable French café was at 72 St James's Street.

Rumpty-tiddley-umpty-ay, singing. 22 p33. I have four candidates for the song sung by Aunt Julia. The first is 'There They Are, There They Are', which Marie Lloyd sang at the Palace Theatre c. 1900:

There they are,
The pair of them on their own.
There they are,
Alone, alone, alone.
They gave me half a crown,
To go away and play,
But umpty-iddle-y, umpty-iddle-y,
Umpty-iddley-y-ay.

Another is a song sung by Dan Crawley around the same period. One verse gives the flavour:

'E fired 'is bullet on the range,
The bullet went astray,
And shot the sergeant-major in
'Is umpty-iddley-ay!

Ellaline Terriss, wife and partner of Seymour Hicks, the actor-manager who gave PGW his first stage commission, wrote that she was once playing in New York in W.S. Gilbert's *His Excellency*. As always, Gilbert drilled his cast ferociously and ensured there was no deviation from the script or action. As soon as Gilbert had left New York, the theatre manager took over and instituted some 'improvements' to Gilbert's ideas. These included Ellaline Terriss dropping the song Gilbert had written and instead regaling her audience with Letty Lind's 'Umpty-umpty-Ay' (my third candidate). She often got seven encores, which was just as well, because she had to stay long enough on stage for the leading man to change out of his costume and come back to do the ventriloquist act which the theatre manager reckoned was far superior to any of Gilbert's highfaluting ideas. She said that if Gilbert had known what was going on, he would have brought the Royal Navy over to blow the theatre to pieces.

Finally, there was also 'Rumpty, tumpty, tiddly umpty, That's the song I sing', from *Little Christopher Columbus* (1893).

Rumtifoo, Bishop of. 6 p55. From Gilbert's *Bab Ballads*.

Run, the Long Run. 6 p276. Hanley Castle Grammar School has a traditional Long Run as part of their Sports Day. See Chap. 26.

Runcible, Johnny. 95 p12. Lear's 'The Owl and the Pussy-Cat': "They dined on mince, and slices of quince, / Which they ate with a runcible spoon." My *Chambers Dictionary* maintains that a runcible spoon is now the term 'applied to a sharp-edged, broad-pronged pickle-fork'.

Rung the bell and was entitled to the cigar or coconut. 59 p268. On British fair-grounds, there was usually a Try-Your-Strength stall where one paid to have three goes at hitting a pivot-lever which, if hit hard enough, would project a ball up a column to hit a bell at the top. I remember burly men like village blacksmiths trying but failing, while the weedy youth in charge did it with a nonchalant one-handed swing. For the prize, see CIGAR OR COCOANUT.

Runyon, Damon. Chap in the Damon Runyon story who always figured if he could bring a little joy into any life … doing a wonderful deed 67 p13. PGW was quoting Sam the Gonoph in Runyon's (1884–1946) story 'A Nice Price'.

Ruritania. 33 p186; 53 p275 and later. Ruritania, the Eastern European country where *The Prisoner of Zenda* (1894) was set, became a popular name for a fictional exotic foreign nation, where everybody seemed to go around in glamorous uniforms (see 65 p46). See also RASSENDYL.

Russell, Lillian. 21 p152; 79 p134. This lady (1861–1922) cut quite a swathe across the American theatre scene from 1879 to 1914. A strong soprano, she was famous, so a reference book said, "for not honouring contracts, for walking out both on her shows and her several husbands", but she attracted audiences everywhere because she was also "a gorgeous, well-proportioned, if ample, blue-eyed blonde". She took the chair at the ship's concert when PGW made his disastrous appearance; see Chap. 17.

Russian ballet. 37 p89 and later. PGW used the term because of the remarkable athleticism of the famous Ballets Russes company (see BALLET RUSSE).

Russian plays. Florence Craye used to take Bertie to Russian plays on Sunday nights 68 p191 and 97 p24. It was and still is, I am told, the custom to stage 'modern', avant-garde theatrical productions at private showings on Sunday nights. In my very limited experience, they tended to be Russian and were always either very gloomy or obscure. If I was foolish enough to ask what they were about, I was immediately classed as a Philistine who probably preferred Gilbert and Sullivan — which I did.

Russian representative at the United Nations issuing … veto. 89 p209. During the Cold War, the Russian delegate on the Security Council vetoed any UN resolution that he felt adversely affected the USSR. The UN only managed to pass the 1950 resolution to send a force to resist Communist North Korea when it invaded South Korea because the USSR delegate was absent.

'Ruth in Exile'. 18 p105; 21 p38. B. Ruth 2.11: "thou hast left thy father and thy mother, and the land of thy nativity and art come unto a people which thou knewest not heretofore."

Ruth, sad heart of (when sick for home etc.). 62 p123. Keats' 'Ode to a Nightingale'.

Rutton. 3 p138. See Chap. 35.

S

(MTT = My thanks to)

***Sacrifice*, plot of the play.** 71 p87–92. This bears a strong resemblance to *Mervyn Keene, Clubman*, which in turn owes something, I believe, to Ouida's *Under Two Flags* (1867). (Mr Lehman's idea to have God on stage comes from *Green Pastures*, a 1930 New York hit which did just that.)

Sad/ saddest words of tongue and pen. See Words of tongue.

Sadder and wiser man, a. PGW ref lost. Coleridge's *Rime of the Ancient Mariner*: "A sadder and a wiser man, / He rose the morrow morn."

Safe Man, the. 60 p47; 81 p165; 87 p133 and later. British bookmakers made a point of advertising their probity, i.e. that they never absconded and always honoured a winning bet. 'The Safe Man' was a common sign on bookies' boards at racecourses.

Safety First. 32 p249 and later. This slogan originated with British railway companies in the 1890s. The London Bus Company then adopted it as an advertisement in 1916 to emphasise how dangerous other bus rival companies were. It entered the popular imagination when the Conservative Party made it their motto in 1922; Stanley Baldwin won the 1924 election with it.

Sailor home from the sea and the hunter home from the hill. 87 p135. See Home from the hunt.

Sailors Don't Care. 36 p30 & p185. 1919 song by A. Rudd.

St Ambrose. Cluniac priory near Brindleford 12 p177. Little imagination is needed to identify the Cluniac (Benedictine) priory at Much Wenlock, near Bridgnorth, Shropshire. See Chap. 35.

St Anthony, a prude. 34 p27 and later. St Anthony (251–356 A.D.) showed his piety by rejecting all weaknesses of the flesh during his twenty years as a hermit. The temptations of Anthony were a source of inspiration for many painters, including Hieronymus Bosch.

St Bernard dogs. Fifty million of them can't be wrong 64 p126. See Fifty million St Bernard dogs.

St Cecilia. 31 p185. In PGW's day, everybody was familiar with Waterhouse's 1895 painting of this lady. Lord Lloyd-Webber bought it for £6.6 million in 2000. For details of St Cecilia's life, see any good hagiography.

St George's, Hanover Square. 28 p91 and later. This church in Mayfair was the customary venue for smart Society weddings. Theodore Roosevelt was married here in 1886.

St James of Compostela. 46 p52. From the 10th to 15th century, this saint was held in very high regard across Europe. He was exactly the saint PGW's two mediaeval chaps would swear by. Hundreds still make the pilgrimage on foot to his shrine in Spain.

***St Louis*, S.S.** 13 p254. The ship in which PGW sailed to America in 1904. See Chap. 17.

St Martin's, Guernsey. 9 p1. This small village in the Channel Islands is 1½ miles from St Peter's Port. PGW holidayed in the Channel Islands in 1905, the year before he wrote *Not George Washington* with Herbert Westbrook.

St Paul's. Hide in the crypt of St Paul's (till the bookies forget) 97 p38. This arcane reference by the 93-year-old PGW goes back over 300 years. In the Middle Ages, churches offered sanctuary to those who sought protection, and St Paul's Cathedral in London was famous as the resort of debtors and bankrupts, since they were immune from arrest within its precincts. The privilege was abolished in law in 1697 but the memory of it lingered on for hundreds of years.

The right of sanctuary is not yet dead. Members of Parliament cannot be served with civil writs within the precincts of the Palace of Westminster since it is, in law, a Royal palace.

St Paul's (school). 4 p275 and later. See Chap. 4.

St Peter's Port. 9 p2. See St Martin's.

St Rocque. 48 p79; 77 p14. See Chap. 20.

St Sebastian. Like the picture of S.S. in the Louvre 36 p186; on receipt of the 15th arrow 51 p131; his reproachful look 65 p230. In 300 A.D., the emperor Diocletian ordered this Roman martyr to be shot to death with arrows. The incident was a popular subject for painters, and the picture in the Louvre is by Henner. (Sebastian recovered and went back to reproach Diocletian, who promptly had him beaten to death with clubs. I cannot help thinking that the saintly Sebastian was pushing his luck.)

St Stephen's Gazette. 9 p155. A London newspaper, now defunct.

St Swithin's hospital. 95 p123. PGW presumably picked this name from the *Doctor in the House* novels/films by Richard Gordon which were very popular in the 1960s. Gordon based the stories on St Bartholomew's in London, where he trained. The oldest hospital north of the Alps, 'Bart's' was founded in 1123.

St Winifred's. 12 p222. This 1862 school story was written with the best of intentions by Dean Farrar (1831–1903), cleric and schoolmaster. Second only to his *Eric, or Little by Little*, it became the book most derided by schoolboy readers. See *Eric*.

Salome dance, a. 18 p249 and later, including the Vision of Salome. Salome danced before Herod to secure the death of John the Baptist (see B. Matt. 14.6–11) and, for some reason which I have been unable to discover, the belief grew that her dancing must have been particularly erotic, i.e. the Dance of the Seven Veils.

The 'free dance'/classical school of dancing (Isadora Duncan etc.) received little popular acclaim till Maud Allan (1873–1956) caused a sensation at the Palace Theatre, London, with her 'Dance of Salome' in 1907. She gave her interpretation dressed in very little and the whole of London flocked to admire her 'technique' and 'artistry'. Edward VII wanted to see her in Marienbad but was advised not to since she appeared wearing "little more than two oyster shells and a five-franc piece". Her success led to Lady Constance Mackenzie (Stewart-Richardson) doing the same thing a couple of years later. There was to have been a repeat performance at the concert in *The Mating Season* "till the Mothers Union blew the whistle on it." See also PSYCHE.

Salvini. 37 p299; 41 p36. Tomasso Salvini (1829–1916) was famous across Europe for his interpretation of Othello.

Samson. Who let Samson in so atrociously 7 p165; and often later. B. Judges chaps 13–16 relate the story, including his bringing the temple down on himself and the Philistines.

San Francisco Earthquake. 39 p171; 95 p124. Because I have so many friends there, I shall just say that San Francisco had a large fire in 1906 which might seem like an earthquake to the uninformed observer. I have a strong suspicion that PGW based 'The Story of William' on the anecdote concerning John Barrymore, who played in *A Thief for a Night*, the stage version of *A Gentleman of Leisure*. It is said that Barrymore was so busy 'entertaining' a young lady that they both ignored the earthquake, and Barrymore blithely emerged from the hotel in the morning in full evening dress to the awed admiration of the other guests huddled outside, who included Enrico Caruso.

Sand and Passion, a tale of desert love. 34 p p51. See SHEIKH.

Sandford and Merton. 3 p23 and later. A moral book for boys by Thomas Day (1789) which made the point, at tedious length, that Good triumphs over Evil.

Sandow system. 9 p146 and later. Eugene Sandow (1867–1925) achieved fame across Europe and America as 'the world's strongest man' and made a lot of money from books telling people how they could become as strong as he was. Charles Atlas ("You too can have a body like mine") was his successor.

Sands of Dee. Those who call cattle home across the Sands of Dee 31 p48; 36p 20 and frequent later. See CALLING CATTLE HOME.

Sands of the desert grow cold, Until the. 33 p120 and elsewhere. Romantic song by Graff & Ball (1911).

Sandwich,satisfying. Cut the satisfying s. 99 p267. G&S *The Grand Duke* Act 2.

Sanger's Troupe of Midgets. 73 p177. Slight error here, maybe a misprint. Sanger's Circus was British, Singer's Circus (and Troupe of Midgets) was American. The British George Sanger (1825–1911) became involved in a lawsuit brought by the American Buffalo Bill Cody around 1898, and Cody's counsel insisted on calling his client "the Honourable Colonel Cody". Sanger didn't think much of this and announced that he was going to call himself Lord George Sanger in future — and did so (see 10 p32). Everybody thought Queen

Victoria would be furious at a showman taking the style of address of a duke's younger son, but apparently she was much amused. The last of the Sangers, Victoria Sanger Freeman, died in 1991, age 96. She and her brother toured the family-owned circus till it closed in 1962 after 117 years.

See also SINGER'S TROUPE OF MIDGETS.

Sans peur et sans reproche. See CHEVALIER BAYARD.

Sapphira. See ANANIAS.

Saraband. Webster tries to dance it 49 p67. A traditional Spanish dance. See also MARIANA, FATHER.

Sardine Sultan. 32 p76. See KINGS.

Sargent. 18 p274; 23 p35 and later. American-born John Singer Sargent (1856–1925) became England's leading portrait painter. As Corky Corcoran tells us, Sargent used to reveal the soul of the sitter on canvas, and Bertie Wooster noted the same effect in *Joy in the Morning* (p177): "It was the work of one of those artists who reveal the soul of the sitter, and it had revealed so much of Aunt Agatha's soul that for all practical purposes it might have been that danger to traffic in person."

Sartor Resartus. 9 p6. A philosophical satire by Carlyle (1834). The title is Latin for 'the tailor re-tailored'.

Saul among the prophets. 12 p226; 42 p170. B. 1 Samuel 10.11: "Is Saul also among the prophets?"

Saul of Tarsus and a sudden bright light. 21 p49 and later. Saul, a fervent persecutor of Christians, got his comeuppance on the road to Damascus when a light from heaven "shined around him", causing him to fall to the earth. This, as well as a few pointed remarks from the Almighty, altered his views considerably. See B. Acts chap 9.

Sausages are done to a turn, Which the. 1 p71. This has a strong ring of Dickens, but I have been unable to find it. Neil Midkiff suggests it comes from chap. 21 of D. *Barnaby Rudge*: "great rashers of broiled ham, which being well cured, done to a turn, and smoking hot, …" Suggestive but not, I think, quite near enough.

Savage Club. See Chap. 21.

Savonarola. 49 p70. This Italian religious and political reformer (1452–98) preached against fine clothes, gambling and every form of idle pleasure.

Saw, dissipated. Less like a hatchet than a d. s. 84 p108. See KNIFE.

Saw the air too much with your hands, Do not. 8 p64. S. *Hamlet* 3.2: "Do not saw the air too much with your hand, thus, but use all gently …"

Say it ain't so (Joe). 88 p205. Famous remark allegedly made by a fan to Shoeless Joe Jackson in the 1920 baseball scandal when the Chicago White Sox were accused of throwing the 1919 World Series. MTT David Landman for pointing out the original remark was "It ain't true, is it, Joe?" By the time they reached the West Coast through Press and radio reports, the words had been altered to the famous version.

Say it with ... Flower-pots 32p 256; eggs 60 p170; bullets 90 p8. PGW gloss on the long-lasting (it began in 1917) advertisement of the American Florists Society: 'Say It With Flowers'.

Sayers, Dorothy L. 46 p62; 49 p252. Miss Sayers (1893–1957) was the creator of Lord Peter WIMSEY.

Sayest to thy brother thou fool. 87 p130. B. Matthew 5.22. "and whosoever shall say to his brother, Raca, shall be in danger of the council; but whosoever shall say, Thou fool, shall be in danger of hell fire." ('Raca' means worthless.)

Scales have fallen from her eyes, the. 44 p309; 59 p13. B. Acts 9.18. This is SAUL OF TARSUS again. "And immediately there fell from his eyes as it had been scales; and he received sight forthwith, and arose, and was baptized."

Scalping really necessary?, Is your. 88 p74. During World War II, travel was discouraged to save on fuel. Every railway station had large notices asking: "Is Your Journey Really Necessary?"

Scarlet Pimpernel (and his Mechlin lace). 59 p195 and later. PGW gave the full reference in the US edition, but not in the UK version since he assumed that, for UK readers, 'Mechlin lace' alone would be enough. The Mechlin lace cuffs clearly refer to Baroness Orczy's famous hero, but are not to be found in *The Scarlet Pimpernel*. They appear in a sequel, *Eldorado*, chap. 11.

Scarlet Woman. I'm the S.W. (of Babylon). 68 p29 and eight times elsewhere. B. Revelation chap 17 describes at length the gory punishments that will come to the Scarlet Woman and those indulging in blasphemy, fornication and other abominations.

Scenic railway. As full of curves as a s. r. 76 p168. See FIGURE.

Sceptred isle. Rather good stuff about this sceptred isle, this demi-Eden 93 p79. John of Gaunt's splendid speech from S. *Richard II* 2.1: "This royal throne of kings, this scepter'd isle, / This earth of majesty, this seat of Mars, / This other Eden, demi-paradise."

Schemes, best-laid, of mice and men. 21 p268 and later. See MICE AND MEN.

Schenk, Nick. 70 p56 & p61. A typo; Nick Schenck (1881–1969) was the financial controller of MGM studios. His brother Joe (1878–1961) became head of 20th Century Fox in 1935.

School most resorted, to which the. See RESORTED.

Schoolgirl complexion. 36 p246 and later. Famous Palmolive Soap advertisement 1917–49: 'Keep That Schoolgirl Complexion'.

Schopenhauer. 9 p6 and later up to 90 p61. 'Pessimistic German philosopher' sums up Arthur Schopenhauer (1788–1860). MTT Dr G.K. Sankaran for the information that the extracts from *The Ethics of Suicide* quoted by Mr Potter in 'Mr Potter Takes a Rest Cure' are from an English translation of Schopenhauer. Perhaps PGW did even more homework on his quotations than I thought.

Schubert brothers. 69 p86. See SHUBERT.

Schuman, Ike, the great. 30 p129. PGW's version of one of the three Shubert brothers. See SHUBERT.

Schwab, Charles. 40 p94; 61 p275. American magnate (1862–1939), founder of Bethlehem Steel.

Schwed, Peter. 83 p134; 86 p173. PGW's compliment to his friend and editor at Simon & Schuster, Peter Schwed (d. 2003, age 92), who was also the dedicatee of 76 (US version). See also next entry.

Schwed versus Meredith. L.R. 3 H.L. 330. 86 p173. A private joke. How many of his readers would have known that the names of the opponents in this fictional law case were those of PGW's agent, Scott Meredith, and his publisher, Peter Schwed? And how many authors can cite an English legal reference correctly? The mysterious LR 3HL stand for Law Reports 3rd House of Lords. This is almost certainly a reference he checked with his barrister grandson, Edward Cazalet, who would become a judge later.

Scotch Express. Honoria Glossop's laugh sounds like the S.E. going under a bridge 31 p67; 41 p66; 48 p55. The Scotch Express train service between London and Edinburgh was inaugurated in 1862. The train still leaves King's Cross Station every day at the original time of 10 A.M. It is the oldest scheduled train service in the world. Although Wodehouse used the correct title, The Flying Scotsman became the popular name for the service in the 1920s after the introduction in 1923 of The Flying Scotsman, the most famous steam engine in the world. It pulled the express train for forty years and still makes occasional outings. See Chap. 17.

Scotch reviewers. One of those Scotch reviewers Byron disliked so much 91 p209. The *Edinburgh Review* was so scathing about his 'Hours of Idleness' that BYRON responded with a satirical poem in 1809: 'English Bards and Scots Reviewers'.

Scots, wha hae. 57p140. Burns' poem 'Scots, Wha Hae'.

Scottish. Promised to play against the S. 23 p187. In this context, this is clearly the London Scottish. Three of London's keenest Rugger clubs are the so-called 'exiles' clubs: the London Irish, London Scottish and London Welsh.

Scotty, Death Valley. 54 p155. Walter Scott (1875–1954), prospector turned promoter, began by driving borax wagons across Death Valley in California and went on to look for gold and to promote rumours of it. This brought in other prospectors who had to buy their supplies from him. His house and store, 'Scotty's Castle', became a tourist attraction.

Screen Beautiful. 54 p48. PGW liked this phrasing. See BOOK BEAUTIFUL.

Scrooge. 70 p38 and elsewhere. Now a common term for any mean, stingy person. See Ebenezer Scrooge in D. *A Christmas Carol.*

Scylla and Charybdis, between. 3 p235; 13 p247. This is heard less often nowadays as teaching of the Classics diminishes. Scylla was the name given by the ancients to the jagged rocks in the channel between Italy and Sicily. The whirlpool of Charybdis is nearby. Today's equivalent is "between a rock and a hard place".

Sea beast among rocks. 12 p134; 32 p212; 43 p283. Wordsworth's 'Resolution and Independence', St 9: "Like a sea-beast crawled forth, that on a shelf, / Of rock or sand reposeth, there to sun itself."

Sea change into something rich and strange, suffered a. 18 p37; Mr Wooster doth suffer a … 73 p59. S. *Tempest* 1.2: "But doth suffer a sea-change / Into something rich and strange."

Sea is boiling hot (and whether pigs have wings). 1 p164. From Lewis Carroll's 'The Walrus and the Carpenter' (*Alice Through the Looking-Glass*).

Sea of troubles … not to take arms against it. 21 p16 and later. 'A Sea of Troubles' is also a short story title from *The Man with Two Left Feet*. S. *Hamlet* 3.1 ('To be or not to be' speech): "Or to take arms against a sea of troubles and by opposing end them?"

Seamore Place from the west, Charles Street from the east. 39 p164. See Chap. 21.

Season of mists and mellow fruitfulness. 59 p7. Keats' 'To Autumn'.

Seaweed, dried. 14 p65; collected by aunts 28 p211. I had not realised that collecting dried seaweed was such a popular Victorian pastime. Queen Victoria began her collection when she was thirteen and kept it up for many years. Strands of different types and colours of seaweed were collected and dried, then stuck to paper in pleasing and intricate patterns. The sheets were then bound in albums and brought out to be admired by visitors. When the Queen of Portugal got married, Victoria's wedding present was her treasured album bound between two enormous shells. ("Gosh! Thanks! Just what I've always wanted!")

Second Division, a mere thirty day in. 59 p298. See Chap. 38.

Secret, I know your. 44 p9; 89 p17. See I KNOW YOUR SECRET.

Secret Nine, the. 35 p179 and five times later up to 97 p14. A favourite PGW thriller title, a reflection of the wildly popular books (Faceless Fiends et al.) written by Edgar WALLACE, Sidney Horler and their fellows. There is no book by this name in the British Library, though they do have five 'Secret Six' thrillers and three 'Secret Sevens' (plus eighteen books of Enid Blyton's famous Secret Seven children detectives).

See — steadily and see him whole. See George steadily and see him whole 38 p128; see life steadily 44 p15; see the postman steadily and see him whole 68 p135; and elsewhere. Matthew Arnold's 'Sonnet to a Friend'. "Who saw life steadily and saw it whole, / The mellow glory of the Attic stage."

See jewness savvay. 54 p82. 'Si jeunesse savoit, si veillesse pouvoit.' See IF YOUTH BUT KNEW.

See than be one, rather. 63 p17. For an explanation of this odd remark by Chimp Twist, see COW, PURPLE.

See themselves as others see them. 36 p129. Burns' 'To a Louse': "O wad some Pow'r the giftie gie us / To see oursels as ithers see us!"

See you on the barricades. 90 p101 and elsewhere. A 1960s catchphrase in both the UK and USA when every public holiday saw protest marches to Stop the

War in Vietnam (USA) or Ban the Bomb (UK).

Seeking whom you may devour. 25 p79 & p186 and frequent later. B. 1 Peter 5.8: "Be sober, be vigilant; because your adversary the devil, as a roaring lion, walketh about, seeking whom he may devour."

Seething the kid in its mother's milk. 44 p311. B. Exodus 23.19: "Thou shalt not seethe a kid in his mother's milk." MTT Dennis Chitty.

Segrave. 43 p144. Henry Segrave, racing driver and speed record-holder (1896–1930), died while setting a new water-speed world record on Windermere.

Seisin. Taking s. of conquered territory 44 p97. Old English legal term to describe taking possession of a piece of land. Mediaeval English law held that land could only be transferred by the new owner symbolically taking a piece of it in his hand. The documentation was secondary in importance. The phrase "he was seised of many acres" was common till recently.

Selfridge, Gordon. 46 p108. This remarkable retailer (1858–1947) made a fortune as a department store manager in Chicago (MARSHALL FIELD), came to London in 1906, decided it needed an up-to-date retail store and opened Selfridge's in Oxford Street in 1909. It set a new standard for the retail trade, and Selfridge is credited with the phrase "The customer is always right." A brilliant salesman, his private life became too extravagant (he kept the Dolly Sisters in luxury), and he was forced to resign as chairman of the store in 1940.

Selfridge's. 33 p11 and later. Famous London store. PGW later merged it with Harrod's to make 'HARRIGE'S'.

Selling platers. Mere s. p. in the way of looks 65 p18; and elsewhere. Horse racing in England has different levels of races. In a selling plate race, the owner of the winning horse has to offer him for sale afterwards. He can always buy him back himself, but I understand classic yearlings (horses capable of great things) are rarely entered in a selling plate race.

Seltzerpore, Rajah of. 2 p55. See Chap. 3.

Senior Conservatives club. See Chap. 21.

Sennett, Mack. 27 p238. This Hollywood producer (1880–1960) gave the world a series of silent movie comedies. He created the Keystone Kops and crazy car chases; directed the young Charlie Chaplin in his first films; and was, so he claimed, the man who saw the possibilities of throwing custard pies in people's faces.

Sensation in court. 30 p114. A newspaper cliché that PGW's early readers appreciated. Criminal trials were followed avidly and whenever a witness made some significant statement, the headline was always 'Sensation in Court'. See also POSITION.

Sense, in a very real. 92 p144. See REAL SENSE.

Sensitive plant, a. 14 p183, 59 p63 and elsewhere. SHELLEY's poem 'The Sensitive Plant': "A Sensitive Plant in a garden grew."

Sentiments deeper and warmer than those of ordinary friendship. 39 p36; 51 p55–6 and later. See Victorian etiquette books and Advice to the Lovelorn columns 1870–1910. I read several, and the phrase was indeed used as often as PGW implied.

September Morn. 63 p200. A painting made famous by a splendid public relations ploy. The 1912 lithograph by the French artist Paul Chabas portrays a nude girl dipping her toe in the water. In 1913 the owner of a small New York art shop bought a thousand copies and put one in his window but, even at ten cents each, there was no interest in it whatsoever. After some weeks, he grumbled about it to a friend, Harry Reichenbach, a public relations man. Reichenbach looked at it and undertook to make it famous. He hired some small boys to come along each day and snigger at it, informed Anthony Comstock about this scandal, and made sure the Press heard of his complaint to Comstock, a well-known crusader against obscene publications of any kind. Comstock, who was incorruptible and zealous, came down to Fifth Avenue and was shocked to see the boys ogling the nude picture. He had the shop owner arrested and prosecuted, and the resultant publicity led to 7 million copies of the picture being sold at a dollar each, while the original was bought for $70,000. It appeared on matchboxes, posters and became the world's first 'glamour calendar'.

Sergeant-major. Retired sergeant-major who came twice a week to teach drill and physical culture at his preparatory school 63 p8; 88 p245; 96 p144–5. This was common at private schools till the 1960s. All the drill and boxing instructors at Dulwich in PGW's time were retired army sergeants or sergeant-majors. Further, his own prep school, the real Malvern House, employed a retired sergeant-major in just such a role. See Chap. 3.

Serio in pink tights. 42 p57. Dolly Henderson, Gally's old love, was a serio. The phrase was shorthand for serio-comic, someone who sang sad songs in a comic way. It sounds contradictory, but there were many in the music halls. A pretty girl would come on and sing a sad song, but did so with a wry humour that made it clear it was all part of life's full rich pattern. 'WAITING AT THE CHURCH' was one of the songs they sang.

Sermons in books, stones in running brooks. 52 p217. Gussie Fink-Nottle can be excused for misquoting "books in the running brooks, sermons in stones and good in every thing" from S. *As You Like It* 2.1.

Serpents. Bite like s. and sting like adders. See ADDERS.

Service and Cooperation. 61 p45 and frequent elsewhere. MTT Nigel Rees, who says it probably comes from J.C. Penney's stores, a nationwide US chain who in 1913 selected their motto as 'Honor, Confidence, Service and Cooperation'.

Servitor dangled me on his knee … and offered me all his savings, no. 26 p53; 42 p233; 46 p221. See Adam, faithful retainer in S. *As You Like It* 2.3: "Here is the gold; All this I give you. Let me be your servant; Though I am old, yet I am strong and lusty." See also GOOD OLD MAN.

Settees, sofas, Chesterfields, desks, hiding behind. 27 p43; Napoleon was always doing that sort of thing 29 p196. See also 37 p306; 43 p137 BW (Bertie Wooster); 51 p245 BW; 55 p215; 56 p88; 61 p90; 68 p143 BW; 85 p151 and p168 BW; 88 p48 (piano) BW; 88 p199 Lancelot Mulliner; 93 p65 BW refers to. In a 1932 letter, PGW wrote: "It's not all jam writing in the first person, what? The reader can know nothing except what Bertie tells him and B can only know a limited amount himself."

I believe it was his theatrical experience that gave PGW the idea of having his characters hiding behind settees and desks. It was good comedy stagecraft, enabling the audience/reader to 'know' what the people on stage do not know, i.e. that there is someone listening to them. It gave him the opportunity to develop four aspects. First, a man diving behind a settee is funny anyway. Second, it enabled him to move the plot forward through the narrator listening to other people discussing the situation — and thus making them narrators as well. Third, the discovery of the hider either by small woolly dogs or Pauline Stoker was comic as well as providing the twist in the plot PGW wanted. Fourth, it allowed the narrator (and the reader) to reflect on his plight. In *Stiff Upper Lip, Jeeves*, for example, it means PGW can give us the splendid sentence: "One was either soaring like an eagle on to the tops of chests or whizzing down behind sofas like a diving duck, and apart from the hustle and bustle of it all that sort of thing wounds the spirit and does no good to the trouser crease."

No wonder he used the ploy so often.

Seven maids with seven mops. 92 p35. Carroll's 'The Walrus and the Carpenter' in *Alice Through the Looking-Glass*: "'If seven maids with seven mops / Swept it for half a year, / Do you suppose,' the Walrus said, 'That they could get it clear?'"

Seven veils, lifting the. 43 p 267. See SALOME DANCE.

Seven years of Famine we read of in Scripture. 97 p72. See FAMINE.

Severest critic. See BEST FRIEND AND SEVEREST CRITIC.

Severn River. 8 p59; 14 p38; 32 p9 and later. England's longest river runs through Shropshire, Worcestershire and Gloucestershire. Since PGW set so many stories in those three counties, when an unnamed 'river' is mentioned, it is usually the Severn.

Shades of evening were beginning to fall pretty freely. 43 p243; shades of night 59 p88; and later. Longfellow's 'Excelsior': "The shades of night were falling fast …"

Shades of the prison house begin to close upon the growing boy. 31 p38 and later. Wordsworth's 'Intimations of Immortality'.

Shadrach, Meshach and Abednego. See FIERY FURNACE.

Shah of Persia. 11 p55; 14 p25. Between 1870 and 1900, Britain was anxious to enlist the Shah of Persia as an ally in keeping the Russians out of India. He was invited on at least two State Visits to Britain, where every effort was made to make him feel an honoured guest. He found certain of our customs strange, and it is recorded that it took all the charm of the Foreign Office to calm his wrath when he was told he could not take the ballet dancers of the Empire Theatre back for his harem. It is rumoured that he made the same demand for the Gaiety chorus. See also DISHPOT.

Shakespeare and Bacon theory. See BACON.

Shakespeare Hotel, where Cloyster lunches. 9 p35. This establishment beside Victoria Station is one of the four London pubs named by PGW still there. See also COAL HOLE.

Shalimar, Pale Hands I Loved Beside The. See PALE HANDS.

Shalott, Lady of. See CURSE HAS COME UPON ME.

Shame or remorse, he burned with. 48 p274. See BURNED, (NOT) WITH SHAME AND REMORSE.

Shape of things to come, the. 61 p55; 67 p91 and later. In general terms: the future is not looking too good. Probably from H.G. Wells' 1933 book of this name, a best-seller which prophesied war in the air and atom bombs.

Sharecroppers. 77 p127. These were American tenant farmers who worked the land and had to share whatever profit they made with the landowner. There were several best-sellers on this theme in the 1930s including *Tobacco Road* by Erskine Caudwell and *I Was A Sharecropper* (1937) by Harry Kroll.

Share-The-Wealth movement. 60 p50 and later. I long thought this was a PGW invention; I should have known better. It was the political slogan of Huey Long, the colourful political leader of Lousiana till he was assassinated in 1935. He believed that since 10% of the US population held 70% of the wealth, the Government should grab it and share it out among the other 90%.

Shark and nothing but the shark, it was. 52 p132. See GAME.

Sharkey, Tom. 36 p154. A leading heavyweight boxer, 1893–1904.

Sharper than a serpent's tooth, how much. 31 p240 and later. S. *King Lear* 1.4: "How sharper than a serpent's tooth it is / To have a thankless child."

Shaw, Artie. How many times A.S. has been married 68 p112. This American bandleader (1910–2004) married eight times. Some names might be familiar to older readers: Jane Cairns, Margaret Allen, Lana Turner, Betty Kern (daughter of Jerome Kern), Ava Gardner, Kathleen Winsor (*Forever Amber*), Doris Dowling and Evelyn Keyes. In 1990 the 79-year-old came out of retirement to form the All New Artie Shaw Orchestra.

Shaw, G.B. 21 p112 and later. This iconoclastic critic and playwright (1856–1950) did not impress PGW. He met him twice (see *Yours, Plum*), and on the second occasion, PGW wrote: "Ethel, silly ass, gave him an opening by saying: 'My daughter is so excited by your world tour', and he said 'The whole world is excited about my world tour.' I nearly said 'I'm not, blast you.'"

She didn't say Yes, She didn't say No. 76 p82. 'She Didn't Say Yes', song from Jerome Kern's 1931 show *The Cat and the Fiddle*.

She is coming, my love, my own etc. etc. 31 p60; 41 p36 and later. T. *Maud* Pt 1.22, last verse.

She never said a word about her love, but let concealment, like a worm i'the bud, feed on her damned cheek. 65 p105; feed on his tomato-coloured cheek (Captain Biggar) 73 p61. S. *Twelfth Night* 2.4: "She never told her love, / But let concealment, like a worm i' the bud, / Feed on her damask cheek."

She sells sea-shells (on the sea-shore). 51 p 201. This 1908 tongue-twister song by Sullivan & Gifford soon became a popular test of sobriety. It was made famous by music hall comedian Wilkie Bard.

She starts. She moves. She seems to feel … 52 p107. See Pig something.

She walks in beauty like the night. 31 p56. Byron's 'She Walks in Beauty'.

Shearer, Norma. 48 p65. Film actress (1900–83) who married Irving Thalberg (see Boy Wonder). When the Wodehouses went to Hollywood in 1930, they rented her house. See Chap. 28.

Sheathe the sword. See Hands to the plough.

Sheaves, bringing back your. 84 p33. B. Psalms 126.6: "He that goeth forth and weepeth, bearing precious seed, shall doubtless come again with rejoicing, bringing his sheaves with him."

Sheep which was lost. 85 p41. Bertie Wooster's phraseology "Rejoice with me, for I have found the sheep which was lost" should read "my sheep that was lost" B. Luke 15.6.

Sheep's Cray, Kent. 33 p14. See Chap. 34.

Sheeted dead who squeaked and gibbered. See Squeaking.

Sheffield Wednesday. Six months come S.W. or thereabouts 56 p34. American readers may need an explanation of Eggy Mannering's little play on words. Most English football clubs began as amateur teams in the 19th century and many have kept their original names. The Wolverhampton Wanderers had no ground of their own so always had to travel to play their matches. Tottenham Hotspur adopted the name to distinguish them from a rival club in the same suburb of north London, while Sheffield Wednesday were, I am told, originally a factory team who were given time off work to play on Wednesday afternoons. Eggy Mannering was simply indulging in topical badinage as to how long it had been since he had met Reggie.

Sheikh, The (stories). 33 p101; 37 p214 & p222; and later. It is difficult today to appreciate the effect of E.M. Hull's book *The Sheikh* (1918). The song 'The Sheik of Araby' and Valentino's film successes were just two consequences. Perhaps it is best described as having an impact similar to Elvis Presley or the Beatles later. Miss Hull (1880–1947) made them the rage across the English-speaking world. Wodehouse used the term 'the Sheik' at least four times. When his heroines sighed over desert romances, 'The Love That Scorches' or 'Sand and Passion', his early readers would all have picked up the allusion. See also Chap. 37 (Rosie M. Banks).

Shellac, chap who wrote poems and was sent down from Oxford. 49 p285. The poet Ronald had in mind was Shelley, who was sent down (expelled) from University College, Oxford, in 1811.

Shelley. "You know your Shelley, Bertie." "Oh, am I?" 59 p63. Poet Percy Bysshe Shelley (1792–1822).

Shell-like (ear). Frequent. Nigel Rees, lexicographer and quotation-finder emeritus suggests the phrase comes from either Thomas Hood's 'Bianca's Dream' — "Her small and shell-like ear" — or, alternatively, from Keats' 'To –': "Be echoed swiftly through that ivory shell / Thine ear."

Sherman. What Sherman said war was 16 p158; 19 p15; and later. Often misquoted as "War is hell". On 11 August 1880, General William Tecumseh Sherman (1820–91) gave an address at Columbus, Ohio, in which he said: "There is many a boy here today who looks on war as all glory, but, boys, it is all hell."

Shield of hides untanned, right good. 47 p74; 67 p64. See HYBRIAS.

Shifnal/Shiffley. 32 p169; 42 p145; 50 p100. See Chap. 35.

Shilling ordinary. 25 p89. This was the term used till c.1914 for the fixed-price (table d'hôte) meals in inns and chophouses. If you wanted something else, you would eventually get it, but at great expense and after a long delay. It was usually far better to take the standard meal that the establishment was serving that day, the 'shilling ordinary', the 'half crown ordinary' and so on. Today the custom is coming back and many pubs offer a 'Roast Beef lunch' on Sundays at a remarkably cheap fixed price. They do very well because so many young mothers today do not have the time to cook roast beef properly and have no idea how to produce the essential light-as-a-feather Yorkshire pudding.

Shimmering through the laurels in the quiet evenfall, came. 52 p189 (Angela with ham sandwiches). T. *Maud* Pt 2.4.11.

Shimmy (dance so popular in the twenties). 83 p220. The shimmy, or shimmy-shake, arrived in the UK in 1920 and horrified the older generation with its lascivious and provocative movements. It was edged out by the Charleston a few years later but was popular enough for the song 'Shimmy With Me' to be a hit in the PGW/Grossmith show *The Cabaret Girl* (1922).

Shine like a good deed in a wicked world. 14 p61; 30 p90. S. *Merchant of Venice* 5.1: "So shines a good deed in a naughty world."

Shine on, thou harvest moon. 18 p43. The words do not occur in the 1908 vaudeville song 'Shine On Harvest Moon', but I have found nothing better. Had PGW forgotten the words, maybe?

Shining evening face. A cloud passed over her s.e.f. 76 p78. I didn't notice this one till February 2009 when chasing another quotation. It was one of the quotations PGW had amended, and it took me a long time to work out that 'evening' was the amendment. It is 'shining morning face' from S. *As You Like It* 2.7 — the 'All's the world's a stage' speech, which contains phrases every Wodehousean will recognise.

Shipbourne, Lord Peter. 61 p12. A private joke. See Chap. 2.

Shipley Hall, Kent. 63 p15; 79 p18. See Chap. 29.

Ship's concerts. See Chap. 17.

Ships that pass in the night. 7 p31 and later. Longfellow's 'The Theologian's Tale: Elizabeth': "Ships that pass in the night, and speak each other in passing; / Only a signal shown and a distant voice in the darkness." The phrase was also the title of a best-selling 1893 novel by Beatrice Harraden.

Shivering on the brink. See BRINK.

Shoe polish, eating. See BOOT POLISH.

Shoot, if you must, this old gray head. 79 p11. See FRIETCHIE.

Shop, village (what it sells). 64 p207; 96 p69. Excellent descriptions, but I'm surprised PGW's observant eye missed knitting wool and tobacco. See Chap. 19.

Shot a flask into the air, I. See I SHOT.

Shot the moon, sir. 7 p227. See SKIPPED BY THE LIGHT.

Show place like the joints you read about … 365 rooms, 52 staircases and 12 courtyards … 85 p40. Enormous Stately Homes like these are known as 'calendar houses'. I suggest PGW was thinking of KNOLE, a stately home in Kent, not far from Leonora's house at Fairlawne.

Shrewsbury clock, a long hour by. 82 pp61 & 113 and later. S. *1 Henry IV* 5.4: "but we rose both at an instant, and fought a long hour by Shrewsbury clock."

Shriner Convention. 48 p96; 73 p71. An American mutual philanthropic society, founded 1886, whose official title is the Ancient Arabic Order of the Mystic Shrine. When looking it up in an American reference book, *Societies and Institutions*, I was surprised by the number of organisations entitled 'Sons of'/'Daughters of' — American Revolution/American Veterans/Settlers of Oregon/Confederate Veterans etc. I was very impressed by one august body: Descendants of Illegitimate Sons and Daughters of the Kings of Britain.

Shrubb, Alfred. 12 p259. UK runner (1879–1964) who once held the world record for every distance from 2,000 yards to 12 miles! Forgotten today, he established a dozen world records on one cold, dark evening in November 1904. He simply set off on his own and ran round the track for an hour. He set world records for 5, 6, 7, 8, 9 and 10 miles and finished the hour having run nearly 12 miles, another world record. It was 50 years before all his times were beaten.

Shubert, J.J. 39 p247 and later. Theatre impresario, J.J. Shubert (1878–1963) and his two brothers broke A.L. Erlanger's grip on the New York theatre world. The Princess Theatre was one of theirs. See Chap. 24.

Shuffle Off To Buffalo, doing a. 76 p74; 77 p95 and later. This syncopated dance came out in 1932.

Sickening thud. Dull, s. t. See Thud.

Sicklied o'er with the pale cast of care/thought. 12 p209; 23 p174 and later. See ENTERPRISES.

Sidcup, Lord. See SPODE and Chap 31.

Siddons, Mrs. In one of her more regal roles 41 p36; Mrs Chavender closely resembles her 62 p10, p12 and p238. This lady (1755–1831) was the leading English actress of her time. When she gave readings, her voice alone could make men cry.

Sidgwick. 3 p237. Classical scholar and philosopher (1840–1920).

Sidney, Sir Philip. 26 p120 and some 14 times later. See especially 68 p34. This remarkable young man (1554–86) was an elegant poet, effective diplomat, skilful soldier and Master of the Horse. His death at the battle of Zutphen in 1586 was widely mourned. The words he spoke at Zutphen, asking that a drink he was offered be given to a wounded soldier beside him, were: "Thy necessity is yet greater than mine." By my reckoning, PGW used the 'his/her need is greater than' line at least twenty times.

It is not only Wodehouseans who revere Sidney's memory. He was at Shrewsbury School and they have a fine statue to him in their grounds (see Chap. 3). At the end of the 1939–45 war, when the Allies liberated The Netherlands, the town of Shrewsbury (still suffering strict rationing themselves) heard the residents of Zutphen were starving and organised special food parcels for them. The two towns have since developed strong links.

Sight for sore eyes. Often. Original version coined by Jonathan Swift in his *Polite Conversation* (1738): "The sight of you is good for sore eyes."

Silence like a poultice comes to heal the blows of sound. 93 p120; 94 p189. From Oliver Wendell Holmes' 'The Organ Grinders', as PGW told us.

Silent tomb, the. Frequent. It has the ring of Shakespeare but comes from Wordsworth's 'The River Duddon': "And if, as towards the silent tomb we go …"

Silent upon a peak in Darien. 81 p76. See NEW PLANET.

Silk-and-satined little treasures she had read about in Ingoldsby legends. 25 p113. See INGOLDSBY LEGENDS.

Silly Symphony. Two-reel S.S. 68 p126. In the 1930s the usual programme in British cinemas was a cartoon, the newsreel and the main feature film. Silly Symphonies was the name Walt Disney (1901–66) gave to the short cartoons which did not feature Mickey Mouse, Pluto or Donald Duck.

Silver bells tinkling across the foam of perilous seas. 79 p 85. As we are told, it is Keats. The 'Ode to a Nightingale' has: "Charm'd magic casements, opening on the foam / Of perilous seas, in faery lands forlorn." I have no idea why PGW changed the words unless it is another case of Keats writing two versions. See WHAT CAN AIL THEE.

Silver lining, look for the. See LOOK FOR.

Silver Ring bookie (Mustard Pott). In Britain, bookmakers were allowed to ply their trade on the course. The difference in their status/reputation was made clear by where they were allowed to operate. None were permitted in the Members' Enclosure, but bookmakers of proven virtue were allowed to set up their stalls adjoining the Enclosure railings. Then there were the bookies allowed to set up their stands in Tattersall's enclosure and the Grandstand enclosure while, at the bottom of the scale, were the bookies who took bets in the Silver Ring i.e. public enclosures. These were so named because it originally cost only two shillings to gain entry, and those who resorted there tended to bet small amounts (in silver coins, not pound notes).

Silver threads among the gold. 44 p134 and elsewhere. This 1873 sentimental song by Danks (lyrics by Rexford) sold 2 million copies. A report in a

Bexhill-on-Sea paper of a local amateur concert in 1930 said someone sang it "with such effect there were few dry eyes among the audience". One line gives the feel of it: "Darling, I am growing old; Silver threads among the gold."

Simeon Stylites. 18 p144. This early and most famous of pillar hermits (390–459 A.D.), the subject of TENNYSON's poem, began with a pillar only three feet high but spent his last twenty years on a column sixty feet high so he would not be distracted by the prayers of his followers. He gave weekly sermons that lasted twelve hours.

Simple faith is more than Norman blood. 7 p123 and often later. See NORMAN BLOOD.

Simpson's in the Strand. 14 p255; 19 p48 (an excellent description). Founded in 1818, this restaurant still serves the best meat in London. I regret to announce, however, that the 'as much as you can eat for half a crown' rule came to an end in 1914.

Sinclair, Upton. 21 p231. American novelist (1878–1961) whose early book, *The Jungle* (1906), on the meat-packing industry in Chicago, led to a Congressional investigation. See also BEEF TRUST.

Sing like the birdies sing — Tweet, tweet-tweet, tweet. 60 p173. 1932 song by Hargreaves & Evans. Do not confuse with 'TWEET-TWEET! SHUSH, SHUSH!' below.

Sing of joy, sing of bliss. 42 p15 and elsewhere. The first words of the chorus of 'Yip-i-addy-i-ay' are: "Sing of joy, sing of bliss, Home was never like this! Yip-i-addy-i-ay." See YIP-I-ADDY-I-AY.

Singer Building. I'll knock you over the S.B. 15A p125. The Singer Building in New York, erected in 1908, was then the tallest building in the world. It was demolished in 1968.

Singer of Saskatoon. Soured and chafing S. of S. 32 p96. PGW changed the usual 'Sweet (Singer)' prefix to emphasise how embittered McTodd was, but reverted to the standard 'Sweet Singer of' later. See Sweet Singer of Garbidge Mews 49 p38; specializing in chipmunks 61 p79; of Kings Deverill 68 p231; of Oakland, San Francisco 88 p155. For their origin, see Chap. 37.

Singer's Troupe of Midgets. 36 p236 and later. This was a famous act of 20 Austro-Hungarian midgets who came to the USA in 1910. They were popular in the two-a-day theatres and vaudeville, after which they became regular circus performers and played the Munchkins in *The Wizard of Oz*. See also SANGER'S.

Singin' in the rain. 51 p16; 92 p157. This song by Arthur Freed and Nacio Herb Brown was first sung in the film *Hollywood Revue of 1929*. It achieved even more success in the splendid Gene Kelly version of 1952 for which Freed and Brown again provided many songs and Freed produced.

Singleton Bros, who turn out books like sausages. 83 p96. Not too difficult to recognise Doubleday, Doran and Co (*Double*day–*Single*ton), who had published PGW's books up to eight years before. In January 1953, Doubleday wanted him to accept a smaller advance and less royalties, so PGW left them for Simon & Schuster. See also SCHWED.

Sing-Sing. 23 p48 and later. The residents of this town in New York State became so fed up with the notoriety of the famous prison, they changed the town's name to Ossining in 1901.

Sinking feeling. 97 p22 and elsewhere. A 1930s advertisement for the meat essence drink BOVRIL showed a man in his pyjamas happily paddling himself along in a rough sea, perched on a large Bovril jar: 'Bovril Prevents That Sinking Feeling' (hunger).

Sinner, miserable. See 'MISERABLE SINNER' BITS.

Sins have found him out, his. 88 p97. B. Numbers 32.23: "But if ye will not do so, behold, ye have sinned against the Lord; and be sure your sins will find you out."

Sins of commission or omission. 87 p154. Infuriatingly, while the term is in constant use among theologians and clerics, I have been unable to find its origin. The Presbyterian cathechism (Q.61) uses the phrase to expand on the fourth commandment and I can only assume that Wodehouse picked it up from his clerical uncles or from sermons at Dulwich. See also WE HAVE DONE THOSE THINGS.

Sins of the Scottie are visited upon its owner, the. 85 p75. BCP. The Communion. The Second Commandment: " and visit the sins of the fathers upon the children unto the third and fourth generation ..."

Sir Nigel (from *The White Company*). 4 p98. *The White Company* (1891) was a popular historical novel by Arthur Conan Doyle.

Sister Anne, scan the horizon like. See ANNE, SISTER.

Sister what-was-her-name, scanning the horizon like. 68 p127; 81 p21. See ANNE, SISTER.

Sisters and his cousins and his aunts, his. 30 p117; 84 p169. Sir Joseph Porter's song in G&S *H.M.S. Pinafore* Act 1.

Sit on his head. 3 p32 and later. This odd method of calming somebody in a rage stems from the time when horses, not cars, were the main form of transport. Horses slipped and fell easily on London's streets, and the accepted wisdom of the time was that a frightened horse lying on its side was best calmed by people sitting on its head.

Sitting Bull. 43 p215. Chief of the Hunkpapa Lakota Sioux (1834–90).

Sitting on top of the world, I'm. 56 p199 and later. 1925 song by Lewis and Henderson.

Sitting Pretty. 83 p125 and elsewhere. A common enough phrase, though it is worth noting it was the title of the 1924 PGW/ Bolton/Kern show on which he based *Bill the Conqueror*. The phrase will also be found in that novel, uttered by the young Horace at p131.

Sitwells. I believe you're one, if not more, of the Sitwells 67 p99. See MULLINER, SACHEVERELL.

Six Characters In Search Of An Undertaker by Tchekov. 49 p231. A clear reference to *Six Characters in Search of an Author* by Pirandello. A newspaper article of 22 March 1987 said: "It is impossible to capture the bewilderment, shock and amazement that his *Six Characters In Search Of An Author* inflicted on its first audiences back in 1921."

Six Hundred Club. 21 p71. Why PGW changed it from the Four Hundred Club, I don't know. See FOUR HUNDRED.

Sixes and sevens, at. 52 p69. This phrase indicating confusion has a splendid origin. In the Middle Ages, the most powerful bodies in London were the trade guilds, butchers, bakers, drapers and so on. They ran a tight ship, and you could not set up in a trade in London until you had served your apprenticeship or otherwise proved your skill and been admitted to the relevant guild. They became known as livery companies because of the robes (livery) they wore, and you still cannot become Lord Mayor of London unless you are a member of a livery company.

The companies have always been very jealous of their seniority, and the phrase 'at sixes and sevens' stems from the big dispute of 1484. In that year, the Merchant Taylors Company and the Skinners Company went to the Lord Mayor seeking a decision on which was sixth in seniority and which was seventh. The Lord Mayor gave his judgement that they take it in turns, changing each year. A very sensible decision which they still follow today.

MTT Rodney Yates, Master of the Tallow Chandlers' Company, for the information that there is one important exception to the rule. If a Merchant Taylor or a Skinner is elected Lord Mayor, then his Company is counted as the senior, sixth in seniority, for that year. The Lord Mayor for 2006 was a Merchant Taylor, and they have therefore been senior two years running. It may seem unimportant to outsiders, but the order of precedence/seniority is taken very seriously among British regiments, and Oxford and Cambridge colleges as well as among the Livery Companies.

Sixpence, taking as much as will cover a. 43 p60. From an advertisement for Kruschen Salts, which were meant to keep your liver clear. Kruschen had enough sense to keep the advertisement going for years, which is why PGW knew everybody would get the reference. You can see the Kruschen advert at page 1 of the June 1926 edition of *The Strand*, which I'm sure every Wodehouse enthusiast has to hand.

Sixty-four thousand dollar question. 81 p74. This 1950s TV quiz programme and its cash prizes attracted vast audiences.

Skeesicks, sensible young. 15 p62. PGW uses it here with the meaning of an ordinary young man. The phrase came into popularity from the long-lived cartoon 'Gasoline Alley', but 'Skeezix' did not appear in that till well after *The Prince and Betty* came out. Apparently it was US slang for a young man from the mid-19th century onwards; another example of PGW's keen ear for New York vernacular c.1909–14. See also RANNYGAZOO.

Skeewassett, Maine. 71 p7. MTT Charles Gould, who has a letter from PGW (19 June 1952) confirming that: "Yes, my Skeewassett in *Angel Cake* is Skowhegan [Maine]. I was there in 1950 with a show I wrote starring Fay Bainter… . I loved Skowhegan. For the purpose of the story I had to put a hotel there [the Lakeside Inn]. Actually there is only an inn that provides meals but not sleeping accommodation [*sic*]."

Skegness is so bracing (as are Bramley on Sea and Margate). 50 p305 and later. See BRAMLEY.

Skin of his/my teeth. 35 p136. B. Job 19.20: "My bone cleaveth to my skin and to my flesh, and I am escaped with the skin of my teeth."

'Skin off your nose.' 'Fluff in your latchkey.' 55 p42. These apparent nonsensical toasts were a natural extension of MUD IN YOUR EYE. The unspoken, mutually-understood prefix was: Let the worst thing that can happen to you be [skin off your nose/ fluff in your latchkey].

Skin you love to touch, the. 38 p64 and later. The 1910 (US) advertisement for Woodbury's Facial Soap ran for years and became part of the language.

Skindle's. 91 p119. A hotel on the Thames once famous, or notorious, as a popular spot for romantic weekends.

Skinner for the book, it would be a. 60 p60. A racing term indicating that no one had bet on the winner.

Skip like a young ram. 41 p195. See SKIPPED IN A MANNER.

Skip ye so, ye high hills, why? 50 p254. I think PGW mixed up his references slightly here. I suggest what Lady Julia should have said were the words from B. Psalms 68.16: "Why leap ye, ye high hills?" PGW probably confused them with the mountains and little hills mentioned at B. Psalms 114.6 (see SKIPPED IN A MANNER).

Skipped by the light of the moon. 73 p84. To leave by night to avoid a creditor or landlord. When you couldn't pay the rent or your bookmaker, you moved out quietly at night-time. Hence also the phrases 'doing a moonlight flit' and 'shooting the moon'.

Skipped in a manner extraordinarily reminiscent of the high hills mentioned in Holy Writ. 41 p203; 60 p293. B. Psalms 114.6. "Ye mountains that ye skipped like rams; and ye little hills, like lambs."

Skipper had taken his little daughter to bear him company, the. 29 p46. Longfellow's 'The Wreck of the Hesperus': "It was the schooner Hesperus, / That sailed the wintry sea; / And the skipper had taken his little daughter, / To bear him company."

***Skippy*.** 56 p260. This 1931 film, based on the strip cartoon of the same name, recounted the efforts of a small boy to help another boy save his dog's life.

Skull. Kid finds a s. and takes it to her grandfather etc. 92 p176. See Robert Southey's 'The Battle of Blenheim'.

Skylark … he would have got on well with Shelley. 94 p96. See SHELLEY's 'To a Skylark'.

Slacker, The Compleat. 3 p239. See Walton's *The Compleat Angler* (1653).

Slang. See ER SUFFIX.

Slave of the Lamp. 41 p174. The genie from the pantomime/fairy tale Aladdin.

Slay this man when he was full of bread, with all his crimes etc. etc. 33 p87. S. *Hamlet* 3.3: "He took my father grossly, full of bread, / With all his crimes" etc etc.

Sleave of care, ravelled. 72 p16. See SLEEP WHICH KNITS.

Sleep. A little s., a little slumber, a little folding of the hands 60 p231; 63 p135. See LITTLE REST.

Sleep of the labouring man is sweet, the. 49 p295. B. Ecclesiastes 5.12: "The sleep of a labouring man is sweet whether he eat little or much, but the abundance of the rich will not suffer him to sleep."

Sleep which knits up the ravelled sleeve of care. 36 p179 and later, although it is sometimes difficult to identify from Bertie Wooster's contorted misquotations, including, at 59 p312, "sleep which does something that has slipped my mind to the something sleeve of care poured over me in a healing wave." S. *Macbeth* 2.1: "Sleep that knits up the ravell'd sleave of care."

Slice her where you like, she's still baloney. 56 p60. See BALONEY.

Sliced bread, biggest thing since. 83 p17. This expression came into common use in the UK in 1969. See BOX FRUIT.

Slide, Kelly, slide. 16 p179. This popular 1889 song by John Kelly, a friend of the man involved, commemorated the baseball player Michael Kelly, who played for Chicago and Boston. He was known as the Ten Thousand Dollar Beauty because that was the cost of his transfer fee. The ability to 'slide' into a base is highly valued in baseball, and Kelly was very good at it. He made a regular income in his retirement signing copies of the song.

Slimmo. Sovereign recipe for obesity 67 p95; 72 p44. I have not found Slimmo, but the *Strand* magazine (February 1930) offered something even better: "La-Mar Reducing Soap … which washes away fat … gently shrinks the skin as it washes away the fat. Results are quick and amazing. No dieting or exercising. Be as slim as you wish … money-back guarantee."

Slings and arrows of outrageous fortune. 2 p36 and frequent later. S *Hamlet.* 3.1 ('To be or not to be' speech): "Whether 'tis nobler in the mind to suffer The slings and arrows of outrageous fortune …"

Slough of Despond. 17 p72 and later. From Bunyan's *Pilgrim's Progress.*

Slumber, sunk in hoggish. See HOGGISH SLUMBER.

Slythe and Sale, Lord. 41 p82; 57 p279; 69 p106. About as near as one can get to the real Lord Saye and Seale, whose splendid family name is Twisleton-Wykeham-Fiennes. Another private Wodehouse joke. He certainly knew Lord Saye and Seale; they signed the Hunstanton Hall Visitors' Book on the same day in 1927 and I believe the fictional version was a compliment to his fellow guest. The present holder of the title tells me his grandfather was fond of atrocious puns; perhaps it was the common enjoyment of playing with words that formed a bond. See Chap. 32.

Smalls. 31 p138. First-year examinations at Oxford.

Smell as sweet. See DINNER FROM ANY HOST.

Smelt a rat (and saw it floating in the air). See RAT SMELT A.

Smile. When you say that, smile 89 p61. Allegedly spoken by Gary Cooper (1901–61) in the 1929 film *The Virginian*. I am told the phrase is another film misquote (see COME UP AND SEE ME), and the actual words spoken were: "If you want to call me that, smile."

Smile and smile and be a villain, One may. See MEET IT IS.

Smile, ghastly. Grinned horrible a ghastly smile, like Death in the poem. See GRINNED HORRIBLE.

'Smile That Wins, The'. 49 short story title. I thought this was from one of those 1920s 'How to Gain Self-Confidence' adverts, but was unable to find it. MTT John Graham, who reminded me of 'The smiles that win' from Byron's 'She Walks in Beauty'. MTT also to Ed Ratcliffe for a 1928 advertisement for the then-new dentifrice 'Pepsodent'. The half-page *Vanity Fair* advert is headed 'Those Winning Smiles'. I think the Byron quote is nearer the mark but would not bet on it.

Smiles' Self-Help. 31 p149. The English social reformer Samuel Smiles (1812–1904) published *Self-Help* in 1859, a book about boys and men who 'got on' by overcoming difficulties and disappointments (the inventors Watt, Arkwright and the like). It became a runaway success, was translated into many languages and the British Institute of Economic Affairs re-published it in 1996. See also ALGER, HORATIO.

Smiling, the boy fell dead. 68 p41. Last line of Browning's 'Incident of the French Camp'.

Smith, Aubrey. A malevolent A.S. 64 p179. C. Aubrey Smith (1863–1948) captained England at cricket, played against PGW in the Actors v. Authors matches, and developed a monopoly of 'grand old English gentleman' parts in Hollywood. He founded the Hollywood Cricket Club (PGW acted as secretary) and set high standards for English actors working in Hollywood. He made a point of flying a Union Jack outside his house, and the weathervane on the roof comprised three stumps, a bat and ball.

Smith had the splendid habit of refusing to read American newspapers, relying on the London *Times*, which took three weeks to arrive. David Niven reported this made things tricky for his English friends, who had to watch what they said. This became nearly unbearable in 1938. Niven said they had to wait in patience till the day Smith threw down his *Times* in disgust and announced in ringing tones: "That swine Hitler has invaded Czecho-Slovakia" — when they were at last able to express shock and horror at news they had known for three weeks. See Chap. 24.

Smith, G.O. 3 p111. This amateur Soccer player (1872–1943) was considered by many to be finest centre-forward in English football till Tommy Lawton many years later. The best way to describe his pre-eminence is to say that, from 1890 to 1910, he and W.G. Grace were the only two sportsmen commonly referred to in newspapers just by their initials. 'G.O.' and 'W.G.' were all that readers needed.

Smithsonian would buy Lord Emsworth's carpet-slippers, the. 91 p187. An odd expression. I assume PGW meant they were so old they should be in the Smithsonian museum.

Smoker. The Trinity smoker 29 p100; smoking-concert 57 p28; and elsewhere. I have included this since I have often been asked what the term means. Smokers (smoking concerts), in the first case one held in Trinity College, Oxford, are informal amateur concerts put on in a college, a club or pub, with smoking and drinking allowed. Usually male affairs, they are highly enjoyable. Savage Club dinners still end with splendid entertainments on the same lines.

Snails. Throwing snails over the fence into his back garden 50 p227; 95 p124. Every reader of A.P. HERBERT's splendid *Uncommon Law* will recognise the reference. In that book, in *Cowfat v. Wheedle*, Mr Justice Wool held that snails count as wild animals (*ferae naturae*) and therefore the laws of trespass and control that apply to domestic animals, dogs, cats, horses etc. do not apply to them. While they are regarded in England only as witty satires on the judicial system, I have read that Herbert's legal arguments are respected in the USA and have been quoted and accepted in American courts.

Snail's on the wing and the lark's on the thorn, or rather the other way round. 93 p190. See GOD'S IN HIS HEAVEN.

Snake in his Path While About to Bathe, Young Man Startled by a. 40 p111; snake in his path 63 p71. I have had great difficulty with PGW titles like these. With a few honourable exceptions, most reference books on paintings list them by painter, not by title. I have a strong recollection of a Victorian painting of some nymph/shepherdess starting back in alarm at a snake in her path, but have been unable to identify it. But see SURPRISED.

Snake, languid. Sunday lunch ... drags its slow length along like a languid snake 12 p267. English grammar books used to have a section on poetic metre, iambic pentameters and that sort of thing. The standard description of the Alexandrine, a line of six iambs, that we all learned was: "That like / a woun / ded snake / drags its / slow length / along." Clearly PGW read it too. It is from Alexander (hence the name) Pope's 'Essay on Criticism'.

Snapping up unconsidered trifles. 4 p133; 21 p44; of cats at random 22 p153. S. *Winter's Tale* 4.2: "A snapper-up of unconsidered trifles."

Snatched up to Heaven in a fiery chariot. 63 p41; 81 p137; the Empress was not 91 p50. Whereas most prophets in the Old Testament died and were buried, Elijah made a more dramatic exit. See B. 2 Kings 2.11.

Sneak the biscuit. See BISCUIT.

Snettisham, Lord & Lady. 43 p201. These two take their names from the village of Snettisham, just up the road from Hunstanton Hall in Norfolk. See Chap. 32.

Snoot. Bust him in the s. 56 p64 & p134 and later. The term 'snoot' achieved notoriety in Britain when Bill Thompson, the anti-British mayor of Chicago, announced that if King George V ever visited Chicago, Thompson would "punch him in the snoot".

Snowden. 46 p194. Labour politician (1864–1937) and Chancellor of the Exchequer in the 1920s, when he imposed a tight financial regime in the UK, making drastic cuts in Government spending.

Snuff, up to. 5 p44. Wide awake, alive, alert to scent like hounds. Said to come from the Dutch word 'snuf', meaning smell. MTT Wim Duk for correcting my Dutch spelling.

Snug as a bug in a rug, You'll be as. 80 p20. Benjamin Franklin in a letter to Miss Georgiana Shipley (1772): "Here Skugg lies snug, As a bug in a rug." (Skugg was a pet squirrel.)

Soapy Syd Hemmingway/ Soapy Molloy. 31 p44; 36 p90 and later. See Chap. 38.

Socage in fief. 55 p211. A form of land tenure in mediaeval England. Your tenure was secure so long as you fulfilled your obligations to the owner of the land, i.e. provided him with so much money/corn each year or provided a specified number of men at arms when called upon to do so.

Society of Authors (had fought Mortimer Busby for many years). 58 p35. PGW was a long-time member and sometime official of the body which looks after authors' interest against publishers like Mr Busby.

Sock and buskin. 68 p13; 89 p161. The distinguishing mark of actors in ancient Greece. The buskin was a high boot worn for tragedy, the 'sock' was a thin-soled shoe worn for comedy. MTT David Landman.

Sock in it, put a. See PUT A SOCK.

Socko, a. 57 p208; 58 p40 and later. See Chap. 24.

Sock-shop. Had kept me from the s. 56 p63. Sock-shop was another term for tuck-shop, a small shop in a school where boys could buy sweets, buns, ice creams etc.

Socrates, (and busts of). 1 p222; 2 p146; 13 p116; 81 p150 and later. The Victorians liked having busts of the ancients around the place and Socrates, the philosopher (469–399 B.C.), was a favourite in academic circles. The fashion started with the Classical revival in interior decoration in the late 18th century (Adam brothers et al.) and became common when 19th-century manufacturing processes made mass production of such things possible. I recall the bust of Socrates, showing his straggly beard and prominent eyes, tended to be seen in headmasters' studies.

Soft sleek ripples hardly bear up shoreward, Charged with sighs more light than laughter. 37 p238. From Swinburne's 'A Word With the Wind'.

Soft word that's supposed to turn away wrath, the. 85 p116. B. Proverbs 15.1: "A soft answer turneth away wrath but grievous words stir up anger."

Soigné river, Way down upon the. 68 p168; 73 p90; 85 p187. See SWANEE.

Sold down the river. 38 p21. Americans will need no explanation of this phrase, but some British readers may not know that, until 1865, slaves in upriver American States were terrified of being sold down the river, i.e. further south down the Mississipi river, where they believed conditions were much worse.

Solemn stillness. 52 p114 and elsewhere. See ALL THE AIR.

Solid flesh (too, too). See FLESH, TOO.

Solomon Eagle. 2 p43. See EAGLE.

Solomon in all his glory. You'd make Solomon in all his glory look like a tramp cyclist 13 p84; and later. B. Matthew 6.28–29. "Consider the lilies of the field, how they grow; they toil not, neither do they spin: And yet I say unto you, That even Solomon in all his glory was not arrayed like one of these." See also TRAMP CYCLIST.

Solomon, King. His habit of marrying 70 p232. B.1 Kings 11.3. says he had 700 wives and 300 concubines.

Solon. 63 p15; 76 p53. This Athenian statesman (639–559 B.C.) gave Athens a strict code of law which they followed for 400 years.

Solvitur ambulando. 1 p118 and later. Latin tag. To solve a problem/question by practical experiment. Literally, it is solved by walking.

Some are born with sprained wrists, some achieve sprained wrists. 8 p147; some policemen are born grafters, some achieve graft and some have graft thrust upon them 13 p28. PGW used the "Some are born X, some achieve X and some have X thrust upon them" often. See 17 p88, 21 p132; 89 p36. S. *Twelfth Night* 2.5. "Some men are born great, some achieve greatness, and some have greatness thrust upon them."

Some wild creature caught in a trap. See CREATURE.

Somebody's Mother. 32 p297; 78 p116. When Psmith uttered these words, he was repeating a popular phrase of the time. In 1878 Mary Brine published a poem in *Harper's Weekly* dealing with the reproof of a young man to his rude friends mocking an old woman. "She's somebody's mother, boys, you know, / For all that she's aged and poor …" This gift to the American music industry was quickly taken up, and six songs with the title appeared in as many years.

Someone, as the poet says, had blundered. 56 p70 and later. T. 'The Charge of the Light Brigade': "Was there a man dismay'd? Not tho' the soldier knew / Someone had blundered."

Something attempted, something done has earned a night's repose. 3 p271. In later references, earned a cigarette; a spot of beer; two penn'orth of wassail in the smoking-room. Longfellow's 'The Village Blacksmith': "Something attempted, something done, / Has earned a night's repose."

Song in his heart, with a. 66 p233 and later. 'With a Song in My Heart', 1929 song by Rodgers & Hart.

Song of Songs. 'Jeeves and the Song of Songs'. B. The Song of Solomon, first line: "The song of songs which is Solomon's."

Song, one grand sweet. See LIFE WAS.

Song was ended. Though the song was ended, the melody lingered on 54 p228. Song by Irving Berlin (1927) 'The Song Is Ended — But the Melody Lingers On'.

Songs of Araby and tales of far Kashmir. 20 p83 and later. Based on Thomas Moore's 'Lalla Rookh' and with music by Frederic Clay, the song was an instant success in drawing-rooms from its publication in 1877.

Songs of Squalor. 32 p173. Nothing firm, but perhaps PGW had in mind Whittier's *Songs of Labour* or *Songs of the Ghetto* by Morris Rosenfeld. Or was it a parody of the series by Ella Wheeler WILCOX: *Poems of Passion, Poems of Pleasure, Poems of Power*?

Sonnets from the Portuguese. 19 p107 and later. By Elizabeth Barrett Browning.

Sonny Boy. 43 p92 and later. I was surprised to find this immortal song (*The Singing Fool* 1928) (and PGW short story title) was written as a joke. Bud De Sylva, Lew Brown and Ray Henderson, decided to write something satirising the sentimental songs that were then all the rage. Their version, they hoped, would emphasise how maudlin these were. To their surprise, 'Sonny Boy' became the most popular sentimental song of all and they had enough sense to keep quiet about it.

Sons of Belial. 7 p14 and later. B. 2 Samuel 23.6: "But the sons of Belial shall be all of them as thorns thrust away …"

Sons of Toil. 50 p298; 87 p27. Term coined or popularised by Denis Kearney (1847–1907), US labour leader, in a speech in 1878. Horny-handed toiler at 25 p10 is probably from James Russell Lowell's poem 'A Glance Behind the Curtain'. "And blessed are the horny hands of toil."

Soothing syrup. Came across with the soothing syrup 93 p99. I had a strong memory of the phrase from Victorian magazines, but it took me a long time to find it. One of the most popular patent medicines in the 19th century in America and, I believe, the UK was 'Mrs Winslow's Soothing Syrup' to ease a child's pain while teething. First sold in 1849, it became wildly popular among young mothers seeking to calm their babies. By the 1880s, it was being advertised everywhere.:

> Advice to mothers. Are you broken in your rest by a sick child? Go at once to a chemist and get a bottle of Mrs Winslow's Soothing Syrup. It will relieve the poor sufferer immediately. It produces natural quiet sleep and the little cherub awakes as bright as a button.

By the turn of the 1900s, many doctors had become suspicious of it. It was at last analysed, and each dose (up to four a day recommended) was found to contain a grain of morphine per fluid ounce. Despite being banned in the USA in 1906, its sale seems to have continued elsewhere till the 1930s. See also PATENT medicines.

Sorrow, man is born to. See MAN IS BORN.

Sorrow, more in. See MORE IN SORROW.

Sorrow's crown of sorrows is remembering happier things. 19 p180 and later.

T. 'Locksley Hall'.

Sorrows of the world had come, on whose head the. 59 p116. From Walter PATER's description of the Mona Lisa in his *Renaissance*: "the head upon which all 'the ends of the world are come,'..." Richard Usborne and others have wondered why PGW misquoted it, but maybe he had simply forgotten it. Pater was quoting B. 1 Corinthians 10.11: " upon whom the ends of the world are come." See also PLATE.

Sotto voce and the silent tomb, she remained. 68 p149; 93 p109; 96 p79. See JABBERJEE.

Soul of the sitter, one of those artists who reveal the. 64 p177. See SARGENT.

Soul's Awakening. 17 p174; 23 p122 (description); and 18 times later! MTT Frank Laycock for the information that this archetypal Victorian painting was done by James Sant (1820–1916). Painted in 1888, it was the hit of the Royal Academy exhibition that year and thousands of prints were sold. The picture shows a thirteen-year-old girl, Sant's great-niece Annie Kathleen Rendle, looking up to Heaven with a prayer book clasped in her left hand. It was still listed in the 1907 Army & Navy Stores catalogue twenty years later. Sant also produced a famous painting of the INFANT SAMUEL.

Sound and fury signifying nothing. 82 p119. S. *Macbeth* 5.5: "it is a tale / Told by an idiot, full of sound and fury, / Signifying nothing."

Sound in wind and limb. 25 p236. A phrase commonly used to describe a horse in good condition. An appropriate term for Reggie Byng to use for his car since they were comparatively new and equine terminology was still in common use.

Sound of a Great Amen. 91 p124. A line from the song 'The Lost Chord' (1877), words by Adelaide Ann Procter, music by Arthur Sullivan. Sullivan wrote the music at the bedside of his dying brother, and the song became wildly popular. I heard it on the radio as I wrote this in December 2001.

Sound of revelry by night, a. 52 p297; 80 p94. BYRON's *Childe Harold's Pilgrimage* 3.21. "There was a sound of revelry by night, / And Belgium's capital had gathered then / Her beauty and her chivalry."

Soup, strengthening. A bowl of s. s. to one of his needy parishioners 68 p102; and elsewhere. See Chap. 11.

Soup to nuts, from. 15 p14 and later. The complete business, the whole thing. From c.1870, formal dinners always began with soup, followed by fish, ending with fruit and nuts with the port. Nowadays there are fewer dinners on this scale, but I would say that, up to 1939, most dinner parties followed this pattern. If I were invited to a formal dinner at an Oxford College, a City livery company or a British army officers' mess, I would be surprised if the rule did not still apply. See also CAVIARE TO NUTS.

Soup-and-fish. Donning the s-a-f. in preparation for the evening meal 43 p23 and p228; and later. This is full evening dress, i.e. black tail coat, white waistcoat, starched shirt with studs and white bow tie. The term probably came into use between 1900 and 1910 to distinguish evening dress from the more informal 'black tie' (dinner jacket). Up to 1939, if you were going to a dance or a formal dinner with ladies present, you wore evening dress. And, since a formal dinner *always* began with soup, followed by fish, the three words became synonymous with full evening dress. I believe that, up to 1939, if you arrived for dinner at the Savoy Hotel wearing a dinner jacket, you would be refused entry to the restaurant and directed to the Grill Room, where such informal dress was permitted.

The term is still in use. Just a couple of years ago, I had to tell somebody I could not attend some function because I was booked for a dinner elsewhere and Royalty was coming. His response was: "Oh! Soup and fish then?"

South American Joe. 68 p19; 88 p27. Maybe based on a specific film/cartoon character. Otherwise I suggest it was a general derogatory term for those Latin lovers in 1930s films who pressed their unwanted attentions on the heroine. They were distinguished by their 'Latin' accent, heavily greased hair and thin moustache.

Southbourne, Countess of. See Chap. 16.

Southmoltonshire. 73 p20. See Chap. 12.

Sower going forth sowing, like a. 56 p188; 67 p149 and later. B. Matthew 13.3: "Behold, a sower went forth to sow."

Sown the wind, we have, and we shall reap the whirlwind. 49 p300; 50 p248 and later. B. Hosea 8.7: "For they have sown the wind and they shall reap the whirlwind."

S.P., better to stick to. See ANTE-POST.

Spade a spade, calling a. See FORD.

Spain. The situation in Spain 58 p236. When PGW wrote that, the Spanish Civil War (1936–39) was at its height, arousing bitter arguments in England at every level of society.

Spaniard who blighted my life, the. 42 p261. Humorous 1911 song by Billy Merson, which was still being sung in the 1960s.

Spanish influenza. 30 p88. The Spanish influenza epidemic of 1918–20 killed more than 40 million people around the world.

Spare the rod, spoil the child. 3 p64. B. Proverbs 13.24: "He that spareth his rod hateth his child; but he that loveth him chasteneth him betimes."

Spartan mother who expected better things of a favourite son. 70 p113. Spartan mothers bred their sons to show no weakness of any kind. See FOX GNAW.

Spartans at Thermopylae. 76 p146. See THERMOPYLAE.

Speaking eyes. One of his speaking eyes was sable (i.e. he had a black eye) 8 p36. From CALVERLEY's 'Gemini et Virgo'.

Speculation in her eyes. Like Banquo's ghost, she had no s. in her e. 18 p260. In 'Deep Waters', when Mary Vaughan rescues George Callender, a crowd of people swoop down "with speculation in their eyes". S. *Macbeth* 3.4: "Thy bones are marrowless, thy blood is cold; / Thou hast no speculation in those eyes / Which thou dost glare with."

Spelvin, Lord George. 36 p196. See next entry.

Spelvin, Rodney; his cousin George is an actor. 37 p219. A semi-private PGW joke. Everybody in the theatrical profession knows it, but not many outside. In the American theatre, George Spelvin is the traditional false name taken by an actor who does not want to use his real name or, more often, where an actor has to play more than one part. Charles Gardner used it in 1886 in *Karl, the Peddler*, but it became popular when Winchell Smith gave it to an actor in *Brewster's Millions* (1906). The show was such a success, he used it as a good-luck charm in every show thereafter. Someone has estimated that George Spelvin has appeared in nearly 10,000 shows over the last hundred years. According to David Jasen's *The Theatre of P.G. Wodehouse*, the part of Professor Appleby in the opening night of *Sitting Pretty* (8 April 1924) was played by George Spelvin.

The UK equivalent is Walter Plinge (or Wendy if female), coined around 1900, commemorating the landlord of the pub next door to Irving's Lyceum Theatre. At Glyndebourne, the music festival, they use an upmarket variation, Walter von Plingenburg or, if female, his sister Waltraut.

At 37 p218, Jane Packard's statement that Rodney Spelvin is "staying with the Wyndhams for a few weeks" would raise a smile among readers with some knowledge of the London theatre. The Wyndhams were a famous theatrical family who built Wyndham's Theatre in 1899 and were still running it when PGW wrote the story.

Spencer, Herbert. 9 p151; would cringe before his old nurse 39 p202. This English philosopher (1820–1903) was one of the Victorian 'giants' who influenced so many 20th-century politicians.

Spenlow. Like Mr. Spenlow, he had a partner 12 p148. In later references, he is named as Mr Jorkins. See D. *David Copperfield*, where Mr Spenlow always evades agreeing to anything, saying his (unseen) partner, Mr Jorkins, would never agree. Up to the 1950s, 'Mr Spenlow' was often used for people who hated making decisions and always blamed somebody else. See HAMLET'S AUNT.

Sphere of influence. 85 p69. This phrase, describing international power politics, became popular in the 1930s when Hitler and Stalin were 'influencing' neighbouring countries by deploying troops along their border and exerting economic pressure.

Spider eating its mate. 74 p150; 77 p57–8. See Chap. 13.

Spies. As single spies, not in battalions 24 p152. S. *Hamlet* 4.5. "When sorrows come, they come not single spies, But in battalions."

Spillane, Mickey. 80 p133. This American writer of tough-guy detective fiction (1918-2006) was very popular in the 1940s–50s.

Spillikens. 3 p242. For those who do not know it, this game (known as Pick-Up Sticks in the US) begins with dropping fifty or so thin sticks/ carved bones in a bundle on the table. The aim is to take off the sticks/bones one at a time without disturbing any of the others. It is far trickier than it sounds.

Spilt milk blows nobody any good. 52 p138. For those unfamiliar with them, this is PGW's twist on the two proverbs: it's no good crying over spilt milk and it's an ill wind that blows nobody good. See also BURNED CHILD.

Spinoza. 64 p11 and later. This Dutch philosopher (1632–77) believed that all life was embraced by an infinite God or nature. His *Ethics* came out in 1677.

Spion Kop ceased with a jerk. 23 p156. Spion Kop was a major battle in 1900 in the Boer War. We lost it.

Spirit, humble and contrite. 32 p179; meek and chastened 61 p137; Dolly Molloy does not have at 36 p89 or at 63 p12. Take your choice of either the BCP Commination Service: "with all contrition and meekness of heart"; or from KIPLING's 'Recessional': "An humble and a contrite heart".

Spirit of '76. 25 p251. This well-known painting was done by Archibald Willard for the centenary of the United States in 1876. It depicts an old man, a young man and a drummer boy marching along in 1776 uniforms.

Spirit was willing but the jolly old flesh would have none of it. 2 p4; 26 p11 and later. The lungs were willing but the memory was weak 36 p22. B. Matthew 26.41: "Watch and pray that ye enter not into temptation; the spirit indeed is willing, but the flesh is weak."

Spiv. 69 p191. This term is dying away now. It came into popular use in Britain in the Second World War for small-time traders who procured rationed goods and items in short supply and sold them at a vast profit on 'the black market'. Since this was not a criminal offence (unless you could prove theft), the authorities had to take a more devious approach. Such persons could be stopped and searched by policemen as a Suspected Person or Itinerant Vagrant — SPIV for short. It soon became a common term for those who did not work for their living, the context in which PGW used it. See also MEANS OF SUPPORT.

Splitting the welkin. 68 p31. See WELKIN.

Spode, Roderick. 59 p21. PGW undoubtedly had in mind Sir Oswald Mosley (1896–1980), leader of the British Fascists in the 1930s. See BLACK SHORTS and Chap. 31 (Sidcup).

Spoiler of Men, A. 8 p52. Novel (1905) by Richard Marsh.

Spondulicks. Frequent. From the ancient Greek word for their early form of coinage which was based on sea shells. The shortened form, 'spon', is, I am told, still used in the UK building trade as a slang term for money.

Sport/sporting with Amaryllis in the shade. See AMARYLLIS.

Sported on the green, together we. 3 p67; 26 p13 and later. An inappropriate reference, I thought, but five dictionaries of quotations all give me "And by him sported on the green / His little grandchild Wilhelmine", the first verse of Robert Southey's poem 'Battle of Blenheim'.

Sporting Times, The. Formal title of *The Pink 'Un*. See Chap. 5.

Sportsman, The. 1 p14 and often later. A small, badly-printed newspaper (1890–1914?) with a wide coverage of football and cricket results, including school matches.

Spread a little happiness. See Happiness, spread a little.

Spring. (1) In s. a young man's fancy lightly turns to thoughts of love 86 p209 and elsewhere. See Livelier iris. (2) S. is here. 51 p17. Song by Jerome Kern for the show *Lucky* (1927) and again in *Sweet Adeline* 1929. (3) Suddenly it's s. 83 p72. 'Suddenly It's Spring' was a song in *Seven Brides for Seven Brothers* (1954) as well as the title of a 1947 film.

Spying out all his ways. That eye which, so to speak, was always "about his bath and about his bed and spying out all his ways" 37 p52; 77 p36; and later. See BCP Psalms 139.2. See also *The Way of All Flesh* (1903) by Samuel Butler and the PGW gloss in chapter 31, which reads: "The heavy hand and the watchful eye of Theobald were no longer about his path and about his bed and spying out all his ways." MTT Elin Woodger & Lord Gladwyn.

Squaler, fling the. 11 p10. 'Squaler' is a good English word for a throwing stick. In rural England, boys used to hunt rabbits, squirrels etc. by throwing sticks at them and developed considerable skill and accuracy. I certainly remember squaler competitions in the 1950s, an outdoor equivalent to darts and a popular pastime in Oxfordshire country pubs. A small object, perhaps three inches high, shaped like a champagne cork, was placed on top of a post about four feet high. The thrower had three sticks, about a foot long and an inch in diameter, and tried to knock the 'sally' — hence 'Aunt Sally' — off the post. The trick was to throw the stick in such a manner that it went through the air without spinning, more of a cast than a throw if you understand me.

Square Deal. See Deal.

Square one two three four. Give me 73 p222. Telephone number of 'Harrige's'. Harrod's, the London department store, were unwilling to let PGW use their name so he called it Harrige's (mix of Harrod's and Selfridge's). Harrod's is near Sloane Square in London and its telephone number was SLOane 1234, so PGW just made it SQUare 1234 instead.

Squeaking and gibbering like the sheeted dead. 60 p123 & p127; 70 p167. S. *Hamlet* 1.1: "The graves stood tenantless and the sheeted dead / Did squeak and gibber in the Roman streets."

Squeal and gibber like the sheeted dead. 79 p80. See entry above.

Stableford, Earl of. 48 p35. See Chap. 35.

Stableford, Shropshire. See Chap. 35.

Stag At Bay, Landseer's. 47 p8; 52 p239; Mr Chinnery looks like such a stag in horn-rimmed glasses 58 p121; and later. It is a moot point whether the most popular painting in Britain in the late 19th century was Landseer's *Stag at Bay* (a stag under attack by hounds) or his *Monarch of the Glen* (another stag looking very full of himself).

Stag at eve. 32 p157 and later; drinking like the stag at eve 56 p12; stag at evening 64 p51. A phrase that needed no explanation to PGW's generation. After the introduction, the first line of the first verse of Walter Scott's 'The Lady of the Lake' is: "The stag at eve had drunk his fill, / Where danced the moon on Monan's rill."

Staggered and would have fallen had he not …, he. 41 p47 and later. PGW loved this phrase and used it often, but I have been unable to trace it. I suggest it was simply a cliché from Victorian novels and melodramas where good/ bad/ surprising news seemed to affect everybody this way. I draw support for this view from 42 p263: "Hugo had often read stories in which people reeled and would have fallen, had they not clutched at whatever it was they clutched at."

Staines, Lord, is heir to Lord Runnymede. 18 p247. A conjunction of titles that English readers appreciated. Runnymede is an island on the Thames, just upstream from Staines.

Stand. Still doing business at the old s. 34 p197. Popular phrase on bookmaker's stands at racecourses implying their business was no fly-by-night affair. See also SAFE MAN.

Standard loaf. Standard loaf containing eighty per cent of the semolina 18 p169. This 1911 reference reflected the attempt of Lord Northcliffe, known to us as Lord Tilbury (see Chap. 7), to win a bet that he could change British eating habits in six months. His papers launched a vast campaign to persuade people to abandon the normal white loaf in favour of 'Standard Bread', a whole-meal loaf of an unappetizing grey colour. It didn't work.

Standing with reluctant feet where the brook and river meet. 38 p48; where the eggs and bacon meet 58 p82; 63 p200; and later. Longfellow's 'Maidenhood'.

Stands alone, he/ she/ you. 60 p229; 66 p69 and elsewhere. A common phrase, and a possible origin is Christina Georgina Rossetti's 'A Study (A Soul)': "She stands alone, a wonder deathly white." But PGW may have remembered the phrase in Robert Ingersoll's 1895 speech on Abraham Lincoln: "He stands alone."

Stands Cosy Moments where it did. 15A p242. S. *Macbeth* 4.3: "Stands Scotland where it did."

Stanley. 97 p41. See DOCTOR LIVINGSTONE.

Stanley, Sir Hubert, praise from. 15A p107; 21 p243 and later. Why this obscure phrase from an obscure play has remained in use for so long is a mystery to me. The line is from *A Cure for the Heartache* 5.2 by Thomas Morton (1764–1838).

Stapleton. The S. road 1 p52; expeditions to S. 3 p108. See Chap. 35.

Star Chamber. 59 p94; 67 p248. This English court was set up by Henry VII in 1486 to try offences for which the law then made insufficient provision. Notorious because of its sweeping powers, it was abolished in the reign of Charles I. Its name comes from the stars painted on the ceiling of the room in which it sat.

Star Spangled Banner. 26 p249 and elsewhere. I was puzzled why so many of PGW's characters were unable to remember the words of this song by Francis Scott Key until I learned that the USA did not adopt it as a national anthem till 1931.

State of man. This is the state of man, Today he puts forth the tender leaves of hope 74 p71. S. *King Henry VIII* 3.2.

State of man suffers the nature of an insurrection. 70 p149. S. *Julius Caesar* 2.1: "and the state of man, / Like to a little kingdom, suffers then, / The nature of an insurrection."

Stately homes of Wimbledon/England (how beautiful they stand). 33 p96; stately home of England 51 p251 and later. PGW twist on the famous poem by Mrs HEMANS which begins: "The Stately Homes of England, how beautiful they stand." Noel Coward's superb parody is now probably better known than Mrs Hemans' original.

Stately pleasure dome. 86 p33. See KUBLA KHAN.

Statue of Right triumphing over Wrong. 53 p136; 62 p237. See also 50 p162 where Beach looks like "Good Citizenship Refusing To Accept A Bribe From Big Business Interests In Connection With The Contract For The New Inter-Urban Tramway System." I have not found a statue with this title, but maybe PGW had in mind the notorious sculpture which caused such a stir in New York. On 21 April 1922, a fountain and statue by Frederick MacMonnie, entitled 'Civic Virtue', was unveiled in City Hall Park, followed by an immediate howl of protest from the women of New York. Civic Virtue was portrayed as a 'robust' male nude brandishing a club, with one foot stamped firmly on the neck of a prostrate female who represented Vice. The row went on till 1941, when the statue was moved to a less prominent position on the lawn of the Borough Hall of Queens.

Steeple Bumpstead. 11 p110. A small town in Essex. PGW knew it and used it to create Steeple Bumpleigh, Steeple Mummery and Market Bumpstead later. See also BUMPLEIGH HALL.

Steggles. I have always assumed that the unscrupulous, cunning Steggles ('The Great Sermon Handicap' and other stories) took his name from the equally unscrupulous, cunning schoolboy of the same name in Eden Philpott's *The Human Boy* (1899), which PGW had certainly read. See HUMAN BOY.

Steichomuthics. 4 p207; 9 p25. The young PGW was showing off a little here. This was a feature of Greek tragedy when the chorus told the audience in different voices/tones what was going on offstage. See GREEK DRAMA.

Stengah. See STINGAH.

Stenographer, dictating to a. See DICTATING.

Stepping high, wide and handsome. 76 p201. I'm sure PGW knew Jerome Kern's 1937 song 'High, Wide and Handsome'.

Stepping stones of his dead self to higher things. 19 p181; 36 p159 and later. See TRUTH WITH HIM.

Stern and rock-bound coast, on the. 60 p189; 93 p79. Mrs HEMANS' poem 'Landing of the Pilgrim Fathers' is the only source I could find: "The breaking waves dashed high, / On a stern and rock-bound coast."

Stick. Motty, who was sucking the knob of his stick, uncorked himself 23 p47;

Eggy Mannering does it at 56 p149. I am not sure when the custom stopped but, up to the 1920s(?), when you paid formal calls on people, you did not leave your gloves, hat or stick in the hall. You took them into the drawing-room with you, lest you could be accused of treating the place like a hotel. I was surprised how many books on etiquette stressed this point.

Stick, a big. (I and Roosevelt.) 15A p154. See BIG STICK.

Sticketh closer than a brother. 25 p178; 26 p16 and later. B. Proverbs 18.24: "A man that hath friends must shew himself friendly; and there is a friend that sticketh closer than a brother."

Stiff upper lip. Frequent. One theory is that this goes back to the old Press Gang days when the only way you could get out of the Navy was by being dead. If you got yourself so drunk that a pin stuck into your upper lip produced no reaction, you were counted as dead. Another view is that the expression began in Boston around 1833, a Puritan desire to restrain one's emotion. A supporter of this theory points out that Harriet Beecher Stowe's Uncle Tom was urged to "keep a stiff upper lip". I suggest this is nearer the mark; a trembling of the upper lip is a sign of fear/emotion which can be prevented by a deliberate effort to stiffen it, to make it rigid. The phrase was popular enough in the 19th century to impel Phoebe Cary (1824–71) to write 'Keep a Stiff Upper Lip'. Also the title of a song by George and Ira Gershwin in the film *A Damsel in Distress*. MTT David McDonough and Tony Ring.

Stiffen the sinews, summon up the blood. 60 p119 and elsewhere. From the 'Once more into the breach' speech in S. *King Henry V* 3.1.

Stig. 21 p77. See DING-BASTED AS A STIG.

Still waters that run deep, one of them. 18 p77. The proverb 'Still waters run deep' has been traced back to the 14th century.

Stilly night, in the. 76 p130. The two words are enough to identify Thomas Moore's 1818 poem, later a popular drawing room song 'Oft in the Stilly Night'.

Sting like adders. See ADDERS.

Stingahs. 73 p139. Captain Biggar, Tubby Frobisher and the Subahdar were drinking whisky and sodas. It was and, I am told, still is the Malayan term for them.

Stirred, something, down at the table/ in the forest. See DOWN IN THE FOREST.

Stirrup. Betwixt the s. and the ground 19 p107. See BETWIXT.

Stockheath, Lord. Cousin of Freddie Threepwood 19 p28. See Chap. 16.

Stockish, hard and full of rage. 93 p141. See MUSIC.

Stoddart. 4 p16. A.E. Stoddart (1863–1915) captained the English cricket team against Australia in the 1890s; he also captained the English Rugger Fifteen.

Stone, Fred. 23 p223. American light comedian (1873–1959), a friend of PGW's.

Stone, Marcus. 58 p115. Painter (1840–1921) best known for his idyllic 'chocolate box' paintings of romantic young men and women in 18th-century dress.

Stone walls do not a prison make nor iron bars a cage. 12 p128 & p311; and later. From Lovelace's 'To Althea, From Prison'.

Stood not upon the order of his going, he. 19 p76; 33 p107; and later; upon the order of his sinking 7 p201. S. *Macbeth* 3.4: "Stand not upon the order of your going, But go at once."

Stop your tickling, Jock. 25 p231. Song made famous by Harry Lauder.

Stopped, looked and listened. Beach did it 84 p107; I stopped and I looked and I listened 93 p43; and elsewhere. 'Stop! Look! Listen!' were notices put up at every railroad crossing in a US Road Safety campaign of 1912. Irving Berlin used it as the title of a song and a show in 1915, and George Robey made the song a hit in Britain.

Storm and stress. 17 p117. Probably better known in the original German *Sturm und Drang,* the play by Friedrich von Klinger (1752–1831).

Stout, Rex. 91 p10 and later. Creator of fictional detective Nero Wolfe.

Strand, Let's all go down the. See Let's all go down.

Strange. 'Twas s., 'twas passing s. 65 p130. S. *Othello* 1.3. "She swore, in faith, 'twas strange, 'twas passing strange; 'Twas pitiful, 'twas wondrous pitiful …"

Strategic retreat (and General Eisenhower). 73 p41. See Eisenhower.

Stray cats, walking through the wet woods … See Cats walking.

Strength was as the strength of ten because his heart was pure. Frequent. T. 'Sir Galahad': "My strength is as the strength of ten, / Because my heart is pure."

Strength's a something something, and a right good shield of hides untanned. 47 p74; 67 p64. See Hybrias.

Strikes a new note. 32 p95 and frequent later. A cliché that seems to have died some time ago. When PGW quoted it in *Bring on the Girls*, it had already become so hackneyed that it was funny to PGW's and Guy Bolton's generation. Its origins lie in the circumlocution of newspapers at the end of the 19th century. As Psmith says in *Psmith in the City*, footballers didn't score goals in newspaper reports, they 'pushed the bulb into the meshes' or 'between the uprights'. Boxers did not make their opponent's nose bleed; they 'tapped the claret'.

I found a serious example of 'strikes a new note' in the *Dover Express and East Kent News* for 8 October 1909 when searching for details of Harvey Hammond, the source of Bertie Wooster's Aubrey Upjohn (see Chap. 3). The paper reported a local charity concert in Dover where all the local big-wigs had done their stuff, just like the Kegley-Bassingtons in the concert in *The Mating Season*. The reporter knew where his duty lay, and every performer had to be mentioned — with different terms of praise for each. Lieutenant Colonel Smythe introduced the programme and "was warmly received". Miss Smythe "delighted the audience" with her singing; Mrs Bostock then came on and "entertained all present" with her monologues. Major Brown's comic songs "induced hearty laughter" while Mr Phipps' recitation "was a touching rendition". The Reverend Mr Smith's songs "evoked much applause" etc. etc. Right at the end, after "Miss May Clarke's songs found much favour", "Johnny

Lawrence struck a new note with his sandwich man's song" …

Stripling smiled, the. To tell the truth the stripling smiled inanely 3 p44. Gilbert's *Bab Ballads*, 'The Ghost, the Gallant, the Gael and the Goblin'.

Strollers Club. 13 p9. Clearly based on the Players' Club, New York, founded in 1888, which is affiliated to the Savage Club of which PGW was a member for some years. From the derogatory term 'strolling player' for an actor — see Mr Jingle in D. *The Pickwick Papers*.

Strong man in his wrath. 52 p189. Elizabeth Barrett Browning's 'The Cry of the Children': "But the child's sob in silence curses deeper / Than the strong man in his wrath."

Strong smoker in his agony, a. 32 p98; some strong swimmer in his agony 63 p59; and elsewhere. BYRON's *Don Juan*, Ct II, St 53 has: "A solitary shriek, the bubbling cry, / Of some strong swimmer in his agony."

Strophe and antistrophe. 4 p207. From Greek plays in which the song sung by half the chorus as it moves to one side is answered by an exact counterpart as it returns.

Struck me divers blows in sundry places. 8 p78. This phrase may have been coined by Pierce Egan the Younger (1814-1880), son of the famous journalist and sports writer Pierce Egan (1772–1849), in his *The Pilgrims of the Thames in Search of the National!* (1837). Pierce Egan the elder was known for recording Regency-era slang, and especially for his extremely successful series of books *Boxiana, or, Sketches of Modern Pugilism* which began to be published in 1813. His *Life in London* sparked a craze for imitating the characters Corinthian Tom and Jerry Hawthorn. In *Pilgrims of the Thames*, Pierce Egan the Younger makes reference to his father's opus magnum: "The Racing Calendar, he pointed out to his friends with delight… the Sporting Magazine, from its commencement, was his 'History of England' as he termed it; and *Boxiana* reminded him of *divers blows in sundry places*!". MTT Chris Paul.

Stuck to him like a brother. 25 p178. See STICKETH CLOSER.

Students' lamps. 40 p42. See CIGARETTES.

Stuffed bosom. 91 p74. See BOSOM.

Style, cramped. 30 p149. See CRAMPED YOUR STYLE.

Style to which he has been accustomed. 22 p122. This seems to have been the standard question put by every Victorian father to a suitor for his daughter's hand. "Can you keep my daughter in the style to which she has been accustomed?" It had already become an over-worked cliché when PGW used it and he treated it as such, similar to SENTIMENTS DEEPER AND WARMER.

Stylites, Simeon. See SIMEON.

Stymie, a dead. 60 p158 and elsewhere. See Chap. 27.

Subdu'd eyes. His subdu'd eyes to drop tears as fast … gum 87 p115. S. *Othello* 5.2.

Submerged Tenth, the. 19 p78; 32 p65; 33 p104. This was a common phrase, akin to the FOUR HUNDRED and the FOUR MILLION. *Who's Who* and Kelly's *Handbook* *of the Titled, Landed and Official Classes* were the leading UK social registers of the late 19th century onwards. I found both invaluable in tracing Wodehouse relatives. Before they came along, you looked people up in Kelly's *Upper Ten Thousand.* If you were listed there, you would not know everybody else in it, but you would have been at school with a cousin of theirs or served in the Army with their father or known someone who married into the family. The title was soon shortened in common parlance to 'the Upper Ten' and people would mock the pretentiousness of their neighbours by saying they imagined they were in the Upper Ten. In his crusade to better the lot of the poor, William Booth (1829–1912), founder of the Salvation Army, emphasised their wretchedness by reversing the phrase which everybody knew. He wrote of the poor as 'the Submerged Tenth' and made that term equally well known.

Subscription dance at Camberwell. 31 p13. See Chap. 18.

Subscription dances at the Empress Rooms, West Kensington. 36 p116. I have a 1924 advertisement for this establishment advertising just these functions. See Chap. 18.

Subsequent proceedings (interested him no more). At 14 p140, PGW gives us: 'In the subsequent proceedings he took no part'. This is clearly a memory of Bret Harte's 'The Society Upon the Stanislaus'. "And he smiled a kind of sickly smile, and curled up on the floor, /And the subsequent proceedings interested him no more.' Harte, who died in 1902, spent the last 17 years of his life in London where his writing was very popular.

Success has not spoiled him. 32 p147; 57 p202 and elsewhere. This newspaper cliché seems to have died at long last. From c.1900 to the 1970s, every interview with successful man used the phrase somewhere.

Such a man, so faint, so spiritless ... Troy was burned. 70 p199. See PRIAM'S CURTAIN.

Sucker. Never give a sucker an even break 61 p158. Various origins have been claimed for this, the most popular being W.C. Fields, who insisted on the words being used in his 1923 show *Poppy.* Another version attributes them to the con man and developer of Palm Beach, Wilson MIZNER, who coined the phrase, which was then taken up and popularised by Fields.

Suffering, we learn in (what we teach in song). See LEARN IN SUFFERING.

Sufficient unto the day was his motto. 3 p50 and later. B. Matthew 6.34: "Take therefore no thought for the morrow; for the morrow shall take thought for the things of itself. Sufficient unto the day is the evil thereof."

Summit meetings. 94 p111. Churchill popularised the phrase in 1953 when calling for top-level talks with the USA and USSR. Dean Rusk warned that 'summit diplomacy' would soon become a drug. He was right.

Sun go down on your wrath, you've let the. 91 p142. B. Ephesians 4.26: "Be ye angry, and sin not; let not the sun go down upon your wrath."

Sun is dark, the ... The skies are grey ... since my sweetie went away. 72 p112. Is this a PGW mix of 'My Sweetie Went Away' (Turk & Handman 1923) and 'Lover, Come Back to Me' (Romberg & Hammerstein)?

Sunken road which dished the cuirassiers at Waterloo. 12 p198; 25 p165; 43

p56. Too complicated to explain fully, but a sunken road allowed a British formation to conceal themselves from Napoleon and then pour in fire from a flank as his forces attacked.

Sunny Jim. You were known as S.J. 50 p14; a racehorse 85 p57. The phrase 'Sunny Jim', still used in the UK for anyone of a cheerful disposition, comes from a century-old advertisement. Force, a breakfast cereal, was launched in the USA in 1901 and in the UK two years later. The picture on the packet showed a thin elderly gentleman wearing a tailcoat and a top hat with the Stars and Stripes on it, with a short pigtail dangling down below it. He was depicted jumping over a fence in an agile and athletic manner. The original advertisement read: "Vigor, Vim, Perfect Trim; Force Made Him, Sunny Jim." In the 1920s the slogan was changed to: "High o'er the fence leaps Sunny Jim. Force is the food that raises him." The packets still have the picture and verse on them. See also BAILEY, BILL.

Sunsets. Their comparison to underdone roast beef 18 p161, 76 p87 and elsewhere. I am sure PGW heard or read this splendid example of bathos somewhere, probably a *Punch* cartoon 1875–1900, but I have been unable to trace it.

Super film/ super super film. He could tell them apart at a glance 32 p30. At 35 p200 ('Fixing It for Freddie'), Jeeves speaks of 'a super-super-film in seven reels'. MTT Brian Taves for a scholarly reply to my request for information. He told me a studio would make so many movies a year, expensive 'A' films and cheaper 'B' films. The 'A' films were then further sub-divided into regular 'A' films, 'specials' and 'supers'. The standard 'A' films would get the standard advertising budget, while a 'special A' would get billboard posters, full-page advertisements and maybe three stars featured in it. The few 'super A' films would have an all-star cast and be based on some famous novel everybody knew (e.g. *Gone With the Wind*), and the advertising ballyhoo meant that everybody went to see it.

Supermen. One of those Supermen one reads about 19 p56 & p171. Not the Comic creation, but from NIETZSCHE's *Thus Spake Zarathustra* of 1891.

Supralapsarianism. 49 p296; 63 p57. The belief that the decree of election and predestination precede the Creation and the Fall. Opponents of this view are Sublapsarians.

Surgit amari aliquid. 17 p113; 49 p180 and elsewhere. Literally, something bitter crops up, something always comes along to spoil things. PGW gives the full version and translation at 93 p192. From Lucretius' *De Rerum,* Bk 4.

Surmise, wild. Looked at each other in w.s. 3 p224 and later. The stout Cortez quote PGW liked so much. See NEW PLANET.

Surprised while bathing / by a snake in her path. Frequent, along with other variations on someone being 'surprised while …' PGW's memory of the popular Victorian paintings of his youth. There were hundreds of these portraying tasteful 'Classical' semi-nude nymphs/goddesses/shepherdesses being surprised by satyrs/shepherds etc. If surprised while bathing, they were even nuder. I have not found 'A Nymph Surprised While Bathing', but Rubens did such paintings as 'Diana and Her Nymphs Surprised by the Fauns', and Watteau did 'Nymph Surprised by a Satyr', 'Nymph of the Spring' and many others like them. Manet, Diaz and Bouguereau all turned out pictures of nymphs bathing or being 'surprised by satyrs'. Most of them were based on the legend of Actaeon, who surprised Artemis bathing and was properly punished for it by being turned into a stag, upon which he was hunted and devoured by his own hounds. That learned him.

Surrey-side villain. 2 p203. See TRANSPONTINE MELODRAMA and TODD, SIR JASPER.

Suspicious, prone to discontent, Men are. 96 p7. Herrick's 'Present Government Grievous'.

Swallowing camels and straining at gnats. 50 p13. B. Matthew 23.24: "Ye blind guides, which strain at a gnat, and swallow a camel."

Swan & Edgar's. 17A p38 and four times later. From 1841 to 1982, this was a large department store on the western corner of Piccadilly Circus. The corner outside their shop was and still is, like the Charing Cross clock, a traditional meeting place for Londoners. See also CLOCK AT CHARING CROSS STATION and CROSSE TO BLACKWELL.

Swan song. 43 p110. It was long believed that a swan only sang just before he/she died.

Swanee (river). 73 p90; soigné river at 68 p168 & later. Despite its importance to America's songwriting industry, you will not find the Swanee River on any map. But you will find the Suwannee River running south from Georgia into Florida. It entered the public consciousness with Stephen Foster's 'Old Folks at Home', which begins: "Way down upon the Swanee River." Foster had never seen it but felt that 'Swanee' had a good yearning sound to it. In 1919, Al Jolson had a terrific hit in the show *Sinbad* with Gershwin's 'Swanee', a far livelier version. It made Jolson famous and led to American songwriters, never ones to miss a trick, producing at least ten more Swanee songs in the next eighteen months — followed by plenty more later. See Chap. 36.

Swanson, Gloria. 38 p102; 53 p302. Leading Hollywood star (1897–1983) for many years. See also DE FALAISE DE LA FOUDRAYE.

Swashing blow, his, like Gregory in Romeo and Juliet. 66 p57. S. *Romeo & Juliet* 1.1: "Draw, if you be men. Gregory, remember thy swashing blow."

Swattesmore Hunt. 46 p139. Even funnier when one recalls that one of England's oldest and smartest hunts is the Cottesmore.

Swatteth one in three. 46 p137. Coleridge's 'Ancient Mariner', who "stoppeth one in three".

Swedish exercises. PGW's characters do them from 22 p119 onwards. One of the many keep-fit exercises popular in the 1890s. See DAILY DOZEN and LARSEN; the contortions involved could apply to either.

Sweet Adeline. 70 p127& p140 and elsewhere. This American song became particularly popular with male groups who, all too often, felt impelled to sing it at the tops of their voices at one o'clock in the morning. Gerard & Armstrong, who wrote it in 1903, were going to call it 'Sweet Rosalie' but noticed a poster announcing Adelina Patti's farewell tour and realised Adeline was a far better word for the long last note. The song became a byword and a public nuisance, but it helped to get J.'Honey' Fitzgerald elected Mayor of Boston twice. Kern & Hammerstein cashed in on it with their show *Sweet Adeline* in 1929. Had Armstrong ever got all the royalties due to him, he would have become a millionaire — he wrote 'Nellie Dean', the equally raucous UK equivalent, a few months later.

Sweet Alice. 60 p212 and later. From 'Ben Bolt', the 1848 song by Thomas Dunn English. George Du Maurier used it in *Trilby* in 1895 and it became famous. "Oh! Don't you remember sweet Alice, Ben Bolt, Sweet Alice whose hair was so brown, Who wept with delight when you gave her a smile, And trembled with fear at your frown."

Sweet bells jangled. Carmyle's emotions, like sweet bells, jangled, were out of tune 30 p278. S. *Hamlet* 3.1. MTT Charles Gould.

Sweet is pleasure after pain. 92 p36. Dryden's 'Alexander's Feast'. "Rich the treasure, Sweet the pleasure; Sweet is pleasure after pain."

Sweet mystery of life. Sung by B. Wooster 76 p8. 'Ah! Sweet Mystery of Life' from *Naughty Marietta* (1910) by Victor Herbert.

Sweet singer of Garbidge Mews (and elsewhere). See SINGER OF SASKATOON and Chap. 37.

Sweethearts still. 42 p41 and elswhere. 1899 song by Harry Freeman.

Sweetness. Wasting his s. on the desert air 2 p215 and later. See GEM OF PUREST RAY SERENE.

Sweetness and light, scatter/spreading. 21 p175 and frequent later. In *Uncle Fred in the Springtime* four times; in *Uncle Dynamite* at least nine times; in *Cocktail Time* ten times. I was puzzled by PGW having Uncle Fred repeat the phrase so often until I looked up the original. Matthew Arnold (1822–88), son of the famous headmaster Arnold of Rugby, was a poet, critic, and highly respected and influential educational reformer. He adopted the phrase 'sweetness and light' from Swift's *Battle of the Book* (1697) and made it his social and literary creed. In his most famous essay, 'Sweetness and Light', he wrote: "The pursuit of perfection, then, is the pursuit of sweetness and light. He who works for sweetness and light, works to make reason and the will of God prevail … [2 lines later] Culture has one great passion, the passion for sweetness and light. It is not satisfied till we all come to a perfect man; it knows that the sweetness and light of the few must be …"

If he could repeat it so often, so could PGW. Although the works of the worthy Arnold do not sound like the young PGW's favourite reading, it is possible they were forced upon him; a Wodehouse cousin married Arnold's daughter.

Swing a cat, room to. In the song 'Nesting Time in Flatbush', a lyric PGW wrote for *Oh, Boy!* (1917), is the line: 'There's room to swing a cat'. For some reason, nearly a dozen American Wodehouseans have asked me to insert this reference. I am still of the opinion that the origin of the phrase is the space required to swing the cat o'nine tails, the nine-tailed whip long used to administer punishment in the Royal Navy. I have read that the phrase pre-dates the introduction of this punishment in the Navy, but no one has produced a better source.

Swoop, The. When this came out in 1909, everybody recognised the satire on two contemporary phenomena — the recently founded Boy Scouts and the craze for war stories, usually involving an invasion of Britain by France and/or Germany. The latter began with the *The Battle of Dorking* (1871) by George Chesney, and the 1890s saw a craze for such invasion scare books. The most popular were written by William le Queux (1868–1927), whose *The Poisoned Bullet* (1894, invasion by Prussians and the French) ran through five editions in a month. In 1906 the newspaper magnate Alfred Harmsworth (see Chap. 7), alarmed by the anti-British speeches being made by the Kaiser, commissioned le Queux to write *The Invasion* of *1910*. With technical advice from Field-Marshal Lord Roberts, le Queux's serial in the *Daily Mail* about a German invasion, culminating in a last-minute victory by the British, was a runaway success. The book sold equally well all over Europe, though le Queux was apoplectic when loose drafting of the contract allowed the German publishers to get their revenge. In their edition, Germany won!

Swoop of the Vulture, The. 11 p36. In *The Swoop*, above, PGW mocked the craze for invasion-scare stories by having nine armies invade Britain and made it clear which book he was satirising. One of the characters, the German general, Prince Otto, is worried about the ensuing confusion and blames it on 'this dashed Swoop of the Vulture business'. Like the celebrated MAISIE, contemporary readers would have enjoyed the reference, which needs explanation a century later. *The Swoop of the Vulture* by James Blyth was the (then) latest invasion story (1909) and described the heroic victory won by ordinary, decent patriotic Englishmen after their army had let them down. By contrast, PGW's satire portrayed ordinary, decent patriotic Englishmen as not a bit bothered — apart from the damage done to putting greens and cricket grounds, or seeing the odd fox shot.

Swooping from a cloud. Like a Homeric god 17 p113. See CLOUD, SWOOPING.

Sword, flaming. 53 p158; 65 p132. See ANGEL WITH THE FLAMING SWORD.

Sword dangling over him, man who sat with a. 76 p159. See next entry.

Sword of Damocles. 34 p264 and often later. Damocles, a flatterer, told Dionysius (431–367 B.C.) the ruler of Sicily, how happy he must be to have so much power etc. Dionysius invited him to sit on the throne to enjoy the same feeling himself. Damocles did so and, amidst all the splendour, saw a sword hanging over his head suspended by a single horse hair.

Sword of Gideon. 84 p86. B. Judges 7.14: "This is nothing else save the sword of Gideon the son of Joash, a man of Israel: for into his hand hath God delivered Midian and all the host."

Syllepsis. I inserted this heading because PGW used syllepsis, the rhetorical figure of speech in which a word relates to two others but in a different sense to each, very effectively. The usual example given in textbooks is: "She went home in floods of tears and a taxi." Two of PGW's usages make me laugh whenever I think of them. In *The Girl on the Boat*, chapter 16 opens by describing Sam Marlowe as "full of optimism and cold beef". In 'The Story of Webster', Webster's look of cold disapproval reminds Lancelot Mulliner of the occasion when he had plugged a senior canon in the leg with his air-gun because "he had been so far carried away by ginger-beer and original sin".

Symplegades. 9 p167. Another Classical reference. These were dangerous rocks at the entry to the Bosphorus, reputedly discovered by the Argonauts.

Synge's *Riders to the Sea.* 68 p89. This work by J.M. Synge in 1904 is commonly held to mark the revival of Irish theatre.

Syrius, Publius. 37 Preface. This Syrian mimic poet (fl. 44 B.C.) was famous for his proverbs. "Necessity has no law" and "He gives twice who gives quickly" are both his. Julius Caesar was one of his patrons.

Syrup, soothing. See SOOTHING SYRUP.

T

(MTT = My thanks to)

Table tennis. See Chap. 18.

Tacitus. 43 p49. A respected Roman historian (55–120 A.D.).

Taft, Bill. A half-portion B.T. (Ogden Ford is). 21 p158. William Howard Taft (1857–1930), president of the United States 1909–13, weighed 300 pounds.

Tagore, Rabindranath. R.T. never had a T-bone in his life 69 p147. Almost forgotten now, this Indian mystic philosopher and writer (1861–1941) was famous for drawing together strands of eastern and western philosophy. He was awarded the Nobel Prize for Literature in 1913.

Take me back, back, back songs. PGW mocked these songs but turned out a few himself. Following Gilbert's example, he enjoyed writing lyrics about prisoners longing for their old Alma Mater. 'Put Me in My Little Cell', 'Dear Old Prison Days', 'Dartmoor Days' are some of them. See Chap. 36.

Take me to your leader. 88 p155. With the interest in space travel in the 1950s, there were dozens of cartoons based on this supposed greeting of aliens landing on Earth. A 'Martian'/'alien' would address a petrol pump or a TV set with an antenna on top of it with these words.

Take up arms against a sea of troubles ... 70 p169. See SEA OF TROUBLES.

Talleyrand. Politicians should write books like a life of T. 80 p25. I think it no coincidence at all that Duff COOPER, the politician who fomented the attack on PGW during the war, wrote a life of Talleyrand (1754–1838) in 1932.

Tambo, Massa. 12 p33. See MINSTREL SHOW.

Tanagra figurine/statuette. As tiny and graceful as a t. f. 62 p151; statuette 73 p27; and later. One does not hear this expression often nowadays. It came into vogue in the late 1890s when the Spitzer collection of Tanagra figurines came up for sale. These Greek statuettes were produced in Boetia from the 3rd century B.C. and nobody had paid much attention to them before. When every millionaire collector started bidding vast sums for them (William Randolph Hearst was unsuccessful), the Press decided the statuettes must be beautiful, and the term became a measure of feminine beauty. While the Spitzer statuettes may have been beautiful, the crudeness of the thousands of modern copies that immediately came on the market killed off the term, which tended to be restricted to people of PGW's age who remembered the original excitement.

Tangled web. See WHAT A TANGLED WEB.

Tank town. 26 p139. An American term for a village or place so small that trains only stopped to draw water from the water tank beside the track. See also JERKWATER.

Tanner. Frequent. Sixpence in English money till 1971, a small silver coin, equivalent to 2½ pence today. See also BENDER.

Tantalus. Torments of T. 13 p170. In Greek legend, Tantalus offended Zeus, never a difficult thing to do, and was punished by being tied to a rock under a fruit tree beside a stream. Whenever he bent to drink, the water level went down so he could not reach it. When he stretched up to pick the fruit, it always evaded his reach. The name is used today for the Victorian invention of a lockable stand containing decanters of whisky, port and sherry. They can be seen but not used unless one has the key.

Ta-ra-ra boom-de-ay. Boom-de-gay 25 p209; and later. This rousing music hall song was written by Henry Sayers in 1891. It did quite well in US vaudeville but was a sensation in British music halls; Lottie Collins (1866–1910) brought the house down with it for years. It became so popular that, up to 1914, Britons visiting Italy always had it played at them because Italian bands were convinced it was the British National Anthem.

Tariff reform. 28 p127; 67 p96. Two late references to the topic that divided the UK in the early 1900s. PGW had great success with his daily poems on Tariff reform in the *Daily Express* in 1903 ('The Parrot'). See THINKING IMPERIALLY.

Tarkington, Mr Booth. Wrote of falling in love at seventeen 25 p62. This is Tarkington's *Seventeen* (1916), which recounted the puppy-loves of 'Silly Billy' Baxter.

Tarzan. Reading the adventures of T. 43 p57. Edgar Rice Burroughs' hero has remained popular since his first adventures were published in 1914. There have been dozens of films made about him, and Tarzan comics have remained a perennial favourite.

Taste lingered, the. 47 p19. See CHEWING GUM.

Tate, Harry. His motoring sketch 46 p95. Tate (1873–1940) was a music hall comedian who specialised in sketches in which the props always went wrong. Fishing lines got entangled, golf clubs disintegrated, and bits fell off the car he tried to repair in his famous motoring sketch. He was the first man in UK to have a personalised car number plate — T1.

Taxation without representation (No). See NO TAXATION.

Taylor, Laurette. 23 p223. This actress (1884–1946) made a hit in *Peg O' My Heart* (1912).

Taylor, Robert. 59 p74 and later. Handsome Hollywood actor (1911–69).

Tchekov. See CHEKHOV.

Tea for two and two for tea. 39 p26. The 'dummy' that became the lyric. When Vincent Youmans and Irving Caesar were writing the songs for the 1924 musical *No, No, Nanette*, Youmans composed the music and either he or Caesar sketched out a 'dummy', i.e. nonsense words that mean nothing but give the lyricist an idea of the rhythm and metre. The impromptu dummy began: "Tea for two and two for tea" — and they both realised this would do very well for the lyric they wanted. Because the show did so well, the following year saw the obvious sequel — *Yes, Yes, Yvette.*

Tear. Every time a fairy sheds a tear, a wee bit star is born in the Milky Way 52 p115. PGW implies that Madeline Bassett is quoting somebody here, but I have not found the source. The nearest I have got is Blake's 'Auguries of Innocence': "Every tear from every eye / Becomes a babe in Eternity."

Teddy bears. 18 p246. The first Teddy bear came out of a Brooklyn store in 1902. The owner, Morris Michton, got the idea from the news story recounting how President Theodore (Teddy) Roosevelt, on a hunting trip, had refused to shoot a small bear cub. Michton made a fortune as American children decided Teddy bears were what they wanted. See also ROOSEVELT, THEODORE.

Teddy boys. 11 p28. This term refers not to the tight-trousered, long-jacketed young men of the 1960s, but was the nickname for the members of the Territorial Army (akin to US militia forces/National Guard) in 1909.

Tediousness of a twice-told tale. 19 p88; 48 p135 and later. Shakespeare and Pope both make the point. S. *King John* 3.4: "Life is as tedious as a twice-told tale." Pope *Odyssey of Homer*, Bk 12, last line: "And what so tedious as a twice-told tale."

Telephone ma baby, I'm going to. 68 p60. See Chap. 36.

Television was not yet in operation on the telephone systems of England. 53 p95. The invention of television by J. Logie Baird in 1925 had aroused great excitement, though public broadcasts were not made till ten years later.

Tell it to the King of Denmark. 18 p120. I have not found the origin of this expression of incredulity. I can only assume it refers to the play within a play in *Hamlet.*

Tell me exactly what occurred ... In your own words ... when the smallest detail may not be important. 49 p15; with minor variations at 52 p149 and elsewhere. See Doyle's 'The Copper Beeches'. A frequent comment by Sherlock Holmes to those who had come to consult him. See also YOU KNOW MY METHODS.

Tell them they mustn't. 2 p174; of incense 39 p104. See MUSTN'T.

Tell, William. Anything W.T. could do I can do better 80 p13. PGW gloss on the song 'Anything You Can Do, I Can Do Better' from the 1946 show *Annie Get Your Gun.*

Telling the Birds, Telling the Bees, etc. See I'M TELLING.

Temper your hilarity with a modicum of reserve. 27 p278; your acerbity with a modicum of reserve 45 p154. The well-known reproof of George ROBEY when the audience laughed was "Desist!" and "Kindly temper your hilarity with a modicum of reserve."

Temple Flower Show 1911. 25 p10. Lord Marshmoreton was right to be proud. This was the annual Royal Horticultural Show, i.e. national show, which began in 1888 and was held in the Temple Gardens before they moved to their present site at Chelsea in 1913.

Temple, Shirley. 60 p131. Wildly popular child film star of the 1930s (b. 1928).

Tempora mutantur, nos et mutamur in illis. 51 p211; 65 p242 has the misprint 'mutumur'; 96 p111. From Ovid's *Metamorphoses*. Times change and we change with them.

Ten Nights In A Bar Room. 96 p46. This temperance novel of 1854 by Timothy Arthur became one of America's biggest theatrical hits when it was dramatized by William Pratt in 1858. It did not do well in cities but it ranked second only to UNCLE TOM'S CABIN in rural areas. The play includes the immortal line: "Father, dear father, come home with me now."

Ten o'clock, a clear night and all's well, Jeeves. 31 p51. Bertie declaiming in the manner of an Elizabethan night watchman has a ring of Shakespeare, but I have not found it.

Tennis, anyone? 83 p101; 88 p141. I have an idea this line was said far less often on stage than is generally thought. However, it came to typify the farces and light comedies that were such a staple of the English stage from about 1892 (*Charley's Aunt*) onwards. One authority says the phrase was first used in a Grossmith-Laurillard show around 1918. It had certainly become a cliché for 'silly ass' parts by the 1920s. It is claimed that it was the first line Humphrey Bogart spoke on stage; he came from a wealthy East Coast family and began in 'Society' roles. It is also reported that Bogart vehemently denied this, but that may just have been to protect his tough-guy image.

Tennyson, Lord. 2 p160; 3 p97. PGW quoted Alfred, Lord Tennyson (1809–92) from his second book to his last — when Lady Florence's mud-pack cracked from side to side — because he was brought up on him. It is impossible to exaggerate the popularity of Tennyson in Victorian England; every middle-class household had his books on their shelves. He dominated English poetry of the day as Dickens dominated the world of fiction. They may not have been the best poems but they were the most popular. Every year the Royal Academy had paintings of scenes from his poems — Lancelot, Galahad, Merlin or Gawaine etc.

It is common knowledge that PGW took Shakespeare with him to the internment camp; he also took his Tennyson. He maintained a scholarly interest in literature far longer than most of us do. In 1948, when he was 67, he told Guy Bolton that he had gone out and bought SHELLEY and Keats because Bolton thought so highly of them. For a man who had English literature at his fingertips as he did, I find this surprising and impressive. How many of us are still anxious to learn at that age? He wrote: "I'm afraid I have got one of those second-rate minds, because, while I realise that Shelley is in the Shakespeare and Milton class, I much prefer Tennyson, who isn't." See also HOME LIFE.

Tenor of her life had been interrupted, the even. 63 p228. See EVEN TENOR.

Tents, cutting/loosening their guy-ropes. 6 p63 & p75; 84 p66. Cutting tent guy-ropes at the schools' cadet camp at ALDERSHOT was a common tactic to show displeasure at another school's behaviour.

Terror by night and the arrow that flieth by day. 97 p13. B. Psalms 91.5: "Thou shalt not be afraid for the terror by night; nor for the arrow that flieth by day."

Terror in your threats. There is no t. in your t. for I am armed so strong. 92 p174. See ARMED SO STRONG.

Terry, Ellen. 30 p165. This actress (1848–1928) was Henry Irving's leading lady from 1878 to 1902.

Tetrazzini or someone who could just pick that note off the roof and hold it ... 27 p272. The coloratura soprano Luisa Tetrazzini (1871–1940) could, so my mother once said, hit a top note, stay there "and play around with it for five minutes".

Teuf teuf. See GOODBYE.

Thanking Heaven, fasting for a good man's love. 70 p131; 94 p95. S. *As You Like It* 3.5.57: "But, mistress, know thyself: down on your knees, And thank heaven, fasting, for a good man's love."

That little more and how much it is. See LITTLE MORE.

That was no lady, that was my wife. See WHO WAS THAT LADY.

Thatcher, Heather. 46 p124. Popular comedy actress (1893–1987) who played in the Grossmith-PGW shows.

That's me all over, Mabel. See MABEL.

That's the way the ball rolls. 82 p119. That's the way the ball bounces, etc. This philosophical cliché became popular in the 1950s; I have no idea why. I suggest golf could be the origin, i.e., a well-struck ball hitting a bump on the fairway and going off course, but I have no evidence.

That's the way the cookie crumbles. 83 p40; 88 p13. A cliché that came into use very soon after the example immediately above. It began in the 1950s and became universally popular when quoted/twisted and misquoted by Jack Lemmon in the 1960 film *The Apartment*.

Thelema. In the spirit of the monks of T. 21 p86. See Rabelais' *Gargantua*. The abbey of Thelema was the reverse of the usual model. The only rule for the 'monks' was: "Do as thou wilt."

Theocritus. 34 p14; 53 p13. Greek poet, fl. 282 B.C., who wrote pastoral poems about shepherds and shepherdesses.

Theophrastus. 9 p15. Greek philosopher who died 288 B.C. at the age of 107.

Theosophist. I've got a cousin who is what they call a T. 23 p19; 32 p227; and later. PGW's brother Armine joined the Theosophists in India when he came down from Oxford and became head of the Theosophical College in Benares.

There are more things in heaven and earth. 8 p80. S. *Hamlet* 1.5: "There are more things in heaven and earth, Horatio, / Than are dreamt of in your philosophy."

There is nothing like a dame. 87 p54; 92 p48. Song from *South Pacific* (1949).

There is some girls that cry ... unto Nancy by and by, says I. 91 p121. This is from Barry Pain's poem "Bangkolidye": "There is some gels whort cry, Says

I.... This unto Nancy by-and-by, Says I." MTT Chris Paul.

There ought to be/have been a law. 73 p160; 85 p76. MTT David McDonough for the information that an American comic strip 'There Oughta Be A Law' ran from 1944 to 1984 and that the artist was, for a long time, Warren Whipple of East Hampton, Long Island. David also points out that he might well have known PGW. David wonders if this acquaintanceship was the reason that Whipple became Whiffle in PGW's later books. Or vice versa, if you look at the dates. An intriguing idea.

Therefore behoveth him a full long spoon (to eat with the devil). 37 Preface. As PGW says, it is from Chaucer's 'Squiere's Tale' Pt 2, l.256. See also S. *Comedy of Errors* 4.3: "Marry, he must have a long spoon to sup with the devil."

There's a light in thy bower. See LIGHT IN THY BOWER.

There's never a law of God or man runs north of fifty-three. 26 p223; 44 p306. Opening words of a chapter in Jack London's 'The God of his Fathers' from *Tales of the Klondyke*. London was quoting a line from KIPLING's 'The Rhyme of the Three Sealers'. MTT Neil Midkiff.

There's no business like show business. 71 p166. Song from *Annie Get Your Gun* 1946.

There's nothing either good or bad but thinking makes it so (as Hamlet very sensibly remarked). 67 p111. S. *Hamlet* 2.2.

Thermopylae, Spartans at. 76 p146. In 480 B.C., in one of the most heroic actions in the history of warfare, Leonidas and his 300 Spartans gave their lives to save Greece.

Thersites recklessly slandering his betters. 18 p198. He poured so much scorn on his fellow Greeks at the siege of Troy that Achilles eventually killed him.

Theseus and the Minotaur. 41 p211. Though Theseus killed the Minotaur, he would never have escaped if Ariadne had not given him a ball of string to trace his way back out of the labyrinth. He repaid her love by doing her wrong — the cad. See ARIADNE.

Thews and sinews. A man of 15A p106; men of 29 p17; a lack of 34 p103. 'Thews' or 'thewes' was used by Shakespeare to denote muscles/ bodily strength, but the first coupled thews-sinews usage I have found is in Sir Walter Scott's *Guy Mannering* (chap. 27).

They also serve who only stand and wait. 24 p83 and later. Milton's Sonnet 16: 'On His Blindness'.

They shall not pass. 37 p91. Mrs Fisher was repeating the defiant comment made by General Pétain on the 1916 German offensive. (It has also been attributed to three other French generals.)

They went away from that place. See WENT AWAY.

They're at the wash. See WHEREABOUTS.

Thing and Thing thing. 77 p10. See BLEAK HOUSE.

Thing that makes the birds forget to sing, you have that certain. 86 p73. See

CERTAIN SOMETHING.

Thing, wild. Some w.t. taken in a trap which sees the trapper coming through the woods 63 p11 (a superb sentence) and elsewhere. See CREATURE.

Things. Could these things be? 8 p106; 18 p146. S. *Macbeth* 3.4:

"Can such things be, And overcome us like a summer's cloud …"

Things in heaven and earth, there are more. 6 p241; 8 p80. See THERE ARE MORE.

Things like that, you know, must be at every famous victory. 92 p175. From Robert Southey's 'Battle of Blenheim'. See also FAMOUS VICTORY.

Things up with which she would not put. Like Mr Churchill, there were … 70 p136. During the Second World War, a civil servant submitted a memorandum to Winston CHURCHILL with a sentence grossly contorted to avoid ending it with a preposition. Churchill promptly returned it with the note: "This is a bastard and stilted form of English up with which I will not put." Berton Braley summed up the matter with:

The grammar has a rule absurd
Which I would call an outworn myth:
A preposition is a word
You mustn't end a sentence with.

Thingummy and what's-his-name. They were (friends) like. 55 p39. Unless my trained senses deceive me, the well-read Egg was thinking of DAMON AND PYTHIAS.

Thinking, high. 63 p55. See HIGH THINKING.

Thinking imperially. 31 p215; 41 p287. PGW was quoting a phrase that ran round the country in 1904. This was a time of tremendous political argument over whether or not Britain should give preferential trade tariffs to her colonies. (See PGW's *The Parrot and Other Poems.*) Joseph Chamberlain (1836–1914) (see above), proponent of Imperial preference, made a powerful speech in 1904 which ended with the words: "Think imperially!" The phrase caught on, much to the fury of his opponents known as 'Little Englanders'.

I have a political banner of the period wishing election success (1906) to Captain Boyd-Carpenter. It is covered with pictures of colonial farmers around the world, all farming away for the good of the Empire with the captions: 'Hands Across The Sea' / 'Help Those Who Help Us, Our Kith and Kin'.

Thinner and thinner. 12 p306. James Deane, a cousin of PGW's, was at Winchester with Rupert D'Oyly Carte, son of the Gibert & Sullivan impresario. It was he who told PGW of the tall, languid schoolboy who, in response to a casual query from a master as to his health, replied: "Sir, I grow thinner and thinner." It was a phrase PGW never forgot, and he must have smiled when he managed to work it in. See Chap. 37.

Thirty cents, feel like. Often in PGW and his emotions when he got his degree at Oxford. Apparently the original term was 'thirty cents shy of a quarter', i.e. less than nothing. PGW's usage probably comes from the poem by George Ade, whom PGW admired. See also MARTINIS.

Thirty-three bites a mouthful crank. 14 p251. See FLETCHERIZE.

This beggar maid shall be my queen. 17 p30 and later. See COPHETUA, KING.

This, if I mistake not, Watson, is my/our client now. See CLIENT.

This is her-r-r. No, it's a rabbut. 31 p186. See RABBUT.

This realm, this England. 83 p114. S. *Richard II* 2.1 (John of Gaunt's speech): "This blessed plot, this earth, this realm, this England."

Thomas, Gus. I'm the young G.T. 22 p153. Thomas (1857–1934) was a successful American playwright.

Thompson, Fred. 31 p55. A private joke. See Chap. 21.

Thorndike Sybil. 49 p227. Dame Sybil Thorndike (1882–1976) was the leading British classical actress of her day. Shaw wrote *St Joan* for her. I had the privilege of seeing her with her husband (Sir Lewis Casson) in their last West End appearance in *Arsenic and Old Lace* in 1966, when she was 84 and he was 91. Like PGW, she was awarded a D. Litt by Oxford.

Thorne, head gardener at Blandings. 19 p48. See Chap. 37.

Thorns under a pot, As the crackling of (so is the laughter of a fool). See CRACKLING.

'Those in Peril on the Tee'. 41 Short story title. The hymn 'Eternal Father, strong to save' is the official hymn of the Royal and American Navies. The first three verses all end with the line "For those in peril on the sea". See also 92 p113.

Thou art the man, Mulliner. 49 p190; 77 p111 and elsewhere. B. 2 Samuel 12.7: "And Nathan said to David, Thou art the man."

Thou wast not made ... to play, infernal ball, 6 p34; for death, immortal bird 62 p123. From Keats 'Ode to a Nightingale': "Thou wast not born for death, immortal bird."

Thought came like a full blown rose, flushing the brow. 20 p111 and often later. Keats' 'Eve of St Agnes'.

Thoughts of youth were long, long thoughts. 25 p134; 60 p30 and later. See Longfellow's 'My Lost Youth': "A boy's will is the wind's will, / And the thoughts of youth are long, long thoughts."

Thoughts too deep for tears. 92 p140. Wordsworth's 'Intimations of Immortality': "Thoughts that do often lie too deep for tears." MTT Charles Gould.

Thousand of bricks, a. See BRICKS.

Thousands Cheer, While. 65 p19; 78 p20. See *As Thousands Cheer*, Irving Berlin's musical of 1933.

Three chaps in the Old Testament ... after sliding out of the burning fiery furnace. 52 p196. See FIERY FURNACE.

Three cheers and a tiger. 21 p22. The 'tiger' was a final yell/ shout to emphasise the cheers.

Three Little Words. 51 p17. Song by Kalmar & Ruby from the 1930 film *Amos and Andy*.

Three Men in a Boat. 14 p90. This immortal book (with the stuffed trout story) by Jerome K. Jerome came out in 1889. Amazing to us today, it attracted much criticism. Critics found it difficult to accept the mixture of lyrical descriptions of the Thames with humorous anecdotes of domestic life. Many felt that such anecdotes should be restricted to the comic papers and not published in a hard-back book. The US equivalent was *The Pike County Ballads*, which came out in 1871; the verses were purportedly written by whisky-drinking, ignorant hillbilly immigrants in California. They began the fashion of 'dialect speech' in American novels and led to the success of Bret Harte and 'Uncle Remus'. Many literati were horrified when these appeared in print and prophesied 'the end of American literature'.

Three Musketeers, ('One for all and all for one'). 58 p187; and 92 p146 for their conflicts with Cardinal Richelieu. See the series of four books by Dumas. Wordy and old-fashioned at first sight, they are still well worth reading. See also ONE FOR ALL.

Three Small Heads. 12 p16. See HIPPODROME.

Three-collar man. Described in the old days as a three-collar man (Tubby Frobisher) 73 p156. As a two-collar man myself, he has my admiration. In the days when dances were dances, you quick-stepped, fox-trotted and waltzed your way round the dance floor for hours, and your stiff dress collar would soon begin to wilt, no matter how heavily starched. So you went and changed it for another and renewed your activity. If the hostess was old-fashioned, you danced Viennese waltzes; if she was modern, you danced Charlestons and Quick Steps, and if you enjoyed dancing, you soon needed the third collar. As a young officer, I remember being detailed off by my colonel to make up numbers at a Hunt Ball. I was also ordered to take a spare collar, which offended my nineteen-year-old pride. To my chagrin, my partner was a lady at least forty years older than I was, and to my even deeper chagrin (I enjoy dancing), she danced me off my feet. Around midnight she instructed me to go and change my collar, checked it was all right when I returned from doing so, told me to see her to her car, informed me that I danced very creditably for my age, and said I could now dance with her attractive granddaughter at whom I had been making eyes all evening.

Three-ee-ee minutes. 76 p75; 85 p39. Before we had automatic telephone exchanges in the UK, long-distance (trunk) calls had a special system of payment. You rang up the operator, asked for the number, and knew you would pay so much for a three-minute call. Beyond that time, the cost doubled so the operator would kindly interrupt to tell you when three minutes was reached. One soon developed a special technique for this. You got the important news over early and then chatted about unimportant matters so the 'Thuree-ee-ee minutes' allowed you both to squeeze in a hurried 'Bye' before you hung up.

Three-volume novel. Something out of a t-v. n. 54 p36, 68 p29. Reggie Tennyson is making it clear he thinks the idea of a three-volume novel is old-fashioned and Victorian. MTT Neil Midkiff for the information that the big commercial lending libraries like Mudie's encouraged the habit since it enabled them to have three volumes on loan to customers for one novel. See also CAINE, HALL.

Throne. Returns to, limping back to, tottering on, etc. See REASON RETURNS.

Throne of kings, this royal, this sceptred isle … 46 p53–4; 81 p138. See SCEPTRED ISLE.

Thucydides. 1 p164. 'Conscia mens recti … revocare gradum', which, very roughly, translates as 'a mind conscious of virtue will, if it is not to endure sorrow, recall the past/ remember past sins'. Why PGW put this in Latin, not Greek, is beyond me. Maybe he was quoting Lucian or Cicero, both of whom admired Thucydides.

This Greek politician and historian, who died 411 or 391 B.C., employed a flowery style of language which made him difficult to translate and therefore highly unpopular with English schoolboys. PGW was writing from the heart here. At 3 p69, Thucydides is awful compared to *Pickwick* and dismissed as 'Thicksides' at p70; his account of the Athenian expedition to Syracuse is referred to at 8 p20.

Thud. Not a dull, sickening thud 68 p146; what some call a dull and others a sickening thud 85 p120. Apparently this does not refer to murders with blunt instruments, but to constant references in the USA to baseballs that did not bounce properly. Until Mr Spalding (1850–1915) managed to produce a standard baseball that bounced as it ought to, players had to cope with dozens of types, many of which were notorious for not bouncing but just 'falling with a dull thud'.

Thurber bloodhound. Questing hither and thither like a T. b. 80 p145. See the superb cartoons of James Thurber (1894–1961).

Tiberius. 30 p83; 79 p10. Tiberius (42 B.C.–37 A.D.), who became emperor of Rome in 14 A.D., retired to Capri where, as my Victorian classical dictionary hints darkly, "he indulged in unlawful pleasures".

Tich, Little. 4 p149. British music hall comedian (1869–1929).

Tichborne business, the. 45 p94. A *cause célèbre* in Victorian England. In 1872, an Australian butcher, Roger Orton, came to England and claimed to be Lord Tichborne, who, it was believed, had been drowned at sea years before. Since there was a large estate involved, the Tichborne family fought his claim. After a series of civil actions, Orton was sentenced to imprisonment for fraud. There are still many who believe he was the real heir.

Ticket-of-leave man. 59 p139. In the UK, a man sentenced to imprisonment who behaved well could have his sentence shortened. He would then be released subject to maintaining good behaviour. We now call it 'on probation'.

Tiddley-om-pom. When you were a tiddley-om-pom and I was a thingummajig 13 p242. For a translation of Lord Dreever's remark, see KING IN BABYLON. 'Tiddly-Om-Pom-Pom' was a music hall song (1907) popularised by Marie Lloyd. Do not confuse with 'RUMPTY-TIDDLEY-UMPTY-AY', which she also sang.

Tide in the affairs of men which, taken at the flood … 14 p194 and later. S. *Julius Caesar* 4.3 "There is a tide in the affairs of men, / Which, taken at the flood, leads on to fortune."

Tidings of great joy. 67 p95; 93 p97. See carol 'While shepherds watched their flocks by night' by Brady & Tate c.1700.

Tie That Binds. *Jeeves and the Tie That Binds* (US title of *Much Obliged, Jeeves*). The American version of this book has an extra two pages at the end in which Wodehouse introduced the phrase. It comes from the 1872 hymn by John Fawcett 'Blest Be the Tie That Binds'. In the UK version, *Much Obliged, Jeeves*, the book ends with: "Much obliged, Jeeves." "Not at all, sir."

MTT Charles Gould for informing me that Peter Schwed, PGW's American publisher, claimed credit for the title: "I wrote the last page or so in our edition and sent it along to PGW for his approval. He did approve, he did rewrite the page." MTT Tony Ring, who says the same thing, adding that Schwed, desperate to justify the change of title (from *Much Obliged, Jeeves*) enclosed the draft change in a letter to PGW of 12 February 1971.

Tigellinus, see it done. 12 p37. Tigellinus was the man appointed by Nero to try conspirators and was himself later found guilty of conspiracy. He died 68 A.D. The quotation was attributed to Nero by Tacitus.

Tiger. Three cheers and a tiger 21 p22. See THREE CHEERS.

Tiger-skin. Might recline on a t-s in the nude 69 p99. This is Elinor Glyn's *Three Weeks* again. See PRINCESS, SCANTILY-CLAD.

Tilbury, ... merely a small town in Essex ... Queen Elizabeth had once held a review there or something. 50 p230. She certainly did. It was at Tilbury in 1588 that she made the stirring speech to her small army gathered to meet the threat of the Spanish Armada. See WEAK WOMAN.

Tilbury House. 84 p119 and elsewhere. The original of Tilbury House, Lord Northcliffe's Carmelite House in Carmelite Street, is still very much as PGW described. Built around the 1870s, it is a fine example of the red-brick Gothic revival office buildings popular at the time.

Tilbury, Lord. See Chap. 7.

Tilden, Back-Handed Slosh. 7 p137. Big Bill Tilden (1893–1953), first American to win Wimbledon, did so in 1920, 1921 and 1930.

Tiled, the meeting is. 25 p127; 45 p71 and later. I am told this is a phrase used at the start of Masonic ceremonies. PGW was a Mason from 1929 to 1934.

Tiller troupe. 49 p284. John Tiller (1854–1926) formed his first highly-disciplined formation dancing troupe in 1895. They became famous around the world and were the inspiration for the New York Rockettes.

Time and change. A friendship interrupted by t. and c. 72 p73. The phrase 'time and change' became popular after Richard Hengist Horne (1802–84) wrote his poem 'Dirge'. It was the theme of the poem; one line reads: "Time and change can heap no more ..."

Time and the place were both above criticism but ... let down by the girl. 32 p169. Very easy to miss this allusion to the popular 1907 musical *The Time, the Place and the Girl*.

Time for all good men to come to the aid. See NOW IS THE TIME.

Time is flying, But. 63 p18. Herrick's 'To the Virgins to Make Much of Time': "Gather ye rosebuds while ye may, / Old Time is still a-flying ..."

Time is money. Frequent in PGW. Coined by Benjamin Franklin in his *Advice to a Young Tradesman* (1748).

Time like an ever-rolling stream. 80 p16; 88 p274 and elsewhere. First line of the last verse of Isaac Watts' famous hymn 'Oh God, our help in ages past': "Time like an ever-rolling stream / Bears all its sons away."

Time the great healer. 7 p191; 23 p240 and later. Possibly from *Troilus and Criseyde*, Book V, by Geoffrey Chaucer: "And for they kan a tyme of sorwe endure,/ As tyme hem hurt, a tyme doth hem cure."

Time will come, a. 6 p88; my time will come 50 p203. Lady Julia's use of the phrase in the second reference, coupling it with the Adelphi (a theatre in the Strand, London), shows the accuracy of PGW's dates. In the 1890s, when Gally was whooping it up with his fellow Pelicans, the Adelphi specialised in melodramas full of villains saying "Hist!" and bold, bad baronets storming off-stage with the ringing declaration "My time will come!" See 58 p182: "He consoled himself, like so many baffled Baronets in the fiction and drama of an earlier age, with the thought that a time would come." See also G&S Ruddigore Act 2: "But a time will come, and then ..." See TODD, SIR JASPER and TRANSPONTINE MELODRAMA.

Timeo Danaos (et dona ferentes). 3 p9; 13 p54 and later. Virgil's *Aeneid*, Bk 2. Literally: I fear Greeks, even bearing gifts. Generally, be very suspicious of devious persons making you tempting offers/ giving you presents.

Times that try men's souls, These are the. 21 p68 and later. Thomas Paine's view of the political situation in America, set out in his *Crisis* of 19 December 1776.

Timms, Jim, the Safe Man. 60 p47. See SAFE MAN.

Tinker in the play whom everybody conspired to delude into the belief that he was a king. 25 p222. MTT Charles Gould, David McDonough and others who have pointed me towards Christopher Sly in S. *The Taming of the Shrew*.

Tinkerty-tonk. See GOODBYE.

Tinney, Frank (at the Trinity smoker). 29 p17 & pp99-100. Tinney (1878–1940), an American blackface comedian, would come on stage and carry on a long argument (cross-talk) with the pianist or conductor of the orchestra. See also FRANK AND ERNEST. For 'Trinity smoker', see SMOKER.

Tinsel town where tragedy lies hid, that. 70 p183. A term for Hollywood coined by the grouchy pianist and actor Oscar Levant (1906–1972).

Tiny Hand (play)/ Tiny Hands (film). 23 p146; 35 p201. I have found two songs with this title (1878 & 1910) but not a play or film. I'm sure there was some late Victorian play with this as the main theme. I have read at least three magazine stories where the proud, unbending duke/earl/millionaire and his equally proud, unbending duchess/countess/wife were reconciled by their golden-haired child calling for them from her bed of sickness etc. etc.

Tiny Tots. 34 p2; 36 p101; 50 p8; 54 p36. See Chap. 7.

Tiptoes through the tulips. 94 p64. 'Tiptoe Through the Tulips with Me' (1926) was still being sung in the 1970s.

Tired Nature's sweet restorer. 68 p41. See NATURE'S SWEET.

'Tis deeds must win the prize. 73 p75. As Jeeves says, it is from Shakespeare. *Taming of the Shrew* 2.1.

'Tis not so deep as a well … 'twill serve. 22p14; 73 p39 and elsewhere. S. *Romeo and Juliet* 3.1: "No, 'tis not so deep as a well, nor so wide as a church-door; but 'tis enough, 'twill serve."

'Tis sweet to hear the watch-dog's honest bark. 13 p50. Byron's 'Don Juan' Canto 1, Stanza 123: "'Tis sweet to hear the watch-dog's honest bark / Bay deep-mouthed welcome as we draw near home …"

Tishbite, you. 27 p302; 33 p139; and later; you greasy Tishbite 63 p240. I do not know why this became a term of abuse. The only Biblical references I can find simply say that Elijah came from Tishbe.

Tit-Bits. 9 p207. A highly successful family magazine started by Alfred Harmsworth (later Lord Northcliffe) in opposition to George Newnes' *Answers*. Wodehouse contributed to it early in his career. See Chap. 7.

Titles. Dukes come first, then marquesses, then earls, then viscounts, then barons, then baronets. These are all hereditary titles. Knights, poor things, only get their knighthood for their lifetime. PGW gives useful guidance in chapter 1 of *Big Money* about forms of address for the female members of the aristocracy, though he got Lady Dora Garland's name wrong later. See NAMES.

Tivoli theatre. 22 p33; 30 p192; 50 p310. This popular music hall in the Strand stood between Durham House Street and Adam Street and closed in 1914. In 1923 it was rebuilt as a cinema and was patronised by Ambrose Wiffin, young Wilfred and Esmond Bates ('Old Stinker') in 'The Passing of Ambrose'.

To — ah — you — ah — beryootiful lady — I. 58 p114. Sam Bulpitt's rendition of 'My Beautiful Lady' from *The PINK LADY*, a show PGW knew very well indeed. David Jasen tells me the song remained popular till the 1950s. See also Chap. 38.

To and fro. In 'How's That, Umpire?', "The somnambulists out in the field tottered to and fro." MTT Robert Bruce for reminding me of the famous cricketing poem 'At Lord's' by Francis Thompson, which concludes with the lines "As the run-stealers flicker to and fro, / To and Fro: / Oh my Hornby and my Barlow long ago!"

To err is human. See ERR.

To the pure all things are pure. 67 p129. Another of those phrases that just stuck. Letter from Charles Lamb to Robert Southey of July 1798, quoting Coleridge: "To the pure all things are pure."

Toad under the harrow. 6 p185 and frequent later including, at 96 p110, Bertie's "as near to being … a toad at Harrow as a man can be who was educated at

Eton". The origin of this is often quoted as KIPLING's 'Pagett M.P.': "The toad beneath the harrow knows, / Exactly where each tooth-point goes." The expression goes back at least 500 years before Kipling; it simply meant anybody under constant persecution or oppression.

Today he is not well. 99 p267. G&S *Patience*, Act 1.

Todd, Sir Jasper. 81 p113. Along with the two other Sir Jaspers in PGW, this man is clearly up to no good. His very name indicates this. I have not found the original but, in Victorian melodrama, when the Good Old Man was evicted from his humble cottage and turned out into the snow, the perpetrator was nearly always the evil baronet Sir Jasper. I recall a Rugger song of the 1950s which dealt with the amatory exploits of 'bad Sir Jasper'. Why Sir Jasper and why a baronet, I have no idea. I do not know the American equivalent. Would it be 'Black Jake', the bearded bully whom the hero always has to thwart? (I spent a long time trying to find a connection with Sir Jasper Murgatroyd, the evil Third Baronet in G&S's *Ruddigore,* but I suspect Gilbert borrowed the bad baronets from Victorian melodrama, rather than the other way round. Although PGW gave us thirteen characters named Murgatroyd, only one was a baddie.) See also BARONETS and TRANSPONTINE MELODRAMA.

Toff, The (boxer). 33p64. See Chap. 4.

Toffee. Tell me, major, are you fond of toffee? 99 p267. G&S *Patience* Act 2.

Toil, son of. See SONS OF TOIL.

Toiled not, neither did they spin. 3 p230; 22 p184 and later. See LILIES OF THE FIELD.

Tolstoy. 26 p120 and later. In my 1922 edition, he is Tolstoi because people were not quite sure how to spell his name. In 'The Clicking of Cuthbert', Vladimir BRUSILOFF respected only two writers, Tolstoy and Wodehouse: "Not good, but not bad." I do not know if PGW read Tolstoy, but we do know, from Ian Sproat, that Tolstoy read Wodehouse. He took *The Captain* to teach his children English, and copies are still to be seen in his house in Russia. On 16 January 1972, PGW wrote to Lord Citrine: "Wasn't that extraordinary. I had never thought of Tolstoy as a Captain reader."

Tom Bowling act. See BOWLING.

Tom Tiddler's Ground. 9 p66 and later. This expression has at least three meanings. PGW uses it in the sense of a place where wealth is to be had by picking it off the ground. Another meaning is debatable land whose ownership is uncertain. The third meaning is a child's game where one boy stands on a pile of stones (Tom Tiddler's Ground) and resists the attempts of other boys to push him off.

Tommy Dodd. A mystic game of T.D. 4 p3. A gambling game in which the bet is whether two coins thrown in the air will come down both odd, both even, or odd and even.

Tomnoddy, Lord. 4 p138. 'Hon Mr Sucklethumbkin's Story' from Barham's *Ingoldsby Legends*. The notable event PGW refers to was a public execution which Lord Tomnoddy and his friends missed because they fell asleep. See also INGOLDSBY LEGENDS.

Tomorrow and tomorrow and tomorrow. 78 p59. S. *Macbeth* 5.5: "Tomorrow, and tomorrow, and tomorrow, / Creeps in this petty pace from day to day, / To the last syllable of recorded time."

Tomorrow was another day. And there would be cabbage leaves in the morning 50 p311. See last page of Margaret Mitchell's *Gone With the Wind.*

Tongue and pen, saddest words of. 12 p184 and later. See WORDS OF TONGUE.

Tonight's the Night. 52 p227; 62 p111. 1914 New York show which came to the Gaiety, London, in 1915.

Tonti, Lorenzo. 79 p10. This Italian-born banker (c.1602–c.1684) introduced the tontine around 1635.

Toodle-oo. See GOODBYE.

Toofer/ toofah. 26 p123; 31 p143. See CIGARETTES.

Tooth and claw, attacked him with. 56 p176; 91 p54. T. 'In Memoriam', St 56: "Tho' Nature, red in tooth and claw / With ravine, shriek'd against his creed."

Top affair. A dashed little t. a., a thing with numbers written round it. 42 p143. These hexagonal gambling toys were called Put and Take (you put money in and took it out). They were a craze in the 1920s, and I remember them in the late 1930s. I never saw the rigged model that Parsloe used.

'Top Hat, White Tie and Tails'. 57 p215. The delightful song that Irving Berlin had written for the Fred ASTAIRE film only two years before the book's publication.

Top of the cupboard, every woman's favourite hiding place. See CUPBOARD.

Top Ten list. The FBI had him on its T.T. l. 89 p14. A nice PGW mix of the FBI's list of Most Wanted Men and the then-new Top Ten music ratings chart. See also PUBLIC ENEMY.

Torquemada. 49 p190 and later. The Dominican monk who created the Spanish Inquisition in 1483 and whose reputation for severity seems completely justified.

Tosti's Goodbye. 25 p240 and later. Francesco Tosti (1846–1916) became music teacher to the British Royal Family. His 'Goodbye', words by Whyte Melville, was published in 1881 and has splendid long notes to hold. It became a popular drawing room song for the next fifty years.

Total gules. 90 p182. Blood. See ADMIRABLE BASHVILLE.

Touch of a vanished hand, the. 18 p136 and later. T. 'Break, Break, Break': "But O for the touch of a vanished hand, / And the sound of a voice that is still.'

Touch of nature. One touch makes the whole world kin. See ONE TOUCH.

Touches the spot, that. Frequent, mainly of a much-needed drink. The term probably stems from the advertisement 'Homocea Touches the Spot'. In 1903 an American-funded patent medicine company was set up in England to sell this cure-all ointment and, following the example of Pears' Soap (see HALLOA!), began with an advertising campaign that swept the country. The ointment had some success, probably due to the extensive advertising, but appears to have been withdrawn in 1929.

Tout comprendre, c'est tout pardonner. 59 p146; 61 p44; 96 p44. See Know all.

Tout Passe waltz. 9 p169. 1902 waltz by Rodolphe Berger.

Townend, Bill. See Chap. 34.

Tracy, Spencer. Imitation of. 66 p34. How does one impersonate this gifted Hollywood star (1900–67)? Try and imitate his distinctive voice? "Not much meat on her but what's there is cherce" from *Pat and Mike* maybe?

Trade gap. Bad for the trade gap. 90 p62. This cliché appeared in the late 1940s, as European nations tried to rebuild their economies after the Second World War.

Trail. Going out on the old trail again 13 p255 and later. Kipling's 'The Long Trail'.

Trail, long, long. See Long, long trail.

Trailing clouds of glory. 50 p296; 72 p41. Wordsworth's 'Intimations of Immortality': "But trailing clouds of glory do we come / From God, who is our home …"

Tramp cyclist. 13 p74 and later, often used of Lord Emsworth. This phrase seems to have died completely, and I am unsure of its origins. As far as I can ascertain, when cycling became popular — and fashionable — in the 1890s, cyclists made a point of dressing smartly. A tramp cyclist was, I believe, simply a tramp who had acquired a bicycle and did not care what he looked like. The *Oxford Companion to the American Theatre* cites Joe Jackson (1880?–1942) as developing "a tramp cyclist act… . He would wander on stage downtrodden and lugubrious, forlornly trying to fix a cuff that would not stay put. Soon he would discover a bicycle which he would ride … until piece by piece it fell apart."

Transpontine melodrama. 3 p13 and later. Since the Romans founded the city of London on the north bank, those living north of the Thames have believed themselves slightly superior to/ more fashionable than those who live south of it. This feeling has faded over the centuries, but there is no doubt that old-fashioned Victorian melodrama hung on far longer on the south bank, the 'Surrey side' of the river. While music halls (variety) became the staple working-class entertainment north of the river from about 1870 onwards, old-fashioned blood-and-thunder plays from the 1820s and earlier, such as *Maria of the Red Barn* and even *Sweeney Todd*, remained popular in south London theatres for another twenty years. Hence PGW'S remark about transpontine melodrama, i.e across the Thames bridges.

In the 19th century, London had no fewer than 300 theatres and people went to the theatre as often as they do to the cinema today. As early as 1887, a theatre critic wrote that although Irving had made Shakespeare popular again, the old sensation days had gone:

> The plays which had real water and sometimes real fire are gone for ever.

The Transpontine melodrama needed no elaborate spectacular effects; its indispensable elements were a villain — and such a villain! And a heroine — and such a heroine!

The playwright would be an employee at three pounds a week who kept to hand, neatly pigeonholed, a large stock of persecuted virtue, rightful heirs discovered by strawberry marks on their left arms, wills bequeathing immense wealth turning up in disused tea-caddies, members of the aristocracy steeped in crime and country farmers with pretty daughters pursued by abandoned squires… . What it always had was plenty of bluster and lots of bellowing, villains strong enough to carry the heroine bodily from the stage, heroines capable of sustained and piercing shrieks, and the occasional discharge of a pistol."

I was lucky enough, as a thirteen-year-old, to see the last gasp of this tradition in a small town in Ireland in 1946. My uncle impressed on me that I was watching one of the very few remaining troupes of strolling players, a tradition that went back to Shakespeare's time. The small company arrived in two battered vans, and the equally battered marquee was set up in a field (free tickets for the farmer). Benches were borrowed from the school (free tickets for the schoolmaster) and the evening began with a farce revolving round a sum of money, eventually found in a teapot. This was followed by songs sung (without the benefit of — or any need for — a microphone) by the heroine while the stage was re-set. Then came a gripping melodrama, culminating in the hero addressing the cowering villainous villain: "You say you would die for Ireland? Then you shall!" followed by a shot from a real revolver! I'd never seen anything so exciting in my life.

See also BARONETS and TODD, SIR JASPER.

Traumatic symplegia. 82 p79; 93 p141. Apparently known as narcolepsy today.

Travels fastest who travels alone. 19 p250 and later. KIPLING's 'The Winners'. Three of the four verses finish: "He travels the fastest who travels alone."

Travis, J. Walter. 18 p121; 37 p310. US amateur golf champion 1900, 1901 and 1903; British amateur champion 1904.

Treacher, Arthur. 70 p67. PGW paying a graceful tribute to an actor (1894–1975) who played butler/gentleman's gentleman parts for thirty years, including that of Jeeves.

Treason, stratagems and spoils. 51 p15; 64 p178 and elsewhere. See MUSIC.

Tree, Beerbohm. 46 p95. British actor-manager (1853–1917) who made Shakespeare so exciting with splendid fighting scenes that he could display 'House Full' notices in August. On one memorable occasion, he took realism too far when he decided to play *Macbeth* in a suit of real (not stage) armour. Everything went well till the scene where he had to kneel before Duncan. At the end of his speech, he found that the armour was so heavy that he was unable to get to his feet and was forced to play the rest of the scene on his knees. The next day the papers were full of praise for his "startling new interpretation of the role".

Trees, singing of. The 'Trees' bird 57 p172. See ONLY GOD.

Trial of Mary Dugan. 59 p55. Famous 1927 New York play about a girl wrongly accused of murder.

Tribes (who talked) in clicks and gurgles. 22 p118. PGW was probably referring to the Bushmen of the Kalahari. He may have heard about these from his cousin James Deane, who served in the Boer War and recounted some of his experiences to PGW.

'Tried in the Furnace'. 55 story title and film at 37 p287. B. Psalms 12.6: "The words of the Lord are pure words; as silver tried in a furnace of earth, purified seven times."

Trilby, brought up on (and therefore feared la vie Boheme). 86 p126. *Trilby*, the famous 1895 play of George Du Maurier's novel, which was based on his own experience, introduced British audiences to the Paris of art students and their models, confirming all their worst suspicions of loose-living Bohemians. The play also introduced Svengali as well as popularising the broad-brimmed hat which took its name from the play. In the US it was even more successful and began a craze for Trilby hats, Trilby coats, Trilby chocolates and Trilby waltzes.

Trimble, Daisy, of the Gaiety. 22 p22. I would not like to speculate on which of the Gaiety girls who married into the aristocracy PGW had in mind. He certainly would have met some of them when working as fill-in lyric writer at the Gaiety. See Chap. 24.

Trinity smoker. 29 p17 & p100. See SMOKER.

Tripoli, Lord of (wife of the). 59 p59. See RUDEL.

Tristan and Isolde. 72 p115. Their tragic love story has been recounted in France and England for 700 years, though the versions by Tennyson and Wagner are now the best known.

Triton blowing on his wreathed horn. 69 p91. In Greek mythology, Triton, son of Neptune, could raise or abate storms by blowing on his shell horn. PGW was quoting from Wordsworth's 'The World Is Too Much With Us': "Or hear old Triton blow his wreathed horn."

Triumph of mind over matter. 25 p177 and later. I am told this is a tenet of Christian Scientists.

Triumphs and disasters, who can meet with (and treat those two impostors just the same). 79 p38. From KIPLING'S 'If'. See IF YOU CAN SOMETHING.

Troilus. On such a night T. climbed the walls of Troy 36 p243. S. *Merchant of Venice* 4.1: "in such a night / Troilus methinks mounted the Troyan walls, / And sigh'd his soul toward the Grecian tents / Where Cressid lay that night."

Trott. 3 p237 and later. The cricketer A.E. Trott (1873–1914) is remembered as the man who, on 31 July 1899, stepped out and hit a ball from the Australian M.A. Noble over the Lord's pavilion, the only player ever to do so.

Trotzky, the prisoner Leon. 35 p159. Trotsky (1879–1940) shared the leadership of the Russian Revolution of 1917 with Lenin. His influence declined after Lenin's death in 1924 and he was banished from Russia by Stalin in 1929. He sought refuge in Mexico but was assassinated there in 1940.

Troubles. Put all your t. in a great big box 34 p30. See PUT ALL YOUR TROUBLES.

Troubles be little ones. 45 p67. See MAY ALL THEIR TROUBLES.

Trousering the fines. All through his years as a magistrate he (Sir Watkyn Bassett) had been t. the f., amassing the stuff in sackfuls 85 p40. Bertie had accused Sir Watkyn, completely unjustly, of the same thing in *The Code of the Woosters* but was merely repeating a common belief. For a long time, 1400?–1750?, fines were retained by magistrates and judges to meet the costs of the court, which would include their expenses. See ST PAUL'S for a similar archaic reference.

Trousers. Losing your trousers is an effective immobiliser; see 29 p35; 36 p208; 58 p269; 85 p151. The same trick was employed to useful effect by Tim Clarke in the last war. Clarke (d. 14 June 1995) was a British Intelligence officer in Syria in the Second World War. Because the loyalty of French troops in Syria was then in doubt (France had surrendered to Germany), the situation was very delicate. Suspecting a French officer was going to initiate action against the Allies, Clarke immobilised him by stealing all his trousers. The French authorities were furious, but CHURCHILL thoroughly approved and saw that Clarke was rewarded for his quick thinking.

After the war, Clarke went on to become a well-known and respected auctioneer for Sotheby's in London. He made his reputation when a group of unruly Turkish carpet dealers set out to disrupt the proceedings. They were reduced to order by Clarke with a volley of fluent Turkish which he had learned during the war. His obituary read: "Nobody knows what he said, but the respect with which the carpet-dealers treated him thereafter spoke volumes."

Trout, papier-maché. As Mr Jerome said of it 4 p70. The story of the stuffed trout that turned out to be a fake made of papier-maché comes from chapter 17 of Jerome K. Jerome's immortal *THREE MEN IN A BOAT* (1889). PGW referred to it again when Mr Bickersdyke told the anecdote in *Psmith in the City*.

True and blushful, A spot more of the. 97 p20. See HIPPOCRENE.

True bill. It is a true bill 2 p24. In the UK, before a serious criminal case was tried, a grand jury had to agree the preliminary charges were valid, a 'true bill' of indictment. This procedure was discontinued in 1930.

True blue. From soup to nuts 67 p29. 'True blue' has altered its meaning over time. Normally used today to signify a stalwart conservative, it comes from the Scottish Covenanters who resolved to fight for their faith against James the Second's introduction of episcopacy in the 1680s. The basic meaning is still reliability and loyalty to a cause. See also SOUP TO NUTS.

True love, path/course of. See PATH OF TRUE LOVE.

True, O King. 3 p133. Daniel 3.24: "They answered and said unto the king, True, O king."

Truefitt's (hairdressers/barbers). 45 p117. Still going strong, Truefitt's began in Bond Street in 1805. I think PGW had Truefitt's in mind for Price's in *If I Were You*, since Truefitt's are proud that they cut the Duke of Wellington's hair before he went off to fight Napoleon at Waterloo.

Trust. Boss of some trust 2 p15. The trusts in the USA were what we call cartels or monopolies in the UK. At the end of the 19th century, about twenty or so men controlled most of the industry of the USA through trusts. When PGW wrote of them, the country was in turmoil as President Teddy Roosevelt began to break their grip with anti-trust laws.

Truth with him who sings to one clear harp in divers tones that men may rise on stepping stones of their dead selves to higher things. 67 p248; 83 p69. T. 'In Memoriam' Canto 1.

Try that on your pianola/bazooka. 45 p41; 55 p211 and later. When I was delving through song titles in the British Library, I noticed that just about every song sheet had, on the back page, an advertisement for some other song the publisher wanted to sell. The song title was followed by a couple of lines of the music and, invariably in large print, the words: "Try This On Your Piano/Pianola". Irving Berlin had noted the usage as well and published a song under this title in 1910. See also BAZOOKA.

Tugboat Annie. PGW used this in an essay, a term for a homely-looking woman that came into popular use after the success of the 1933 film of that name. The veteran actress Marie Dressler played the tugboat skipper trying to keep her feckless husband (Wallace Beery) off the drink, so their son (Robert Young) could fulfil his ambition to become captain of a luxury liner. As one critic put it: "The all-stops-out emotional climax, with Annie tooting to the rescue of her son's stricken liner, won't leave a dry eye in the house."

Tulip Time in Sing Sing. This lyric from *Sitting Pretty* (1924), another of Wodehouse's prison songs (see TAKE ME BACK), was popular because his audience recognised the satire on 'Tulip Time', the hit song in ZIEGFELD's *Follies* of 1919.

Tumult and the shouting had died, the. 32 p239; 43 p113, p223 & p307; and later. KIPLING's 'Recessional': "The tumult and the shouting dies; / The Captains and the Kings depart."

Tunney, Gene. 82 p110; and Dempsey in Chicago 96 p74. See EUGENE.

Tuppenham School. 6 p228. I suggest this rival school is clearly PGW's gloss on Uppingham, whom Dulwich played at Rugger. See GEDDINGTON for another disguised reference to it.

Tuppy (Glossop and three other PGW characters with the same nickname). I have been unable to find any source for this cognomen. See Chap. 30.

Turbot ... obscene-looking mixture of bones and eyeballs and black mackintosh 50 p260. MTT Prof. Owen McGee for pointing out that the *Oxford Dictionary of Quotations* has: "'Turbot, Sir' said the waiter, placing before me two fishbones, two eyeballs, and a bit of black mackintosh." From *The Dinner Knell* by Thomas Earle Welby.

Turbulent butler. Will no one rid me of this t. b.? 63 p229. See BECKET.

Turkish Baths, twenty yards from the Senior Conservatives Club, in Cumberland Street. 14 p194 & p203. See Chap. 21 for the establishment PGW had in mind. There are, I understand, only two Turkish Baths now left in London. The well-known Jermyn Street establishment where Bill West and Judson Coker spent the night (chap. 5 of *Bill the Conqueror*) closed some years ago.

Turkish this side,Virginian that. 40 p41; 51 p209 and later. See CIGARETTES.

Turn. When X says 'Turn', we all turn. See WHEN COMRADE JACKSON SAYS 'TURN'.

Turn my face to the wall. 68 p68. B. Isaiah 38.2: "Then Hezekiah turned his face toward the wall and prayed unto the Lord." PGW used the phrase to instil a general sense of gloom because he assumed his readers would know that the previous verse had said Hezekiah was "sick unto death".

Turpin, Dick. 3 p108 and later. This highwayman (1706–39) occupied a position in cheap fiction in the England similar to that of Jesse James in the USA. There were still stories about him being published in the 1920s, all of which mentioned his legendary ride from London to York on his mare Black Bess. It was only recently I discovered this feat was, in fact, done by the highwayman Dick Dudley about 1675. He held somebody up at Barnet, just north of London, at 5 A.M., then rode the 150 miles or more to York, appearing on a bowling-green there at 6 P.M. When tried for the robbery, the jury acquitted him since the feat was clearly impossible. Why the story was credited to Turpin fifty years later, I do not know.

Tush, not to say pish. 31 p118. Presumably from Pish-Tush in G&S *The Mikado*, but maybe from Gilbert's *Bab Ballads* or *More Bab Ballads*.

Tussauds, Madame. 33 p113 and up to 97 p33. This famous waxworks exhibition has drawn crowds in London since 1802. PGW was highly flattered when they did a waxwork of him in 1973.

Tutankhamen's tomb, something excavated from. 58 p200 and later. The finding of this Egyptian king's tomb and the beautiful gold artefacts buried with him caused a sensation in 1922.

Tuttle. 37 p33; 49 p246 and later. Tuttle's Lane, Bensonburg 77 p158; Loretta Tuttle 88 p94 & Lana Tuttle at 88 p263. See Chap. 23.

'Twas now the very witching time of night. 73 p163. See WITCHING TIME OF NIGHT.

'Twas strange, 'twas passing strange. See STRANGE.

Tweet, tweet! Shush, shush! Now, now! Come, come!, I lifted up your finger and said. 43 p130; 50 p85. PGW was quoting the recently-published (1929) popular song by Leslie Sarony 'I Lift Up My Finger and I Say Tweet-Tweet, Shush-Shush, Now-Now, Come-Come.'

Twentieth Century Limited. See CORNISH EXPRESS.

Twenty-one today (I'm). 25 p171; Stanwood Cobbold serenades Lord Shortlands with a similar version 66 p63. I was surprised to find this song, by Alec Kendall, was not written till 1911.

'Twere well 'twere done/smacked into quickly. See IF 'TWERE DONE.

Twerp. 58 p69. This term of abuse now seems to have died at last. My dictionaries give different meanings for it. One says it is a caddish person, another says it means a stupid person, a third says it is a foolish or unimportant person. The term seems to have been coined in the 1920s, and the first meaning, a cad, would fit very well with PGW's description of Adrian Peake. My school friends and I used it constantly during the 1940s in the third sense, to describe someone as being stupid or of no importance. I do not think I've heard it in more than ten years.

Twice-told tale. 34 p7. See TEDIOUSNESS.

Twig snap beneath their feet, letting not. 20 p140 and later. See COOPER, FENIMORE.

Twist, dancing the. 88 p119. This vigorous dance, akin to the Charleston, was very popular in the 1960s.

***Twisted Lives* (play).** 55 p276. Not too difficult to identify Noel Coward's *Private Lives*.

Two cars in the garage, two chickens in the pot. 93 p78. "A chicken in every pot and a car in every garage" is a slogan often attributed to Herbert Hoover (1874–1964) in his successful presidential campaign of 1928. It is now believed he never said it, though a pamphlet of his did have the heading 'A Chicken in Every Pot', a phrase originally coined by Henry IV of France.

Two chins grow where one had grown before. 87 p22. Probably from "two ears of corn grow where one had grown before" in *Gulliver's Travels* 2.7.

Two eyes, like stars, start from their spheres. 67 p109. See PORPENTINE.

Two hearts that beat as one,. 28 p105; 31 p215; two minds with but a single thought 41 p146; and later. Friedrich Halm's *Der Sohn der Wildness* (1842) Act 2: "Two souls with but a single thought, Two hearts that beat as one."

'Two lovers built this nest.' 85 p41. In a letter to Bill Townend in 1932, Wodehouse wrote about H.G. Wells and the woman he was living with. He said: "By the way, when you go to his residence, the first thing you see is an enormous fireplace, and around it are carved in huge letters the words: 'TWO LOVERS BUILT THIS HOUSE'." MTT Sophie Ratcliffe.

Two Macs, The. 52 p263. See Chap. 24.

Two strong men face to face. 63 p237. See WHEN TWO STRONG MEN.

Two voices. There are two voices, as Wordsworth wrote 8 p98. Wordsworth's 'Two Voices Are There': "Two voices are there; one is of the sea. One of the mountains ..."

Tyldesley. 2 p198; 12 p15. Cricketer. From the dates, this has to be J.T. Tyldesley, who played for Lancashire 1895–1923. E. Tyldesley and R. Tyldesley did not play for Lancashire till 1909.

***Types of Ethical Theory*.** 35 p10; 64 p15. The words Bertie quotes are at page 124 of the 1885 edition of the book (MTT Jack Stewart). It was written by James

Martineau D.D., LL.D, Principal of Manchester New College, who had also published *A Study of Spinoza* in 1882. In support of Bertie Wooster's comment as to what a small world it is, I happened to be dining with a senior officer of the Harriet Martineau Society (Harriet was James' sister) when an e-mail arrived from an American Wodehousean asking him for his views on Bertie's allusion.

U

(MTT = My thanks to)

Uffenham, Lord. See Chap. 37.

Ukridge, Stanley Featherstonehaugh. See Chap. 34.

Ultry-violet rays, must avoid its. 87 p72; 97 p53. From Noel Coward's witty 1932 song 'Mad Dogs and Englishmen', which he wrote after a stay in the Malay States. It was allegedly inspired by the eccentric behaviour of the Governor, Sir Hugh Clifford. The first verse ends:

> Because the sun is much too sultry
> And one must avoid its ultry-violet rays.
> The natives grieve when the white men leave their huts
> Because they're obviously, definitely nuts!

Ulysses at Ithaca. 12 p244; 20 p52. He had been away for twenty years and his reunion with his faithful hound Argos is at 21 p192. Why PGW used the Latin name Ulysses instead of Odysseus, and why he called the faithful dog Argos instead of Argus, is beyond me. In any event, Homer tells us that, having kept watch for his master all those years, Argus recognised Ulysses/Odysseus despite his disguise, licked his hand, and then died happy. Aaaaah! See Homer's *Odyssey*.

Umbrella Club. 74 p173; 77 p20 & p30. Guy Bolton explained the concept to PGW in *Bring on the Girls* (p173). An interesting idea, and I am surprised no one has tried it. It would be particularly useful if one could hire those big golf-umbrellas which are too large to be carried to the office every day.

Umustaphas. 4 p235. Because expensive cigarettes were made from Turkish or Egyptian tobacco, many cheaper (Virginian tobacco) brands were sold under Turkish/Egyptian-sounding names: Umustaphas, Mustaphas, Queen of the Harem, etc. There is also a popular English joke here. One of the traditions of English pantomime is the perpetration of appalling puns. So, in pantomimes like *Ali Baba* or *Aladdin*, some comic character will always be given the name Mustapha. This can then lead to endless jokes about 'Mustapha cuppertea'; 'Mustapha drink'; 'Mustapha nother' etc. See also CIGARETTES.

Uncertain, coy and hard to please. In my hours of ease this aunt is sometimes 76 p184 and variations elsewhere. See WOMAN IN OUR.

Uncle Tom's Cabin. 13 p237; 93 p54. This book by Harriet Beecher Stowe came out in 1852 and symbolised the anti-slavery movement in the USA. It was turned into a play the following year and was an instant success; I cannot think of anything in England which achieved the same popularity. In 1879 there were no fewer than forty-two companies touring it in America, all doing good business. Many actors, known in the profession as 'tommers', spent their lives playing it, and there were still twelve companies touring it on a permanent basis in 1927. One reference book says that 1930 was the only year when it was not showing somewhere in the USA and notes that some troupes enthralled their audiences by featuring a real bloodhound. In Tombstone, Arizona, in 1883, a cowboy was so carried away by the sight of one chasing poor ELIZA across the stage that he jumped to his feet and emptied his revolver into the unfortunate animal.

Uncle Woggly to His Chicks. 50 p18. I wonder if this is PGW's version of the long-lasting American series of Uncle Wiggily stories written by H.R. Garis. He published the first in 1910 and went on to produce another 12,000 over the next fifty years. See also Chap. 7.

Underdone beef. Sky looked like it 18 p161, 76 p87 and elsewhere. See SUNSETS.

Understood all and pardoned all, He. 60 p14. See KNOW ALL.

United States, relationship with United Kingdom. 20 p21 gives a masterly historical summary, culminating in Miss Edna May and *The Belle of New York*, which cemented good relations in 1898.

Universal (a step up from Wonderland). 33 p118. This was the National Sporting Club. See Chap. 4.

Unkindest cut of all, the most. 53 p39 and later. S. *Julius Caesar* 3.2: "This was the most unkindest cut of all."

Unsweetened, six pennorth of. 14 p100. Until around 1920, 'unsweetened' was the usual working-class term for unflavoured cheap gin. The term goes back to the 18th century and the horrors of Hogarth's 'Gin Lane', when gin was cheap and became the popular spirit drunk by the poor. Conversely, this caused it to be despised by the Victorian middle classes. Gin was *not* drunk in polite society until cocktails became socially acceptable in the 20th century.

Untamed gazelle. Bingo dancing like an u. g. 31 p29. This has a strong ring of a quotation, but the nearest I have found is a comment that this is how BYRON viewed Lady Caroline Lamb.

Unto the what-d'you-call-it generation, don't you know? 22 p23. See SINS OF THE SCOTTIE.

Unwashed, the Great. 24 p106. See GREAT UNWASHED.

Unwritten Law, the. 23 p195. As far as I can ascertain, this phrase held good in certain states in America where, if a cad trifled with your sister's affections or had an *affaire* with your wife, you could shoot him and plead the Unwritten Law.

Up and doing with a heart for any fate, Let us then be. 29 p135 and later. Longfellow's 'A Psalm of Life'.

Up from the depths. Story title in 69; 88 p157. English translation of De Profundis. B. Psalms 130: "Out of the depths have I cried unto thee, O Lord."

Up, Guards, and at them. 94 p119. This order by Wellington to the Guards at

Waterloo (1815) was attributed to him by a young officer who was there. Many years later, Wellington acknowledged he might have said: "Stand up, Guards" and then ordered the division to advance. The version Wodehouse quoted remained in popular use for 150 years.

Up Lyme (Lyme Regis). 7 p102. See Chap. 12.

Up to snuff. See SNUFF.

Up to the mark. Can a pig keep up to the mark 91 p5. The expression goes back to the days of bare-fist boxing when a fight could last for a hundred rounds or more. A line was drawn across the middle of the ring, and if a boxer could not 'come up to the mark' when the bell rang for the next round, he had lost. The present system of counting a man out if he cannot get to his feet in ten seconds is the same basic idea.

Upas tree. 18 p106; 85 p81. There was a legend that this tree from Java poisoned all around it.

Upjohn, Aubrey. 59 p82 and often later. See Chap. 3.

Upon what meat doth this, our — feed? Our Fillmore 30 p196; our Clutterbuck 77 p196; our Horace 81 p11; and elsewhere. S. *Julius Caesar* 1. 2: "Upon what meat does this our Caesar feed, / That he is grown so great?"

Upper crust. Synonymous with the Upper Ten (see SUBMERGED TENTH). I only learned recently that the term comes from late mediaeval England when everybody baked their own bread. The dough was placed in a small opening beside the kitchen fire, and the base of the loaf was always blackened and rough from the ashes on which it sat. When the bread was cooked, the loaf was sliced horizontally, not vertically. The most junior vassal got the burned, ash-covered bottom crust. The best of the bread, the upper crust, was given to the head of the household or the most important guest.

Upper Ten. See SUBMERGED TENTH.

Upton Snodsbury. 40 p233; 55 p161. A small village six miles east of Worcester. See Chap. 26.

V

(MTT = My thanks to)

Valentine, Jimmy (safe cracker). 70 p129; 90 p120 & p155. The hero of the short story 'A Retrieved Reformation' by O. Henry. The play *Jimmy Valentine* (1910) swept America.

Valentino. 71 p9. This handsome film hero (1895–1926) made women round the world swoon with films like *The Sheik*. His full name was Rudolpho Alfonzo Raffaelo Pierre Filibert Guglielmi di Valentina d'Antonguolla. See also SHEIKH.

Valley of the shadow of death. 21 p294; and scrambled out safely the other side 54 p126. B. Psalms 23.4: "Yea, though I walk through the valley of the shadow of death, I will fear no evil ..."

Van Dyke beard. 81 p22. See Frans Hals' painting 'The Laughing Cavalier' to get an idea of what a Van Dyke beard looked like.

Van Meegeren. 79 p107. This brilliant picture faker (d. 1947) caused chaos in the art world with his superb imitations which deceived everybody.

Van names. Van Alstyne / Van Nugget / Van Brunt / Van Tuyl. There is an important difference between the London 'Vans' and the New York 'Vans' in PGW's stories. When he wrote of the London 'Vans' (Van Nugget, Van Alstyne), he had in mind the South African millionaires who came to London from 1890 onwards to spend the money from their diamond and gold mines. Building enormous mansions in Park Lane, similar to the millionaires' palaces in Newport, Rhode Island, they were definitely vulgar 'new' money and were accepted for their wealth, but rarely respected. In New York, the reverse applied. The prefix 'Van' meant the holder was 'old New York' and came from the original Dutch families who had settled New York before the British took over. They looked down upon Mrs Astor and those like her as social upstarts. PGW had a very good sense of such social distinctions. See also next entry.

Van Tuyl, Reggie. 27 p94. This languid young man was a member of New York's old aristocracy, the Dutch families who settled it in the 17th century. I find it no coincidence at all that, among the contributors to *Vanity Fair* in 1916 (much of it written by PGW), was Captain Prescott van Tuyl, who wrote articles about millionaires' yachts (175-ft long, staterooms for ten and staff quarters included etc.) and American Stately Homes. He clearly had all the right connections.

Vancutt, the muffin baker, a landlord in Rupert Street. 9 p64. My 1907 London Directory shows that a muffin baker, William Forscutt, had his premises on the corner of Rupert Street/Rupert Court with the pub across the alleyway from it.

He let rooms to Herbert Westbrook; see Chap. 34.

Vanguard. Engine of a stationary V. 9 p218. The Vanguard was an early English motor car.

Vanished face. The tragedy of a v. f. 44 p109. See TOUCH OF A VANISHED HAND.

Vanished hand, touch of a (and the sound of a voice that is still). See TOUCH OF A VANISHED HAND.

***Vanishing Lady, The* (film).** 85 p50. The 1938 film *The Lady Vanishes* by Hitchcock still grabs the attention. MTT Dr Tim Healey for pointing out the film was based on *The Lady Vanishes* by Ethel Lena White (1936).

Vardon, Harry. 28 p28. One of the Great Triumvirate (Vardon, Taylor and Braid), Harry Vardon (1870–1937) is the only golfer to have won the Open six times.

***Variety* magazine.** 30 p138 and later. See Chap. 24.

Varium et mutabile semper femina. 82 p125. Roughly: a woman is always changeable and fickle. Virgil's *Aeneid* Bk 3, l.359.

Vasty deep. 21 p20. S. *1 Henry IV* 3.1: "I can call spirits from the vasty deep."

Vaulting ambition. 8 p64. S. *Macbeth* 1.7: "Vaulting ambition, which o'erleaps itself, / And falls on the other."

Vehmgericht. 4 p46. A secret mediaeval German Imperial court who carried out punishments on the spot.

Veils, seven. 43 p 267. See SALOME DANCE and PSYCHE.

Vengeance of Heaven, this is the. 51 p220. Choose from either B. Jeremiah 50.28 — "the vengeance of the Lord our God" — or Cowper's 'Boadicea': "Heaven awards the vengeance due."

Venus rising from the foam. P.C. Oates emerging from a ditch 59 p90. A favourite subject among painters from Botticelli's 'The Birth of Venus' onwards. The goddess is invariably depicted in the nude, although long tresses of her hair preserve most of her modesty as she rises out of the sea.

Verbum sapienti satis. 56 p16. An epigram by Terence: A word is enough to a wise man. In the UK, the phrase is often abbreviated to 'Verb. sap.'

Vere de Vere, the caste of. 13 p234. See REPOSE.

Verily, as a jewel of gold in a swine's snout is a woman which is without discretion. What Ecclesiastes wrote in the good book 80 p66. Nanny misquoted the source. It is B. Proverbs 11.22. "As a jewel of gold in a swine's snout, so is a fair woman which is without discretion." See also 39 p95, where the Bishop of Stortford had to have his reference corrected.

Verisimilitude to an otherwise bald and unconvincing narrative, It gives. 95 p156. G&S *The Mikado* Act 2.

Veto, lost my. 18 p247. In 1911 the House of Lords lost its power of veto over finance Bills passed by the House of Commons. This was a radical change in the British constitution.

Vice Chancellor of the County Palatinate of Lancaster. 67 p54. One of PGW's few factual errors. My 1911 Burke's *Peerage* and 1952 Kelly's *Handbook* both state that an earl's younger son goes into dinner before not just the Vice

Chancellor of the Duchy of Lancaster, but before the Chancellor himself. I notice, however, the younger sons of Viscounts fall in behind the Vice Chancellor. Perhaps Wodehouse was confused.

Vice in Spiller, there is no. 12 p187; in Skinner 21 p196; in J.G. Miller 63 p174. Until c.1920, there were more horses than cars in England. This meant that PGW's generation grew up using terms applicable to horses, which are now forgotten (see also SIT ON HIS HEAD). Buying and selling horses was a complicated matter, and a buyer would stipulate that the horse was "guaranteed free from vice", i.e. had no bad habits. A good, willing horse "had no vice in him".

Vice is a monster of so frightful mien etc. etc. 37 p159. Pope's *Essay on Man*, Epistle 2.

Vice Versa. 3 p247; 4 p70. This 1882 book by F. Anstey describes the complications that arise when a father and son find themselves in each other's bodies. *Laughing Gas* transposed the idea to Hollywood.

Vicente y Blasco What's-his-name stuff. 31 p35. See BLASCO.

Vicissitudes of Vera. 39 p39. See *DANGERS OF DIANA*.

Victory, famous. 21 p82. See FAMOUS VICTORY.

Victory or Westminster Abbey now, It was. 12 p150. At the start of the Battle of Cape St Vincent (1797), Nelson gave the order to attack and added "Westminster Abbey or victory", i.e. by the end of the battle he would either be dead or victorious.

Victrola. Biggest thing since Marconi invented the v. 38 p102. Because the large horns on top of gramophones (see PUT A SOCK IN IT) were believed to be unsightly, the Victor gramophone company created the Victrola in 1901. It had an elegant cabinet in which the amplifying horn was housed below, not above, the record, but gave the same resonance. For background music, you kept the doors of the cabinet shut; for full volume, you opened them. See also MARCONI.

Vie de Boheme, La. 97 p26. See TRILBY.

Vile body. What the hymn-book calls your vile body 47 p96. B. Philippians 3.21: "Who shall change our vile body, that it may be fashioned like unto his glorious body ..."

Village blacksmith. His brow which was like the village blacksmith's 22 p115. PGW used the term often to describe someone of burly build. Longfellow's 'The Village Blacksmith': "The smith, a mighty man is he, / With large and sinewy hands; / And the muscles of his brawny arms / Are strong as iron bands." The second verse has the line "His brow is wet with honest sweat."

In 'Pig-hoo-o-o-o-ey!', Angela's "clear soprano rang out like the voice of the village blacksmith's daughter". In Longfellow's poem, the blacksmith thinks his daughter's voice is "like her mother's voice / Singing in Paradise."

Village Mothers. 55 p52. I regret to say this is PGW's version of the Mothers' Union, a very worthy Church of England organisation founded in 1878. It is stronger in rural districts of Britain than in more ungodly, sophisticated urban areas. See Chap. 17.

Vine leaves in his hair. 42 p105 and later. Someone intent on enjoying himself. From the habit of Roman men putting vine leaves in their hair to attend a formal banquet; akin to donning a black tie today.

Vine Street police station. 25 p60; 31 p86 and later. The old Vine Street police station, just off Piccadilly, would indeed be the appropriate place to take a miscreant arrested in the Haymarket.

Vinton Street police court. 73 p53. Clearly Vine Street, but PGW had been away from London for over fifteen years and had probably forgotten the name.

Violets, it ain't all/ lavender?/violets? 96 p145. It was lavender. See IT AIN'T ALL LAVENDER.

Violets, It's raining. 32 p258. See RAINING VIOLETS.

Viollet-Le-Duc. 19 p110. Eugène Viollet-le-Duc (1814–79), French architect and noted writer on achitecture.

Vision of Salome (till the Women's Institute toned it down). 68 p194. See SALOME DANCE.

Vision of Sir Launfal. 63 p47 — Penguin edition. Why this line is in the Penguin edition and not in my first reprint of the first edition is beyond me. In any event, it is from James Russell Lowell's poem 'The Vision of Sir Launfal'.

Visits of Elizabeth. 9 p153. This 1900 book by Elinor GLYN was considered very daring.

Vitellius. 69p14; 70 p174 and later. Roman emperor who enjoyed food so much that he would eat four or five large epicurean meals every day, making himself sick after each to make room for the next. He was assassinated in 69 A.D. See also GALBA.

Vivian, Sir Walter. All a summer's day, etc. 89 p138. Opening lines of T. *The Princess*: "Sir Walter Vivian all a summer's day / Gave his broad lawns until the set of sun / Up to the people etc.

Vo-de-o-de-o. A gay song with a good deal of v. about it 61 p9. A term used for the syncopated rhythms of songs and dances that came into fashion after the success of the Charleston in the mid-1920s. It came to represent fast, lively, cheerful songs as opposed to slower sentimental ballads.

Voice I heard this passing night was heard … clown. 78 p154. Keats' 'Ode to a Nightingale'.

Voice that breathed o'er Eden. 20 p82 and later. Synonymous with marriage ceremonies, this 19th-century hymn was written by Keble and Stainer.

Voices, beyond. See BEYOND THESE VOICES.

Volga boatman. Slow dragging step like a V. b. 59 p180; and later. This sad, slow Russian folk song was first noted in 1869. Feodor Chaliapin (1873–1938), the great bass, recorded his arrangement in 1922 and made it popular round the world. It became as closely associated with him as 'Ol' Man River' was with Paul Robeson. I sang it in a choir of eight-year-old trebles at school which must have sounded incongruous, to say the least.

Volstead Act. 48 p48; 71 p142. This introduced Prohibition in the USA in 1919.

von Moltke, a man of few words. 15A p197. Helmuth von Moltke (1848–1919; Prussian Army chief of staff 1889–91). It was said that his "silence in five languages was more expressive than a thousand words".

Vorticist sculptor. 38 p1. See NEO-VORTICIST.

Vowing he'd ne'er consent, consented. 38 p32 and later. Byron's *Don Juan* Ch 1, cxvii: "A little still she strove, and much repented, / And whispering 'I will ne'er consent' — consented."

'Voyage of Maeldive', Tennyson's. 15 p9. Misprint. See 16 p15 where the correct reference is given, i.e. Tennyson's 'Voyage of Maeldune'.

V-shaped depression ... would shortly blacken the skies, a. 61 p171; 68 p95 and later. When UK newspapers started printing weather forecasts in the 1930s, the areas which would see a 'depression', i.e. a fall in barometric pressure and rain, were marked on the map by a line with V-shaped black marks along it.

Vulgar brawl, mere. See BRAWL.

Vultures gnawing at his bosom. 53 p36 and later. See PROMETHEUS.

W

(MTT = My thanks to)

Wabble and I vacillate, I. 59 p43. This sounds Shakespearean, but the only source quoted in the *Oxford Dictionary* is *Harper's Magazine*, which used 'wabble' in 1881 as a variant of 'wobble'.

Waddington's Ninety Seven Soups. 45 p19. PGW gloss on Heinz 57 Varieties. Mr Heinz (1844–1919), whose popularity in the UK began in 1886 when Fortnum & Mason's bought his entire stock, produced far more than 57 soups, but felt '57 Varieties' sounded right.

Wages of sin. Trousered 42 p14; and three times later. B. Romans 6.23: "For the wages of sin is death ..."

Wailing and gnashing of teeth. See WEEPING AND GNASHING.

Wailing for her demon lover. 58 p74; 68 p227 and elsewhere. Coleridge's *Kubla Khan*: "As e'er beneath a waning moon was haunted / By woman wailing for her demon lover!"

Wait and see. We must wait and see 43 p17; 59 p210. ASQUITH made this comment in Parliament in 1910. The Opposition was anxious to get some indication of the Government Budget and badgered Asquith ceaselessly on it. He adopted "Wait and see"' as his standard reply and the phrase became famous.

Wait till the clouds rolled by. 72 p174. The song 'Till the Clouds Roll By', music by Jerome Kern, words by PGW, featured in the 1917 show *Oh, Boy!* David Jasen adds that it was also the title of the 1946 biopic of Kern, screenplay by Guy Bolton.

Waiting at the Church. There was I 72 p77; 84 p52. Vesta Victoria popularised the 1906 sad/comic song 'Waiting at the Church' by Fred Leigh.

'Waiting for Percy, I'm.' That sounds like the title of one of those avant garde off-Broadway shows 86 p74. Beckett's *Waiting for Godot* had come out nine years before and every avant-garde/experimental theatre company in the world was playing it.

Waiting for the Robert E. Lee. 20 p26. Popular song by Gilbert & Muir (1912).

Waitresses instead of waiters... . I thought that went out with the armistice. 31 p233. In most London clubs, it had. One of the shocks London clubmen suffered in the 1914 war was seeing women (waitresses) in their all-male establishments. They were forced to employ them because all the men were conscripted. As soon as the war was over, most clubs got waiters back as soon as they could, so waitresses were unusual.

Wake up, England. 10 p15; 46 p174. On 5 December 1901, the Prince of Wales, later George V, returned from a trip to Australia and made the comment in a speech at the Guildhall criticising British industry for becoming complacent. In 1911 it was reprinted with the title 'Wake up, England', a phrase that became popular. Do not confuse with 'Wake up, America', a speech by Augustus Gardner in 1916.

Walking-race to Brighton. See BRIGHTON.

Wall Street. Show Wall Street some high finance that would astonish it 24 p19. See ASTONISH IT.

Wallace, Edgar. 43 p152 and later. PGW stayed with Wallace (1875–1932) for a weekend and was very impressed by his two butlers, one for day, one for night. Wallace wrote his books extraordinarily fast, dictating four different stories to four secretaries, allotting an hour to each story and picking up the plot of the next without a pause. A famous cartoon of the period showed an eager magazine stall clerk offering a traveller 'the midday Wallace'. In 1929 he produced one-quarter of all the fiction published in the UK! He did not write detective stories, he wrote thrillers in which the goodies and baddies were clear from the start. They were exciting, action-packed, and his Faceless Fiends and Master Criminals were beloved by all.

Wallace, Nellie. 39 p141; 49 p227. This music hall singer (1870–1948) made her name by stressing her sad lot in dozens of humorous songs.

Wallingford, Get-Rich-Quick. 17 p19. George Chester's short stories about this ingenious American con man came out in the *Saturday Evening Post* in 1908. George M. Cohan produced a successful play based on them in 1910.

Walls do have ears. 70 p58. "Walls have ears" is a 14th c. proverb.

Walls, Lady Evelyn, daughter of the Earl of Ackleton. 25 p267. In the same way that Lord Runnymede has a natural connection with Lord STAINES, Ackleton is a small village about a mile away from the hamlet of Walls. Both lie down the road from PGW's boyhood home in Shropshire. See Chap. 35.

Walls of Jericho. 9 p153. This play by Sutro opened at the Garrick, London, in 1904.

Walpole, Hugh. 7 p97; 46 p41; 74 p207. PGW knew this novelist (1884–1941), but they were acquaintances rather than friends. Like many serious writers of the time, he was puzzled by PGW's success. When Hilaire Belloc gave the talk on the BBC in which he said Wodehouse was the master of his profession, Walpole was completely at a loss. He did, however, pay PGW the compliment of imitation. Impressed by PGW's *Mike,* he decided to write a boy's story himself. It was the start of the Jeremy series — good books but very different from PGW's.

Walpole Street, No 23. 9 p50. See Chap. 25.

Walpurgis Night. A sort of W.N., phantoms whizzed to and fro 34 p109; 57 p115. This is the eve of May Day when witches in Germany held high revelry. Walpurgis was the saint who brought Christianity to much of Germany. She died 779 A.D.

Walrus. As the Walrus said, the time has come to talk of may things 71 p123. From Lewis Carroll's 'The Walrus and the Carpenter' (*Alice Through the Looking-Glass*).

Walsingford Hall, Walsingford Parva, Berkshire. 58 p7. Walsingford Hall, described in detail at the start of 58 chap. 2, is unmistakeably the Chateau Impney Hotel in Worcestershire. As he did in *Money for Nothing*, PGW described a building so accurately he had to move it. In any event, he needed somewhere within easy reach of London. See Chap. 26.

Walsingford-below-Chiveney-on-Thames. 49 p280. The name derives from Wallingford, a town on the Thames, fifty-five miles from London. In *Summer Moonshine*, Walsingford possesses the Booth & Baxter biscuit company, a clear reference to the famous Huntley & Palmer's biscuit factory in the nearby Thames-side town of Reading. See also WALSINGFORD HALL and REDBRIDGE.

Walter, don't falter. 63 p20; 81 p147. Unconfirmed, but the Victorian music hall song 'Walter, Walter, lead me to the altar' seems a good source.

Walton Heath. 20 p33 and later. See Chap. 27.

Wambler. You wretched, pie-faced w. 43 p145. An odd term of abuse for Aunt Dahlia to use. The *Oxford Dictionary* states that to wamble is to feel nauseous; to twist one's body; to roll about while walking. Perhaps Aunt Dahlia was using it in the sense that Bertie's intransigence made her feel sick? At 49 p210, in 'Open House', Marcella Tyrrwhitt stigmatised Eustace Mulliner as a wambling misfit.

Wand of Death, the. 19 p12. A story in the tradition of 'The GREEN EYE OF THE LITTLE YELLOW GOD'.

Wandered through a world of women, seeking you, I. 77 p167. See I WANDERED THROUGH.

Wandered through dry places seeking rest, he. 3 p68. B. Matthew 12.43: "When the unclean spirit is gone out of a man, he walketh through dry places, seeking rest, and findeth none."

Wanderer on the face of the earth, a. 9 p91. All I have found are Biblical commentaries saying this was Cain after he killed his brother Abel. At Genesis 4.14, Cain says: "I shall be a fugitive and a vagabond in the earth …"

Wandering boy. See BOY, WANDERING.

Want but little here below, one of those men who. 7p58. From 'A Ballad' in Goldsmith's *Vicar of Wakefield*. MTT Nigel Rees.

Want what they want when they want it. 24 p91; 86 p45. 'I Want What I Want When I Want It' was a song from the 1905 New York show *Mlle Modiste*, words by Henry Blossom, music by Victor Herbert.

War horse saying Ha Ha among the trumpets. Frequent, especially 92 p109, which has a fuller version. B. Job 39.25: "He saith among the trumpets, Ha, ha; and he smelleth the battle afar off, the thunder of the captains, and the shouting."

War to the knife (niblick). 28 p47 and later. BYRON's *Childe Harold's Pilgrimage*, Canto 1. A term applied to battles where the warriors involved really hated each other and would continue to fight with knives if they had lost their other weapons.

Ward, Artemus. Quoted A.W. 15A p204. Artemus Ward was the pen name of the American C.F. Browne (1834–67). He became famous as a humorist through 'Artemus Ward's Sayings', describing the adventures of an itinerant showman. Noted for his deliberate misspellings and grammatical errors, he came to London and gave a series of popular talks, as well as contributing to *Punch.*

Waring, Stewart, owner of tenements. 15A p164. See Chap. 23.

Warner, cricketer. 6 p20. P.F. ('Plum') Warner, captained England against Australia in 1903. He met PGW in Hollywood years later.

Warrior taking his rest. 17 p107. MTT Jim Linwood for reminding me of this one. "He lay like a warrior taking his rest" from 'The Burial of Sir John Moore at Corunna' by Charles Wolfe.

Washburn, Bryant. 27 p159. Romantic hero (1889–1963) of silent films.

Wasting his sweetness on the desert air. 2 p215 and later. See GEM OF PUREST RAY SERENE.

Watch. Called the rest of the watch together and thanked God they were rid of a knave 80 p69. S. *Much Ado About Nothing* 3.3.

Watch Committee, local. 93 p77. See BANNED IN BOSTON.

Watchdog. Tis sweet to hear the w.'s honest bark 13 p 50. See 'TIS SWEET TO HEAR.

Watcher of the skies when a new planet swims into his ken. 15A p105; 29 p277 and later. See NEW PLANET.

Watchman, What of the Night? 53 p180. Clifford Gandle used this phrase from B. Isaiah 21.11 probably because it had become popular as the title of a splendid Victorian song. Get it sung by a really strong baritone (four of them are even better) and you are in for a treat.

Water Rats, the. 11 p72. A British theatrical charity, it got its name when the original committee went to enlist someone's support. They travelled in an open carriage and arrived soaking wet from the rain, whereupon their host told them they looked like water rats.

Watering her couch with her tears. 'Watering the geraniums with her tears.' 67 p159. B. Psalms 6.6. "I water my couch with my tears."

Waterloo, Battle of. Like the B. of W., it was going to be a close-run affair 13 p154; it had been a devilish close-run thing 81 p25. 'It had been a devilish close run thing' was the remark commonly attributed to the Duke of Wellington. There is good evidence of his saying: "It was the nearest thing you ever saw in our life." "A near thing" became a popular phrase.

Waterloo Station. 9 p31 and later. Until its rebuilding in the 1920s, Waterloo was a dark and murky place exactly as PGW described, and until the 1960s/70s, there was a marked contrast between Waterloo and PADDINGTON STATION. As

Lord Ickenham told us (60 p107–8), Paddington was a quieter, more dignified station whose clientele was very different from the suburbanites who made up most of the Waterloo customers.

Watier's. 13 p61; 89 p37. A famous gambling club in Regency days.

Watson. And this, if I mistake not, Watson, is my client now. See CLIENT. PGW had a tremendous respect for Arthur Conan DOYLE and quoted him constantly. My difficulty was how to index quotations like this. I have done the best I can, but if Watson is in a PGW quote, it is always Doyle — except for the example immediately below.

Watson, Watson, Watson, Watson and Watson. 81 p111. No surprise to find that PGW's American lawyer was Watson Washburn.

Watts, Dr. Quoted 6 p41; 12 p307; 37 p*v*; and often elsewhere. Isaac Watts (1674–1748) was a clergyman and writer of hymns who, in 1715, produced his *Divine Songs — Attempted in Easy Language for the Use of Children*. The Songs comprise twenty-eight hymns with such titles as 'Against Lying'; 'Against Quarrelling and Fighting; 'Against Scoffing and Calling Names'. It remained in print for over 200 years. They were certainly drilled into the infant PGW and his fellows, and many of Watts' phrases became embedded in the language. I have set out three examples of his verses below.

> Let dogs delight to bark and bite
> For God has made them so.
> Let bears and lions growl and fight
> For it is their nature to.
> But children, you should never let
> Your angry passions rise.[1]
> Your little hands were never made
> To tear each others eyes.[2]
> ....
> When children in their wanton way
> Served old Elisha so[3]
> And made the prophet go his way,
> 'Go up, thou baldhead, go'.
> God quickly stopped their wicked breath
> And sent two raging bears
> That tore them limb from limb to death
> With blood and groans and tears.
> ....
> How doth the little busy bee
> Improve each shining hour
> And gather honey every day
> From every opening flower.

---

[1] See PASSIONS 3 p22.

[2] Commonly changed to: "To black each other's eyes."

[3] See ELISHA 21 p114.

Waugh, Evelyn. 77 p127; his *Vile Bodies* 80 p23; and later. Waugh (1903–66) was an enthusiastic admirer of PGW. He regarded him as 'the Master' and justified the title by saying: "One has to regard a man as a Master who can produce on average three uniquely brilliant and entirely original similes to every page."

Waukeesis/ Waukeesy. 7 p16; 18 p13 and later. I am told this is/was an American shoe firm.

Wax to receive and marble to retain. 36 p235 and elsewhere. BYRON's 'And Wilt Thou Weep', but from Cervantes' *Don Quixote* before that (in Motteaux's translation). See Chap. 38.

Way of an eagle, the. 42 p275; 67 p236. *The Way of an Eagle* was a 1912 best-seller by Ethel M. Dell. See Chap. 37.

***Way of the World, The* (play).** 3 p201. Do not confuse with the play of the same name written by Congreve in 1700.

Way they have in the Army, a. 7 p225. Because PGW reminded us often that BEALE had been in the Army, it would be natural for Corky to link Beale's actions to the popular song written by John Blockley and J. Geoghegan in 1863. 'A Way We Have in the Army' was also quoted by KIPLING in *Stalky & Co*. The chorus is:

For the way we have with our Army
Is the way we have with our Navy
An' both of them lead to adversity
Which nobody can deny.

Ways and Means, a discussion of. 60 p95. Ways and Means is the name of the main finance committee in both the House of Commons and the US Congress.

We are lost, the captain shouted as he staggered down the stairs. 85 p46. From 'The Captain's Daughter'(1858), a poem by James Thomas Fields. MTT Helen Murphy.

We are not amused. 62 p179; 70 p8; 92 p56. This famous quotation, attributed to Queen Victoria, was long held to be apocryphal. It has recently been learned from a diary of one of her Ladies-in-Waiting that she once so expressed her disapproval of a jocular comment made about another reigning monarch. Alternatively, Bartlett's *Dictionary of Phrase and Fable* suggests she made the remark on seeing an imitation of herself by the Honourable Alexander Yorke, one of her equerries.

'We Are Seven', Wordsworth's. 41 p303. A sad and touching poem (see next entry) which only Hollywood, as satirised by PGW, could have changed into the feature film *Where Passion Lurks* with Oscar the Wonder-Poodle and Professor Pond's Educated Sea-Lions.

We, as Wordsworth might have said but didn't, are five. 1 p99. Wordsworth's poem 'We Are Seven'.

We can't do nothing till Martin gets here. 50 p38; 78 p137. 'You Can't Do Nothing Till Martin Gets Here', 1913 song popularised by Bert WILLIAMS.

We don't want to fight, but by Jingo if we do! 71 p52. See BY JINGO.

We fell out, my wife and I. 18 p113; 21 p314. T. *The Princess*, Pt 2: "We fell out my wife and I, / O we fell out I know not why. / And kiss'd again with tears, / And blessings on the falling out, / That all the more endears …"

We have done those things which we ought not to have done (and left undone those things which we ought to have done). 6 p207 & p243; 7 p61; and later. BCP. Morning Prayer, the General Confession.

We leave our country for our country's good. 31 p212. One of those infuriating phrases everybody knows, but which you will not find in many dictionaries of quotations. It comes from the days when Britain got rid of its felons by transporting them to the colonies. America was the favourite till 1776, when Australia replaced it. The line was written by a notorious forger, Barrington, for a play in New South Wales in 1796. "True patriots all, for be it understood, We left our country for our country's good."

We left the lovers loving and the parents signing cheques. 50 p306. I thought PGW was satirising KIPLING here, but he was quoting correctly from Kipling's 'The Three-Decker' (1894).

We shall meet at Philippi. 17 p50 and frequent later. One of the (mis)quotations that was common in popular speech, certainly up to the 1970s. S. *Julius Caesar* 4.3: "We'll along ourselves, and meet them at Philippi."

Weak and sinful. Kay Shannon's golf is weak and sinful 70 p74. The phrase does not appear in the Bible nor in the BCP. It is, however, in *HYMNS ANCIENT & MODERN*. The fifth line of the hymn 'I love to hear the story which angel voices tell' reads: "I am both weak and sinful."

Weak woman, I am only a. 59 p266 & p267 and elsewhere. Queen Elizabeth's splendid speech to her small army at Tilbury when the Spanish Armada was sailing to invade England in 1588. "I know I have the body of a weak and feeble woman, but I have the heart and stomach of a king, and of a king of England too, and think foul scorn that Parma or Spain, or any prince of Europe should dare to invade the borders of my realm."

Wealth beyond the dreams of avarice. 33 p128; 46 p260; 69 p233 and later. From Edward Moore's *The Gamester* c.1750. The phrase was famously used by Dr Johnson later.

Weariest river winds somewhere to the sea, the. 32 p201; 61 p181 and later. Swinburne's 'Garden of Proserpine': "That even the weariest river / Winds somewhere safe to sea."

Web, tangled. See WHAT A TANGLED WEB.

Webleigh Manor. 40 p148. See WEOBLEY.

***Webster's Dictionary*.** 18 p135; 81 p142. Noah Webster (1758–1843), who caused so many problems for Americans and Britons trying to communicate with each other, published his dictionary in 1828. He set out to eliminate what he considered English affectations in spelling; even American reference books admit that "in the introduction to his speller (he) issued a literary declaration of independence" and comment that "the great weakness (of the dictionary) … lay in its etymologies." No doubt he meant well.

Wedding Bells Will Not Ring Out, Those. 52 p170 and elsewhere. See 'Those Wedding Bells Will Not Ring Out', song (1896) by Rosenfeld.

Wedding Glide, The. 23 p184. Song from *The Passing Show* (1912).

Wedding Guest. He was engaged in beating his breast like the W.G. 60 p273; 66 p186; the w.g. who heard the loud bassoon 79 p81. Coleridge's *Rime of the Ancient Mariner*: "The Wedding-Guest here beat his breast, / For he had heard the loud bassoon."

Wedding Guest … who, having omitted to dress the part, got slung out on his ear. 64 p193. B. Matthew 22.12: "And he saith unto him, Friend, how camest thou in hither not having a wedding garment? And he was speechless." In the next verse, the miscreant was bound hand and foot and cast into the outer darkness.

Wedding of the Painted Doll. 49 p217; 51 p16. Lively song from the early talking film *Broadway Melody* (1929). See also VO-DE-O-DE-O.

Wedding presents, both numerous and costly. 28 p81. Another UK newspaper cliché popular between 1880 and 1920. Press accounts of weddings *always* described the presents as "both numerous and costly". In the Shropshire local newspapers 1890–1910 that I read, reports of weddings listed every present with the name of its donor. I was surprised to see how many young couples started off their married lives with embroidered bookmarks, models of the Parthenon or St Paul's Cathedral, or the complete works of Shakespeare, Lord Tennyson or Mr Browning. The *Shrewsbury Chronicle* describing the wedding of the Earl of Bradford's daughter in 1898 (see Chap. 39) listed all 300 wedding presents received and their donors. I noted six volumes of the works of Mr Ruskin, an embroidered blotter, a silver bookmark, a pair of china vases and so on. Practical gifts like blankets, furniture, glass or china were notable by their absence. See also FISH SLICE.

Wedge, flying. 63 p17. See FLYING WEDGE.

Wee sleekit timorous cowering beasties. 93 p147. Robert Burns' 'To a Mouse': "Wee, sleekit, cow'rin, tim'rous beastie, / O what a panic's in thy breastie!"

We-e take him from the city or the plough. We-e dress him up in uniform so ne-e-e-at. 1 p107. First and second lines of Henry Hamilton's 1893 patriotic song 'Private Tommy Atkins', which achieved tremendous popularity during the Boer War 1899–1902. "O, we take him from the city or the plough, Ta-ran-ta-ra / And we drill him, and we dress him up so neat, Ta-ran-ta-ra."

Wee Tots. 61 p47 and later up to 88 p119. See Chap. 7.

Weeping and gnashing of teeth. 43 p250 and elsewhere. "Cast into (the) outer darkness and there shall be weeping and gnashing of teeth" only occurs in B. Matthew, who has it three times, at 8.12, 22.13 and 23.50. But, at 94 p85, PGW uses the variation "there shall be wailing and gnashing of teeth." Again, only Matthew uses this phrase, at 13.42 and 13.50, both of which read: "And shall cast them into a furnace of fire: there shall be wailing and gnashing of teeth."

Weighed in the balance (and found correct). 1 p18. B. Daniel 5.27: "Thou art weighed in the balances, and art found wanting." See also WRITING ON THE WALL.

Weight of this unintelligible world, the heavy and weary. 93 p167. Wordsworth's 'Lines Composed above Tintern Abbey': "That blessed mood, / In which the burthen of the mystery, / In which the heavy and the weary weight / Of all this unintelligible world, / Is lightened."

Welkin. Splitting the w. 68 p31; causing the w. to ring 91 p93. Making a very loud noise (the welkin is the air/ sky). The expression has the ring of Shakespeare, but it is simply a once-common phrase that has gone out of use. See also TOAD UNDER THE HARROW.

Well. Not so deep as a well. See 'TIS NOT SO.

Well became her, womanly candour/sympathy that. 28 p41. See BECAME HIM/ HER WELL.

Well met by moonlight, proud Oakshott. 67 p84; proud Phipps 70 p119; proud Wisdom 80 p164. S. *Midsummer Nights Dream* 2.1: "Ill met by moonlight, proud Titania."

Weller, Sam. 74 p129; 96 p96. Pickwick's servant in D. *The Pickwick Papers.*

Weller, Tony, on alibis. 4 p203. See D. *Pickwick Papers*, chap. 33.

Wellington, Duke of, dictum of. "When in doubt, retire and dig yourself in." 29 p277. An accurate summary of Wellington's tactic of retiring behind the Lines of Torres Vedras (1809–10) and defeating Marshal Massena by the simple process of waiting and starving him out.

Wembley. "This is Wembley", and the other chap said "I thought it was Thursday", and the first chap said "Yes, so am I" 68 p51. PGW's recollection of a well-known comic picture postcard of the 1920s. These 'saucy' postcards are still to be found at every British seaside resort; they are childish, smutty and wildly popular. The most famous artist was Donald McGill (1875–1962); a typical McGill card depicts a large fat anxious father in a bathing costume telling a startled bikini-clad blonde that he has lost his son with the caption: "I've lost my little Willie." It was probably McGill who drew the postcard PGW had in mind. It depicted two drunks on the Underground and the caption read: "Is this Wembley?" "No, it's Thursday." "So am I. Let's have another drink."

Wembley Empire Exhibition. 35 p146. The 1924 Exhibition was exactly as described in 'The Rummy Affair of Old Biffy', including the 'Palace of Beauty' sponsored by Pears' Soap. Though many believe the great football stadium was the only relic of the 1924 Exhibition left, the area around the stadium has several factories and offices with some very odd facades. They are the old pavilions and exhibition halls converted to other uses. See Chap. 38 for the recipe for Green Swizzles consumed at the Exhibition.

Wenlock Edge. An hour away from Rudge 40 p181. This scenic tree-covered ridge in Shropshire is indeed about 'an hour away' from Droitwich, whither PGW had moved 'Rudge Hall ' (Hunstanton Hall) from Norfolk. See Chaps

26 and 32.

Wensleydale's (Lady) 'Sixty Years Near the Knuckle in Mayfair'. 50 p16. Another reference to Lady Cardigan's famous autobiography. See BABLOCKHYTHE.

Went away from that place, they. 19 p191. When I first read this phrase, I remembered it immediately as part of an Easter Gospel reading, referring to the disciples discovering the empty sepulchre. But *Cruden's Concordance* to the Bible has only seven references to 'that place' and none of them are relevant to this event. The Authorised Version has Luke 24.9 saying of the discovery of the empty sepulchre: "And (they) returned from the sepulchre, and told all these things unto the eleven." But, by sheer chance, I found that the Basic English version of the Bible has: "And they went away from that place and told ..." Exactly the phrase PGW and I knew.

I checked my 1589 Geneva Bible, my Book of Common Prayer, my Catholic prayer-book and they all agree with the Authorised Version. So where did PGW (and I) get the phrase? Like one of PGW's curates, I am beginning to have doubts. What sort of Bible was used by his clerical uncles or at Dulwich? Or did it come from one of those innumerable Bible *Commentaries* and just entered PGW's subconscious as it entered mine? Or is it from somewhere else entirely?

Weobley. A small town in Herefordshire which PGW used under a number of guises — 'East Wobsley'; 'East Wibley', 'Webleigh Manor'. He knew it from his time as a boy in neighbouring Worcestershire and adopted it as a 'good' name.

Wept with delight when she gave him a smile, he. 76 p83. See SWEET ALICE.

West, Mae. 54 p65 and later. This lady (1892–1980) is summarised in Halliwell's *Filmgoer's Companion* as "the archetypal sex symbol, splendidly vulgar, mocking, overdressed and endearing. Wrote most of her own stage plays and film scripts, which bulge with double meanings."

Westbrook, master at King-Hall's, a good slow bowler. 12 p23. See Chap. 34.

Westbury. 34 p25. Westbury, an area southeast of Great Neck, Long Island, was once noted for its large estates and the wealthy people who lived there.

Western front. So much for the western front. We now turn to the eastern 52 p159. In World Wars I and II, newspapers popularised the phrases 'Eastern Front' (Russia) and 'Western Front' (France).

Westhampton. See Chap. 23.

We've drifted apart ...you've broken my heart. 94 p95. See YOU'RE BREAKING MY HEART.

Whalen, Grover. 62 p110; 66 p10. Whalen (1886–1962) was a businessman who became chairman of the Committee for Reception of Distinguished Visitors to New York, i.e. its official greeter. This role meant he constantly appeared in newspaper photographs, which made his luxurious drooping moustache famous.

Whammy. Adela gave him a full w. 70 p173; double whammy 76 p205. See FLEAGLE, EVIL EYE.

What? 26 p85 (Freddie Rooke); Lord Hunstanton says it because it is expected of him 38 p26; and often later. The habit of adding an interrogative 'What?' at the end of every sentence became fashionable in England in 1906. The origin is not known, but Gretton's *Modern History of the English People* (1913) is definite as to the year. It was probably simply a change from 'Don't you know', which had been the previous affectation. As late as 60 p169, Lord Bosham says "Eh?", "adding a 'What?' to lend the word greater weight." For *The Rose of China* (1919), PGW wrote a song entitled 'What! What! What!', unused, I regret to say. See also DO YOU KNOW? and HALLOA!

What a go is life! 8 p52. See GO LIFE IS.

What a hole it is. 40 p81. See WHOLE.

What a tangled web we weave, Oh. 42 p66; 57 p58 and later. Walter Scott's 'Marmion' C.6.17: "O what a tangled web we weave, / When first we practise to deceive."

What bloody man is this? 79 p59. S. *Macbeth* 1.2: "What bloody man is that? He can report, / As seemeth by his plight, of the revolt / The newest state."

What can ail thee, wretched wight, alone and palely loitering. 70 p31. First line of Keats' 'La Belle Dame Sans Merci'. When Denis Mackail told PGW he had misquoted and it should be "O what can ail thee, knight at arms, Alone and palely loitering", PGW tore out the page in his copy and sent it to Mackail (letter of 24 May 1951). Apparently 'knight at arms' are the words Keats wrote in his manuscript of 1819 but, what with one thing and another, the published version of 1820 said 'wretched wight'. There has been much deep academic discussion on the significance of the alteration, Keats changing his mind and his reasons for doing so etc.etc. Perhaps it was just bad subediting? Look at the way PGW's publishers changed his Biblical references.

'What Fun Frenchmen Have'. 48 p64. Probably from Cole Porter's 1929 show *Fifty Million Frenchmen'* (Can't Be Wrong). See also FIFTY MILLION.

What ho! Often in PGW as a greeting. Partridge's *Dictionary of Slang* states it began c.1860 as a lower-class greeting to call attention to something. Perhaps a forerunner of 'Hallo' (see HALLOA!).

What, in other words, of the Future? 42 p69; 53 p9 and later. There were dozens of books with the title *What of the Future* or something very like it. Mrs Hignett's *What of the Morrow?* (in *The Girl on the Boat*) was one. H.G. Wells wrote on the theme from his 1895 *The Time Machine* to *The Shape of Things to Come* in 1933.

What is a pleasant voice if the soul be vile? See EVERY PROSPECT.

What is wrong with this Picture? 34 p273; 37 p145. See PICTURE.

What news on the Rialto? See RIALTO.

What shall it profit a man (that he do the long hole in four). 37 p268 and later. B. Mark 8.36: "For what shall it profit a man, if he shall gain the whole world, and lose his own soul?"

What the well-dressed man is wearing. Article by B. Wooster 35 p208; advertisement of 62 p172; 81 p206. Every smart magazine used to have articles of this sort. My copy of *Vanity Fair* of 1916 (of which PGW wrote a third) has a regular column entitled 'Shopping for the Well-Dressed Man'.

What though the spicy breezes blow soft o'er Steeple Bumpleigh. 64 p79. See EVERY PROSPECT PLEASES.

What was Baxter to him or he to Baxter now? 42 p237. See WHAT'S HECUBA TO HIM.

What will he [the boy] become? See BOY, WHAT WILL HE.

What words that tongue could utter could even give a sketchy idea of how one feels about you, Jeeves. 64 p251. T. 'Break, Break, Break': "And I would that my tongue could utter / The thoughts that arise in me."

What would the harvest be? 53 p19; 56 p120; 62 p79 and elsewhere. I have not found the direct quote, but I favour B. Hosea 8.7: "For they have sown the wind, and they shall reap the whirlwind." Or maybe Galatians 6.7: "Whatsoever a man soweth, that shall he also reap."

What'll I Do? 58 p175; 72 p126. 1924 song by Irving Berlin.

What's Hecuba to him or he to Hecuba? 2 p57. S. *Hamlet* 2.2: "What is Hecuba to him or he to Hecuba?"

What's My Line? 89 p127. An early TV quiz game in which the team had to find a person's occupation in twenty questions.

What's the matter with …? With biscuits 8 p25; with England 11 p13; nothing the matter with Freddie 26 p66; and later. This US catchphrase was also used in the UK: "What's the matter with Gladstone? He's all right. Who's all right? Gladstone!!!"

The reference books say that "What's the matter with Kansas?" was coined by the *Emporia Gazette*, Kansas, in 1896. What worries me is that the remark about Mr Gladstone was in *Diary of a Nobody*, which came out in 1884. A probable explanation is that the later "What's the matter with Kansas?" was famous as an ironic twist on a common phrase. "What's the matter with X?" was a popular expression of admiration. However, William White, the editor of the *Emporia Gazette*, was so outraged at Kansas supporting William Jennings Bryan against William McKinley in the presidential election that he turned the phrase around. Far from admiring Kansas, he condemned it for supporting the wrong man. The phrase was taken up around the country and helped McKinley win.

Whatsoever thou takest in hand, remember the end. 49 p297. This is from Ecclesiasticus 7.36 in the Apocrypha, not from Ecclesiastes. Probably a sub-editor's error. MTT Dennis Chitty.

Wheelock, John Hall. Black panther caged within his breast 78 p146. This poet and publisher (1882–1978) published 'The Black Panther' in 1922.

Wheels of juggernaut. Some unfortunate Hindu beneath the w. of J. 50 p72.

Juggernaut is a Hindu god whose devotees hold a festival in his honour each year. A feature of the festival is an enormous wheeled vehicle dragged to the temple by fifty men. It was common for worshippers to throw themselves under the enormous 'wheels of Juggernaut.'

When a man's afraid, a beautiful maid is a cheering sight to see. 18 p38 and later. G&S *The Mikado* Act 2.

When beauty fires the blood, how love exalts the mind. 39 p162. Dryden's 'Cymon and Iphigenia'. See LOVE IS EVERYTHING.

When Comrade Jackson says 'Turn', we all turn. 15A p31; when Father says 'Turn', we all turn 66 p25. Probably from a music hall comic song or monologue, but I have not found it. I have, however, seen a brightly-coloured comic picture postcard c.1905, perhaps reflecting the song/ monologue. It shows a father, mother and eight children squeezed side by side into a bed. The caption reads: "When Father says turn, we all turn."

'When Doctors Disagree'. 18 p 54. This short story title comes from Pope's *Moral Essays Ep.III* (To Lord Bathurst. 1732): "Who shall decide, when doctors disagree, / And soundest casuists doubt, like you and me?"

When Father says 'Turn', we all turn. 66 p25. See WHEN COMRADE JACKSON.

When I takes the chair at our harmonic club. 1 p98. Nearest source found is 'Our 'Armonic Club' by Albert Chevalier 1886.

When Irish Eyes Are Smiling. 72 p116. Popular song by Chauncey Olcott, 1912.

When it is red … stingeth like an adder. 70 p146. See ADDERS.

When It Was Lurid. 9 p146 & p216. PGW's gloss on the sensational best-seller of 1903, *When It Was Dark*, by Guy Thorne.

When pain and anguish wring the brow, a ministering angel thou. Often, including "When something something something brow, a ministering angel thou" at 42 p95. See WOMAN IN OUR.

When they buried him. 69 p89. See AND WHEN THEY BURIED HIM.

When two strong men stand face to face. Two strong men face to face, rolling about on the carpet 63 p237; each claiming to be Major Brabazon-Plank 67 p204; and later. KIPLING's 'Ballad of East and West': "But there is neither East nor West, Border, nor Breed, nor Birth, When two strong men stand face to face, though they come from the ends of the earth!"

When you say that, smile. 89 p61. See SMILE.

When you were a tiddley-om-pom. 13 p242. See KING IN BABYLON.

Where am I?, he asked. 70 p160. I can confirm people say this when recovering from concussion, fainting or a Micky Finn. I was dancing for the first time with the girl I was later to marry and, anxious to demonstrate my grace and expertise, did a particularly tricky step just as some idiot barged into me. This caused my partner to fall backwards onto the stone floor and go out like a light. We carried her out of the room and put her on a sofa till she recovered. She opened her eyes and asked "Where am I?" At least I was able to say that, on our first date, I had swept her off her feet.

Where are the boys of the bulldog breed? 64 p162 and later. Song by Atkins & Handyman c.1900. The popular identification of Britain with the gallant, tenacious bulldog began during the wars against France 1790–1815. The newspapers then were full of cartoons showing brave, honest (if stupid) John Bull and his bulldog facing up to the slippery, deceitful French.

Where did you get that hat? 5 p47. This popular vaudeville comic song was written either by Joseph Sullivan in the US in 1888 or by James Rolmaz in the UK 1890s. (Song-stealing was common in those days). The song did so well, Rolmaz cashed in with 'A New Hat Now' in 1891.

Where every prospect pleases. 30 p199. See Every prospect.

Where falls not hail (or rain) nor any snow, nor ever wind blows loudly. 46 p233. This is Tennyson's island-valley of Avilion again, though PGW omitted 'or rain'.

Where is my Wandering Boy tonight? 22 p106 and later. See Boy, wandering.

Where men are men. See Men are men.

Whereabouts. Do you know anything of my husband's whereabouts? (They're at the wash.) 25 p81; inquiring as to my whereabouts 95 p154. The standard reply — "They're at the wash/at the laundry" has been a staple of English pantomime for over a century.

Whiffle/ Whipple/ Wipple. See Chap. 40.

While there is Life, there is hope. See Life.

Whimper. The world seemed to come to an end not with a w. but with a bang 91 p161; how betrothals end 92 p94. In 1925 T.S. Eliot's poem 'The Hollow Men' was very popular and everybody quoted the lines: "This is the way the world ends, / Not with a bang but a whimper." Many were outraged by the sentiment and G.K. Chesterton wrote a splendid response in 1927 and recited it in a broadcast in 1936:

Some sneer; some snigger; some simper;
In the youth where we laughed and sang,
And *they* may end with a whimper
But *we* will end with a bang.

MTT Tim Murphy.

Whiskers, tore off. Tore off his whiskers and it was Jim. See Jim.

Whisper in the ear, The place is haunted. 99 p101. Thomas Hood's 'The Haunted House'.

Whistler, Mr. Set to paint sign-boards 7 p124. James Whistler (1834–1903) was a brilliant but short-tempered painter.

Whistler's Mother. 73 p44; 94 p190. This famous 1872 painting of his mother by Whistler is officially titled 'Arrangement in Grey and Black', but Jeeves used the popularly accepted name. The painting became well known in 1934 when it featured on a special three-cent stamp as a tribute to the mothers of America. The sombre expression on the lady's face has led to many facetious comments, ranging from her unhappiness at having a son like the famously irascible Whistler to the alternative caption: "When is that no-good son of mine going to send some money home?"

Whistling Rufus. 3 p144. A catchy two-step written in 1899 by Kerry Mills.

White City and its fairground attractions. 18 p62; 22 p127. Like Wembley later, this 40-acre site in west London was built for an exhibition, the 1908 Franco-British Exhibition. The sideshows included the Flip-Flap, the Roly-Poly, Screamers, Witching Waves, Wiggle-Woggle, Boomerang and the Whirlpool. The 1908 Olympics were held there and the running track was used for the national championships for many years.

White Company, The. 4 p8. Adventure story by Arthur Conan DOYLE.

White Feather, The. Book title. A common term for cowardice, 'showing the white feather' comes from the ancient pastime of cock-fighting. Game cocks were very carefully bred and a single white feather in the tail was taken as a sign of bad breeding. It was believed that such a bird would not fight but turn tail — and show the white feather.

White Hart/ Stag at Barnes. 33 p59; 81 p183. Why PGW changed the name of this real pub at Barnes from the White Hart to the White Stag in the second reference is not known. Since there were thirty-two years between the two references, I imagine he just forgot. See also COAL HOLE.

White Hope, the. 19 p192; 24 p90 and later. In today's climate of political correctness, the term may be unacceptable, but it was in use for a very long time. When Jack Johnson (1878–1946) won the heavyweight boxing championship in 1908, it was a tremendous shock to many who saw it as a threat to the white race. For years there was a frantic search for what the Press called a 'White Hope' to defeat Johnson; this was eventually done by JESS WILLARD in 1915. The phrase, however, continued to be used for any promising performer in any sport for thirty years, long after the original racist connotation had been forgotten.

White man has not trod, where the foot of, nor the Gospel preached. 44 p97. See FOOT OF THE WHITE MAN.

White man's burden. 73 p12; 76 p90. See BLACK MAN'S BURDEN.

White rabbit heated in the chase, like a. 80 p188. A splendid combination of *Alice in Wonderland* and Tate and Brady's hymn: "As pants the hart for cooling streams, When heated in the chase." See also PANTS THE HART.

White Ship, King Henry and the. 19 p7. See KING HENRY.

Whiteley's. 7 p59. A large London department store, founded by William Whiteley (1831–1907), who advertised himself as the 'Universal Provider'.

Whites of their eyes. 80 p12. See DON'T FIRE.

Whitest man I know, the. 78 p13. In addition to the 'GREEN EYE OF THE LITTLE YELLOW GOD', J. Milton Hayes also gave us the stirring poem 'The Whitest Man I Know', which owes much to Kipling's 'GUNGA DIN'. In *Over Seventy*, PGW uses the phrase as a footnote to thank himself for an extract of his *Louder and Funnier* of thirty-five years before.

Whither thou goest, I will go. 71 p54. B. Ruth 1.16: "For whither thou goest, I will go; and where thou lodgest, I will lodge …"

Whitman, Walt. 81 p22; 89 p27. This American poet (1818–92) was indeed as heavily bearded as PGW says.

Whizzo. Fairly whizzo I call it. 81 p114. This term of appreciation has vanished now. It came in during the war when British fighter pilots adopted the word 'wizard' as their standard term of approbation. It soon became shortened to whizzo, and its very popularity and consequent overuse soon killed it off.

Who ever loved that loved not at first sight. 52 p123. S. *As You Like It* 3.5.

Who is it/he? 33 p88; 52 p37. This comes from an advertisement that ran for many years in English magazines up to 1939. It showed a restaurant or hotel lounge, full of beautiful women, each accompanied by a distinguished-looking gentleman, and all eyes are fixed on the handsome young man who has come through the door. He is wearing the costume beloved of Victorian novelists, 'faultless EVENING DRESS'. As the accompanying text makes clear, it is his superb clothing that has given him such an air of distinction and causes all the beautiful women to ask, "Who is it?" If the reader only had the sense to patronise Messrs Whoeveritwas, Bespoke Tailors, then he too would have everybody asking "Who is it?" when he attended social functions.

Who is your stuffed friend? 79 p105. A superb PGW twist on a phrase that embedded itself in the popular memory. During the Regency period in England, the leader of fashion, when fashion was all that mattered, was Beau (George Bryan) BRUMMEL. Tailors paid him to wear their coats and waistcoats, and the Prince of Wales (later George IV) came to him for lessons in tying a cravat. So sure was he of his social supremacy that, when a creditor asked him for the fifty pounds he owed, Brummel replied: "I've paid you twice over. I let you take my arm as we walked in Piccadilly and I nodded at you from the window of White's. What more do you want?"

Eventually Brummel made the mistake of offending the Prince of Wales, who was grossly overweight and sensitive of the fact. One morning, in 1813, Brummel walked down St James's Street and met Lord Alvanley with the Prince of Wales. His greeting became famous: "Morning, Alvanley. Who's your fat friend?" Brummel at once became persona non grata and was later declared bankrupt.

Who lost Mark Antony the world? 7 p165 and later. From Thomas Otway's poem *The Orphan*.

Who ran to help me when I fell … 21 p197 and later. See MY MOTHER.

Who steals my/his lordship's purse steals trash. 73 p124; 93 p49. See PURSE.

Who stole my heart away? 53 p82. 'Who?' (stole my heart away), a song from Jerome Kern's 1925 show *Sunny*.

Who was it I did see thee coming down the road with? 18 p241. See next entry.

Who was that lady I saw you coming down the street with? That was no lady, that was my wife. 27 p209; That wasn't a man. That was my literary agent 49 p229; 55 p39; no gentleman but an old friend 59 p92; 68 p48; no lady, that was my fiancée 69 p95; and later. The *Oxford Companion to the American Theatre* has traced this back to the 1880s. Joseph Weber (1867–1942) and Lew Fields (1867–1941) joined forces as ten-year-olds to form a 'Dutch' cross-talk act and were successful for fifty years. It was during the 1880s that they produced 'one of the most famous of all American jokes: "Dat vas no lady. Dat vas my wife."' It became one of the most-overworked jokes in UK cross-talks acts as well. I could have given the correct reply when I was eight years old.

Who Will O'er The Downs With Me? 68 p187. Song by Robert Pearsall (1853).

Whoever-it-was, Madame. 93 p77. See DEFARGE.

Whole. Rudge must be looked upon as a whole. And what a whole it is 40 p81. PGW got this from Baron Coleridge (1820–94), who made this immortal gaffe at Oxford in a speech in the Sheldonian Theatre. "I speak not of this college or of that, but of the university as a whole — and, gentlemen, what a whole Oxford is."

Whole raft of gems of something something the something caves of ocean bear. 94 p45. For the lines Grayce Llewellyn was trying to remember, see GEM OF PUREST RAY SERENE.

Whose Baby Are You? 51 p17. Song by Jerome Kern and Anne Caldwell in the 1920 show *The Night Boat*.

Whose heart hath ne'er within him burned ... 21 p117. Scott's *The Lay of the Last Minstrel*, C.6. The verse begins: "Breathes there a man, with soul so dead." See BREATHES THERE A MAN.

Whose name led all the rest. See ABOU BEN ADHEM.

Whoso findeth a wife. See FINDETH A WIFE.

Why beholdest thou the mote that is in thy brother's eye ...? 93 p86. See BEAM.

Why does a chicken cross the road? 11 p48; 52 p212. This timeless cliché of a joke, to which the audience always knew the answer, originated with the black-face minstrel shows of the 19th century. See also BONES; MINSTREL SHOWS; WHO WAS THAT LADY.

Why skip ye so, ye high hills? 50 p254. See SKIP YE SO.

Whyte-Melville. 2 p227. G.J. Whyte-Melville (1821–78), a retired Army officer, wrote novels and poems on racing and field sports.

Wicked man in the Psalms, fleeing like the. See FLEEING.

Wicked may flourish like a ruddy bay tree, as the Good Book says. 66 p139. See BAY TREES.

Widgeon and a gentleman, like a. 83 p84. See OFFICER.

Widgery on Nisi Prius Evidence. 29 p193 & p224 and later. I have not found a book under this title, but a Widgery became Lord Chief Justice forty years after PGW wrote of him.

Widow and orphan (doing down/taking advantage of etc.). 51 p12 and elsewhere. B. Exodus 22.22: "Ye shall not afflict any widow or fatherless child."

Wife of Bath, she reminds me of his (Chaucer's). 89 p57; 92 p28. In Chaucer's *Canterbury Tales*, we learn this forthright lady has had five husbands, thinks virginity is highly overrated, and thoroughly enjoys the married state.

Wife won't let me, my. 17 p215. From the song 'WAITING AT THE CHURCH': "Can't get away to marry you today, My wife won't let me."

Wilcox, Ella Wheeler. Knew E.W. by heart 18 p122. This American poetess (1850–1919) was read across the English-speaking world, and her books of verse, with such titles as *Poems of Pleasure*, *Poems of Passion*, *Poems of Progress* and *Poems of Cheer* etc., were best-sellers. When she died, the London *Times* said she was " the most popular poet of either sex and of any age".

Wild asses of the desert. See BACHELORS.

Wild surmise, looked at each other in. See NEW PLANET.

Wild thing taken in a trap, some. 33p154. See CREATURE.

Wildingesque tennis player, a. 22 p44. Tony Wilding (1883–1915) was Wimbledon champion 1910–13.

Wilhelm. 11 p42. See KAISER.

Willard, Jess. 20 p143. World heavyweight champion (1915–19) who beat Jack Johnson but lost his title to Dempsey. See Chap. 4.

Williams, Bert. 29 p115; 74 p11. Williams (1874–1922) is described in the *Oxford Companion to the American Theatre* as the greatest of black American comedians.

Willie, Little. 12 p128; 14 p254 and later. It is difficult to define/describe the term 'Little Willie' as used by PGW and other writers of the time. It was an ironic congratulatory term (see *Psmith in the City* p254) for a boy who had done something brave/remarkable/worthy of congratulation. The most likely origins are the countless Victorian stories where the young hero, though despised and bullied by his fellows, saves the school from fire/the headmaster's daughter from drowning/the local squire from being gored by a bull etc. etc. The sad 'Willie' songs by Stephen Foster (his admired elder brother was named William) probably provided the name. One half of the American literary world insists that Little Willie stems from the poem 'Lament on the Death of Willie' by the Sweet Singer of Michigan, Julia Moore (see Chap. 37). The other half points out that, twenty years before, Stephen Foster had written 'Willie, My Brave', 'Willie's Gone to Heaven', 'Willie, We Have Missed You' and 'Willie's Gone to the War'.

I favour Foster, whose tributes to Willie were followed by some 150 other songs about this gentleman over the next 70 years. Typical titles were 'Our Willie Dear Is Dying', 'Willie's Gone to the Angels', 'Willie's Joined the Guards'; 'Little Willie's Coming Home'; 'Waltzing Willie'; 'Waltz Me Willie in Ragtime'; 'Willie, What Would Piccadilly Say?' and 'Won't You Come Over to Philly, Willie'. See also Chap. 36.

Willow the King. 3 p267. Written by John Snaith in 1899.

Wimbledon Common. 33 p11 up to 86. See Chap. 25.

Wimpy, the well-known moocher in Popeye. 89 p149. This hamburger-eating cartoon character gave his name to the hamburger chain.

Wimsey, Lord Peter. 55 p87 and later. Detective, creation of Dorothy L. SAYERS.

Win friends and influence people. Not at all the sort of chap likely to 68 p178; 86 p96. See CARNEGIE, DALE.

Winchell, Walter. Peep at the home life of the rhinoceros 63 p226; I'll write to W.W. 70 p105; and later. Winchell (1897–1972) was an American institution for more than thirty years. Over 50 million people listened to his radio programme or read his column. He invented the modern 'scandal' gossip column and convinced Americans that they 'had the right to know' every detail of anyone's private life. He was at least fearless and incorruptible, though he admitted he had no scruples, decency or conscience, but "I've got the readers".

Winchester. 26 p12 and later. See Chap. 3.

Wind. A mighty rushing wind 7 p197; 43 p137; 52 p38 and later. B. Acts 2.2: "And suddenly there came a sound from heaven as of a mighty rushing wind, and it filled all the house where they were sitting."

Wind which I respect not. Bothering passes me by as the idle wind which I respect not. 65 p214. See ARMED SO STRONG.

Windles in Hampshire. 29 p12 & p238. See Chap. 16.

Windsor, Duke of, danced with. 69 p98. See DANCED WITH.

Wine is a mocker and strong drink is raging. 70 p140; 86 p50. B. Proverbs 20.1. The verse continues: "and whosoever is deceived thereby is not wise."

Wings. Hear the beating of its w. 26 p174 and later. See BEATING.

Wings of a dove, O for the. 39 p129; 51 p170 and later. B. Psalms 55.6. "And I said, Oh that I had wings like a dove! For then would I fly away, and be at rest." The version by Mendelssohn, when sung by a choirboy treble, is guaranteed to reduce everybody in the audience over fifty years old to tears (female) and hard blowing of handkerchiefs (male). The famous 1927 recording by Ernest Lough was the first HMV record to sell a million copies.

Winkle, Mr. An excellent sportsman in theory 3 p263. See D. *The Pickwick Papers*.

Winnie the Pooh. 68 pp38 & 183. This 1926 creation of A.A. MILNE's needs no introduction. What is needed is a wider appreciation of the superb illustrator E.H. Shepard, whose drawings made the bear so memorable.

The toy bear has now taken his place in European history. The final bulletin of the European Parliament in 1979 included a summary of its recent session at Luxembourg. One section read: "The House also discussed Mr Shaw's report on company audits and budget carry-overs… . Mr John's report on environmental carcinogens, Mr van der Gun's report on Winnie the Pooh …" The *Daily Telegraph* (24 May 1979) explained that the report dealt with the sociological aspects of promotion of education contacts between European colleges. The committee producing the report debated what to call it for hours, but were unable to produce a title less than a paragraph in length. When a voice at last cried out, “Oh, call it Winnie the Pooh” — they did.

Winning friends and influencing people. 84 p13. See CARNEGIE, DALE.

Winstone Court. Not ten miles from Blandings 32 p19. See Chap. 39.

Winter of my discontent made glorious summer by this J.B. Butterwick, now is. 94 p84. S. *Richard III* 1.1. “Now is the winter of our discontent / Made glorious summer by this sun of York.”

Winter Garden. Two seats for the W.G. 36 p176. A minor reference, but when PGW wrote this line in *Sam the Sudden*, the show at the Winter Garden theatre in London just happened to be the Wodehouse/Grossmith show *The Beauty Prize*.

Wired for sound, she was. 68 p97. When talking films were introduced in the late 1920s, cinemas rushed to fit sound equipment. ‘Wired for sound’ became a popular cinema advertisement.

Wisden. 6 p4; 12 p141 and later. This magisterial Cricketer’s Almanack was first published in 1864.

Wisdom lingers. Knowledge comes, but w. l. See KNOWLEDGE COMES.

Wisely. Playit never so wisely. See ADDER, DEAF.

Wisions limited, my. 6 p209. Sam Weller at the trial in D. *The Pickwick Papers*.

Witching time of night, ’Twas now the very. 73 p163. S. *Hamlet* 3.2: “’Tis now the very witching time of night.”

With all her faults, I love her still. See LOVED HER STILL.

With knobs on. See KNOBS.

Withdrawn his countenance from me, My uncle has definitely. 32 p77. This sounded very Biblical but it isn’t in the Authorised Version, though many Biblical commentators use the phrase. In the BCP, the nearest I could find was the Deus Misereatur in Evening Prayer: “God be merciful unto us, and bless us and shew us the light of thy countenance.” (See also chap. 50 of D. *Pickwick Papers* where Mr Ben Allen withdraws his countenance from his son.)

Without a check. A pursuit that had lasted fifty minutes 1 p115. A fox-hunting term for a good run, i.e. hounds not distracted by rabbits or losing the scent. Aunt Dahlia uses the same term later.

‘Without the Option’. Short story title. The magistrate was being tough here. For such offences, the court would usually fine a chap and send him to jug if he could not pay. Circa 1910, failure to pay a fine up to £5 meant seven days inside; if you wouldn’t/couldn’t pay a fine of £20, you got a month. But if the magistrates realised that a financial penalty would mean little to the culprit, they jugged him ‘without the option’ of paying a fine.

Wodehouse Glide. Denis Mackail and others referred to the Wodehouse Glide, i.e. PGW’s well-known habit of quietly vanishing at the end of an evening or surreptitiously leaving a room when he was bored. I have heard of Leonora using the term and had always wondered if PGW knew people spoke of this habit of his. Thanks to Mr Michael Meakin (see Chap. 32), I now possess a photocopy of a letter from PGW to Charles le Strange in which he apologised "for the recent Wodehouse Glide".

Wolf, big bad. See BIG, BAD WOLF.

Wolf of Wall Street. Oofy Prosser resembles one 60 p60; Jimmy Schoonmaker is probably one 84 p24. *Wolf of Wall Street* was a 1929 film starring George Bancroft as a ruthless financier who gets his just deserts.

Wolf will always be near or about the vestibule. 61 p15 and elsewhere. PGW gloss on the phrase 'to keep the wolf from the door', i.e. to be hungry.

Wolfe, Nero. 64 p330; his fatness 88 p218; and later. Fictional fat detective created by Rex Stout, whose stories PGW much enjoyed, commenting that they could be re-read so often with so much enjoyment. Having recently come to read and enjoy Rex Stout (1886–1975), I know exactly what he meant. Stout is the only writer I know whose stories can be re-read within three months and enjoyed just as much the second time around. I was puzzled by this till it was pointed out to me that the stories are narrated by a likeable, cheerful young man and deal with his sometimes difficult relationship with an older, cleverer individual who solves seemingly insoluble problems (c.f. Bertie/Jeeves). MTT Elin Woodger, who introduced me to Rex Stout and pointed out the similarity.

Wolff-Lehmann. 53 p69; 84 p10; 91 p12, dead at p 63. See Chap. 40.

Woman, good. 39 p 94. See GOOD WOMAN.

Woman, I am only a weak. See WEAK WOMAN.

Woman in our hours of ease, uncertain coy and hard to please. 29 p15 and often later. Walter Scott's 'Marmion' c.6.28. All Wodehouseans will recognise the first two lines and the last two, but maybe not the two in the middle.

O Woman! In our hours of ease,
Uncertain, coy, and hard to please,
And variable as the shade
By the light quivering aspen made;
When pain and anguish wring the brow,
A ministering angel thou!

Woman is only a Woman, but a hefty drive is a slosh. 28 p57 and variations of this later: a smoke is a smoke, a pint is a pint, etc. See GOOD CIGAR.

Woman, O Woman, Woman. 7 p162; 29 p36 and later. Thomas OTWAY's 'The Orphan'.

Woman of iron, a. 70 p191. See MAN OF BLOOD AND IRON.

Woman scorned, a. See HELL HATH NO FURY.

Woman whom God forgot. From topknot to shoe sole 68 p11. There is a strong Biblical ring to this description of Madeline Bassett, but it will not be found in the Authorised Version. Robert W. Service wrote 'The Land God Forgot' and I have found a 1920 film entitled *The Wife Whom God Forgot*. Its title in the UK was *Tangled Hearts* (see *Nothing Serious*).

Womanly candour/ sympathy that became her well. 28 p41. See BECAME HIM/ HER WELL.

Women he had seen at Le Touquet groping their way out into the morning air after an all-night session in the Casino, like. 80 p119. In a letter to Bill Townend, PGW recounted how he had a good evening in the casino and gone home early. When he got up, he went for an early walk and met Ethel coming home. She had lost as much as he had won.

Women Who Shouldn't Have Done But Took A Pop At It. 49 p226. See MEN WHO DID.

Women's Institute. 68 p194. This organisation, founded in Canada, has become an important institution in Britain. All too often dismissed in the Press as 'jam and Jerusalem', its members have found practical solutions to many problems of country life. I remember my wife Charlotte summing up their efficiency: "The parish council discusses something and then wonders who can do something about it. We decide if something needs to be done and then we go and do it."

Wonderland (boxing venue). 33 p59 & 118. See Chap. 4.

Wooden nickels, don't take any. Frequent. I thought this was just a meaningless catchphrase, but learned that these were wooden tokens, covered with a veneer of metal, for use on machines and sideshows at fairs, carnivals etc. They were used widely at the 1893 Chicago World Fair and, though they were of no commercial value, con men used them in rural areas where they would be unrecognised. The caution became a cliché.

Woodward of Chelsea preserved his skill in spite of his advanced years. 22 p130. V.J. Woodward, a remarkable amateur footballer, earned and kept his place in Chelsea's (professional) team for some five years (1905–10) and played for England during the same period. He was reckoned to be even better than the legendary G.O. SMITH.

Wool. All wool and a yard wide. See ALL WOOL.

Woollam Chersey. Country residence of Aunt Agatha 43 p15, 59 p178; of Bill Bannister 47 p87. See Chap. 2.

Woollcott, Alexander. 86 p149. See ALEXANDER OF THE *TIMES*.

Woolworth Building. Lean over the edge of the W.B. and spit into Broadway 48 p199. When *Hot Water* was written, the Empire State Building was not yet built and the top of the Woolworth Building was the popular spot for tourists.

Wooster Number Five. 82 p156. See CHANEL.

Worbury/Worfield. 3 p136; 12 p64. See Chap. 35.

Worcestershires, Loyal Royal. 44 p128. See Chap. 2.

Word Beautiful, the. 38 p4. See BOOK BEAUTIFUL.

Word in season, the. 1 p260; 81 p90. B. Proverbs 15.23: "and a word spoken in due season, how good is it!"

Word is their bond, whose. 84 p41. "My word is my bond" is the centuries-old motto of the London Stock Exchange.

Words carved/graven on the heart. See GRAVEN ON HER HEART.

Word(s) like a knell. 33 p45; 40 p62. See FORLORN.

Words of tongue or pen, sad. Of all sad w. of tongue or pen, The saddest are these: 'It might have been' 12 p184; 18 p170; and later, including the poignant lines in *Big Money* (p 270): "... the saddest are these: 'He knew something good but could not make a touch.'" From Whittier's 'Maud Muller'(1856). The poem describes the encounter between a wealthy judge and a girl raking hay. They converse politely and he walks on, but both think how nice the other is and regret they are poles apart socially. Whittier said he had indeed once met a country girl raking hay and thought how delightful she was. He let it be known later that he had in mind his own unrequited love for Mary Emerson Smith, whom he could not marry because he was poor and socially inferior to her. Bret Harte satirised the poem with the lines: "More sad than these we daily see. It is, but hadn't ought to be." See also I KNEW HIM WHEN.

Words to that effect, or. 85 p120 and elsewhere. Phrase commonly used in policeman's evidence to a court, when they are asked to report the tenor of the accused's remarks. See also ALARM AND DESPONDENCY.

Wordsworth, when he saw a flower, experienced thoughts too deep for tears. 90 p98. Wordsworth's 'Intimations of Immortality': "To me the meanest flower that blows can give / Thoughts that do often lie too deep for tears."

Work of a moment. Was with him the w. of a m. 4 p136; and often later. I long thought this had a ring of Conan Doyle, but it is 200 years older. See Chap. 38 (Motteaux).

Worker, World's. 19 p233; 35 p11 and later. See end of Marx's 1848 Communist Manifesto: "Workers of the world, unite."

Working-girl, protect the. 21 p175. See HEAVEN PROTECTS.

World ended not with a whimper but a bang. 91 p161. See WHIMPER.

World is too much with us, the. PGW ref lost. Wordsworth's *Miscellaneous Sonnets* No. 33, 'The World Is Too Much With Us'.

World knows little of its greatest men/women. See GREATEST MEN.

World of women, a. I wandered through a w. of w., seeking you 77 p167. See I WANDERED THROUGH.

World so full of beautiful things, In a. 44 p15; where he felt we should all be as happy as kings 50 p51; and later. R.L. Stevenson's 'Happy Thoughts'.

Worlds, best of all possible. See ALL IS FOR THE BEST.

World's Sweetheart. Even if I were the W.S. 40 p77; 54 p65. This was the title with which the film studio publicised Mary PICKFORD (1893–1979). They were reluctant to do so since it paid them to keep their staff anonymous (it saved wages), but Pickford's following was so strong, they had to give way. She invested her money wisely and became one of the richest women in America.

Worm i' the bud. See SHE NEVER SAID.

Wormwood Scrubs. 32 p125; 68 p223 and later. A prison in London which enjoys the distinction of being built by prison labour (1874–90).

Worplesdon, Lord. 35 p11. Florence Craye's father takes his title from the golf course west of London where PGW used to play with E. Phillips Oppenheim.

Worthless cheque, I'm a (a total wreck, a flop). 71 p159. Song 'You're the Top', for which PGW wrote some of the lyrics, from *Anything Goes*.

Wotwotleigh, Lord. 51 p62. I have not found this character or the play he appeared in, but I am pretty sure it existed. I suggest it was staged after 1906 (see What?) and before 1914. The theme of a penniless aristocrat trying to marry American money was common enough, since so many (118) American heiresses married into the peerage in the period 1874–1910. The best candidate I have found is the 1907 play *The Man from Home*, by Booth Tarkington and Harry Leon Wilson, in which an American lawyer comes to England to rescue his ward from a disastrous attachment to the venal son of an even more venal aristocrat.

Would never smile again, like a famous English king. 71 p131. See King Henry.

Would you buy me with your gold? See Gold.

Wrangler. The Rev. Septimus was a w. 3 p195. At Cambridge, the student who is awarded most marks in the mathematical tripos is named the senior wrangler. Those below him/her are named second wrangler, third wrangler etc. I am told tenth wrangler is normally the last named. The term goes back to the time when students won their degrees by disputing a point of theology, law, philosophy, mathematics etc. with their examiners.

Wrath, man of. See Man of wrath.

Wreck of the Hesperus, The. 19 p108 and often up to 91 p65. Longfellow's poem was reluctantly recited by many children from PGW's time to mine. See also Skipper had taken.

Wrecking Crew, The. 37 p115; 57 p111; 81 p31. See Chap. 27.

Wrekin, the, not Bredon. 91 p185. See Housman.

Wretched man felt his position deeply, the. See Position.

Wretched wight. See What can ail thee.

Writing on the wall. 52 p97; 53 p37 and later. B. Daniel 5.5. and 5.25–28. After a hand had written mysterious words on the wall at Belshazzar's feast, Daniel interpreted them, including the phrase 'Thou art weighed in the balances, and art found wanting'. See also Belshazzar's feast.

Wrykyn. See Chaps 3 and 35.

Wyatt. 12 p12. See Chap. 3.

Wymondham-Wymondham, Algy. 41 p13. This member of the Drones Club is notable because of his name. It is the only time PGW referred to Wymondham, Norfolk, the seat of the Earl of Kimberley, the head of the Wodehouse family. See Chap. 32.

Wynn, Ed. 35 p110. American comedian (1866–1966). He is not mentioned in 'The Aunt and the Sluggard' in *My Man Jeeves* but does appear in the same story in *Carry On, Jeeves* later, presumably because the latter was published in America.

X-Y-Z

(MTT = My thanks to)

Xenophades' 'Lyrics from a Padded Cell'. 3 p251. I suggest this is a misprint for Xenophanes the Greek philosopher (6th c. B.C.), whose bizarre ideas on astronomy and the relationship of gods and men so outraged his fellow Greeks that he was judged to be either mad or evil. He was exiled for being one or the other.

Xenophon's Ten Thousand. 48 p34 and later. Xenophon — soldier, writer and philosopher — was in the army of Greeks who, in 401 B.C., found themselves supporting the wrong side in a rising in the Persian Empire. With remarkable bravery, diplomacy and leadership, Xenophon brought the army back across modern-day Turkey against tremendous odds till at last they reached the Aegean Sea and safety ("Thalassa! Thalassa!" [The Sea! The Sea!]). See also PARASANGS.

Yahoo. 48 p37. The Yahoos were depicted as savage brutes with human bodies in Swift's *Gulliver's Travels*. The term came to mean a boor, a lout. I remember people being described as Yahoos in the 1960s, but I think Swift's term has now finally faded as a term of abuse.

Yam. That yam, Pilbeam 42 p133. Clearly a term of abuse, but my dictionary of American slang offers no explanation.

Yea be Yea, Let your. See LET YOUR YEA BE YEA.

Year's at the spring, the, … God's in his Heaven. 59 pp310 &311. See GOD'S IN HIS HEAVEN.

Years, might/may be for. See MIGHT BE FOR YEARS.

Years that the locust has eaten. See LOCUST.

Yellow and few in the pod, you are so. 33 p43. Ukridge is clearly accusing Teddy Weeks of cowardice, and I assume 'few in the pod' expresses some deficiency of character, but I have been unable to find the source. Something to do with beans perhaps?

Yellow journalism. 15A p2. The term stems from the circulation battles between sensational New York newspapers of the 1890s. See Chap. 7.

Yellowback novels of fifty years ago. 41 p13. I have an idea, no more, that these novels died away around the 1890s when Northcliffe's (Lord Tilbury) magazines replaced them. I possessed a few. The back covers were always of a bright yellow and the front always showed some dramatic scene, the abduction of a heroine or the hero horsewhipping some villain who clearly deserved it.

They were at the upper end of the 'sixpenny horrors' or the 'penny dreadfuls'. See Chap. 7.

Yeoman's Wedding Song. 25 p240 and later up to 95 p173; B. Wooster's memories of singing it at 68 p15, 82 p16 and 93 p91. This song was written by Josef Poniatowski (1816–73). Related to the Polish Royal Family, he became a famous tenor in Italy, wrote his own operas, and was given a title by the Duke of Tuscany. He then became Tuscan ambassador to Brussels, London and Paris, and Napoleon III was so impressed by him, he made him a Senator. Poniatowski followed Napoleon into exile in England, where, his biography says, his Yeoman's Wedding Song "became very popular". It was probably written in 1871.

Yes … he had no mananas. 54 p223. PGW gloss on the popular song 'Yes, We Have No Bananas'. Written by Silver & Cohn in 1923 after Cohn heard a Greek greengrocer in New York with a poor grasp of English telling a customer what he had available for sale.

Yes, love indeed… . our low desire. 39 p161. From BYRON's 'The Giaour'. See LOVE IS EVERYTHING.

Yes, sir, that's my baby (No, sir, I don't mean maybe). 39 p12; 40p44 and later. 1925 song by Kahn and Donaldson.

Yes-Men. 53 p222; 63 p66. The phrase originated in a newspaper cartoon of 1913 by T.A. Dorgan entitled: 'Giving the first edition the once-over.' It showed the editor looking at the first proofs coming off the press, surrounded by assistants all praising it, each with a label saying 'Yes-man'. The phrase took off and entered the language.

Yesterday has faded from its pages. 74 p209. See PHOTOGRAPHICALLY LINED.

Yip-i-addy-i-ay. 74 p72. The first two lines of verse are from the song by Flynn and Cobb (1908) but the remainder were written by PGW. I have no idea why. Perhaps he thought his version was better than the original. It is certainly far wittier. Few people knew the verses but, up to c.1970, everybody knew the rousing chorus 'Yip-i-addy-i-ay-i-ay, Yip-i-addy-i-ay'.

George Grossmith Jnr (see Chap. 13) introduced this into the Gaiety show *Our Miss Gibbs* (1909), in which he played the juvenile lead. The song was wildly successful, but George Edwardes was suspicious of his actors branching out in this way and was reluctant to feature it. Because of the enthusiastic response from the audience, however, Grossmith continued to sing it. Its popularity for raucous audience participation was equalled only by 'TA-RA-RA BOOM-DE-AY'.

Grossmith wrote some of the lyrics for the Wodehouse/Grossmith 1922 musical *The Cabaret Girl*, and it is clear that he was trying to repeat his earlier success with a song called 'Whoop-de-oodle-do'. It had the same format, with a preliminary chorus to work up the audience by repeating "Whoop-de-oodle-do! Whoop-de-oodle-do! Whoop-de-oodle-do!" three times before launching into: "One-Two-Three! Pull up your socks and shout it! Whoop-de-oodle, whoop-de-oodle, Whoop-de-oodle-do!" It didn't work.

Yo Ho Ho and a bottle of Slimmo. 72 p100. Better known as 'Yo Ho Ho and a bottle of rum' from R.L. Stevenson's *Treasure Island* (1883).

York Mansions, Battersea Park Road. 22 p168. See Chap. 25.

You ain't heard nothing yet. 71 p88. See JOLSON.

You can lead a horse to the altar, but you can't make it drink. 51 p171. Another spendid mixed proverb. See BURNED CHILD.

You can tell him by his hat. Father/He's in the pigstye/pig sty. See PIGSTYE.

You can't do that there here. 65 p24; 68 p187 and later. Traditional admonition by a policeman when he comes across activities not actually illegal but causing annoyance to others. Boys playing cricket in the road, someone singing in the street at the top of his voice at midnight would be told: "You can't do that there here." If the miscreants persisted, they could be arrested for "causing a breach of the peace".

You can't keep a good man down. 69 p228 and later. 1900 song by M.F. Carey, followed in 1920 by the PGW version, 'You Can't Keep a Good Girl Down' in the musical *Sally*.

You can't take it with you. 62 p234; 68 p122. This traditional reproach to a man who refuses to lend you money was the title of George Kaufman's 1936 play. My favourite usage is the true Pelican Club story when, having had his request for a loan turned down, the rejected suppliant retorted: "You can't take it with you. And if you did, it would melt!"

You don't know (as the song hath it). 1 p181. Wodehouse was quoting a popular song written two years before, 'You Don't Know, They Don't Know and I Don't Know' by Sam Richards (1900).

You have done the state some service. See DONE THE STATE.

You have lit a candle etc. See CANDLE.

You kid/boss. 13 p108 and later. See OH YOU KID.

You know my methods, Jeeves. Apply them. 52 p91. See Conan DOYLE's *The Hound of the Baskervilles*, chap. 1, third page.

You made me what I am today! I hope you're satisfied. 21 p240. See CURSE OF AN ACHING HEART.

You may boast of the pride of your ancient name … Love that conquers all. 58 p206 & p274. This song should have been easy to find, but I was unsuccessful. One of Jerome Kern's or Cole Porter's? Perhaps PGW wrote it, one of the many lyrics he produced that were never used?

You pain me. 13 p107. See DESIST.

You want the best seats, we have 'em. 32 p29. Freddie Threepwood expresses his exultation in *Leave It to Psmith* by repeating the advertisement to be seen all over London from 1921 to 1950. It advertised London's biggest and oldest theatre ticket agency — Keith Prowse. PGW also used it as a title for a song he wrote for the Grossmith/Wodehouse show *The Cabaret Girl*, during whose London run he just happened to be writing *Leave It to Psmith*.

Young Artists' Exhibition in Dover Street. 48 p37. This would certainly have taken place at the Arts Club in Dover Street, the only club still there today from PGW's time.

Young blood. 38 p23. From Charles Kingsley's poem 'Young And Old': "Young blood must have its course, lad / And every dog his day."

Young but not so young as that, he may have been. 2 p94. See GRAND DUKE.

Young England. 3 p15; 52 p211. A boys' magazine of the 1890s, the title of several songs 1886–1906, a musical comedy of 1916 and, in this case, a generic term for schoolboys.

Young lady from Natchez. See NATCHEZ.

Your need is greater than mine (As what's-his-name said to the stretcher case). 50 p108 and often elsewhere. See SIDNEY.

You're breaking my heart, we're drifting apart, as I knew at the start it would be. 72 p107; 94 p95. 1948 song 'You're Breaking My Heart'.

You're the cream in her coffee. See CREAM IN HER COFFEE.

You're the Sort of Girl That Men Forget. 36 p30. Al Dubin's 1923 song 'Just a Girl That Men Forget'.

You're the Top. 63 p141 and p147; 83 p28. From the Cole Porter musical *Anything Goes*, original book by PGW and Guy Bolton. PGW wrote some of the verses for this song for the UK version and updated them later for a revival.

Youth but knew, If. See IF YOUTH BUT KNEW.

Youth on the prow and Pleasure at the helm. 54 p122. 'The Bard' by Gray.

Youth, rash. For know, r. y., that in this star crost world … 64 p212. G.B. Shaw's *The Admirable Bashville*.

Youth, thoughts of (long, long thoughts). See THOUGHTS OF YOUTH.

Zacharaiah (prophet). 84 p74. An error, apparently due to a typo by PGW himself. It is Zecharaiah, not Zacharaiah, who was wounded. B. Zecharaiah 13.6: "And one shall say unto him, What are these wounds in thine hands? Then he shall answer, Those with which I was wounded in the house of my friends."

Zadkiel. 32 p84. Pen name of Lieutenant Richard James Morrison (1794–1874). He published his astrological almanac (*Prophetic Almanac*) in 1838 and yearly thereafter. It proved amazingly popular.

Zam-Buk. Put your nose right in a day 12 p111; 15A p227. This ointment, very effective for spots and sore skin, is still on sale after a hundred years. My father used to tell his patients to use this rather than come to him with minor scratches.

Zampa, overture to. 69p50. A fine rousing piece for brass bands. Written by Louis Herold in 1831.

Zanuck, Darryl. 70 p178. Hollywood mogul (1902–79). I have read he was the only studio head happy to speak and write in English.

Zbysco. 12 p179; 22 p54. Stanislaus Zbyszko (1879–1967), famous wrestler c.1910–20 when the wrestling craze had gripped Britain. See also

HACKENSCHMIDT.

Zend Avesta of Zoroaster. 73 p71. Sacred texts of the Parsees.

Zenda stories. 16 p52. *The Prisoner of Zenda* and *Rupert of Hentzau* were very popular novels by Anthony Hope (1863–1933). See RASSENDYL.

Ziegfeld, Florenz. 70 p199. This extravagant American theatrical impresario (1867–1932), with whom PGW worked, created the immortal Ziegfeld Follies in 1907 and could charm money out of the pockets of the most reluctant businessmen. His ten-page telegrams described by PGW in *Bring on the Girls* were well-known; he had talked Western Union into allowing him to send up to 3 million words a year at a reduced rate. He died a million dollars in debt — and those who knew him were surprised it wasn't more.

Zola. 18 p104 &p145. The French writer Émile Zola (1840–1902) wrote realistic (i.e sad/sordid) stories of French rural life.

Zowie. The *Oxford Dictionary of Modern Slang* attributes the word to PGW and I believe it is wrong. 'Zowie' was a common term in America, but perhaps the Oxford editors, as with so many of their attributions of American words to PGW, felt it didn't really count till PGW used it. Who can blame them?

Index

E

F

G

H

I

J

K

L

M

S

T

U

V

Lightning Source UK Ltd.
Milton Keynes UK
UKHW041254070621
385079UK00007B/1739